D1598363

THE TERMINAL CLASSIC
in the Maya Lowlands

THE TERMINAL CLASSIC
in the Maya Lowlands

COLLAPSE, TRANSITION, AND TRANSFORMATION

EDITED BY

Arthur A. Demarest

Prudence M. Rice

Don S. Rice

UNIVERSITY PRESS OF COLORADO

Published by the University Press of Colorado
5589 Arapahoe Avenue, Suite 206C
Boulder, Colorado 80303

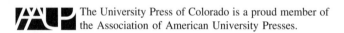 The University Press of Colorado is a proud member of
the Association of American University Presses.

The University Press of Colorado is a cooperative publishing enterprise supported, in part, by
Adams State College, Colorado State University, Fort Lewis College, Mesa State College,
Metropolitan State College of Denver, University of Colorado, University of Northern Colorado,
and Western State College of Colorado.

The paper used in this publication meets the minimum requirements of the American National
Standard for Information Sciences—Permanence of Paper for Printed Library Materials. ANSI
Z39.48-1992

Library of Congress Cataloging-in-Publication Data

The Terminal Classic in the Maya lowlands : collapse, transition, and transformation / [edited by]
Arthur A. Demarest, Prudence M. Rice, and Don S. Rice.
    p. cm.
Includes bibliographical references and index.
  ISBN 0-87081-739-6 (hardcover : alk. paper)
  1. Mayas—History. 2. Mayas—Politics and government. 3. Mayas—Antiquities. 4. Social
archaeology—Central America. 5. Demographic archaeology—Central America. 6. Central
America—Antiquities. I. Demarest, Arthur Andrew. II. Rice, Prudence M. III. Rice, Don Stephen.
  F1435 .T383 2003
  972.81'016—dc21

                                                                                          2003010948

Designed and typeset by Daniel Pratt

13   12   11   10   09   08   07   06   05   04   10   9   8   7   6   5   4   3   2   1

CONTENTS

Figures

TABLES

EDITORS' PREFACE

This collection of chapters on the transitions from Classic to Postclassic-period lowland Maya civilization had its origins in a series of symposia Arthur Demarest organized in the late 1990s at annual meetings of the American Anthropological Association and the Society for American Archaeology. He invited Don and Pru Rice to co-organize one of the last of these symposia, at which point we began talking about publishing a volume of selected contributions. As might be expected, it has not been easy for three editors with administrative responsibilities and field projects to gather and edit a volume of twenty-three chapters written by multiple authors with various international affiliations, who also are frequently in the field.

Furthermore, we suffered a setback when our originally contracted publisher experienced its own transition in publishing and marketing goals. We are very grateful to Darrin Pratt at the University Press of Colorado for immediately and enthusiastically stepping into the breach and for providing constant encouragement as our efforts lurched along. He and his staff have been wonderful partners in this endeavor.

In compiling this volume, we opted not to impose an internal organizational structure of formal sections based on areal, topical, or other commonalities and distinctions, with introductory editorial commentary. The issues tackled in each chapter are complex—ceramic and other artifactual data, architecture, chronological concerns, cultural processes—and are addressed in varying ways depending upon the authors' theoretical inclinations and the history of research in the particular site and region in question. Instead, we organized the chapters on a roughly geographical basis, from Petén through Belize to northern Yucatán, opting to let the authors address the topics in their own ways and speak in their own voices.

Related to this, the editorial staff at University Press of Colorado decided, and we agreed, that the most appropriate editing strategy for the papers in this volume was to aim for internal (that is, within chapter) consistency in orthography (spelling) and diacritics (accent and other marks, such as glottal stops) for site names and words in the Mayan languages, rather than to impose a consistent style throughout all chapters. Many of these decisions relate to differences in indigenous language orthography between Mexican and Guatemalan scholars, and also among linguists and epigraphers.

For example, one issue concerns the specific Mayan language in which the Classic inscriptions were written: Ch'olan was used in the west and south, while Yukatekan was used in the north, but there were times and areas in which these distinctions are unknown or when the two overlapped. An immediate signature of this distinction is the use of "ch" as opposed to "k", as in *"chan"* versus *"kan"*, which is often seen in rulers' names. In addition, some scholars discern differences between long and short vowels, which are indicated by variant spellings as, for example, Nuun versus Nun. Also, plurals in Mayan languages are indicated by *-ob,* and some scholars prefer to retain that spelling while others simply invoke the English and Spanish plural designator "s", as in *sacbeob* versus *sacbes.* As a result of all these differences, references to one particular site of interest may be seen in these chapters as "Chichen Itza," or as "Chich'en Itza" *(chi ch'en,* transliteration of the Yukatekan Maya language), or as "Chichén Itzá," following Spanish conventions on modern maps.

The list goes on, but the point has been made: to be faithful to the original voices and intellectual contexts of the authors of each chapter, it is not proper for us to arbitrarily impose uniform editing rules. We acknowledge with regret that this approach may create some difficulties for readers who are not intimately acquainted with the technical linguistic, epigraphic, and political arguments so entailed.

Last but certainly not least, we express our tremendous appreciation and gratitude to Allison Price and Matt O'Mansky at Vanderbilt University. The *kuch,* or burden, of physically organizing this volume and communicating with authors fell on Matt's able shoulders, with Allison aiding and abetting him at every turn, and he accomplished these tasks with skill, dedication, professionalism, and humor. We trust he will chalk it up as a useful learning experience.

THE TERMINAL CLASSIC
in the **Maya Lowlands**

1

THE TERMINAL CLASSIC AND THE "CLASSIC MAYA COLLAPSE" IN PERSPECTIVE

Prudence M. Rice, Arthur A. Demarest, and Don S. Rice

he alluringly alliterative notions of the "mysterious Maya" and the "mysterious Maya collapse" have been enduring icons since the very beginnings of archaeology in the Maya lowlands. A century and a half of exploration and public interest in Maya archaeology was spurred by the vision of towering temples and palaces suddenly abandoned, swallowed by the jungle as their inhabitants fled for parts unknown. Despite more than a century of scholarship and accelerated archaeological investigation, the engaging "mystery" of the Maya collapse has not succumbed to the brutal truths of cold, hard, scientific fact. Even by the turn of the millennium, we still had not come to any agreement on what caused the Maya collapse or precisely how to integrate the vast amount of data, often contradictory, that pertain to this issue.

Part of the problem might have been that we were asking new questions about the Maya collapse, but our attempts to answer them were bound to outmoded concepts that no longer yield useful insights and explanations. Here we introduce the contributions to this volume by revisiting some of these time-honored concepts, like "collapse," that have guided thinking over the decades. We offer a varied set of perspectives—not necessarily right or wrong, but simply varied—on the Maya Terminal Classic period, the collapse, and related issues, to establish the deep background within which the research reported in these chapters was carried out.

Although the contributions in this volume do not resolve the many controversies, they do indicate that the discussion of the Classic to Postclassic transition has moved to a new level of detail in culture-history and of sophistication in concepts and approaches. Some scholars here still think in terms of a general collapse of Classic Maya civilization and of one or two "global" causes of this alleged cataclysm. Yet the editors and most scholars in this volume now reject such notions of uniformity of the nature or the causes of Classic- to Postclassic-period changes. Instead, we see this volume as the beginning of a more sophisticated process of reconstructing, region by region, the changes that occurred between A.D. 750 and 1050 and led, through varying paths, to the different societies and settlement distributions of the Postclassic period. The broader patterns and linkages that emerge in these regional sequences are discussed in our concluding chapter.

Be forewarned, however, that the variability and complexity of this Classic to Postclassic transition have increased with our greater knowledge of the archaeological and historical evidence. The plotting of these changes will tell us a great deal about the culture and political systems of both the Classic- and Postclassic-period kingdoms of the ancient Maya. Sadly, however, this volume also ushers in a new period in the archaeological study of this transition: the mundane and difficult work of building and linking regional histories that we have begun here will replace the romantic search for the "secret" to a presumed uniform and simultaneous catastrophe that never occurred.

PERSPECTIVES ON THE END OF THE CLASSIC PERIOD
Early Historicism

Explorers of the Maya lowlands in the late nineteenth and early twentieth centuries discovered carved, dated stone monuments at southern sites, simultaneously noting that their erection ceased in the late ninth century A.D. Along with cessation of the stelae-altar complex and hieroglyphic texts, there was also a decline of polychrome ceramics, sumptuous burials, and apparent abandonment of many of the Classic southern cities. And at about the same time, they noted, occupation began to flourish at new and different sites in the northern lowlands.

In these early years, archaeological and anthropological thinking on cultural change was relatively unsophisticated, and explanations tended to be couched in terms of fairly dramatic scenarios of rises and falls of empires, or collapses of civilizations (see Yoffee and Cowgill 1988; Cowgill 1988). Probably only the fall of the Western Roman Empire has been discussed more often than the Maya as an example of the decline of a civilization. One result of this thinking was the notion of the collapse of lowland Maya civilization, that is, the "Old Empire" of the south, followed by the establishment of a "New Empire" in the north (Morley 1946; Thompson 1954). And thus was established a holy grail for subsequent archaeological research: If this was the collapse of Classic-period civilization, now we must discover its causes.

By the mid-twentieth century, numerous causes had been proposed to explain the decline and collapse of what had been envisioned as a ruling priestly hierarchy at the southern sites. These causes included (Morley and Brainerd 1956: 69–73; see also Adams 1973a): earthquake activity, climatic change (drought), epidemic diseases such as malaria and yellow fever, foreign conquest, "cultural decadence," agricultural (soil) exhaustion, and revolt of the lower classes. The last was viewed as the most plausible.

The Notion of the Terminal Classic

The concept of a lowland Maya "Terminal Classic" period was formally introduced into the archaeological lexicon at the 1965 Maya Lowland Ceramic Conference in Guatemala City, Guatemala (Willey, Culbert, and Adams 1967). This meeting was held for the purpose of discussing and visually comparing ceramic complexes, particularly to compare chronologies, as published ceramic data were not widely available. The focus was primarily on relatively large sites where major research projects had earlier been carried out.

The Terminal Classic concept was intended primarily as a mechanism for separating and marking the Classic to Postclassic transition (Culbert 1973b: 16–18) in the lowlands, and was initially defined on the basis of its ceramic content. Its name, Tepeu 3, was borrowed from the Uaxactún ceramic sequence, although the sphere designation, Eznab, is drawn from that of Tikal. The Terminal Classic thus referred to both a time period (roughly A.D. 830–950) and a particular set of cultural circumstances: specifically, cessation of the cultural practices that characterized the Classic pinnacle of Maya civilization. Although the term was adopted "in the hope that it [would] connote both the continuity and the destruction of previous patterns . . ." (Culbert 1973b: 17), emphasis has more often been on their endings than their continuities. The Terminal Classic concept was always inseparably connected to the termination of Maya "Classicism"—its collapse and the attendant abandonment of the southern and central lowlands.

Participants in the 1965 ceramic conference also identified the Terminal Classic as an archaeological "horizon." A horizon is characterized as "a spatial continuum represented by the wide distribution" of recognizable artifacts, styles, or practices, defined most saliently by "its relatively limited time dimension and its significant geographic spread" (Phillips and Willey 1953: 625; Willey and Phillips 1955: 723, 1958: 38). Choice of the horizon label for the lowland Maya Terminal Classic was dictated not by the widespread prominence of a distinctive artifact style, then and now the most common basis for defining archaeological horizons (D. Rice 1993a), but rather by the perception that the lowland Late Classic period ended everywhere with a societal collapse so widespread that it constituted a bona fide cultural horizon. As T. Patrick Culbert (1973b: 16) later noted, the Tepeu 3 horizon was "the period during which the processes of the downfall worked their course."

Collapse-centrism

Not long after the Maya Ceramic Conference, leading Mayanist scholars met in a seminar at the School of American Research in Santa Fe, New Mexico, in 1970 for the first attempt to systematically compare and synthesize the data that had accumulated on the causes of the collapse. The conference, organized because "a series of major research projects [had] been undertaken in the Maya Lowlands in the last two decades that provide important masses of new data" (Culbert 1973d: xiv), revealed some of the complexity of the lowland Late Classic Maya world and the emergence of different regional patterns of change in the eighth through tenth centuries. But it is important to recognize that the data presented at the conference and published in the resultant volume, *The Classic Maya Collapse* (Culbert 1973a), represent a rather biased sample of the lowlands. Robert L. Rands's (1973a) effort to provide the chronological summary for the volume was based on data from only eight sites—essentially those from the earlier ceramic conference—particularly in the west along the Pasión and Usumacinta Valleys (Seibal, Piedras Negras, Altar de Sacrificios, Palenque, and so forth).

The Classic Maya Collapse concluded with a characteristically skillful summary by the "Great Synthesizer," Gordon Willey, assisted by Demitri Shimkin. These authors (Willey and Shimkin 1973) wove the seemingly contradictory interpretations and diverse data sets into a summation that included "structural" considerations (subsistence, population density, sociopolitical organization, religion, militarism, urbanism, trade, and markets) and dynamic features (role of the elite, social distinctions, intersite competition, agricultural problems, demographic pressures, disease burdens—especially malnutrition—and external trade). Significantly, they downplayed the role of militarism, either as internal revolt (earlier favored by Sylvanus G. Morley and J. Eric Thompson) or external invasion (see Rice n.d.). They concluded with a descriptive model of sorts that uncomfortably forced integration of all these possible causes and, as such, was unsatisfactory (Culbert 1988: 76 calls it a "kitchen-sink model"). The fissions in our visions of a uniform "Classic Maya collapse" were already apparent.

Subsequently, in the late 1970s and 1980s archaeological research in the lowlands began to legitimize a new focus—the Postclassic period—and this brought about completely different perspectives on the Classic collapse. Instead of viewing the ninth and tenth centuries as the sudden ending of something (that "something" being Late Classic civilization, privileged as the principal period of Maya history worthy of study), archaeologists began to consider the view that these centuries simultaneously represented a transition and, possibly, the beginnings of something else that was also of importance (Chase and Rice 1985; Sabloff and Andrews 1986). Indeed, one conclusion drawn from such perspectives is that, in the Maya lowlands, the truly dramatic transformations "came with the fall of Chichen Itza in the thirteenth century A.D. and not with the fall of the Classic centers in the South" (Andrews and Sabloff 1986: 452).

In the years following the 1970 conference, additional scrutiny of the collapse included new approaches such as computer simulation (Hosler, Sabloff, and Runge 1977), general systems theory (Culbert 1977), catastrophe theory (Renfrew 1978), trend-surface analysis of the distribution of dated monuments (Bove 1981), and new or revised causal mechanisms, including peasant revolt (Hamblin and Pitcher 1980), decline of Teotihuacan influence (Webb 1973, 1975; Cowgill 1979), and agricultural-subsistence stress (Culbert 1988). At the same time, growing interest in settlement surveys, combined with the interpretations of massive depopulations in the ninth and tenth centuries, sparked closer attention to regional demographics and more realistic population estimates (Culbert and Rice 1990). It has been estimated that by A.D. 800 the population density was about 145 people per square kilometer, falling into the low 40s per square kilometer by A.D. 1000 (Turner 1990: 312). In terms of numbers, by A.D. 800 the population peak is estimated to range between 2.6 and 3.4 million, falling to "less than 1 million or so" by A.D. 1000, a depopulation rate of 0.53–0.65 (Turner 1990: 310). Also during the 1980s and 1990s, rapid advances in glyphic decipherments brought about new interpretations of events of the Late Classic period, principally leading to an emphasis on militarism and intense intersite warfare as factors in the collapse in some regions (Demarest, Valdés, et al. 1991; Demarest 1996, 1997; Schele and Miller 1986; Schele and Freidel 1990; also Cowgill 1979).

Culture Change

Earlier considerations of the so-called Classic Maya collapse were plagued by the assumption of a common "cause" and by vague terminology (see, e.g., Cowgill 1988). Here, in our consideration of what constitutes the decline, collapse, or transformation of a political system, such as that of the Maya, we follow recent discussions and debates of the epistemology of such considerations of culture change (e.g., Eisenstadt 1967, 1968, 1986; Tainter 1988; Yoffee and Cowgill 1988).

In particular, as Norman Yoffee (1988: 14) explains, the various meanings assigned to the word "collapse" can be grouped into two categories. One category consists of words like fall, collapse, fragmentation, and death, which imply "that some meaningful entity ceased to exist." The second category implies a change to something that is "morally or aesthetically inferior," as in the words decline, decay, and decadence. Here, when we speak of a "decline," it is in reference to a particular political system that experiences a notable decline in the degree of complexity.

In addition, Cowgill (1988: 256) urges a careful distinction between the kinds of entities that are in transition, such as state, society, and civilization. The term "state" refers to a type of political organization, and its ending, unless achieved by force, should be referred to as "fragmentation" rather than collapse or fall. Civilization should be used "in a specifically *cultural* sense, to mean . . . a 'great tradition.' To speak of the collapse of a civilization, then, should be to refer to the end of a great cultural tradition" (Cowgill 1988: 256).

Some of these specific distinctions are difficult to apply to the lowland Maya, however. The term "political fragmentation" may or may not be inappropriate, as it depends on the degree to which Maya states are viewed as centralized or decentralized. Similarly, "civilizational collapse" is inappropriate unless one postulates a "southern lowlands variant of the Maya great tradition" (Cowgill 1988: 266).

Postmodernism and Postprocessualism

The collapse of the Maya, like that of any other civilization, is a gripping metaphor for contemporary fears of individual death or societal decline, and has always been a subjective, reflexive reading of an imagined past in the present. As recent trends in social philosophy have emphasized, the ancient past has never been "objectively" or "scientifically" studied. The ancient past has always been, at best, a Rorschach test for contemporary concerns, and at worst, a text constructed in a metanarrative with a conscious or subconscious agenda of legitimating the conquering Western capitalist tradition. Clearly, the "mystery of the Maya collapse" falls somewhere between these subjective extremes as a contemporary, emotional reading of the past (cf. Montejo 1991; Castañeda 1996; Hervick 1999).

The notion of a collapse of Maya civilization has been viewed as offensive by some scholars and a few Maya activists, given the vigor of the Maya cultural traditions of millions of speakers of Maya languages in Mexico and Guatemala today. Both the intellectual confusion and political insensitivity can be attributed to careless terminology about what constitutes a "transition," "decline," or "collapse" and *what it is that experiences* the transition, decline, or collapse. Clearly, Maya civilization as a general cultural and ethnic tradition—a "great tradition"—did not experience any "collapse" or "decline." The Postclassic Maya kingdoms of northern Yucatán, Belize, and Guatemala were large, vigorous polities, and the Maya tradition of more than ten million indigenous citizens of Guatemala and Mexico is currently experiencing a great cultural, linguistic, and political florescence (e.g., Fischer and Brown 1996). Indeed, this contemporary Maya resurgence is challenging our conceptions of what is "Maya" and how anthropologists and archaeologists view these societies (e.g., Warren 1992; Watanabe 1995; Nelson 1999; Montejo 1991; Fischer 1999; Cojtí Cuxil 1994).

In this regard, our referring to or describing a "collapse," "decline," "transition," or "transformation" of Classic lowland Maya kingdoms is neither a moral/aesthetic judgment nor a denigrating statement about Postclassic Maya polities or the later societies and cultural formations of speakers of the Maya languages and their traditions (although some earlier authors may have placed such connotations on these terms). Rather, these are more specific interpretations about what happened to particular *political and economic systems* in the ninth and tenth centuries. Similarly, talking of the decline of the Western Roman Empire or the collapse of the Austro-Hungarian hegemony is not a broader denigrating statement on the European Western tradition or modern Western society; it is a generalization about changes, some rapid, some gradual, in particular political systems.

While acknowledging the inevitably reflexive nature of archaeology, many of us still remain dedicated to the mundane, traditional task of ordering artifacts from different regions, dating them using a variety of methods, comparing them, and then attempting to construct culture-history consistent with those data sets and sequences. Our dedication to this task may simply be due to a lack of intellectual courage; that is, we are lackeys in the capitalist metanarrative construction system and this is our job! Alternatively, however, one could argue that despite the efforts of Jacques Derrida, Michel Foucault, and a host of French philosophers (and their British archaeological "translators," Ian Hodder, Michael Shanks, Christopher Tilley, et al.), some of us still cling to the seemingly outdated concepts of linear time, subject/object distinctions, and other credos of modern science.

A volume such as this must be viewed as traditionalist construction and comparison of regional culture-histories, together with some initial attempts at interpretation of causality in terms of traditional Western scientific "metanarrative." We did not seek in this volume to debate the epistemology or terminology of discourse as applied in archaeology, in Mayanist archaeology, or, specifically, in the study of the final centuries of Classic Maya civilization. We share concerns regarding the admittedly problematic terms used in interpretive discourse here and in general in the Maya field, such as *civilization, tradition, decline, collapse*, etc. These concerns are touched upon briefly in several articles in this volume and also in Chapter 2 by Diane Z. and Arlen F. Chase. We do not necessarily agree with the Chases' negative presentation of much earlier research, nor with their approach to "hermeneutics." Nonetheless, we do believe that awareness of postprocessual critique has enriched some of these chapters. In general, however, we leave to future forums the worthy debate and general re-evaluation of our essentialist views of "Maya civilization" and its culture-history, and the necessarily subjective and value-laden ways in which we interpret such abstractions in the archaeological record.

New *Balche'*, Old *Ollas*

Since the 1970 Santa Fe conference, the concept of civilizational collapse has stirred enormous disagreement among Mayanists, particularly because such an event did not occur simultaneously in the north, where cities were flourishing. In the thirty years since the conference, an enormous amount of research has provided a wealth of data, stimulating a need for a new look at the ninth- and tenth-century changes taking place in the lowlands. This research has also revealed considerable variability in the timing of these processes and in the extent to which they took place. Most archaeologists' discussions now highlight (rather than suppress) variability within and among Classic Maya kingdoms during this period.

Wholesale abandonment versus slow decline, sudden versus gradual economic change, population dispersion, endemic warfare, destruction, reorientation, and florescence—all are represented in the interpretations of change and transformation in regional lowland cultures during these centuries. In addition, the whole notion of "collapse" as the defining event of the ninth and tenth centuries in the lowlands is being rethought, and major shifts in theoretical approaches to culture-history and causality prompt similar reviews.

We adopted the term "Terminal Classic" in accumulating these papers, largely because of tradition: this is what it has been called in the southern and central lowlands. The Terminal Classic in the southern lowlands was dated ceramically from a beginning at about A.D. 800/830, to an ending around 950/1000. In the northern lowlands, however, the temporal interval of the Terminal Classic is subsumed with a longer (ca. A.D. 700–1050/1100) period usually known as "Florescent" or "Pure Florescent," alluding to the flowering of the Puuc centers in the northwestern corner of the Yucatán peninsula (see Brainerd 1958). For the northern lowlands, then, the term "Terminal Classic" is a rather ill-fitting and restrictive label for this longer period.

Consequently, we have taken the period under consideration here to be an interval of some three hundred years, from approximately A.D. 750 to 1050. This is not a conscience-stricken attempt to force-fit the southern chronology into the northern, but rather recognition that, overall, the focus of interest for Mayanists is no longer simply a political collapse in the south. Instead, research has revealed that the end of divine kingship—the termination of a key element of "classicism" in the south—is only one strand in a complex web of events and processes of intra- and intersite dynamics and broader, continuing inter-regional interactions between the north and the south. While still flawed, the "Terminal Classic" designation at least remains more neutral than terms like "collapse," "fall," or "decline."

The reader will find even greater chronological variation in the periods covered by these articles. To some degree, this reflects the great chronological variability in the changes in material culture in different regions. For example, the events and processes leading to a population decline and emigration in western Petén began before A.D. 750 and in some areas (such as the Petexbatun, and possibly the Copán Valley) were all but over by A.D. 830. Yet in some other areas, in Belize and the northern Yucatán peninsula, a variety of differing shifts and changes continued through A.D. 1100, before the material culture and institutions associated with the Postclassic were firmly in place. This variability is especially notable in Chapters 19–22 on the northern lowland sites.

Other variations in the chronological framing of chapters is due to the interpretive approaches and theories of the authors, which draw on earlier, or later, parallel processes. For example, in Chapter 15, Richard Adams et al. envision a true global "collapse" that is the last of three earlier global "disasters" driven by climatologically caused droughts and famines. They trace their regional culture-history, then, back to the Preclassic to try to demonstrate such a repeating pattern. Conversely, Christopher R. Andres and K. Anne Pyburn (Chapter 18) and Marilyn A. Masson and Shirley Boteler Mock (Chapter 17) try to elucidate the changes involved in the Classic to Postclassic transition by working backward from Postclassic evidence in Belize that helps define the new, yet vigorous, Maya tradition in Belize after A.D. 1100.

What is really of interest to anthropological archaeologists, after all, are the processes underlying a broader cultural transformation, a Late Classic to Postclassic transition, taking place in this period. In the southern lowlands, the focal transition has long been the end of divine kings and the large cities they ruled. In some areas, this was an abrupt political collapse of the type that is traditionally identified with the Terminal Classic period and is certainly worthy of scholarly attention. However, contributing factors can be traced back to at least the sixth century, carved stelae continued to be erected in some sites into the early tenth century, and the aftermath—population movements and new alliances—all demand that at least several decades immediately preceding and following the Terminal Classic proper be considered in any genuine effort to understand these broad processes of cultural transformations.

TRANSITIONS, TRANSFORMATIONS, AND COLLAPSES IN THE TERMINAL CLASSIC: THE CHAPTERS IN THIS VOLUME

What actually collapsed, declined, gradually disappeared, or was transformed at the end of the Classic period was a specific type of political system and its archaeological manifestations: a system of theater-states, identified by Emblem Glyphs, dominated by the *k'ul ajawob* (holy kings) and their inscribed stone monuments, royal funerary cults, and tomb-temples, the political hegemonies of these divine lords, and their patronage networks of redistribution of fineware polychrome ceramics, high-status exotics, and ornaments. This system ceased during the late eighth and ninth centuries in most of the west and some areas of central Petén. Its ending was often accompanied within a century by the depopulation of major cities, drastic reduction of public architecture, and other changes. Notably, however, in other areas, such as Belize, the Mopán Valley, and the northern lowlands, the close of the Classic period saw more gradual change or even florescence. There clearly was no "uniform" collapse phenomenon, but rather a sequence of highly variable changes. Yet in all cases there was a pronounced change in the Classic Maya sociopolitical order by the end of the Terminal Classic (varying from A.D. 950 to 1100), with the "termination" of the divine *k'ul ajaw* institution and most of its distinctive, archaeologically manifest features of elite culture.

The intention of this volume was not to find common cause(s) of these phenomena, but rather to plot this very variability as a starting point for future interpretations of the transition from Classic to Postclassic Maya lowland political and economic systems. The modest goal was to compile and compare summaries of the Terminal Classic and Florescent period (circa A.D. 750–1050) archaeological evidence and culture-histories from excavations and interpretations in the 1970s, 80s, and 90s. With only brief epistemological digressions here and in Chapter 2, then, most chapters are archaeologists' culture-historical summaries of their data on the late eighth to eleventh centuries from their regions of research. *Most* scholars in the volume implicitly or explicitly apply their reconstructions (regional or pan-lowland) of decline, transition, or transformation to the *political systems* of Classic Maya lowland kingdoms. And most of the chapters end with some speculative discussion of the broader nature of the end of the Classic Maya kingdoms and the beginnings of the Postclassic in their respective regions. Indeed, several move more broadly beyond the period under discussion to describe the Postclassic florescence (e.g., Chapters 17 and 18) or to posit a more gradual transition to Postclassic political and economic systems (Chapter 2). In our final summary (Chapter 23), we argue that some chronological patterns and parallels can be discerned in the wide array of evidence presented. There we also try to more clearly delineate the nature of the disagreements about data or interpretation seen in these many chapters.

RESULTS AND PROSPECTS

We did *not* expect any manner of consensus to arise from these chapters—and none has! What we did expect was that intriguing patterns might emerge, that directions for future research might be better defined, and that disagreements could be clarified as to their degree and nature. In general, the chapters in this volume provide summaries of regional archaeological evidence and culture-histories, a snapshot of the "state of the art" in Maya research on the centuries of the Classic to Postclassic transition, A.D. 750–1050. These summaries and interpretations allow comparisons and contrasts between the assemblages, the events, and the processes proposed for the many subregions of the Maya lowlands. Some contributions describe depopulation and political disintegration in their regions, while others present evidence for a more gradual change in institutions with less dramatic shifts in demography, economy, and political order. It is hoped that this compilation of data and ideas will provide an overview of the highly variable archaeological record and the wide range of scholarly interpretations of the evidence on this period, upon which research and syntheses can build.

Yet we do believe, as stated previously, that the volume represents a watershed in studies of the Classic to Postclassic transition, moving away from global projection of local evidence or grand theories to hypothesize a uniform pan-Maya catastrophe. The evidence presented here largely argues against the concept of a uniform, chronologically aligned collapse or catastrophe in all regions of the lowlands or even a uniform "decline" in population or political institutions. (Note that some recent climatological theories run counter to this trend and return to catastrophism, e.g., Chapters 9 and 15; Hodell et al. 1995; Haug et al. 2003). In light of the data and perspectives in most of these chapters, the enigmas of the Terminal Classic become more manageable and less value-laden problems. We can plot the various collapses, declines, or transformations of Classic Maya regional culture across the political landscape of the Maya lowlands and note the common underlying structural problems, the varying proximate "causes" and external forces, and the different results in each region. The beginning of such a comparative plotting was the principal goal of this volume and the meetings, correspondence, and debates that generated these papers.

We hope that these chapters will provide a baseline that will stimulate, clarify, and direct the continuing systematic compilation of regional culture-histories of the end of the Classic and beginning of the Postclassic period. This new epoch of research on the problem should leave behind the myth of global, pan-Maya catastrophism and the "mystery" of *the* collapse. Instead, the specifics of the varying regional sequences, and linkages between them, may lead to a more sophisticated understanding of the changes in lowland Maya political and economic systems.

2

HERMENEUTICS, TRANSITIONS, AND TRANSFORMATIONS IN CLASSIC TO POSTCLASSIC MAYA SOCIETY

Diane Z. Chase and Arlen F. Chase

opular views of the Classic Maya collapse and of the changes between the Classic and Postclassic Maya are due as much to past paradigmatic factors, including research perspective and methodology, as they are to actual data or distinctions. The Classic and Postclassic Maya have often been viewed in terms of polar oppositions. The break between the two eras frequently has been described as temporally and culturally abrupt. However, the Maya survived the collapse at many sites in the southern lowlands. And, cultural distinctions once drawn between the two eras are not as clear-cut as once thought. Changes once believed to coincide with the inception of the Maya Postclassic period actually took place much earlier during the Classic period. These new interpretations may be used to critically re-examine the transitions and transformations that occurred between the Maya Classic and Postclassic eras and to reconsider the Classic Maya collapse.

A recurrent theme for discussion among scholars and the lay public alike is the inevitability of the rise and fall of civilizations (e.g., Tainter 1988; Yoffee and Cowgill 1988). Whether the interest in the rise and fall of past cultures is ascribed to an inherent fear of collapse and decay in contemporary culture or to an insatiable curiosity about the past, in many of these considerations the "mysterious" collapse of the southern lowland Maya of Guatemala, Mexico, and Belize is considered to be a case in point. Occurring during the eighth and ninth centuries A.D., the Classic Maya collapse is defined primarily by the end of erection of stone monuments with royal hieroglyphic inscriptions and the presumed coeval abandonment of many major architectural centers. Explanations for its occurrence range from internal factors involving peasant revolt to external intervention by foreign invaders to environmental factors, particularly related to drought and the overuse of land. Popular conceptions of the Maya who survived the collapse are of a lessened or almost nonexistent civilization (Gallencamp 1985).

Continued research on the Maya suggests many factors that obscure a simple rise-and-fall scenario and place Maya collapse discussions squarely within current debates in archaeological theory—particularly concerning the way the past is constructed in the present. It is now evident that the Classic Maya "collapse" was neither total nor uniform throughout the Maya area and that the collapse and the transition between the Classic and Postclassic periods was in many places a very lengthy and even a continuous process. A further unexpected development is the discovery that a number of features previously thought to characterize the Postclassic Maya actually had their origins substantially earlier in the Classic period.

HERMENEUTICS: PERCEPTIONS OF THE POST-COLLAPSE MAYA

Inherent to discussions of the Classic Maya collapse are considerations of what came before it and what happened after it—or, in other words, the relationships between the Maya of the Classic (A.D. 250–900) and Postclassic (post-A.D. 900) periods. As scholars researching the Postclassic period have long noted (Chase and Rice 1985; Pendergast 1990b: 169), the Postclassic Maya often have been viewed with a Classic-period ethnocentrism. Descriptions and interpretations of the late Maya are frequently based on contrasts with the Classic period, usually consisting of lists of items missing from the Postclassic cultural repertoire that are thought to be prominent characteristics of the preceding Classic era. Thus, the Postclassic period has been characterized by a *lack* of finely carved monuments, a *lack* of tall impressive pyramids, a *lack* of slipped polychrome pottery, a *lack* of sumptuous tombs, and a *lack* of extremely large and densely populated centers.[1] All of this tended to make the Postclassic "less" than the Classic. And, as the modern Maya have also been portrayed as being but a shadow of their former glory (Morley and Brainerd 1956; Thompson 1954), these differences in material culture have been utilized to confirm the existence of a dichotomous picture between the Classic and Postclassic Maya.

Hermeneutics, the study of interpretation and meaning, has been incorporated into contemporary archaeology (Whitley 1998: 13). In discussing archaeological interpretation, Shanks and Tilley (1987: 107–108; see also Shanks and Hodder 1998: 76) have argued that a fourfold hermeneutic exists in archaeology (see also Binford 1989: 28). Interpretive problems exist in: (1) "understanding the relation between past and present;" (2) "understanding other societies and cultures;" (3) "understanding contemporary society, the site of archaeological interpretations;" and (4) "understanding the communities of archaeologists who are performing interpretations." This fourfold hermeneutic is sometimes condensed into a "double hermeneutic" (Preucel and Hodder 1996: 13) and other times is referred to as a "hermeneutic spiral" (Shanks and Hodder 1998: 82). Regardless of the specific terminology, hermeneutic analysis is concerned with both searching for patterns in past contexts and considering the impact of research prejudice and prejudgments in the quest for meaning.

Knowledge of the Maya collapse and, by extension, interpretations of the Maya Terminal Classic and Postclassic periods has been conditioned by the social context in which it has been constructed, and compounded by attempts to view the Postclassic Maya from a Classic-period Maya perspective. For the most part, perceptions of the Postclassic Maya were set prior to substantial excavation of late Maya sites. Long-term work at Classic-period sites, such as Copán and Palenque, began prior to the onset of the twentieth century. In contrast, large-scale, long-term excavations of Postclassic sites were unheard of until the Carnegie Institution of Washington's work at Mayapan in the 1950s (Pollock et al. 1962) and were not common until the last twenty-five years (D. Chase and A. Chase 1988; Pendergast 1981a; P. Rice and D. Rice 1985). Without a solid body of excavation data, interpretations of the late Maya were largely limited to the above-mentioned contrasts with the Classic period and to applications of statements found in historical writings. For example, certain commonly quoted ethnohistoric statements, such as those suggesting that the Maya maintained numerous "idols" (e.g., Tozzer 1941: 11), have led to views of late Maya religion as being nonunified. However, many of these descriptions may themselves have been conditioned not only by the sixteenth-century European—as opposed to Maya—mind-frame of the writers, but also by the way in which the information was gathered from local Maya; it has been suggested that in some cases Maya respondents were tortured as a means of generating "complete" responses (Tedlock 1993). The research preferences of individual scholars also may have played a role in negative characterizations of the Postclassic Maya; this seems implicit in Shook's (1990: 252) retrospective lamentation that the final Carnegie Project could not work on "early material and big sites," but was instead relegated "to rock piles in Mayapan!" One must also consider the frame of reference or meaning for the ancient and modern Maya, the social settings of both contemporary and earlier archaeologists, as well as the ethnographic skills of sixteenth-century European writers (who evince many of the same problems with ethnographic interpretation that have been identified for modern ethnographers [Tedlock 1991]). Thus, there is clearly a double (Preucel and Hodder 1996: 13) and/or quadruple hermeneutic (Shanks and Hodder 1998: 76) involved in archaeological interpretation of the ancient Maya of the Postclassic era.

In spite of continued scholarly work and new interpretations concerning the Postclassic Maya (D. Chase and A. Chase 1988; A. Chase and P. Rice 1985; Sabloff and Andrews 1986b), *popular* interpretations of Postclassic Maya society often continue to reflect models from earlier writings (Coe 1993; Gallenkamp 1985), following the early Greco-Roman comparison used by Proskouriakoff

(1955) in which the term "Postclassic" was applied in a developmental sense indicating the fall from a "Classic" age. But, how could this still be the case? Answering this question requires a review of literature on the collapse itself.

THE CLASSIC MAYA COLLAPSE

The "Classic Maya collapse," correlated by many with the Terminal Classic period, was once thought to be a very rapid event occurring throughout the southern Maya lowlands from roughly A.D. 830 to 889 (Culbert 1988: 74; Morley 1946; Sharer 1993; Thompson 1954, 1970). The perception of a rapid and sudden collapse was closely tied to epigraphic interpretation in which dates for the collapse were derived from a cessation of Maya hieroglyphic history on stone stelae and altars (Lowe 1985). Within this interpretive context, the collapse also became correlated with the widespread cessation of monumental architectural construction, a decline in the use of elaborate tombs, and large-scale site abandonment (Culbert 1988). Frequently associated with this view of the Maya collapse is a conjoined idea of cultural decay or decline that occurred in conjunction with drastic change (Adams 1991; Thompson 1954).

Explanations for the collapse are numerous (Adams 1973b; Culbert 1988; Sharer 1977; Willey and Shimkin 1973) and varied. Single and combined explanations include demographic and ecological stresses, natural disasters, internal social change and/or upheaval, foreign intrusion, and warfare. But this great diversity of explanations has often been subsumed within a paradigm of a relatively rapid and catastrophic end to Classic Maya society. Becker (1979) once related Thompson's popular interpretations of the Maya collapse (which still form the dominant paradigm in Maya studies) to a romanticized Western view of the Russian Revolution (cf. Marcus 1982). Other modern events have been used to recast and interpret the Maya collapse. When Guatemala endured a massive earthquake in 1976, such natural disasters were resurrected as triggers for a sudden collapse (Bevan and Sharer 1983; see also Mackie 1961). More recently, analysis of Yucatán lake sediments has been used to return to a consideration of drought as a potential trigger for the Maya collapse (Sabloff 1995).

Although catastrophic events may have played a part in the "Classic Maya collapse," scholars researching the Maya have shown that the "collapse" was neither simultaneous nor uniform (Chase and Rice 1985; Marcus 1995). Hieroglyphic texts carved in stone ceased to be erected at various times at southern lowland sites (A.D. 761 at Dos Pilas [Houston 1993; Demarest 1993], A.D. 859 at Caracol [Houston 1987c], A.D. 869 at Tikal [Jones and Satterthwaite 1982], A.D. 889 at Seibal and Xultún [Sharer 1993], and A.D. 909 at Toniná [Sharer 1993]). The loss of texts was not sudden; it instead covered a span of 148 years. At many sites, furthermore, populations continued well beyond the last dated monuments, often for several hundred years, such as at Copán (Webster and Freter 1990b) and Caracol (D. and A. Chase 1996). Thus, the once cataclysmic "Maya collapse" actually spanned several centuries. And, while stone monument erection with attendant Long Count dates was no longer common in the Maya lowlands, some lowland Maya continued to use the Long Count system on Classic-period monuments dating to the ninth and tenth centuries (Tedlock 1992).[2]

It is perhaps even more important to note that not all parts of Maya culture were transformed in unison, or even in conjunction, with the "collapse" and/or the cessation of monument erection. Some aspects of Maya culture changed well before and some well after A.D. 900. Perhaps most significant, many of the changes once believed to correlate exclusively with the onset of the Postclassic period (specifically many of those cited by Thompson [1954, 1970] that form the heart of the popular paradigm) can now be seen to have had their origins substantially earlier in the Classic period. This is true not only for some of the more mundane aspects of Maya material culture, such as construction techniques, but also for more aesthetic Maya ceremonialism, evident in ritual caching practices. A re-evaluation of the continuities and disjunctions between the Maya Classic and Postclassic periods is key, then, to understanding and reconstituting an interpretive frame for the Classic Maya collapse and the continuation and evolution of Maya culture.

VIEWS OF CHANGE IN THE ARCHAEOLOGICAL RECORD

Archaeological interpretations of culture change are of necessity based in considerations of change in material culture, combined with written materials when these are available. Although few archaeologists or anthropologists would argue that the initial appearance of a single artifact—in and of itself—indicates change in an entire culture, cumulative or conjoined changes are often thought to coincide with cultural transformations. But, there are no hard or fast rules to guide the precise correlation of material change with social or cultural behaviors. Thus, a consideration of hermeneutics is also key in considerations of culture change. This is particularly true for Maya Terminal Classic material remains, as these are easily viewed comparatively from both earlier and later perspectives. Differences of opinion on the inevitability of collapse also may be based in semantics as easily as in historic or archaeological data, especially because the term "cultural collapse" enjoys a variety of meanings ranging from the total death of a civilization to institutional restructuring (e.g., Erasmus 1963; Yoffee 1988: 15). However, just as the complete death of a civilization is a rarity in the archaeological record, so too is total disjunction between one time period and the next. More usually, distinct artifact types and classes are seen as varying and changing at different times and rates. In cases where near total disjunctions in material culture are initially posited, later work may reveal greater continuities than previously thought.

TIME AND SPACE SYSTEMATICS AND THE ROLE OF NORTHERN BELIZE

Part of our constructed archaeological reality with regard to the Terminal Classic period is the result of a series of early culture-historical perceptions and interpretations. Most importantly, Chichen Itza in the northern lowlands (though now known to date to the Terminal Classic) was initially thought to postdate the Classic-period occupation in the southern Maya lowlands. Although some early researchers commented on this distinctive temporal placement (Pollock 1965), Chichen Itza was viewed as an Early Postclassic site (Tozzer 1957). Thus, initial views of the Terminal Classic in the Maya lowlands largely derived either from discoveries of the latest remains at Classic-period sites in central Petén or from attempts to move backward in time from the Postclassic northern lowlands using the direct historical approach. Almost by default, the Terminal Classic period became an analytical construct focused on specific artifacts and material traits rather than on any complete archaeological assemblage that could be either processually or contextually situated.

The Terminal Classic period has proved difficult to identify until relatively recently. Southern lowland Postclassic material remains were not successfully isolated from Classic remains until the late 1960s and early 1970s (Adams and Trik 1961; Bullard 1970, 1973; Sharer and Chase 1976) in spite of work at Tayasal by Guthe in the 1920s (A. Chase 1990; A. Chase and D. Chase 1985). By this time, an established paradigm of "collapse" had already been set in place (Morley and Brainerd 1956; Thompson 1954). In the northern lowlands there was an early focus on the Postclassic (Berlin 1953; Sanders 1960; Pollock et al. 1962), but the temporal frame of reference was dominated by iconographic and ethnohistoric interpretation relating to the Postclassic "Mexicanization" of Chichen Itza and the Yucatán peninsula (Tozzer 1957) derived largely from the native Maya histories known as the books of "Chilam Balams" (Roys 1933); these materials overshadowed any archaeologically established frameworks (A. Chase 1986; Lincoln 1986) and were used to establish the culture history. In fact, time and space systematics for the Terminal Classic in both the northern and southern lowlands were extremely varied and problematic (Ball 1979a; A. Chase and D. Chase 1985).

Archaeological work in northern Belize during the 1970s began to change the disjunctive perspective by squarely situating the Terminal Classic within viable, vibrant, and continuous contexts. At this time, in spite of substantial research in the country (especially by Pendergast [1969, 1970a, 1971] and Hammond [1975, 1983]), Belize was considered to be a "cultural backwater" for Maya studies (Hammond 1981). The ceramics from northern Belize did not match those known from the southern lowlands (Adams 1971; Culbert 1993a; Sabloff 1975a; R. Smith 1955), from the northern lowlands (Brainerd 1958; R. Smith 1971), or even from farther south in Belize (Thompson 1939; Gifford 1976), thus lending themselves to independent analytical sequencing (Pendergast 1970a). Even within the analytical constraints of a type-variety approach (A. Chase 1994), at minimum four distinct ceramic traditions were recognized in the relatively small area of northern Belize during the Late Classic (Pring 1976). Postclassic materials, however, were widespread within this region (Gann 1900; Sidrys 1983). How then were these various Late Classic and Postclassic complexes integrated in time and space?

Eventually, the space-time systematics in northern Belize proved crucial for aligning diverse regional sequences found in the northern and southern lowlands (D. Chase and A. Chase 1982, 1988). There are a number of reasons for this. Northern Belize proved to be an area with a great variety of inter-regional contacts over time (D. Chase 1981, 1984, 1985a; D. Chase and A. Chase 1989; Hammond 1991; Pring 1976; Robertson 1983), especially during the Terminal Classic (D. Chase and A. Chase 1982). There was also an early concern with "contextual" analysis in the archaeology of northern Belize, especially as represented in the work of David Pendergast (1979, 1981a, 1982, 1990a) at Altun Ha and Lamanai. And, unlike central Petén, there were clear continuities in ceramic traditions from the Terminal Classic into the Postclassic—to the point where it sometimes can be difficult to distinguish time periods (Pendergast 1986a; Graham 1987b). Thus, there was no recognized disjunction in northern Belize. Instead, the archaeological focus shifted to looking at temporal continuities within discrete contexts.

Work at Nohmul, undertaken by us in 1978 and 1979 (and subsequently amplified [Hammond et al. 1985]), also was crucial in establishing a contextual, rather than analytical, typology for both ceramics (D. Chase 1982a) and other remains (D. Chase 1982b). Excavations at Nohmul Structures 9 and 20 provided both architectural and ceramic data that helped correlate northern and southern sequences. Primary refuse associated with Structure 20 permitted the linking of San Jose V materials (Thompson 1939) with a variety of northern lowland slate wares and also *molcajetes* (D. Chase 1982a). Architectural associations with these ceramic materials also helped place the bulk of "Mexican" Chichen Itza architecture into the Terminal Classic (D. Chase and A. Chase 1982)—at the same time strongly supporting what was called an "overlap" model for the northern lowlands in which the Puuc sites and Chichen Itza were seen as being coeval (Ball 1979a). At the time, the placement of Chichen Itza squarely into the Terminal Classic period was a relatively novel idea, but one that is now commonly accepted based on a reinterpretation of data largely deriving from Chichen Itza (Andrews 1990; Cobos, Chapter 22, this volume; Lincoln 1986; Schele and Freidel 1990). These spatio-temporal realignments also had implications for the Terminal Classic events and processes that engulfed the southern lowlands (A. Chase 1985b; D. Chase and A. Chase 1982; Kowalski 1989), but the full linkages still have not been worked out or fully explored.

CONTINUITIES IN CLASSIC TO POSTCLASSIC MATERIAL CULTURE

In the Maya area, Classic-period monumentality once was thought to represent a nearly total departure from the architecture of the preceding Preclassic period; however these ideas now have been almost completely overturned (Hammond

1985). Architectural complexes once thought to be hallmarks of the Early Classic period, such as E Groups, are now known to have their origins much earlier in the Middle Preclassic period (A. Chase 1985a; Laporte and Fialko 1995; Chase and Chase 1995; Hansen 1992). Likewise ceramics are no longer viewed as totally disjunctive between these two periods; both forms and slips crosscut any previously perceived boundary (Brady et al. 1998; Lincoln 1985). The Maya Preclassic to Classic ceramic traditions are linked. A similar situation can be suggested to exist for the transition between the Classic and the Postclassic periods. Not only is the "collapse" both variable and long-lived, but any changes that occurred in Maya material culture can now be seen as more complex and less disjunctive than a simple Classic-Postclassic dichotomy would suggest. Perhaps the best example of this may be seen in the one class of material culture thought to be among the most sensitive to change—ceramics. At Maya sites where occupation continues smoothly into the Postclassic period, it has proved nearly impossible for researchers to distinguish between Terminal Classic and Early Postclassic pottery, prompting a number of researchers to identify a large group of ceramics as "Terminal Classic-Early Postclassic" (Pendergast 1986a; Graham 1987b; D. Chase and A. Chase 1988).

Postclassic architecture often has been viewed as very distinctive from the preceding Classic period (Thompson 1954; Pollock et al. 1962). However, it is possible to view Postclassic construction techniques as continuations of trends that also were evident during the Maya Classic period. One hallmark of Postclassic architecture has been the occurrence of low "line-of-stone" buildings, constructions consisting primarily of foundations or base-walls for perishable edifices. Such buildings are observed initially only by flattened areas of soil and are sometimes included within so-called "vacant terrain" constructions (Bronson 1966; D. Chase 1990; Pyburn 1990). However, low constructions are not an innovation of the late Maya, but rather were made by the early Maya as well (Webster and Gonlin 1988; Willey et al. 1965). Line-of-stone buildings, in fact, characterize the majority of non-epicentral residences at many sites during the Classic period. For instance, at Caracol, Belize, fewer than 20 percent of buildings outside the site epicenter were vaulted and most of these are located in or near Caracol's administrative causeway termini; the vast majority of residential group structures consist of "line-of-stone" and/or "base-wall" constructions (although many are on raised foundations). Likewise, other construction techniques frequently found at Postclassic sites, such as upright stone facings, also have antecedents earlier in the Late Classic at Caracol.

Postclassic architecture has been called "shabby" (Thompson 1954) in contrast to that of the preceding Classic period. Some scholars (Sabloff and Rathje 1975a) have suggested that "reduced-time" modifications in construction techniques were intentionally used as cost-saving measures. However, "shabby" construction techniques and "reduced-cost construction," which included the application of a thick slather of stucco over poorly constructed walls (for surface beautification), are not Postclassic inventions. At Caracol, Belize, Late Preclassic and Early Classic buildings are exceedingly well bedded, bonded, and constructed; intact examples of this early architecture still stand after nearly two thousand years. In contrast, Late Classic Caracol buildings are less solidly constructed and are rarely found intact; fully half of all Late Classic building walls have collapsed and fallen off the backs and sides of pyramids because of construction techniques that did not focus on long-term permanence. Thus, Postclassic architecture is simply the culmination of a long tradition of construction changes.

This is not to say that there are no distinctions between Classic and Postclassic material culture. There are differences. For example: Postclassic architecture is generally less massive than that found in the Classic period; small arrow points are far more common in the Postclassic than in earlier eras; and decorative techniques used on Postclassic pottery may include more modeling and post-fire painting. However, much of Postclassic material culture may be seen as comprising modifications and logical outgrowths of Classic-period precedents. And, in some cases, patterns previously thought to be Postclassic "innovations" can be shown to be in evidence much earlier in the Classic period.

THE CHANGING ROLE OF MAYA WARFARE

Proskouriakoff (1955) contrasted a militant Postclassic Maya era with a serene and peaceful earlier Classic age. Since her 1955 work, substantial research conducted on the Classic and Postclassic Maya suggests that any simple dichotomous distinctions in warfare activity between Classic and Postclassic Maya peoples are inappropriate. Hieroglyphic texts make reference to battles, wars, and the taking of captives and cities long before the end of the Classic period. The earliest "star-war," dating to the sixth century, is known from Caracol, Belize, and foreshadows more than three centuries of frequent and hieroglyphically documented warfare (Webster 1977, 1993, 2000; Schele and Miller 1986: 209–210; A. Chase and D. Chase 1989, 1998a; D. Chase and A. Chase 2002; Chase, Grube, and Chase 1991). Archaeological evidence may be used to illustrate shifts in the technology and tactics of warfare, especially during the Late and Terminal Classic (A. Chase and D. Chase 1989; D. Chase and A. Chase 1992; Demarest 1993; Hassig 1992). Even later, Maya warfare during the Postclassic underwent yet another shift in tactics and weapons (Hassig 1992).

It is true, however, that by the very end of the Classic period, activities and relationships throughout the Maya lowlands appear to have been changing. This may be seen in the Terminal Classic iconography of both the northern and southern lowlands. Burning and sacking of towns is visible in murals at Chichen Itza, Mexico. There are also increased indications of human sacrifice. A platform just outside the ballcourt at this site depicts layers of human skulls, implying a similarity to later Aztec *tzompantli*, or skull racks. Such a skull platform is also known from Classic-era Copán, and less elaborate versions surely existed at other sites. Art relating to war events in the northern lowlands—especially at Chichen Itza—portrayed a great many participants (Krochock 1988; Wren and Schmidt 1991), perhaps related to a suggested emergence of warrior societies or military orders at this time (Thompson 1943, 1970: 328). Southern lowland sites are similarly replete with increased and changed warfare imagery, which appears on both ceramics and monuments (Chase, Grube, and Chase 1991). Throughout the lowlands a change in weaponry occurred toward the end of the Late Classic. Atlatl became the weapon of choice. Although previously known to the Maya (e.g., Early Classic Stela 31 at Tikal), the atlatl does not appear to have been heavily employed by the Maya until the Terminal Classic period, when it became a prominent weapon in both the iconography (Hassig 1992: 178) and the archaeological record (D. Chase and A. Chase 1992; Coe 1965a; Sabloff and Rathje 1975a: 76). Evidence of aggression is also visible in the construction of Terminal Classic fortifications in both the northern and southern lowlands (Dahlin 2000; Demarest 1993; Demarest et al. 1997; Webster 1977, 1979). Within these changing venues, we have suggested that the Terminal Classic Maya were increasingly concerned with regional territorial control and that some polities (such as Chichen Itza) may have been attempting to create large-scale empires (D. Chase and A. Chase 1982, 1992). Thus, the concern with warfare seen in Postclassic Maya society developed from long-standing Maya cultural traditions.

INDIVIDUALIZED WORSHIP AND
THE BREAKDOWN OF ORGANIZED RELIGION

In contrast to the highly organized state religion often attributed to the Classic Maya (Thompson 1950, 1954, 1970), Postclassic Maya religion has been portrayed as having broken down into a system of privatized or individualized worship (Proskouriakoff 1955; Freidel and Sabloff 1984). Ethnohistoric support for a system of dispersed worship has been derived from accounts such as those of Bishop Landa, who describes the existence of numerous idols in Maya houses (Tozzer 1941: 110). Archaeological evidence that has been used to bolster this view of Postclassic religion are the broken pieces of incense burners found throughout Postclassic sites and the widespread distribution of caches and presumed household shrines in residential groups (Pollock et al. 1962, but cf. D. Chase 1992). Proskouriakoff's (1955, 1962) interpretation of these phenomena was that the Postclassic Maya had a plethora of gods, a marked departure from the Classic period, which she viewed as having a single dominant deity (following Thompson's 1954 and 1970 conceptions of Itzamna). In more recent literature, the widespread distribution of Postclassic incense burners has sometimes also been taken to suggest a decentralization of Maya religious practices within a still extant state system (Sabloff and Rathje 1975a; Andrews 1993: 59).

That these bodies of data indicate the breakdown and privatization of late Maya religion is not at all clear. The ethnohistoric evidence itself is not without ambiguity; Dennis Tedlock (1993: 145–146), for example, has pointed out that descriptions of numerous idols in early historic "confessions" may have been exaggerated in response to fear of torture. Postclassic cache and censer deposition patterns have also been viewed as reflecting organized rituals centered on the calendar year rather than as reflecting a fragmented society characterized by dispersed individualized worship (D. Chase 1985a, 1985b). Differences between Classic and Postclassic religion, however, do exist. Data from Postclassic Santa Rita Corozal, Belize, suggest that Maya religion was characterized by a trend toward broadening and popularizing the extant symbolism of the Classic period, something particularly evident in Postclassic caches (D. Chase 1988; D. Chase and A. Chase 1998). From our perspective, Postclassic Maya religion was broad-based and had a large constituency. Nearly identical offerings were made at distant sites, as can be seen in cached deposits at Mayapán in Yucatán and Santa Rita Corozal in northern Belize (D. Chase 1986); intriguingly, both sites also are thought to have been the governing seats of distinctive regional political units. To some extent these Postclassic cache similarities may be viewed as comparable to the similarities in Classic-period caches found at separate Classic-period sites like Tikal and Piedras Negras in Guatemala (Coe 1959). But, there are significant differences. Although residential caches are found in some Classic sites, they usually comprise different items than those found in caches associated with Classic-era nonresidential monumental architecture (for example, compare Culbert 1993a with Coe 1990 and Becker 1999). Similar Postclassic caches can be found both in central locations and throughout residential units.

Regardless of whether or not the characterization of dispersed ritual reflects Late Postclassic society, the basic archaeological patterns upon which these interpretations are made—specifically the widespread distribution of caches, incense burners, and shrines—are found not only in the Postclassic period, but are also common among certain Classic-period Maya sites. Late Classic residential-group caches are ubiquitous at Caracol and form a very distinctive pattern. Caches with modeled and appliqued faces and small lip-to-lip bowls containing human finger bones are found in the eastern structure in the majority of groups that have been tested (D. Chase and A. Chase 1998). Censerware is found throughout the Late Classic settlement and is not restricted to the Caracol site epicenter (A. Chase and D. Chase 1996d). Specialized shrines also occur in many Classic-era residential groups at Caracol and elsewhere (Becker 1982; Leventhal 1983, Tourtellot 1983: 47; A. Chase and D. Chase 1994b). Thus, practices presumed to be uniquely Postclassic actually have antecedents much farther back in the Classic period. And, continuity, rather than disjunction, may be found between the Classic and Postclassic patterns. Indeed, as indicated above, if a shift from centralized to dispersed ritual practices may be discerned in the archaeological record, it occurred prior to A.D. 600 at sites like Caracol.

TRADE, EXTERNAL TIES, AND UPWARD MOBILITY

It has been suggested that the Postclassic Maya may have been "pragmatic mercantilists" (Sabloff and Rathje 1975a: 79) with an ascending merchant class who perfected masonry false-fronts on buildings, employed mass-production methods in pottery production, and conducted extensive long-distance trade. The Late Postclassic Maya also have been projected as being more cosmopolitan in their external ties; this is particularly visible in their somewhat more uniform art styles (Robertson 1970). Evidence for an extremely wide distribution of similar or identical material remains—including ceramics (Plumbate: Shepard 1948), lithics (tanged points: Rovner 1975), art (Mixteca-Puebla: Nicholson 1960), and architectural styles (plaza plans: Rice 1986; Rice and Rice 1985; Tourtellot, Sabloff, and Carmean 1992)—in and following the Terminal Classic, ethnohistoric descriptions of traders (Roys 1957; Sabloff 1977), and comparisons to the dendritic Aztec economic system (Hassig 1985; Santley 1994) have all led to suggestions that both upward mobility and a cosmopolitan outlook were made possible among the Postclassic Maya by an increased emphasis on trade.

Cozumel may have had a focus on trade that was more pronounced than anything that existed in the Classic period (Freidel and Sabloff 1984; Sabloff and Rathje 1975a, 1975b). Yet it is clear that the Maya had a long history of involvement in trade. Studies indicate that even the Preclassic Maya were active traders (Cobos 1994; Hammond 1976; Sidrys 1976). Stackable vessels and standardized vessel forms, thought to be indicative of mass production during the Postclassic era (Sabloff and Rathje 1975a), also can be considered as a hallmark of the Late Preclassic (labial flanged bowls) and Late Classic (ring-based plates) Maya lowlands. Throughout the lowlands during the Early Classic period, contact was maintained and trade goods obtained from distant areas such as the Guatemalan and Mexican highlands (Ball 1974a, 1983b; Coe 1967; Pendergast 1970b). Thus, the Postclassic era is not the only Maya time-span that may have focused on trade and mass production.

Arguments about trade and economics are integral to considerations of Mesoamerican social complexity. Sanders (1992: 291) has noted that "only within a large mercantile class and its related economic elements, the *tlameme* and elite craft specialists who processed the raw products brought by the merchants, could a significant, well-defined middle class emerge in setting as energetically and technologically limited as Prehispanic Mesoamerica." Research at large Maya sites like Caracol (A. Chase 1992; A. Chase and D. Chase 1987a, 1996c; D. Chase and A. Chase 1994), Dzibilchaltun (Kurjack 1974; Andrews IV and Andrews V 1980), and Tikal (Haviland and Moholy-Nagy 1992) have produced archaeological data suggesting that such a level of institutional complexity was, in fact, met during the Late Classic era.

Various archaeological data indicate the growth of a middle social level beginning minimally in the early part of the Late Classic period. Investigations at Caracol, Belize, indicate that most residential groups were engaged in the manufacture of items for trade. These same data demonstrate that material well-being and upward mobility were widespread during the Late Classic period (A. Chase 1992; Chase and Chase 1996b). Tombs, polychrome pottery, marine shell, jadeite, and other ritual items were found throughout the excavations at Caracol (D. Chase 1988; A. and D. Chase 1994b, 1996d; D. Chase and A. Chase 1996). Dental inlays, sometimes thought to be indicative of status (Krecji and Culbert 1995), are also relatively widespread (D. Chase 1994: 131–132). Even hieroglyphic texts—at least the portable ones—were apparently shared by non-elite individuals; in fact, portable artifacts with hieroglyphic texts have been found largely in non-elite contexts at Caracol. The widespread distribution of all these items is indicative of a highly integrated economic system at Caracol.

Sabloff and Rathje (1975b: 19–20) argued that effective internal communication combined with a homogenized artifactual assemblage and a centralized bureaucracy characterized Cozumel Island as a trading center during the Postclassic era. In actuality, what they defined is consistent with an administered economic system (e.g., C. Smith 1974, 1976b) where distribution is controlled by a central elite or bureaucracy. It is also consistent with archaeological data from Caracol that have been used to argue for an administered economic system (A. Chase 1998). Caracol's radiating causeways not only served as passage routes for the site's population, but also, in conjunction with the causeway termini, as a framework for distributing goods throughout the city (A. Chase and D. Chase 1996a, 1996c). Thus, the emergence of internally complex economic institutions and of a middle socioeconomic level, once argued to mark only Postclassic society, as typified by the Aztec (Sanders 1992), appears to have occurred among the Late Classic Maya and is another indication of cultural continuity between the Classic and Postclassic periods. Regardless of whether the discussion revolves around trade, mass production, status levels, economic systems, or upward mobility, antecedents to Late Postclassic Maya patterns may be discerned in the earlier Classic period.

LINKING THE CLASSIC AND POSTCLASSIC

Viewing the Terminal Classic–period Maya from multiple perspectives and with a concern for hermeneutics helps make understandable heretofore undiscernible or controversial areas of Maya culture. Moreover, such analyses help make the Postclassic Maya appear substantially less unique and the "collapse" even less uniform.

The Postclassic Maya maintained some aspects of Classicism and modified others. The texts on Classic stelae and altars recorded predominantly political activity, neglecting other aspects of culture and history. Yet the extant Postclassic Maya codices indicate that Classic-era writing must have been used to record a much wider range of more practical information. None of the known Maya codices bear close resemblance to Classic monuments, as none record dynastic history. However (and contrary to popular belief), Long Count notation continued long after the ninth century in the lowlands (Tedlock 1992: 247–248). The very striking examples of Postclassic art—innovative work that stressed different media than those generally favored in earlier eras—indicate that a vibrant culture still existed (D. Chase 1981; Pendergast 1986a). Postclassic Maya religion continued to have both pan-Maya symbolism and household distribution of ritual items (seen in the Classic period). Widespread Postclassic caching practices (D. and A. Chase 1998) can be seen as an attempt to involve more people in the detailed aspects of religious activity and have Late Classic precursors. In general, trends begun in the Late Classic period continued with greater emphasis in the Postclassic; mass-production techniques were used (especially with regard to ceramics) and internally complex economic institutions were established. Upward mobility was also apparently an option in the Classic era and is not restricted solely to the Postclassic.

All this is not to deny that discontinuities existed between the Classic and Postclassic eras. Populations moved away from many of the old cities to areas where important resources—especially water—were more readily available. Residential groups became less visible and were seemingly not as evenly dispersed over the landscape as were their Classic counterparts; rather, Postclassic house groups were densely "clustered" into what appear to be numerous small towns. Architectural constructions also involved less intensive building techniques in combination with exterior adornment of building facades in more perishable plaster and paint, building modes (with origins much earlier in the Classic period) that were certainly not inappropriate for an established society (see also Andrews 1993: 58–59).

Situating Terminal Classic events and activities within a continuous, rather than disjunctive, frame of reference sheds additional light on the Classic to Postclassic transition. Information pertaining to eighth- and ninth-century events in the Maya lowlands is suggestive of factors that were important to the Maya of the Terminal Classic. Many sites do show evidence of both increased warfare and alliances (A. Chase 1985b; D. and A. Chase 1992). Stone monuments portray warriors, exhibit captives, and tell of battles as well as of alliances (Grube 1994a). Like the late monuments, molded-carved pottery also shows both bound captives and scenes of alliance. Terminal Classic murals depict warriors and battles. Some lowland sites show evidence of fortification. Although there may have been rapid abandonment of the epicentral locations at some sites, there is also increasing evidence for continued occupation of certain outlying areas. Terminal Classic trade routes survived into the Postclassic and so apparently did many elite. We believe that there were significant political changes in Maya society at the end of the Classic period, but that these alterations merely reinforced cultural variations and traditions put into place centuries earlier.

Was the transition from the Classic to Postclassic really a devolution? Does it represent the "fall" or "collapse" of a formerly great civilization? We think not. More than any other point in Maya prehistory, the Classic to Postclassic transition requires hermeneutic considerations to illuminate understanding of this transformation. What is seen in Postclassic society is the continued adaptation of the Maya to a shifting reality (e.g., Rathje 1975). This adaptation generally followed traditionally established Maya patterns, but with modifications conditioned by social and political events that link the Classic and Postclassic periods. Importantly, many of the culture changes generally associated solely with the Postclassic in past literature and interpretive frames (summarized in Chase and Rice 1985)— the appearance of a middle status level, privatization of worship, pragmatic mercantilism, and expansive warfare—had their roots squarely in the preceding Classic period. Thus, the basic developmental trends toward Postclassic lifeways were already in place well prior to the Terminal Classic. The Postclassic Maya cultural transition was not solely the result of a specific, or a series of specific, disjunctive Terminal Classic events, whether cast in terms of warfare, climate change, or environmental degradation. Postclassic Maya and their cultures are not disjunctive with their Classic ancestors; they are the product of a long tradition of transformations, including those taking place during the minimally two-hundred-odd years of what was once termed the Maya "collapse."

NOTES

1. The utility of these features in characterizing even the Classic-period Maya is a point that can certainly be debated. Use of trait-lists obscures the variability in culture during all time horizons. Finely carved monuments do not occur at all Maya sites; they are conspicuously absent, for example, at the majority of Classic-period sites in northern Belize. Tall pyramids are now known to exist during the Preclassic period not only at El Mirador, but also at sites such as Caracol, where they are generally obscured by later construction activities. And, like Postclassic house pads (D. Chase 1990), much Classic-period occupation occurs in relatively low-lying residential constructions. Similar to the Postclassic, the absence of polychrome pottery in many Early Classic contexts has, in the past, led researchers to assume incorrectly that there was little or no occupation during this time (see A. and D. Chase 1995; Lincoln 1985). While tombs are thought to characterize Classic Maya society, they also occur in Postclassic contexts at Mayapán (Pollock et al. 1962) and Lamanai (Pendergast 1981a). Finally, Classic Maya centers also varied substantially in size from huge, densely populated cities to much smaller hamlets and centers.

2. Apparent cessation of monument erection is also not limited to the "collapse" but is found at other times in Maya prehistory. Some of these occasions are attributed to ancient monument destruction (such as at Tikal, presumably by Caracol [A. Chase 1991] or at Naranjo, presumably as a result of warfare [Houston 1991]) associated with political turbulence. In other situations a lack of stone monuments may be an inten-

tional act by an otherwise successful polity; for instance, we believe Caracol's Late Classic non-use of stone monuments must have been politically expedient (A. and D. Chase 1996c). In still other situations, the stone monument record may have been purposefully replaced with stucco building decoration, as at Copán (A. Chase 1985b).

ACKNOWLEDGMENTS

Parts of this paper derive from a presentation at the 94th Annual Meeting of the American Anthropological Association in Washington, D.C., in November 1995 entitled "Management Strategies and Cultural Change: The 7th Through 9th Centuries at Caracol, Belize," and from a presentation at the 61st Annual Meeting of the Society for American Archaeology in New Orleans during April 1996 entitled "Smoke and Mirrors: Before and After the Classic Maya Collapse." We hope that some of the constructive comments made by Pru Rice, Don Rice, and Arthur Demarest on an earlier version of this paper are included in the present version. Support and funding for the work synthesized in this paper has come from numerous sources. The University Museum of the University of Pennsylvania helped sponsor the Tayasal research and analysis (1977, 1979, 1982), originally undertaken by the museum in 1971. The Nohmul research was partially sponsored by Norman Hammond's Cuello Project (1978) and partially sponsored by our own Corozal Postclassic Project with funds from the University Museum and the Anthropology Department of the University of Pennsylvania (1979). Research at Santa Rita Corozal was first sponsored and funded with the assistance of Peter Conn, Robert Dyson, and Ward Goodenough of the University of Pennsylvania (1979, 1980, 1981, 1984) and the Explorers' Clubs of Philadelphia and New York, and then by National Science Foundation grants (BNS-8318531 and BNS-8509304) and private donations in 1984 and 1985. Work at Caracol from 1985 through 1999 has been sponsored by the University of Central Florida, the Miami Institute of Maya Studies, the Harry Frank Guggenheim Foundation, the National Science Foundation (BNS-8619996, SBR-9311773, SBR-9708637), the United States Agency for International Development, the government of Belize, the Dart Foundation, the Stans Foundation, the Foundation for the Advancement of Mesoamerican Studies, Inc., the Ahau Foundation, the Kislak Foundation, and extensive donations to the University of Central Florida Foundation, Inc.

3

TERMINAL CLASSIC-PERIOD LOWLAND CERAMICS

Prudence M. Rice and Donald W. Forsyth

he Terminal Classic period in the Maya lowlands was originally described and defined at the 1965 Maya Lowland Ceramic Conference, held in Guatemala City, Guatemala (Willey, Culbert, and Adams 1967). The basis of the definition was ceramic content, although overall the period was seen as reflecting the collapse or cessation of multiple kinds of cultural evidence in the southern lowland region. Nonetheless, pottery remains one of the most important archaeological markers for readily recognizing and periodizing such changes. At the time of the 1965 ceramic conference, detailed ceramic reports were available for only a few sites and discussion of key characteristics of ceramic chronologies was thus fairly limited. Most of the data presented at the conference were the personal observations of the archaeologists present: Richard E.W. Adams, E. Wyllys Andrews IV, William R. Coe, T. Patrick Culbert, James C. Gifford, Robert L. Rands, Jeremy A. Sabloff, Robert E. Smith, Bruce W. Warren, and Gordon R. Willey. Not long after that conference, when Rands prepared his chapter on ceramic chronologies for the 1970 School of American Research publication on the Maya collapse in the southern lowlands (Rands 1973a; Culbert 1973a), he was able to work with materials from only eight sites or areas: the Belize Valley, Trinidad/lower Usumacinta, Tikal, Uaxactún, Seibal, Altar de Sacrificios, Piedras Negras, and Palenque.

Participants in the 1965 conference highlighted important trends evident in Terminal Classic ceramic complexes. One such trend is that Tepeu 3 represented an intensification of the process toward increasing "divergence" and regionalization of ceramic complexes that began in Tepeu 1 and continued through Tepeu 2 (Willey, Culbert, and Adams 1967: 301). Another is an accelerated decline in the apparent quality and quantity of the polychrome painted decoration evident in Tepeu 1 to Tepeu 2 times (ibid.). Rands (1973a) later elaborated this point, noting that there were in Late and Terminal Classic times two lowland ceramic traditions: a polychrome tradition in the south-central area plus a fine paste tradition in the west, which gradually moved eastward.

These trends are pertinent primarily with reference to the southern lowlands and their ceramic complexes, however. In early summaries the complexes of the northern lowlands received only scanty attention. Fortunately, there has been a great deal more work at northern lowland sites in the past three decades, and a third lowland tradition—slate ware—clearly should be added to Rands's earlier list. Comparative study of ceramic complexes of both areas is now possible (with due caution), contributing to a clearer picture of Terminal Classic events throughout the lowlands.

INTEGRATIVE CONCEPTS

Over the years Maya archaeologists interested in ceramic systematics have occasionally attempted to compare contemporaneous assemblages using spatially larger integrative units than the site-specific ceramic complex. Such units recognize not merely similarities in typological and formal content of the complexes but permit their interpretation in broader socio-politico-economic terms. Among such comparative units are the concept of horizon, ceramic sphere, and a third, which might be called a ceramic "supercomplex."

Cultural Horizons

In the 1965 lowland ceramic conference the Terminal Classic was identified as an archaeological "horizon." Although a horizon is typically characterized by a broad spatial, rather than long temporal, distribution of distinctive artifacts or styles (Phillips and Willey 1953: 625; Willey and Phillips 1955: 723, 1958: 38; Rice 1993b), the Terminal Classic was deemed to be a horizon because of the perception that the lowland Late Classic period ended everywhere throughout the lowlands with societal collapse.

The problem with this conceptualization is that it pertains to only a portion of the Maya lowlands, the south and central zones. In the northern lowlands, patterns of "classicism" varied regionally and changed at different times and in different ways than those of the south. The focus on the cessation of Classic traits in the southern region was primarily a result of several factors related to the vagaries of archaeological investigation and assumptions about the Maya area in general. By 1965, more research had been carried out, with more data available to researchers, concerning the southern and central zones than in the north or other areas peripheral to the southern region. Moreover, much of this work was done in the western region—the Usumacinta and Pasión River Valleys—where collapse *did* occur (Demarest, Chapter 6, this volume). In addition, the detailed research had been concentrated on a few relatively large sites that tended to draw a natural interest in the elements of elite classicism. Thus there was a general tendency to see the southern region as constituting the center or "core" of the Maya lowlands in a cultural, and not merely a geographical, sense. These factors plus others, such as a reliance on dated monuments and standing architecture for assessing occupation at most Maya sites, had led many researchers to see the termination of long-established Classic traits and behavior as a rapid and catastrophic process that affected the whole southern region more or less simultaneously. The horizon concept for Terminal Classic lowland ceramics may have been a valid one thirty years ago, but it certainly is not now.

Ceramic Spheres

One of the more useful comparative and integrative concepts in Maya ceramic studies is that of the ceramic "sphere." The sphere concept was originally developed and elaborated to permit correlation of ceramic complexes into horizons, in order to resolve questions of priority and contemporaneity (Willey, Culbert, and Adams 1967: 306). Its definition emphasized typological similarities and dissimilarities between ceramic complexes: a ceramic sphere "exists when two or more complexes share a majority of their most common types" and "makes possible the recognition of two degrees of content similarity: high . . . and little or no . . ." (ibid.). It follows, then, that the content of a ceramic sphere "is the sum total of all the types and modes of its member complexes. The diagnostic content of the sphere consists of those elements shared by all or some of the complexes upon which decisions about membership in a sphere are based" (Willey, Culbert, and Adams 1967: 307; basically, these "elements" constitute the "horizon markers"). The idea was that information on the total number of "elements" and the proportions of those that are shared, partially shared, and unique would be useful for studying the development and spread of ceramic traditions. Further, variations in spheres' areal extent could reveal the direction and intensity of culture contacts.

In contrast to its originally intended use, as a building block for defining horizons, the sphere concept has proven to be informative in and of itself. Spheres and their cultural inferences have been operationalized most effectively by Joseph Ball (1976) in his summary discussion of the pottery of Barton Ramie in the Belize River Valley in west-central Belize. Sphere identifications begin with recognition of diagnostic versus nondiagnostic (or general) ceramic types in the complexes in question. Diagnostic types are abundant and widely shared among the ceramic complexes that constitute a sphere, and a given type can be part of the content or affiliation of more than one sphere (Ball 1976: 324). Consequently "[C]eramic spheres essentially are *quantitatively* rather than *qualitatively* defined"; in other words, spheres are defined not by the mere presence of a particular type but by its abundant, shared presence in numerous complexes (ibid.). Thus it is not ceramic types or groups that have a sphere affiliation, but rather entire complexes. Finally, it is important to remember that ceramic spheres are "spatiotemporally dynamic rather than static constructs. . . . [they] should be expected to move, expand, and/or contract over the course of their existence" (ibid.).

Using what he called a "more or less arbitrary standard of judgment," Ball (1976: 323) created three categories of sphere membership (or exclusion) into which a given complex can be placed:

1. "Definite, full sphere membership" means that a complex has roughly 60 percent or greater content similarity (via either typological identification or the equivalent) between two complexes. It means that "a significant proportion of locally produced or imported, domestic utilitarian pottery (such as would include water-carrying and storage vessels, dry storage vessels, everyday service vessels for food preparation and presentation, and so on) as well as, or in contrast to, more specialized and rarer fine and/or ceremonial wares was common to the compared complexes."

2. "Peripheral sphere membership or exclusion" can occur when there is roughly 40–50 percent content similarity between two complexes. In this ambiguous situation, decisions about sphere membership depend on the subjective judgment of the analyst.

3. "Definite exclusion from a sphere" occurs if there is roughly 40 percent or less content similarity. As Ball notes, this circumstance demands careful attention, because it may reflect a variety of possible cultural situations, including importation of luxury, funerary, ceremonial, or specialized utilitarian pottery; reciprocal exchange; foreign intrusion; common derivation from an earlier shared tradition; and so forth.

The 1965 Guatemala City Maya ceramic conference participants identified, with very limited data, characteristics of southern lowland Terminal Classic pottery in terms of spheres, and many of their observations are still useful today. In particular, the conferees noted that the period reflected loss of the widespread "ceramic unity" evident in the preceding Late Classic period, particularly in its Tepeu ceramic sphere, and this gave way to

three separate spheres of limited areal extent. . . . A striking characteristic of all of the spheres is the drastic reduction or total disappearance of the tradition of polychrome painting . . . [and] a high degree of local differentiation after the disappearance of polychomes. . . . [This] 'ceramic disruption' . . . correlates . . . with the breakdown of the stela cult, monumental construction . . . [and] loss of cultural cohesiveness (Willey, Culbert, and Adams 1967: 311).

Ceramic "Supercomplexes"

A different but complementary picture comes from a recent synthesis of Terminal Classic ceramic continuity and change in the southern lowlands (Forsyth 1997, 1999). Donald Forsyth focused not so much on the elite polychromes that were the hallmark of the collapsing elites, but rather on the ordinary utilitarian pottery that would have been used by common people. In so doing, he identified a set of ceramics that he initially referred to as a "Petén Subcomplex." However, because the term "subcomplex" already has a different meaning and Forsyth's intent was integrative, this entity may be more appropriately termed a "super-complex." Thus the "Petén supercomplex" consists of three form classes: large bowls/basins, tripod dishes, and tall-necked jars, all usually red slipped and with fairly standardized but minimal decoration. These are found in the same types and sometimes varieties throughout Petén, from the Usumacinta to Río Azul, and even peripherally into northern Belize. However, they appear to be much less dominant in central Belize, where Terminal Classic complexes contain only some aspects of the Petén supercomplex (see below), while the northwestern area of the lower Usumacinta, from Piedras Negras northward, lacks it nearly entirely.

Forsyth divided this Petén supercomplex into two groups, a Western group and an Eastern group. The Western group covers the Pasión and middle Usumacinta regions, including the Petexbatun area, Seibal, Altar de Sacrificios, and perhaps as far north as Yaxchilán and southeast into the Mopán River basin. It is characterized by the types Subín Red and Chaquiste Impressed, and by Fine Orange and Fine Gray ceramic wares. The Eastern group of the Petén supercomplex comprises the Eznab sphere, best known from Tikal and Uaxactún and the various types of the Tinaja (red) ceramic group. In the central Petén lakes area, the Western and Eastern groups overlap, with types of the Western group more common at sites in the western lakes (e.g., around Lake Petén Itzá), while Eznab sphere types dominate to the east at Yaxhá.

Forsyth closed by noting that central Petén is unusual in the widespread homogeneity of its utilitarian wares, in contrast to their heterogeneity in the complexes of both the northwestern and eastern zones. This suggests to us some level of politico-economic integration operating in Petén but absent in surrounding areas; it also indicates a certain stability and continuity in production from Late Classic times into the Terminal Classic.

Static Concepts and Dynamic Change

The interpretive and inferential value of ceramic spheres and ceramic super-complexes has not been thoroughly explored by lowland Mayanist ceramicists to date and we do not attempt such a daunting task here. Instead, we attempt to summarize and describe the ceramic changes that mark the Late to Terminal Classic to Early Postclassic transition on a region-by-region basis.

We employ this approach for several reasons. For one, since archaeologists' earliest efforts at synthesis, the Late and Terminal Classic periods have been characterized ceramically as exhibiting change, or more specifically, increasing regionalization. In this context, it is worthwhile to consider the subject of ceramic change in general. Archaeologists have devoted substantial effort to understanding patterns of artifact change, particularly ceramic change, which has of course long been the basis for establishing chronologies. Chronology-building was also a major goal of the 1965 Maya Lowlands Ceramic Conference. But in the decades since that meeting was held, lowland chronologies have been better elaborated by means of more excavations, inscriptional data, and radiometric methods. Hence, it is time to look at Maya ceramic change with an eye toward its social, political, and economic contexts.

For study of change in lowland Maya ceramics during the Terminal Classic period, several studies are instructive. One is David Clarke's (1968) *Analytical Archaeology,* which focuses on analyzing and understanding variability in artifacts and artifact assemblages. Variability can be studied comparatively in many ways; when we study variability through time, we are addressing the topic of "change." Changes can be studied in terms of individual attributes of artifacts, which for analytical purposes may be characterized as key, essential, and inessential (compare with Ball's discussion of sphere diagnostics). Using an analogy with terms more familiar to Maya ceramicists, in the type-variety system we tend to identify technological attributes (paste and surface characteristics) as key variables at the ware level of analysis, while decorative techniques or motifs usually are inessential variables. However, at the type and variety levels (and also modally) decoration is often the key variable, while paste characteristics are far less discriminatory. At the same time, there are many different *kinds* of change:

> substitution of one element for another, addition of new elements, or subtraction of elements; change may mean a change in numbers or a change in kinds; or it may simply be an increase in variety, but without any fundamental alteration of the developmental course of the system. . . . Does change mean that something *new* or just something *different* occurs? Change . . . may be a difference in total variety (numbers of things) or morphogenetic (differences in kinds of things) (Rice 1984: 237–238).

Another useful perspective on ceramic continuity and change comes from study of archaeological pottery in ancient Nubia (Adams 1979). The researcher found no correlation between major political or religious transformations—new imperial rule and the introduction of Christianity—and stylistic changes in native wheel-made wares (see also Wright 1991 on Harappa). Earlier studies (e.g., Tschopik 1951; Charlton 1968) similarly had drawn attention to the apparent noncorrelation of societal and ceramic change, even in the contextual extremes of conquest and depopulation. Still other analyses (e.g., Reina 1963; Foster 1965) called attention to the presumed "conservatism" of traditional potters, especially in closed corporate communities, pointing to their reluctance to innovate in forms or styles, largely as a consequence of perceived social pressures to conform. All these observations are relevant to analysis of Terminal Classic pottery in the Maya lowlands, especially in the southern lowlands, given the prevailing sense of dramatic political and elite collapse accompanied by the disappearance of distinctive elite ceramics (certain polychromes) while utilitarian wares display continuities.

Against the background of these studies, we acknowledge that attempts to outline patterns of ceramic change in the lowland Maya Terminal Classic period carry a number of limitations. Our knowledge of the ceramic inventories of lowland regions is still spotty and there are enormous areas about which we have little or no information at all. Moreover, even in areas where such data are available, the quality and quantity vary considerably, from full-scale ceramic reports to little more than brief descriptive accounts of sequential complexes. With these caveats in mind, we nonetheless attempt such a comparative study of ceramic change, focusing on questions about what traditions were ended, what innovations were introduced, and what continuities can be discerned. For the sake of convenience, we organize our discussion around the archaeological "zones" defined by Culbert (1973b: 4–11).

SOUTHERN LOWLANDS

In general terms, the crucial questions posed in studies of pottery pertaining to the Terminal Classic period in the southern and central lowlands concern the nature of ceramic change and continuity during the region's sociopolitical "collapse." Questions relating to individual ceramic complexes are phrased in terms of continuities (or lack thereof) between Late Classic and Terminal Classic complexes, between and among contemporaneous sites in a region (essentially questions of sphere membership), and between Terminal Classic and Early Postclassic complexes.

Central Zone

The Central Zone of the southern Maya lowlands is the area of Forsyth's "Eastern (sub-)supercomplex," the home of the Eznab ceramic sphere. It was here—essentially the area of northeastern Petén, Guatemala—that the ceramic markers of the Terminal Classic were first defined, initially at Uaxactún and later at Tikal. Data of varying utility have subsequently become available from Calakmul, the Petén lakes region, and the El Mirador basin. This entire region manifests considerable continuity in its ceramic inventory from Late Classic through Terminal Classic times.

As originally understood, the transition from Tepeu 2 to Tepeu 3 in what might be thought of as the "central Central Zone," that is, the area of Tikal and Uaxactún, was characterized primarily by: (1) the disappearance or diminution of the polychrome tradition, both in terms of quantity and quality, especially human-figure polychromes; (2) the occurrence of small amounts of Altar Group Fine Orange (and some Fine Gray) pottery, or its local imitations; and (3) the addition of some new forms in the continuing red monochrome (Tinaja ceramic group) tradition that mimic those of some of the new fine paste ware forms (Smith 1955: Fig. 50a 10–13, b; Culbert 1973c: Fig. 13). Note, however, that the Tepeu 3 complex at Uaxactún was initially defined as a residuum, essentially the leftovers after Tepeu 1 and 2 materials were separated out (Smith 1955: 161).

Around the central Petén lake chain, south and east of Tikal/Uaxactún, Terminal Classic complexes are difficult to characterize. One reason is that they differ from Late Classic complexes primarily by a decline in the quality and quantity of the polychromes; also, fine paste wares and local imitations of fine paste shapes are quite rare. Another reason is that Terminal Classic complexes exhibit localized and also east-west clinal variability. For example, Terminal Classic pottery at Yaxhá and Topoxté, in the easternmost lake basins, is very similar to that of the Tikal/Uaxactún Eznab sphere, and Yaxhá's Tolobojo ceramic complex is a full member of the Eznab ceramic sphere (see Rice 1979; Hermes and Noriega 1998). Moving westward through the lakes zone, however, sites are only peripheral members of the Eznab sphere, as there is increasing presence of Boca sphere diagnostics characteristic of the Pasión region to the southwest (see below). These diagnostics include the types Subín Red, Chaquiste Impressed, and Pantano Impressed, and the ubiquitous large, incurved-rim bowl form that continues into the Postclassic. Also, around Lake Petén Itzá, polychromes are replaced by greatly reduced numbers of less elaborate polychromes, such as Lombriz Orange-polychrome (Adams 1971: 39; Chase and Chase 1983: 99; Forsyth, personal observation), while in the middle of the lake chain Jato Black-on-gray is particularly notable as funerary furniture (Rice 1987c).

Although it is often difficult to separate Late and Terminal Classic complexes in the lakes area, it also has proven difficult to separate Terminal Classic from Early Postclassic complexes at sites like Ixlú and Zacpetén. This is because the distinctive clays used for manufacturing Postclassic Paxcaman-group pottery—fine, silty, organic, lacustrine clays with snail inclusions—were used with Tinaja-like forms and slips, and frequently were tempered with volcanic ash, typical of Late Classic technology (Rice, personal observation). All this is suggestive of significant Classic to Postclassic continuities in the lakes area, in contrast to what was believed at the time of the 1965 Maya ceramic conference.

The site of Calakmul, lying on the northern edge of the Central Zone, had significant occupations during both Tepeu 2 and Tepeu 3 times. Ceramically, the site exhibits strong relations with those of the Central Zone, although sharing features with Río Bec and particularly the El Mirador basin in Calakmul's Late Classic Ku complex. In the Terminal Classic Halibé complex, the introduction of small quantities of slate ware suggests intensified interaction with the northern lowlands. However southern and western monochrome types (Subín, Chaquiste, Cameron) also make their appearance, as do small quantities of Fine Orange, Fine Gray, and imitations of these wares in the local monochromes. Calakmul is a full member of the Eznab sphere, with less than 1 to 2.1 percent of the complex representing pottery from areas other than Petén (Braswell et al., Chapter 9, this volume). As they note, Late Classic Calakmul participated in an "essentially Petén-focused interaction sphere," an intriguing observation given the wealth of epigraphic data interpreted as highlighting intense warfare between that site and Tikal.

In the northern portion of the Central Zone, the El Mirador basin so far has yielded no evidence of a significant Terminal Classic occupation, but the Tepeu 2 and very rare Tepeu 3 examples recovered (Forsyth 1989: 119ff) are more like those of the Tikal/Uaxactún area.

East of the Mirador Basin, at Río Azul, the Late Classic to Terminal Classic transition was apparently one of considerable change (Adams and Jackson-Adams 2000: 270). As at other Central Zone sites, it was marked by the appearance of small amounts of Fine Orange pottery, Tres Naciones group Fine Gray ware, and imitation Fine Orange. In addition, small amounts of Puuc Slate Ware and vessels influenced by northern lowlands styles also occurred. Many of the monochrome and unslipped types continued, however, sometimes in new varieties. Río Azul differs from other sites, nevertheless, in maintaining a strong polychrome production during the Terminal Classic, albeit with somewhat different varieties and styles from those of the Tepeu 2 horizon.

Belize Zone

Sites along the upper Belize River and some its tributaries have the longest history of ceramic research, although the data are of varying quality and comprehensiveness. The site of Benque Viejo, now known as Xunantunich, was excavated in the 1930s and reported by J. Eric S. Thompson (1940a), who analyzed the pottery by ware/form classification. William Bullard (1965) described only the whole or partial vessels from Baking Pot, but provided the type names and related information for Barton Ramie (see also Ricketson 1929) for the final type-variety analysis by James Gifford (1976). Ceramics from the Mopán-Macal Triangle Project, as well as the recent Xunantunich investigations, have been reported primarily in summary form (Ball 1993b: 255; LeCount 1992). At the site of Naranjo, across the border with Guatemala to the west, Marcus's collections suggest that the site shares numerous diagnostic types with the Belize Valley (Forsyth 1980: 75–79, 81).

The Belize Valley area is generally seen as highly diverse ceramically, differing typologically and modally from other southern lowland areas. By early Late Classic (Tiger Run = Tepeu 1) times, the ceramic inventory was distinct from other nearby areas, linked to Petén primarily by its polychromes. After about A.D. 700 west-central Belize had its own ceramic sphere, Spanish Lookout (Gifford 1976;

Ball 1976: 328), with the Spanish Lookout complex having early and late facets. The Terminal Classic period, represented by late-facet Spanish Lookout, is marked by the disappearance or marked reduction in locally produced polychromes and ash-tempered wares. In fact, most forms of decoration on vessel surfaces, common in the Late Classic, virtually disappear. Monochrome types of the carbonate-tempered Vaca Falls ceramic group, Roaring Creek Red and Mount Maloney Black (especially incurved-rim basins), characterize this late facet (Willey et al. 1965: 373; LeCount 1992: 135–136). The substantial problems in the published report of Barton Ramie ceramics—including the fact that Belize Red, the red-slipped ash-tempered group of the upper Belize Valley, is typologically and technologically identical to Tinaja Red in Petén—force us to question the existence of a distinct Spanish Lookout sphere and wonder whether these materials would be better considered peripheral Tepeu/Eznab. Regardless, the succeeding New Town (Early Postclassic) ceramic complex (Sharer and Chase 1976) in the Belize Valley, with the predominance of the red-slipped, carbonate-tempered Augustine ceramic group, constitutes a significant break with the previous complex, whatever its sphere affiliation.

At the large site of Caracol, south of the Belize Valley, it is difficult to know how to situate ceramics of the site's final Terminal Classic occupation. Most of the published pottery is from special deposits, primarily caches and mortuary contexts, and largely lacks type-variety classification and sphere identification (A. Chase 1994). The Late Classic ceramic assemblage, basically in place by A.D. 537, represents a "profound change" from the Early Classic complex. It appears to have strong ties to Tepeu, with "Holmul-style" red-on-cream polychromes, Belize/Tinaja Red, and other Petén gloss ware components (A. Chase 1994: 170). The most diagnostic Terminal Classic form is a small tripod bowl with in-slanting rim and oven-shaped feet, a form also present in the Eznab sphere in Tinaja/Belize Red type. Molded-carved decoration is known from both true Fine Orange and its imitations; cylindrical vessels typically show prisoner-presentation scenes (ibid.: 173). Unslipped wares occur in the same forms as those in central Petén (ibid.: 175).

In far southern Belize, the site of Lubaantun was occupied during the Late and Terminal Classic, roughly A.D. 700–890. Hammond (1975: 296) sees a "basic unity" in the pottery of the site and identified it as the Columbia ceramic complex, with early and late facets. The early facet is affiliated with the Tepeu sphere of central Petén and is characterized by the presence of gloss wares and cream-based polychromes, plus ash-tempered Belize/Tinaja Red. The late facet is primarily affiliated with the Boca sphere of the Pasión zone, but also has "strong links" with Eznab; it is characterized by the presence of Altar Fine Orange and reduced quantities of polychromes.

To the north of the Belize River, the San Jose/Lamanai region constitutes another ceramic subregion, more closely related to the Spanish Lookout sphere, perhaps, than to Tepeu, but probably still distinct from it (Graham 1987b; Thompson 1939). San Jose V differs from the preceding Tepeu 2-related San Jose IV complex by the virtual disappearance of polychromes and changes in vessel forms in red ware ceramics (see Graham 1987b: Fig. 2; Thompson 1939: Fig. 93), and by the addition of vessel forms and decorative techniques in local pottery that duplicate or are reminiscent of Fine Orange/Fine Gray pottery (Thompson 1939: Figs. 79a, 80b, 83–84). At Lamanai the Terminal Classic ceramic complex continues uninterrupted into the Early Postclassic (Graham 1987b; Pendergast 1985: 95).

In the far northern portion of Belize, the ceramic situation is complex as two, perhaps overlapping, patterns apparently occur here (D. Chase 1985b: 123). The northernmost of these, best known from Santa Rita Corozal and Nohmul, constitutes a significant change in the ceramic inventory (Chase 1987: 68) as evidenced by new ceramic complexes that extend into the Early Postclassic. That is, the major break seems to be between the Late Classic and the Terminal Classic periods in this region. Ceramically it is marked by distinctive regional ceramics—for example, the double-mouthed jar (Sidrys and Krowne 1983)—and by the appreciable occurrence of slate wares and trickle decoration related to the northern lowlands.

A very different situation seems to mark the region around Colhá. There the Late Classic to Terminal Classic Masson complex ceramics seem to fit fairly strongly into the Tepeu sphere and link the region more closely to Petén than to any other Belize site (Valdez 1987: 249–251). Few ceramic markers appear to separate the Terminal Classic from Late Classic: much of northern Belize seems to lack Fine Orange/Gray pottery, although some slate ware vessels seemingly occur. Unlike the situation farther north, there is a dramatic break at the end of the Classic, with a completely new complex replacing the Masson complex after, perhaps, an interval of abandonment. Thus Colhá seems to have experienced a set of cultural processes more similar to those in parts of Petén.

At La Milpa it is likewise difficult to separate the Terminal Classic from the Late Classic ceramically, and the strength of the Terminal Classic occupation is not clear (Kosakowsky et al. 1998: 661). Apparently both Fine Orange ware and northern slate wares show up in small quantities; however, unlike Colhá, La Milpa is more closely tied to the Belize region than to Petén during this period.

Southeastern Zone

Except for the site of Copán (Longyear 1952; Viel 1993a, 1993b), the Southeastern Zone is not well reported ceramically. Nevertheless, Copán's Terminal Classic and its aftermath are still a matter of some dispute. According to René Viel (1993b: 141), the Coner phase marks the Tepeu 2 equivalent at Copán as well as the apogee of the site. Although typical Maya gloss polychromes are not common here, distinctive Copador polychromes are found over a wide area of western El Salvador and parts of Honduras along with Surlo group pottery, decorated primarily by surface penetration, and these constitute the Coner fine wares. A few Ulua-Yojoa polychromes appear as imports.

In one view, the end of the Coner phase marks the "collapse" of elite activity at Copán. In fact, Viel suggests a final phase of Coner "characterized by the decadence of the ceremonial pottery and by the presence of fine paste [pottery] similar to that in Tepeu 3 [Fine Orange] after the fall of the hierarchical order" (Viel 1993b: 142). Fash and Manahan (1997) have expressed an essentially similar viewpoint, with Viel's Ejar phase representing a Postclassic occupation characterized by dramatic changes in ceramics, lithics, and settlement. They argue for an abandonment of the Acropolis at the end of the Coner phase, and a Postclassic Ejar phase reoccupation. Webster and others, however, argue that Coner phase ceramics continue on, minus the fine wares and with the addition of some Terminal Classic and Early Postclassic ceramics, for three or four more centuries after the collapse of elite culture (see Webster, Freter, and Storey, Chapter 11, this volume). This continuation model would seem to imply that the manufacturing and distribution systems of Coner-phase ceramics for fine and ordinary wares were distinct. That is, when the fine pottery ceased to be made, the production of utilitarian pottery continued. Regardless of how the debate is resolved, there does seem to be agreement that the Terminal Classic is marked by a decline in fine wares and the import in small amounts of Fine Orange and other tradewares such as Nicoya/Las Vegas polychromes and Tojil Plumbate.

Although there are as yet no comprehensive data on Quiriguá pottery, it would appear that there is considerable ceramic continuity into the Terminal Classic. Nevertheless, the period is apparently marked by dramatic and significant changes in the fine ware pottery at the site, which Sharer (1985: 250; see also Schortman 1993: 174ff) attributes to a new elite group from outside the Southeastern Zone.

Slightly farther northeast, the Lake Izabal region appears to have participated in ceramic exchange with highland and lowland sites, meanwhile having its own distinctive ceramics (see Hermes 1981). At many sites the Late and Terminal Classic Manatí ceramic complex (A.D. 650–950) represents a reoccupation after Early Classic abandonment. Some sites in the lake basin have yielded examples of Petén gloss wares and/or imitations of Tinaja Red, leading to a peripheral Tepeu sphere assignment, but the major affinities are with ceramics of Verapaz (Hermes 1981: 113, 116, 118). Small quantities of imitation Pabellon Molded-Carved are also evident in the area, testifying to occupation into the Terminal Classic period.

Pasión and Usumacinta Zones

The Pasión and Usumacinta Zones, named after the major rivers on the western and southwestern borders of Petén, constitute Forsyth's (1997, 1999) Western ceramic sub- or supercomplex in the Terminal Classic. During the Late Classic period, sites in this region were closely linked to the Tepeu sphere in the Central Zone, although they exhibit some regional characteristics that differentiate them from that zone. In the southwest, the Subín, Chaquiste, and Pantano variants of the red Tinaja group are overwhelmingly dominant.

Terminal Classic pottery in the Pasión/Usumacinta Zones is markedly distinct from that of central Petén and is identified as the Boca sphere (after the complex from Altar de Sacrificios; Adams 1971). Boca sphere complexes are marked at most sites by the same widespread diminution of polychrome wares that is seen elsewhere. But Terminal Classic Boca complexes differ significantly from those of other zones by the appearance of considerable quantities of fine wares, specifically Fine Orange and Fine Gray (Sabloff 1975: Figs. 370–423; Adams 1971: Figs. 66–73; Foias 1996: Figs. 6.85–6.89) as well as local imitations in non-fine pastes. All these have stylistic and typological ties to pottery from the Middle/Lower Usumacinta River area. This pattern may extend as far north as Yaxchilán in the Usumacinta area (López 1989), but is only well documented in the northwestern Pasión region. At Altar de Sacrificios, Terminal Classic Boca sphere pottery was followed by fine wares of the Early Postclassic Jimba complex (Adams 1971).

Because of the importance of fine paste wares and their imitations in Terminal Classic ceramic sequences, it is useful to give more attention to their manufacture and occurrence. These wares usually occur with untempered orange or gray pastes, apparently representing variations in the firing atmosphere. Provenience studies of these fine paste wares through neutron activation analyses have revealed two general zones of fine ware manufacture (Sabloff et al. 1982; Bishop 1994: 20–24; Foias and Bishop 1994). Wares found in the upper Usumacinta River Valley were produced within the zone, and therefore do not represent imports to the region. Fine paste wares recovered from sites in the lower Usumacinta valley to the north were likewise manufactured locally. Patterns by which these fine paste wares came to be introduced into southern lowland assemblages are not well understood and seem to vary considerably. One distinct class of fine paste pottery, the Chablekal group (a Fine Gray variant), appears to have been introduced into Piedras Negras and the Petexbatun region toward the end of the Late Classic (Holley 1983; Foias 1993, 1996: 429, 967). Later Fine Gray of the Tres Naciones ceramic group and Fine Orange of the Altar and Balancan ceramic groups only appear during the Terminal Classic, where they postdate the collapse of the Petexbatun system (Foias 1996: 626ff).

To the east of the Pasión, in the Dolores area in the upper Mopán River Valley, ceramics of the Fine Orange and Fine Gray groups occur in the Terminal Classic, but in very small quantities. The fact that any is present at all is somewhat surprising, as proximity to Belize might suggest that the area would be part of the Spanish Lookout sphere, but inscriptional evidence suggests broad dynastic and linguistic ties across southern Petén.

Although we do not as yet have comprehensive data, it appears that the ceramic pattern seen in the Pasión zone extends down the Usumacinta at least as far as Yaxchilán (López 1989, 2000). Similar to other known Pasión/Petexbatun sites during the Late Classic, the Terminal Classic Yaxmuc complex exhibited the heavy influx of Altar Group Fine Orange and Tres Naciones group Fine Gray pottery, in a manner analogous to Altar de Sacrificios and Seibal. Although the exact nature of the Yaxmuc complex is not yet entirely clear (see Foias 1996: 631–632), the quantities of Terminal Classic fine paste wares are large, indicating that Yachilán was participating in the same pattern of ceramic production and use as the better-known Pasión sites to the south.

Farther north, the site of Piedras Negras in the far northwest corner of Petén constitutes a distinct ceramic zone from the area farther upriver and also from the general Petén region, as it was only marginally related to the Late Classic Tepeu sphere (Holley 1983; Forsyth et al. 1998; Forsyth 1997). Holley's (1983) inter-pretation of the 1930s evidence correlates the collapse of the site with the intro-duction of Chablekal group Fine Gray ceramics at the end of the Late Classic or beginning of the Terminal Classic. The Fine Orange and Tres Naciones com-plexes, so common at Altar and Seibal, were only weakly represented at Piedras Negras, introduced well after the site collapsed. The 1997 and 1998 field seasons at Piedras Negras, under the direction of Stephen Houston and Héctor Escobedo, have recovered only scattered amounts of Chablekal Fine Gray pottery and virtu-ally no Fine Orange or Tres Naciones (Forsyth, personal observation, 1997; René Muñoz, personal communication, 1998). Holley's view may well be correct, but needs further corroboration.

All in all, the Terminal Classic in the Pasión/Usumacinta Zones seems to present a complicated pattern of ceramic and cultural change. In some cases the later fine paste ceramics seem to represent a squatter settlement of no great extent (Piedras Negras) or a remnant, holdout community (Punta de Chimino; Foias 1996: 626ff). In others it seems to be an add-on to the normal range of Late Classic ceramics (Seibal [see also Tourtellot and González, Chapter 4, this volume]; the Petexbatun); and if the Yaxchilán data are as they have been reported, then a complete replace-ment takes place there with little or no overlap at all. The Altar de Sacrificios example is more equivocal. Adams (1971: 162) argued for a complete replace-ment model like that described by López (1989) but others have questioned this conclusion (Sabloff 1973: 121–122; Demarest, personal communication, 2000), suggesting instead that the Altar situation was more similar to the pattern at Seibal. But given the fact that the only comprehensive data we have bearing on this issue from the whole region is from the Pasión/Petexbatun (Foias 1993, 1996; Foias and Bishop 1994), it may be unwise to make too much of these discrepancies until we have more secure data from the area downriver from the Pasión zone.

Western Zones

Apart from the upper Usumacinta/Pasión area, most of the western region of the Maya lowlands along the middle and lower Usumacinta River is very poorly known ceramically but appears to constitute a number of small distinct spheres.

For purposes of discussion here, we separate the Western Zone into two parts, southwestern and northwestern.

In the southwestern Western Zone, only Toniná has been reported in detail (Becquelin and Baudez 1979), although a ceramic report has been prepared for Chinkultic (Ball 1980). During the Late Classic, Toniná probably constituted its own ceramic sphere, but with important links to the Tepeu sphere (Becquelin and Baudez 1979: 218). Although polychromes were prominent in the Ocosingo Valley during the Late Classic (Becquelin and Baudez 1979), they are nonexistent at Chinkultic during this interval. As in the upper Usumacinta and Pasión Zones, small amounts of Chablekal Fine Gray occur as imports. The Terminal Classic is apparently a continuation of the Late Classic pattern with the addition of small amounts of Fine Orange and Fine Gray pottery of the Tres Naciones group. The ceramics of the Postclassic occupation, perhaps after a break in the sequence, are no longer related to the lowland Maya, but rather to the highlands of Chiapas.

At Chinkultic, which surely belongs to a distinct ceramic sphere, the reoccupation of the site, after a long break, occurred during the Terminal Classic, around A.D. 700–900. Apparently the acropolis at Chinkultic was built during this period and the site came to prominence at this time. It would appear that the southwestern zone (including Toniná), like parts of the northern lowlands, underwent a period of growth at precisely the time that Petén and the Usumacinta region were experiencing considerable difficulty. Ceramically, the transition from Classic to Postclassic was marked by the appearance of some examples of Altar and Tres Naciones fine paste ceramics (Ball 1980: 95).

The northwestern Western Zone is also poorly investigated, with the exception of the site of Palenque. What information we do have suggests that, in comparison to the archaeological zones examined thus far, this region was highly heterogeneous ceramically, especially compared to the more homogeneous pattern of Petén.

Palenque represents a completely distinct ceramic sphere during the period under consideration and, in reality, throughout the whole ceramic sequence (Rands 1973b, 1974, 1987). Moreover, in contrast to the situation in Petén, Palenque was not part of a relatively widespread and uniform ceramic area. Rather, the area surrounding Palenque was highly diverse (Rands 1967a, 1987). Ceramically, the latest clearly Classic complex at Palenque (Balunte or, alternatively, early Balunte) is marked by the introduction of a subcomplex of buff/brown/gray paste wares, which includes Chablekal Fine Gray and local variants, alongside the earlier paste tradition. According to Rands (1973b: 192, 1974: 68, 1987: 230), evidence of elite activity and population decline dramatically by the end of this period. The Terminal Classic period (late Balunte or, sometimes, Huipale) is poorly represented and marked by very small quantities of Fine Orange ware. Thus, like Piedras Negras, Palenque would seem to have gone into decline before the substantial introduction of fine ware pottery. Whatever the causes of the site's demise, it is clear that Palenque maintained its ceramic uniqueness until the end (Rands 1987).

Farther north in the flatlands of the lower Usumacinta River, the pottery from the Jonuta and Tecolpan region (Berlin 1956) is considerably different from that of Trinidad, upriver (Rands 1969, 1987), which, in turn, is different from both Piedras Negras (Holley 1983) and Palenque (Rands 1967a, 1967b, 1973b, 1974, 1987). Calatrava apparently is similar to the Jonuta-Tecolpan region (Rands 1967a: 130, 1987: 232), as is Tierra Blanca (Ochoa and Casasola 1978: 33, 38). All these complexes are marked by large quantities of Fine Orange ware of the Balancan and/or Altar groups, but Calatrava and Tierra Blanca are known only from surface collections.

Still farther north, the site of Aguacatal (Matheny 1970), on the western margin of the Laguna de Terminos, seems to represent yet another ceramic region distinct from the others. There is a general modal similarity to the Late Classic pottery of the Petén region, but the overall pattern is quite divergent, not only from Petén but also from the other complexes in the northwestern zone. It would appear that there existed a coastal ceramic sphere surrounding the Laguna de Terminos (Matheny 1970; Ruz 1969; Ball 1978). Interestingly enough, Terminal Classic fine paste wares, although present, do not seem to be very common, at least in comparison to the later Mangle and Plantación complexes that represent the Postclassic period. This seems to be true of other Laguna de Terminos sites with the exception of Los Guarixes, where fine wares are common (Ruz 1969: 89–105; Ball 1978: 82).

In the extreme northwestern portion, Comalcalco and the surrounding area (e.g., Huimango; Berlin 1956: 127–129) constitute still a different ceramic pattern from other regions (Peniche 1973). As outlined by Piedad Peniche, the ceramic chronology places the major occupation at Comalcalco in the Terminal Classic period after an occupational break of nearly seven hundred years, although more recent investigations at Comalcalco have encountered evidence of Classic-period occupation of the site (López V., personal communication). Moreover, the presence of Campeche Late Classic polychromes now known to pertain to both the Tepeu 1 and 2 spheres (see Ball 1978: 97–98) also supports the likelihood of a Late Classic occupation. Likewise, the architectural similarity between Palenque and Comalcalco would suggest contemporaneity of the two sites (Andrews 1967: 99ff; Peniche 1973: 170). Peniche, on the other hand, argues that Comalcalco came into full flower as Palenque went into decline, and that Comalcalco may have served as a refuge for a population from Palenque. However this all sorts out, if Peniche's chronology is correct, Comalcalco experienced a major occupation during the Terminal Classic, which consists of a local ceramic inventory that, although including some Balancan Fine Orange trade pieces, reflects its own rather unique regional character, but with considerable interactions with the Campeche coast.

NORTHERN LOWLANDS

The interval from roughly A.D. 800 to 1000, which is known as the "Terminal Classic" in the southern lowlands, does not have the same name or connotations to the north. In the northern lowlands, this interval is at the core of a slightly longer (ca. A.D. 700–1050/1100) period usually known as "Florescent" or "Pure Florescent," alluding to the flowering of the Puuc centers in the northwestern corner of the Yucatán peninsula (see Brainerd 1958).

Just as the timing of cultural florescence in the north varies from that in the south, so too does the focus of ceramic inquiry. The major issues that have preoccupied ceramicists in the northern lowlands are not related to societal "collapse," but rather concern the cultural and chronological relations of its two major Terminal Classic ceramic spheres, Cehpech (previously Copo) and Sotuta, and the sites with their constituent complexes. During the Classic period, much of the pottery in the northern lowlands demonstrated relations with the southern lowlands and its gloss wares and polychromes. By the end of the Late Classic, however, sometime around ca. A.D. 700–800, these ties to Petén diminished and there began what can be seen as either the "general homogenization of ceramic [slate ware] production" (Ringle et al., Chapter 21, this volume) or the "regional differentiation" of Cehpech complexes (Cobos, Chapter 22, this volume) throughout the northern peninsula.

Most chronological, political, and socioeconomic inferences are based on the distribution of several kinds of ceramics known as slate wares or *pizarra*. Named after the "slaty" gray-brown color of their slipped surfaces, these ceramics are found throughout the northern lowlands in the Terminal Classic/Early Postclassic period(s). These wares seem to have their origins considerably earlier than the Late Classic, however, according to evidence from northwestern Campeche (Williams-Beck 1998: 28–31; see also Brainerd 1958: 52–53) and Ek Balam (Bey et al. 1998: 114). Slate wares represent a significantly new and relatively standardized set of forms and technological styles. Different kinds of slate wares, recognizable by slip color, paste color, and temper, are characteristic of the Cehpech and Sotuta spheres, and lingering questions concern degrees of geographical and temporal "overlap."

Many of the problems with existing "Terminal Classic" ceramic chronology in the north can be traced back to the site of Chich'en Itza and the work of Carnegie Institution of Washington archaeologists there (see Anderson 1998). From the time of Sylvanus Morley and even earlier, lowland Maya prehistory had been reconstructed in terms of the "Old and New Empires." In the north, this was recognized in the building sequence of Chich'en Itza as an indigenous Maya occupation with Puuc-style architecture, followed by a foreign, "Toltec" occupation (see Tozzer 1930, 1957; Valliant 1927, 1933). Consequently, the Terminal Classic Cehpech ceramic complex, associated with sites in the Puuc hills to the west, was seen to be followed by the Early Postclassic Sotuta complex of "Toltec"

Chich'en Itza, which was then followed by Hocaba, representing the Middle Post-classic occupation of Mayapán (see Smith 1971).

Shortly after the Mayapán ceramic report was published, this simple linear and ethnic sequencing was challenged by Ball (1979a, 1979b), who suggested temporal overlap of the Cehpech and Sotuta complexes. In a "partial overlap" model, Cehpech and Sotuta were largely coeval, succeeded by Hocaba; in the "total overlap" model all three complexes overlapped to some degree (see discussions in Lincoln 1986, 1990; Schmidt 1994; Anderson 1998). What is of concern here (and in several papers in this volume) is not the late end of this sequencing, involving Early and Middle Postclassic complexes, but rather the beginning of it in the Terminal Classic. Of particular interest is the degree of chronological overlap and the likelihood that the ceramic spheres were contemporaneous regional variants, Cehpech largely in the west (Puuc Maya) and Sotuta in the east ("Toltec" Chich'en Itza). Ball's questions about chronological overlap were stimulating formulations on which to base new investigations. In turn, the fruits of these new investigations are seen in more detailed reconstructions of, and still more questions about, the geographical and temporal variability evident in Terminal Classic ceramic assemblages throughout the northern lowlands.

Cehpech Ceramic Sphere

Cehpech sphere ceramics are found throughout most of the Yucatán peninsula, especially in the west in the Puuc hills region, with a distribution extending as far southward as Champoton and the Río Bec area (Ball 1979a; Andrews and Robles 1985: 65). Cehpech also has an eastern manifestation seen at Ek Balam and Yaxuná and extending to Cobá near the coast, and southward into northern Belize (Chase and Chase 1982).

First defined at the Puuc sites of Uxmal and Kabah, the Cehpech complex and sphere is particularly identified with Thin Slate ware and Fine Orange of the Balancan and Altar groups. On this basis, the complex has been said to resemble an elite or fine ware subcomplex, that is, the domestic service ware and/or mortuary pottery of a socially elite group (Ball 1976: 328–329). Its distribution, in turn, has been thought to represent "the actual movements of a small, mobile group of warrior-merchants, ultimately of southern Campeche-Tabasco coastal plain origin" (ibid.). Most of the characteristic wares, groups, and types have names drawn from the Puuc geographical area: Puuc Slate ware (Tekit Incised), Puuc Unslipped ware (Yokat Striated), Puuc Red ware (Teabo Red), Ticul Thin Slate, and so forth.

Cehpech slate wares such as Muna Slate from the Puuc region, described most succinctly by Kepecs (1998: 125–126; see also Smith 1971: 28; Robles and Andrews 1986: 77–78), have primarily gray or brown pastes and a slightly translucent, waxy-feeling, gray or brown slip. In contrast, eastern (Coba) Cehpech slates have brown or reddish paste and a brown slip, and slightly different forms.

Cehpech slate wares from both eastern and western regions are usually calcite tempered, although they sometimes may have volcanic ash temper like the Sotuta wares. The western Cehpech sphere also has an imitation slate ware, the sherd-tempered Cauich Coarse-cream ware.

One of the earliest well-defined ceramic sequences within the Cehpech sphere comes from the site of Becan in the Río Bec region (Ball 1977). In the equivalent of Tepeu 1, the region participated peripherally in the Tepeu sphere, but the trend toward regionalization was increasingly evident through time. Becan's Late Classic Chintok complex was not abundant, usually occurring in poor condition and in mixed lots. Overall, it showed "more differences than similarities" to Tepeu 2, with the major monochrome being brown-slipped (Traino Brown; Campeche gloss ware) and the beginnings of slate wares replacing gloss wares (Ball 1977: 161).

Becan's Terminal Classic Xcocom complex, beginning in the early ninth century, is a member of the Cehpech sphere and, even in the early facet, represented a considerable break with the previous Petén-related complex. Characterized as "a radical revitalization and reorientation of the local ceramic tradition" (Ball 1977: 7), the Xcocom complex featured "an entire battery of new types and modes," including graters, Ticul Thin Slate, and Fine Orange ware (Ball 1977: 162–163). Early-facet Xcocom is similar to Cehpech in types, forms, and decoration; late-facet Xcocom is contemporary with Sotuta but shows little in common with it (Ball 1977: 164). Late Xcocom continues many of the same types and groups as before, but with later imports such as Silho Fine Orange and Tohil Plumbate (ibid.).

In the extreme northwestern part of the Yucatán peninsula, Dzibilchaltun's Terminal Classic Copo ceramic complex was originally seen to have "strong linkages" to complexes in Petén, both Eznab and Boca (Willey, Culbert, and Adams 1967: 303). Copo is now regarded as a member of the Cehpech sphere by virtue of the presence of Puuc Slate, Muna Slate, Teabo Red, and Chablekal Gray (Fine Gray). The end of the late facet, Copo II, saw the addition of some Sotuta ceramics. Sotuta may have been restricted to certain groups or strata within the site of Dzibilchaltun, because the ceramics were found mostly near main *sacbes* (Bey et al. 1998: 116).

To the northwest of Becan, Edzná shares the typical western or Puuc Cehpech sphere Terminal Classic diagnostics, including Puuc Unslipped, Puuc Slate, Thin Slate, Puuc Red, Cauich Coarse-cream, and Fine Orange wares (Forsyth 1983: 212). Slate types frequently bear trickle decoration in red or black. There are few polychromes and virtually no apparent ties to Petén spheres such as Eznab or Boca.

In the eastern part of the peninsula, the Cehpech sphere presents a different picture. The east coastal variant of Cehpech is best known from the Oro complex (A.D. 730–1100) of Cobá in northern Quintana Roo. During much of the Late Classic and into the Terminal Classic, Cobá had pronounced architectural as well as ceramic ties to central Petén. However, the dominant Terminal Classic ceramics of Cobá and other contemporaneous complexes, such as the San Miguel complex at Tancah (Sanders 1960), are slate wares, particularly those associated with western Cehpech. These include Puuc Slate and Thin Slate, as well as non-slate types like Puuc Red ware and Vista Alegre Striated. Eastern Cehpech slate wares are distinctive, as noted above, by virtue of their brown or reddish paste and brown slip, rather than gray colors.

Inland, the Terminal Classic complex at Yaxuná, twenty kilometers southwest of Chich'en Itza, is referred to as Yaxuná IV and has two facets. The Yaxuna IVa or Initial Terminal Classic complex (A.D. 730–900) is believed to represent colonization from the Puuc area; ceramics include a mix of eastern and western Cehpech influences, with eastern forms predominating (Suhler, Ardren, and Johnstone 1998: 178). During Yaxuná IVb, the Late Terminal Classic facet (A.D. 900–1100), the site is believed to have been taken over by Chich'en Itza, and Sotuta complex ceramics were recovered, though largely from ritual contexts (ibid.).

Ek Balam, located almost equidistant from Cobá and Chich'en Itza, reached its apex during the late facet of the Yumkab phase, roughly A.D. 700–1050/1100. The late Yumkab ceramic complex shares considerable similarity with the Puuc Cehpech sphere, with Muna Slate and Chum/Encanto Unslipped wares accounting for 69 percent of the material (Bey et al. 1998: 114). However, there is comparatively little fine paste ware or Ticul Thin Slate, characteristic of western Cehpech, while Vista Alegre Striated, which is common at Cobá and eastern Cehpech sphere sites, is nearly absent also (ibid.). Significantly, the site's investigators note that "Itza influence [in the form of Sotuta sphere ceramics] is barely detectable in the archaeological record of Ek Balam" (Bey et al. 1998: 118).

Sotuta Ceramic Sphere

The Terminal Classic to Early Postclassic ceramic sphere encompassing much of the northern and eastern Yucatán peninsula is the Sotuta sphere, associated with Chich'en Itza's "Toltec" florescence and its allied sites. Sotuta ceramics are found from Tabasco and western Campeche across northern Yucatán to northeastern coastal Quintana Roo, at least as far south as El Meco and possibly Cozumel (Andrews and Robles 1985: 69–70). This area includes Isla Cerritos on the north coast, and a corridor of sites between Chich'en and the northeastern coast, including the Chikinchel province (Kepecs 1998). They are not known from Cobá, however, in the east coastal peninsula. Nonetheless, farther to the south in Belize, Sotuta sphere ceramics are present at Ambergris Cay and possibly at Nohmul.

The principal diagnostics of the Sotuta complex at Chich'en Itza and the Sotuta sphere as a whole are a series of slate wares and red-slipped wares, plus some distinctive trade wares. These include Chichen Slate (some with black "trickle" decoration), Dzitas Slate, and Chichen Red, along with Tohil Plumbate and Silho Fine Orange. Sotuta slate wares, such as Dzitas, have a red paste that almost invariably has volcanic ash temper and a lighter, cream-colored slip (Kepecs 1998: 125–126; see also Smith 1971: 28; Robles and Andrews 1986: 77–78). Although eastern Cehpech slates sometimes may have volcanic ash inclusions, "Chichen Itza and the western sites had a type of [volcanic] ash temper that is markedly distinct from that of Coba and Yaxuna, suggesting separate sources of supply" (Andrews and Robles 1985: 69). The Sotuta sphere also includes an "imitation" slate ware, calcite-tempered Peto Cream ware.

With respect to Cehpech-Sotuta overlap, questions are still very much alive, although most archaeologists seem to have accepted the reality of some degree of overlap. As additional scientific excavations are done, the greater the likelihood that considerably more local, regional, and chronological variability will be discerned and understood. For example, at Yulá, only five kilometers south of Chich'en Itza, Cehpech and Sotuta ceramics were found together in the same stratigraphic levels. While sherds of Sotuta types were clearly dominant (by counts), they occurred in the same relative percentages in upper and lower strata, with 10–12 percent Cehpech and 88–90 percent Sotuta (Anderson 1998: 158). And, as Rafael Cobos explains in his contribution to this volume (Chapter 22), there may be early and late facets of Sotuta at Chich'en Itza and elsewhere. The early facet is marked by the presence of Thin Slate, Chichen Unslipped, Chichen Red, and Fine Orange wares; the late facet is characterized by Chichen Slate ware and Plumbate, while Chichen Unslipped and Fine Orange wares continue.

So, at the end, what can be said about the overlap issue? It appears that Cehpech and Sotuta are largely coeval spheres that share what might be called similar "technological styles" of wares (slate wares, red wares) but different resources (red- versus gray-firing clays, calcite versus volcanic ash). Careful stratigraphic excavations and ceramic analyses appear to have revealed that in some sites/areas there are geographical subspheres of Cehpech (eastern and western) as well as chronological faceting that can be correlated with different architectural styles. It also appears that Sotuta either lasts longer than Cehpech or replaces it at several sites. In a number of sites/areas (Dzibilchaltun, Uxmal, Ek Balam, Yaxuná), Sotuta appears at the very end of a Terminal Classic occupation that had been Cehpech-affiliated, and a chronological division of Sotuta into early and late facets is therefore highly probable. Given the fairly restricted distribution of these late-Sotuta ceramics at Dzibilchaltun and Yaxuná, it is also likely that they represent a socially or functionally specialized subcomplex.

CONCLUDING OBSERVATIONS

This overview of Terminal Classic lowland Maya ceramics emphasizes breadth rather than depth of coverage, which makes it risky to attempt any substantial conclusions. Our review does, however, permit us to tease out some observations that are relevant not only to the ceramics themselves but also to the Terminal Classic period and its before-and-after processes.

In returning to the integrative concepts with which we began this discussion, we note that the early idea of a Terminal Classic horizon in the lowlands has for a long time lacked sufficient supportive data and should be abandoned. We note simultaneously that the ceramic sphere concept has been around for an equally long time but has failed to be utilized optimally. Here we address in more detail the concept of lowland Maya ceramic spheres and discuss their implications for the Terminal Classic. In particular, we focus on the need to integrate artifactual (i.e., the abundant ceramic) evidence with inscriptional, architectural, and settlement data in a more holistic interpretation of Maya cultural history. It is our conviction that Maya ceramic classificatory units can bring useful perspectives to bear on the history of Maya civilization, but their potential has been sadly underutilized.

Ceramic Spheres Through Time

During the Late Classic period, one ceramic sphere clearly dominated most of the lowlands: the Tepeu sphere of north-central Petén. Even in the northern lowlands, ceramic ties to Petén were evident in the early Late Classic period (Tepeu 1, ca. A.D. 600–700). Although these broke down during the subsequent century, elsewhere throughout the southern and central lowlands during the period from roughly A.D. 700 to 830, the red-slipped and gloss ware polychrome types characteristic of Tepeu 2/Imix pottery occurred widely. Full members of the late Late Classic Tepeu sphere (Figure 3.1) include core region sites of Tikal, Uaxactún, Yaxhá, the Petén lakes, and Calakmul, along with a number of more distant sites having links ranging from perhaps peripheral sphere membership (Lubaantun, Colhá, El Mirador, Cobá, Becan, the Izabal region) to marginal participation in the sphere (the Pasión area, Caracol, and much of the western Usumacinta region). Even the early facet of the Spanish Lookout sphere in the upper Belize Valley exhibits strong ties as evident in Tinaja/Belize Red type.

In the Terminal Classic period in the southern lowlands, the core area of the former Tepeu (2) sphere constricted, as the ceramic traditions of the more distant regions evolved in such different directions that separate sphere designations become warranted. Archaeologists studying the pottery of this period have highlighted discontinuities, either by identifying temporal variants or facets of the Late Classic complexes or by naming distinct Terminal Classic complexes with different sphere identifications. Examples of the latter—identification of Terminal Classic ceramic complexes distinct from the Late Classic—can be found at sites and regions around the western and eastern margins of the former Tepeu sphere: in the Pasión and parts of the Usumacinta areas, as well as at Cobá, Becan, northern Belize, and southeastern Petén. Farther to the east and southeast, more distant from central Petén, sites have faceted Late Terminal complexes that all maintain ties to Tepeu/Eznab. These include the faceting of the Lubaantun Columbia complex

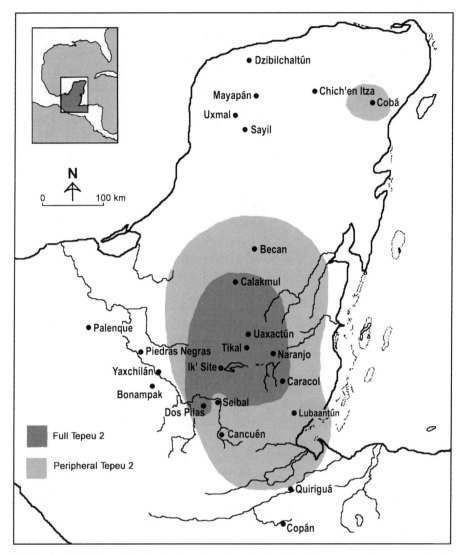

3.1 Map of the Maya lowlands showing the extent of the Tepeu ceramic sphere in the Late Classic period.

(the late facet having primary affiliation to Boca and secondary to Eznab); the Izabal region's Late and Terminal Classic Manati complex (peripheral Tepeu/ Eznab); and Colhá's Late and Terminal Masson complex (full Tepeu/Eznab?). Only Tikal, Uaxactún, Yaxhá, Calakmul, and possibly Colhá constitute full members of the Terminal Classic Tepeu 3/Eznab sphere (Figure 3.2), while El Mirador has no Terminal Classic complex but only a handful of clearly Eznab Terminal

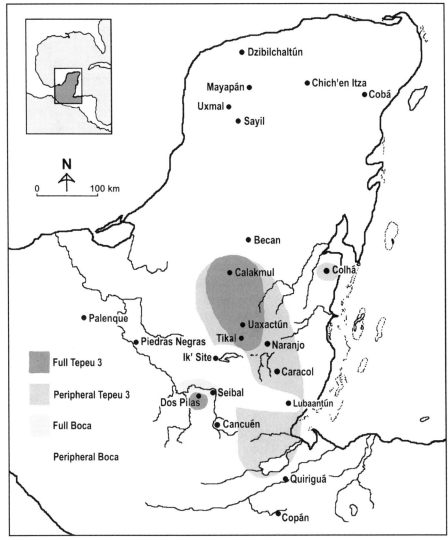

3.2 Map of the Maya lowlands showing the extent of the Tepeu and Boca ceramic spheres in the Terminal Classic period.

Classic examples; the Petén lakes region and the Izabal area exhibit peripheral membership.

Archaeologists have identified four major Terminal Classic ceramic spheres in the lowlands: Cehpech (Eastern and Western) plus Sotuta in the north; Eznab and Boca in the south (ignoring Spanish Lookout for the moment). These circumstances demand attention to the significance of ceramic spheres in social, cultural, economic, and political terms. What do spheres actually "mean" in terms of real human behavior? What kinds of interactions are represented by full, peripheral, and marginal memberships in a ceramic sphere? The most immediate answers to these questions would seem to lie in the economic realm, that is, ceramic production organization, trade networks, and regional economic integration.

The most obvious interpretation of the ceramic sphere concept is that participants in a sphere shared similar ideas of what constituted appropriate or customary ceramics. In many cases, the translation of these ideas of the appropriate or customary was not simply a matter of local copying of vessel shapes, colors, or decorations, but rather the actual circulation of certain distinctive vessels (known to archaeologists as wares, groups, types, and even varieties) within a region through trade or exchange. Proceeding from this line of argument, then, full membership in a ceramic sphere would seem to indicate close economic relations that include direct exchange of goods. Such exchanges, in turn, could—but do not necessarily—implicate some sort of politico-economic affiliations and/or interactions as, for example, control of (re)distribution mechanisms and/or trade routes, dynastic intermarriage, and sharing of politico-religious material symbols. The kinds of pottery involved in the Late and Terminal Classic—both red-slipped serving wares and various kinds of polychromes—could, in theory, be interpreted as consequences of elite-cum-political relations involving ritual and/or gift-giving behavior in a so-called "prestige goods economy." However, the spatial and quantitative distributions of ceramic types and forms implicated in the sphere identifications seem too substantial for such largely individual actor-based behavior. Unfortunately, very little is known of Classic Maya economic organization by which to postulate centers of ceramic production and routes or mechanisms of exchange (but see Masson and Freidel 2002).

Other questions about political and economic relations in the south-central lowlands loom large here. For example, why were two of the supposed "enemies" of Tikal, which engaged in repeated "conquests"—as suggested by inscriptional evidence, i.e., Calakmul and Caracol—affiliated with Tikal's ceramic sphere in the Late Classic? To judge from the material evidence, these sites were apparently copying or importing (or both) ceramic wares, types, forms, and decorations characteristic of the Tikal area in north-central Petén, with which they were supposedly at war. Were lowland Maya "political" and "economic" realms of behavior so discrete that sites engaged in "battles" while at the same time exchanging basic goods? As is often true in historical archaeology, the interrelationships described in documents do not always conform to the reality of the material evidence uncovered by archaeology. It will be necessary to conduct more detailed examinations of lowland Maya pottery dating to the Terminal Classic period to determine if the materials were locally produced, directly exchanged, or obtained through some other mechanisms.

In addition, for integrative purposes it may be useful to pay more attention to even larger units that might be thought of as "super-spheres" or supercomplexes. In his contribution to *The Classic Maya Collapse* volume, Rands noted two elite ceramic traditions in the southern lowlands—fine paste wares and polychromy—that were largely sequential but had distinct east-west (respectively) geographic centers. Related to this, Foias (1996: 572) noted east-west geographical distinctions based on polychromy, with a cream slip base favored in central and northeastern Petén/Belize and orange background in the west (Pasión region and northward). Most recently, Forsyth noted a similar east-west separation of non-elite utilitarian complexes in Petén. There are also, of course, distinct eastern and western divisions of the temporally overlapping Cehpech ceramic complexes to the north in the Yucatán peninsula, where there seems to be a parallel distinction in patterns of obsidian sources as well. Obsidian at sites in the eastern Cehpech sphere is primarily from the Ixtepeque source (as is Terminal Classic obsidian in the Petén lakes), while in the west obsidian seems to be primarily from El Chayal (Braswell 1996b); sites with Sotuta ceramics tend to have obsidian from central Mexican sources. In the north, at least, it is tempting to see these Terminal Classic east-west divisions as antecedents of the Late Postclassic ethno-social split between the Itza and Xiw groups.

Ceramic Change: A "Quasi-Modal" Analysis

One lesson to be learned from this examination of ceramic change from Late Classic through Terminal Classic into Early Postclassic periods in the Maya lowlands is that differences in the spatial distribution of elite trade wares may not be matched by corresponding changes in utilitarian wares. As researchers have long noted in contexts outside the Maya area (see Rice 1987: 449–468), and as Forsyth has noted within the southern lowlands, elite wares may change rapidly (through exchange, gift-giving, or other mechanisms), but basic utilitarian cooking and serving subcomplexes tend to be less susceptible to the whims of fashion. Partly as a result of dietary conservatism, plus the basics of culinary needs and techniques—boiling, toasting, dry storage, etc.—utilitarian forms and wares tend to maintain their integrity through all manner of political, religious, and social upheavals.

One way to look at ceramic continuity and change in the Terminal Classic is to move from classificatory units such as spheres, types, and varieties and instead, consider ceramic modes. It is not possible here to do a complete modal analysis of all ceramic modes throughout the lowlands, but some attention can be given to different "kinds" of modes, and whether they were added, dropped, or substituted during the Terminal Classic. By "kinds of modes," we refer to general modes of surface treatment, form, and technology. The prevailing sense has been that from the Late to the Terminal Classic, variability decreased as pottery became simpler in decoration and more "homogeneous." While on the one hand this kind of reduction in variability could be read as the kind of increasing standardization that often accompanies mass production, the context in which it occurred—an apparent elite collapse in the south, and considerable population dislocations throughout—suggests this was not likely the case.

What can be said about variability in surface treatment in the Terminal Classic? The entire lowlands experienced a cessation of production of human-figure, gloss ware polychrome decoration, and polychromy in general declined. In place of painting, in the southern and central lowlands, decorative treatments moved toward techniques of surface penetration or displacement such as incising/excising, striation, and the like. With the exception of molded-carved decoration, these surface treatments certainly represent a process of simplification and most likely reflect the loss of skilled artists, although a decline in patronage and/or certain resources could also be involved. Monochrome red slipping continued (from the Late Classic) as the most common surface color for serving wares in Petén, while black became more common to the east in the Belize Valley. In the northern lowlands, new slipping in grayish-brownish colors resulted in the widespread Terminal Classic slate wares.

Variability in form—including vessel size—also is evident during the Terminal Classic. In the southern and central lowlands, one evident change is in monochrome serving plates and bowls, which became somewhat smaller than those of the Late Classic. This raises the issue of whether dietary patterns were changing—perhaps either different foods were served or different patterns of dining were followed, perhaps in smaller groups. The former calls to mind the presence of grater bowls in the Terminal Classic Xcocom complex at Becan (Ball 1977). Another distinctive form in the southern and central lowlands is a large basin with incurving rim, often bolstered and decorated. Although present in the Late Classic, these vessels are particularly common in the Terminal Classic from the Pasión area across into the Belize Valley, and seem to continue into the Early Postclassic in the Petén lakes region. Finally, it is worth noting that there were changes in the ritual subcomplexes, too. The JGIII (Jaguar God of the Underworld) incense burners and/or pedestals, so common as part of Late Classic royal funerary ritual, disappeared and were replaced by simpler ladles or hourglass vases in the Terminal Classic (see Ball 1977; Rice 1999).

Changes in ceramic technology were also evident in the Terminal Classic period in the lowlands. One dramatic addition to the region's ceramic inventories comprises the series of untempered fine paste wares, specifically the types and varieties of the Fine Orange and Fine Gray groups. Manufactured apparently as firing variants in the lower and middle reaches of the Usumacinta River on the western periphery, these vessels were traded widely—and also prompted numerous imitations—throughout the lowlands in the Terminal Classic and Postclassic periods. Another set of technological innovations can be seen in the slate wares of the northern lowlands. Although accumulating evidence suggests that slate wares began to be made prior to Late Classic (see Bey et al. 1998: 114), they became widespread throughout the northern lowlands in the Terminal Classic and had numerous imitations as well. There are eastern and western variants of slate wares (primarily evidenced through color of paste and slip) as well as Cehpech and Sotuta variants of slate wares (primarily evidenced through use of volcanic ash tempering), but they do appear to register some striking technological similarities (see Kepecs 1998: 126 for discussion of slate ware technology). The consistent use of volcanic ash temper in Sotuta slate wares, and its comparative rarity in Cehpech slates, is intriguing, for in the southern lowlands volcanic ash tempering declined sharply during the Terminal Classic period. As in the case of obsidian procurement, this raises questions about sources of supply and trade routes, because the obsidian at Sotuta-related sites seems to be primarily from Mexican sources (Braswell 1996b).

Ceramic Change: Transitions

Finally, a very different way to look at ceramic change in the Terminal Classic period in the Maya lowlands is through comparative systematics: comparing the kinds of classificatory units archaeologists have used to organize ceramic variability in the Late to Terminal Classic and the Terminal Classic to Early Postclassic transitions. At some sites and in some regions, archaeologists have identified continuities between these periods and separated them only by facets, while at others there seem to be marked disjunctions. We conclude with a chart summarizing these differences (Figure 3.3).

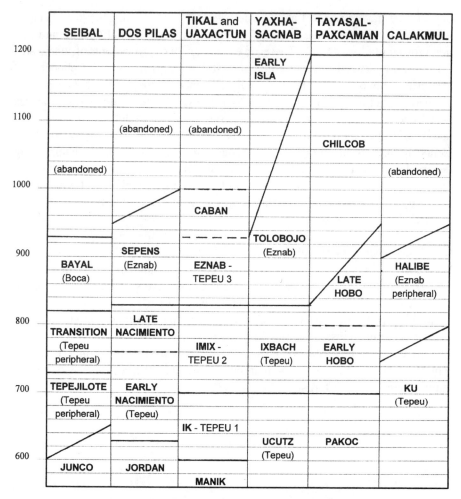

3.3a Comparative ceramic chronologies for the Late Classic through Early Postclassic periods (from left to right). Seibal: Sabloff 1975; Tourtellot and González, Chapter 4, this volume. Dos Pilas: Demarest, Chapter 6, this volume. Tikal and Uaxactún: Smith 1971, Culbert 1993a. Yaxhá-Sacnab: P. Rice 1979; Hermes 2000. Tayasal-Paxcaman: A. F. Chase and D. Z. Chase 1983. Calakmul: Braswell et al., Chapter 9, this volume.

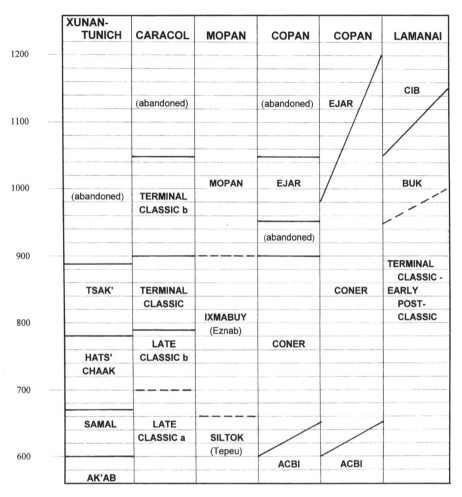

	XUNAN-TUNICH	CARACOL	MOPAN	COPAN	COPAN	LAMANAI
1200						
1100		(abandoned)		(abandoned)	EJAR	CIB
1000	(abandoned)	TERMINAL CLASSIC b	MOPAN	EJAR		BUK
900				(abandoned)		TERMINAL CLASSIC - EARLY POST-CLASSIC
800	TSAK'	TERMINAL CLASSIC	IXMABUY (Eznab)		CONER	
	HATS' CHAAK	LATE CLASSIC b		CONER		
700						
600	SAMAL	LATE CLASSIC a	SILTOK (Tepeu)	ACBI	ACBI	
	AK'AB					

3.3b Comparative ceramic chronologies for the Late Classic through Early Postclassic periods (from left to right). Xunantunich: *Ashmore et al., Chapter 14, this volume*. Caracol: *A. Chase, personal communication, August 2003*. Mopan: *Laporte, Chapter 10, this volume*. Copán: *Fash et al., Chapter 12, this volume*. Copán: *Webster et al., Chapter 11, this volume*. Lamanai: *Graham 1987b*.

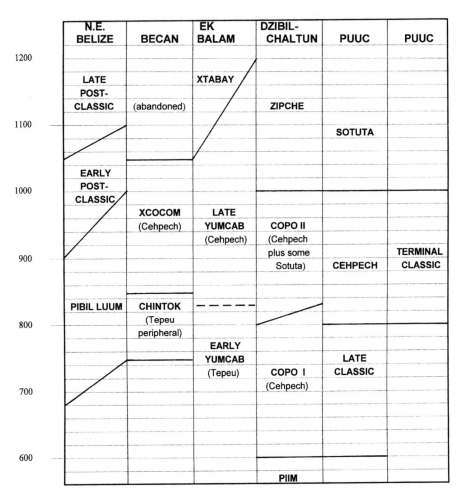

	N.E. BELIZE	BECAN	EK BALAM	DZIBIL-CHALTUN	PUUC	PUUC
1200						
	LATE POST-CLASSIC	(abandoned)	XTABAY	ZIPCHE		
1100					SOTUTA	
1000	EARLY POST-CLASSIC	XCOCOM (Cehpech)	LATE YUMCAB (Cehpech)	COPO II (Cehpech plus some Sotuta)		
900					CEHPECH	TERMINAL CLASSIC
800	PIBIL LUUM	CHINTOK (Tepeu peripheral)	– – – – –			
700			EARLY YUMCAB (Tepeu)	COPO I (Cehpech)	LATE CLASSIC	
600						
			PIIM			

3.3c Comparative ceramic chronologies for the Late Classic through Early Postclassic periods (from left to right). Northeast Belize: *Masson and Mock, Chapter 17, this volume.* Becan: *Ball 1977.* Ek Balam: *Bey et al. 1998; Ringle et al., Chapter 21, this volume.* Dzibilchaltun: *Ringle et al., Chapter 21, this volume.* Puuc: *Bey et al. 1997; Suhler et al., Figure 20.3, this volume.* Puuc: *Pollock 1980. (For Dzibilchaltun and Puuc sites, see also Suhler et al., Figure 20.3, this volume; Cobos, Table 22.3, this volume.)*

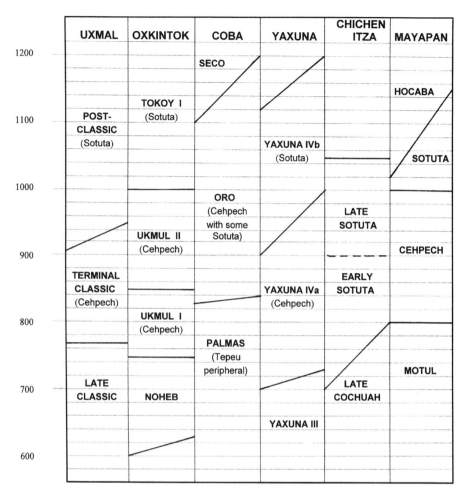

3.3d Comparative ceramic chronologies for the Late Classic through Early Postclassic periods (from left to right). Uxmal: Carmean et al., Chapter 19, this volume. Oxkintok: Carmean et al., Chapter 19, this volume; Varela 1996. Cobá: Bey et al. 1998; Ringle et al., Chapter 21, this volume; Robles 1990. Yaxuna: Suhler et al. 1998; Suhler et al., Chapter 20, this volume. Chich'en Itza: Cobos, Chapter 22, this volume. Mayapán: Bey et al. 1998; Milbrath and Peraza 2003. (See also Suhler et al., Figure 20.3, this volume; Cobos, Table 22.3, this volume.)

4

THE LAST HURRAH
CONTINUITY AND TRANSFORMATION AT SEIBAL

Gair Tourtellot and Jason J. González

CONQUERING SEIBAL

The Terminal Classic period (A.D. 830–1000) is important in Maya studies because it is transitional from the Late Classic (A.D. 650–830) to the Postclassic (A.D. 1000–1500) periods; exhibits radical change in the Maya lowlands both intra- and inter-regionally, including much elite "collapse"; and introduced numerous "foreign" elements in architecture, sculpture, hieroglyphics, and ceramics, possibly carried by migrating people (Rice and Puleston 1981; Rice 1986; Rice and Culbert 1990; Sabloff and Andrews V 1986a; Sabloff and Henderson 1993a; Stuart 1993; Willey 1986). Much of the debate over the fate of Late Classic society during the Terminal Classic has invoked population movements. Some theories, or scenarios, focus on the movement and intrusion of small "non-Classic" elites foreign to the Classic Maya tradition (e.g., Ball and Taschek 1989; Kowalski 1989; A. Miller 1977; M. Miller 1993; V. Miller 1989; Sabloff 1973; Thompson 1970), while others invoke broader population movement and replacement (e.g., Adams 1973b, 1980; Chase 1985b; Fox 1987; Sabloff and Willey 1967). Because Seibal lies at the crux of these highly diverse (and thereby suspect) theories, it is imperative to come to a fuller understanding of this site, located in the Río Pasión region of the southern lowlands in Petén, Guatemala.[1]

Seibal is strategically located one hundred meters above river level on the inside of the great bend of the Río Pasión (Figure 4.1). A pivotal Terminal Classic site, it has long been renowned for its many well-preserved and vigorous sculptures, their many characteristics outside the Classic Maya canon, as well as their

60

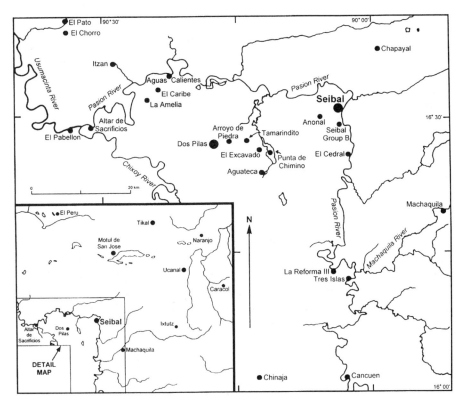

4.1 Seibal and the Pasión Region in Petén, Guatemala. (Modified from a map by Peter Mathews with permission of the Pre-Columbian Art Research Institute.)

late (post–A.D. 830) dates, defying the general collapse of lowland Petén Classic culture (Maler 1908; Morley 1937–1938; Proskouriakoff 1950; Spinden 1913). New elements include non-Classic Maya figures, long hair, strange costumes and regalia, and cryptic hieroglyphs. Stimulated by these features, the 1964–1968 Seibal Archaeological Project (SAP) added to this list phallic "Atlantean" dwarfs, a "Toltec" prowling jaguar, a circular pyramid, ballcourts, radial temples, cause-ways, a remote stela platform, house plans and burial patterns, masses of "west-ern" fine paste pottery (also showing people with long hair), a decrease in polychromes, and flat metates, among other things (Graham 1990; Sabloff 1975; Smith 1982; Tourtellot 1988b; Tourtellot 1990; Willey 1978, 1990).

The late community of Seibal passed through three phases. First came the rapid reoccupation and growth of a former Preclassic–Early Classic settlement area, in the Late Classic Tepejilote Tepeu phase (A.D. 600/650–770, equivalent to Tepeu 1/early Tepeu 2). Second, growth of Late Classic culture and settlement continued in the Tepejilote–Bayal Transitional phase (A.D. 770–830, equivalent to late Tepeu 2).[2] Finally, the comparatively powerful florescence of Seibal, with its many stelae, arrived in the Terminal Classic Bayal Boca phase (A.D. 830–930+, equivalent to Tepeu 3). That climax shortly ended in a delayed version of the Classic Maya collapse (Willey 1990). The SAP thesis was that many of the Terminal Classic Bayal features were the consequence of foreign conquest by non-Classic or "Mexicanized" Maya from near the Gulf of Mexico to the west.

Troubling aspects of the conquest hypothesis were the problematical degree to which Bayal analytically represented a replacement of Tepejilote, a nucleated enclave, or an elite overlay; the temporal and spatial isolation of Seibal; and the widely dispersed sources for the alleged foreign influences and imports. Our Seibal-centric view hardly recognized the absence of critical data on nearby sites (Graham 1973: 211): besides Altar de Sacrificios (Willey 1973), fifty-five kilometers downstream, SAP was reliant on scanty evidence from the rest of the Río Pasión and Laguna Petexbatun. Almost by default, any resemblances found were likely to be "foreign" to the Pasión region, although similarities over similar distances into northeastern Petén were not so designated. A specific shortcoming of theories proclaiming migration has been inattention to the full context for Seibal, in favor of cherry-picking "foreign" traits (Adams 1973a: 156–158, Appendix B).

Because the issue of identity is central to discriminating migration in the Terminal Classic, we take a broad and contextual look at Seibal in its region. Identity in this sense is the perceived notion of self-identification with a biologically or socially bounded group (Barth 1969: 9; Bourdieu 1977: 17; Giddens 1987; Glazer and Moynihan 1975: 3; González 1998: 10; S. Jones 1997: 84; Kelly and Kelly 1980: 134; Sackett 1990: 33; Shennan 1989: 6; Weissner 1990: 107). Among the concrete (archaeological) dimensions of cultural identity that have the most potential are burials, where we may find biological differentiation, and material cultural systems of mortuary practice and intimate everyday housing and ritual largely dependent on family socialization (Barth 1969; Bourdieu 1977: 89; Henderson and Sabloff 1993: 465–467; S. Jones 1997; Shennan 1989; Snow 1997). Hieroglyphic text statements and beliefs expressed in iconography can be of great heuristic value in identifying people, although learned formally and more readily subject to conscious manipulation (Houston 1993: 95–97; Kelley and Kelley 1980: 138; Sackett 1990: 39; Wiessner 1990: 110). Although there is arguably good agreement among these lines of evidence at Seibal, we shall find, ironically, that the best evidence for both migration and conquest at Seibal applies to the Late, not Terminal, Classic period.

NEW INFORMATION

Much new information in Maya archaeology has become available in the decades since SAP. These decades have witnessed the successful decipherment of Maya hieroglyphics and texts—incidentally inverting the prime position of Seibal in its region. Neighboring sites in the Laguna Petexbatun subregion twenty kilometers west of Seibal (Figure 4.1) have been investigated by Yale and the Vanderbilt Petexbatun Regional Archaeology Project (PRAP). They provide antecedents and history for some changes previously observed in isolation at Seibal.

Human Remains

The most direct data on population changes into the Bayal phase should derive from burials. Analysis, along eight dimensions of mortuary practice, of thirty-two Bayal individuals compared to seventeen Tepejilote people appeared to show that the Bayal invaders differed from the Tepejilote inhabitants (Tourtellot 1990). However, when tested against a seriation of burial vessel types, "[t]his comparison does not confirm that we have identified the remains of two distinct ethnic groups. . . . At best, we may have found a scale by which to measure acculturation of the groups. . . ." (Tourtellot 1990: 139–140).

Subsequently, Wright (1994) of PRAP has reanalyzed the Seibal skeletons, finding deficiencies in the original biological data and cultural samples and denying Bayal differentiation away from Classic norms.[3] The Seibal burial samples from each period are simply too small to be reliable and sampling bias is likely due to limited trenching, a focus on patios and plazas, a scarcity of elite burials, and under-representation of females. Finding many of the "normal Maya" antecedents for Bayal burials only at other sites suggests local Tepejilote burials are comparatively impoverished (or undersampled), more "non-Classic" than Bayal! The same sampling problems will work against identifying migrants who might have fled the Petexbatun collapse (Demarest 1997: 220).

The only elite burial SAP found is the Bayal "cached" female Burial 1 on Str. A-14 (confirmed by Wright 1994: 138, 152). New analysis by Wright (1994: 161) finds that Burial 4 (parts of eleven people, some bones burned in a green state, in radial platform A-13 on line with the A-19 ballcourt) includes two women and a child, and thus cannot be a sacrificed ball team (Smith 1982: 62). Instead, it is a mass (not multiple) burial foreign to Classic practice (Lori Wright, personal communication, January 1999; Ruz Lhuillier 1968; Welsh 1988). Perhaps significantly, Burial 4 has a calibrated radiocarbon date of A.D. 930 (Smith 1982: 62), which might place it very late in Bayal, in the context of a siege village (see below).

Bayal burials beneath small class C platform-altar/shrines in house patios anticipate a common Postclassic practice (Leventhal 1983). Possible antecedents to such altars at Seibal are forty-nine class C structures listed for Dos Pilas (Houston 1993: Table 2.2), and possibly two others at Tamarindito (Chinchilla 1993), but few are comparably placed in the center or east of patios and apparently none contain burials (Emery 1995c; Lori Wright, personal communication, January 1999). In sum, Bayal burials do not clearly show "foreign" inspiration, let alone migration.

Faces and Facies

Seibal sculpture offers a second chance to identify distinctive foreigners. The Bayal sculptures, mostly located on the South Plaza of Group A (Figure 4.2), are a remarkably varied lot for such a short span of time (some eighty years), and hint at a more complex series of events than "a Bayal conquest" (see Graham 1990). Graham (1973, 1990) proposed that two different groups of people are depicted on the Bayal stelae. His Facies A individuals, most of them dated A.D. 849 (10.1.0.0.0), are said to differ from normal Classic ones by facial features more than by a few articles of dress (Figure 4.3). The overwhelmingly traditional kit of Facies A is attributed to "cultural aspirations" (Graham 1973: 213); at what point must not "aspirations" become "identity," recognizing that Classic Maya exhibited temporal as well as regional and site variation?

Graham's Facies B figures (Figure 4.4) are recognized especially by very long hair, vertical foreheads, minimal garb, and large bead necklaces, along with squared cartouche glyphs and non-Classic (non-period ending) dating (Graham 1973: 213). Facial hair may appear in either facies. Although frequently adopted and theorized by others, no exhaustive listing of the two facies has been compiled. The *outré* Facies B people are only one facet of Bayal, appearing on later monuments like Stelae 3, 13, and 17 with likely dates of 10.2.0.0.0 to 10.3.0.0.0+ (A.D. 869–889+) (Graham 1973: 213–217). This Facies B is the one group at Seibal that may be truly non-Classic in origin as well as date. Some have seen Facies B as foreign mercenaries (from along the Gulf of Mexico) who accompanied the Facies A ruler, but eventually took over (Graham 1973; Ringle et al. 1998; cf. Fox 1987: 83), possibly amid fractious turmoil (three rulers in twenty years; Mathews and Willey 1991: 58). The proposed identification of Stela 17 as depicting a confrontation scene between the two facies about A.D. 899, with Facies B ascendant (Graham 1973: 215), is concordant with this suggestion, but Stuart sees the reverse occurring (Stuart 1993: 337). Stuart remarks a general change during the Late Classic to depicting an increased range of statuses, besides the ruler (cf. M. Miller 1993: 407), and suggests Facies B people simply possessed lower status rather than a distinct cultural identity. The absence of the Seibal Emblem Glyph from these later monuments is consistent with inferior status (among other explanations). Clearly, the significance of these two facies remains controversial.

The key attribute of long hair as indicating foreigners has four strikes against it. First, it is easily changed, an item of culture not genes, as is also true of most Facies B traits. Second, while it can point to origins in Acalan along the Gulf of Mexico (Graham 1973: 213), in fact long hair was also worn in Petén and northern Yucatán (G. Jones 1989: 107, 147), eliminating long hair as uniquely western. Third, Schele and Mathews suggest that the longish and "impossibly high" hair seen on the Facies A monuments is a wig (Figure 4.3; Schele and Mathews 1998: 185, 192). The quintessential long and free-flowing hair of Facies B individuals

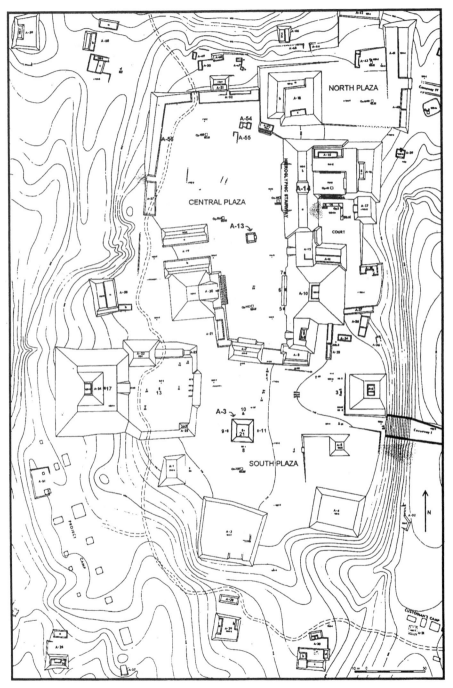

4.2 Seibal Group A. (Adapted from Willey 1990: Figure 4.)

might find the same explanation (masks and a "babushka" on Stela 3, perhaps appended to natural neck-length hair on Stela 13). If a wig, then we cannot really tell whether people have a Classic sloping forehead or a "non-Classic" erect one. Fourth, long hair may not even be new in the Pasión region: longish hair occurs on Machaquilá Stelae 3, 4, and 8, east of Seibal (Proskouriakoff 1993: 174), and long (clubbed or ponytail) hair may be depicted on Dos Pilas Stelae 2 and 11 and Aguateca Stela 2 (see Houston 1993: Figures 3.27, 3.28, 4.20). Is it only coincidence that the Petexbatun stelae depict Ruler 3, conqueror of Seibal in A.D. 735 (Houston and Mathews 1985; Houston 1993; Mathews and Willey 1991)? Hirsute faces had also been shown earlier on Copán Stela C (A.D. 711) and Piedras Negras Stela 12 (A.D. 785) (Schele and Mathews 1998: Figure 4.9; John Montgomery, personal communication, February 1999).

Names and Actions

Before reviewing the Bayal people named in hieroglyphic decipherments, we must begin with two earlier sets of monuments, for breakthroughs at Petexbatun sites have completely upended our understanding of Tepejilote history (Houston and Mathews 1985; Demarest 1997). One set consists of the Hieroglyphic Stair (HS) panels re-erected on the west stair of

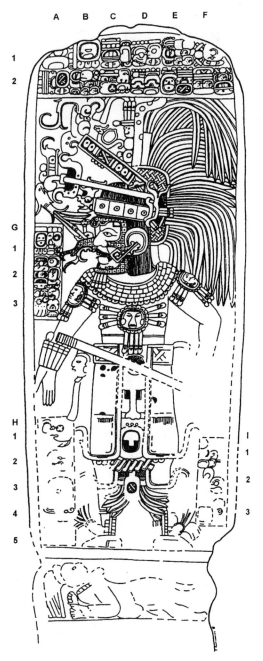

4.3 Stela 11. Facies A: Wat'ul Chatel. (Drawing courtesy of John Montgomery.)

4.4 Stela 13. Facies B. (Drawing by Ian Graham. Copyright by Harvard University.)

outer Structure A-14 on the Central Plaza of Group A (Figure 4.2; Graham 1990; Smith 1982). Four facts about the hieroglyphic text, introduced by an Initial Series, are particularly relevant. First, it commemorates the conquest of Seibal in A.D. 735 (9.15.4.6.4) by Ruler 3 of the Dos Pilas dynasty and was erected by Ruler 4 in A.D. 751 (9.16.0.0.0) (Houston and Mathews 1985; Houston 1993). The defeat was a blow to the pride of Seibal and to SAP. Second, native Seibal rulers are mentioned, the Early Classic Macaw-Jaguar and Yich'ak-Balam, the ruler sacrificed by Ruler 3 of Dos Pilas (Houston 1993). Third, on Dos Pilas Stela 2 and Aguateca Stela 2 it is proclaimed "they chopped the writing of the statues that were made" at Seibal, which is to say that "the Seibal dynasty lost its history when it lost the war" (Schele and Mathews 1998: 177). In fact, no monument predating the HS was found, except perhaps miscellaneous bits and some of the thirty-four "plain" stelae (Smith 1982: 151, 244, Table 2; Tourtellot 1988b: 105, 451, 458). Monuments so lost may account for a misleading lack of antecedents for the "new" Bayal stelae (cf. Stuart 1993: 339). Fourth, the HS panels are the only early monuments that display the Seibal Emblem Glyph, until it reappears ninety-eight years later on a forest of Bayal stelae.

The second Tepejilote set consists of three later monuments associated with the temple A-10 stair (Stelae 5, 6/22, 7; Graham 1973: 16–24). They are notable on four counts here. First, the Petexbatun Emblem Glyph is repeatedly expressed, but never the Seibal Emblem. Second, the dating system employs the short Calendar Round rather than full Initial Series, anticipating the practice continued on the Bayal monuments. Third, they feature depictions of a ballplayer, although it is uncertain whether a ballcourt yet existed at Seibal (Smith 1982: 77–82, 157–162). Fourth, the ballplayer, Ruler "D" (Mathews and Willey 1991), ascended his throne in A.D. 771 (9.17.0.0.0), dedicated the stairway in A.D. 780 (9.18.10.0.0), and bore the title Ah-Bolon-Abta (Graham 1990:21, 23).[4] We note that Ruler D's title, which appears here during the Tepejilote–Bayal Transition phase, is also featured prominently on Bayal Stelae 8–11 (Graham 1990: 28. 33, 36, 41). Schele and Mathews note (1998: 179, Footnote 5) that it is a type of title also held by Petexbatun kingdom rulers. In sum, the lord memorialized on the A-10 stairway was in charge of a city previously conquered by the Petexbatun kingdom and he still claimed some relationship to it, via title and Emblem Glyph, despite the disarray and decline that realm suffered after A.D. 761. We suggest the conquest by Dos Pilas is the explanation for the character of the subsequent Transition phase during which Ruler D held sway: an historical time when Seibal was relatively impoverished and unable to acquire polychrome vessels or special ritual architecture, and was also suffering during the late Nacimiento-phase dissolution in the Petexbatun (Demarest 1997; Houston and Mathews 1985; Houston 1993).

The Facies A people of Structure A-3, dated A.D. 849 (10.1.0.0.0), are the key Bayal people at Seibal. Radial temple A-3 possesses five stelae in a unified composition of extraordinary innovation (Smith 1982: 12–59). The stelae apparently depict a single lord of Seibal, Wat'ul Chatel or Wa-ba-lu-K'a-?-le (Schele and Mathews 1998: 175–196; Stuart 1993: 339), who is engaged in five different ceremonies. If his role can be clarified, much else becomes clear. Two aspects of Wat'ul as the leader of the alleged Bayal invaders are particularly damaging to migration hypotheses. First, he is perhaps sometimes rendered with a Classic sloped forehead (Stelae 8, 9, 21?), other times with a non-Classic undeformed visage (Stelae 10, 11?), thus confounding factional attribution (native or foreign) versus artistic license (or different artisans [Graham 1990: 25]). Proskouriakoff (1993: 181) believed that these sculptors came from Machaquilá. Second, Wat'ul appears to have been sent by one Kan Ek', "He of Ucanal" (Figure 4.3, glyph C2a; Schele and Mathews 1998: 183). If correctly read, Wat'ul Chatel was sent by someone from Ucanal—in the heart of the Classic realm, northeast of Seibal— and is likely neither non-Classic nor non-Maya. This is the same Classic region from which come three "witnesses" listed on Stela 10 (Hun . . . Kawil of Tikal[?], Kan-Pet of Kalak'mul, and Kan-Ek' from Motul de San José [Ik' site]; Marcus 1973; Schele and Mathews 1998: 185–187). The only way to save Wat'ul's role as the leader of a non-Classic invasion from the west is to claim Facies B is a genetically distinct faction of the invading forces (as in "mercenaries").

Decipherments of Wat'ul's texts also strike the general conquest hypothesis (Schele and Mathews 1998: 183–195). Wat'ul Chatel appears to make no accession statement, no claims of victory or conquest, and shows hardly a weapon. On Stela 11 alone, he stands above a captive (unnamed). Moreover, nor did Wat'ul "destroy history" as Ruler 3 of Dos Pilas had done. Instead, Wat'ul revives the Seibal Emblem Glyph rather than use a Petexbatun Emblem or introduce one of his own. Wat'ul also continues the use of Calendar Round dating, first seen on Stelae 5–7, but does not employ "Puuc" dating (Graham 1973; Graham 1990), thus pointing to Classic Petén rather than the west. Nor does Wat'ul use the Ucanal emblem in any other context. Yet this one mention is a pregnant one, for Ucanal was another Classic Maya site still erecting stelae, recently under the thumb of Naranjo (an ally of Tikal), possibly associated with the peripatetic Itzá, and having "important links" to the Seibal stelae (Chase 1985b; Graham 1973; Schele and Freidel 1990: 189–194, 386; Thompson 1970: Chapter 1). While Ucanal Stela 4 at 10.1.0.0.0 shares a non-Classic squared glyph cartouche with (later) Stelae 3 and 13 at Seibal, squared cartouches are widespread and found as much as four centuries earlier (Graham 1973; Graham 1990: 63; Proskouriakoff 1993: 186). Thus, like fine paste pottery, they may be a gross diagnostic of the Terminal Classic horizon and not much use to identify "foreign" homelands (Schele and Mathews 1998: 179, Footnote 6).

The personage appearing on Stela 1, erected near Str. A-3 in 10.2.0.0.0, is identified as "Knife-Wing," a name also known from Chichén Itzá (Kowalski 1989). He (of no designated facies) may have been memorialized as an advisor or powerful visitor (or the power behind the throne [Ringle et al. 1998: 219]). A case might be made that his appearance at Seibal antedates his presence at Chichén, for the calendrical dates cited by Kowalski (1989) for the Chichén connection are later than Wat'ul and "Knife-Wing" at Seibal.[5]

Overall, the sculpture of Seibal is remarkably subdued and unsupportive of the allegedly militaristic and foreign conquerors invoked to explain the Bayal phase, particularly in comparison to the martial art of Yaxchilán or Piedras Negras. Only one captive is depicted and a subordinated figure occurs only on Late Classic Stela 5. The confrontation scenes on late Stelae 3 and 17 seem more verbal than military, people actually breaking into speech scrolls on Stelae 19 and 13 (Figure 4.4; Graham 1990: Figures 24, 26, 35).

Clothing

Facies A individuals are still Classic in their esoteric knowledge of writing and iconography because much of their regalia and rites have significant, direct, and deep roots in the Classic (Schele and Mathews 1998: 182–195; Stuart 1993: 339). Tepejilote, Petexbatun, Classic, or "archaic" antecedents for most Bayal elements and poses have been recognized, if underplayed, in favor of the exotic non-Classic ones (usually read as "foreign" rather than "late") (Graham 1973; Graham 1990; Schele and Mathews 1998; Stuart 1993). Facies B stelae may show more "exotic" traits simply because they are generally decades later than Facies A, or perhaps show statuses (like holders of "curved sticks") not previously represented (Stuart 1993: 336–344). Indeed, Schele and Mathews (1998) appear to be "untelling" earlier views (Mathews and Willey 1991; Schele and Freidel 1990: 385–389) by arguing that it was true Classic Maya, arriving at Seibal, who brilliantly innovated the Facies A embodiment of the Classic tradition.

Another conclusion is that the alleged uniqueness of the large corpus of eleventh-cycle monuments at Seibal is part and parcel of the non-Classic qualities of its art. It is not trivial that these monuments postdate the great bulk of Classic Maya stelae (and are chronologically "post-Late Classic"): one would expect differences to appear through both error and innovation, particularly while situated in the historical and processual forces at play in the wider Epiclassic world (Diehl and Berlo 1989).

Graham's (1990) analysis and grouping (seriating) of the stelae at Seibal argue for stylistic change from Tepejilote to late Bayal. Rather than speculating on four different elite-level "foreign" migrations (Tepejilote, Petexbatun, Facies A, Facies B), the sequence may represent stylistic evolution, possibly within a single group, in parallel with an accelerating rate of change elsewhere in the later Classic period (cf. Stuart 1993). Graham notes (1990) that the artistic and technical qualities expressed in the monuments become less Classic, less competent, less graceful, more distorted, flatter, cruder, and laconic in the compass of only 40+ years.[6] Technical skill to handle large structures and monuments may have been lost, for Graham (1990: 6) thinks that some of the final monuments were inspired by miniature art, like amulets of the sort found in the Cenote of Sacrifice at Chichén Itzá (Ringle et al. 1998: Figure 20), or on fine paste pottery (Sabloff 1970: 403).

Finally, we infer from the widely dispersed "sources" of the art of Seibal that it is an historical, perhaps experimental, syncretism of diverse inspiration, rather than an elite- or site-unit intrusion from any one place. For example, the presence of Chichén Itzá "slipper" footwear on Stela 14 is curious, for it is only at Seibal that the "complete" pair of them is shown, the Chichén examples are always worn with a sandal of another type (Proskouriakoff 1950: 86; Graham 1973; Kowalski 1989), as if a misunderstanding, or melding, of the Seibal original. Of course, if one were partial to the "Great Man" theory of history, Wat'ul is the named individual who is situated at the base of the Terminal Classic, clearly a charismatic, erudite, and innovative agent, who would have reigned a *k'atun* before "Knife-Wing," and two *k'atunob* before Kak'upacal appeared at Chichén Itzá, the alleged source of so many similarities (dates from Kelley 1976, cited by Kowalski 1989: 177).

Architecture

In a sense, the new architecture of Seibal is easy to discount (Figure 4.2). Ballcourts (Strs. A-19, C-9), radial pyramids (A-3, A-13), range-type buildings (A-14), and causeways (I–IV) might be new at Seibal, but they are not new to the Late Classic Maya (Kubler 1975; Pollock 1965). All but the ballcourts and little A-13 are built over earlier constructions. Fill ceramics and stratigraphy allow that the ballcourts and causeways could be pre-Bayal constructions; a fifth causeway in Group D (Op. 38) certainly is (Smith 1982). The internal sequences and ceramics allow construction lasting through a century, or still more if the A.D. 930 radiocarbon date for A-13 is correct (Berger et al. 1974; Smith 1982).

More noteworthy is the possible absence of similar types of Classic rituals and architectural settings in Tepejilote (Smith 1982), not their presence in Bayal. Aside from problematical datings (Sabloff 1975: 12–19), the answer may lie in Seibal's subordination to the Petexbatun between A.D. 735 and 800+, coetaneous with the Tepejilote–Bayal Transition.

This is not to denigrate Terminal Classic Seibal. Wat'ul skillfully built himself a charter with richly stuccoed temple A-3 and its five stelae (Smith 1982: 12–63; Schele and Mathews 1998: 179–182). The combination of "one of the most ancient and sacred temple forms—the radial pyramid—with a new and highly inventive use of stela placement, imagery, and message" (Schele and Mathews 1998: 179–180) is stunning and "new," but it is not thereby "foreign." Temple A-3 might be viewed as "simply" the conflation into one k'atun-ending structure of many elements of an entire twin-pyramid complex at Tikal (C. Jones 1969, 1996), including the translocation of the stela enclosure and southern building atop a bare radial pyramid.

Other "foreign" influences are possible. The specific forms of the ballcourts resemble ballcourts 2D9 and 3D4 at Chichén Itzá (Smith 1982: 231), but the latter may have been erected after 10.2.0.0.0 (Kowalski 1989: 175), perhaps forty years after Bayal began. It has been suggested that engaged columns of masonry or one-piece (pseudo-) three-member binder moldings at Seibal (A-14) are comparable to ones at Chichén Itzá or in the Puuc (Smith 1982: 240; or closer Bonampak Str. 1 [Kubler 1975: 173]). However, the resemblance is superficial and, more importantly, identical one-piece three-member moldings are now known from Late Classic Dos Pilas (Chinchilla 1990), proving local precedence instead.

Only Structure 79, a circular terraced platform at a causeway terminus, was unexpected at Seibal and in Classic Petén (Smith 1982:164–173). No sherds later than Tepejilote–Bayal Transition are definitely associated with its fill, or in the plaza around it, or in Causeway II leading to it; consequently a Terminal Classic style date on Altar 1 in front of Str. 79 was applied to the structure as well (Smith 1982: 172–174).[7] Construction dating the quasi-attached caretaker group 81 might also be pre-Bayal, but rare Early Postclassic pottery was found on its surface (Sabloff 1975: 228; Tourtellot 1988b: 153). Direct evidence for a Bayal dating is thus tenuous (cf. circular Str. 1 in Late Classic group Ixtonton 87, sixty-five kilometers east of Seibal [Laporte 1994: 110]). Regardless, round structures have no special foreign source and the perishable building on top of Str. 79 is unlikely to have been round, as for Ehecatl (cf. Pollock 1936), because the building platform on Str. 79 is rectangular.

Turning to elite housing, Wat'ul Chatel and his successors probably lived in the courtyard fronted by Str. A-14, the grandest Bayal assemblage. Several aspects of A-14 suggest a significant link between the Bayal rulers after A.D. 830 and earlier rulers of Seibal. Structure A-14 is located not in the South Plaza near the pristine new A-3, but over earlier remains, facing on the Central Plaza, which was the ancient heart of Seibal (Smith 1982: 118, 243; Tourtellot 1988b: 372). The Hieroglyphic Steps were reinstalled here in Bayal times (Smith 1982: 65), although they record the crushing defeat of Seibal in A.D. 735. The consociation of palace and text cannot be an accident. Because both Seibal and Petexbatun rulers are mentioned on the HS, it is moot with whom Wat'ul wished to associate himself. The consociation is there and leads one to question whether this is an act of a foreign conqueror; it is certainly not the act of an ignorant one. We can only speculate that it could have been astute self-protection by ingratiating himself with his new subjects—or was it an acknowledgment of his kinsmen who had once ruled over Seibal (cf. Mathews and Willey 1991: 58)? Nowhere does Wat'ul make parentage statements; perhaps the HS was his substitute.

Alternatively, his disinterest in parentage could mean he was turning away from divine kingship and adopting the earlier experiments with governance and councilor rule (W. Fash 1988; B. Fash et al. 1992; Grube 1994b; Viel 1999). Perhaps the diversity of people on the Bayal monuments is a reflection of a more diverse governing body as well as varied statuses. Carved "mat" designs on the walls of a Class K "headman's house" close to Group A suggest it might have been a *popol na* ("mat" or council house) for such a group (Norman Hammond, personal communication April 1998; Tourtellot 1988b: 53, 293, 364, Figures 223, 224).

Housing

Housing is closely related to the culture and beliefs of people living at a site, can be expected to change with them, and is visible in the archaeological record (Glassie 1975; Stanish 1989; Sutro and Downing 1988; Yates 1989). If invaders lived at Seibal in Bayal times, the types of houses or nature of occupation might change from Tepejilote, the social strata of the people living in the new types might be identified, and thus the extent of population change might be revealed.

The Late Classic Tepejilote reoccupation of the Seibal plateau appears to have gone quickly, spreading into all areas of the site, followed by even more people whose ceramics are classified as Tepejilote–Bayal Transition (Tourtellot 1988b: 395, Maps 10 and 11). Bayal occupation may have decreased in number and perhaps area, but it increased in central density. Bayal house construction is concentrated near Groups A and C, in contrast to Tepejilote houses dispersed everywhere. This concentration raises the possibility of a Bayal elite enclave in a sea of Transitional commoners (Tourtellot 1988b: 401–406, Map 12; cf. Ringle et al. 1998: 219).

Innovative statistical analysis can reinforce cultural distinctions suggested by qualitative differences in house plans (González 1998: 103; Stanish 1989; cf. Tourtellot 1988b: 339–341, for groups of houses). The excavated ground plans for perishable Seibal houses (excluding the rare masonry buildings) form a consistent and characteristic cultural identity, expressed in size, shape, plan, and detail, that cannot be differentiated into Tepejilote versus Bayal (González 1998: 186–305, 384–394). For example, the percentage by phase of all excavated houses built with diagnostic Seibal broad C-shaped bench plans (classes G, I, K) rose from 65 percent of Tepejilote to 86 percent of new Bayal houses, while C-shapes as a percentage of total house occupations per phase remained fairly constant, at 65 percent of 26 Tepejilote houses, 76 percent of 25 Transitional, and 63 percent of 84 Bayal houses (from González 1998: Tables 80, 82). Statistical comparison of the Seibal pattern with Late Classic Tikal and Terminal Classic Copán house platforms conclusively shows that all three express different cultural identities (Figure 4.5; González 1998: 305–344).

The Seibal house pattern—despite its characteristic broad C-shaped benches that somewhat resemble the C-shaped wall-and-bench buildings of the Early Postclassic (Bey III et al. 1997; Rice 1986: 306–309)—is not late or foreign, however, for the entire typology of domestic structures at Seibal is virtually duplicated at Dos Pilas (Houston 1993: Chapter 2). The only question still open—to

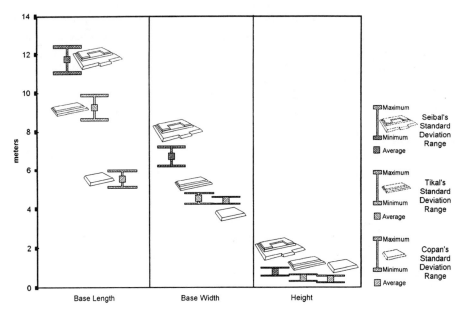

4.5 Site-specific architectural patterns: dimensions of ordinary Seibal, Tikal, and Copán house platforms. (Chart by Jason J. González.)

account for some differences in emphasis (Inomata 1995: 467–482, 518)—is whether Seibal developed in parallel with Dos Pilas (from Tikal origins?), or whether its vernacular house form arrived as a consequence of the Petexbatun's victory.

Any mass migrations from the Petexbatun to Seibal will be difficult to detect against the background of similar house plans. One clue may lie in curious stair or bench stones bearing a raised disk (Solar God?). A number were found at Seibal, placed on temples, ballcourts, and houses in Groups A and C (Smith 1982: 235; Tourtellot 1988b: 454). Examples have now been found on a Late Classic structure at Dos Pilas (Chinchilla 1990). Because raised-disk orthostats are shared between Dos Pilas and Seibal, their installation in several west-facing (and possibly Transitional) houses in central Seibal may indicate the area where a Petexbatun-emulating leader resided (large group C-1 with its own causeway stub and plain stela), and perhaps began the causeway system that radiates from there. Raised-disk stones on Bayal phase house C-19b may signal a destination for still others fleeing the Petexbatun collapse. Raised-disk stones on two big pyramids (A-20 and A-24) with Bayal outer construction (and Facies B stelae) comprise another hint of a continuing Petexbatun influence at Bayal Seibal.

The possibility of decline in population already occurring during the Bayal florescence (Tourtellot 1988b: 400–407, 426) suggests abandonment processes affecting the common people perhaps more than the elite (cf. Pendergast 1992), and would also argue against massive immigration. A decline in the labor pool might also account for the singular Bayal focus on the area of Groups A and C, for the relatively small volume of elite Bayal constructions—often merely new skin on old structures (Smith 1982)—and for the perceived decline in sculpture. Flight is a common Maya response to elite or foreign oppression (Farriss 1984). However, the real trajectory of late population change is still unresolved because SAP was unable to convincingly discriminate between Bayal artifacts as representing a shrunken and nucleated replacement for all Tepejilote or a high density elite facet added to the center of the expansive and continuing Transitional settlement (see also previous burial discussion).

Production

Ceramics are the key basis for distinguishing the Tepejilote Late Classic from the Bayal Terminal Classic phases, dated by monument associations and ceramic cross-dating (Sabloff 1973, 1975). The contrast of Tepejilote polychromes and flanged censers with Bayal fine paste pots and spike censers is well known (Sabloff 1973, 1975; Willey 1990), but in the Transitional phase all of these seem absent. Bayal complex ceramics of Seibal form two groups, the fine paste wares of presumed "foreign" origin and Late Classic "local" monochrome, striated, and unslipped types continuing and developing from the Tepejilote ceramic complex (Sabloff 1975: 153–222; Willey 1990: 250). The diagnostic Bayal types tend to be concentrated in the core area of Seibal, appearing in new construction almost exclusively there, and few of them are seen farther out (Tourtellot 1988b: 401–406).

Recent analytical sourcing of fine paste clays have found sources both more widely scattered and closer to Seibal than originally thought (Foias and Bishop 1997; Sabloff 1982). Fine Gray vessels appear in Late Classic Petexbatun after A.D. 750 (Foias 1992: 272–276), but not at Seibal. The key point is that production of fine paste wares already had worked its way into the lower Pasión River, and perhaps Seibal, by Bayal times (Foias and Bishop 1997; Willey 1990: 257–258). Although local to the region, it did not displace local domestic tempered wares.

The procurement of Bayal highly decorated pottery is not systemically different from Tepejilote's pattern, for each complex "obtained most of its [fine] serving pottery from outside its sustaining area" (Sabloff 1973: 116). Like Bayal, Tepejilote is not exclusively Petén-centric but already had some westward affiliations to the lower Usumacinta, via Altar de Sacrificios (flanged censers and much domestic ware [Sabloff 1975: 236]).

Pabellon Molded-Carved is the critical fine paste type because it shows the same types of people and regalia as appear on Bayal monuments at Seibal, particularly those of Facies B ("long-hair") type (Sabloff 1970, 1973). However,

Adams showed that twice as many of the style traits in common between Pabellon vessels and Seibal sculpture have Classic antecedents as those that do not, marking a very substantial "Classic" component in the allegedly non-Classic style, the remainder of which Adams concludes is also distinct from "Mexican" styles (Adams 1973b: 146, 153–155, Appendix B).

Among other classes of artifacts, molded pottery figurines continue through with no detectable changes, significantly including the warrior type (Willey 1978: 12–35, 1990: 258). No particular significance can be assigned to new tool forms like exotic thin-flat metates and laurel-leaf projectile points/knives (Willey 1990) because they occur in Late Classic Petexbatun as well (Brady 1994: 613, 617–621; Holtman 1991; Stiver 1992). The one arrow point is likely to be part of a tiny Postclassic occupation (Willey 1990: 260).

Defense

Although horrific signs of defensive construction and destruction fill the Petexbatun subregion (Demarest et al. 1997; Inomata 1997), Seibal seems placid in comparison. Seibal does have great natural defense potential and Group D, hidden above the river frontage, is a strongly built fortress and area of refuge (Tourtellot 1988b: 432–436). Ironically, Group D was clearly rebuilt and most heavily occupied in Tepejilote times (Smith 1982: 223), so it is the part of the site most likely to have suffered the defeat by Dos Pilas in A.D. 735. By Bayal times some defensive structures in Group D had been abandoned and it was only a light residential area (Smith 1982: 223; Tourtellot 1988b: 406–407).

The Group D fortifications most likely date to the Tepejilote–Bayal Transition, contemporary with the fractious decline of the Petexbatun kingdom. Although the fortification might have been useful as early as Seibal's dated defeat in A.D. 735, fortifications in the Petexbatun do not definitely appear before the changed dynamics of warfare and siege following A.D. 761 (Demarest 1997; Inomata 1997). Curiously enough, Dos Pilas' nearest neighbor and most bitter rival, Tamarindito, never did build dedicated defense works (Demarest et al. 1997; Valdés 1997).

Group A may have been less formidably defended. Its potential defensive works consist of very wide "parapet" structures A-40–42, A-52, and A-56–57, closing off the North and Central Plazas of Group A (Figure 4.2; Adams 1963; Smith 1982: 232; Tourtellot 1988b: 432–436). Not thoroughly tested by SAP, they are of indeterminate Tepejilote-Bayal date and might have been parts of a large marketplace, as also represented by traces of low platforms scattered over the plaza surface, like Strs. A-54 and A-55 (Smith 1982: 106–108, 232; Tourtellot 1988b: 308).

In view of the discovery of a siege village at Dos Pilas (Demarest et al. 1997), could the alleged Seibal marketplace in Group A instead be another example of a siege village? A siege village, or refuge, at Seibal would consist of the parapets, low "market stalls," and perhaps the A-13 mass-burial platform (Smith 1982: 59–

63). Such a village could date from A.D. 830 (Wat'ul) to perhaps A.D. 930 (Burial 4 in A-13).

Seibal appears to differ from the Petexbatun (especially Aguateca) in the extent of its settlement defenses (Demarest et al. 1997; Tourtellot 1988b). Seibal lacks the fortified hilltop house groups seen on the Petexbatun plateau, in part due to flatter mapped terrain. Some Seibal house groups were built on defensibly tall basal platforms (Preclassic "tells"), and some patio groups had low masonry footing walls connecting their adjacent structures, but these have innocuous explanations. Field walls, property walls, or extended defensive walls were not seen within two kilometers of Seibal, nor did they show up in limited trenching of open areas (but see Dunning and Beach 1994: 60; Dunning et al. 1997: 261). Admittedly, outlying wooden palisades may have been footed invisibly in deep soil rather than on stone foundations, as were some wall sections in the Petexbatun (Inomata 1997). However, eliminating the need for still visible one-meter-high stone foundations requires that Seibal had much deeper soils than on the Petexbatun escarpment. It is not clear that it did (for example, Dunning 1993; Dunning and Beach 1994: 56; Dunning et al. 1997: 263; Tourtellot 1988b: Chapter 3).

TERMINAL CLASSIC TRANSFORMATION

On the basis of the foregoing summary and analysis of data, we outline the shape of an answer to the question of the nature of the Bayal "conquest" at Seibal. First, Bayal looks special in part because Tepejilote does not. Clearly, part of the answer to why Bayal stands out is that the Tepejilote-cum-Transition phases exhibit relative impoverishment in sculpture, epigraphy, architecture, ceramics, and burials; that is, Tepejilote is more "non-Classic" than Bayal in significant respects. A relatively impoverished Tepejilote seems real, witness the destruction proclaimed by Dos Pilas Ruler 3, but other contributing factors may include sampling bias and SAP reconstruction imperatives for the latest architecture.

Second, only a Late Classic Tepejilote immigration can be documented with considerable certainty. It is an initial reoccupation migration, rather than a partial (elite) or complete (replacement) migration (Snow 1997), as shown by sterile soil layers and absence of Middle Classic occupation preceding it, by the enormous amount of new construction, new house plan, rapid growth in population, and by high ceramic counts (Sabloff 1975: 234; Tourtellot 1988b: 256, 272, 392, 394, 422). Already the Late Classic Petexbatun-Seibal region was stepping away from its Tikal-centric identity and was developing along its own course of architectural, ceramic, and sculptural evolution—perhaps even the "long hair" trait—under the Petexbatun kingdom.

Third, the only provable conquest at Seibal is not Bayal, but the surprise discovery of an earlier one in A.D. 735 for which we do have broadly trumpeted events, date, actors, point source, and consequences. The later Bayal "conquest," on the other hand, has now become more complex and less certain. We know who was probably involved (Wat'ul Chatel), and whence he may have come (Ucanal), but it is not stated that there was a war, who lost, in what kind of an event, or what happened to the loser. For a leader who publicly flaunted his personage, he is surprisingly reticent about how he might have gained the throne. This alone should make us suspicious of an armed conquest against opposition, and ready to consider alternatives. House, burial, domestic pottery, and artifact types hardly change, but closely linked sculpture and elite ceramics do, as the defining criteria.

Besides foundering on the Petexbatun data, a number of systemic problems exist within the theories that invoke long-distance migrations, whether of elite groups or whole populations. Underlying them is a degree of essentialism, as if the Classic Maya were essentially like Tikal, never mind Yaxchilán in the "west." Nor are non-Classic foreign "sources" in turn unitary. Furthermore, many of these theories smack of unexamined biological determinism, as if Classic and non-Classic Maya cultures were carried by the biology of their origins: ethnic biology was destiny. The proposal for a new Epiclassic world-religion (Ringle et al. 1998) has in its favor the strong recognition that new ideas also moved by means other than conquest and migration.

Oldetyme Leadership

Clearly, Seibal saw major changes in certain aspects of its life during Bayal, but most of its citizens probably changed little and in limited ways. The complexity of their reaction—as shown by the poor correlations of status with house types and sizes and with artifact and ceramic inventories (González 1998; Tourtellot 1988b)—suggests not only a varied array of social classes, but different degrees of acculturation rather than sharp distinctions based on biological origin (cf. Ringle et al. 1998: 219). In addition, PRAP and others are now finding Classic Maya antecedents for some "new" Bayal characteristics.

On Seibal Stela 11 Wat'ul Chatel declares that he arrived accompanied by four palanquin lords, two of whom might be Kan-Ek' and Ho-Pet (Figure 4.3, glyph D1; Schele and Mathews 1998: Figure 5.9). Two men with similar names are among the five lords who witness Wat'ul's ceremonies. The home realms of the three witnesses on Stela 10 point to central Petén once again influencing Río Pasión affairs, as Tikal and Kalak'mul had when the Dos Pilas dynasty was first established (Houston and Mathews 1985; Houston 1993; Mathews and Willey 1991). Their presence here may signal that they actively attempted to restore a former state of affairs.

In any case, the Ah-Bolon-Abta title, frequently cited by Wat'ul, is already prominent on earlier Stelae 5 and 7. The "Ah . . . Abta" title is characteristic of the Petexbatun and is adopted by Wat'ul, along with the old Seibal Emblem. Although perhaps only a wily ploy on his part, it certainly means he was not a stranger ignorant of local traditions, and might even mean that he was legitimately adopting the old title. By this we mean he may have been a descendant, directly or collaterally, of the Petexbatun dynasty, or of the Seibal branch in particular (Mathews and Willey 1991: 58).

If Wat'ul built palace A-14, then he was also associating himself with the reinstallation of the Hieroglyphic Staircase panels there, which show not only the old Seibal Emblem Glyph but also the Dos Pilas Emblem. Given the lack of monuments between A.D. 800 and 830, yet an apparently large population of farmers, we wonder if the demise of the Petexbatun kingdom did not produce a power vacuum, or a vacancy into which Wat'ul was invited, coming from the eastern Petén because many Maya sites continued strong through 10.1.0.0.0 in that area (Laporte 1994; Mathews and Willey 1991). Perhaps he married in and was "adopted" into the local dynasty.

The point is that the traditional leadership first associated with the Seibal Emblem Glyph had already been interrupted by the Dos Pilas conquerors, and Wat'ul's stelae seem compatible with a restoration. We do not expect the use of the emblem by a conqueror who was truly foreign, not connected to a long-defeated (if not discredited) dynasty, unaffiliated with the Classic Maya, or just passing through.

Evolution

The Pasión region exhibits internal change, or evolution, during the Late Classic, as shown above for Seibal. Not least is the discovery that outsiders founded the Dos Pilas dynasty and that it then underwent a pernicious evolution of warfare (Demarest 1997). This evidence from the Petexbatun plays two principal roles at Seibal. In the Late Classic the Petexbatun is either parallel, or a donor through conquest, to the Tepejilote and Transition phases at Seibal. In the Terminal Classic the Petexbatun is largely broken, reduced to the island site of Punta de Chimino (see Demarest, Chapter 6, this volume) and unlikely to have played a leading role in either the alleged foreign invasion or the ultimate collapse of Seibal. A third body of evidence is the attribution of sources of fine paste ceramics to the "lower Pasión" (see Foias and Bishop 1997), weakening the critical ceramic basis for Bayal's "foreign" origin. Ironically, then, earlier arguments (that Facies B sculptural images imitate pottery) may now be inverted to argue for local development.

Rather than seeing late invasions as disrupting Classic Maya civilization, serious trouble may already have developed in the Late Classic from internal processes, producing conditions under which people eventually sought and developed an alternative form of rule and worship that offered them hope. All those who witnessed Wat'ul Chatel's rites are from the Classic Maya area, and Knife-Wing of Chichén's Stela 1 is later than Wat'ul; does Knife-Wing represent foreigners attracted by Watul's charisma, or do they instead originate and spread quickly from Seibal itself? While the quantity of representation elsewhere is against this local evolution, the later calendrical dates on significant elements support it. Perhaps, instead of being agents of Chichén Itzá first, individuals like Knife-Wing eventually contributed to the *mul tepal* (council) government there instead. Perhaps it was Chichén that owed something to ". . . family ties, and political connections with the new rulers in the south" (Kowalski 1989: 183), more than the reverse. A key aspect of the Terminal Classic is that it seems a cultural stew, taking its ingredients from far-flung sources, and equally partitively ladling them out again to different sites and regions (cf. Ringle et al. 1998). One wonders if the auspicious close of the *bak'tun* at 10.0.0.0.0 played a role, Wat'ul celebrating not only himself but surviving the "millennium bug." He was arguably a founding agent in the widespread cultural uniformity of the Epiclassic period.

THE END

The end and abandonment of Seibal remains a problem. Demarest (1997) has effectively removed the most likely explanations by arguing that the earlier collapse of the Petexbatun kingdom was not due to drought, agricultural imbalances, overpopulation, disruption of trade and economy, nutritional or biological decline, or fragile kinship relations, but to the systemic consequences of an evolution of internecine local warfare (cf. Dunning et al. 1998; Foias and Bishop 1997; Wright 1997). Non-Classic Maya play no role and Terminal Classic occupation is small, except at Seibal and its Lake Petexbatun outlier, Punta de Chimino (Demarest 1997: 220). If none of these potential causes can apply to Seibal, because it prospers instead, then why does it eventually fade away, too?

We see little evidence for Seibal's end in a continuing swirl of social and political violence, from which Seibal had recovered very well. A social revolt is not the answer, for as John Graham shows (1990), there is virtually no destruction of any of the late monuments, nor did SAP find late destruction layers or valedictory rites, although the aforementioned three rulers in just twenty years may hint that not all was entirely tranquil. There is also the scant possibility of (still another) "conquest" suggested by the hypothetical siege village in Group A, or of a confrontation perhaps memorialized on late Stela 17.

There could be other ways to explore the end of Seibal. For one, occupation may have continued stronger and longer than is presently believed. A scattering of Early and Middle Postclassic ceramics and simple houses occurs (Sabloff 1975: 222–228; Tourtellot 1988b: 223, 407). These might be the mere shadow of stronger Postclassic-period settlement, followed by a Late Postclassic village at Punta de Chimino (Demarest 1997: 220). Because some of the rare Postclassic sherds at Seibal are themselves exotics, the bulk of a complementary domestic assemblage may have consisted of analytically Bayal types continuing into Postclassic times. Some "illiterate" stela rites may have occurred at this time as well (Graham 1990: 17). Willey (1990: 197, 260) observes that three equivocal radiocarbon bone dates in as many "Bayal" burials actually "fall in the A.D. 1000–

1050 range, or a century or so later than our Bayal closing estimate of A.D. 928," up to a century and a half later than the last dated monument.

Of the alternative outcomes (M. Miller 1993: 405), Seibal appears to have simply "fizzled out" rather than to have experienced a "dramatic cessation" as at La Milpa (Hammond and Tourtellot, this volume). Perhaps we need seek no catastrophic explanation, but see only another pulse of "normal Maya" settlement dispersal or flux (Tourtellot 1993: 225), rebounding from previous overcentralization (cf. Komchen, El Mirador, Blue Creek). Possibly, the presence of Postclassic exotics at Seibal even signals increased peasant mobility and extraregional interaction. We do not know the settlement pattern history along the entire Seibal ridge, whether Bayal nucleation gave way to dispersal or field houses became permanent abodes. Perhaps the recent agricultural clear-cutting and looting is an "opportunity" for rapid survey and collection. In a still broader view, Seibal may have been reoriented from the Petexbatun basin eastward, where boom times were occurring during the Terminal Classic and may well extend in greater strength for a century later (Laporte 1994).

Or perhaps Seibal declined for no internal reason, but because of world-altering strategic events outside of the Pasión basin that, instead of pushing people to Seibal, drew natives off instead. For example, Webb (1964) argued for grand international developments on the Epiclassic horizon, Sabloff (1977) for the rise of seaborne trade, Kowalski (1989) for a shift in external trading networks, and Ringle et al. (1998) for the spread of a new religion. To the extent that Seibal functioned as a major trade inflection point (Tourtellot 1988b: 431–432), its reason for being may have disappeared along with its customers.

NOTES

1. The authors are solely responsible for the contents of this paper. The views of other authors cited here are historical and may not reflect their present views. While we cite competent epigraphers and iconographers, they should not be held responsible for our inferences regarding historical events at Seibal.

2. Largely defined negatively, the problematical Transition has been treated as a middle phase in the development of late Seibal, although it might be an analytical residual, assignable either to Tepejilote (Tourtellot 1988b; Willey 1990) or to Bayal (Sabloff 1975; Smith 1982). We favor late Tepejilote now that PRAP provides a strong historical context.

3. Three of Wright's (1994: 159–162) specific criticisms invoke irrelevant Preclassic Seibal burials as local antecedents (for cranial deformation[?], Tabular Erect deformation, and extended position). Two other criticisms assume that no deep excavation was conducted in suitable locations (only Bayal burials are either in structures or axial). Wright is correct that change in stature over time is statistically indistinguishable; that dental mutilation did not in fact vanish; and that sampling error due to the small burial series (and only one elite) may account for much of the apparent difference in burials from one phase to the next.

4. This title and the similar ones on Stelae 8–11 were all originally transcribed as Ah-Bolon-Tun by Graham (1990; Schele and Freidel 1990: 287) and subsequently changed to Ah-Bolon-Abta, perhaps "he of nine works" (Schele and Mathews 1998: 179, Footnote 5).

5. "Knife-Wing's" depiction on Seibal Stela 1 is dated 10.2.0.0.0 (A.D. 869), while his name on Chichén's Yula Lintel 1 is apparently four years later at 10.2.4.8.4, and the Temple of the Four Lintels' Lintel 1 is apparently twelve years later at 10.2.12.1.8 and 10.2.12.2.4 (Kowalski 1989: 174). Other Chichén and Uxmal dates adduced by Kowalski (1989) in his comparisons with Seibal and the Comitán Valley extend past 10.3.0.0.0. Smith (1982: 240) compared the form of the two ballcourts at Seibal with ballcourts 2D9 and 3D4 at Chichén Itzá, and Kowalski (1989: 175) now proposes Chichén ballcourt 3D4 probably postdates 10.2.0.1.9, and adds Uxmal's ballcourt at 10.3.15.16.14 to the comparison. Note that the dating of Seibal ballcourt A-19 is uncertain and might be as early as Tepejilote (Smith 1992: 82) and thus possibly contemporary with ruler D, the ballplayer-without-a-court on Stelae 5 and 7 (in the second set of Tepejilote monuments).

6. Some circularity of reasoning may occur, because many of the stelae do not bear dates. For example, the "prowling jaguar" altar-receptacle associated with Stela 17, style-dated A.D. 869? (Graham 1990: 70–73), seems similar to the image and position of the jaguar on Late Classic La Amelia Stela 1 dated A.D. 807 (Schele and Freidel 1990: Figure 10:3a).

7. Altar 1 is circular, with the head and tail of a jaguar carved onto its edge. Three legs, two sculpted in the shape of dwarves, supported it. These were called "the Atlantean trait" and compared with Maya-Toltec Chichén Itzá and Tula (Smith 1982: 151–152, 239, Figure 140). They do not resemble the familiar figures with upraised arms, but bear the altar on their heads; they might be called "Caryatids" instead, if the Classic Maya did not already provide a suitable name: *bacab*.

5

SETTLEMENT AND LATE CLASSIC POLITICAL DISINTEGRATION IN THE PETEXBATUN REGION, GUATEMALA

Matt O'Mansky and Nicholas P. Dunning

The Petexbatun region, located in the Pasión region of the western Petén, Guatemala, was the first lowland zone to experience a dramatic ending of Late Classic Maya civilization. Eight years of multidisciplinary research there at major sites, smaller centers, and intersite villages, beginning in the late 1980s, investigated many different aspects of ancient Maya civilization in order to address the ongoing debate regarding the radical changes in the Late and Terminal Classic (e.g., Sabloff and Willey 1967; Culbert 1973a, 1988; Sabloff and Andrews 1986b). The researchers sought to elucidate proximate and root causes underlying these changes. They discovered that, after 150 years of unprecedented expansion through militarism and strategic alliance, the Petexbatun kingdom collapsed in a state of endemic warfare beginning in A.D. 761. Within little more than a half century, the region was nearly completely abandoned.

Note that these changes represent the earliest and, perhaps, the most drastic cessation of the Classic-period political system yet uncovered in the lowlands. For that reason, it is important to trace the sequence of shifts in settlement strategy back to the beginning of the Petexbatun sequence and to provide specific evidence (beyond the historical inscriptions) for the nature of change linked to eighth-century militarism. As sketched below, the evidence from settlement patterns and ecology tallies with the historical record. These settlement and paleoecological data reflect profound *political* processes associated with the end of Classic-period society in the Petexbatun region.

83

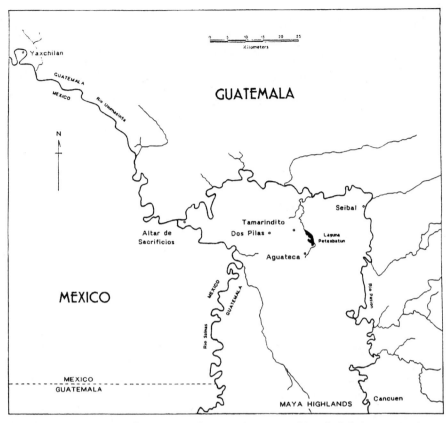

5.1 The Pasión River Valley region of Petén. Courtesy of Vanderbilt University Press.

PREVIOUS RESEARCH IN THE REGION

The Petexbatun region is part of the Lower Pasión region and is located in the Chapayal Basin between the Pasión River to the east and north and the Salinas River to the west (Figure 5.1). The region was visited by a number of explorers and archaeologists—sometimes in the course of oil explorations—in the middle of the twentieth century (Grieder 1960; Vinson 1960; Navarrete and Luján Muñoz 1963). Ian Graham (1961, 1963, 1967) explored Dos Pilas and Aguateca (among other Pasión sites) at approximately the same time, producing sketch maps of the latter site. He was the first to report on wall systems at these sites.

The first systematic archaeological research in the region was undertaken by the Peabody Museum of Harvard University at Altar de Sacrificios in the late 1950s through early 1960s (Willey and Smith 1969; Willey 1973) and at Seibal in the 1960s (Sabloff 1973; Willey et al. 1975; Willey 1978, 1990; Tourtellot 1988b).

The Seibal project discovered important data from the Terminal Classic that fueled debate regarding the role of foreign invasion in the fall of Classic Maya civilization (see Tourtellot and González, Chapter 4, this volume).

Epigraphic research on the corpus of Petexbatun monuments began in the 1970s by Ian Graham and Peter Mathews (Graham 1967; Mathews n.d., 1985; Mathews and Willey 1991). This work was continued and expanded by Stephen Houston (Houston and Mathews 1985; Houston 1987b) who, along with Boyd Dixon and Kevin Johnston, produced a map of Dos Pilas and preliminary maps of several other Petexbatun sites.

THE VANDERBILT PETEXBATUN
REGIONAL ARCHAEOLOGICAL PROJECT

A large-scale, regional multidisciplinary project was carried out by Vanderbilt University from 1989 to 1994 under the initial direction of Arthur Demarest and Stephen Houston and later Demarest and Juan Antonio Valdés (Demarest 1997). This was followed in 1996 by the Punta de Chimino Project directed by Demarest and Héctor Escobedo (Demarest et al. 1996). The Petexbatun region was selected in order to continue, test, and refine the work of the earlier Harvard Seibal and Altar de Sacrificios projects on the nature of events and processes involved in the end of Classic Maya civilization in the southern lowlands. Numerous specialists, including archaeologists, epigraphers, ecologists, ceramicists, lithicists, osteologists, paleobotanists, and geographers, participated in intensive research over the course of the project in order to examine all related aspects—political, ecological, social, economic—of eighth- and ninth-century Classic-period Maya civilization in the Petexbatun region. The approach was explicitly ecological and regional, in keeping with the processual paradigms dominant in field archaeology. However, research directions and considerations of agency were concomitantly humanistic reflecting the rich epigraphic data available in the region (Demarest and Houston 1989, 1990; Houston and Stuart 1990).

Field research began in 1989 at Dos Pilas, the Late Classic capital of the Petexbatun kingdom. The scope of research soon expanded to include the other large sites in the region in addition to minor centers, villages, and intersite areas (Figure 5.2). Mapping and excavation was undertaken at all of the major sites in the region, including Dos Pilas (Demarest 1991; Palka 1995, 1997), Aguateca (Inomata 1995, 1997, 2004; Tamarindito (Houston et al. 1990; Chinchilla 1993; Valdés et al. 1994; Valdés 1997), Arroyo de Piedra (Stuart 1990; Escobedo 1994b, 1997), and Punta de Chimino (Wolley 1993; Demarest et al. 1996). Subprojects examined many aspects of ancient Maya civilization, including economy (Foias and Bishop 1997; Foias 2004; Emery 1997, 2004; Wolley 1997), ecology and subsistence (Wright 1994, 1997a, 2004; Dunning et al. 1997; Dunning and Beach 2004), cave ritual (Brady et al. 1997), settlement patterns and demography (Killion et al. 1991; Van Tuerenhout et al. 1993; Van Tuerenhout 1996; O'Mansky and

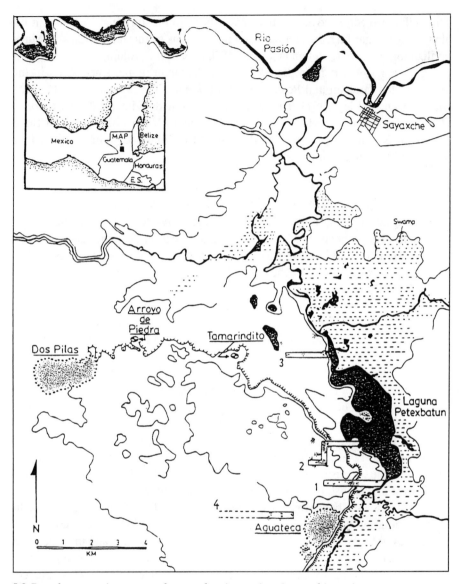

5.2 Petexbatun project research area showing major sites and intersite survey transects. Courtesy of Vanderbilt University Press.

Demarest 1995; O'Mansky, Hinson, Wheat, and Demarest 1995; O'Mansky, Hinson, Wheat, and Sunahara 1995; O'Mansky 2003), and epigraphy (Houston 1987b; Houston and Stuart 1990). Together, these various specialists assembled a remarkably complete picture of ancient Maya civilization in the Petexbatun region, especially the Late and Terminal Classic periods, when the Petexbatun kingdom first expanded and then disintegrated before being abandoned in the late eighth and early ninth centuries, as discussed below.

RESEARCH ON SETTLEMENT PATTERNS AND ECOLOGY

The dominant natural feature in the karst Petexbatun region is a series of uplifted horsts and dropped grabens along faults in the underlying limestone (Dunning et al. 1997; Dunning and Beach 2004). The most dramatic of these is the Petexbatun escarpment, which runs in a roughly northwest-southeast direction, rising nearly one hundred meters from the adjacent graben that contains the Laguna and Río Petexbatun, themselves tributaries of the Pasión River. The low-lying grabens include large areas of uninhabitable swampland, while the horsts are well drained and dotted with springs, along with sinkholes with rich, deep deposits of soil lining their bottoms. The land at the foot of the escarpment along some sections of the Laguna and Río Petexbatun is among the richest in the region, with bedrock lying two to four meters below the modern ground surface. It is in this fertile ecozone that the earliest inhabitants of the region settled. Atop the escarpment, much of the bedrock is covered by only ten to fifty centimeters of soil, although deep, cumulic soils are found within the numerous *rejolladas* (sinkholes) that dot this elevated terrain. Yet it is along this ridge that nearly all of the Classic-period occupation was located, centered primarily around natural springs and caves and exploiting the deep soils in sinkholes.

It was apparent from the start of the Petexbatun project that, in order to understand the nature of Late Classic changes in the region, a program of mapping, sampling, and excavation outside of the large sites was needed. Thus, the Intersite Settlement Pattern Subproject (ISPS) was initiated in 1991 under the direction of Tom Killion (Killion et al. 1991). Dirk van Tuerenhout took over this work in 1992 and 1993 (Van Tuerenhout et al. 1993) and the field research was completed under the guidance of Matt O'Mansky in 1994 and 1996 (O'Mansky and Demarest 1995; O'Mansky 1996). The primary goals of the ISPS were to determine chronologies and spatial variation of regional settlement, calculate demographic estimates for all periods, document evidence of warfare in intersite zones, and examine how all of these factors interacted with local ecology and subsistence systems. Toward these goals, four transects were mapped and tested in order to produce a complete overall picture of regional settlement in relation to ecology and changes in settlement strategy over time. These transects included areas within each of the seven ecozones described by Dunning and colleagues (Dunning et al. 1991; Inomata 1995: 43–45).

Each transect was oriented east-west and was mapped in a "fishbone" pattern wherein a central line was cut along the length of the transect. Every fifty meters along this line, 90-degree angles were turned to the north and south. One-hundred-meter-long side trails were then cut perpendicular to the central line, resulting in a total transect width of 200 meters. Archaeologists and local workers, spaced at intervals between five and twenty meters (spacing varied according to foliage and visibility), then walked parallel to the main line between side trails. All structures and features encountered were flagged, cleared, and mapped. Finally, a minimum sample of 10 percent of these features within each transect was tested, primarily through 1×2–meter excavations.

The first transect, Transect 1, began on the western shore of the southern tip of Laguna Petexbatun approximately two kilometers northeast of the epicenter of Aguateca. The two-kilometer-long transect, which was mapped in 1991 (Killion et al. 1991) and excavated in 1993 (Van Tuerenhout et al. 1993), ran west up and onto the escarpment. A total of sixty-seven structures and several walls were discovered within the transect. The main concentration of settlement was the fortified village Quim Chi Hilan, which contained twenty-nine structures and a series of defensive walls. Sinkholes dotted the terrain west of Quim Chi Hilan and a number of structures, walls, and terraces were located in that area. A second, smaller village, Tix Li Poh, was located at the base of the escarpment (Van Tuerenhout et al. 1993; Van Tuerenhout 1996).

Transect 2 was mapped initially in 1991 (Killion et al. 1991) and was extended in 1996 (O'Mansky and Wheat 1996a). It was excavated during the 1994 and 1996 field seasons (O'Mansky, Hinson, Wheat, and Sunahara 1995; O'Mansky and Wheat 1996a). It began just south of Punta de Chimino on the western shore of Laguna Petexbatun at the modern village of Excarvado. The first 800 meters of the transect proved to be largely uninhabitable as it crossed perennial swampland before climbing the escarpment. Atop the escarpment, the transect turned south for 300 meters before returning to a west heading for an additional 800 meters. Several small villages were discovered along the transect and reconnaissance by Dunning and Killion to the north of the transect discovered additional clusters of settlement. This fairly dense occupation may be due to the presence of the minor center of El Excavado just to the north. An additional three structures were located at the foot of the escarpment near a spring.

In general, settlement in Transects 1 and 2 followed upland ridges in the rolling terrain, leaving the lower-lying areas clear for agricultural fields. Extensive wall systems were encountered along these two transects, most obviously field or property boundaries, quite distinct in form and placement from the defensive walls found elsewhere in the region. Dunning, Beach, and Rue (1997: 261) suggest that these walls, which often are associated with agricultural terraces, were used to partition the land, indicating that this productive land was controlled and managed at the household or corporate group level. This area between Tamarindito and Aguateca had some of the most fertile and valued lands in the region and the presence of low boundary walls here indicates intensive use for gardening. Soil phosphate analysis also suggests intensive cultivation within walled areas, as well as in rejolladas.

Transect 3 began on the western shore of the northern tip of Laguna Petexbatun east of Tamarindito (Van Tuerenhout et al. 1993). This was the only transect that did not map areas on the escarpment. It began on a small bluff above the modern village of El Faison and gradually descended to the west over its 1.2-kilometer length before terminating near the eastern shore of Laguna Tamarindito. Two villages, dubbed Bayak and Battel, were mapped along the transect (Van Tuerenhout et al. 1993) and, to the surprise of the ISPS team, no walls, defensive or otherwise, were identified.

Transect 4 was mapped and tested in 1994 and 1996 in order to more completely sample the variety of environmental zones in the Petexbatun region (O'Mansky, Hinson, Wheat, and Demarest 1995; O'Mansky and Wheat 1996b). It began atop a hill 120 meters west of Cerro de Mariposas, one of a series of north-south running hills west of Aguateca. The terrain in the region consists of steep karst towers with very thin soils and no conveniently located water sources. Despite such unfavorable conditions, a total of seventy-nine structures in three villages, in addition to several terraces and wall systems, were discovered within the 1.75-kilometer-long transect.

Within intersite zones members of the ecology subproject examined ancient land-use practices. This research consisted of both informal reconnaissances and field and laboratory soil phosphate analysis. The reconnaissances, at times in conjunction with the transect work of the ISPS, identified ancient modifications to the landscape, including wall systems and terraces. Soil phosphate tests were conducted within each of the first three transects (save for the Transect 2 extension mapped in 1996) at intervals ranging from ten to fifty meters in order to identify human activity areas overlooked in other analyses (see Dunning and Beach 2004: Chapter 6 for a complete discussion of the methodology, limitations, and results of soil phosphate testing).

CHANGING SETTLEMENT AND SUBSISTENCE STRATEGIES IN THE PETEXBATUN

A brief review of period-by-period settlement strategies highlights the changing rationale of site placement and subsistence uses over time. In the Petexbatun, the evidence indicates almost a reversal of the culture-historical sequence often posited as leading to the Classic Maya "collapse": that of continuous anthropogenic ecological degradation resulting in crisis and collapse at the end of the Classic era. Instead, Preclassic uses of soils and subsistence systems were probably the most ecologically damaging, with agricultural adaptation to the local ecology improving during the Classic period to result in a stable, sustainable adaptation (Dunning et al. 1997; Dunning and Beach 2004). As we briefly document here (see also O'Mansky 2003), from the Preclassic to the Terminal Classic there is a gradual shift from ecological factors as the major determinant of settlement strategy to an increasingly political rationale for settlement, culminating in a purely defensive site-placement strategy.

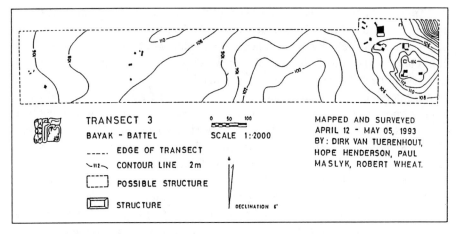

TRANSECT 3
BAYAK - BATTEL
..... EDGE OF TRANSECT
∼₁₁∼ CONTOUR LINE   2m
[___] POSSIBLE STRUCTURE
[□□] STRUCTURE

0   50   100
SCALE 1:2000

MAPPED AND SURVEYED
APRIL 12 - MAY 05, 1993
BY : DIRK VAN TUERENHOUT,
HOPE HENDERSON, PAUL
MASLYK, ROBERT WHEAT.

DECLINATION 5°

5.3 Map of Transect 3. Courtesy of Vanderbilt University Press.

Preclassic Settlement Strategies

The earliest evidence for settlement in the Petexbatun region dates to the Middle Preclassic. Lake cores from Laguna Tamarindito suggest the initial settlement of the region occurred between 2000 and 1000 B.C. (Dunning et al. 1997; Dunning and Beach 2004). The earliest evidence from material culture indicates that these inhabitants selected those econiches with the most abundant natural resources in which to build their homes.

The soils between the northern tip of Laguna Petexbatun and the escarpment are deep and well suited for agriculture. The land at Punta de Chimino is similarly fertile. It is in these locations that the first Maya settled. The village of Bayak on Transect 3 (Figure 5.3) consists of seventeen mounds and terraces and is located on a low rise overlooking the waters of Laguna Petexbatun. One of these structures, Structure 10, covers an area of 400 square meters and rises more than three meters in height. A terrace or patio extends an additional seven meters from the south side of the structure. This building may be the earliest structure of elite and/or ritual function in the region. The second group, Battel, is located 900 meters west of Bayak by the edge of Lagunita Tamarindito. This small village consists of nine additional housemounds. All excavations conducted in Transect 1 yielded ceramics dating to the Middle and Late Preclassic periods (the lone exception is an intrusive Late Classic burial at Bayak) (O'Mansky, Hinson, Wheat, and Sunahara 1995). In fact, more than 99 percent of the Middle Preclassic pottery and almost 60 percent of Late Preclassic pottery discovered over the course of the Petexbatun project comes from these excavations (Table 5.1). Other foci of Preclassic settlement in the Petexbatun include Punta de Chimino and Aguateca, representing approximately 30 percent and 10 percent, respectively, of the recovered Petexbatun Preclassic pottery assemblage (Foias 1996, 2004).

Table 5.1.

Site	Excarvado 600–300 B.C.	Faisan 300 B.C.–A.D. 350	Jordan A.D. 350–600	Nacimiento A.D. 600–830	Sepens A.D. 830–950
Dos Pilas	0	41	1,115	92,531	6,364
Aguateca	0	681	42	40,371	7
Tamarindito	0	15	1,253	14,190	261
Arroyo de Piedra	0	3	1,816	21,279	17
Punta de Chimino	28	1,801	29	0	7,498
Survey Transects	4,856	3,743	173	16,980	3
Total	4,884	6,284	4,428	185,351	14,150

The earliest Petexbatun inhabitants chose zones with abundant natural resources and high agricultural potential for their houses and villages. Both Punta de Chimino and the Transect 3 villages are well situated to exploit aquatic resources and both areas have rich, fertile soils several meters deep, in contrast to the thin soils atop the escarpment, which were favored by Classic-period populations. Preclassic pottery at Aguateca is known from cave locations, suggesting early ritual use of these sacred features. Middle to Late Preclassic settlement strategy here, as in most areas of the Petén, was based on access to water sources and rich soils. Notably for settlement in the region, except for Aguateca, these early Petexbatun sites were not especially well situated for defensive purposes.

By the end of the Preclassic, the once rich environment chosen by the first settlers in the Petexbatun was suffering from the effects of a millennium of *milpa* farming. Soils were eroding and becoming less fertile as the forests were cleared back to the base of the escarpment. Lagunita Tamarindito, below Battel, was increasingly filled with sediment (Dunning et al. 1998; Dunning and Beach 2004). Recent research at Laguna Las Pozas on the southern margins of the Petexbatun region also indicates significant environmental degradation during the Preclassic (Johnston et al. 2001). Faced with decreasing productivity in their fields and a resultant shortage of arable land, the Petexbatun Maya shifted the focus of settlement up onto the escarpment in ensuing periods.

Early Classic Settlement

In the Early Classic, Tamarindito emerged as the primary center in the Petexbatun region. Located on the escarpment immediately above the Preclassic villages of Transect 3, the site was strategically situated atop the highest section of a series of hills. Below the site are two springs and three small lakes. Toward the end of the Early Classic, the inhabitants of Tamarindito began to implement strategies to increase agricultural production. To the west of Tamarindito was the smaller site of Arroyo de Piedra, a secondary capital to Tamarindito founded in the sixth century. The Early Classic shift in settlement strategy seems to have resulted from Late Preclassic population growth, leading to the settlement of less ecologically exhausted escarpment areas, which then became the focal area for larger centers.

The Early Classic Petexbatun ceramic assemblage suggests an overall decrease in population from Preclassic times, as well as the shift in settlement location. Although the total number of diagnostic Early Classic Jordan sherds is smaller than that of the Late Preclassic Faisan assemblage, Tamarindito and Arroyo de Piedra, while still fairly small centers, had significant population increases. Punta de Chimino, Aguateca, and intersite zones—the foci of earlier settlement—show reduced Early Classic occupation (Foias 1996; Foias and Bishop 1997). This apparent shift in settlement strategy, however, may be an artifact of sampling, as many intersite areas were not tested and some centers were tested more completely than others, or it may reflect the nucleation of settlement around Tamarindito and Arroyo de Piedra. It may also be a result of Mayanists' difficulties in securely separating Early Classic ceramics from those of the Late Preclassic (Lincoln 1985). In central Petén and some other zones, Early Classic markers are well defined. In the Petexbatun we suspect that many Late Preclassic types and modes continued after the third century Thus, the apparent demographic decline may be, to some extent, a methodological, not culture-historical, problem. The presence of architectural caches in "late Proto-Classic" (i.e., Early Classic) style at Punta de Chimino tends to support this thinking (Escobedo 1996). In any case, settlement expansion to the escarpment and areas farther inland indicate a shift in settlement with the onset of the Classic period, possibly accompanied by some degree of population decline.

By the middle of the seventh century, the Petexbatun was characterized by a small but growing population base well in tune with the local environment. The foci of occupation were situated to exploit natural springs and deep soils that lined the bottoms of sinkholes. Work then began on ecological adaptations that would sustain higher populations. Contrary to scenarios of Late Classic anthropogenic degradation of the environment, the sixth to eighth centuries here saw the construction of terraces, rejollada depression gardens, household gardens, and a variety of other systems. These adaptations contrast with the ecological degradation of the Late Preclassic period and created highly productive fields and gardens with lower levels of erosion (Dunning and Beach 2004). These adaptations were most evident in the Tamarindito area, where the Classic-period populace constructed check dams and terraces to increase agricultural productivity and a reservoir dam to provide ready access to fresh water for gardens (Beach and Dunning 1995; Dunning et al. 1997; Dunning and Beach 2004).

SEVENTH-CENTURY EVENTS AND SETTLEMENT CHANGE

Into this stable setting came a new, unsettling force early in the seventh century A.D., when a royal lineage from Tikal arrived at Dos Pilas but soon thereafter fell under the sway of Calakmul. Recently recovered hieroglyphic evidence demonstrates that the first Dos Pilas ruler arrived early in the seventh century when he was only a child (Demarest and Fahsen 2003). Presumably guided by a regent, the young prince and his followers settled at Dos Pilas (Demarest and Fahsen 2003; Houston 1987b). The strategy for choosing Dos Pilas was the presence of water (the two springs for which the site is named) and the absence of any large local population that would have had to be confronted. It has been posited that the site was established by Tikal as a military base to reassert Tikal's dominance of the Pasión River trade route and defend it from the expanding Calakmul alliance (Demarest 2004; Demarest and Fahsen 2003). Such a military function seems probable given that the earlier lack of a sizable local population had a reason: the soils in the area are either extremely thin over bedrock or waterlogged, in either case very difficult for productive cultivation (Dunning and Beach 2004). The newly arrived Tikal leaders rapidly constructed an impressive capital at Dos Pilas, retaining the Tikal Emblem Glyph because they were an outpost of the Tikal dynasty. A newly uncovered hieroglyphic stairway at Dos Pilas places this *entrada* at A.D. 632 (Demarest and Fahsen 2003). Monumental constructions were rapidly raised as the new ruling lineage consolidated its power base, increased its local prestige and influence, and supplanted Tamarindito as the regional capital. Unfortunately for Tikal's strategic designs, in A.D. 652 Calakmul conquered Dos Pilas and turned the now vassal center into its ally and agent.

Because the site of Dos Pilas was ill suited for agriculture, it was never host to a sizable population prior to this period. In fact, settlement studies and associated phosphate fractionation analyses indicate that Dos Pilas may never have been the locus of any significant agricultural activity, even in the eighth century when its population numbered in the thousands (Dunning et al. 1997; Dunning and Beach 2004). To sustain their population in this marginal setting, the leaders of Dos Pilas, their elites, and even non-elites must have relied heavily on regional transport of foodstuffs and on tribute. In contrast, Tamarindito, Arroyo de Piedra, and the rural areas inventoried on Transects 1 and 2 had intensive and extensive agricultural systems that could have provided substantial surplus, perhaps partly rendered as tribute to Dos Pilas.

Turning to the epigraphic evidence, within a century the predatory Dos Pilas tribute state controlled an area of fifteen hundred square kilometers and controlled much of the Pasión River trade route from near Mexico to the head of navigation far to the south at Cancuen (Mathews n.d.; Mathews and Willey 1991; Demarest 1996, 1997; Martin and Grube 2000; Williams 2002; Demarest and Fahsen 2003; Demarest 2004). According to epigraphic evidence, this expansionism first occurred under the aegis of Calakmul (Martin and Grube 2000: 54–67; Demarest and Fahsen 2003). Yet after the defeat of that powerful rival by Tikal in A.D. 695, the subsequent Dos Pilas rulers reasserted and expanded this hegemony.

The success of the rapid seventh- and eighth-century expansion of the Petexbatun hegemony is manifest throughout the Petexbatun region, but especially at its capital, Dos Pilas. Large temples and elaborate palaces were rapidly built there while monuments were erected and hieroglyphic stairways constructed. Abundant rich offerings (including tribute from wars) were placed in sacred caves beneath the site as the population reached its peak size, despite the area's lack of fertile agricultural lands. The early eighth century was a period of wealth, power, and prestige at Dos Pilas. A secondary capital and palace for the Dos Pilas rulers was seated at Aguateca and the ruler and his court apparently moved between these dynastic seats.

EIGHTH-CENTURY WARFARE BETWEEN THE PETEXBATUN CENTERS

Both epigraphic and archaeological evidence confirm that the Late Classic florescence of the Dos Pilas hegemony came to an abrupt end in A.D. 761. After a century of successful expansion the overextended kingdom dramatically collapsed when Tamarindito and other centers rebelled against Dos Pilas, defeating and exiling Ruler 4, K'awiil Chan K'inich, the last known ruler of Dos Pilas, sacking the site, and sending the region into a spiral of intensifying warfare.

The archaeological evidence of warfare has been thoroughly excavated at Dos Pilas. There, defensive walls of stone footings and wooden palisades were rapidly constructed at several key locations using stone ripped from existing nearby structures, including the facades of palaces, hieroglyphic stairways, a ballcourt, and even the funerary shrine of Ruler 2, Itzamnaaj K'awiil (Demarest et al. 1991, 1997). Extensive excavations of these defenses discovered baffle gates, killing alleys, and a cache of decapitated heads of adult males—presumably captured warriors (Demarest 1989, 1990; Demarest et al. 1991, 1995; Escobedo et al. 1990; Inomata et al. 1990; Wright 1994; Symonds 1990; Palka 1991; Brandon 1992; Rodas 1995). Ceramics recovered in these excavations date the walls to late Tepeu 2 (the ceramically distinct Late Facet Nacimiento complex), coinciding with the date of the fall of Dos Pilas (A.D. 761) based on epigraphic decipherments (Houston and Mathews 1985; Houston 1987b; Houston and Stuart 1990). Mapping and excavations within the plaza area enclosed by the walls discovered a dense grouping of low platforms for thatch-roofed huts. Ceramics from associated middens date this "squatters village" in the ceremonial heart of Dos Pilas to just after the capture of Ruler 4, from the A.D. 760 to 830 Late Facet of the Nacimiento phase (Foias 1996, 2004; Foias and Bishop 1997; Palka 1995, 1997).

After the defeat of Ruler 4 ceremonial construction and the erection of monuments at Dos Pilas ceased and the city was largely abandoned; it had lost the tribute that had allowed it to thrive in the Late Classic and was therefore no longer a rational place for human settlement, nor a safe location for investment in public architecture or even settlement. The remaining elites may have then relocated to the more defensible site of Aguateca, high on a steep eroded fragment of the

Petexbatun escarpment, with a deep natural chasm bisecting the site center. To further secure the city, six kilometers of stone-footed wooden palisades were constructed in and around it. Some of the wall systems extended out to enclose field areas, rejolladas with probable intensively cultivated gardens, and access to potable water from springs (Inomata 1995, 1997, 2004; Dunning and Beach 2004). Despite such extensive defenses, Aguateca fell by about A.D. 810 (Graham 1967; Houston and Mathews 1985). Inomata (1995, 1997, 2004) discovered evidence for burning and rapid abandonment in the site center.

By the early ninth century, the last remaining major center of population in the Petexbatun was at Punta de Chimino. There, the naturally defensible peninsula had been fortified through the construction of three wall systems and the excavation of three moats, the largest of which was twelve meters deep. The other two moats protected arable land between the mainland and the tip of the peninsula. Research at the site in 1996 revealed that this neck of land was used for intensive agriculture, including stone box gardens (Beach 1996; Dunning and Beach 2004). The construction of the moats and the erection of palisaded walls atop the moats gave Punta de Chimino the most formidable defensive system in the Maya lowlands (Webster, personal communication to Arthur Demarest, 1993).

LATE CLASSIC REGIONAL SETTLEMENT

The settlement and paleoecological evidence closely parallels historical and archaeological reconstructions that indicate the population of the Petexbatun region reached its peak in the eighth century. At that time, not only did the large sites, such as Dos Pilas, Aguateca, and Tamarindito, achieve their maximum populations, but many intersite areas along the escarpment were densely occupied. Beyond the patterns observed in Transects 1 and 2, informal reconnaissance indicates that Late Classic population covered most of the length of the Petexbatun escarpment between Aguateca and Dos Pilas. Dense clusters of house mounds extend at least three kilometers west of the escarpment's edge. Given this observation, the total area encompassed by the Late Classic settlement pattern in intersite areas is approximately twenty square kilometers. The data from Transects 1 and 2 indicate that only approximately 35 percent of the land was directly occupied, a dense but not unsustainable population, given the region's skillfully applied agricultural and erosion control systems (Dunning and Beach 2004).

Late Classic Demographic Estimates

The issue of estimating population figures from archaeological remains is notoriously difficult and an inexact science at best. Yet it is an important question and there have been significant attempts in recent years to make estimates of ancient populations more accurate (see, for example, Culbert and Rice 1990 for methodologies for estimating populations in the Maya area). Adams (1983) made the first estimate of ancient population for the entire Río de la Pasión region, including the Petexbatun, based on assumed population ranges across various land cover types; his estimates ranged from a conservative figure of 482,692 to a maximum of 1,542,167. However, Adams's figures were partly dependent on the assumption that wetland agriculture was an important part of the regional subsistence system, an assumption that has proven to be invalid (Dunning and Beach 2004). Using redefined land uses, Dunning (1991) estimated the range of the carrying capacity of the Río de la Pasión region to be between 255,100 and 318,875.

In the Petexbatun region, the first attempt at estimating the ancient population based on settlement remains was conducted by Inomata for central Aguateca (Inomata 1995: 794–808). For that site he assumed that all structures were occupied at the same time because central Aguateca has a very short occupation history. Inomata also assumed that there were few hidden structures because the soils were quite thin, and that 46 percent of structures were nonresidential (rather than the more commonly used figure of 16.5 percent [Haviland 1965]). Finally, he applied the figure of 4.5 people per household. Based on these figures, he calculated a population of 1,480 people for central Aguateca, or a density of 2,027 people per square kilometer of habitable land.

For the intersite zones in the Petexbatun, we follow Inomata for comparative purposes and make calculations based on 4.5 individuals per household and no hidden structures (because soils in intersite zones are so thin that platforms would have been necessary for solidly footing even thatch structures). However, since the Nacimiento Complex (approximately Tepeu 2) extends for a period of more than two centuries, we assume only 75 percent contemporaneity. Also, as these zones are quite different in function than that studied by Inomata—the ceremonial core of Aguateca—we assume, based on Rice and Culbert (1990), that 25 percent of structures were nonresidential. Using these variables, we arrive at a figure of 486 people per square kilometer, or a total population of 9,720 in intersite areas in the Late Classic (based on structure counts for Transects 1 and 2 that yield 192 structures per square kilometer, less 25 percent correction for contemporaneity and an additional 25 percent for nonresidential structures, and 4.5 individuals per household) (Table 5.2).

In sum, the Late Classic marked a peak in regional population in the Petexbatun. At that time 99 percent of all structures tested in the region were occupied (Foias 1996, 2004). By the middle of the eighth century, the larger Petexbatun centers were at their maximum occupation levels and continuous clusters of population spanned the upland ridges from Dos Pilas in the northwest to Aguateca in the southeast.

Late Classic Ecology and Settlement Changes

Yet high population levels in the Petexbatun during the Late Classic were not harbingers of ecological and economic disaster. Analysis of sediment cores by

Table 5.2.

Transect	Mounds/ km²	Pop./km² 75% contemp. 4.5 people	Pop./km² 75% contemp. 5.6 people	Pop./km² 90% contemp. 4.5 people	Pop./km² 90% contemp. 5.6 people
1 Late Classic	168	425	529	510	635
2 Late Classic	215	543	676	652	811
3 Preclassic	104	263	328	316	393
4 Late/Terminal (?) Classic	357	905	1,126	1,085	1,351

the Petexbatun Ecology Subproject indicates that rates of erosion were relatively slow due to the use of terracing, check dams, and a wide range of sustainable agricultural systems (Dunning and Beach 2004). The skillfully applied mix of milpas, box gardens, intensively cultivated rejolladas, orchards, probable forest preserves for game hunting, and aquatic resources provided plentiful food. Investigations of ancient animal bones (Emery 1997, 2004) and human skeletal remains (Wright 1994, 1997a, 2004) also indicate that forest, game, and foodstuffs in general remained abundant in the Late Classic. In contrast to areas in the central and southeastern region of the lowlands where cultural decline occurred much later, the Petexbatun showed no evidence of an approaching or ongoing subsistence crisis of any kind (Dunning et al. 1997; Dunning and Beach 2004; see Demarest, Chapter 6 this volume).

Late Classic warfare and settlement changes are well documented at the larger centers, and even small villages were fortified. Excavations at the village of Quim Chi Hilan on Transect 1 discovered defensive walls with a baffled gateway (Van Tuerenhout 1996). There it appears that fortifications were built to protect field systems that would have sustained the remaining royal capital of Aguateca after the defeat of Dos Pilas (Inomata 1995; Dunning and Beach 2004). The findings at Quim Chi Hilan represent an extraordinary record of endemic warfare at a level not seen in earlier evidence from the Petexbatun or, indeed, from anywhere in the Maya lowlands. The extensive fortifications and baffled gateway enclosed only a few houses that clearly functioned to protect the food supply of Aguateca, to which they were linked by an extensive system of defensive walls (Demarest et al. 1997; Inomata 1997, 2004). Significantly, excavation of the baffled stone gateway recovered burned daub impressions of the wooden palisades and gate that were, at some point, destroyed, confirming the apparently unsuccessful defensive function of this extensive fortification system (Van Tuerenhout 1996; Van

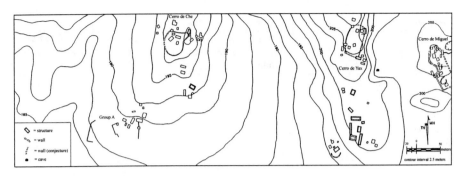

5.4 Map of Transect 4. Courtesy of Vanderbilt University Press.

Tuerenhout et al. 1993, 1994; Demarest et al. 1997). Meanwhile, excavations and survey of Transects 1 and 2 indicated that these areas were abandoned shortly after the fall of Dos Pilas. Note that landscapes on most of these transects were not well suited for defensive purposes.

In order to give a more accurate overall sample of regional subsistence, ecology, and demography, Transect 4 was mapped and tested in 1994 and 1996 (Demarest et al. 1995; O'Mansky, Hinson, Wheat, and Demarest 1995; O'Mansky and Wheat 1996b). A summary of the Transect 4 findings demonstrates the political and settlement changes at the end of the eighth century. The terrain of Transect 4 (Figure 5.4) consists of karst towers and very thin soils ill suited for agriculture. Despite this, population was clustered atop each of the steep hills in Transect 4, which extended for almost two kilometers from Cerro de Mariposas, a small hilltop fortress located approximately one kilometer north-northwest of the Aguateca epicenter (Inomata 1991; O'Mansky, Hinson, Wheat, and Demarest 1995; O'Mansky and Wheat 1996b). Within the first 600 meters of the transect, three additional steep hills were crossed before the terrain began a gradual, gentle descent over the last 1.15 kilometer. This descent continued all the way to the modern village of El Jordan more than two kilometers farther west. Despite the inhospitable conditions in the area—extremely thin soils, karst hills, and lack of nearby potable water sources—we discovered dense clusters of occupation atop the three hills encompassed within the transect. Each of these small villages was highly defensible and fortified.

The first village encountered was dubbed Cerro de Miguel. It consists of fourteen small structures and agricultural terraces clustered within a defensive wall (Figure 5.5). Most of the village is situated on the northern portion of the hill with ten structures densely packed within the defensive wall. On the upper portion of the southern slope of the hill, three additional structures stand within the wall while a nearly circular terrace wall lies between the structures. A single

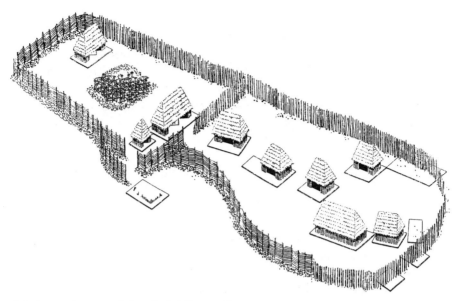

5.5 *Cerro de Miguel fortified hilltop village reconstruction drawing. Courtesy of Vanderbilt University Press.*

structure is located just west of the defensive walls at Cerro de Miguel and is the lone unfortified structure there.

A second fortified village, Cerro de Yax, is located 150 meters west of Cerro de Miguel. Like the first village, Yax consists of a tightly clustered settlement atop the hill and additional structures on the southern slope. The northern settlement consists of fourteen small structures, eight of which are within or bisected by a defensive wall that rings the hilltop. Of the six remaining structures, five are part of a pair of patio groups that include structures passed through by the defensive wall. The southern settlement cluster consists of nineteen structures with a central plaza group. Only one wall segment was discovered while mapping this group and its location—downhill from all structures and parallel to the face of the hill—suggests that it may have been an agricultural terrace.

A third fortified hilltop village, Cerro de Che, is located at the 600-meter mark of the transect. Like the other cerros, it consists of a walled settlement atop the hill, with additional settlement to the south. The northern settlement includes twenty-one somewhat dispersed structures and a single defensive wall strategically ringing the hilltop. Only four structures, however, lie within the wall, while three more are connected to it. The remaining fourteen appear to be unfortified. The southern cluster of settlement consists of eleven structures and is the only low-lying settlement on Transect 4.

Note that the form and fortifications of all three of these hilltop fortresses is similar to the nearby fortified village of Cerro de Mariposas (Demarest et al. 1995). All appear to be small hamlets in defensible locations that were rapidly encircled with crude palisade walls. Another hilltop redoubt a few kilometers away at Cerro de Cheyo was a much more massive fortress with well-planned walls more than four meters high and no significant residential occupation (ibid.). Cerro de Cheyo appears to have been a part of the extensive Aguateca defensive system.

Pottery recovered from excavations at the Transect 4 hilltop villages dates entirely to the Late Classic Nacimiento phase, probably to its final decades. The extremely inhospitable nature of the environment in Transect 4 suggests that the villages may have been a last refuge for a segment of the rural population.

Applying the same variables for estimating population as used in Transects 1 and 2, we arrive at a figure of 357 structures, or 904 people per square kilometer—a density nearly twice that of Transects 1 and 2 (O'Mansky 1996, 1999, 2003). However, the actual population density is probably considerably higher. A very short duration of occupation in the Transect 4 villages (perhaps on the order of just a few decades, at most) is suggested by the relative dearth of artifacts and middens recovered in excavations (as compared to those from other transects). We suspect that all structures were occupied contemporaneously for a short period. Also, only approximately 45 percent of the land within Transect 4 is habitable—the remainder consists of steep ravines between the karst towers. It would appear, then, that at the end of the eighth century, populations abandoned nearby fertile areas to cram themselves atop these defensible hilltops, despite the ecologically unfavorable setting of these eroded karst hills.

Thus, by the end of the Late Classic period in the Petexbatun, there had been yet another significant shift in settlement strategies, even among the rural peasant population. No longer were the usual factors for settlement location—fertile soils, abundant natural resources, and potable water—important. Instead, a single factor, defensibility, determined where people lived. As the surviving population from the larger sites sought ever more secure locations—from Dos Pilas to Aguateca to the Punta de Chimino island fortress—in the face of endemic warfare in the late eighth and early ninth centuries, the non-elite population moved from prime locations for agriculture to forbidding, but remote and defensible, locations. Yet by the Terminal Classic, even these zones were completely abandoned. During this period and the subsequent century, some populations may have migrated elsewhere on the Pasión River system (Demarest and Barrientos 2000) and lakes (Johnston et al. 2001)

CONCLUSIONS

Shifting, distinct settlement pattern strategies in the Petexbatun reflect social and political events in the course of the history of the region. The earliest inhabitants entered a virgin landscape and logically chose the fertile zones with the most abundant natural resources in which to build their homes. As soils became less productive through the Late Preclassic, Early Classic inhabitants moved up onto the escarpment but still focused settlement on locations that were well situated to exploit the environment. Natural springs and deep soils in sinkholes were used in combination with increasingly complex subsistence strategies to support a small but growing population. The Petexbatun region experienced a population boom during the first half of the Late Classic. Population figures reached their height at all centers, and even the landscape between centers filled with small villages interspersed with agricultural fields delimited by walls and terraces. Despite heavy occupation, there was little appreciable ecological decline. While deforestation did occur, it was ameliorated by a well-managed system that included check dams, terraces, field walls, box gardens, reservoirs, managed forests, and other features that controlled ecological deterioration (Dunning et al. 1997; Dunning and Beach 2004).

However, settlement strategies shifted yet again with the fall of Dos Pilas. In the late eighth century, virtually the only deciding factor in settlement location in the Petexbatun was defensibility. At Dos Pilas and Aguateca, energy was focused on building complex defenses. Nearby, fertile intersite zones were abandoned in favor of remote, resource-poor hilltops that could be more easily defended. Only at Punta de Chimino, where box gardens were established on a fortified portion of the peninsula, was subsistence clearly considered in addition to defensibility. By the ninth century, the Petexbatun escarpment was virtually devoid of occupation, with only very small villages located near the springs of Tamarindito and Dos Pilas. The last center with public architecture was the low-lying, fertile peninsula of Punta de Chimino with its deep soils and access to the abundant aquatic resources of Laguna Petexbatun. The population decline in the Petexbatun was the result of warfare and population shifts in the Late Classic. Despite debates about ultimate causality, here this final settlement shift and the simultaneous demographic collapse occurred in the context of ongoing endemic warfare.

One of the most significant facts in the abandonment of the Petexbatun region is that, in comparison to the Late and Terminal Classic changes elsewhere in the lowlands, the Petexbatun decline was the earliest—yet one of the most rapid—shifts, a true "collapse" in the terms defined by Tainter (1988) and Yoffee and Cowgill (1988). This leaves us to ponder the impact of the Petexbatun abandonment on the remainder of the Maya world. As described in the next chapter of this volume (Demarest), recent data from other western areas suggest that the early political collapse of the Petexbatun kingdom may have set in motion or, more likely, accelerated, Late and Terminal Classic changes elsewhere in Maya civilization (see also Barrientos et al. 2000; Johnston et al. 2001; Demarest 2001; Demarest and Escobedo 1998). In the Petexbatun itself, the settlement (O'Mansky 2003) and paleoecological evidence (Dunning and Beach 2004) reflect a nearly complete abandonment of most zones by A.D. 830.

6

AFTER THE MAELSTROM
COLLAPSE OF THE CLASSIC MAYA KINGDOMS
AND THE TERMINAL CLASSIC IN WESTERN PETÉN

Arthur A. Demarest

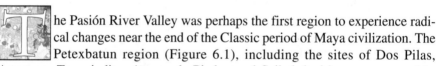he Pasión River Valley was perhaps the first region to experience radical changes near the end of the Classic period of Maya civilization. The Petexbatun region (Figure 6.1), including the sites of Dos Pilas, Aguateca, Tamarindito, Arroyo de Piedra, and Seibal, had become engaged in intense internecine warfare in the eighth century (O'Mansky and Dunning, Chapter 5, this volume; Tourtellot and González, Chapter 4, this volume). The roots of the intensification of warfare in this region really began with the sixth- and seventh-century wars and campaigns between Tikal and Calakmul for control of the Pasión River trade route (Demarest and Fahsen 2003). As described in Chapter 5 of this volume, these earlier wars left as their heritage a center at Dos Pilas, supported by the tribute, and compelled economic and ecological circumstances to continue that strategy.

The breakdown of this system began with wars against this predatory tribute state of Dos Pilas during the late seventh century. By the late eighth century Dos Pilas had been defeated, its remnant population besieged, and the region was plagued by intensive warfare (O'Mansky and Dunning, Chapter 5, this volume; Demarest 1996, 1997).

First, these wars may have been between the local dynasties of Tamarindito, Aguateca, Seibal, and the other contenders for dominance of the Petexbatun kingdom. By the end of the eighth century these conflicts had degenerated into what Dunning and Beach have dubbed as a "landscape of fear" (Dunning and Beach 2004). Siege and fortification warfare is evidenced by walls and palisades sur-

102

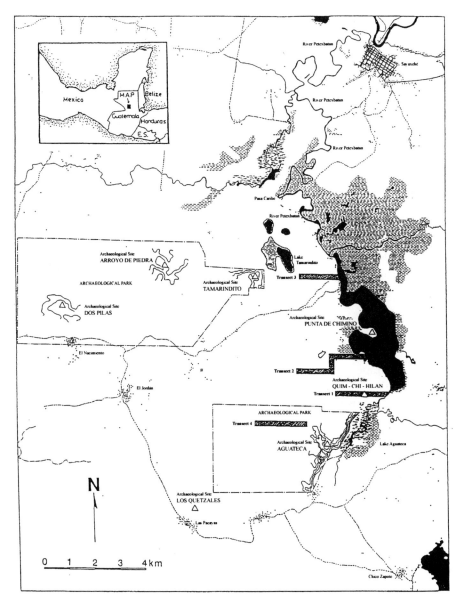

6.1 Petexbatun region showing major centers and settlement transects. Courtesy of Vanderbilt University Press.

rounding remnant epicenters and hilltop refuges throughout the region (O'Mansky and Dunning, Chapter 5, this volume; Demarest et al. 1997; Inomata 1995, 1997; Palka 1995, 1997). Although we can still debate the causes of this warfare and other underlying problems, there is no longer any question that in the Petexbatun, and the Lower Pasión Valley in general, the Classic Maya kingdoms politically collapsed during a period of endemic war.

LATE TO TERMINAL CLASSIC CHANGES IN PETEXBATUN CERAMICS, SETTLEMENT, AND POPULATION

Terminal Classic changes and the decline of Classic-period kingdoms is probably more precisely reconstructed for the Petexbatun than for any other region of the Maya world. This more complete view is due to the combined efforts of forty years of researches in the region, which have refined our understandings of ceramics, chronology, epigraphy, art, and regional culture-history (e.g., I. Graham 1967; Willey and Smith 1969; Willey 1973; Houston 1987a; Demarest 1989, 1990, 1997; Demarest and Escobedo 1998). By the end of the Vanderbilt University Petexbatun and Punta de Chimino projects, ceramic sequences closely linked to historical and architectural chronologies were able to subdivide the Late and Terminal Classic into three distinct periods:

1. Full Tepeu 2 (Nacimiento phase, Early Facet) from about A.D. 630 to 760

2. Late Tepeu 2 (Nacimiento phase, Late Facet) from about A.D. 760 to 830

3. Terminal Classic (Sepens phase, Tepeu 3) from A.D. 830 to A.D. 950/1000.

Ceramic markers distinguishing the Late Facet of the Tepeu 2 Nacimiento phase include not only decorative attribute and form frequencies, but the presence of new pastes and types (Figure 6.2), particularly imported Chablekal Fine Gray and local imitations of this fine paste ceramic (Foias 1996; Foias and Bishop 1997). Note that significant quantities of Chablekal, as well as their own local imitations, have been found in the recent excavations at Cancuen more than sixty kilometers to the south in the Upper Pasión (Demarest and Barrientos 1999, 2000, 2001, 2002). Ultimately, it should be possible to use these late Tepeu 2 markers to subdivide chronologies throughout western Petén. In turn, such chronological refinement would illuminate our comparative understanding of the eighth-and ninth-century processes throughout the western Maya world.

Changes in ceramics allow assessment of shifts in settlement, population, architecture, and economy at the end of the Classic period, Terminal Classic, and the initial Postclassic. The eighth-century historical inscriptions record wars, alliances, and dynastic struggles, and then fall silent as public architecture and monuments cease, first at Dos Pilas and later at other centers in the region. Paralleling the political fragmentation, ceramic production becomes more localized and less standardized, as conflicts disrupted patterns of exchange (Foias 1996; Foias and Bishop 1997). Other eighth-century changes in the Petexbatun and Pasión region include the development of new house forms, such as those with C-shaped benches, once believed to be a Postclassic development or a "foreign"

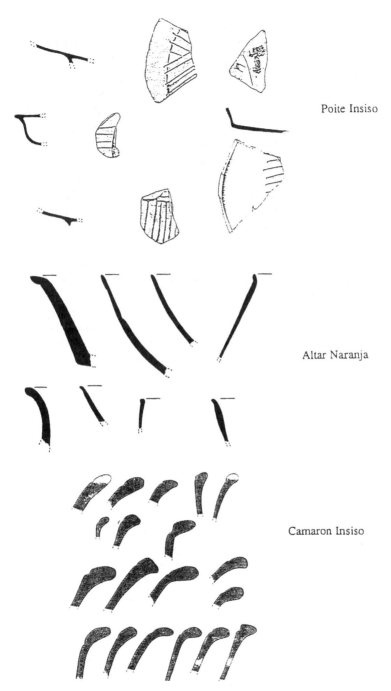

Poite Insiso

Altar Naranja

Camaron Insiso

6.2 Some Terminal Classic ceramic types of the Petexbatun. Courtesy of Vanderbilt University Press.

element introduced at the time of the "collapse." The Petexbatun evidence shows that many such elements were present in the eighth century at Dos Pilas and at other sites in the Pasión before the Terminal Classic (Palka 1995; Tourtellot and González, Chapter 4, this volume). The salient change in settlement in the late eighth century is concentration of settlements on natural defensible locations and the conversions of major site epicenters and even villages into palisaded forts (O'Mansky and Dunning, Chapter 5, this volume).

Major site epicenters were in ruins with only small remnant populations present by the early to middle ninth century, as marked by the shift to Tepeu 3 ceramic forms, modes, and wares. These include Fine Gray, Fine Orange, characteristic Terminal Classic incurved wall tripod bowls, and other clear diagnostics (Foias 1996). By the beginning of the Terminal Classic period, reduced populations are found in scattered households or small hamlets inland. Population at Dos Pilas was reduced to 20 percent of previous levels by the end of the eighth century (Palka 1997), and by the Terminal Classic, small hamlets of a few households were located near the springs in the ruined epicenters of Dos Pilas, Tamarindito, and Arroyo de Piedra.

The only major Tepeu 3 epicenters with substantial population still construct-ing monumental architecture were located in defensible positions along the Pasión and its tributaries. Seibal, Altar, and the smaller island fortress of Punta de Chimino are the best excavated of these Terminal Classic enclaves. Excavations at these three centers, together with the Petexbatun Project study of the hamlets and houses inland, allow a characterization of the economy and material culture of the Terminal Classic and a contrast with the Classic period. Comparisons of the full range of changes in the Late to Terminal Classic allow speculations on the causes for the eighth and early ninth century acceleration of warfare, depopulation, and the political collapse of the inland centers.

LATE TO TERMINAL CLASSIC STABILITY IN
PETEXBATUN ECOLOGY AND SUBSISTENCE

Evidence from Punta de Chimino, the Terminal Classic hamlets at Dos Pilas and other sites, and regional comparative material culture studies together have pro-vided a characterization of Terminal Classic ecology and economy. There is no evidence of environmental deterioration or radical environmental change. Paleo-ecological studies by Nick Dunning, Timothy Beach, David Rue, and others, including phosphate analyses and analysis of pollen cores, do show some evi-dence of deforestation throughout the Classic period, but with considerable re-gional forest cover intact through both the Late and Terminal Classic (e.g., Dunning, Beach, and Rue 1997; Dunning et al. 1998; Dunning and Beach 2004). While land use was intensive at the end of the Late Classic, Petexbatun farmers were inge-nious in their application of a wide variety of agricultural systems and conserva-tion measures, including check dams, foot slope terraces, fertilized household gardens, terraced sinkholes, stone box terraces, and artificial reservoirs (Beach and Dunning 1997; Dunning and Beach 1994; Dunning, Beach, and Rue 1995, 1997; Dunning et al. 1993, 1998). By the time of the Petexbatun political collapse, the agricultural potential of the region was far from exhausted and, moreover, farmers were perfectly aware of a wide variety of conservation and intensification measures to further extend this potential (see O'Mansky and Dunning, Chapter 5, this volume).

Osteological and paleofaunal evidence support this picture of a stable rainforest and milpa environment in the Late to Terminal Classic period. Wright's osteological studies found neither significant change in diet nor deterioration in health from the Late Classic into the Terminal Classic period (Wright 1994, 1997a, 1997b, 1997c; Wright and White 1996; Wright 2004). Emery's paleofaunal studies show no *chronologically linked* variability in dietary patterning. Emery's studies of isotopes in deer bone collagen show no significant change in the diet of the deer themselves between the Late and Terminal Classic (Emery 1997, 2004; Emery et al. 2000). Deer diet indicates a stable Terminal Classic environment of mixed rainforest and milpa, the latter representing the mainland population of scattered farming and hunting households.

The absence of any evidence of widespread famine or increased malnutrition and disease in the late eighth to early ninth centuries contradicts some popular theories of widespread drought as a major cause of the decline of Classic Maya kingdoms in the western Petén (e.g., Gill 2000; Hodell et al. 1995; Adams et al. Chapter 15, this volume; Dahlin 2002; Haug et al. 2003). The unraveling of the Petexbatun kingdoms was, in any case, a process of the eighth century. Before hypothesized ninth and tenth century climate changes and droughts would have began, the Petexbatun kingdoms already were in ruins or under siege. The absence of evidence of an *increase* in disease or malnutrition in the Late Classic or in the subsequent Terminal Classic in this region negates hypotheses that the Classic Maya "collapse," decline, or transformation in the Pasión and Petexbatun regions was driven by *either* anthropogenic or climatological deterioration of the environment (Wright and White 1996; Wright 2004). The combined array of Petexbatun studies of paleoecology, osteology, and fauna revealed diverse, viable, and well-adapted agricultural regimes and unchanged overall health and nutrition throughout the Late and Terminal Classic periods.

Note that recent articles revising catastrophism as a simplistic explanation of the Classic to Postclassic transition have strenuously avoided addressing the detailed data of the many Petexbatun project publications (see for example Chapters 9 and 15, this volume; Dahlin 2002; Haug et al. 2003; Gill 2000; Hodell et al. 1995). Although most of the Petexbatun reports and articles have been published in Spanish, many have also appeared in English, and results have been presented at every professional meeting for the past decade. Instead, emphasis has been placed on the far northern Petén/southern Campeche/Quintana Roo region where the drought hypothesis does seem to have explanatory value. I refer the readers to Chapters 1 and 23 for an assessment of the revival of catastrophism. Once again, archaeologists are globally projecting presumed "causes" for a mythical uniform "collapse" phenomenon from interpretations appropriate only for their regions of research. No major ecological change in nutrition, vegetation, diet, health, or any other parameter of the material well-being of humans or animals is evidenced in any of the many independent Petexbatun studies (see especially Dunning et al. 1997; Dunning and Beach 1994, 2004; Wright 1994, 1997a, 1997b, 1997c, 2004; Wright and White 1996; Emery 1997, 2004; Emery et al. 2000; O'Mansky and Dunning Chapter 5, this volume; O'Mansky 2003).

Despite any significant ecological or subsistence changes, the region experienced one of the few true "collapses" in the Maya lowlands, a subregional political breakdown that climaxed at 750/760, before or just as climate shifts have been proposed to begin (e.g., Hodell et al. 1995; Gill 2000; Haug et al. 2003). The deus ex machina of climate catastrophe is inappropriate for a number of regions— which do not experience the proposed true "collapse"—but is simply irrelevant (and contradicted by the evidence) for the well-documented, earlier sequence of events in the Petexbatun and elsewhere in the west.

STATUS RIVALRY, THE K'UL AJAW SYSTEM, AND UNDERLYING FORCES IN THE CLASSIC MAYA COLLAPSE

For causal pressures underlying the endemic warfare of the eighth century, the Petexbatun evidence points instead to political factors. These include elite status rivalry, the growth of the elite class through polygamy, the growing economic burden on society of increased noble and royal consumption, and the intensification of warfare for limited positions of power and for access to exotic goods (Demarest and Valdés 1995, 1996; Demarest 1996, 1997, 2004). Throughout the southern lowlands, a proliferation of elites was manifest in massive Late Classic investment in public architecture, an increase in the number of Emblem Glyph–bearing centers, a dramatic rise in the number of monuments celebrating the lives and achievements of the ruling "holy lords" of these centers, and an intensification of all forms of elite interaction (e.g., Schele 1991; Schele and Mathews 1991; Mathews and Willey 1991; Demarest and Fahsen 2003; Demarest 2004).

Competition or "status rivalry" between the growing class of "holy lords" was also manifest in more direct terms in warfare, especially in the west (e.g., Webster 1998). Yet the specific form taken by status rivalry in other regions probably varied greatly—larger-scale architectural projects, increased trade for status-reinforcing exotics, and encouragement of demographic growth were potential forms of competition with the ruling lords of other major centers and potential rivals at vassal centers or even within their own dynasties. Warfare was only one of these options, the one clearly manifest in western Petén. Yet in other regions, status rivalry would have stimulated increased investment in public monuments and rituals, as well as demographic growth and the agricultural intensification to support such growth. Demographic growth and economic intensification also may have been stimulated to support increased construction and ritual display. While not violent, all of these forms of status rivalry came at great cost to the fragile economic infrastructure of this rainforest civilization. The growth of elites and the increasing burden of their support and activities can be seen, then, as a probable common factor (not a "cause," but a structural vulnerability) in the variable manifestations of collapse, transformation, or transition in differing regions of the Maya world.

Another common factor in the varied forms of the eighth- to tenth-century changes in Classic Maya civilization in the southern lowlands may have been the limitations of the K'ul Ajaw (holy or divine lord or king) system itself. Classic Maya kingdoms were dominated by the cult of divine kingship, with political power and religious authority focused in a single charismatic figure and the royal line. Royal ancestor worship and much of the public ritual and expense of elite maintenance were part of this politico-religious system. Yet findings from most regions, certainly from the detailed Petexbatun studies, indicate that direct royal involvement in economics and infrastructure may have been limited in many kingdoms to specific projects near epicenters (Dunning et al. 1997) and to management of exchange and production of high-status elite goods (e.g., Ball 1993b). Such a limited economic role would have made it difficult for Late Classic rulers to respond to the very stresses and demands generated by their own inter-elite status rivalry. The *may* cycle system of rotation of power described by P. Rice (Rice and Rice, Chapter 7, this volume; P. Rice 2004) could have mitigated such status rivalry and provided more orderly transitions of power. Yet this system itself also would have added costs in great periodic burdens on the new centers chosen to "seat" a k'atun cycle of rituals, or the longer 256- or 128-year may and half-may periods of ritual (P. Rice 2004).

The focused authority, but limited economic role, of Classic Maya holy lords might also have become anachronistic by the eighth century. It may have been increasingly difficult for southern lowland kingdoms to compete in the greater Mesoamerican world. Economies and concepts of power were changing in the wake of the decline of Teotihuacan and other Classic-period societies. Multiple institutions of economic, religious, and political authority were becoming characteristic of highland and Gulf Coast polities, as was a greater reliance on tribute and on long-distance exchange of major commodities.

Thus, the endemic warfare and political fragmentation in the Petexbatun can be seen as only one manifestation—albeit a dramatic and early one—of the common underlying factors that led in many areas of the Petén to either the decline of Classic Maya kingdoms or to their transformation to systems with significantly different political, economic, and ideological strategies. In other subregions climate change, overuse of soils, shifts in trade routes, and other proximate factors may have been involved in the later declines, transitions, transformations, and/or florescences involved in the Terminal Classic. Yet in the west (and probably central Petén), by the mid-eighth century, the burden of the top-heavy and energetically costly elite status rivalry had placed unsupportable stresses on the productive but fragile rainforest subsistence base and archaic economic structure of many kingdoms.

In the Petexbatun and Pasión regions, the political system came apart in the earliest manifestation of radical change in widespread warfare. In other regions, at somewhat later dates, differing responses to these same underlying stresses ranged from warfare and abandonment (e.g., Yaxchilán, Piedras Negras, Xunantunich,) to political fragmentation and decline (e.g., the Tikal and Copán kingdoms), to reorientation and florescence (e.g., the Puuc, parts of Belize, Chich'en Itza), as detailed in the articles in this volume. In all cases, however, the K'ul Ajaw system of divine kingship disappeared, be it suddenly or through a more gradual transition or replacement. As detailed in this volume (e.g., Chapters 2, 3, and 23), continuities were many and great between the Late Classic and Postclassic in many zones, especially in the northern lowlands and Belize. In western Petén, in contrast, the large centers ceased to erect public architecture except for the Terminal Classic enclave centers at Seibal, Altar, and Punta de Chimino. Population throughout the west remained minimal through the Postclassic, with later light settlement of only some zones by immigrants from central Petén and only a few minor centers (Morgan and Demarest 1995; Foias 1996, 2004; Johnston et al. 2001; Demarest 2004).

AFTER THE PETEXBATUN COLLAPSE: TERMINAL CLASSIC SUBSISTENCE AND SETTLEMENT

In the Petexbatun, the "proximate" manifestations of these common stresses broke out in the intercenter warfare and political fragmentation of the Late Classic political system. Between A.D. 760 and 830, first major centers and then even villages had been fortified and besieged—or were simply abandoned (see O'Mansky and Dunning, Chapter 5, this volume). The *aftermath* of this process and the nature of surviving population centers may provide insights into the end of Classic Maya civilization in general, as well as the possible impact of Petexbatun events on other regions of the lowlands.

By the end of the Late Classic and into the Terminal Classic, reduced settlement location and economic systems had adapted to the militarized landscape of the Petexbatun. Localized intensive food production systems, including box terraces, sunken gardens, dams, and intensive household gardens have been found near the defensible royal epicenter at Tamarindito and on the periphery of the extensive defensive system of Aguateca (Dunning et al. 1993, 1995, 1997; Dunning and Beach 1994, 2004; Van Tuerenhout 1996; Inomata 1995, 1997). Slope terraces have also been tentatively identified near hilltop village forts at the end of the eighth century (O'Mansky and Dunning, Chapter 5, this volume). By the beginning of the Terminal Classic, marked by Fine Orange and the Tepeu 3 diagnostics, most of these defensible or fortified locations had been abandoned. Only riverine enclaves like Punta de Chimino, Seibal, and Altar de Sacrificios continued to erect public architecture as part of the problematic Cycle 10 Terminal Classic occupation of those centers (see Tourtellot and González, Chapter 4, this volume).

The best evidence of Terminal Classic subsistence and coordination of site defenses with food production systems was recovered at the site of Punta de Chimino. There, massive earthworks constructed in the eighth century formed three sets of walls and deep moats excavated into the limestone bedrock. The moats cut off the peninsula, creating an artificial island fortress (Figure 6.3). While the outer island itself was densely occupied in the Terminal Classic, the only occupation in the two adjacent moated zones of the peninsula was one residence near the third moat. The intermediate zone had crude low walls forming closed areas or terraces that were not associated with houses or middens.

Excavation of these features led to identification of these zones as areas of intensive food production, including low stone box gardens (Figure 6.4). Then, technical soil phosphate studies were applied to test this hypothesis. Mapping of soil phosphate field values in the Petexbatun has been used to identify areas of net phosphate depletion (which can be agricultural fields) and areas of phosphate enrichment (often midden deposits or fertilized gardens). Soil use can be further hypothesized through fractionation of constituent mineral phosphates with phosphate fractions occluded with iron and hydrous oxides (fraction 2), an indicator of possible artificial phosphate enrichment of soils through fertilization (Dunning et al. 1997; Dunning and Beach 2004; Beach 1996). Phosphate analyses from these two unoccupied Punta de Chimino perimeter zones were consistent with the hypothesis of intensive fertilization. Even more intriguing was the fact that the loci with the highest overall phosphate enrichment (and the highest fraction 2 ratios) were probable stone box gardens excavated in 1996 (Beach 1996; Dunning and Beach 2004). These were areas of dark soil and clay enclosed in crude stone walls with no other associated features or middens. Organic material from the bajo area on the south side of the peninsula could have been easily dredged up and used in these gardens. It is also probable that fertilizer included "night soils" generously contributed by the occupants of the heavily populated island center (Beach 1996).

Food production and distribution from these two zones may have been centrally managed. This pattern does not represent a radical change from Late Classic subsistence in the Petexbatun, or elsewhere. Small, state-managed intensive agricultural systems have been found adjacent to Late Classic site epicenters, although overall the agricultural landscape was decentralized (Dunning et al. 1997; Dunning and Beach 2004). As with other aspects of the economy, subsistence systems in the Terminal Classic show great continuity from the Late Classic

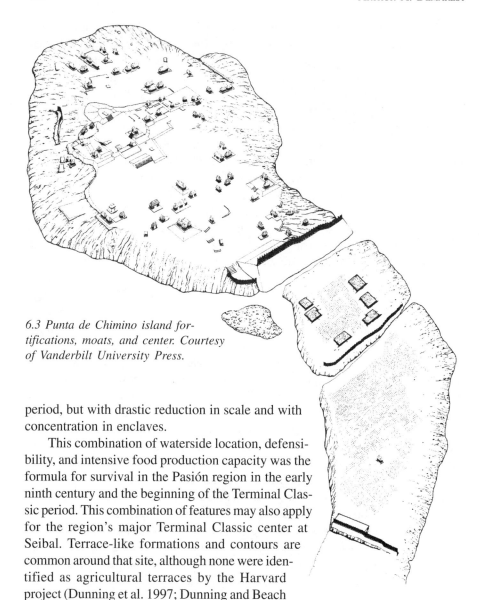

*6.3 Punta de Chimino island for-
tifications, moats, and center. Courtesy
of Vanderbilt University Press.*

period, but with drastic reduction in scale and with
concentration in enclaves.

This combination of waterside location, defensibility, and intensive food production capacity was the
formula for survival in the Pasión region in the early
ninth century and the beginning of the Terminal Classic period. This combination of features may also apply
for the region's major Terminal Classic center at
Seibal. Terrace-like formations and contours are
common around that site, although none were identified as agricultural terraces by the Harvard
project (Dunning et al. 1997; Dunning and Beach
2004). Most inland centers were abandoned by the beginning of the ninth century, probably because such intensive investments in architecture or agricultural
systems could not be protected from episodic predation by enemies (O'Mansky
1996, 1999; O'Mansky, Hinson, Wheat, and Demarest 1995; O'Mansky and Wheat
1996a; O'Mansky and Dunning, Chapter 5, this volume).

Inland occupation in the Terminal Classic was limited to just a few scattered
hamlets in the entire region. Terminal Classic hamlets at Tamarindito and Dos

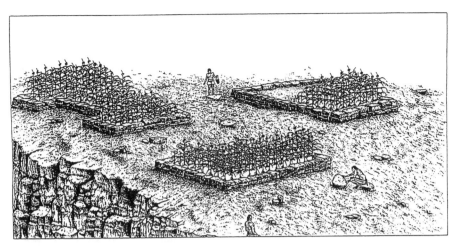

6.4 Stone box gardens in protected zones of Punta de Chimino. Courtesy of Vanderbilt University Press.

Pilas may represent later reoccupation in more peaceful intervals after the end of the eighth-century period of war and massive population reduction. Hamlets of several houses were located near springs in prime positions for hunting and agriculture. At the Dos Pilas hamlet, Emery excavated and studied a bone workshop that seems to have specialized in the highly efficient production of tools from deer bone using a standardized Terminal Classic technology (Emery 1992, 1995a, 1995b, 1997). Yet at these two sites and the few scattered Terminal Classic occupations elsewhere there is no investment in public architecture or intensive food production. With investment at a minimum, the occupants, if attacked, could simply flee.

Terminal Classic Production and Exchange

Terminal Classic production and exchange systems in ceramics have been studied by Foias and Bishop (e.g., Foias 1996; Foias and Bishop 1997; Foias 2004). In the Terminal Classic assemblages at Punta de Chimino and at the larger Pasión centers of Altar and Seibal, most Tepeu 2 polychromes were replaced by fine paste wares, including Altar Fine Orange and Tres Naciones Fine Gray. Contrary to earlier hypotheses of the foreign, "Putun," or Mexican importation of these ceramics, compositional studies now show that they were produced within the Pasión region (e.g., Foias and Bishop 1997; Foias 2004).

Fine paste style and technology may reflect influence from the Lower Usumacinta region, where there was a long tradition of fine paste ceramics and figurines (Bishop 1994; Foias and Bishop 1997). Even such a diffusion of style and technology, however, probably occurred earlier in the eighth century. In fact, it is the earlier Late Facet of the Nacimiento phase (late Tepeu 2, A.D. 760–830) that is the period of greatest long-distance exchange and Petexbatun contacts with the west and northwest. During that period, early fine paste Chablekal Fine Gray ceramics were being imported from the Palenque region, along with some fine brown and fine cream wares (Foias 1996; Foias and Bishop 1997). We might hypothesize that, during this period of endemic warfare, trade routes within central Petén were disrupted and alternative elite ceramics were sought from the west. By Terminal Classic times, the Petexbatun and Pasión regions were producing their own distinctive fine paste gray and orange ceramics, with very few imports of any kind.

Pasión region parochialism in Terminal Classic material culture can also be seen in evidence of ceramic specialization and standardization of production. Both monochrome and polychrome ceramics show *less* standardization in the Terminal Classic as evaluated by statistical study of quantifiable modes such as vessel diameter, wall thickness, and vessel height. Foias and Bishop (Foias 1996, 2004; Foias and Bishop 1997) cite this evidence to refute earlier theories of a Terminal Classic period of great commercialization of Maya economies, greater mass production, and wider exchange systems. Their neutron activation compositional studies show no dramatic shift in exchange patterns and less, not more, standardization (Foias and Bishop 1997). Continuity is also observed in the style of most Terminal Classic ceramics and artifacts at Seibal, Altar, and Punta de Chimino.

Neither foreign invasion nor radical economic transformation were registered in the economies of the remnant Terminal Classic public centers of the Pasión and at Punta de Chimino in Lake Petexbatun. Careful assessment of the Petexbatun burials, osteology, architecture, and artifacts have negated the scenarios of a new economic order managed by mercantile, militaristic "Putun" warrior elites (Demarest 1997; Foias and Bishop 1997; Stuart 1993). Instead, at both Seibal and Punta de Chimino, the Terminal Classic economies appear to be a more regionalized and reduced re-entrenchment of Classic-period patterns (e.g., Tourtellot and González, Chapter 4, this volume).

TERMINAL CLASSIC ENCLAVES
AND THE CYCLE 10 "PSEUDO-FLORESCENCE"

Thus, the evidence from the most thoroughly excavated centers in the Lower Pasión region indicates that the Terminal Classic period was one of reduction of population, but without evidence of radical environmental change, economic transformation, or foreign invasions. Instead, Terminal Classic enclaves at Punta de Chimino, Seibal, and Altar were reduced and concentrated remnants of Late Classic Maya kingdoms. Only in these few locations did major public architecture continue. Elsewhere, depopulation was dramatic.

At Punta de Chimino, a massive ballcourt, large plastered palace platforms, and a corbelled vaulted masonry shrine (Morgan 1995) were erected during Terminal Classic times (Figure 6.5). The ballcourt, the largest in the Petexbatun, was

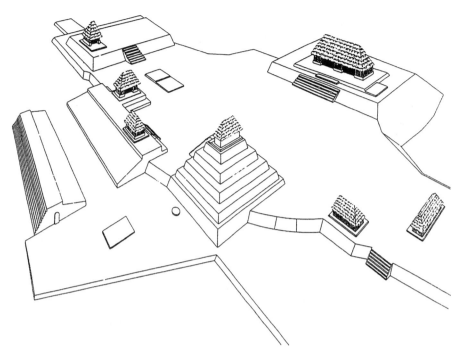

6.5 Punta de Chimino Terminal Classic ballcourt and epicenter. Courtesy of Vanderbilt University Press.

similar in dimensions and architectural form to the Terminal Classic C-9 ballcourt at Seibal (Smith 1982: 157–162). Terminal Classic elite residences at Punta de Chimino (Quezada 1996; Morgan 1996) had broad platforms (10 x 20 meters) covered thickly in plaster, an unusual display of wealth for the Petexbatun. A large "Plaza Plan 2" compound with a fine masonry corbelled vaulted roof indicated the elite status of some Terminal Classic residents. A cache with Altar Fine Orange and Plumbate confirmed the Terminal Classic date of the shrine, and its distinctive carved cornices were similar to those on Bayal phase structures at Seibal (e.g. Tourtellot 1988b: 79; Morgan 1996: 72). Unmistakable Tepeu 3 diagnostics in the ballcourt and residences, including Fine Orange and tripod interior incised "grater bowls," dated these remarkable constructions (Morgan 1995, 1996; Castellanos 1996). The florescence at Punta de Chimino was surprising in light of the Terminal Classic landscape elsewhere in the Petexbatun, which consisted of tiny hamlets and scattered homesteads amid the ruins of the Classic-period centers. Punta de Chimino's island fortress, the last ceremonial center and elite occupation in the Petexbatun, remained a refuge in the Terminal Classic behind its massive moats, sustained by its protected zones of intensive agriculture (Demarest, Escobedo, and O'Mansky 1996).

Of course, even more impressive were the temples, Cycle 10 monuments, and ballcourts of Seibal and Altar de Sacrificios to the north on the Pasión River itself. This elite monumental propaganda was successful in its original intent: to impress and awe with ancient Maya elite imagery mixed with new, exotic foreign elements. Yet I suspect that this display has been even more successful with modern archaeologists. It has inspired three decades of speculation on the Cycle 10 florescence in the Pasión, which has been envisioned as being led by Mexican warriors, Putun warrior/merchant-elites, or a more mercantile, "new" order of society.

The problem in interpretation comes, obviously, from relying too heavily on various aspects of elite imagery and monumental art and architecture. Tourtellot's original studies of residential settlement, which are too often ignored, had argued for a probable Terminal Classic population *decline* (Tourtellot 1988b: 402). While the difficulty of estimating Tepeu 3 population sizes is considerable (see Tourtellot 1988b: 367–372; Chase and Chase, Chapter 2, this volume), the Terminal Classic markers in the Pasión region are fairly widespread and include non-elite as well as fine ware ceramics (Foias 1996). Tourtellot also had observed that the new imagery and Cycle 10 monuments of Seibal are striking, but the total volume of earlier full Classic-period architecture was much greater (1988b: 402). The pattern at Seibal may, then, be the same as that at Punta de Chimino, but on a larger scale: reduction of population into defensible locations and an attempt at public revitalization by the new elite.

Reassessment of the Seibal settlement and architectural data (Tourtellot and González, Chapter 4, this volume), like the Petexbatun settlement patterns and fortifications (O'Mansky and Dunning, Chapter 5, this volume), show the eighth century to have been a period of intensified warfare across the entire Pasión region. Evidence of possible defenses and a siege village can now be identified at Seibal (see Tourtellot and González, Chapter 4, this volume). The subsequent Pasión-center Terminal Classic architectural constructions, shrines, ballcourts, and monuments might be interpreted as part of a program by the region's elites to politically maintain the diverse remnant population that had concentrated at these fortified enclaves.

The eclectic nature of Seibal iconography, ceramic styles, and inscriptions could reflect such an effort by its elite at revitalization in the postapocalyptic landscape of the Pasión region. The "Facies A" and "Facies B" styles at Seibal are now recognized to be fundamentally Classic Maya, rather than "foreign," "Putun," or Mexican as once believed (Graham 1973, 1990; cf. Stuart 1993; Schele and Mathews 1998: 179–184). Nonetheless, the Terminal Classic elite stressed their distant affiliations, including ties to Ucanal far to the east (Schele and Mathews 1998: 183) and to distant Chichen Itza (Kowalski 1989). The unusual headdresses, costumes, and sculptural style of Graham's "Facies B" monuments at Seibal, new architectural elements, and foreign associations in "Facies A" inscriptions all may reflect a conscious program of ideological legitimation. Bayal-phase leaders were invoking prestigious and traditional Classic Maya associations, but also new pan-Maya affiliations.

Ringle et al. (1998) have suggested that many of these new stylistic elements may be part of a Quetzalcoatl cult that spread through the Maya world in Terminal Classic times. Similarly, A. Chase and Chase (1985) identified some possible Terminal Classic pan-Maya iconographic elements, indicating political associations of remaining elites. Both interpretations would be compatible with the hypothesis that leaders of Seibal, Altar, and Punta de Chimino were consciously legitimating their remnant kingdoms by combining Classic Maya political ideology with new associations and symbols. The prevalence of fine paste wares with new vessel forms and modeled carved imagery may also have been part of this attempt at elite redefinition.

These efforts of revitalization now must be viewed in the light of the more extensive settlement and historical data from the Petexbatun. These centers may have represented a last gasp of Classic Maya K'ul Ajaw political ideology after a period of endemic warfare, political devolution, depopulation, and probable massive emigration. These efforts to maintain power failed within a century, leading to the dwindling of populations at Seibal, Altar, and Punta de Chimino. Indeed, the failure of Terminal Classic political formations in the region was also reflected in the unusual paucity of Postclassic population in the Pasión and Petexbatun. At Seibal, the Petexbatun centers, and nearby scattered intersite areas, Postclassic occupation is limited to a few scattered households, with little or no public architecture. Pollen core data indicate another area of possible Postclassic occupation to the south of the Petexbatun at Laguna Las Pozas (Johnston et al. 2001), but again no public architecture has been found. A small center to the north of the Petexbatun (near Sayaxche) may have included some minor public structures with some Postclassic use. The hieroglyphic stairway at Punta de Chimino itself was buried by one of the larger Postclassic occupations: a sheet midden of fishermen's net weights, fish bones, and Postclassic ceramics (Morgan and Demarest 1995). These ceramics show no continuity with earlier Petexbatun forms, but represent a later small reoccupation by central Petén groups (Morgan and Demarest 1995; Foias 1996, 2004).

EIGHTH- AND NINTH-CENTURY MIGRATION AND ITS POSSIBLE IMPACT IN THE WEST AND BEYOND

The political competition and warfare of the eighth and early ninth centuries appear to have nearly depopulated the Petexbatun and probably much of the Pasión region. In the Petexbatun the change could not be more dramatic: a half dozen major centers, many minor centers, and high levels of population were reduced to less than 10 percent of earlier levels within a little more than half a century (A.D. 760 to 830).

Such rapid and large-scale population reduction would have involved migration to other regions. Petexbatun warfare by the late eighth century required even defensive positioning and fortification of small hamlets and agricultural field systems (O'Mansky and Dunning, Chapter 5, this volume). Locations suitable for settlement were greatly reduced, and even those would have difficulty protecting their fields and water sources. Emigration elsewhere would have been the best option for Petexbatun populations after A.D. 760 and it appears to have been the option generally chosen.

It is notable that during this same period some regions elsewhere in Petén experienced radical and erratic population changes. While most of the Petexbatun was depopulated in the late eighth to early ninth centuries, some populations moved to the Seibal, Altar, and Punta de Chimino enclaves or farther afield to other lakeside and riverine loci. For example, up the Pasión River in the Cancuen region to the south, new residences were constructed outside that site's epicenter in areas that had previously been unoccupied alluvial farmlands (Barrientos et al. 2000). This occupation at Cancuen introduced distinctive middle Pasión ceramic modes and types, including Pantano and Chaquisite impressed in middens and imported Chablekal Fine Gray vessels in burials (Bill 2000; Bill and Callaghan 2001).

Meanwhile, farther *down*river (north) on the Usumacinta system, Yaxchilan, Piedras Negras, and Palenque suffered decline or abandonment early in the ninth century. In part this probably was due to warfare and emigration, as in the lower Pasión. Note, however, that intensified warfare and the formation of the Seibal and Altar conquest states also had effectively blocked the Pasión/Usumacinta River trade artery and the highland/lowland exchange networks in obsidian, pyrite, jade, shell, and other exotics. The great river portage kingdoms of the west, including Cancuen, Yaxchilan, and Piedras Negras, would have been deprived of a major segment of their distribution and patronage networks. Composition and production studies have confirmed that in the Terminal Classic, long-distance exchange systems were disrupted (Foias and Bishop 1997; Foias 1996, 2004). Combined with intensified warfare and major military defeats, the loss of patronage networks may have driven the rapid decline of these western centers (Martin and Grube 2000: 116–175).

Some recent interpretations have attributed the decline at Piedras Negras and elsewhere to a failure of leadership to meet with expectations of "moral community" needed to retain population. With this failure of the ruler's "moral authority" at Piedras, "the moral community, now inverted into a community of despair, would potentially transform itself into an expulsive force," resulting in the emigration of its sustaining population (Houston et al. 2001; Sharer and Golden in press). Yet the decline at Piedras Negras, and later Yaxchilan and Palenque, can be more economically explained as an expected response by the population to historically recorded humiliating military defeats, political fragmentation, and the disruption of elite access to many exotics brought by the Pasión/Usumacinta trade routes. Loss of faith in leadership and emigration elsewhere would be expected in kingdoms that could no longer provide physical security or prized exotics to their elite subordinates and the sustaining population. The pattern of abandonment at these great western centers of Piedras, Yaxchilan, and Palenque was perfectly consistent in nature and timing with the disruptions we have described here to the south and east on this same western river system during this same period (Demarest and Fahsen 2003).

Elsewhere in Petén, population increases in the late eighth century were sometimes accompanied by political fragmentation and a proliferation of Emblem Glyphs. In the northeast Petén and northern Belize the picture is complex and difficult to align with other regions. Adams et al. (see Chapter 15, this volume) record great population increases in some centers, while others decline or are abandoned. There, as in most of Petén, ceramic chronologies are less refined than in the Petexbatun, and so difficult to align for processual or culture-historical interpretation. Still, the general late-eighth-century picture throughout central Petén, Belize, and to the north in the Puuc zone appears to reflect population increases, but in an irregular pattern, accompanied by political disruptions and re-entrenchment (e.g., Dunning 1992; Chapters 14–21, this volume). In my view, this highly variable pattern does not correspond to the great "collapse" expected from drought/famine models, especially given that Belize as a whole maintains large populations into the Postclassic period.

Ceramic markers for Tepeu 3 in many areas are dependent upon the presence of types or traits from the lower Pasión region. In addition to trade, migration to the east of small groups and families, as well as migrations along the Pasión itself, could explain both the general spread of Pasión ceramic markers to the east and north and the changes upriver to the south at Cancuen. Rapid population growth in some regions in the eighth century also might, in part, reflect the direct or indirect impact of gradual immigration from the west. As indicated by Ashmore et al. (Chapter 14, this volume), agriculturally rich areas in Belize may have attracted families and small groups from the depopulating kingdoms of central and western Petén. We can speculate that the stresses associated with overpopulation in late Tepeu 2 times would have been exacerbated by such population displacements, even if the units involved were very small. Migration might also have contributed to the political disruptions, re-entrenchment, and transformations taking place in other regions. As we know from many modern examples, immigration can be positive or negative in its effect, depending on the nature and timing of movements, and especially on economic, ecological, and political conditions of the region receiving migrants.

WAR, MIGRATION, AND POLITICAL RECONSTRUCTION

Over the past decade, data from the Petexbatun project have helped fuel a growing interest in the role of warfare in the end of Classic Maya civilization. Some scholars, however, have responded with skepticism that war could be a factor in the many changes involved in the Classic/Postclassic transition of lowland kingdoms referred to as "Classic Maya civilization." The mortality rates associated with warfare are, indeed, usually insufficient to explain presumed widespread and rapid depopulation, and ecological causes have been sought instead. Yet such responses indicate a stereotyped view of the Classic Maya "collapse" as a uniform process involving widespread abandonment of the lowlands. As the diverse papers in this volume demonstrate, the end of the Classic period of lowland Maya civilization was a highly varied phenomenon with population decline in many regions, but with political florescence and transformation in other zones. Peak population areas were redistributed in new patterns with new affiliations.

Precisely these types of realignments do occur after periods of large-scale warfare and population displacement. As the United Nations Refugee Commissions have demonstrated (e.g., Hakovirta 1986; Anan 1997; Cohen and Deng 1998), massive population displacement and its consequences can be the most devastating cost of war. The movement of refugees caused by war often has a profound impact on regional ecology, leading to overexploitation of water and soil resources and eventually to famine (e.g., Black and Vaughan 1993; Bellos 1997; Black 1998). Exhausted emigrating groups are susceptible to disease, which can spread with their movement (e.g., Cohen and Deng 1998). Alternatively, smaller-scale migrations can have a positive impact on regions that have economic and political systems capable of absorbing and utilizing new sources of labor and skills (see below). What is most consistent is the political impact of population movements, which can change stable neighboring systems and transform neighboring polities (e.g., Rogge 1987; Cohen and Deng 1998). Recent events in Somalia, Yugoslavia, and central Africa have driven home this point. Disease, famine, ecological decline, and the contagious spread of warfare or other forms of political disruption often follow in the wake of regional wars and subsequent migrations. Again, however, migrants can simulate political systems infused with this new, generally subordinate, source of labor.

At the end of the Classic period, shifts in population are accompanied by both declines and florescences of polities in the lowlands, some with new political forms. Political fragmentation in central Petén was followed initially by increased occupation in defensible locations in the lake region (Rice and Rice, Chapter 7, this volume). Subsequent Postclassic alliances occupied central Petén more widely, but vied in regional wars for control. Belize witnessed an erratic ninth- to tenth-century pattern, with some kingdoms continuing with general stability while other centers were abandoned, grew dramatically, or continued successfully, absorbing both northern and Pasión-region influences (e.g., Pendergast 1986a; Adams et al. Chapter 15, this volume; D. Chase and A. Chase 1982; A. Chase and D. Chase 1985, Chapters 3 and 16, this volume).

Meanwhile, to the north, the Puuc region and central Yucatán witnessed cultural transformation, florescence, and population growth, but accompanied by an increase in siege and fortification warfare. Notably, western Petén ceramic influences, political titles, and even identical epicenter fortification layouts appear in Yucatán at this time (Stuart 1995; Schele and Mathews 1998; Schele and Grube 1995; Carmean et al. Chapter 19, this volume; Suhler et al. Chapter 20, this volume). The low defensive walls encircling Yaxuna, Ek Balam, Uxmal, Chacchob, Dzonot Ake, Cuca, and many other northern sites in the ninth to tenth centuries were virtually identical to those encircling the architectural epicenters, small sites, and villages in the Petexbatun in the late eighth and early ninth centuries (Suhler et al. Chapter 20, this volume; Carmean et al. Chapter 19, this volume; Ringle et al. Chapter 21, this volume; Webster 1980). Meanwhile, to the southeast in the Mopán region (Laporte, Chapter 10, this volume), Classic-style kingdoms continued to thrive, but registered strong influences from the north and west. They only later declined in a gradual, as yet poorly understood, process.

It is probable, then, that warfare and collapse in the Petexbatun and lower Pasión regions affected processes in other regions through migration and its consequences. This is not to say that the Maya lowlands collapsed through a "domino effect" of warfare. Rather, the movement of peoples from the western Petén would have simply impacted processes of change already beginning elsewhere. The common problems of the K'ul Ajaw system, the competitive pressures from other regions of Mesoamerica, and in some regions ecological stresses, already were guiding kingdoms elsewhere to the various types of changes that they experienced later in the ninth and tenth centuries. The political collapse of the western lowland kingdoms and subsequent migrations may help explain the chronological sequencing of these changes and their concurrence within a century and a half. Notably, while Terminal Classic manifestations in each region differed, in all areas the K'ul Ajaw system (and its monumental accoutrements) was abandoned or transformed into the varied *multepal* political systems characteristic of the Postclassic era.

IDEOLOGY AND ENCLAVE FORMATION

Modern research and humanitarian studies of refugee displacement have shown that such migrations are a highly varied and complex phenomenon. Only rarely do they involve movements of large groups retaining political and social identity. The archaeological standards for identification of "site unit intrusions" would only be met by such coherent large-scale movements. Furthermore, this is *not* the most common form of war-related refugee displacements. Instead, individual households, extended families, or small villages seem to be the most common units for migration, often without some males who perished in war, were captured, or who were still involved in conflicts. As cogently argued by Ashmore et al. (Chapter 14, this volume), small communities appear to have retained significant autonomy utilizing their own local economic and ideological programs for cohesion or division. The Xunantunich region data cited by these authors also help to explain the rapid abandonment of that region during the Terminal Classic period (which was parallel to events at Piedras Negras, the Petexbatun, Cancuen, and other earlier abandoned cities of the west). With the inability of local rulers in the Pasión/Usumacinta region to respond to stresses of immigration and overpopulation, to disrupted trade routes, and to warfare, local groups at the small community or extended family level may have merely exercised their option to move away to other areas in the north or east.

Recent regional endemic warfare in central and east Africa provides some insights into these issues. In Somalia, warfare between major powers later degenerated into intensified conflict between villages and even between fortified districts within the capital city of Mogadishu. A process of rapid political devolution reduced the nation to rule by rival factions under petty warlords. Throughout this process, emigration was under way as populations moved within the nation or to adjacent countries. The units of migration varied from whole towns to fragments of families (mothers and some children) (McKinley 1997). Yet, this gradual small-scale emigration came to total hundreds of thousands of individuals within two decades (Hampton 1998: 81–84).

A more peaceful northern zone that received continuous small group migrations was the northwestern region around the town of Bossaso. The population of Bossaso alone increased from 10,000 to 80,000 during the 1990s (McKinley 1997). It is also interesting to note attempts at political reformulation in the face of such population movements. While warlords vied savagely in the south, leaders in Bossaso attempted to consolidate the diverse elements in their region, including refugee populations, by experimenting with new unifying political concepts, especially "experiments in clan-based government" (McKinley 1997). For a period, a thirteen-member council of elders was established by Bossaso military leaders drawing upon heads of sub-clans and even minority groups. Disputes were mediated by this council, which itself was legitimated by the ancient Somali principles and ideology of clan-based rule.

It is not difficult to see the parallels between these political efforts at postwar adaptation in Somalia and the experiments in council rule in the Puuc, Copán Valley, and elsewhere (see Carmean et al. Chapter 19, this volume; Fash et al. Chapter 10, this volume; Fash et al. 1992). There were probably a variety of new, old, and revitalized political formations in the Terminal Classic Maya landscape, like that of Somalia today or as in early medieval Europe. The diversity of political formations helps to explain the extreme regionalism of Terminal Classic culture and styles. It may explain the eclectic mixture of ancient and foreign elements in art, artifacts, and architecture at sites such as Seibal, Nohmul, and the Puuc centers, as leaders drew upon both traditional and exotic symbols to try to legitimate their power and consolidate their polities in the midst of chaos (e.g., Ringle et al. 1998; A. Chase 1985b).

Without drawing analogies too closely, we should view Altar, Seibal, Punta de Chimino, Nohmul, the Puuc sites, and even Chichen Itza with an awareness of this complexity of processes of warfare, migration, and political innovation. It now appears that Seibal, Uxmal, and Chichen Itza might all be best regarded as such "experiments in government" drawing upon traditional Classic Maya concepts, but with a new amalgam of ancient cults and exotic elements. These and many other Terminal Classic polities may not have represented a new Postclassic order of society, nor Mexicanized invaders. Instead, they might have been a reoriented "last gasp" of Classic Maya politics and ideology in a world disrupted by war, population movements, and economic change (e.g. Robles and Andrews 1986).

THE END IN THE WEST AND ITS IMPACT

These regional political formulations had varying degrees of success—some ending by the early tenth century, others perhaps surviving until A.D. 1050, others becoming the basis of Postclassic society. Most of these polities slowly declined. In Belize, northern Yucatán, and the central Petén lake district, they were replaced in gradual transitions or rapid transformations into new Postclassic states and alliances. The K'ul Ajaw complex and its monumental propaganda were, however, conspicuously absent from these Postclassic states.

In the Pasión and Petexbatun regions, the splendid Terminal Classic political experiments rapidly declined. These late centers at Altar, Seibal, and Punta de Chimino had looked inward and to the past for most of their legitimating symbols. While a millennium later their monuments would awe—and utterly confuse—modern scholars, the kings of the late eighth and ninth centuries would see their populations slowly dwindle and disperse. By the Early Postclassic there were much-reduced and scattered populations and few centers with public architecture.

While the pattern in the western Petén is clear, a broader speculation about the Terminal Classic has also been presented in this chapter. I have argued that stresses and problems were experienced by other Late Classic states, but that emigration from early collapsing western polities effected change in other regions. Yet the validity of such a hypothesis must be verified (or rejected) by future researches and especially chronological studies. At present this remains a circumstantial argument, since the chronologies in the eastern and northern lowlands are still too imprecise to allow more specific, testable hypotheses on direct or indirect culture-historical or processual linkages between these regions.

What is certain is that the end of the Classic period of Maya civilization *in western Petén* was indeed a "collapse" in any normal use of that controversial, colloquial term. In most kingdoms there was "a rapid loss of sociopolitical complexity," a political collapse as defined by Tainter (1988) and Cowgill and Yoffee (1988). In many cases, in *western* Petén, warfare, site destruction, and/or declines in population accompanied these changes. Not only the Petexbatun but the entire far-western region seems to have experienced these changes. A limited counter-current to this decline was created by the Terminal Classic enclaves at Seibal, Altar, Punta de Chimino, and elsewhere with their reformulated version of low-land political ideology. Yet these failed attempts to hold together some of the western communities only reinforce the general pattern of a radical and rapid change in the west.

For at least part of the Maya world (though perhaps *only* that zone!) the end of the Classic period still can be seen as the end of the Classic Maya political order, the economic system that maintained it, and the elaborate art and ideology that legitimated it. These early events in the west certainly would have had an impact on the declines, transitions, transformations, and florescences in other lowland regions in the Terminal Classic period. Vigorous and populous Postclassic societies would arise from those transformations in many other regions. Yet in many zones of western Petén itself, state-level societies would never re-emerge.

7

LATE CLASSIC TO POSTCLASSIC TRANSFORMATIONS IN THE PETÉN LAKES REGION, GUATEMALA

Prudence M. Rice and Don S. Rice

ince 1994, we have been involved in Proyecto Maya-Colonial, an archaeological and historical investigation into the development of the seventeenth-century political geography of the lakes region of the Department of Petén, Guatemala (Rice, Rice, and Jones 1993; Rice, Rice, and Pugh 1998; Jones 1998; Cecil 2001; Pugh 2001). The lakes region (Figure 7.1) includes, from east to west, lakes Sacnab, Yaxhá, Macanché, Salpetén, Petén Itzá (including the small lakes of Quexil and Petenxil to the east of Petén-Itzá's small southern arm), and Sacpuy. This area's uninterrupted record of Maya settlement spanning two millennia provides unparalleled opportunities to analyze critical intervals of Maya history, such as the Terminal Classic period, from both early-to-late, or beginning-to-end, approaches ("bottom-up") as well as retrospectively from a late-to-early (or "top-down") view.

The Maya Terminal Classic has been viewed most often as exactly what the term implies: the termination of the florescence of Classic civilization. However, continuity of occupation in the lakes area of central Petén from Classic through Postclassic periods allows us to consider the Terminal Classic from a different perspective, one that witnesses the *beginnings* of Postclassic developments in polity and society. We use both approaches here, because this allows us to frame the political geography of the central Petén Terminal Classic period in terms of the origins of the region's Postclassic inhabitants.

In addition, Terminal Classic central Petén was both a center and a crossroads, the nexus of transitions both geographic (from east to west, and north to

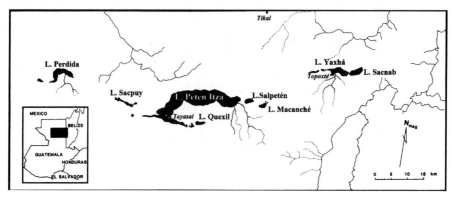

7.1 Map of the Petén Lakes region.

south) and temporal (from Classic to Postclassic). The substantial interactions and population movements occurring within Petén and between southern and northern lowlands—movements taking place in both directions—are revealed in material culture distributions, settlement and architecture, and monumental sculpture.

TOP-DOWN AND BOTTOM-UP: THE ITZA OF PETÉN AND YUCATÁN

At the time of European contact (A.D. 1524–1697) with the indigenous peoples of what is now Petén, the lakes area was dominated by a group of Maya known to the Spaniards as Itza. The identity and origins of the Itza have been long debated (see Rockmore 1998 for a historical review), but recent studies by the late Linda Schele, Erik Boot, and colleagues have shed new light on the situation. These scholars suggest that the origin of the Postclassic lowland Maya group known as the Itza was in north-central Petén, more specifically in the region around Tikal and its allied centers near what is now known as Lake Petén Itzá. The data supporting this conclusion are summarized below (drawn from syntheses in Schele and Mathews 1998: 187, 203–204, 352 n10, 363 n30–368 n31; also Schele, Grube, and Boot 1995: 10; Schele and Grube 1995: 113, 120; Boot 1996, 1997).

The ethnic identifier "Itza" began to appear in central Petén as early as the Early Classic period, although unfortunately much of the evidence comes from unprovenienced material. A text on a stela from Motul de San José mentions the Emblem Glyph or title *k'ul itza ajaw* 'Holy Itza Lord', and the text on a looted pot from Petén names its owner as a *yune itza ajaw* 'child of the Itza lord'. Furthermore, the name of Lake Petén Itzá may originally have been *itz ha* 'enchanted water' (Schele and Mathews 1998: 362, citing personal communication from Nikolai Grube); if so, this could have been the origin of the name of the group known as Itza.

Another important bit of information on the Classic-period occupants of the region comes from a looted pot (perhaps from the Xultún area; Houston, personal communication) bearing a text that mentions the name Kan Ek'. Kan Ek' (*kan* 'four, snake, sky'; *ek'* 'star, black') was the name of the ruler of the Itza at their island capital, Tayasal/Nojpeten (modern Flores Island, in Lake Petén Itzá), from A.D. 1524 to 1697. The reference on a Classic-period ceramic vessel suggests that this name/lineage/title goes back centuries in the region. Central Petén rulers named Kan Ek' are also identified on two Terminal Classic monuments from Seibal: Stela 11, which names Kan Ek' as 'he of Ucanal' and Stela 10, where the name occurs with the Motul de San José Emblem Glyph. The name Kan Ek' also appears on Yaxchilán Stela 10 and in inscriptions at Chich'en Itza. On the basis of these findings, Schele and colleagues (Schele 1995: 4, emphasis added) concluded: ". . . [that] the Itza were always in the Southern Lowlands and that the name came north with them during the [Late Classic] migrations. This new interpretation suggests that the retreats of the Itza [back to Petén] at the fall of Chichen Itza and Mayapan . . . *represented a return to a homeland.*"

Although we differ in assessment of this scenario—one of us (P. Rice) thinks it likely; the other (D. Rice) is more skeptical—our purpose here is not to identify the Itza or specify where in Petén their homeland lay. Rather, we wish to explore certain aspects of the Terminal Classic and Postclassic sociopolitical situation in the northern lowlands and attempt to trace them into the Late and Terminal Classic southern lowlands.

We take as our starting point one important generalization about the Postclassic and early Colonial period northern lowlands. This is that sociopolitical relations in the region were polarized into two broad regional divisions, largely based on elite lineages or lineage groups: the Xiw in the west and the Kokom-Itza in the east. Despite the *multepal* or "joint rule" government of multiple lineages centered at Mayapán in the Late Postclassic, the Xiw and the Itza did not necessarily coexist peaceably. They harbored substantial enmity, as evidenced in various ambushes and murderous plots. They wrote different "prophetic histories," the *Book of Chilam Balam of Chumayel* being Xiw-written and the *Book of Chilam Balam of Tizimin* being Itza. They observed different calendars, which were finally fused into a compromise calendar in A.D. 1539. And they participated in different trade and material culture systems. These regional differences in the northern lowlands are recognizable at least as early as the Terminal Classic period on the basis of differing distributions of Cehpech- and Sotuta-related ceramic spheres.

Significantly, we have found a similar east-west ethno-political or ethno-social division in the Late Postclassic central Petén lakes region. While our surveys have covered all of the central Petén lake basins, our excavations in Postclassic towns have thus far been concentrated primarily to the east of Lake Petén Itzá, in an area identified by Grant Jones (1998) on the basis of ethnohistoric documentation as occupied by people known as Kowoj. The studies of three of our students have isolated discrete sets of identifiers—architectural (Pugh 2001), ceramic (Cecil 2001), and mortuary (Duncan 1999a, 1999b, 2001)—common to sites in this eastern area, and which are either lacking or are different in the western part of the lakes region. We hope to test this proposition in future fieldwork.

For the present purposes, it suffices simply to note that such a division appears to exist in the Late Postclassic lakes region. Here, we are interested in its earlier manifestations and antecedents and the more general flows of people, goods, and ideas in central Petén in the Terminal Classic.

MATERIAL CULTURE: POTTERY AND OBSIDIAN

In his contribution to *The Classic Maya Collapse* volume, Robert Rands (1973a) identified two elite ceramic traditions in the Late Classic southern lowlands: polychromy and fine paste wares. These were largely sequential but had distinct east-west geographic centers. More recently, Donald Forsyth (1997, 1999; Rice and Forsyth, Chapter 3, this volume) identified a similar east-west separation of non-elite utilitarian "supercomplexes" in Late and Terminal Classic Petén. An eastern group comprises the Eznab sphere of central Petén and western Belize, while a western group stretches from the middle Usumacinta and Pasión regions, from Yaxchilán southeast into the Mopán River basin. Similarly, in the northern lowlands, there are distinct eastern and western divisions of the Terminal Classic Cehpech sphere, and this is particularly evidenced in the pastes and slips of slate wares.

Returning to the Petén lakes area, it is in this region that the western and eastern traditions of both utilitarian and elite wares overlap in an east-west clinal distribution. The Late and Terminal Classic ceramic assemblages of the eastern lakes, Yaxhá and Sacnab, clearly fall into the Tepeu 2/Eznab spheres, with some ties farther to the east in the Spanish Lookout phase of Barton Ramie (e.g., Benque Viejo Polychrome, blackwares). To the west, however, from the Lake Macanché basin (P. Rice 1987c) and beyond, Terminal Classic assemblages show decreasing similarities with Eznab and increasing relationships with the Boca sphere of the Pasión area (P. Rice 1996). Yet the fine wares of the Pasión area made their way, albeit in small quantities, to the Yaxhá region, where demand stimulated the production of imitation Pabellon Molded-Carved in at least four distinct pastes (P. Rice 1986).

This localized variability has complicated efforts to make clear distinctions between Late Classic, Terminal Classic, and Early Postclassic ceramic complexes in our excavations in the lakes area, a problem also evident in the Chases' (A. Chase 1983; A. Chase and D. Chase 1983) study of pottery of the Tayasal-Paxcaman portion of the lakes region. Several observations common to both our and the Chases' studies are of particular interest here. One is that Augustine Red, a common Early Postclassic type in the Belize Valley, is also present around Lake Petén Itzá, but is increasingly rare moving eastward through the intervening lake basins (Salpetén, Macanché, Yaxhá-Sacnab). Another is that the slightly "waxy"-feeling slips of the Trapeche ceramic group, another Early Postclassic type common around Lake Petén Itzá (Chase 1983) and Lake Macanché (Rice 1987c), look suspiciously like local copies of the slate wares known in the north. A few sherds of probable slate ware imports, identified by their "trickle" decoration, have been noted in the Petén Itzá portion of the lake chain, but these are quite rare.

From the viewpoint of ceramic technology, this spatial and temporal intermingling of the wares, types, forms, and decorations characterizing multiple ceramic spheres is extremely frustrating. As of this writing, Late Classic (Tepeu 2) ceramic assemblages are relatively clearly defined in the area, and Late Postclassic (beginning ca. A.D. 1200?) types also are clearly defined (Rice 1979, 1996; Cecil 2001). But the ceramic situation in the intervening four centuries or so is extremely difficult to sort out. The most intractable problem yet to be solved is tracing the beginnings of the most widespread Postclassic pottery type/group/ware in the lakes region, Paxcaman Red and its constituent units.

There also seems to be a parallel east-west distinction in patterns of sources of obsidian in the northern lowlands during the Terminal Classic (Braswell 1996b). Obsidian at sites in the eastern Cehpech sphere is primarily from the Ixtepeque source in eastern Guatemala, while sites with Sotuta-sphere—Chich'en Itza–related—ceramics tend to have obsidian from central Mexican sources. Some similarities to this pattern can be seen in the Petén lakes area, although the differences are more temporal than spatial (Rice et al. 1985). X-ray fluorescence analysis of nearly 300 obsidians from sites in three of the lake basin pairs, Yaxhá-Sacnab, Macanché-Salpetén, and Quexil-Petenxil, revealed a dramatic decline from the Late Classic dominance of the El Chayal and San Martín Jilotepeque sources to a Terminal Classic resurgence of Ixtepeque.

In any case, ceramic and obsidian artifacts from sites in the Petén lakes region suggest that it was an area of considerable interaction in the Terminal Classic period, with populations moving in, out, and around, and local and exotic goods moving with them. In particular, the Late and Terminal Classic east-west divisions in the southern lowlands seem to parallel those in the north, and, given the growing evidence for migrations between the two areas, might relate to the Late Postclassic ethno-social split between the Xiw and Kokom/Itza groups.

SETTLEMENT AND MIGRATION

The role of conflict and endemic warfare has been increasingly highlighted in some reconstructions of the Maya Late Classic period. We believe that much of what has been read as "battles" and "star wars" among southern lowland Maya sites are instances of ritualized combat for the purpose of obtaining the captives so prominently trampled by rulers on period-ending monuments (P. Rice n.d.). Furthermore, it is likely that many of these so-called "battles" were actually ballgame contests and the captives—losers of the game—were sacrificial victims, trussed as a ball, as seen at Yaxchilán on Structure 33, Hieroglyphic Stair 2 (see Freidel, Schele, and Parker 1993: 356–362).

That being said, we also acknowledge that there *is* evidence of real conflictive relationships in the southern lowlands during the Late Classic period. At least one, and perhaps more, disaffected factions of elites existed within Tikal. It seems fairly clear that one such group moved to the Petexbatun and began displaying the Tikal Emblem Glyph (Demarest, Chapter 6, this volume). Possibly others—leaving voluntarily or being ousted; perhaps joined by like-minded groups from other Petén sites—moved northward, and were responsible for the introduction of Petén-like architectural and iconographic traits to the northern lowlands. It is apparent that throughout Petén the Terminal Classic saw a dramatic demographic loss (Culbert and Rice 1990).

The lakes area also experienced population decline, as settlement data reveal a drop in the number of architectural constructions datable to the Terminal Classic and Postclassic periods relative to the Classic. Nonetheless, central Petén—in particular the region of the central Petén lakes—was not completely depopulated (D. Rice and P. Rice 1990). There is evidence for continuity of occupation from the Classic period, through the collapse of royal dynasties, and into the subsequent Postclassic period in all lake basins that have been surveyed. In addition, it is evident that during the Terminal Classic period, groups of people were moving into central Petén from the northern lowlands, the Pasión region, and perhaps the Gulf Coast.

Furthermore, the Terminal Classic period in the lakes area witnessed the beginning of a marked change in location of settlements between the Classic and Postclassic. Small, densely settled and nucleated Postclassic communities are found primarily on naturally defensible islands or peninsulas in the lakes. Postclassic constructions exist on the mainland slopes of the basins, but they are much reduced in number and density relative to Classic-period patterns. The choice of easily defended sites for focal settlements suggests that conflict was a key feature of the political environment, and perhaps also that the nature of warfare had changed during the later centuries of the Classic period. It is significant here that the Terminal Classic to Historic–period peninsular site of Zacpetén, on the north shore of Lake Salpetén (Figure 7.2), was fortified at its narrow join with the mainland by a wall-and-moat complex (Pugh 2001).

Also during the Terminal Classic, that is, ca. the tenth and eleventh centuries, new settlements were founded at the site of El Fango in the savanna region south of Lake Petén Itzá (P. Rice and D. Rice 1979; D. Rice and P. Rice 1980), and at the sites of Pasajá in the southern Petén Itzá basin and Chachaclún on Petén Itzá's north shore. Contemporaneous, intrusive domestic structures also have been identified in the site peripheries of Nixtun Ch'ich' on Petén Itzá's western San Jerónimo peninsula and at Michoacán in the basin of Lake Quexil, south of the main body of

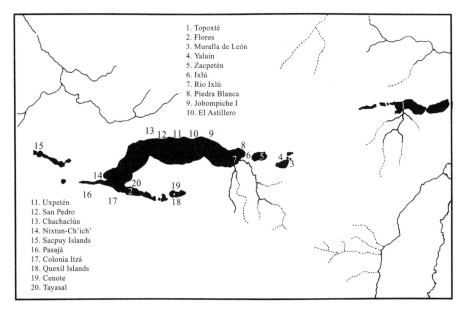

1. Topoxté
2. Flores
3. Muralla de León
4. Yalain
5. Zacpetén
6. Ixlú
7. Rio Ixlú
8. Piedra Blanca
9. Jobompiche I
10. El Astillero

11. Uxpetén
12. San Pedro
13. Chachaclún
14. Nixtun-Ch'ich'
15. Sacpuy Islands
16. Pasajá
17. Colonia Itzá
18. Quexil Islands
19. Cenote
20. Tayasal

7.2 Map of Petén Lakes region sites.

Lake Petén Itzá. Each of these sites, save Nixtun Ch'ich', is located on relatively impoverished soils formed over hard and nutrient-poor limestone bedrock, low in organics, high in clay content, and ferrogenic. Historically these soil suites have supported vegetation communities dominated by grasses, low oaks, and xerophytic or fire-resistant herbaceous species (P. Rice and D. Rice 1979; D. Rice and P. Rice 1980), and they were not the focus of Maya settlement in the Classic period.

The location of these late sites in zones of poor agricultural potential, areas devoid of prior settlement, and the peripheral nature of intrusive residential architecture at the established sites of Nixtun Ch'ich' and Michoacan, suggest the migration of small groups into the Petén Itzá zone at the close of the Classic period, groups forced to settle in marginal pockets of an established settlement system. The residential structures are poorly constructed, largely consisting of unworked chert cobbles that are ubiquitous in Petén's grasslands and seemingly plastered with savanna clays as opposed to limestone-based plaster.

ARCHITECTURE

The forms of the structures in these new settlements are not characteristic of Classic central Petén, but rather introduce features that are standard in later Postclassic architecture. Postclassic structures typically consist of a low, square-to-rectangular, single-level platform for a masonry or perishable superstructure.

Masonry superstructural foundations are common and appear to conform to a limited number of plans in Petén (D. Rice 1986, 1988): a single room or portico composed of a masonry back wall and/or bench, or a back wall with one (L-shaped) or two (C-shaped) side walls and/or benches, and an open front. Some "tandem" structures apparently had a second room of masonry and/or perishable materials constructed directly behind the masonry fore-room, which then functioned as a portico to the house.

C-shaped structures are known in the Petexbatun region in the eighth century (Demarest, Chapter 6, this volume), but in central Petén these distinctive structural forms appear later, showing up first at the savanna site of El Fango south of the lakes district. Here the arrangement is conspicuous on the northern edge of a small community of late Late Classic plazuela groups scattered throughout the El Fango grassland. At the time of our mapping of El Fango, however, we did not know that the pattern would be repeated elsewhere by later Late Postclassic populations. C-shaped structures are also found in the southern Lake Quexil basin at Michoacán, at the site of Ixlú, and at the site of Chachaclún on Lake Petén Itzá's north shore. They share features with Terminal Classic, non-Maya construction in the Petexbatun (Demarest, personal communication), at Seibal (Tourtellot 1988b), in the Chontalpa region of México (Fox 1980, 1981, 1987), and in the Guatemalan highlands (Ichon and Grignon 1981). Structures and formal architectural complexes similar to those in Petén have also been defined as residences and civic-ceremonial groups at Chich'en Itza (Cobos 1999a, 1999b; Lincoln 1990), and at the later Postclassic Yucatán sites of Cozumel (Freidel 1981a; Freidel and Sabloff 1984) and Mayapán (Smith 1962).

The source area(s) for these Terminal Classic architectural innovations is unknown, but their associated ceramic inventories and bench forms suggest that they represent migrants from the Petexbatun region (Demarest, personal communication 2002) or the Río Pasión riverine zone (Tourtellot 1988b). These groups may well be "refugees" of late Late Classic raiding and endemic warfare in this riverine zone. These immigrants to the central Petén lakes region are assumed to have been forced from their homelands under threat to personal safety and/or crops and subsistence, and there is some evidence in the form of a defensive wall-moat complex at Nixtun Ch'ich' (and also to the west at Zacpetén) that they were not received hospitably by all residents of the Petén Itzá basin. This episode is the first in a Postclassic history punctuated by in-migration, defensive posturing, and warfare in central Petén.

While the above architectural features point to relations between the Petén lakes region and the Petexbatun to the southwest, there are also suggestive links to the north, to the Puuc region. The site of Nixtun Ch'ich' on the western edge of Lake Petén Itzá has a very large ballcourt complex most closely comparable to that of Chich'en Itza in size, shape, and superstructural elements, making it the largest and most likely the latest ballcourt in Petén. No other Postclassic site in the central Petén lakes region has a recognizable ballcourt save Ixlú, which has two, but the ballcourts at Ixlú appear to date to the late Late Classic occupation and construction of the site, and they bear no resemblance to those at Chich'en and Nixtun. While the ballcourt at Nixtun Ch'ich' has not yet been excavated, we believe it suggests strong and early influence, if not in-migration, from Chich'en Itza and/or the Puuc zone.

MONUMENTS AND ICONOGRAPHY

Among the more interesting aspects of the Late to Terminal Classic transition in central Petén are the changes evident on the sculptured monuments. Evidenced by different monument shapes, layouts, images, and glyphs, they point to considerable diversity within Petén and contacts with other areas. This was first drawn to our attention during project surveys, when we noted several monument fragments cemented into the courtyard of the "Escuela Normal Rural 'Julio E. Rosado Pinelo' " in Santa Elena, on the south shore of Lake Petén Itzá, where a Classic-period site was reportedly destroyed. Santa Elena Stela 1 is the upper portion of a stela with carving on both faces, suggesting a Late Classic date. What is distinctive about this monument is its non-Petén-style pointed shape, with both upper "corners" removed. Similar monument shapes occur in the Puuc area in the north, at sites such as Sayil and Oxkintok, where stelae often have narrow, pointed tops as well as unusual (in Petén) features, such as decorated borders and multiple registers (Pollock 1980). These northern features also appear on some Terminal Classic monuments in the Petén lakes area and elsewhere, for example at Jimbal, Ixlú, and Ucanal.

The presence of unusual iconographic features has long been known from western Petén, where the Terminal Classic appears to witness the incursions of "foreigners." Seibal is most frequently cited (Graham 1971, 1990; Tourtellot and González, Chapter 4, this volume) because of its many stelae showing individuals with "non-Classic Maya" facial features and attire. In addition, some Terminal Classic monuments at Seibal and other sites have unusual square glyph cartouches. Unusual day glyphs in squared cartouches also occur on Seibal Stela 13, Ucanal Stela 4, Jimbal Stelae 1 and 2, El Zapote Stela 5, Flores Stela 5, and Calakmul Stela 86. Edmonson (1988: 229–230) says these glyphs "are certainly not Mayan," and instead considers them to be Gulf Coastal, most likely "Late Classic (and provincial) Olmec."

In addition to squared glyphs and unusual iconography, many Terminal Classic stelae in central Petén show seated figures conversing. The figures are simply dressed, conspicuously without kingly regalia and accoutrements of office, suggesting that they are not flaunting symbols of status and power. Similar conversation scenes also appear on Terminal Classic Fine Orange (Pabellon Molded-Carved type) pottery bowls and vases, perhaps vessels used for serving food and beverages as part of the hospitality of such gatherings. Together, these scenes accentuate what might be of paramount interest at this time: the fact that discussions are taking place, as opposed to displays of the power and charisma of individuals. The putative "foreigners" moving into Petén seem to have been peacefully assimilated and perhaps even expected and welcomed. These scenes plus another new emphasis, all-text stelae and altars, suggest that these extended monuments could record outcomes of "summit meetings" of leaders from different areas meeting in Petén.

Finally, it is interesting to consider the shape of Terminal Classic stelae at Tikal and other nearby sites. Terminal Classic stelae at Tikal and other sites in its realm were "top-heavy"—asymmetrical and wedge-shaped. The expanded upper area depicted the Paddler gods, royal ancestors floating on clouds/serpents and nearly smothering the ruler below. The explanation for the pointed tops of the Puuc stelae could be that the sculptured monuments are modeled after the painted end walls of corbel-vaulted structures, where the in-slanting walls of the vault cut off the upper corners of the scene. On the other hand, it could be a specific repudiation of the Tikal program and its glorification of dynastic ancestors. Whatever the explanation, this new iconographic program of the Terminal Classic outside of the Tikal realm explicitly rejects royal display, ancestors, and dynastic rule, and instead appears to celebrate conversation, diplomacy, and less flamboyant interactions.

CALENDARS AND POLITICAL ORGANIZATION

Analysis of the texts and iconographic programs of stelae in the Petén lakes area, broadened to include adjacent regions and other categories of data, particularly architecture, suggests that the Classic Maya in the southern lowlands had the same calendar-based political organization as that known in the northern lowlands during the Late Postclassic and early Colonial period. The basis for this geo-politico-ritual structuring was the interval of thirteen *k'atuns*, or approximately 256 Gregorian years, known as the *may* (P. Rice 2004).

The *may,* and its possible applicability to the Classic Maya, was first explored by Munro Edmonson (1979, 1986: 4–5) on the basis of his translations of the prophetic histories known as the "books of the *chilam b'alams*." In the northern lowlands, the calendrical cycle known as the *may* was ritually "seated" in an important city, which became the *may k'u*, or cycle seat, for 256 years. The city holding this honor was sacred or divine (*siyah kan*). Within its realm, other towns competed to seat the thirteen k'atuns that constituted the cycle, an honor that conferred substantial political powers for the twenty-year interval. There is considerable agreement among early Colonial sources as to which cities seated which cycles and k'atuns (Edmonson 1986: 275–276).

Key to the applicability of this Postclassic- and Colonial-period *may* model to the Classic Maya are the stelae in Tikal's twin pyramid complexes. It is well known that these complexes, with their paired radial structures, date to a series of

Late Classic k'atun endings (Jones 1969). A second clue to the presence of a calendrically based political organization comes from apparent cycles of events based on 256-year intervals. These were noted by Puleston (1977, 1979), who referred to an "epistemological pathology" in the repetition of declines, collapses, and conquests—particularly the so-called "hiatus" and the "collapse"—on the basis of repetitive cycling of k'atuns of the same "name," for example, a K'atun 8 Ajaw or a K'atun 11 Ajaw. He concluded by suggesting "that the collapse of Classic Maya civilization was triggered by an internal mechanism. I am not denying that the system in which the Maya participated was under various forms of stress, but the timing of this ultimate event seems to have been linked to very specific and deeply rooted assumptions that the Maya had about the nature of time."

The third and final element, the mechanism explaining how this system might have "worked," comes rather indirectly from Bishop Landa's *Relación* and Tozzer's (1941: 168 n885, citing Roys) commentary on it. Landa noted the significance of half-periods and successively overlapping decades of rule of the "k'atun idols" in the Maya temples, which we extend to the workings of longer cycles of 256-year period of the *may*. For the 20-year k'atun, each "idol" actually had a thirty-year period of responsibility. During the first ten years it acts as "guest" (B) of the idol in place (A), gradually drawing power from A. A "retires" at the end of this ten-year interval, at which point B begins to rule alone, which it does for ten years until a new "idol," C, joins B as "guest" and begins absorbing B's power.

Putting these (and other; P. Rice 2004) components together, then, it is possible to suggest that the Classic Maya observed politico-ritual cycles of 256 years, in which key cities such as Tikal, Calakmul, and other sites seated the *may*, with subsidiary centers around them seating the constituent k'atuns. For a given *may k'u*, such as Tikal, during the first half or 128 years of its seating it might have been, like a k'atun idol, a "guest" of a current seat. Then it took over as the sole seat, providing political and ritual leadership for 128 years. At that point, Tikal was joined by a "guest," the new seat of the next cycle, and for the last half or 128 years of its seating it "lost power," or ceased to dominate ritual and politics.

Interestingly, this is exactly what is seen at Tikal, which is postulated to have become a *may* seat in A.D. 426 (or 8.19.10.0.0), in the ten-year midpoint of a K'atun 8 Ajaw (A.D. 416–435), the last k'atun of the thirteen-k'atun cycle, under the rule of Siyaj Kan K'awil II. During the first half of this seating, from 426 to ca. 554, or 128 years, Tikal actively participated in regular k'atun celebrations marked by the erection of period-ending stelae. The second half of this *may* seating, from ca. 554 to 692, marks the infamous and enigmatic "hiatus," a 128-year period in which no monuments were erected at Tikal. Later, in the Late Classic period, a similar pattern can be seen: Tikal regularly erected stelae during the first 128 years of its next term as *may* seat, from A.D. 692 to 810, but not, with one exception, thereafter. The second half of Tikal's Late Classic *may* seating is known, of course, as its "collapse." We suggest that instead of being evidence of Tikal's declines, these intervals without monument erection were known and anticipated changes in politico-ritual practice accompanying the co-rule and transfer of "power" between one *may* seat and another. Other sites demonstrating 128- (or 129-)year patterns of stelae erection include Dos Pilas and Machaquila.

CONTINUITY AND CHANGE

We deliberately chose to use the word "transformations" in the title of our chapter, because we believe that is the operative term for the period in question, certainly in the central Petén lakes region if not elsewhere in the lowlands. Rather than marking solely the "termination" of Classic civilization, it is also a period of initiation of numerous patterns that are distinctly Postclassic. At the same time, it is generally an interval of flux—population movements and material exchanges— that play a role in those endings and beginnings, but also have their own dynamic. We see the Terminal Classic in the central Petén lakes area as a "Transformational Classic," a time of continuities and changes between the Classic and the Postclassic.

Discussions about the Classic "collapse" and the end of the institution of divine kingship in the southern lowlands tend to imply, if not state outright, that the entire system of Classic Maya politico-religious organization (cum "government") collapsed and died. However, while divine kingship and Long Count dating may have ceased, other components of the underpinnings of Classic lowland civilization and geo-politico-ritual organization were maintained through the Postclassic period. These include calendrics, cosmovision, shared architectural programs, period-ending rituals, as well as calendrically based political organization based on celebration of k'atun and *may* cycles. In this regard it is useful to remember an often ignored point: Mayapán revived the Classic period–ending stela complex, with at least thirteen sculptured stelae and twenty-five or more plain monuments (Proskouriakoff 1962: 134). Landa's informants (Tozzer 1941) told him that they were accustomed to erect these monuments every twenty years. One stela per k'atun for thirteen k'atuns equals 256 years, a *may* cycle. After this span of stela erection, Mayapán experienced the foreordained "collapse" and "abandonment"—or ritual termination— of a *may* center, in a scenario not unlike that of the southern lowlands in the Terminal Classic some 500 years (two *may* cycles) earlier.

Thus we find it difficult to accept the idea that lowland Maya civilization "collapsed." Following the reasoning in Chapter 1, the Maya "civilization as 'great tradition'" neither ended nor necessarily became less complex or fragmented. Rather, it transformed itself into something different—perhaps describable as a transition from more theocratic and less secular, to less theocratic and more secular. And even though it might be argued that "collapse" pertains primarily to elite ruling authority (especially divine kings), occurred at only the largest sites, and did not result in complete depopulation, it is evident from the data above that the k'atun- and *may*-based political organization of the Preclassic and Classic periods survived through the Terminal Classic and Postclassic periods and up to the time that it was recorded during the Colonial period in the books of the *chilam b'alams*.

At the same time, by the end of the Late Classic period there is evidence for intersite conflict in many parts of the lowlands, and surely such hostilities would have played a major role in transformations of the Terminal Classic period. There is, for example, considerable evidence in Classic Maya art of the capture and sacrifice of elites by their counterparts from other kingdoms, with the Bonampak murals (Miller 1986) being the archetypical illustrations of battles between such factions. While there is disagreement over the degree to which war was ritualized competition, and the degree to which success in combat yielded ideological versus material gain for the victors (e.g., Demarest et al. 1997; Webster 1993, 1998, 2000), it is clear that Classic-period wars began at a small scale, with a limited number of individuals involved.

In the late Late Classic period, however, the nature of warfare was transformed. The construction of fortifications in site centers (Wolley 1995), the relocation of population centers to physiographically isolated locations such as islands and peninsulas (Demarest, Chapter 6, this volume; Demarest and Escobedo 1997; Pugh 2001; D. Rice 1986), and the construction of massive moat-wall complexes at defensible boundaries of sites (Pugh 2001; Rice, Rice and Pugh 1998; Wolley and Wright 1990) suggest to us that local populations were increasingly involved in and the focus of warfare, and that motivations for hostilities included control over territory.

One implication of this level of Late Classic warfare is that it would have resulted in vast numbers of refugees and displaced persons. Regardless of time and circumstances, displaced and migrating populations change social and political landscapes. Disfranchised and dispossessed, they abandoned fields and stores, and often have been denied access to food. They are invariably suffering malnutrition, diseases, and fertility problems related to living in impoverished circumstances. They are susceptible to diseases that can spread with their movement (*The Morbidity and Mortality Weekly Report* [MMWR] http://www.cdc.gov/mmwr/). Displaced persons and refugees put added stress on soil and water resources, altering the natural ecology and often creating famine conditions (Bellos 1997). Most consistently, however, they disrupt the economic, social, and political systems of neighboring regions, exacerbating problems those polities and populations may be already facing and forcing redefinition of in-group and out-group boundaries. As of December 31, 2000, the estimate of refugees worldwide was 14,544,000, with the largest numbers coming from Africa—3,346,00—and the Middle East—6,035,000 (*World Refugee Survey* 2001: Table 2). An additional twenty million persons were estimated to be internally displaced worldwide. Causes of this out-migration and displacement include: alleged armed insurgency; border war; civil war; foreign occupation; lawlessness resulting from a breakdown of civil and moral authorities; and religious and political violence. Units of population movement varied from whole towns to fragments of families (mothers and their children).Warfare between ethnic factions in Somalia in 1988–1994, for example, produced more than 500,000 deaths from the violence and population displacement (http://www.refugees.org/world/countryrpt/africa/somalia.htm). In the southern zone of the country, factional disputes degenerated into intensified conflict between villages, as well as between fortified districts of the capital city of Mogadishu, producing a rapid political devolution that reduced the nation to rule by rival petty warlords (Anan 1997; McKinley 1997). During the worst of the turmoil in 1992, an estimated 800,000 Somalis were refugees in neighboring countries and two million were internally displaced. In the more peaceful northern zone of Somalia, which received continuous small-group migrations of internally displaced people, the city of Bossaso alone increased from 10,000 to 80,000, pushing leaders of Bossaso to attempt political reformulations, experiments in clan-based government focused upon ancient Somali principles and ideology, in an effort to consolidate the diverse elements of incoming refugee populations (McKinley 1997).

We reference these details here because we see in them an analogy to the situation in the central Petén lakes region during the Terminal Classic period. The lakes region seems to have been an intermediate or final destination for numerous groups of people on the move between about A.D. 800 to 1000. The reasons for the movements may be varied, including political factionalism, ideological or "religious" disputes, social or ethnic strife, agricultural stresses, or other causes. We can refer to these groups as refugees—fleeing something in their homeland—or more neutrally as migrants.

Whatever the causes and whatever the terminology, it is clear from multiple sources of evidence that, while the Petén lakes region experienced some population loss during the Terminal Classic, it also saw considerable in-migration. Architectural styles (the introduction of C-shaped structures) and ceramics (including Fine Orange) bespeak the arrival of migrants from the war-torn Pasión region, while architecture (the Nixtun-Ch'ich' ballcourt), stelae (glyphs and styles), and ceramics (imitation slate wares?) indicate contacts with—and probably migration from—the Puuc region. In this context of movements and interactions in central Petén, the erection of monuments emphasizing extended texts and scenes of conversations (diplomacy? negotiations?), rather than individual rulers' power, seems highly appropriate.

Elsewhere (Rice and Rice n.d.) we have discussed the Petén lakes area in terms of its constituting a frontier, particularly in the Contact period. As we noted there,

> [i]nterpretations of frontier-type situations tend to be couched in terms of
> dichotomies: frontier as place vs. frontier as process. . . . They may be

regarded as spatially dynamic and socially open, or as static and closed backwaters. They may be occupied and contested or an empty no man's land, close to a homeland or distant from it, permeable or impermeable, inclusive or exclusive, long-term or short-term. Frontiers may be conceived as repositories of tradition or as arenas of innovation. Through time, they may expand or shrink. They may be literally "front lines" in a wave of movement of something new ... or they may be "last lines of defense" in the conservation of cultural traditions. Often, they are all these at once.

Frontiers are places, but what makes them interesting are not so much the characteristics of place but rather the processes played out within them. We see the Petén lakes area during the Terminal Classic period as a frontier in the sense of being "spatially dynamic and socially open" to in-migration and new ideas, but also "occupied and contested" as evidenced by settlements on islands and peninsulas, sometimes fortified. It was a region of dynamic and contested social and political identities, simultaneously a "repository of tradition" (the role of the Kan Ek' dynasty and stelae glorifying ancestors) and an "arena of innovation" in architectural and iconographic styles. It seems to have maintained this frontier status well into the Early Postclassic period, perhaps up to ca. A.D. 1200 or so.

It is doubtless significant—although the nature and implications must await further fieldwork and testing—that the evidence for population incursions, new iconographic styles, new architectural forms, and imported ceramics in the Terminal Classic is found in the western part of the lakes district, specifically around Lake Petén Itza. The eastern extreme of the region, that is, Lakes Yaxhá and Sacnab, seems to have been relatively isolated from these intrusions. It appears, therefore, that what we have identified as an east-west ethno-political or ethnosocial differentiation in the Late Postclassic period in the Petén lakes region— Kowoj in the east and Itza in the west—may trace its roots into the Terminal Classic period and the many transformations occurring during these centuries.

It is also significant that there existed eastern and western ethno-socio-political divisions in both northern and southern lowlands for nearly seven centuries beginning in the Terminal Classic period. We cannot resist the temptation to suggest that this might represent a new Postclassic quadripartition of the geopolitical landscape, something on the order of what Marcus (1976) presented for the Classic period.

8

DISASTER IN SIGHT
THE TERMINAL CLASSIC AT TIKAL AND UAXACTUN

Juan Antonio Valdés and Federico Fahsen

ikal and Uaxactun were known in antiquity as Mutul and Sian-Kan (Schele and Mathews 1998: 63–66), two cities that, because of their proximity and prosperous development, saw themselves involved in a long rivalry that began in the Preclassic period, when Uaxactun appears to have been more impressive in the eyes of visitors with its beautiful acropolis in Group H. This changed starting in the Early Classic, when the army commanded by K'ak' Sih (Smoking Frog) entered the site at the complex identified by Fahsen (1992: 2) as Shell-Kawak (the famous Str. A-5), which was the true heart of the city, and took Uaxactun under his power. From this point on, the history of both cities was closer and more parallel, as K'ak' Sih remained ruler of the city and his descendants were the sovereigns during the ensuing centuries until the Terminal Classic (Valdés and Fahsen 1995: 206–218).

During the last part of the Early Classic and during the centuries of the Late Classic, Tikal imposed a harsh control over the conquered land, because the blood of the victorious royal family coursed through the veins of all the sovereigns that followed Smoking Frog, as they recorded in their sculptured monuments through the centuries. Nevertheless, the high prestige enjoyed by Uaxactun always remained, and proof of this is that at this site the last carved monuments of these two cities were erected.

Without doubt, both cities were responsible for the process that led to the growth of Maya civilization and for the success that allowed the Maya of central Petén to remain in the vanguard, though with battles and falls along the way. One of their best weapons was their astuteness in creating and modifying continuously the ideological strategy that provided the population with a divine order, and that harmonized life into an axis and allowed them to understand how all the diverse components of life functioned, including the continual regeneration of the universe. The rulers transmitted this ideology that influenced the population that supported them for a millennium. There is also no doubt that their best "ally" during Classic times was the sophisticated use of architecture, sculpture, and painting, in which the plazas became theater stages where spectators, priests, and kings mixed with ceremonial paraphernalia, music, and the fragrant incense smoke dedicated to the gods.

In the central Maya area, this ideology began to crumble during the second half of the ninth century, when Tikal was governed by Hasaw Kan K'awil II and Uaxactun by his homologue, K'al Chik'in Chakte, in the year A.D. 889 (Valdés et al. 1999). Throughout the tenth century, chaos prevailed and, although Tikal maintained a more prolonged occupation, the inhabitants of Uaxactun migrated to other lands, possibly to the east and northeast in the direction of Belize, where human occupation lasted longer (Willey et al. 1965; Pendergast 1985). Interpretation of this process is under revision due to recent archaeological discoveries and epigraphic decipherments, reformulating the frequent political activity in the region during the last centuries of the Late and Terminal Classic. The relationships of dependency were as complex as the causes of the collapse, a phenomenon presently seen as a consequence of internal factors (Sabloff and Henderson 1993; Demarest and Valdés 1995; Foias and Bishop 1997), not of external influences over the Maya area, as suggested twenty-five years ago.

ANOTHER ENCOUNTER WITH THE FAME OF THE EIGHTH CENTURY

Multiple models have been presented in the last decades to explain the political organization of the Classic Maya, and their acceptance or critique have been derived mainly from the theoretical orientation of the scholars themselves. However, the new epigraphic decipherments propose a territorial structure of macrostates, with political hegemonies that incorporate smaller polities, at least in the case of Tikal and Calakmul (Martin and Grube 1995; Martin 1996; Lacadena and Ciudad Ruiz 1998). In contrast to the numerous titles related to dependency that have helped determine the relationships between sites in the Usumacinta-Pasión region (Mathews 1985; Houston 1993; Schele and Freidel 1990), the same situation does not occur in central Petén. Here, the growing wealth of the nobles was translated into sumptuous palaces and the acquisition of exotic goods, but monumental inscriptions are not so explicit about the system of sociopolitical organization, although more information about noble titles is being discovered on painted vessels that circulated as "social currency" (Reents-Budet 1994, 1997).

In the central area, the internal organization of the Late Classic is understood now through epigraphy, and through the same source we can observe that since the Early Classic, the hopes of the nobles were partially satisfied, since some of them were permitted to sculpt monuments and carve their own names, as seen in the "Tikal Ballcourt Marker" and the "Man of Tikal," from the beginning of the fifth century. In Uaxactun, a similar process possibly took place when two personages with different nominals erected their own monument on the same date as early as A.D. 357. It is possible that this denotes a strategy of "democratization" in favor of the closest relatives of the rulers.

During the eighth century, the sovereigns of the central area focused on developing a complex network of social, economic, and political alliances, which constantly shifted depending on multiple variables. The glyphic inscriptions reflect wars, indicate the relations established with neighboring cities, and record important events in the lives of their leaders. This century, which we can call the "Golden Century," shows the works of grandeur and stability as the product of sage governments. Polychrome vessels, the smaller masterpieces, have become a principal avenue for discovering details of the identities of the elites, as their painted palace scenes display images ranging from daily life to an internally stratified society.

The destiny of Tikal was driven from A.D. 633 until around A.D. 800 by great statesmen who had long reigns: Nun Bak Chak (Shield Skull, ca. A.D. 633–679) and his son, Hasaw Kan K'awil I (Ruler A, Ah Cacau, A.D. 682–734), and grandson, Yik'in Kan K'awil (Ruler B, A.D. 734–750), who was followed by *his* son, Yax Ain II (Ruler C, A.D. 768-ca.790) (Jones and Satterthwaite 1982; Schele and Grube 1994). Recent studies confer on Nun Bak Chak responsibility for initiating the revitalization of Tikal and the hegemonic powers of its sovereigns. Although Nun Bak Chak's reign was agitated by wars (Houston 1993: 108; Schele and Mathews 1998), it is clear that he took very seriously his desire to place Tikal at the forefront with his program of transcendental works. The proof of this rests on the recent ceramic dating of the construction of Temple V during the Ik phase (Laporte and Gomez n.d.), revealing that Nun Bak Chak must have ordered the construction of this building around A.D. 600–650. From our viewpoint, this dating is perfectly supported by the architecture of the pyramidal base of Temple V, which exhibits certain elements fashionable during the Early Classic, such as rounded corners and wide balustrades framing the stairway that climbs to the top. The use of these elements denotes the persistence of a previous period's tradition, also exposed in the earlier versions of Strs. 5C-49, 5D-22, and 5D-35. Furthermore, the simultaneous construction of two ballcourts, one in the East Plaza and another in the Complex of the Seven Temples (Jones 1991: 116; Laporte and Fialko 1995: 83), indicates the importance of commemorating the creation myth and the rebirth of the people of Tikal into a prosperous future.

The extensive growth program was continued by Hasaw Kan K'awil and his descendants during the eighth century, proclaiming their qualities as magnificent statesmen and authors of ambitious constructions, while at the same time access to foreign materials increased via commercial networks, and the polychrome pottery industry was reactivated (Dahlin 1986: 84–112), confirming the supremacy of this site and the glory of its local dynasty. This corresponds to the Imix phase, which is widely known for the beauty of the pottery types Palmar Orange Polychrome and Zacatel Cream Polychrome, many decorated with palace scenes and courtesans accompanied by hieroglyphic texts, distributed all over the lowlands. The monumental constructions of the Great Plaza, Central Acropolis, Lost World, and the rest of the architectural complexes of the city were enlarged. Also, religious rituals were revived and Tikal's external relations were expanded through political and marriage alliances to regions as far away as Piedras Negras, Yaxchilán, and Copán. Tikal was a beautiful metropolis, and its population increased dramatically to 90,000–120,000 persons (Culbert et al. 1990).

This golden age persisted even during the rule of Yax Ain II, around A.D. 800, as he ordered extensive architectural works in the city, including the building of courtyards and structures in the Central Acropolis, especially in the area around Toh Chak Ich'ak's palace (Great Jaguar Paw, ca. A.D. 317–378). Possibly the most beautiful edifice was his royal palace, known today as the Maler Palace, where a date corresponding to July 4, 800, was found written, indicating that the residence was still in use at that time (Schele and Mathews 1998). The continuous bellicose manifestations that affected this region at the end of the eighth century were also documented by the graffiti inscribed on these structures' walls, as seen in the Maler Palace and the contemporaneous palaces of Group G, reflecting the preoccupation of their occupants with involvement in these actions, leading them to reproduce drawings of prisoners and the capture of palanquins of enemy rulers (Figure 8.1).

The only inscription dated for this time is Stela 24 in A.D. 810, but it was found so deteriorated that it was impossible to decipher the name of the ruler who erected it. Nevertheless, the glyphic text of Lintel 2 of Temple III ends by affirming that the construction was the work of the Supreme Priest or "Prayermaker of the People," who is also identified by the titles of K'inich Nab Nal and Chakte. The interesting part of this case is that when the nominals of the sovereign in this panel are studied, they are almost identical to the glyphs used by Yax Ain II. For this reason, without a doubt his rule must have been responsible for the construction of Temple III around A.D. 810 and for Stela 24, which commemorates his reign. After this date, there is no glyphic information from Tikal until fifty-nine years later.

In the case of Uaxactun, recent studies (Valdés, Fahsen, and Escobedo 1999) have permitted full identification of four rulers boasting their power during the eighth century and the beginning of the ninth. It is known that one or two more rulers existed, because they are mentioned in Stelae 8 and 11, but their names have been completely destroyed by the erosion of the monuments. The first ruler appears on Stela 14, dated A.D. 702, and is named Chaan K'an Ko. The next ruler,

8.1 Graffiti from Group G (5E-11) of Tikal, showing captives tied and humiliated, a frequent theme on the structure walls during the eighth and ninth centuries.

represented on Stela 2 fifty years later, was called Oxlahun Koxba, followed by another sovereign mentioned on a vase dated A.D. 759; although the first part of his name cannot be read, it concludes with Chik'in Chakte. Next ruled the two personages mentioned on Stelae 8 and 11. During the final part of the Late Classic, however, power was clearly in the hands of ruler K'an Ko, whose image was carved on Stela 7 in the year A.D. 810.

Of Chaan K'an Ko, we know that he was in power at the same time as Hasaw Kan K'awil in the neighboring metropolis, and it is notable that on Stela 14 this ruler makes reference to the founder of the Tikal lineage, Yax Moch Xoc. This mention and the erection of this stela in Group B of Uaxactun suggest the particular interest of this governor in maintaining the memory of his family's place of origin and in proclaiming that he was the descendant of K'ak' Sih of Tikal (Smoking Frog), who 300 years before had erected monuments commemorating his triumph in the same group (Mathews 1985; Schele and Freidel 1990; Valdés and Fahsen 1995).

Several decades later, Stela 2 was erected, also in Group B, demonstrating the intention to honor this space again. The glyphs are clear in naming ruler Oxlahun Koxba, displaying his power and the date of celebration of the end of the *k'atun* in 9.16.0.0.0, which corresponds to August 5, 751. At that moment, the destiny of Tikal was in the hands of Yikin Kan K'awil, who had erected Stela 20 to celebrate the same event.

The next ruler was identified through the restudy of the so-called "Vase of the Initial Series," which formed part of the mortuary offering of Burial A-2, discovered in Group A. According to this text, the new Uaxactun sovereign used the title "Chik'in Chakte," although his complete name is unknown. The details of the burial (R. Smith 1937: 207) indicate that it was a male individual interred with a rich offering that included exotics, such as jade and marine artifacts, from faraway regions. After its placement, it was covered by fill, including hundreds of obsidian and chert flakes and blades, perpetuating an ancient tradition employed in royal tombs in Tikal and Uaxactun since the Early Classic. The custom of placing burials within bedrock, painting the walls and roofs of the vault of the tomb with a red color, and including jaguar skins is part of a funerary tradition of central Petén known from the North Acropolis and Lost World Complex at Tikal (Coggins 1975; Laporte and Fialko 1995), Uaxactun (L. Smith 1950), and Río Azul (Adams 1986; Graham 1986), which may begin as early as the Late Preclassic with the burials in Tikal's North Acropolis. For these reasons, the suggestion that it was a funerary tradition that arrived at Tikal from Caracol during the events of the Middle Classic (Chase and Chase (1987: 61) seems strange.

After the ruler Chik'in Chakte, mentioned on the "Vase of the Initial Series," there were one or two additional leaders during the eighth century at Uaxactun who continued the work of aggrandizing the site and, in particular, ordering the construction of new plazas. At this point Stelae 8 and 11 were carved, but both are impossible to read, so it is unclear if they make reference to one or two separate individuals. Of great importance is the discovery that the construction of the Main Plaza in Group A took place between the years A.D. 760 and 770, because in 771 Stela 8 was the first to be erected in this plaza (Valdés, Fahsen, and Escobedo 1999). This new public space was the location of all monuments carved after this time, and in this way it perfected the processional avenue that united Groups A and B through a wide and beautiful sacbe oriented north-south. In this manner, the history of Uaxactun and its protagonists became joined symbolically, as two of the oldest edifices built before the conflict with Tikal (Strs. B-2 and A-1) were at this avenue's extreme north and south ends. To complete the scene, Stela 9 (A.D. 327), pertaining to one of the first rulers of the fourth century, was raised in this plaza as a sign of respect for the ancestors and their millenarian traditions that continued to be valid even at the end of the eighth century.

During the dawn of the ninth century, the Main Plaza of Group A had become the most sacred space of Uaxactun, so the new ruler K'an Ko had erected Stela 7 (A.D. 810) in front of the stairway of Temple A-1. This monument was placed in its position at the same time that Stela 24 was raised at Tikal, celebrating in both cases the end of k'atun 19. The construction projects in the Main Plaza begun by the previous sovereign were continued by K'an Ko, and new edifices were built at this time, such as the remodeling of Str. A-5.

THE TERMINAL CLASSIC IN THE CENTRAL MAYA AREA

The dates assigned to the Terminal Classic in our region of study correspond to the ceramic sphere Tepeu 3. Equivalent complexes for this period include the Eznab phase in Tikal, Tepeu 3 in Uaxactun, and Tolobojo in Yaxhá, all beginning around the year A.D. 830. However, because the ceramic assemblage of the Tepeu 3 sphere shows significant regionalization in comparison to Tepeu 2, this has led to dating discrepancies for the end of this period in the different subregions of the central Maya lowlands (Rice 1986). Although several scholars continue to consider concluding the Classic period in the year A.D. 900 in locations as distant as Yaxhá (Hermes, Noriega, and Calderon 1997), La Milpa (Hammond et al. 2000), and the Maya Mountains (Dunham and Prufer 1998), at the present time this position is being re-evaluated based on ceramic materials, with the proposal that the Terminal Classic of the central area and eastern regions continued until A.D. 950–1000, depending on the characteristics presented by each site (Laporte and Fialko 1995; J. Braswell 1998; G. Braswell 1998; Rice, personal communication).

The term "Terminal Classic" is restricted exclusively to the Maya area and was first employed with the study of the post-construction deposits of Temple I at Tikal (Adams and Trik 1961). According to Culbert (1993, 1997), Eznab pottery at Tikal is similar to the earlier material of the Ik and Imix phase of the Late Classic, and reflects a general decadence in variability, although Rice (1986) adds that the ceramic changes related more to the pastes. Without a doubt, two of the clearest diagnostics in the ceramic industry are the appearance of Fine Orange ware, which reflects ties between the central area and the Pasión-Usumacinta drainages (Foias 1996; Foias and Bishop 1997: 283), as well as the sudden disappearance of polychrome pottery. These features accompany more significant changes used as markers of the Terminal Classic in central Petén, such as political organization, disappearance of inscriptions, dramatic change in funerary patterns, and demographic decline and shifts in settlement patterns.

The Terminal Classic represents a critical stage, a product of deficiencies and failures in the government and its system of administration that could not judge the cost of the political wear due to an exaggerated centralized power in the hands of the supreme sovereign and his reduced elite group. As a consequence, in Tikal, Uaxactun, and neighboring cities, processes of leadership and economic and social instability were unchained during the second half of the ninth century, increasing over time until the collapse of these centers. However, this phenomenon of instability manifested itself in central Petén almost a century after the wars of disintegration in the Petexbatun region and many decades after the collapse in the Usumacinta zone. For these reasons, the time span assigned to the Terminal Classic varies according to the region under study.

The investigations undertaken in Dos Pilas and other Petexbatun centers have discovered that the local crisis and collapse began with the process of regional disintegration in this zone. This occurred, in part, when minor polities, such as those of the Petexbatun, had to fulfill the pact supporting Calakmul in its continuous wars against other sites. Without doubt, the minor polities were ruined by the conflicts and wars commanded by the major states of Calakmul and Tikal (Martin and Grube 1995; Demarest and Valdés 1995, 1996; Demarest 1997). The continuous battles undertaken by the rulers of Dos Pilas since its founding also took them to their final destruction, because the last leader, K'awil Kan K'inich (Ruler 4) was captured by the army of Chanal Balam, ruler of Tamarindito, in the year A.D. 761. At the death of this sovereign, he was interred with honor in a funerary temple. His mortuary offering included two sacrificial knives, one of obsidian placed over his pelvis, and another larger (0.50 meter in length), sharp knife of chert deposited over his chest and between his arms as a symbol of the great warrior-chief of vanquishing armies. Iconographic evidence of this time period shows that these knives served to extract the hearts and to decapitate sacrificial victims (Valdés 1997: 327). The defeat of Dos Pilas without a doubt altered relationships in this riverine zone and led to the questioning of the supreme power of the traditionally respected major centers by the small dependent sites, affecting the scheme of alliances maintained by the ruling elites.

This disequilibrium affected commercial routes as alliances were suddenly broken, interrupting the right of passage from one place to another and access to sumptuary goods for religious ceremonies. This weakness, and the rapidity with which the conflicts propagated, caused one site after another throughout the region to stop sculpting monuments during the eighth and ninth centuries. But, in the same conservative manner that they sculpted their rulers during the eighth century, the traditional and hierarchical society of Tikal responded with more confidence to the worrisome news from afar, showing that it possessed a better or more complex organization that permitted the cities of the central area to last longer. However, this changed at the end of the ninth century and at the beginning of the tenth century, when the cessation of inscriptions, the disappearance of the polychrome pottery with palace scenes, the absence of exotics due to the interruption of commercial routes, and the dramatic change in the placement of burials show the decline of the traditional political dynastic system. Thus, in Tikal the last carved monument dates to A.D. 869, while twenty years later, the last monuments were inscribed at Uaxactun, Jimbal, Ixlú, and La Muñeca. Stela 6 of Xultun (A.D. 899) was the last monument sculpted in stone in the central zone. This same phenomenon also clearly affected the sites located to the north of Uaxactun, in the Mirador basin (Forsyth 1989: 134; Hansen 1996: 4–11), where the densest settlements, such as Nakbe, ceased producing Codex-style polychrome pottery, and the weak regional interaction cracked, destroying minor sites at the same time.

With this perspective of crisis and exhaustion, the elite could not confront the changes, nor did it have sufficient force to plant a new model with enough validity to reorient their lives and activities. During the tenth century, the sites of central Petén were rapidly abandoned, sometimes in a dramatic manner, leaving behind their old objects of daily use in the palace rooms. The lower-class city dwellers and farmers continued to live at Tikal and Uaxactun but moved from their original homes toward the center of these cities to occupy the vaulted edifices abandoned by the upper class (Ricketson 1937; Smith 1950; Puleston 1974; Valdés 1985; Laporte and Fialko 1995). After the collapse, little is known about the fortunes of the elite families, as they disappear from history without ever again using written records.

It is interesting to note that archaeological investigations undertaken in southeast Petén and in northwest Belize have detected an irregular pattern of settlement for Tepeu 3. According to these studies, many major and minor centers in southeast Petén declined and the population became concentrated, especially in the zone of Dolores, where the site of Ixtonton centralized a large part of ritual and residential activities (Laporte and Quezada 1998: 732). On the other hand, R. Adams (Demarest and Escobedo 1987: 703) indicates that some sites in northwest Belize experienced great growth during the Terminal Classic, and others only increased in a modest way, while a third group of sites suffered a strong decline. These inconsistencies are notable in the pottery of La Milpa, where Tepeu 3 ceramics are more similar to sites in southern Yucatán and the rest of the Belize region than with the sites of central Petén (Kosakowsky et al. 1998: 661).

A general opinion among Maya archaeologists signals that it is impossible to define the exact moment when the Terminal Classic ends and the Early Postclassic begins, mainly because of the continuing lack of refinement in the ceramic analyses of the late materials. In spite of this problem of temporal definition, it is possible to suggest that the irregular pattern in the demographics of the Terminal Classic reflects migrations from the polities that were declining in all parts of the Maya lowlands. In Uaxactun, there is no ceramic evidence later than Tepeu 3, no doubt because of an extremely reduced population remaining at the site. Almost all the sites of the central area remained abandoned, and chaos and despair must have ruled. Nevertheless, some communities of the central Petén lakes region, others in southeast Petén, as well in the Belize area, including Lamanai, were able to provide refuge and security to the migrating people, which allowed them to continue and cross that frontier of cultural time marked as the arrival of the Postclassic period.

THE TERMINAL CLASSIC IN TIKAL

The arrival of the ninth and tenth centuries is associated with Eznab ceramics (A.D. 830–1000), a time tied with the collapse phenomenon in the central Maya area. The projects undertaken by the rulers who directed Tikal's destiny during

8.2 Tikal Stela 11 carved with the image of the last sovereign of the Terminal Classic: Hasaw Kan K'awil II.

the ninth century are poorly documented because of the scarcity of glyphic texts. What is certain, though, is that sixty years passed before another monument was carved, in this case Stela 11, pertaining to the ruler Hasaw Kan K'awil II in A.D. 869, representing the last glyphic inscription at the site (Figure 8.2). We can read with some security that he was thirty-second in the line of succession, indicating the existence of one or two sovereigns before him who do not appear in the epigraphic record, possibly because their monuments were later destroyed.

It is known that there was a strong demographic decline during the Eznab phase, but due to the lack of a more detailed ceramic chronology, it is not possible to determine precisely the temporal events of this decline. At the beginning of the ninth century a large labor force was used for the construction of Temple III, indicating that the power of the ruler remained solid. Later, there were no other monumental projects, reflecting the early debility of the system, for which we propose that the cultural and demographic decline must have started a little before A.D. 869 when Hasaw Kan K'awil II was on the throne.

Based on the information available, we have been able to discern that there are two factors that impede us from better understanding this historical moment: 1) the lack of refinement of the Eznab phase, and 2) the absence of hieroglyphic inscriptions. Nevertheless, thanks to the excavations of the Pennsylvania Tikal Project and the Proyecto Nacional Tikal, it is known that during the ninth century construction projects continued in different sectors of the city and that significant changes must have occurred at the transition to the tenth century (Fry 1969; Culbert 1973; Puleston 1974; Coe 1990; Jones 1991; Laporte and Fialko 1995). In the East Plaza, a group of residences was built in the north, and the ballcourt was arranged so that its use continued, although the market appears to have already been abandoned. Eznab-phase ceramic deposits were found in the Central Acropolis, while burials and refuse were present in the Lost World. It is notable that the population of the Terminal Classic, possibly during or after Hasaw Kan K'awil II, was mostly concentrated in the palace areas adjacent to the Great Plaza, at a time when the site was occupied by only 1,000 to 2,000 persons.

As already described, the last ruler known at Tikal erected his monument in A.D. 869 and continued as the head of state in the year A.D. 889, as we know from the reference made to him on Uaxactun's Stela 12. This demonstrates that some sites continued to have divine rulers decades after their last written text, but in the middle of the impending social and political crisis, the sovereigns possibly feared writing their nominals in stone. It must be taken into account that this Tikal ruler was last named on a monument of Uaxactun, not in his own city, twenty years later. This fact, although strange, is not unique, as Yax Pasah of Copán participated in a bloodletting rite in Quirigua when he was no longer named in his own city. Furthermore, the last ruler of Palenque appears mentioned on a painted sherd found in a modest residential group in the plains north of the ceremonial center (Schele and Freidel 1990: 342, 381–382).

The instability of the great region of Tikal is manifested on Altar 1 of Ixlú, which commemorates the date 10.2.10.0.0 (A.D. 879) by a ruler who used the Tikal Emblem Glyph, as did the sovereign of Jimbal ten years later on Stela 2 (Figure 8.3). This leads us to propose two possibilities: 1) by this time, Tikal's central authority was seriously questioned by the neighboring secondary sites and their governors, possibly relatives of the royal family of the primary center, wanted to affirm their independence, but without forgetting the glorious lineage that legitimated them; and 2) the Tikal lord made a last effort to save his kingdom, implementing a new political model formed by small, semiautonomous polities that replaced the old centralized system. It seems to us that the second option is more likely and would help explain why these secondary centers were permitted to use the Tikal Emblem Glyph, since at both Ixlú and Jimbal the sovereign proclaimed himself as "K'ul Mutul Ahaw." There remains a chance, however, that in his eagerness to reconstruct his power, the last leader may have held a type of regency shared with the governors of secondary centers, similar to what happened at Copán (Schele and Freidel 1990). Unfortunately, it was too late to implement political changes and the model did not have the desired success, without leadership support. Even so, the Tikal Emblem Glyph was still used on Stela 6 (at C5) of Xultun in the year A.D. 889 (10.3.10.0.0), this being the last known glyphic reference to the great metropolis.

The impact of this instability caused the palaces with multiple rooms and built in monumental groups to be abandoned by their original inhabitants, in a wave that increased after A.D. 900 and in the following decades. The decrease in or disappearance of population in the rural sectors during the Eznab phase indicates a mobilization toward the administrative center, where the inhabitants arrived to reoccupy the palaces of the elite groups (Puleston 1973). This same situation was occurring in the secondary centers around Tikal, as observed in Bobal, Chikin Tikal, Jimbal, Uolantun, Navajuelal (Fry 1969), and maybe Corozal, which concentrated their populations in the central sector. In very few instances the new occupants worried about fixing or remodeling the invaded edifices, because they did not have the means or the labor for the necessary work. When they did renovate, the difference in architectural quality and finish was notable, as they used very thin walls, and with the passage of time sporadic wall falls would occur in the interior of the rooms as well as on the exterior facades of the structures. The reservoirs and deposits of water were, of course, magnets for human occupants. These migratory shifts left the fields without workers, however, and the subsistence system must have suffered several production losses, especially the maize crop that needed permanent care, from the preparation of the soil to the planting and harvest.

The dramatic change in funerary patterns has particularly attracted our attention. While during the centuries a transcendental respect for death and its significance existed, during the Terminal Classic no cists or tombs were prepared for

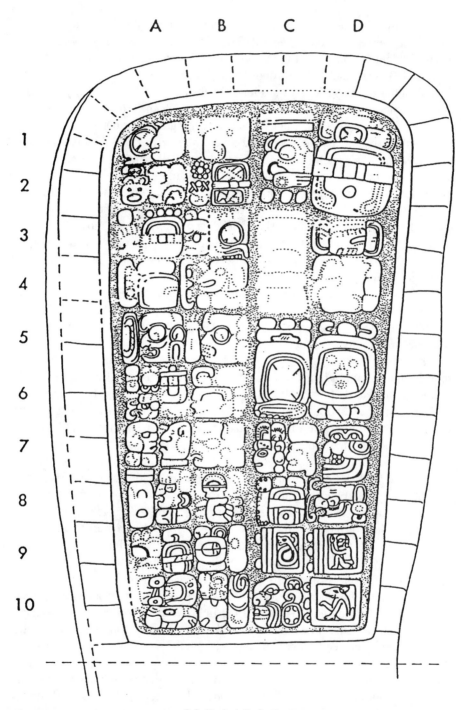

8.3 *Jimbal Stela 2.*

the placements of human burials, but rather these began to be deposited within the existing constructions, such as stairways, floors, rooms, or even over collapsed residences. An example comes from Group 6C-15 (Valdés 1983, 1992), a small ceremonial complex that included an oratory on the east side (Str. 6C-50) and where three priests of the Late Classic (Imix phase) were interred ceremoniously, following the traditional customs of using the main axis of the building. However, after the abandonment of the building, a flexed burial was placed in the stairway access, and the body was partially covered by the same stones of the staircase, although the cranium was left in the open. The putrefaction of this body and the other burials left half-exposed in the Lost World and other groups at Tikal probably were odiferous at some distance and may have resulted in the appearance of contagious diseases.

The young adult male buried in Str. 6C-50 maintained the old tradition of cranial deformation, and next to his body was placed a mortuary offering of predominantly lithic objects. Among these were 18 fine obsidian blades, 2 obsidian knives, 3 chert lance points, a greenstone, and 3 ceramic vessels. Other burials of this epoch also showed a preference for lithic offerings, leaving pottery in second place. Following the same abandonment process, in Str. 6C-50 a cylindrical censer and various bowl fragments were deposited in the interior of a niche that remained open and untouched for centuries, until the arrival of archaeologists. The censer is of the type Pedregal Modeled, decorated with the image of the solar deity of the Underworld. We consider that its use must have been of primordial importance in the rituals carried out by the priests during the night, because the use of this type of incensario was frequent by the end of the Terminal Classic (Rands and Rands 1959) as the priests maintained the relation between the Jaguar-Sun deity of the Underworld in his manifestation of the night sun with the rituals of fire (Stuart 1998: 408).

In Tikal, the Caban phase was defined for the Early Postclassic, beginning around A.D. 1000, with the presence of Pabellon Molded-Carved pottery. The most important manifestations of this moment in time are marked by continued occupation in the debris of the ancient palaces, the movement of carved monuments, the pillaging of tombs, and the celebration of rituals in the ancestral temples. Cases that implicate the replacement of sculpted monuments have been reported from the Great Plaza and Temple VI (with some monuments reutilized as grinding stones). Signs of Postclassic rituals were found in the upper precincts of Temples I and II with the deposition of burials and offerings that included blue-painted copal balls. (Adams and Trik 1961; Coe 1975). Such activities also took place in an oratory located immediately south of Temple III, where quantities of sherds and broken Postclassic censers (Coe 1975: 77) were discovered, and on the stairway of Str. 3D-43 in the North Zone, where a tripod censer with rattles of Paxcaman Rojo type appeared. The censer was used and abandoned in this structure, so that the archaeologists found it complete, but it was covered by debris from the upper part of the edifice.

According to Culbert (1973), only a dozen dispersed localities present signs of Postclassic occupation within and around Tikal. This was confirmed by the excavations undertaken in residential groups south of the Lost World, where only two (6C-12 and 6D-20) of sixteen groups yielded Caban pottery (Valdés 1985; Laporte and Iglesias 1999).

THE TERMINAL CLASSIC IN UAXACTUN: ARCHAEOLOGY AND HIEROGLYPHS

During the Tepeu 3 phase, activities at Uaxactun were associated with minor construction projects, while in the peripheral and central areas a marked demographic decline is noted. Few burials of relative importance were detected in the majestic palatial group formed by A-5, but it is known that the local elite preserved its power as they erected carved monuments in A.D. 830 and 889, when the last glyphic inscription was dedicated at this site. The presence of these monuments indicates a stable sequence of rulers residing in the monumental Groups A and B, which had become a sole administrative and ceremonial complex. Although the population decreased rapidly, the elite pursued their lives—no doubt with anxiety, given the fatal news of the events taking place in nearby polities. They continued celebrating their traditional rituals, although with a smaller public. Uncertainty about the future must have reigned everywhere while they awaited a means to salvation that never arrived.

The two rulers who had the reins of Uaxactun's leadership during the Terminal Classic were Olom Chik'in Chakte and K'al Chik'in Chakte (Valdés, Fahsen, and Escobedo 1999). The dates of their accession to the throne are unknown, but monuments record events and dates from their reigns between A.D. 830 and 889.

Here it is of primary importance to emphasize that the design of Strs. A-2 and A-4, built during Tepeu 3, included stone pillars in their facades (Smith 1950: 47–48). Their presence is vital, because it permits identification of examples of this trait in central Petén before the Early Postclassic. The dating of these edifices corresponds with the presence of Stelae 13 and 12 erected in front of A-2 in A.D. 830 and 889. So there remains no doubt that constructions of this type were made in Uaxactun during the ninth century, when the Main Plaza was remodeled. This proposal is reinforced by the recent dating that J. Braswell (1998: 722) assigned to a similar structure in Xunantunich, proposing that it predates A.D. 950, or during the Terminal Classic. The presence of architectural elements traditionally considered foreign to the Petén style, such as the use of pillars and columns in the facades, should allow the re-evaluations of these structures because they have now been discovered to pertain to earlier dates than those assigned previously. It is important to note the recent discovery of rounded columns in the facade of Str. M8-37 at Aguateca, dated to ca. A.D. 800, demonstrating once again the early presence of these elements in the Maya zone (Diaz Samayoa and Valdés 2000).

Stela 13 commemorates the date 10.0.0.0.0 (A.D. 830) and was erected in an epoch in which many Maya sites were involved in wars and political conflicts, principally in the zone of the Usumacinta and Pasión Rivers, as well as at Ucanal and Naranjo in the central area. Uaxactun does not escape, as the text of Stela 13 (Figure 8.4) concluded by mentioning a military event, but lamentably the inscription is not clear enough to know against whom the conflict took place. The nominal of the sovereign who erected this monument was clearly written as Olom Chik'in Chakte. With respect to this lord, we must add that years later there is reference to a personage named Olum on Stela 1 of the nearby site Jimbal (A.D. 879). The nominal of this latter stela's subject is erased, but in position B8 appears a clause that reads "son of Olom," for which reason we propose the governor of Jimbal was the son of the Uaxactun ruler Olom.

In support of this argument is the difference in the years between both monuments, the geographical proximity of the two sites, and the fact that the lord of Jimbal names his father but does not include the Tikal Emblem Glyph. The only ruler known at this moment with the name Olom is that of Uaxactun, and it would be very rare that another existed in the same area. In any case, we know that the name of the Tikal sovereign was different, for which reason the father could not have been from this site. Therefore, the governor who ruled Jimbal in A.D. 879 was the next descendant of the sovereign of Uaxactun, which

8.4 Uaxactun Stela 13 erected by the ruler Olom Chik´in Chakte in A.D. 830.

must have been convenient for reinforcing alliances between these two neighboring centers.

The last monument dated is Stela 12 (Figure 8.5), also erected in the Main Plaza in Group A in front of Str. A-2, and commemorates a bloodletting ritual and the placement of this monument by the rulers K'al Chik'in Chakte of Uaxactun and Hasaw Kan K'awil II of Tikal in A.D. 889 (Valdés, Fahsen, and Escobedo 1999). The text concludes by recording the arrival of a third unidentified personage, but the celebration of this ceremony by the two rulers together can be interpreted as a sign of solidarity, as the two lords continued to share a common destiny.

Another important detail contributed by the inscriptions of the last two stelae and by the "Vase of the Initial Series" is that these rulers carry the title of Chik'in Chakte, translated as "Lord of the East," which apparently is a noble title or office used at that time. According to the epigraphic information, K'al Chik'in Chakte was the last sovereign of Uaxactun, and it is probable that he was still in charge in the year A.D. 900. The final population of this site shows a minimum number of inhabitants in Groups A, B, and E, as Ricketson (1937) and L. Smith (1950) report evidence of use of these abandoned ancient palaces as well as the deposition of burials in the debris of the rooms (as it occurred at Tikal). No trace of occupation corresponding to the beginning of the Postclassic has been recovered in Uaxactun, demonstrating that it was abandoned before its neighbor Tikal.

THE POPULATION OF TIKAL AND UAXACTUN DURING THE LATE AND TERMINAL CLASSIC

Evidence unearthed by archaeologists of the University of Pennsylvania's Tikal Project allowed them to argue that during the equilibrium of the eighth century, Tikal had reached a population of 50,000 to 80,000 individuals (Fry 1969: 160; Puleston 1973: 201–207). However, later studies undertaken by Patrick Culbert and his colleagues (1990: 103–121) have suggested that during its apogee, Tikal extended over 120 square kilometers, and Turner (1990: 303) adds that the area under its control came to extend over 12,600 square kilometers. The city's limits were marked to the north and south by the presence of two defensive trenches or moats built during the Early Classic. Nevertheless, as a reflection of the stability reached during the Late Classic, these were filled in and the city continued beyond these limits, as much to the north as to the south.

Demographic studies for the epoch of major occupation at Tikal consider that within these 120 square kilometers were approximately 62,000 inhabitants, although another 30,000 could be added when we take into account the number of residences discovered up to a distance of ten kilometers outside the center. Thus, when both areas are considered, Tikal was a large urban center composed of no fewer than 90,000 inhabitants. To this estimate we can also add the structures of the rural space, which permits raising the population to 120,000. These

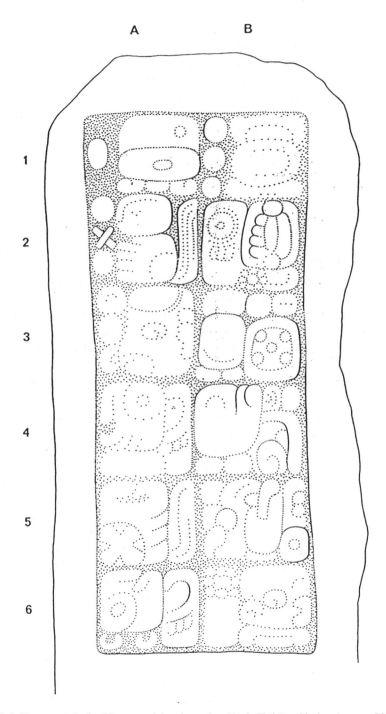

8.5 Uaxactun Stela 12 erected by the ruler K´al Chik´in Chakte in A.D. 889.

calculations show that we were certainly facing the largest and most populous city of the Late Classic in the Maya area.

For Uaxactun, R. Acevedo and A. M. Paz (1991: 157–159) undertook a detailed settlement pattern study, with reconnaissance, mapping, and test pitting in a sixteen-square-kilometer area, detecting preferential levels of occupation on dry land and very little in the low areas of the Bajo Juventud. This demonstrated the tendency, originating in the Preclassic, to place residences on higher land free from flooding. Apart from the monumental architecture in the center of the city, Acevedo and Paz discovered 131 residential groups, of which 118 were occupied during the Late Classic.

The ceramics from the test-pitting program permitted a more detailed understanding of each complex's temporal occupation, by which it is known that twenty-four groups were occupied during Tepeu 1, representing 20.3 percent of the population. For Tepeu 2, there was an increase in construction, with 106 groups (89.9 percent) dating to this time. This is the time when Uaxactun reached its apogee in residential occupation, which reflects the stability attained by its rulers. However, during Tepeu 3, the panorama changed abruptly, as Terminal Classic pottery was found in only seven groups (5.9 percent), representing a population dramatically reduced in comparison with the previous phase. These facts demonstrate that the population of Uaxactun was significantly lower than that of Tikal, as it was a site of lower rank, for which it has been proposed that it could have reached a population that fluctuated between 10,000 and 15,000 inhabitants (Turner 1990: 318).

The information furnished by excavations shows that this growth was interrupted in both cities during the Terminal Classic, when the population declined dramatically as much in the center as in the periphery. The demographic shifts of this last period are not known in detail, but some consider that the population abruptly fell by 90 percent. According to Turner (1990: 321), the number of inhabitants in the entire Tikal region of 12,600 square kilometers reached 1,520,000 in its period of highest splendor for the year A.D. 800. During the following time period of the Terminal Classic, this population was reduced dramatically to only 276,659 individuals in the entire region, contrasting the density of 120.6 persons per square kilometer for Tepeu 2, with 22.0 persons per square kilometer for Tepeu 3. After this period, the occupation continued falling to 13.4 inhabitants per square kilometer, which means that the whole region of Tikal must have numbered only 168,732 after the year A.D. 1000.

ARCHITECTURE OF THE LATE AND TERMINAL CLASSIC: CONTEXT AND FUNCTION

As the Late Classic progressed, the rulers decided to centralize the main activities of the government, especially of the administrative and religious type. The administrative duties were executed in the epicenter of the sites, but this led to the leading class' isolation when they began to close off their plazas with palaces and temples. In Uaxactun, this happened particularly in Groups A and B, while at Tikal it is notable in all major groups: in the Great Plaza, which was closed by the construction of Temples I and II; in the Central Acropolis, where new palaces were built to close off plazas; and in the Lost World complex, where new structures were constructed to restrict access more and more. Everywhere, the entrances were reduced in size and strictly watched by guards, and nobody could, therefore, freely enter or exit.

To compensate for the restriction of public spaces, the government devised a plan to construct new cult places, as in the case of the twin pyramid complexes, reserving in this manner the Great Plaza of Tikal exclusively for the elite. It is considered that from this moment on, the general population had access to this plaza only during celebrations of festivities and specific ceremonies, such as the enthronement of a new ruler or mortuary rituals for their leaders. This practice required, then, a decentralization of rites and religious offices toward other groups, recognized archaeologically by the groups that include an eastern temple or oratory. Complexes of this nature were defined typologically as Plaza Plan 2 by Becker (1971), and subsequent excavations have supported this idea, demonstrating their high frequency and use in all sectors of the city and in elite groups, as well as in peripheral groups of lower rank (Valdés 1985). Investigations in Uaxactun also supported the presence of groups using the Plaza Plan 2 in the central part as well as in the periphery, although with a lower frequency than at Tikal.

We believe, therefore, that the government allowed the coexistence of an "official religion" that corresponded to the interests of the leaders, together with a "popular religion," practiced by the city's inhabitants, that included the worship of minor deities of daily life. This proposition is supported by the popularity and diffusion reached by the construction of groups with eastern religious precincts used as subsidiary cult locales, as in Tikal 105; such groups are documented for the Late Classic (Valdés 1985: 60). During the Eznab phase, these were slowly abandoned as the population moved toward the epicenter.

Another radical change in the original building function is observed in the Central Acropolis of Tikal during the late times of crisis. Schele and Mathews (1998: 84) point out that when the palace 5D-51 was partially falling down, it was used as a prison for captives, with wooden poles crossing the entryway. Maybe they were defending themselves from the same intruders who were arriving in groups from the periphery. Thus, the palace was transformed from its original function as a conjuring house, as it is believed to have been conceived.

Some structures changed in use because doors were sealed and the inhabitants forced to reduce the width of the entryways to make them more restricted and more easily guarded. A clear case is seen in the palace of Great Jaguar Paw in the Central Acropolis, which was left with only one door when all the others were closed off, giving the structure the aspect of a fortress hard to conquer.

CONCLUSIONS

At the beginning of the ninth century, the rulers K'an Ko of Uaxactun and Yax Ain II of Tikal had contemporary reigns when their cities still enjoyed the splendor reached in earlier centuries. However, this situation changed a few decades later, around A.D. 830–850, when the pressure on the central area and especially on Tikal must have been very strong. Its last inscription is from A.D. 869, although we know that its lord was in Uaxactun celebrating a bloodletting ritual twenty years later as a witness to the end of the third k'atun of the tenth *baktun*. Without a doubt, the major part of this crisis fell on the shoulders of the both cities' last sovereigns, Hasaw Kan K'awil II and K'al Chik'in Chakte, at the end of the ninth century. The years of the tenth century saw the end of this culture in the center of Petén, as testified by the inscriptions of Jimbal, Uaxactun, and La Muñeca, dated A.D. 889, with the last text in the central area from A.D. 899 found in Xultun. The last three known texts in the Maya area are from Toniná, Uxmal, and Dzibanché, all pertaining to the year 909, only ten years after Xultun, curiously forming a triangle in the extreme periphery of the great Maya territory.

Starting in A.D. 810, commemorative inscriptions became scarce and sporadic, although other neighboring cities, such as Ixlú and Jimbal, had commemorative celebrations similar to those of Tikal and Uaxactun. In the case of Ixlú, a monument was erected in 10.2.0.0.0 (A.D. 869), at the same time as the last stela at Tikal, while at Jimbal, the end of the period 10.3.0.0.0 (A.D. 889) was ritually celebrated at the same time as the last date from Uaxactun. These two minor sites hold a special importance in the final crisis because their rulers titled themselves K'ul Mutul Ahaw, that is, they shared the royal title with the last king of Tikal.

Here, then, another question resurfaces about why Hasaw Kan K'awil II of Tikal celebrated the end of the third k'atun in Uaxactun and not in his own land. This reference appears to indicate the willingness by the Tikal sovereign to share his great ancient kingdom with other lords of the secondary centers. However, we should not forget that in the particular case of Uaxactun it could represent a demonstration of the solidarity between both cities, which is interesting because it means the continuation of tight ties, both political and familial.

The final noose of the collapse was tightening and the last years were not at all peaceful. In Tikal there are no texts or information for sixty years, and in Uaxactun, the monumental inscriptions bespeak bellicose conflicts. The continuation of a monumental record at Uaxactun until 10.3.0.0.0, or twenty years after Tikal, only shows a slower agony, as K'al Chik'in Chakte competed for scarce resources and power with the lords of Xultun to the north and of Jimbal to the south. The instability reported since the defeat of Dos Pilas at the hands of Tamarindito in A.D. 761, the burnings of Ixkun in 779, Ucanal in 780, and Caracol in 865, as well as the continuous conflicts of Yaxhá and Naranjo, on top of those of Bonampak, Yaxchilán, Piedras Negras, and Seibal, laid the foundation for the gradual destruction of a centralized system that could not continue any longer due to the interruption of political and economic networks. The governing elites demonstrated their incapacity to deal with these circumstances and lost effective control, setting in motion the final result.

9

DEFINING THE TERMINAL CLASSIC
AT CALAKMUL, CAMPECHE

*Geoffrey E. Braswell, Joel D. Gunn, María del Rosario Domínguez Carrasco,
William J. Folan, Laraine A. Fletcher, Abel Morales López,
and Michael D. Glascock*

or more than one thousand years, Calakmul, located in southeastern
Campeche, Mexico, was the capital of one of the largest and most
powerful regional states in the Maya lowlands (Folan, Marcus, Pincemin
et al. 1995; May Hau et al. 1990). At its peak during the Classic period, the
territory under the direct control of the *k'uhul kan ajawob,* as the kings of the
Calakmul polity were known, extended over an area of approximately 13,000
square kilometers (Figure 9.1; Domínguez Carrasco et al. 1997; Folan 1988;
Marcus 1973, 1976). In fact, the kingdom of Calakmul was at least as large in
area and population as any other Late Classic state of the central Maya lowlands,
including Tikal (Fletcher and Gann 1992; Folan 1988).

The importance of Calakmul in the Classic Maya world also is reflected in the
architecture and hieroglyphic texts of sites far beyond its direct control. The
architectural program of central Calakmul, already established by the Late
Preclassic period, may have been the model for the central precincts of Classic-
period Naranjo and Xunantunich (Ashmore 1998: 174–175). The Calakmul Emblem Glyph appears more often in ancient Maya texts and its spatial distribution is
greater than that of any other Classic Maya site, including Tikal (Folan, Marcus,
Pincemin et al. 1995). The political and military prowess of the Calakmul polity is
recorded at sites like Palenque (which was sacked at least twice by Calakmul in
the late sixth and early seventh centuries); Dos Pilas and Caracol (both lesser
allies of Calakmul who, in concert with their stronger partner, claim to have killed
two important kings of Tikal); El Perú, Naranjo, Piedras Negras, and Yaxchilán

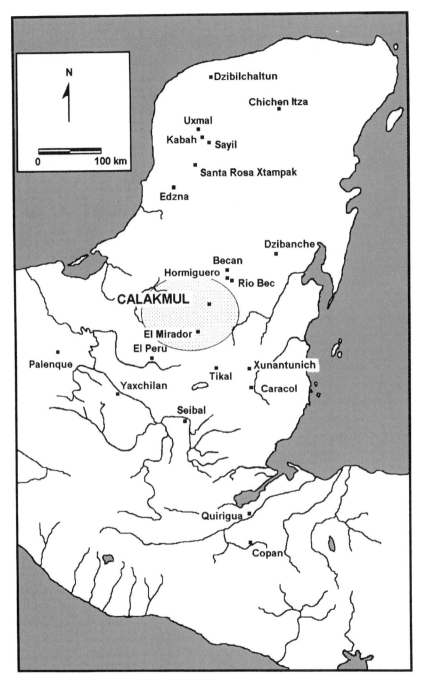

9.1 Approximate extent of the Calakmul regional state during the Late Classic period.

(all subordinate allies of Calakmul); Quiriguá (whose king, K'ahk' Tiliw Chan Yopaat, captured and sacrificed the important Copán king Waxaklajuun U B'aah K'awiil in A.D. 738, apparently with the blessing of a k'uhul kan ajaw); Copán (where Stela A mentions Calakmul as one of four important Maya cities in A.D. 731); and Seibal (where the last explicit mention of Calakmul, still considered one of the four great Maya polities, appeared on Stela 10 in A.D. 849) (Marcus 1973, 1976; Schele and Mathews 1998; Looper 1995).

The central role played by Calakmul in so many battles, marriages, accessions, and commemoration events has led Martin and Grube (1995) to call the polity a "superpower." Although we are unsure that the term can be applied legitimately to any Maya kingdom, it is clear that no model of Classic Maya political process that ignores the fundamental importance of Calakmul is viable (Marcus and Folan 1994; Pincemin et al. 1998). If warfare or other aspects of political intrigue were factors in the complex processes leading to the collapse of state-level society in the central Maya lowlands (see Demarest 1997 and Chapter 6, this volume), there can be no doubt that the k'uhul kan ajawob were pivotal actors at the center of this drama. We argue, therefore, that an understanding of the events and conditions of the Terminal Classic at Calakmul is central to any discussion of the Classic Maya collapse.

In this chapter we characterize the changes that took place at Calakmul during the ninth and early tenth centuries. Like many other large Maya centers, Calakmul suffered a dramatic decline of population during this period. We have evidence, however, in the form of continued elite residence and the erection of dedicatory monuments at least as late as A.D. 899, that the political structure of the Calakmul kingdom continued to function into the period of demographic crisis. The changing fortunes of the ninth century also are reflected in the establishment of new trading alliances outside the central Maya lowlands, specifically with emerging polities in the northern Maya lowlands and the Gulf Coast. There was, then, an economic response to the collapse, an adaptation that was successful for a time despite adverse environmental and political conditions. A third point we stress is that during the Terminal Classic, the use of space in the epicenter of Calakmul changed; formerly sacred structures were modified to serve as loci for more quotidian activities. This shift should not be described simply as a process of secularization: the sacred role of temples was not abandoned but combined with residential, administrative, and economic functions in a new way characteristic of sites in the northern Maya lowlands. Finally, we present evidence that one of the catalysts in the changing fortunes of Calakmul was climatic deterioration. We think that a prolonged drought was a contributing factor to the decline of the largest, and arguably most important, Classic Maya polity.

INVESTIGATIONS AT CALAKMUL

The data and interpretations presented in this chapter are the result of ongoing archaeological research that began more than two decades ago. Field investigations conducted by the Proyecto Calakmul of the Universidad Autónoma de Campeche include the detailed survey and mapping of the thirty square kilometers that form the inner core of Calakmul, the excavation and consolidation of several monumental structures in the site epicenter, limited excavations in other sectors of the city and its environs, study of the hydraulic system surrounding the city center, environmental studies of the site and its sustaining area, and a wide variety of survey and mapping operations conducted within the Calakmul kingdom. In the laboratory we have conducted analyses of ceramics, stone tools and debitage, figurines, and other artifacts recovered from excavated contexts, and also have analyzed settlement and demographic data derived from our surveys. Because much of this work—particularly aspects of our settlement and demographic studies—continues, the results presented here should be considered preliminary.

Much of our discussion of the Terminal Classic occupation of Calakmul is derived from excavations in Structures I, II, III, and VII in the site epicenter. Survey and mapping operations in less imposing portions of the site and in its sustaining area have not revealed the existence of Terminal Classic and Early Postclassic structures similar to those described at other sites in the central Maya lowlands. Moreover, Terminal Classic ceramics are uncommon outside the site center. For these reasons, it seems likely that the Terminal Classic occupation of Calakmul was concentrated in the epicenter of the city. Although many of the ninth- and early-tenth-century inhabitants probably were commoners who moved into the elite architecture of the site center, there are strong indications of the persistence of a privileged class until A.D. 900 or later. A wide variety of imported goods—including pottery, obsidian, shell, jade, and metal—were recovered from Terminal Classic contexts in Structures I, II, III, and VII. These types of goods, though more broadly distributed in the Maya area during the Terminal Classic than in earlier periods, suggest the presence of an economic elite. Significantly, the erection until at least A.D. 899 of stelae with both hieroglyphic inscriptions and depictions of divine kings demonstrates the continued existence of royalty until a time that cannot be distinguished from the abandonment of Calakmul.

ENVIRONMENTAL AND CULTURAL SETTING
OF LATE CLASSIC CALAKMUL

Calakmul is located in the northern Petén region of the central Maya lowlands in an area that today is heavily forested. Recent analyses indicate that the millennium in which Calakmul thrived was characterized by moderate but dependable rainfall (Gunn et al. 1994, 1995). Compared to the rainforest of Guatemala, however, little surface water is available in the region. For this reason, the ancient Maya of Calakmul built and relied on thirteen public reservoirs to supply water throughout the dry season. The largest of these reservoirs, Aguada 1, encompasses an area of five hectares (Figure 9.2). We estimate that the minimum total capacity of these reservoirs was 200 million liters (Domínguez Carrasco and Folan 1996;

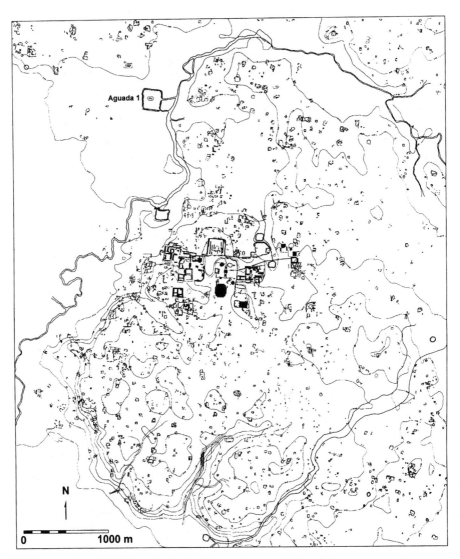

9.2 Inner core of Calakmul, showing reservoirs, canals, and structures (after May Hau et al. 1990).

Gates and Folan 1993; Zapata Castorena 1985). Thus, if filled to capacity each rainy season, the hydraulic system of Calakmul easily could have supplied enough water to support 50,000–100,000 individuals. We could find no evidence that the reservoirs of Calakmul were used to irrigate crops (Domínguez Carrasco and Folan 1996).

The urban center of the city was called Ox Te' Tuun ('Place of Three Stones'), perhaps a reference to the massive triadic pyramid Structure II as the place of the fourth creation (Marcus 1987; Martin 1996; Pincemin et al. 1998). The many triadic structures built throughout the site center served as constant reminders of the identity of the city. Calakmul is organized in a strongly concentric fashion on the margin of the large seasonal swamp called El Laberinto. The initial Middle and Late Preclassic occupation was situated along the perimeter of the bajo, and the majority of large Classic structures were built in the ecotone up to twenty or thirty meters above its edge (Fletcher et al. 1987; Folan, Marcus, and Miller 1995). The rich and moist soils of the bajo margin were heavily planted and chert deposits in the heart of the swamp were exploited as the source of lithic material for stone tool production (Domínguez Carrasco and Folan 1996). The inner thirty-square-kilometer core of Calakmul, much of which sits on an artificially leveled limestone dome, has been mapped. A total of 6,250 structures and other stone constructions have been identified. The most striking architectural features within the urban core are a central plaza containing an astronomical commemorative group similar to Uaxactún Group E (Figure 9.3: Structures IV and VI), two of the largest pyramidal structures ever built in Mesoamerica—each more than fifty meters high (Figure 9.3: Structures I and II)—and the Great Acropolis, a complex of buildings currently under investigation by Ramón Carrasco Vargas of INAH (Carrasco Vargas 1998).

Late Classic Ceramics

We have identified twenty ceramic types characteristic of the Late Classic Ku-phase occupation of Calakmul (Domínguez Carrasco 1994a: 122–181; 1994b: 52). The high percentage of ceramics from this phase (36.4 percent of all analyzed sherds) and the great variability in utilitarian types reflect the maximum economic extension of the kingdom. As in earlier times, the strongest ceramic ties were with sites to the south, particularly those in the El Mirador basin. The Late Classic ceramics of Calakmul and El Mirador share a considerable number of formal attributes that distinguish them from pottery produced in other parts of the central Maya lowlands (Domínguez Carrasco 1994a: 301–315; 1994b: 51).

In our analysis of 22,639 Late Classic sherds from excavations into Structures I, II, III, and VII, only 151 (0.67 percent of the Ku phase total) pertain to types and varieties produced outside the Petén Tepeu II sphere.[1] Three of these (Traino Brown: Traino variety [Traino Group], Moro Orange Polychrome: Moro variety [Chimbote Group], and Pelota Modeled: Pelota variety [Corona Group]) are known principally from the Río Bec zone, located sixty kilometers northeast of Calakmul (Ball 1977a). An additional twelve sherds, all from Structure VII, are Cui Orange Polychrome: Cui variety, a funerary ware known primarily from the Chenes region and Jaina, but also found at Edzná, Acanceh, and Dzibilchaltún (Ball 1975; Ball and Andrews 1975: 232–233; Forsyth 1983: 90).

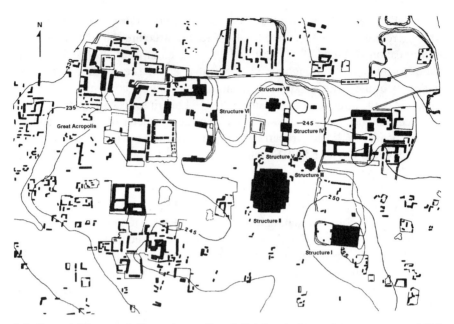

9.3 Central Plaza and Great Acropolis of Calakmul. Area shown measures 1000 x 1500 meters (after May Hau et al. 1990).

Boucher and Dzul (1998: Cuadro 1), who have analyzed an additional 64,629 Late Classic sherds recovered during recent INAH consolidation excavations at Calakmul, have noted the presence of eight more ceramic groups and thirteen types produced in the Río Bec and Chenes regions. Two additional ceramic groups, Petkanché and Azcorra, each with two types represented at Calakmul, seem to suggest economic relations with northwest Belize. Since these types also are found in the Río Bec zone (Ball 1977a), their presence may indicate only indirect contact with that region. Boucher and Dzul (1998) also identified the type Egoísta Resist (which has a wide distribution in the northern lowlands, Belize, and Petén [Ball 1977a: 82]), and found one sherd of a type that might come from the Río Motagua zone or Baja Verapaz, Guatemala. Still, all these types account for only 2.1 percent of the Ku-complex sherds analyzed by Boucher and Dzul (1998). Thus, both of our analyses support only weak ceramic similarities with Late Classic sites outside the Tepeu sphere, with the strongest external ties linking Calakmul with both the Río Bec and Chenes zones. Late Classic Calakmul partici-pated in an essentially Petén-focused interaction sphere, with only limited quanti-ties of ceramics, obsidian, jade, basalt, and shell entering the kingdom from other regions.

Classic-Period Monuments and Architecture

Approximately 120 stelae, dating from A.D. 431 to some time after A.D. 830, have been found within the site core of Calakmul (Marcus 1987; Pincemin et al. 1998). Only two of these, Stelae 43 and 114, clearly date to the Early Classic period. Despite the paucity of early texts at Calakmul, we know that the Early Classic was a period of significant expansion. The masks on Structure II, the largest pyramid at the site, probably were dedicated during the reign of the king who ordered the carving of Stela 114 (Carrasco Vargas 1998: 381). In addition, Structure IV of the astronomical commemorative group was remodeled as a funerary monument to the great k'uhul kan ajaw Tuun K'ab' Hix (?). A lintel from this building displays the king as the resurrected maize god sitting above a cleft in the earth, an identity later chosen by K'inich Janaahb' Pakal of Palenque for his sarcophagus lid. At the end of the Early Classic period, Structure V was converted into the most important stelae shrine at the site.

Although the architecture of Calakmul is best described as Petén style, a few stylistic elements from the Río Bec region and the northern lowlands were added to some buildings dating to the end of the Late Classic period. These include decorated benches or altars with niches (e.g., Structure II-B and Structure VII [Figures 4b, 6b]) and cord-holders incorporated into door jambs. The latest superstructures of Structures V and VI also contain Río Bec features (Carrasco Vargas 1998). Conversely, the influence of Calakmul can be found in Río Bec architecture dating to this period. Becán Structure 4, very similar to the much earlier Calakmul Structure III, was built near the end of the Late Classic period.

At least 100 stelae date to the century between A.D. 652 and 752, the apogee of the political and military power of the Calakmul state (Folan, Marcus, Pincemin et al. 1995: 327; Marcus 1987). Many of these relate events that occurred during the lifetime of Yukno'om Yich'aak K'ahk' (nicknamed "Jaguar Claw the Great"), a ruler who became k'uhul kan ajaw in A.D. 686 in a great public ceremony attended by B'alaj Chan K'awiil ("Ruler 1") of Dos Pilas (Marcus 1987; Mathews and Willey 1991). King Jasaw Chan K'awiil ("Ruler A") of Tikal claimed to have defeated Yukno'om Yich'aak K'ahk' on Lintel 3 of Temple 1, but it is unlikely that the Calakmul king actually was captured. The stucco frieze from Tikal Structure 5D-57 shows the Tikal ruler with a bound captive, but he is a secondary lord named Aj B'olon Oon Aj Sa (?) (Marcus 1997; Marcus and Folan 1994). It is not entirely clear that this individual came from Calakmul.[2] Similarly, a carved bone from the tomb of Jasaw Chan K'awiil depicts Uux Ja Te' Hixil Ajaw (?), another secondary lord, and not Yukno'om Yich'aak K'ahk' himself (Pincemin et al. 1998; Schele and Friedel 1990: 213). The recent discovery of Tomb 4 in Structure II of Calakmul suggests that Yukno'om Yich'aak K'ahk' died at Calakmul and was not captured and taken to Tikal. A plate from this tomb identifies its owner, the deceased, as Yukno'om Yich'aak K'ahk' (*Arqueología Mexicana* 1997: 77; Carrasco Vargas et al. 1999).

An additional 362 stelae have been found at secondary and smaller sites in the Calakmul kingdom, including a *bak'tun* 8 monument from Balakbal (Pincemin et al. 1998). But like most of the carved monuments from the capital, the majority of these stelae date to the Late Classic period. The earliest of eighty-two known references to Calakmul found outside the kingdom was carved on a hieroglyphic stairway at Dzibanché dating to A.D. 495. Most appearances of the Calakmul Emblem Glyph, however, date to the late seventh and eighth centuries, the period of greatest power of the kingdom.

Late Classic Demography

Using a 55 percent contemporaneous occupancy rate for the habitation structures found in the urban core of Calakmul, we calculate a Late Classic population density of some 1,000 per square kilometer for the center of the city. Greater Calakmul, consisting of 122 square kilometers, supported an average population density of 420 individuals per square kilometer. Hence, we estimate that the total population was approximately 50,000 souls during the Late Classic period (Fletcher and Gann 1992; Fletcher et al. 1987, 2001). Calakmul was a true city, and not simply a well-developed central place consisting of a royal household surrounded by the dwellings of lesser nobles and commoners. Although it is certain that few Maya centers approached the size or functional complexity of Calakmul, the notion that the Classic Maya world lacked urban cities is mistaken.

A total of twenty secondary sites, including large centers such as Oxpemul, La Muñeca, Naachtún, Uxul, and Sasilhá, are located within the Calakmul kingdom. Based on previous publications (Ruppert and Denison 1943; Turner 1990) and our own surveys, we estimate that the total population of these sites during the Late Classic period was 200,000 people.

The *El Petén Campechano: Su Pasado, Presente y Futuro* project continues to survey rural areas of the Calakmul kingdom where numerous third- and fourth-level sites are located. For example, the recently concluded survey transect running south from the Escárcega-Xpuhil highway to the Centro Chiclero Buenfil and Calakmul has located fifty-two sites. This 400-meter-wide transect, which crosses 16.5 kilometers of bajo, is fifty kilometers long. Many of the sites along the transect are relatively small, consisting of multiple courtyard groups inhabited during the Late Classic period. Larger sites contain palaces, temples, and stelae, and were occupied during several periods. These larger rural sites tend to be located on elevated ridges emerging from the bajo margins, that is, in ecotones very similar to that of Calakmul.

After deducting that portion of the terrain left unoccupied, using a 68 percent contemporary occupation rate (see Robichaux 1995), and an estimate of 5.6 individuals per residence, we calculate that the Late Classic rural population of the Calakmul kingdom was 1.5 million people.[3] Turner (1990: Table 15.5) has estimated that the rural-intersite population density of the Calakmul kingdom was

96.3 people per square kilometer (515,484 people in 5,355 square kilometers), a figure slightly lower than our calculation of 120 people per square kilometer but in general accord with it. Incorporating our population estimates for the city of Calakmul (50,000), the twenty secondary sites (200,000), and the rural population (1.5 million), we derive a total population of 1.75 million individuals for the 13,000-square-kilometer Late Classic kingdom of Calakmul. This value is larger than the Late Classic population (1,520,107) calculated by Turner (1990: Table 15.4) for the 12,600-square-kilometer Tikal polity. Thus we see no reason to think that the Tikal regional state was either larger in territory or more populous than the Calakmul kingdom (Folan 1988: 157).

CALAKMUL DURING THE TERMINAL CLASSIC (A.D. 800–900/950)

Excavations in the Site Center

Excavations conducted by the Centro de Investigaciones Historicas y Sociales of the Universidad Autónoma de Campeche in 1984–1985, 1988–1989, and 1993–1994 focused on three buildings: Structures II, III, and VII. Additional excavations were undertaken in Structure I. All four structures evince substantial occupation during the Terminal Classic period.

Significant quantities of artifacts were recovered from in situ floor contexts in three of the four structures. These include incense burners and other items used in rituals, but the majority of the artifacts are related to mundane domestic and economic activities. Although we are aware of the recent emphasis placed by archaeologists on termination rituals (e.g., Freidel 1998; Freidel et al. 1998; Mock 1998d), few of the floor assemblages recovered from Structures II, III, and VII appear to be offerings of any kind, let alone termination offerings. Items such as Postclassic incense burners were found in some rooms, but they cannot be linked to termination rituals conducted at the end of the Classic period. Instead, we interpret the vast majority of the artifacts found in primary floor contexts at Calakmul as representing certain aspects of the last use of a building before abandonment. We caution, however, that we have no evidence that these collections resulted from a hurried and unplanned abandonment, as has been noted at Aguateca and Joya de Cerén (Inomata 1997; Inomata and Stiver 1998; Inomata et al. 1998; Ponciano Alvarado et al. 1998; Sheets 1992, 1997). Thus, the artifacts found in the rooms of Structures II, III, and VII are those items left behind—perhaps deliberately—by a population preparing to leave the site. They form an incomplete assemblage that may not represent the full range of behaviors conducted in the buildings. We presume that other items were carried off by the last inhabitants of Calakmul.

Structure II

Like many other important Preclassic Maya temples, Structure II is a triadic construction (Figure 9.4a). The structure, measuring 140 meters to a side and

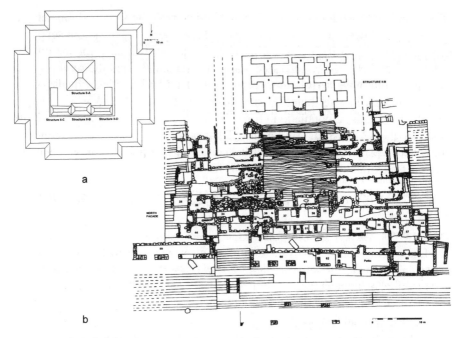

a

b

9.4 *Calakmul Structure II: (a) plan, (b) detail of north facade.*

rising to a height of 55 meters, is one of the largest buildings in Mesoamerica extensively occupied during the Classic period. Early Classic modifications to the building did little to change its fundamental appearance. But beginning in the middle of the eighth century, an important building program forever altered the original Late Preclassic triadic pattern of the temple-pyramid. At this time, the Early Classic masks of Structure II were buried, a large central staircase was raised, and Structures II-B, II-C, and II-D were built on the northern edge of the platform. The construction of these superstructures, which served as a palace complex, altered the basic function of Structure II. Somewhat later, a series of crude rooms were built on the facade of Structure II. Thus, in the late eighth and ninth centuries, Structure II was both a sacred temple and a secular residence.

Structure II-B originally consisted of three vaulted, parallel rooms. During the Terminal Classic period, the inner space was divided, creating a total of nine rooms (Figure 9.4b). The building once supported a stuccoed and painted roof comb. The front two rows of rooms (Rooms 1–6) in Structure II-B were used for food preparation, cooking, and sleeping. Each room contained two or more hearths and at least one trough-shaped *metate* fragment (Folan, Marcus, Pincemin et al. 1995: 317). More metates and hearths were found outside Structure II-B and on the platform associated with the center stairway. A few hearths were found in the darker recesses of Rooms 7–9, but no evidence for food preparation was found, presumably because these rooms are farthest from light and ventilation. Sleeping benches with niches were discovered in Rooms 1 and 6, Room 8 contained what may be a ceremonial altar with Río Bec–style niches, and Room 7 was a sweat bath. A small stone slab found in situ in this room was used to seal the restricted entrance (Folan et al. 1989, Folan, Marcus, Pincemin et al. 1995: 317–318).

A Terminal Classic burial was found beneath the floor along the south side of Room 5. It contained an adult male in supine position oriented with his head toward the east. All the bones were articulated, but his tibiae and femora had been removed (Coyoc Ramírez 1989a, 1989b; Folan, Marcus, Pincemin et al. 1995; Pincemin 1999, 1994; Tiesler Blos et al. 1999). Burial goods included a metate fragment covering the cranium, a bone needle and imitation stingray spine, and a small stone. Two vessels, a tecomate placed inside a dish, also were recovered. The dish is of Fine Orange ware and is similar to the Terminal Classic type Provincia Plano-Relief (Ball 1977a: 101; Forsyth 1983: Figure 32gg; 1989: 124, Figure 50g; Smith 1971: Figure 9d). The tecomate, assigned to the type Tinaja Red, contained a cord covered in red pigment and a small cloth bag enclosing bone fragments and ash (Folan, Marcus, Pincemin et al. 1995: 318–319; Pincemin 1989).

A series of small, crudely built masonry rooms were added to the north facade of Structure II at the end of the Late Classic and in the Terminal Postclassic period (Figure 9.4b). Activities such as preparing *nixtamal*, cooking, serving and consuming food, weaving, stone knapping, and shell working are demonstrated by the stone tool kits, ceramics, faunal remains, and lithic and shell debitage recovered as in situ floor assemblages (Domínguez Carrasco et al. 1996, 1998a, 1998b; Folan et al. 2001). These assemblages have allowed the identification of activity areas.[4] A concentration of *Spondylus* debitage in Facade Room 7 is evidence that shells were worked somewhere near this midden. Facade Rooms 9, 42, 43, and 53–58 contained hearths, cooking vessels, and metates. For this reason, we have identified them as food preparation areas. Large storage vessels found in open patios were used for storage and perhaps for the collection of water. Facade Rooms 36–42 tentatively have been identified as sleeping quarters. Fine stone tools, including obsidian instruments, encountered in situ in Facade Rooms 50–51 and 59–62, suggest that detailed precision work was carried out by the occupants of these rooms. Spindle whorls and obsidian blades found together in sets in Facade Rooms 34 and 58 indicate that these spaces may have been places where textiles were produced. Rooms 25–26 contained large quantities of partially worked bone and shell beads as well as fine stone tools. Numerous resharpening flakes from chert bifaces had accumulated in Rooms 59 and 62, consistent with their use as lithic production loci or temporary disposal sites. Similarly, 7,000 chert waste flakes were recovered from a floor context in Room 61. Finally, crude lithic instruments, deer antler billets, and discarded cores were found in association with animal bones on the floors of Facade Rooms 44, 65, and on the lower patio. During this final occupation, tons of ash containing domestic and household production waste were deposited at the base of Structure II, further demonstrating the daily use of a structure that had once served a purely sacred function.

Importantly, the floor assemblages from the Structure II rooms demonstrate production activities traditionally associated with both men and women. We therefore suggest that the building was occupied by one or more extended families. It is difficult to imagine that so much garbage would have been stored for long periods in occupied rooms. Hence the debris, particularly lithic debitage and other dangerous waste material, is indicative of the final use of the structure shortly before its abandonment in the tenth century (cf. Clark 1991).

The rooms on the north facade of Structure II stand in stark contrast to the structures surmounting the pyramid. With the exception of food preparation in the front of the Structure II-B elite residence and to the sides of Structure II-A, there are few indications of production activities on top of the platform. Despite significant functional changes to other parts of the building, Structure II-A served as a temple throughout the Late Classic and Terminal Classic periods. Most of the ceramics associated with Structure II-A were polychrome serving vessels; no cooking vessels were found in the temple. Significant quantities of elite serving wares also were present in Structure II-B, but as predicted by the numerous hearths and metates in this building, utilitarian ceramics were more numerous. The rows of rooms constructed on the north facade of Structure II, on the other hand, contained very few imported finewares. We therefore interpret these lower rooms as places where artisans, servants, and less important elite lived and conducted everyday activities during the Terminal Classic period. In contrast, Structures II-B, II-C, and II-D constituted a palace compound. Structure II-A, at the summit of the pyramid, continued to serve as an important temple, with access limited to those elite living in the palace compound.

At the time of abandonment in the tenth century, Structure II was still undergoing renovation. In particular, the stair leading to Structure II-B was being rebuilt, as was the upper stair leading to Structure II-A. The inner floor of the temple was being replastered, and several plaster-covered earthen additions at the rear and west side of Structure II-B were under construction. These ongoing construction projects, the accumulated debris in occupied rooms, the deliberate placement of metates in inverted positions, and the careful storing of obsidian blades, cores, and projectile points in niches, all suggest to us that the final abandonment of Structure II was sudden but orderly, and that the Terminal Classic occupants planned to return.

Structure III

Lundell's Palace, or Structure III at Calakmul, is a twelve-room residential structure located east of the Central Plaza (Figure 9.3; Alvarez Aguilar and Armijo

Torres 1989–1990). The western facade, originally adorned with stucco masks, contains three doors. Three roof combs, positioned on the north, south, and east sides of the structure, imitate the triadic summit of the earlier Structure II (Figure 9.5a). This design not only tied the royal family who lived in Structure III to religious events held in Structure II (Folan et al. 2001), but also served to identify the city as Ox Te' Tuun.

Lundell's Palace, built early in the Early Classic, was occupied continuously until the Terminal Classic period. Although some minor changes, such as the opening of a door between Rooms 1 and 9, were made during the Terminal Classic, the building never was significantly altered. This demonstrates its importance to the ruling family of Calakmul. One reason Structure III was maintained for so many centuries is that it served as a funerary monument to an important ruler. Tomb I, one of the most elaborate burials known from the site, was found beneath a raised section of Room 6 (Figure 9.5b). A nine-meter-long "psychoduct" connected the tomb to the northern facade of the building, outwardly indicating that the palace contained an important burial (Coyoc Ramírez 1989a; Pincemin 1999; Tiesler Blos et al. 1999). The funerary goods accompanying this late fourth or early fifth century k'uhul kan ajaw have been described in detail elsewhere (Folan, Marcus, Pincemin et al. 1995; Pincemin 1994). We suspect that he may have been a predecessor to the king who dedicated Stela 114, the earliest known monument at the site (Pincemin et al. 1998: 323).

As was the case in excavations of Structure II, numerous artifacts were recovered from in situ floor contexts within the rooms of Structure III and on the stairs and platform in front of the superstructure. The greatest concentration of ceramic material was found in the latter area, particularly in the northern and southern corners. Most of these vessels were large *ollas* and jars assigned to the type Tinaja Red. These may have been used for food storage, but also could have been placed outside to collect rainwater. Evidence for Terminal Classic household activities within the superstructure includes the presence of hearths and cooking wares, metates, carbonized seeds, stone tools, and gastropods in Room 9. It probably served as a kitchen. The Terminal Classic doorway in the wall between Rooms 1 and 9 probably was opened to allow more light and better ventilation into this cooking space. Hearths, cooking vessels, and metates also were found in the northern half of Room 1, and so it too may have been used for food preparation. Room 10 has a sleeping bench, and Room 4 contained significant quantities of lithic debitage, including casual percussion cores made of chert. It may have served as a temporary storage place for hazardous lithic debris or even as a production space. Several metates were found in situ in Structure III. As for Structure II, we interpret this pattern as indicating that the last occupants of the building intended to return.

Figurines, nearly all of which were musical instruments, were left on the stairs and in the center of Room 12, on the platform in front of the central and

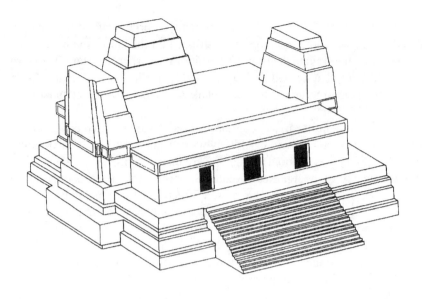

a

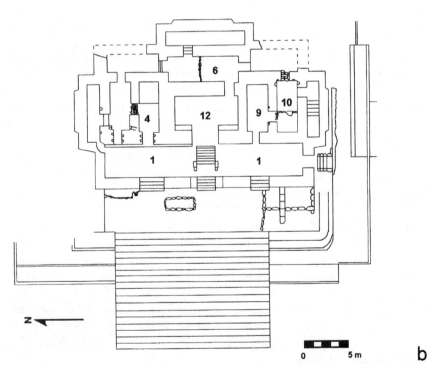

b

9.5 Calakmul Structure III: (a) reconstruction drawing, (b) plan (after Folan et al. Figures 9–10).

southern entryways, and on the upper risers of the main stairs (Braswell et al. 1998; Domínguez Carrasco et al. 1998a, 1998b; Ruíz Guzmán 1998; Ruíz Guzmán et al. 1999). These artifacts, no doubt, were placed in front of the superstructure during ceremonial activities at the end of or postdating the Terminal Classic occupation of the building. Although there are other possibilities, it is conceivable that they represent termination rituals. Oddly enough, all the figurines are of Late Classic style. We suspect that they were heirlooms or finds left on the stair as offerings.

Structure VII

Like its much larger counterpart on the southern extreme of the Central Plaza, Structure VII is a pyramid surmounted by three superstructures placed in a triadic arrangement (Figure 9.6a). The earliest construction phase dates to the Late Preclassic period, the central superstructure dates to the Late Classic, and a final building episode dates to the Terminal Classic period.

The central temple contains an important burial dating to about A.D. 780 (Coyoc Ramírez 1985; Domínguez Carrasco 1992b). The burial was found under a Río Bec–style altar containing a niche (Figure 9.6b). It consists of the remains of an adult male who was wrapped in a mat, which then was exposed to fire. Jaguar claws, skull fragments, and a portion of a tail also were associated with the funerary bundle, suggesting that the noble was buried with his jaguar cloak. The elaborate tomb furnishings contained 2,147 pieces of jadeite, including a mosaic mask, shells, a pearl, and ten Late Classic vessels. An offering of six obsidian blades also was found in the tomb, and fifty-eight additional complete blades were found with chert eccentrics in an associated cache (Domínguez Carrasco and Gallegos Gómora 1989–1990; Folan, Marcus, Pincemin et al. 1995: 319–320). All sixty-four obsidian blades, probably bloodletters, are made of obsidian from the El Chayal source, and many appear to have been struck sequentially from the same core.

Floor assemblages from Structure VII included numerous *incensario* fragments found along the central axis of the structure. Some of these are Chen-Mul Modeled Mayapán-style incense burners dating to the Late Postclassic period. Terminal Classic cooking vessels recovered from the eastern half and a *patolli* board scratched into the western half of the outermost room suggest that the superstructure was inhabited for a time (Domínguez Carrasco 1992b, 1994c; Domínguez Carrasco et al. 1998b; Folan, Marcus, Pincemin et al. 1995: 320).

Structure I

Limited clearing and test excavations were conducted on the summit of Structure I, a temple-pyramid structure fifty meters high. Excavations concentrated on two platforms and a small temple. The superstructure was found to be in poor condition, and almost all cultural material was recovered from slump and fall

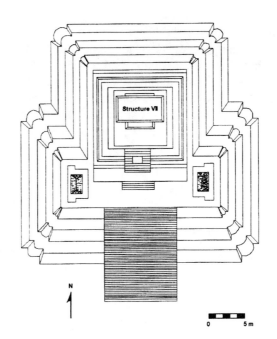

a

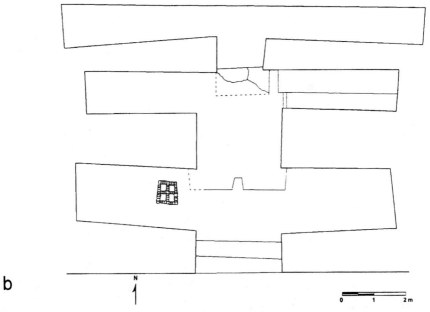

b

9.6 Calakmul Structure VII: (a) plan, (b) detail of central temple (after Folan et al. 1995: Figures 7–8).

contexts. For this reason, it is difficult to conduct a functional analysis of the structure based on the associated artifacts (Zapata Castorena and Florey Folan 1989–1990). Still, nearly half of the ceramics from the temple were large ollas and jars dating to the Terminal Classic Halibé phase. These are utilitarian vessels used predominantly for cooking and storage (Domínguez Carrasco et al. 1998b: 607). It seems likely, then, that Structure I served as a residence during the Terminal Classic period.

Interpretation: The Terminal Classic Palace-Temple Pyramid

Excavations in Structures I, II, and VII reveal that the simple characterization of pyramidal structures as "temples" does not hold for the Terminal Classic occupation of Calakmul. Instead, a variety of activities including cooking, eating, sleeping, and craft production were conducted in architectural space that in previous periods was reserved for ritual activities. The earliest evidence we have for this shift in the use of temple-pyramids is the construction of Structures II-B, II-C, and II-D in the mid-eighth century. These buildings, elite residences of the highest order, formed a small palace compound. Terminal Classic residential debris also was collected from Structures I and VII, suggesting that they, too, were inhabited. We stress that these Terminal Classic occupants were not squatters, but members of an elite class that had access to high-status goods including imported finewares and jade. Evidence of cooking, shell working, lithic reduction, bead production, and textile manufacture was recovered from the series of rooms and patios on the north facade of Structure II. These rooms contained far fewer polychrome or imported serving vessels than their counterparts on top of the platform. We conclude, therefore, that by the end of the Late Classic period, temple-pyramids served as palace compounds where everyday production and consumption activities were conducted by the elite and their retainers.

This important functional shift toward the secular use of pyramidal structures should not be interpreted as indicating a decline in the use of buildings as temples. Incense burners, whistle figurines, and other offerings were recovered from Structures I, II-A, and VII. They also were found in Structure III, an archetypal palace structure. These artifacts indicate that certain portions of the buildings, particularly interior rooms and stairs leading to the highest superstructures, retained their sacred function. For this reason, we choose to call such structures "palace-temple pyramids."

Structures like the palace-temple pyramids of Terminal Classic Calakmul are not widely known in the central Maya lowlands, though the Caana of Caracol may be another example (see A. Chase and D. Chase, Chapter 16, this volume). Such structures are more common, however, in the northern lowlands of Campeche and Yucatán. Williams-Beck (1995, 1996) has called them "linear (vertical) complexes." They include such well-known buildings as the Cinco Pisos pyramid at Edzná (as well as the entire elevated Great Acropolis at that site), the palaces of Santa Rosa Xtampak and Halal in the Chenes region, numerous palaces of the Río Bec region (e.g., Becán Structure I, Xpuhil Structure I, Río Bec-B Structure I, and Hormiguero Structure II), and the Palace of Sayil. In all these Late and Terminal Classic structures, temple-pyramids and palaces are conflated. The Late to Terminal Classic modifications of both the form and function of temple-pyramids at Calakmul suggest to us that the elite maintained important cultural ties with the Río Bec, Chenes, and Puuc regions.

Terminal Classic Stelae

The last Period Ending recorded as a Long Count date at Calakmul was 9.19.0.0.0 (A.D. 810), appearing on Stela 16 and Stela 64 (Marcus 1987: Table 1). Three additional monuments (Stelae 15, 17, and 65) are assigned to the range 9.17.0.0.0–10.1.0.0.0 (A.D. 771–849) for stylistic reasons (Marcus 1987: Table 1; Proskouriakoff 1950). Two very late monuments, Stelae 84 (west of Structure IV-B) and 91 (north of Structure XII), have been attributed to bak'tun 10 on stylistic grounds and date to around A.D. 889 (Marcus 1987: Table 1; Proskouriakoff 1950: 152). Stela 61 contains an abbreviated date of either A.D. 899 or 909, as well as a reference to Aj T'ok' (?), the last identified ruler of Calakmul (Martin 2000: 44–45). Two other monuments, Stela 50 and Stela 93, may date to an even later period. Proskouriakoff (1950: 152) noted similarities between the sandals on Stela 50 and footwear depicted at "Toltec Period" Chichén Itzá. We see broad affinities between the late stelae of Calakmul and ninth- and tenth-century monuments found in the northern lowlands, and are particularly intrigued by similarities with carved columns at Chichén Itzá. The Cycle 10 stelae of Calakmul also are notable for what they lack: depictions of so-called "Chontal Maya" or other immigrants (as at Seibal) carved in a noncanonical style (Folan, Marcus, Pincemin et al. 1995: 330).

Terminal Classic stelae are known from secondary sites within the Calakmul kingdom. Several are firmly dated by Initial Series dates. These are Oxpemul Stela 7 (10.0.0.0.0, A.D. 830), La Muñeca Stela 13 (10.2.10.0.0, A.D. 879), and La Muñeca Stela 1 (10.3.0.0.0, A.D. 889; Folan, Marcus, Pincemin et al. 1995: 330; Proskouriakoff 1950; Ruppert and Denison 1943).

There is clear evidence, then, that despite significant demographic decline, Calakmul and some of its dependencies continued to be occupied well into the Terminal Classic period. Moreover, the continued commissioning of carved stelae by rulers demonstrates that divine kingship continued in some form until at least the last decade of the ninth century.

Terminal Classic Ceramics

A total of 22,795 Halibé-phase sherds have been identified, accounting for 36.7 percent of the ceramics in our collection (Domínguez Carrasco 1994a: 357). These have been classified into thirty-nine types and thirteen ceramic groups

(Domínguez Carrasco 1994b). The vast majority of the Terminal Classic ceramics, as in the Late Classic period, are types and varieties known from Petén. The most striking difference between the Petén Gloss ware ceramics of the Ku and Halibé phases is the great reduction in variation of elite ceramics and the complete cessation of polychrome production.

Although the quantity of Terminal Classic ceramics imported from outside the central Maya lowlands is relatively small, economic ties with sites in the northern Maya lowlands and lower Usumacinta were substantially more important than in the Late Classic period. A total of 873 sherds, representing 3.8 percent of the Halibé-phase collection, come from these regions (Domínguez Carrasco 1994a: 357). These imported ceramics include Fine Orange wares of both the Altar and Balancán groups, also known from the Río Bec region (Ball 1977a: 163) and El Mirador (Forsyth 1989: 134). A few sherds of Chicxulub Incised, a Fine Gray ware, also were recovered. Unlike at El Mirador, the Terminal Classic assemblage from Calakmul contains a variety of Cehpech slate wares of the Muna, Ticul, and Dzitas groups. All types of these groups represented at Calakmul occur in the Río Bec region in greater frequencies. It is possible, then, that trade connections with the Puuc, the lower Usumacinta, and Chichén Itzá were indirect and mediated by Becán. Another possible intermediary, particularly for access to goods produced in the Gulf Coast region, is Edzná (Boucher and Dzul 1998).

A peculiar ceramic grinding pestle dating to the Halibé phase was recovered from Structure II-F (Florey Folan and Folan 1999). To our knowledge, the only other examples are from Sotuta contexts at Chichén Itzá in the Group of the Phalli, the Caracol, the Temple of the Atlantean Columns, the House of the Grinding Stones, and the Northeast and Southeast Colonnades (Brainerd 1958: 256, Figure 72g). Brainerd proposed that the punched surfaces of the artifacts were used to grind chile on grater bowls. He further suggested that their closest known relatives are found among the Tairona of Colombia (see Mason 1939: 373), and may have diffused to Yucatán along with gold artifacts (Brainerd 1958: 256). It is significant that the only copper ring known from Calakmul was found at the same floor level as the pestle. More recently, Smith (1998a) has linked the distribution of grater bowls (and presumably the pestles used with them) to ethnic identity in Terminal Classic Yucatán.

Two previously undocumented ceramic types, which we have named Calakmul Slate and Calakmul Slate Impressed, also were identified in the Halibé complex (Domínguez Carrasco 1994a: 288–291). The surface treatment of the second type is similar to that of the Pantano Impressed: Pantano variety of the Tinaja group. We therefore suspect that Calakmul Slate Impressed was produced somewhere in the *petén campechano*. Recent geochemical analyses of sherds belonging to both types support our hypothesis that Calakmul Slate and Calakmul Slate Impressed—the two most common types of slate ware found at Calakmul—were local products.

Boucher and Dzul (1998: Cuadro 1) have identified 6,407 sherds belonging to fifty-two types and fourteen ceramic groups assigned to the Halibé phase. In addition to the types we have noted, their collection also contains thirty-one polychrome sherds of the types Zanahoria Scored and Droga Roja (Ball 1977a: 63–64, 90), best known from the Río Bec region. They also found Altar Group Fine Orange ware in the form of tripod *molcajetes*, perhaps used in conjunction with the effigy pestles discussed here. Finally, Boucher and Dzul (1998: 12) identified ten sherds belonging to the Hontún and Chencán groups, previously reported only at Edzná and Jaina (Forsyth 1983: 113, 123). For this reason, they suggest that economic ties with Gulf Coast peoples may have been mediated by Edzná (Boucher and Dzul 1998: 12).

Although the details of our analyses differ somewhat, Boucher and Dzul's (1998) results support our earlier conclusions (Domínguez Carrasco 1994a, 1994b, 1996). During the Terminal Classic Halibé phase, few elite polychromes of Petén style were produced or consumed at Calakmul. Instead, these were replaced by Fine Orange, Fine Gray, and Slate wares originating in the north and in the Usumacinta region, and by two types of locally produced Slate ware. Because most of the imported wares also are known from Terminal Classic contexts in the Río Bec zone, it seems likely that trade between Calakmul and the northern lowlands was indirect. Nevertheless, it is clear that during the Terminal Classic period, economic ties with the northern lowlands became more important than in any earlier period.

Terminal Classic Obsidian

A total of 515 obsidian artifacts were recovered during excavations in Structures I, II, III, and VII. With the exception of the sixty-four prismatic blades from Tomb I and an associated cache in Structure VII, all were subject to three kinds of study: geological or geochemical provenience analysis, typological classification, and metric analysis.[5] Although many of these artifacts undoubtedly come from fallen architectural fill, 140 were recovered from floor assemblages in Structures II, III, and VII. As ceramic analysis continues, we are beginning to separate Terminal Classic obsidian from artifacts of earlier periods. In addition, certain characteristic technological traits and source procurement patterns recently have been shown to be diagnostic of the Terminal Classic period (e.g., G. Braswell 1997a, 1997b, 1998a). These also can be used to identify Terminal Classic obsidian artifacts.

All 451 analyzed obsidian artifacts were first assigned to geological sources according to visual criteria. We have found that using this method, we can attribute artifacts to sources with a 95 percent or better success rate (G. Braswell 1997a, 1997b, 1998a, 1998c, in press; Braswell et al. 1994, 2000). As a test of these assignments, thirty-nine artifacts were assayed by neutron activation analysis (Figure 9.7). One small piece had been given an erroneous assignment, sug-

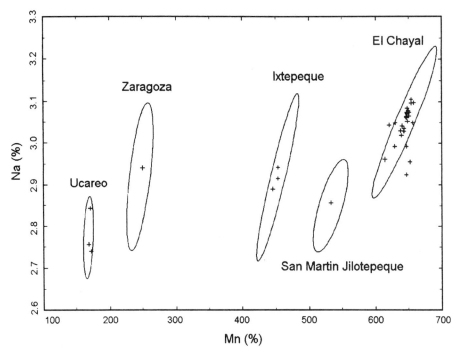

9.7 Sodium and manganese contents of thirty-nine obsidian artifacts from Calakmul. Ellipses indicate 95 percent–confidence intervals for assignments to each geological source.

gesting a success rate for visual sourcing of the entire collection of about 97 percent. This is a conservative estimate, because only those pieces judged difficult to assign to a source were subject to neutron activation analysis.

Results of the combined sourcing methodology indicate that obsidian from El Chayal, Guatemala, accounts for 86.3 percent (N=389) of the collection. The remainder consists of obsidian from Pachuca, Hidalgo (4.7 percent, N=21); Ixtepeque, Guatemala (4.4 percent, N=20); Ucareo, Michoacán (2.4 percent, N=11); San Martín Jilotepeque, Guatemala (1.6 percent, N=7); and Zaragoza, Puebla (0.2 percent, N=1). Two additional pieces (0.4 percent) were not assigned to sources and are unique artifacts that could not be assayed by a destructive technique. The first, a fragment of a ground and polished earspool, is probably of Otumba obsidian and is certainly from a Mexican source; we know of no such artifacts produced in the Maya area. It was found associated with Structure II-A.

The vast majority of Late Classic obsidian from sites in the Petén and southern Campeche comes from El Chayal. In comparison, assemblages from throughout the Maya area dating to A.D. 800–1000 show a more diverse pattern of resource procurement. At the beginning of the Terminal Classic, obsidian from the Ucareo, Zaragoza, and Zacualtípan sources reached the Maya region for the first time (Aoyama 1996; Braswell 1997b; Stiver et al. 1994). Pachuca obsidian, famous for its gold-green color, also is found in significant quantities at many Terminal Classic sites. Although obsidian blades were imported from this source during the Early Classic period, there is very little evidence that Pachuca polyhedral cores were worked in the Maya area until after A.D. 800. Thus, green core-reduction debitage, which is not found at Early Classic Maya sites (with the exception of Tikal), is occasionally present in Terminal Classic contexts.

Obsidian from the San Martín Jilotepeque and Ixtepeque sources also is found commonly in Terminal Classic contexts in the central Maya lowlands. Material from the former source was used frequently during the Preclassic period, but is uncommon in Early and Late Classic assemblages. Ixtepeque obsidian, though found in trace amounts at Petén and southern Campeche sites dating to the Early and Late Classic periods, grew rapidly in importance after A.D. 800. At sites in the Petén lakes region such as Topoxté, Ixtepeque obsidian serves as a clear diagnostic of Terminal Classic and later contexts (G. Braswell 1998a; Rice et al. 1985). By A.D. 1050–1200, Ixtepeque obsidian became the chief source of obsidian utilized in the northern Maya lowlands, Belize, and Petén.

The most diagnostic feature of Terminal Classic and Postclassic prismatic blades is the presence of ground platforms, a modification that allows the tip of the pressure crutch to find solid purchase on the core. Platform grinding is a production step in the preparation of macrocores for export; that is, it is conducted at or near quarry workshops. Most blades manufactured in the central Maya lowlands during the Early and Late Classic periods have scratched platforms, a modification made as sequential rings of blades were removed from the core. Pachuca obsidian blades from Early Classic contexts in the Maya area have smooth, unmodified platforms, as do Classic-period blades found at Teotihuacan. In contrast, the vast majority of highland Mexican blades found in Terminal Classic and later contexts have ground platforms. Some time between A.D. 800 and 1000, macrocore producers in the Guatemalan highlands also began to grind their platforms.

Ground platforms on proximal prismatic blade fragments of El Chayal, Ixtepeque, Pachuca, and Ucareo obsidian recovered from Structures II and III indicate that these buildings were occupied during the Terminal Classic period. The presence of Ucareo and Zaragoza material also is diagnostic of a Terminal Classic date, as is the presence of significant quantities of Ixtepeque and Pachuca obsidian. Finally, a stemmed prismatic blade point made of Pachuca obsidian was recovered from Structure VII. This type of artifact is particularly diagnostic of the Terminal Classic and Postclassic periods.

The highland Mexican sources represented in the collection suggest that Terminal Classic inhabitants of the site participated in a trade network that also included sites belonging to the Sotuta ceramic sphere of the northern Maya lowlands. Ucareo and Pachuca material together account for more than half of the obsidian consumed at Chichén Itzá (G. Braswell 1998c), but these sources are infrequently represented at Cehpech-sphere sites (G. Braswell 1997b, 1998c). Furthermore, the distribution of Ucareo and Pachuca obsidian within the Cehpech ceramic sphere is limited to late occupations (after A.D. 900) at the largest sites. And many of these late Terminal Classic contexts—at sites like Uxmal, Kabah, and Dzibilchaltún—also contain significant quantities of Sotuta ceramics. Thus Chichén Itzá seems to have been the principal, if not sole, importer of Ucareo and Pachuca obsidian to the peninsula during the ninth century. The presence of material from these sources in the Calakmul collection suggests at least indirect contact with that important economic and political power.

Comparison of the samples from Structures II and III reveals an interesting difference in procurement patterns. While only 4 percent of the artifacts recovered from Structure II are from sources in highland Mexico, 13 percent of the obsidian from Structure III is Mexican. In fact, the relative proportion of Ucareo material in Structure III is nearly six times greater than that of Structure II. In contrast, Structure II has considerably more obsidian from the Ixtepeque, Guatemala, source. These patterns and the fact that a greater proportion of Terminal Classic ceramics were recovered from the rooms in Structure II suggest that occupation was more intensive at a later date in Structure II than in Structure III.

ECOLOGICAL CRISIS:
CALAKMUL AND A TERMINAL CLASSIC DROUGHT

A prominent result of an extensive and rapidly expanding program of climatological research is that the tropics are strongly affected by changes in global temperatures (e.g., Broecker 1995). The notable record of the rise and fall of state-level political organization in the Maya lowlands makes it an important area for studies of the interaction of climatic change and cultural patterns. Although studies of Maya lowland ecology and how it relates to climate have appeared during the last two decades (e.g., Dahlin 1983; Folan 1981; Folan et al. 1983; Gunn and Adams 1981; Gunn and Folan 1996; Gunn et al. 1994, 1995; Messenger 1990), interest in global climate change is now increasing. The Maya lowlands also have attracted the attention of limnologists (e.g., Curtis et al. 1996; Deevey 1978; Dunning et al. 1998; Hodell et al. 1995). Their data, derived from cores extracted from lakes in the northern and central lowlands, provide a wealth of information on climate fluctuation on the regional level that has verified our earlier findings.

Modeling Terminal Classic Climate in the Calakmul Basin

The dynamics of climate in the central and northern lowlands are driven by shifts in the boundary between the southeastern tropics and the northwestern subtropics (e.g., Folan et al. 1983; Gunn et al. 1994, 1995). The regional atmospheric mechanism that causes this change is a double sea-breeze effect that normally brings rainy season precipitation through the convergence of eastern and northern air streams (see Folan et al. 1983). The former, supported by the eastern trade winds, carries moist air and tropical storms from the Caribbean. Dry air comes from the north and has its origins in the Bermuda-Azores high. During the rainy season, the collision of these two sea breezes over the course of the day creates a line of northeast to southwest precipitation. Global warming leads to greater amounts of moisture, an earlier rainy season, and a northwest shift in the tropical-subtropical boundary. Conversely, cooling leads to a later rainy season, less precipitation, and southeast movement of the tropical-subtropical boundary.

One approach to assessing the regional effects of global warming on the climate of the Maya lowlands is to analyze the discharge of rivers. The Calakmul Basin forms part of the Río Candelaria watershed. We have found that a comparison of the annual discharge of the Río Candelaria with global temperature fluctuations during the period 1958–1990 strongly supports the double sea-breeze model (Gunn et al. 1994, 1995). This model, abstracted as a regression equation predicting river discharge from mean global temperature, was projected over the last three thousand years to estimate the impact of global temperature regimes on local climate. The model indicates extended droughts at the end of the Preclassic, Classic, and Postclassic periods, and overly moist conditions during the Early Postclassic period (Figure 9.8; Gunn et al. 1994, 1995). The longest period of extended drought during the Classic period began about A.D. 750 and lasted for approximately 200 years.

Subsequent analyses of lake sediment cores provide an empirical assessment of the double sea-breeze model. Hodell et al. (1995) analyzed a core from the northern Maya lowlands that records a very strong drought during the Terminal Classic period. Another core studied by Curtis et al. (1996) also shows a drought at the end of the Classic period. Nonetheless, a sample taken from Laguna Tamarindito, located in the Petexbatún region of southwestern Petén, Guatemala, does not provide unambiguous evidence for a Terminal Classic drought. Increased charcoal levels and a shift from gilled to gilled-and-lunged snails were observed in the core. These indicate a local drying trend in the Terminal Classic, but there is no evidence that climatic change—rather than human action—was responsible (Dunning et al. 1998: 147).

Subregional variation may reconcile our double sea-breeze model and data from the northern lowlands with the Laguna Tamarindito core. The Petexbatún receives some of its water from an uplift of the Maya Mountains and the northern foothills of the Sierra Chamá. These hills may have continued to generate precipitation despite generally drier conditions to the north. Alternatively, global cooling may not have been sufficient to push the tropical-subtropical boundary far enough to the south to affect southern Petén. Laporte (Chapter 10, this volume; Laporte and Quezada 1998) has documented a heavy Terminal Classic occupation of south-

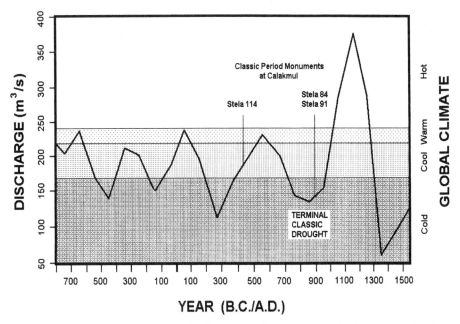

9.8 Fluctuations in the annual discharge of the Río Candelaria during the late Holocene (after Gunn et al. 1995: Figure 7).

eastern Petén, precisely that area predicted to be least affected by southeasterly shifts in the boundary.

If a regional drought contributed to the decline of Calakmul during the ninth century, why did the Chichén Itzá and Puuc regional states thrive in the even drier northern lowlands? Although the northern lowlands also experienced decreased precipitation levels, a southern shift in the tropical-subtropical boundary did not affect this area to the same extent because it lies to the northwest of the boundary. Conversely, global warming, resulting in greater precipitation, would have more impact on climatic conditions in the north than in the central Maya lowlands.

One of the most important conclusions of our climatological research is that global changes in temperature often create different climatological effects on regional and local levels (Gunn and Folan 1996). In the case of the Terminal Classic, global cooling may have adversely affected sites located in the Candelaria watershed. But without further data, we should not extrapolate a drought at Calakmul to sites in other watersheds within the Maya lowlands (see Ringle et al., Chapter 21, this volume). Discharge studies of the Río Champotón (to the north of the Candelaria) and Usumacinta (to the south) watersheds indicate highly variable responses to global conditions. The Usumacinta shows no effects from moderate changes in global temperature (Gunn and Folan 1996). This provides a partial explanation of why Terminal Classic centers along the lower Usumacinta continued to thrive at a later date than some cities in the central lowlands. The Tamarandito core, drawn from the upper Usumacinta region, may reflect the buffering effects inherent to that watershed. Analyses of osteological remains from the Petexbatún region do not suggest any undo subsistence failure (Wright 1997; Wright and White 1996), a result that also is inconsistent with a drought in the upper Usumacinta watershed. For these reasons, and because the processes of political fragmentation and depopulation were underway in the Petexbatún before the Candelaria drought, we are particularly hesitant to apply a dessication model to that region.

The Río Champotón, on the other hand, is extremely flood-prone during periods of global warming, which makes its lower reaches virtually uninhabitable (Gunn and Folan 1996). In other words, precisely the same global conditions that contributed to the demise of Calakmul may have fostered the continued occupation and florescence of Edzná during the Terminal Classic period. But anthropogenic factors play an equally important role in the Champotón watershed. Deforestation in the upper Champotón also causes flooding of the lower reaches of the river. Scenarios that posit a drought as the unique cause of a pan-regional Classic Maya "collapse" must be viewed with caution. We stress that regional and local environmental factors (including human-induced changes to the landscape), as well as cultural responses to deteriorating conditions, must be incorporated in any environmental model of the Maya "collapse."

Terminal Classic Demography

One issue worthy of study is the suggestive evidence that drought was an important factor in the demographic decline of the Calakmul kingdom during the Terminal Classic. Despite ample proof of a significant Terminal Classic occupation in the epicenter of Calakmul, and evidence—in the form of carved monuments—for a late occupation at secondary sites within the kingdom, most rural sites were abandoned early in the period. We have recovered only trace quantities of Terminal Classic ceramics from our recent survey transects, and so far have identified only two C-shaped and no "Petén veneer" structures known to be diagnostic of the Terminal Classic and Postclassic periods (e.g., Bey et al. 1997; Orrego Corzo and Larios Villalta 1983; Tourtellot 1988b; D. Rice 1986; P. Rice 1987c; Tourtellot et al. 1992). Although our demographic analyses are still in their initial stages, we believe that the rural zone lost 90 percent of its population during the ninth century.

Why did occupation, albeit diminished, continue at Calakmul and certain secondary sites after much of the rural zone was abandoned? We suspect that the principal reason was access to water. Calakmul and many of the larger sites in the kingdom have elaborate reservoir systems and are built along the bajo margins. Our ethnographic investigations indicate that planting in artificially and naturally raised areas in the bajo is a viable strategy in years when the rainy season is too short to support agriculture in the uplands (Folan and Gallegos Osuna 1992). Reconnaissance and excavations in the El Laberinto bajo have discovered not only lithic extraction and reduction stations, but also house platforms and raised agricultural fields bounded by stone walls (Figure 9.2; Domínguez Carrasco 1992a). The ecotone of the bajo margin, when complemented by a functioning reservoir system, is therefore the best local environment for habitation during periods of drought. Calakmul and many of the secondary sites of the kingdom were the last places to be abandoned during the Terminal Classic because they were the most habitable.

THE "COLLAPSE" OF CALAKMUL
AS AN EXAMPLE OF PAN-REGIONAL PROCESSES

The political and demographic processes that led to the "collapse" of Calakmul during the Terminal Classic period have parallels elsewhere in the Maya region (e.g., Culbert et al. 1990; Fash et al., Chapter 12, this volume; Fash and Sharer 1991; Fialko et al. 1998). As at Copán, the political decline of the Calakmul regional state began long before a period for which there is any evidence of population loss. We date the beginning of this political process to A.D. 695, when, after a series of spectacular victories (some of which were won through lesser allies such as Caracol) lasting almost 200 years, Calakmul suffered an important defeat at the hands of Jasaw Chan K'awiil of Tikal. The recent discovery of the tomb of Yukno'om Yich'aak K'ahk' in Structure II makes it highly unlikely that Jasaw Chan K'awiil captured and sacrificed the great Calakmul king (Carrasco Vargas et al. 1999; Pincemin et al. 1998). Nevertheless, at least two important lords of Calakmul seem to have been captured in this action. Moreover, it is certain that the Calakmul king did not live long after this event and it is conceivable that he died as a result of the battle. Thus the end of the "hiatus" at Tikal, the beginning of which was signaled by a defeat of that site orchestrated by Calakmul in A.D. 562, marks the beginning of the political decline of Calakmul (cf. Marcus 1998: Figure 3.1). Although we can find no evidence linking this loss in war to a loss of population, we concur in a general way with Demarest (Chapter 6, this volume). Success in warfare played an important role in the rise of Calakmul, and a reversal of fortunes contributed to its political decline.

But early eighth-century Calakmul was still one of the two greatest political forces of the Maya lowlands. In A.D. 736, a lord of Calakmul visited K'ahk' Tiliw Chan Yopaat at Quiriguá, apparently extending the influence of the Calakmul regional state to the southeastern periphery. The defeat of Waxaklajuun U B'aah K'awiil of Copán less than two years later may have been accomplished with the consent of this k'uhul kan ajaw (Looper 1995). Thus the first event in the political decline of Copán may have been precipitated by the machinations of a still powerful Calakmul.

By A.D. 750 Calakmul began to forge stronger political and economic ties with polities to the north. This, as Carrasco Vargas (1998) has speculated, may have been a response to the waning political strength of the ruling dynasty. Alternatively, we suggest that this change in external relations represents a shift away from the weakening political and economic sphere of the south, toward the vibrant and emerging system of the north. In our view, this change of focus was an attempt by the ruling elite to reinforce the political and economic strength of Calakmul. These new connections are manifested in the archaeological record by the first appearance at Calakmul of ceramics from the Río Bec, Chenes, and Edzná regions. Northern affinities also can be seen in Calakmul architecture, particularly in modifications to Structure II, which became a palace-temple pyramid with the addition of Structures II-B, II-C, II-D, and the rooms on the north facade. Such buildings that integrate the economic, residential, and administrative functions of palaces with the sacred role and architecture of temple-pyramids were common in the northern lowlands during the eighth century.

At about the same time that Calakmul began to engage in significant interaction with sites in the northern lowlands, global cooling started to affect rainfall in the Río Candelaria watershed (Gunn and Folan 1996; Gunn et al. 1994, 1995). Although we do not know the precise date when climatic deterioration became serious enough to lead to population loss—either through lowered birth rates, migration, or starvation—much of the rural area of the kingdom was abandoned in the ninth century. By A.D. 900, the population of the Calakmul regional state had declined by at least 1.3 million individuals from its Late Classic maximum.

We have identified two general adaptive strategies to waning political power and the first century of the drought (A.D. 750–850). First, economic ties with the northern Maya lowlands and the lower Usumacinta region became more important. As the Petén economic sphere became less important to Calakmul, greater quantities of goods like Fine Paste ceramics and Mexican obsidian were received from trading partners to the north and west. In particular, trade connections were formed with the Puuc region and Chichén Itzá, and access to Gulf Coast trade may have been mediated by Edzná. Second, existing populations within the kingdom became focused on bajo margins, particularly in areas with existing reservoirs. The abandonment of drier uplands and the construction of slightly raised fields in the moister bajos served as a maximization strategy during a period of diminishing agricultural returns (cf. Fialko et al. 1998).

Despite significant political setbacks, climatic deterioration, and a subsequent demographic crisis, a political system based on the precepts of divine rulership continued to function until at least A.D. 899 or 909, when the last dated stelae were erected in the kingdom. Calakmul Stelae 61, 84, and 91, Oxpemul Stela 7, and La Muñeca Stelae 1 and 13 all depict individuals dressed in the trappings of divine kings. These all are coeval with the last dated monuments at Toniná and Dzibanché.

Terminal Classic Calakmul, Tikal, and Copán:
Shared Political and Demographic Processes

Although the event that marked the gradual ebbing of the political importance of Calakmul ushered in a Late Classic revival of Tikal, the ninth-century demographic declines of both sites were contemporary. By the beginning of the Eznab phase about A.D. 850, central Tikal and its sustaining area already had suffered an 80–85 percent depopulation (Culbert et al. 1990: Tables 5.1 and 5.2). The last dated monument at that site, erected by a second king named Jasaw Chan K'awiil, was raised two decades later, and carved monuments continued to be produced within the Tikal kingdom until A.D. 889. Here, too, some semblance of divine kingship continued into the period of demographic crisis. Like the Halibé phase at Calakmul, the Eznab phase is marked by increasing economic ties with the north and northwest. As production of Petén polychromes decreased, increasing quantities of Fine Paste wares were imported for use by the Terminal Classic elite (Boucher and Dzul 1998; Domínguez Carrasco 1994a).

At Copán we see a similar pattern of slow political decline in the early eighth century followed by rapid depopulation, a restructuring of economic ties, and an eventual dynastic collapse (Braswell 1997c). There is no credible evidence that the demographic crisis at that site began after A.D. 800.[6] Instead, it is likely that population levels began to drop before that date. The first *k'atun* (A.D. 763–783) of the reign of Yaax Pasaj Chan Yopaat saw a renaissance at Copán, but very few monuments or buildings were raised during the last four decades of his life. In fact, the only substantial addition to the acropolis dating to after A.D. 775 is his tomb. The cessation of artistic and architectural elaboration at Copán during the last decades of the eighth century may indicate the decay of dynastic power, but also may reflect population loss. By A.D. 800, the workforce necessary to cut and erect stone blocks and to carve monuments in honor of a decrepit king already may have dispersed. Yet the royal dynasty of Copán continued to survive for at least another twenty years.

There also is evidence for the decline in local ceramic variation and richness at Copán by A.D. 800, suggesting the loss of production loci and perhaps population (Bill 1997, 1998). An economic response of the late Coner phase (A.D. 800–850/900) was the strengthening of trade relations with partners in northwestern and central Honduras. The last decades of dynastic Copán saw an influx of Ulúa/Yojoa polychromes replacing locally produced Cream Paste ceramics (Bill 1997: 406–408, Table 2.28). Thus, as the elite of Calakmul and Tikal were turning to the northern lowlands and Gulf Coast region, the royalty of Copán fashioned stronger economic bonds with their non-Maya neighbors.

Investigations at Calakmul, Tikal, and Copán suggest a similar series of events and an analogous pattern of economic response to the changing conditions of the Terminal Classic period. The political decline of both Calakmul and Copán began as a result of a military setback in the Late Classic period. All three sites probably suffered significant population losses by the first decades of the ninth century, though reliable demographic data for this period still are lacking for Copán. A major factor in the process of demographic decline at all three sites appears to have been environmental degradation, stimulated by natural or human causes. Calakmul and perhaps Tikal suffered from a drought caused by global cooling (see Fialko et al. 1998). Anthropogenic factors played an important role in the deterioration of the local ecology of Copán (e.g., Fash and Sharer 1991; Fash et al., Chapter 12, this volume). Nonetheless, the political institution of divine kingship seems to have survived at all three sites into the period of demographic crisis. The Terminal Classic elite of each polity reacted to political, environmental, and demographic stresses by forming new (and strengthening existing) economic alliances beyond their kingdoms.

Despite these stresses, and perhaps because of economic adaptations to them, the k'uhul ajawob of Calakmul and Tikal were able to maintain the airs of divine rulership until the waning years of the ninth century. The Copán dynasty, in contrast, was less successful, lasting only to A.D. 820. At that site, the entire history of political decline from first defeat to fragmentation was condensed to an eighty-two-year span.

Finally, at all three cities, the end of dynastic rule was followed quickly by abandonment. The sequence and nature of events surrounding the abandonment of each site, though, were different. The last inhabitants of Tikal seem to have been squatters inhabiting abandoned palaces and remnant populations living in buildings constructed in a new architectural style. Central Copán and its residential suburb of Sepulturas were burned, destroyed, and abandoned between A.D. 820 and 900 (Andrews and Bill in press; Fash et al., Chapter 12, this volume). But there is no evidence that the last Terminal Classic inhabitants of Calakmul were squatters or were forced violently from their homes. There are no indications of widespread burning as found at Copán, and there is no evidence of warfare—in the form of fire, defensive works, the repositioning of population, and large quantities of projectile points—as has been noted for the Petexbatún region. In contrast, domestic artifacts left in Structures II and III of Calakmul were carefully stored in ways suggesting that their owners hoped to return.

Differences in their last days of occupation notwithstanding, we are struck by the generally similar sequence of processes shared by Calakmul, Tikal, and Copán. Calakmul and its two Terminal Classic contemporaries endured analogous political and environmental stresses and adapted to them in similar ways. It is not surprising that their historical trajectories also were parallel.

NOTES

1. The tallies presented here come from our analyses of ceramics recovered through the 1989 field season. They do not include materials from our 1993 and 1994 excavations. In our original examination (Domínguez Carrasco 1994a) we assigned Traino

Brown: Traino variety and Encanto Striated: Encanto variety to the Terminal Classic Halibé phase because they both were found in lots containing typical Terminal Classic diagnostics. In contrast, Boucher and Dzul (1998) place both in the Late Classic Ku phase. This difference in interpretation is particularly significant for Encanto Striated: Encanto variety, the predominant utilitarian ceramic used at Calakmul, accounting for 18.7 percent of our total collection and 11.6 percent of Boucher and Dzul's (1998). We now strongly suspect that both varieties straddle the arbitrary boundary between the Ku and Halibé phases. In fact, neither our own collections nor those of Boucher and Dzul (1998) contain varieties that we have assigned to more than one ceramic phase. Although we recognize that both Encanto Striated: Encanto and Traino Brown: Traino probably were used during both phases, we nonetheless have opted to assign these two ceramic taxa to the Ku phase, enabling easier comparison with Boucher and Dzul (1998).

2. Marc Zender (personal communication 2000) points out that this title or name, which means 'He the ninth noble, he of Sa,' suggests a connection with Naranjo. The toponym Sa is found commonly in inscriptions related to that site.

3. While writing this chapter, we conducted a demographic analysis of the northern twenty-five kilometers of the survey transect running from Conhuas to Calakmul. Although a substantial portion of this ten-square-kilometer area is bajo, a total of 559 structures were recorded. Applying the same adjustments as Robichaux (1995), this is equivalent to a Late Classic population density of 340 inhabitants per square kilometer for land outside the bajo. Using this result for the entire Calakmul kingdom, a total rural population of three million people is calculated. Caution should be used in extrapolating from such a small sample, but this result, the only population estimate for the Calakmul rural area generated from data gathered in the field, should not be ignored.

4. We use the general term "activity area" because the location of production debris reflects discard patterns and does not necessarily indicate the actual locus of production. Moreover, we avoid the word "workshop" because we are uncertain of the scale and organization of craft production associated with Structure II.

5. The prismatic blades are on permanent display in the Baluarte San Miguel in Campeche and were not available for detailed study.

6. The only data that have been mustered to support a demographic decline after A.D. 800 are a series of highly suspect obsidian hydration dates (e.g., Webster et al., Chapter 11, this volume). These dates have been rejected by most Copán researchers for a wide variety of reasons. First, they were generated from external rinds. External surfaces of obsidian artifacts at Copán have been proven to be significantly eroded (Braswell 1997c). That is, if the correct values are used for hydration rate constants and environmental variables, external rinds always will yield late dates. Second, the hydration rate constants used to generate these dates were determined by a process demonstrated to cause surface erosion (Stevenson et al. 1989; Tremaine and Frederickson 1988), and in fact yield rates that are off by a factor of two (Braswell et al. 1996b). Third, effective hydration temperatures were estimated using air-temperature data from two distant meteorological stations and integrated using the most inaccurate method known (Jones et al. 1996). A later thermal cell program demonstrates that these estimates are seriously in error, as is the assumption that all archaeological soils in the Copán pocket have a relative humidity of 100 percent (Braswell 1997c). Fourth, the hydration dates

were not treated as a statistical data set, and the probability of having outliers in a very large sample was underestimated (Braswell 1992; Cowgill and Kintigh 1997). Fifth, ceramic types recently recovered from Early Postclassic structures were not reported for contexts that yielded Postclassic hydration dates, that is, there is no ceramic evidence supporting the late dates (e.g., Fash et al., Chapter 12, this volume; Manahan 1996). Sixth, although some of the more than seventy radiocarbon dates from Copán concur with some of the hydration dates, there are only a small number of radiocarbon dates later than A.D. 900. These come from samples collected from contexts that contain typical Early Postclassic Ejar ceramics (Kan ware, Tohil Plumbate, and Las Vegas Polychrome), and not from Coner-phase contexts (Fash et al., Chapter 12, this volume; Manahan 1996). Seventh, ceramics collected from recently re-examined sites—which, according to obsidian hydration dates, were first occupied during the Postclassic period—are types assigned not only to the Coner phase, but also to the earlier Acbi and Bijac phases (Canuto 1997, 1998).

Given the unreliable nature of these obsidian hydration dates and the now discredited method used to generate them, we concur with Andrews and Bill (in press), Fash et al. (Chapter 12, this volume), and Manahan (1996) in their dismissal of a prolonged demographic collapse at Copán. All credible evidence suggests that the Copán region was abandoned sometime before A.D. 900, and perhaps as early as A.D. 822. A brief reoccupation, conceivably by Lenca peoples native to Honduras, dates to the Early Postclassic Ejar phase (A.D. 950–1050).

ACKNOWLEDGMENTS

We are grateful for the support received by the Proyecto Calakmul from the Universidad Autónoma de Campeche, the Gobierno del Estado de Campeche, INAH, Conacyt, and the National Geographic Society. Funding for neutron activation analysis was granted by the National Science Foundation and the Foundation for the Advancement of Mesoamerican Studies, Inc. (Gr. 95004). We thank Jennifer Briggs Braswell and Joyce Marcus for their insightful comments and skillful editing of an earlier draft of this chapter. We also thank Marc Zender for his aid with the emerging orthographic conventions of Southern Classic Mayan.

10

TERMINAL CLASSIC SETTLEMENT AND POLITY IN THE MOPAN VALLEY, PETÉN, GUATEMALA

Juan Pedro Laporte

outheastern Petén, a large territory covering about five thousand square kilometers, has been less explored than other parts of Petén. Since 1987 the Atlas Arqueológico de Guatemala project has recorded many sites in this region with a distinctive sociopolitical organization and a wide chronological spectrum (Figure 10.1). These surveys, plus those in the adjacent Belize Mountains since 1992 (Dunham 1993), allow southeast Petén to be placed into the overall picture of the Maya lowlands.

SOUTHEASTERN PETÉN SUBREGIONS AND RESOURCES

Southeastern Petén is clearly delineated by two major physical divisions: southern mountains and northern savannas. Due to the geographical complexity of such a large and diverse area, it is necessary to give a more elaborated description of the different valleys that have divided the region into sectors (Table 10.1). The fluvial valleys are subdivided according to their elevation: upper valleys in mountain zones and lower valleys in the savannas. This discussion of change and continuity between the Late and Terminal Classic in southeastern Petén uses as an example the middle and upper Mopan Valleys, supported by results from other related mountain valleys (Sacul, Xaan, and Poxte Rivers) and savannas (San Juan and Salsipuedes Rivers).

The Maya Mountains Subregion

To the south, the Maya Mountains zone is associated with the origin of the major rivers of southeastern Petén (Machaquila, Pusilha, Mopan, and Chiquibul).

195

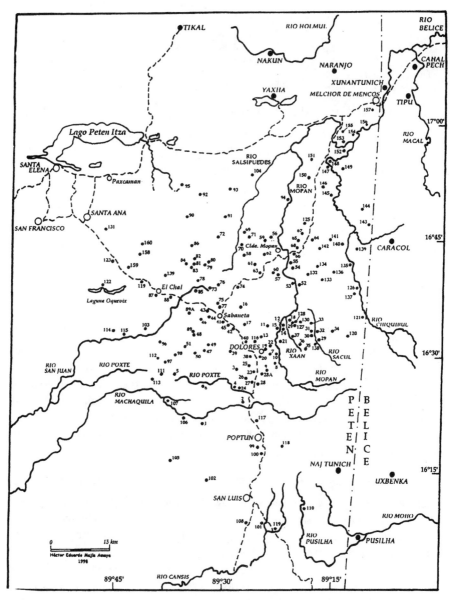

10.1 Location of archaeological sites in southeastern Petén.

The Maya Mountains extend into southeastern Petén, Guatemala (municipios of Dolores, Poptun, and San Luis), from the Stann Creek district in Belize, where the central and highest cordillera is located (Dunham and Prufer 1998). This mountainous zone, measuring approximately 150 to 100 kilometers wide, has

Table 10.1.

Division by Hydrographic Valley	Municipality
A. Cuenca alta del río Cansís	San Luis
B. Cuenca alta del río Pusilha	San Luis
C. Cuenca alta del río Machaquila	Poptun
D. Cuenca del río Poxte	Poptun
E. Cuenca alta del río Mopan	Dolores
1. Cuencas de los ríos Sacul and Xaan	
2. El río Mopan hasta su resumidero	
F. Cuenca alta del río Chiquibul	Dolores
G. Parte aguas de los ríos Poxte, San Juan, and Mopan	Dolores
H. Cuenca media del río Mopan	Dolores
I. Cuenca del río Salsipuedes	Melchor de Mencos
J. Cuenca baja del río Chiquibul	Melchor de Mencos
K. Cuenca baja del río Mopan	Melchor de Mencos
L. Cuenca alta del río San Juan	Dolores
1. Área de Santa Cruz-La Puente-Santo Toribio	
2. Área de El Ochote-El Muxanal	
3. Área de El Chal	
4. Área inferior del río en el extremo oeste	
M. Zones not associated with fluvial valleys	Santa Ana
1. El parte aguas Mopan–Petén Itza	
2. Área de sistema de aguadas y lagunetas	

been widely studied in its physical aspects (Ford and Williams 1989; E. Graham 1987a; Jennings 1985; Laporte 1996; Ower 1928).

Overall, this mountain chain is characterized by low elevation (below 1100 meters above sea level) and consists of a volcanic core of igneous and metamorphic material surrounded by a heavily eroded limestone cliff, situated along a sedimentary plain. Elevation varies, creating micro-niches in small basins and plateaus with good agricultural soil. The area has a high degree of biodiversity, usually indicating mature and undisturbed tropical forests (Miller and Miller 1994: 15). It has two well-differentiated vegetation sectors: pine forests and tropical rainforest. Fields of corozo palms (*Orbignya cohune*) are also common, and may be part of the region's original vegetation. The karstic nature of this landscape is appropriate for the formation of sinks (*resumideros* or *siguanes*) and caves, as a consequence of soil, bedrock, and water. Lagoons (bajos or *ponors*) form in some areas where these sinks do not have enough water flow. Residual limestone hills or domes also emerge through the alluvial plains.

The Guatemalan sector of the Maya Mountains is subdivided into four areas: the San Luis Mountains, the Dolores-Poptun Plateau, the eastern high mountains, and the northern Yaltutu sierra. Although all four areas have been surveyed, only the Dolores Plateau and high mountain areas have relevant Terminal Classic components for discussion here.

The Wet Savanna Subregion

To the north, humid savannas occur in the extensive valleys of the region's rivers, along with other drier zones (Figure 10.1). Many climatic, edaphic, and floristic features must be considered in defining savannas (Bartlett 1956; Cole 1986; Furley 1992; Hammond 1980; Harris 1980; Hopkins 1992; Laporte 1996; Lundell 1937; Snow 1988; Stevens 1964). Although different types of tropical savannas can be defined, they share structural and functional characteristics that allow them to survive seasonal droughts, while their vegetation is favored by a high degree of light intensity, temperature, and evaporation.

The term "wet savanna" identifies certain conditions of precipitation (>1000 millimeters), water table, and soil texture (more clay than sand). Wet savannas in southeastern Petén are mixed tropical forest zones and fluvial valleys with permanent rivers (Mopan, Salsipuedes, and Chiquibul to the east and San Juan to the west). Here I do not consider the Chiquibul and lower Mopan Valleys, both surveyed in the 1998 and 1999 seasons of the Atlas Arqueológico project. A good part of the settlement is already known, with large centers like Naranjo, Caracol, and Xunantunich.

Another wet savanna area in southeastern Petén lies in the municipio of Santa Ana. It is not associated with the fluvial valleys mentioned above and lacks surface water. Edaphically, the area responds to a drier climatic pattern than other wet savannas, with fewer and smaller islands of tropical forest. Despite previous indications of low settlement potential in this zone (D. Rice and P. Rice 1979; P. Rice and D. Rice 1979), recent surveys indicate more complex occupation.

Productive Resources

A wide variety of raw materials rare in other central lowland zones are found in the mountain area. The area itself consists of a block of metamorphic sediments with volcanic intrusions. Rocks include granite, sandstone, and quartzite, as well as schist and slate (Bateson 1972; Hall and Bateson 1972; Healy et al. 1995). In Belize, several resources have been documented: porphyritic andesite, diorite, porphyry, and conglomerate cemented by silica, materials used for making grinding stones and identified in samples from Papayal and Ruina Martín in Belize (Dunham 1996: 329) and Uaxactun and Seibal in Petén (Shipley and Graham 1987). Massive beds of hematite, pyrite, goethite, limonite, and manganese oxide in the granite intrusions were used for making red, orange, and yellow pigments (Bullard 1963; Dunham 1996; E. Graham 1987a; Ower 1928). Furthermore, high quality clays for ceramic production have been found in many caves or in surface contexts, resulting from the erosion of volcanic materials.

Similarly, the pine forests and tropical forests of the Maya Mountains offer varied botanical and zoological resources (Dunham and Prufer 1998), because the annual rainfall is higher than in any other part in the region and the temperature is more moderate. Resources obtained from the pine forests include resins and *ocote* for illumination. Moreover, the soils in the mountains allowed production of corn and beans, just as today (Laporte 1993), as well cacao cultivation.

The location of some sites is ideal for exploitation and exchange of resources, that is, maximizing the access to mineral and biotic resources, permanent water, dry and plain terrain, and soils for agriculture (Dunham and Prufer 1998). Networks of exploitation and exchange existed along the rivers. Such exchange could have been internal and short range, and helped to establish more distant contacts. This territory's location also had economic importance for regional trade routes that crossed the central lowlands (Lee and Navarrete 1978). Some centers are located in sectors where the long-distance routes must have passed, as suggested by the preference for the same route in the Colonial period and today. Routes through the mountains were favored in order to avoid the lower zones, where rivers and flooded areas are larger. The mountain routes allow an east-west passage, linking the Caribbean with the Usumacinta system, as well as north-south movement, favoring communication between the lowlands and highlands.

PREDOMINANT POLITICAL FORMATIONS IN SOUTHEASTERN PETÉN

In the territory covered in this analysis, twenty-six Late Classic polities have been determined as contemporaneous (Figure 10.2; Laporte 1996, 1998). All of them have an analogous structure and similar size, averaging sixty-six square kilometers in area, and include between one and eight sites. This situation contrasts with the generalized concept of major polities, which has been used mostly for the lowlands and especially northern Petén. Therefore, it is clear that we are dealing with diverse political zones and not all central lowland sectors had a similar organization, being different in vital structural aspects: population level, subsistence basis, extent, degree of urbanization, and political decentralization (Houston, 1987a; Leventhal 1992a). Thus, it is evident that various levels of cohesion and development coexisted in Maya polities.

A specific type of political organization predominated in southeastern Petén, based in polities of reduced scale, whose spheres of influence intersected and were superimposed. The variables for determining this peculiar political formation have been previously presented (Ball 1993a; Culbert 1992; Dunham et al. 1989; Hodges 1987; Laporte 1996; Montmollin 1989, 1995; Smith 1976a) as segmentary entities in one extreme and as unitary states in the other, designated according to the degree to which the territorial units are related to a main core. These different forms of political organization are not mutually exclusive and can be superimposed throughout the Maya area. They did not differ culturally, only in political integration.

In the type of political organization with multiple centers, each had equal political and economic access to resources. They also belonged to a regional organization where interaction was fundamental and did not depend on specific control by any of the centers. The sociopolitical processes that created limits

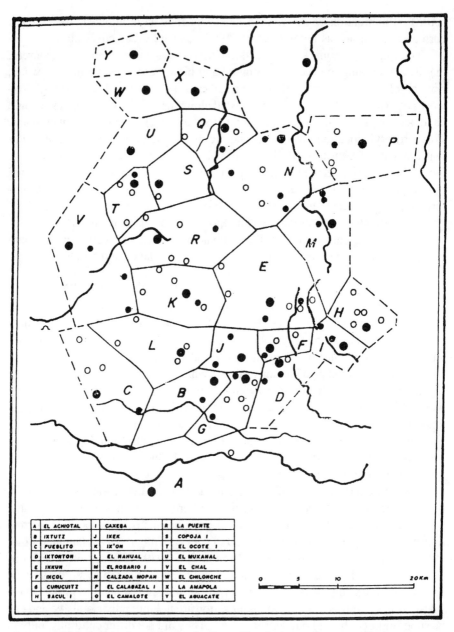

A	EL ACHIOTAL	I	CAXEBA	R	LA PUENTE
B	IXTUTZ	J	IXEK	S	COPOJA I
C	PUEBLITO	K	IX'ON	T	EL OCOTE I
D	IXTONTON	L	EL NAHUAL	U	EL MUXANAL
E	IXKUN	M	EL ROSARIO I	V	EL CHAL
F	IXCOL	N	CALZADA MOPAN	W	EL CHILONCHE
G	CURUCUITZ	O	EL CAMALOTE	X	LA AMAPOLA
H	SACUL I	P	EL CALABAZAL I	Y	EL AGUACATE

0   5   10   20 Km

10.2 *Political entities in the Late Classic in southeastern Petén.*

between coexisting polities were complex, overlapping, and changed frequently. Prehispanic settlement in southeastern Petén corresponds to this type of sociopolitical organization.

Under the unitary state perspective, if a major polity in another lowland sector dominated the smaller polities in southeastern Petén, it must have been limited to economic control, given that the political system was not highly integrated. Furthermore, it is not possible to determine what site could have maintained control over the southeastern Petén region and its productive benefits. It could have been one single state through time or a changing situation depending on expansionist actions by other states. However, because of its geographic location, this region could have been controlled by centers in northeastern Petén and Belize such as Tikal, Yaxha, Naranjo, Xunantunich, and Caracol.

Nevertheless, there are other alternatives: one is that not all polities in southeastern Petén were dominated or allied with only one major center; another is that the wet savanna and mountain zones did not have the same political affiliations. Whatever the real situation, the cultural unity of southeastern Petén polities is evident in multiple ways: 1) the settlement pattern is similar among the savanna and mountain centers, with predominance of the Public Ritual Complex as the core in each one; 2) the distance between each center, and the area of control in each one, is constant when sharing a clear political tradition; 3) there are no differences in the production and use of materials among these centers, with shared ceramic sequences, lithic artifact classification, and aspects of funerary tradition; 4) the scarce historical data known from monuments in the region only record events that occurred between savanna and mountain centers; 5) none of the texts in the region mention any of the major states of northern Petén or Belize, with the exception of a stela from Ixtutz, which has a reference to Dos Pilas, a Pasión River center (Laporte and Escobedo 1992).

One trait used to define main centers in the southeastern Petén surveys is a predominant architectonic compound known as the Public Ritual Complex (Cohodas 1985; Laporte and Morales 1994). Structurally and functionally, these complexes have two elements: a west pyramid and an east platform. This composition recalls the diagnostic characteristics of the assemblages known as the Group E Complex (Chase 1985a; Chase and Chase 1995; Rathje et al. 1978; Ruppert 1940), observatories (Aveni and Hartung 1989), and Commemorative Astronomic Complex (Fialko 1988).

In the absence of any explicit indication of political hierarchy in a region, as in the southeastern Petén case, the distribution of contemporary sites must be analyzed and a landscape division created. This was done using the Gravity Model and a version of the Thiessen Polygon technique (Ball and Taschek 1991; Cherry 1987; Christaller 1972; García 1992; Hodder and Orton 1990; Hodges 1987), in that the spatial limits are determined according to the relative weight of the centers. For establishing such relative weights, several variables were used, integrating information in a scale of values for public plazas, functionality, monuments, ter-racing, residential units, useful areas, and other areas with sociopolitical impor-tance (Ashmore et al. 1987; Dunning and Kowalski 1994; Laporte 1996).

Centers with unitary structure are located in a west-northwest arc formed by various sites associated with the upper San Juan Valley: San Luis Pueblito, El Chal, and El Muxanal (Figure 10.1). To the north, the Salsipuedes Valley is delin-eated where centers of nucleated nature predominate, like El Chilonche, La Amapola, Ucanal, La Blanca, Holtun, and San Clemente (Mayer 1993, 1994a, 1994b; Quintana 1996). The southern limit of this political tradition is clearly delimited with an irregular and unpopulated geographic zone of the Maya Moun-tains that begins in the Poptun zone. Southernmost, only poorly defined settle-ments are found, which do not follow the pattern noted elsewhere in southeastern Petén. To the east, this segmentary phenomenon is bounded by Caracol in the mountain sector of Belize, which suggests a polity that became unitary after a long nucleation process (Chase and Chase 1996b: 68).

In the upper Mopan Valley, in the northern extreme of the Dolores-Poptun Plateau, clearly hierarchized sites created four polities (Figure 10.2): Ixtonton to the east (four sites), Ixcol in the center (four sites), Curucuitz to the west (six sites), and Ixkun to the north (eight sites). Detailed studies of this archaeological area are found in previous studies: Ixtonton (Laporte 1994), Ixcol (Laporte et al. 1995), Curucuitz (Laporte and Alvarado 1997), and Ixkun (Laporte et al. 1994).

The Sacul and Xaan sub-valleys in the eastern high mountains belong to the upper Mopan drainage system. Sacul shows a more broken landscape, with el-evations that reach 650 meters above sea level. In the survey carried out in the plains and hills that surround the Sacul Valley, six archaeological centers were identified (Figure 10.2; Laporte and Ramos 1998), which correspond to only one polity. On the other hand, the Xaan River is located in the central portion between the Mopan and Sacul Valleys. Three archaeological centers are associated with this valley: Canahui, Xaan Arriba, and Caxeba (Suasnávar 1995), the latter being the polity core in the Late Classic.

The middle Mopan Valley corresponds to the wet savanna geographical area. Research permitted the identification of four specific polities (Figure 10.2): 1) El Rosario in the southern extreme, consisting of five sites; 2) Calzada Mopan in the intermediate section and the west bank of the river, with eight sites; 3) El Calabazal in the same sector, but on the east bank, with five sites; and 4) Ucanal in the northern limit of this valley, consisting of only the main center. Other studies have covered this zone too (Laporte, Gómez, and Corzo 1999).

Five polities have been defined in the Salsipuedes sub-valley sector: El Chilonche, La Amapola, El Aguacate, Los Lagartos, and El Camalote (Figure 10.2). In addi-tion, it has been determined that the first four fit the unitary polity model and only El Camalote is clearly of segmentary nature, composed of four sites (Mejía et al. 1998; Samayoa 1996).

The upper San Juan Valley, due to its large size, can be divided into four sections, all of them with evident Late Classic occupation. For the present, especially for comparison with the middle Mopan Valley, only two sections will be described (Figure 10.2): 1) the northern zone, with two polities: El Ocote (consisting of five sites) and El Muxanal, a unitary center (Morales 1997); and 2) the El Chal area in the eastern valley (Morales and Laporte 1995), with the polity of El Chal, formed by five sites, including the major Preclassic settlement of El Retiro.

Evidence of Terminal Classic occupation in the Mopan Valley is relatively abundant, though the data have not yet been processed at the same analytic level. Hence, this discussion has been reduced to four categories: 1) the changes in construction manifested in monumental architecture; 2) the general use of ceramic materials according to surface contexts, midden concentrations, funerary offerings, and other ritual actions; 3) historic events recorded in monuments in the region; and 4) changes in political organization in a nucleation process absent in Late Classic polities.

TERMINAL CLASSIC ARCHITECTURE

Given that the intensity of research in each site has not been the same, the architectonic sample presents an evident bias, and Terminal Classic architectural data will be presented only from the sites of Ixtonton, Curucuitz, Sacul, El Chilonche, and El Chal. Other excavated sites that still do not have a clear Terminal Classic architectonic sample include Ixkun, Ixtutz, Grano de Oro, Ixek, Yaltutu, and Xaan Arriba (Figure 10.1). The remaining centers have been only tested or the excavations have been focused only on Public Ritual Complexes, and others are still in excavation processes, especially Calzada Mopan.

Ixtonton in the Upper Mopan Valley

After a long occupation beginning in the Late Preclassic, new constructions and modifications of earlier buildings occurred at Ixtonton during the last part of the Late Classic, probably around the end of the eighth century A.D. (Laporte 1994). Afterward, new forms appeared and new floor levels in the plaza area indicate maintenance and alterations. These Terminal Classic evidences are strong in the central area and in residential units as well. In the latter, these frequently include the addition of basal features to the original plan and burials.

At the end of the Late Classic, the East Temple was built in the East Platform of the Public Ritual Complex, the most complex building at the site, integrating two levels (Figure 10.3). Other important features are the masonry vault in the upper room and a carved stela—now exfoliated—that was part of the precinct upper wall. At the same time, small lateral temples were built on the same foundation, probably with corbelled vaults, this being the only case of this building type known in southeastern Petén. Although these buildings do not seem to have been altered in the Terminal Classic, the abundance of ceramic material in the room

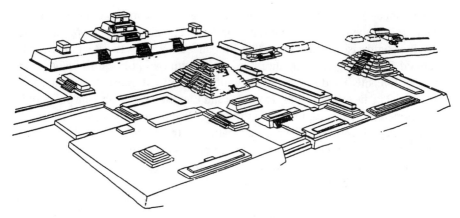

10.3 Ixtonton, East and West Plazas at the end of the Late Classic.

interior may indicate continuous use and ritual activities reaching into the Postclassic. The West Pyramid, a complementary structure of this complex, had multiple modifications and activities, including a possible residential function, due to the high number of ceramic material and human bone remains burned or scattered.

The Northwest Plaza is located in this sector of the central area, consisting of a group of three low platforms that adjoin the west structure of Ballcourt 1 (Figure 10.3). This group has unique residential characteristics for the central area, suggesting an elite nucleus. Close to the high *taludes* that elevate the plaza, a Terminal Classic midden was found, with abundant figurine fragments, *rodelas* and other worked potsherds, chert, obsidian and slate tools, granite grinding stones, ornaments and artifacts made from shell, snails and bone, serpentine beads, and so forth. Some Postclassic materials were recovered in the midden's upper levels, indicating a continuous, though less intensive, occupation in this residential area.

Another component of Ixtonton's central area is the West Plaza. Its architectonic scheme during the Late Classic includes the South Pyramid, which has six frontal steps decorated with masks made with stone core and covered with stucco. They represent an anthropomorphic water deity figure (Figure 10.4) with large earflares, square eyes, headdress, pronounced nose, and an open mouth with a square enlargement. Remains of stucco indicate that they were painted in green, red, black, and yellow. During the Terminal Classic the South Pyramid was decorated with new masks that show a mosaic technique not seen before. These masks are built with small carved blocks in low relief, representing earflares, beads, and parts of the teeth and mouth, all part of an anthropomorphic figure (see Figure 10.4 for a partial reconstruction).

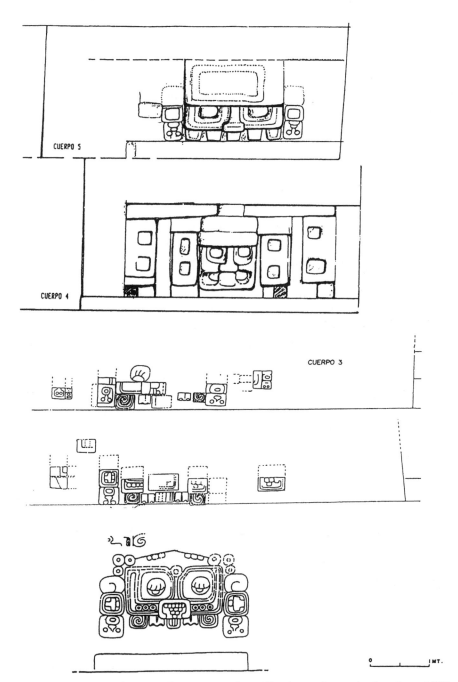

10.4 Ixtonton West Plaza, south structure: Late Classic masks on the fourth and fifth terrace levels; Terminal Classic masks on the second and third terrace levels; reconstruction of a Terminal Classic mask.

These anthropomorphic masks are restricted to the South Pyramid, thus suggesting that this structure had a main role in the site core ritual activities. The stylistic changes shown in the last two construction stages and stone masks are difficult to evaluate given the absence of similar elements in the region. The Late Classic masks resemble the ones built in other central lowland zones, while the Terminal Classic ones have a mosaic style, unusual in the central lowlands. A similar case was recently reported at San Luis Pueblito, west of the Dolores region (Laporte et al. 1997), and Calzada Mopan, thus defining the regional style in masks during this period.

Furthermore, the Ixtonton Acropolis is located on top of a modified hill, and consists of two plazas (Figure 10.5). Plaza A has seven structures, four of them of major size, with their location and function already formalized in the Late Classic. During the Terminal Classic, the arrangement of this group was altered in successive stages by modifying structures and constructing new ones. Abundant surface material indicates that some structures were residences, although it is evident that the group maintained an administrative function. Some architectonic features are of interest for the Terminal Classic. For example, the front and back corners in the North Structure are rounded, raised by drum quarters. A similar application was observed in one structure at Ixtonton Group 64, associated with the West causeway. Another case has been reported from the Calzada Mopan Acropolis.

The Late Classic phase corresponds to the construction of the two initial stages in the South Structure, when three structures were built on top of the high basement that can be reached through separated stairways. The east and west lateral temples are of similar form, and separated from the central temple by an alley, with a difference in level; each has only one chamber. There are remains of the cornices, decorated with small carved blocks.

The final plaster coat in the three temples clearly indicates a new construction stage during the Terminal Classic. The new structure had only one long chamber; no access or other details are known. This building caused the partial destruction of walls and vaults of the previous temples. Some undefined steps seem to represent the stairway that reached the new chamber. Abundant carved stones came from the excavations, probably as part of earflares and beads of an anthropomorphic figure that could correspond to a frieze from this last epoch. The presence of mosaic sculpture during the Terminal Classic is confirmed by similarity with the South Pyramid masks in the West Plaza last stage.

Another important element was found in the West Structure. Carved stone elements were found in the structure walls, notably some kind of prominent or "flowery" noses (Figure 10.6), a feature that recalls the styles in the northern Maya area.

Plaza B is a group of four structures (two palace-type) located in the Acropolis' lower basal platform (Figure 10.5). The West Structure has a rectangular

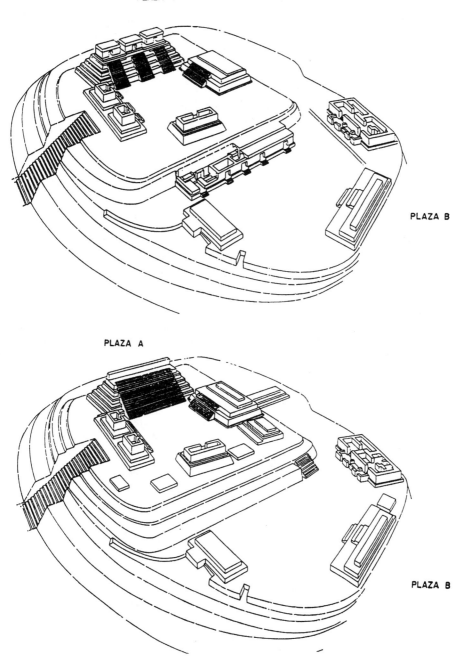

PLAZA A

PLAZA B

PLAZA A

PLAZA B

10.5 Ixtonton Acropolis: architectural development in the Late and Terminal Classic.

shape, with four vaulted rooms arranged in two sectors and joined by an alley. Modifications include construction of new rooms, separation and reduction of spaces, and blocking accesses. A good part of the cornice was destroyed, given that pieces of stucco sculpture were found in the construction fill, including a tenoned anthropomorphic head.

The South Structure has a complex plan, with three frontal rooms. The central one allows passage to a second row of rooms, from which one enters the lateral ones. A modification added three benches. During the Terminal Classic, the foundation and rooms were covered by sloping walls around the limestone hill of Plaza A, in order to hide the previous palace.

If Plaza B had a residential function, it was of an elite nature. Nevertheless, the Terminal Classic occupation seemed to be less exclusive, with more people living in the ancient precincts. Even during the Postclassic, these structures continued to be occupied, with some indications of ceremonial activity, such as fragments of carved monuments brought from the site center ceremonial plazas. Some activity areas with chert debitage were found too. To conclude, life in the ruins of ancient buildings was evidenced at various central sectors of Ixtonton.

Curucuitz in the Upper Mopan Valley

After long settlement beginning in the Middle Preclassic, Curucuitz became a polity core in the Dolores-Poptun Plateau during the Late Classic, lying near other polities like Ixtonton to the east, Ixtutz to the west, and Ixek to the northwest (Figure 10.2; Laporte and Alvarado 1997). Its architectonic development created a complex plan consisting of various central groups and abundant residential ones.

Unlike Ixtonton, where after a long Late Classic development only a few minor units were built in the central precincts, and others were modified in the Terminal Classic, at Curucuitz a population decline is noted, especially in the periphery area. Given the persistence of Ixtonton as a Terminal Classic core in the Dolores zone, Curucuitz must have been dependent on this latter. Nonetheless, Curucuitz maintained a stable population into the Postclassic period. Indeed, a settlement that depended on Curucuitz during the Late Classic—Ixcoxol 2—represents the best Postclassic sample for the Dolores-Poptun Plateau. At that point, after a fifteen-century trajectory of occupation, Curucuitz was abandoned.

Sacul in the Eastern High Mountains

Although its location differed during the Preclassic, Sacul's Late Classic development represented the core of this polity (Laporte and Ramos 1998). The site core consists of several plazas, two arranged in a Public Ritual Complex and one a monumental acropolis, all dated to the Late Classic. During the Terminal Classic new plaza floors were built, associated with a dense occupation indicated by abundant surface materials, including incense burners. Many structures were altered by covering stairways or adding new elements, including circular basal platforms.

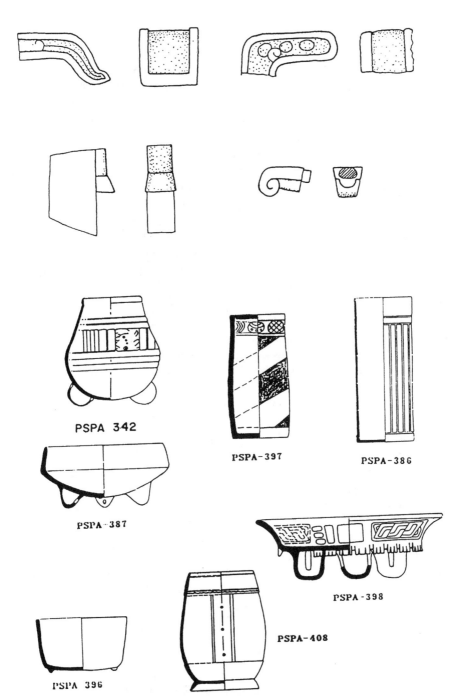

PSPA 342

PSPA-397

PSPA-386

PSPA-387

PSPA-398

PSPA-408

PSPA 396

10.6 Fragments of sculpture from architecture, Plaza A, Acropolis of Ixtonton. Ceramic material from Terminal Classic funerary offerings at Ixtonton.

The Terminal Classic occupation had distinctive ritual elements, too. Plaza A is notable for its Late Classic stone monuments. Stela 10 is one of the latest monuments in Sacul, if not the final one, with a dedicatory date that may correspond to 9.18.0.0.0 10 Ajaw 8 Zek (A.D. 800; Escobedo 1991, 1993). Terminal Classic modification in this plaza area included deposition of a burial inside a large precinct partially carved in bedrock and covered by limestone slabs. The offerings consisted of ten vessels that included bowls, plates, and an incense burner.

The three buildings in Plaza C, built in the Late Classic and continuously modified until the Terminal Classic, are arranged in a clear example of a triadic architectural pattern. During the exploration of the East Structure frontal walls, two plain, circular limestone altars were found, probably moved from elsewhere at the site (Figure 10.7). The importance of this building is due in part to its funerary use in the Terminal Classic. A cist covered with slabs was created under the higher platform, with a dedicatory cache consisting of eleven vessels and an obsidian blade placed above it. The cist contained a youth or adolescent accompanied by a rich offering consisting of an alabaster vase, two ceramic vessels, and varied ornaments that included a spindle whorl, nine rings made of snail, twenty-four ring-like artifacts, mother-of-pearl shell and pyrite beads, and a greenstone pendant. This offering more closely resembles northern Petén patterns than the known burials in the Dolores region, though this situation may be the result of differences in the social status of the individuals excavated, which come mainly from residential areas.

Other ritual activity during the Terminal Classic includes a vessel cache discovered in the North Structure of Plaza E (Laporte and Torres 1987), consisting of several hundred simple plates and various kinds of incense burners. The plates, all very similar, were stowed and tied with some kind of vine, suggesting transport activity and thus reinforcing Sacul's important role in the trade routes through the Maya Mountains. The cache was probably placed by traders.

Although minor, Postclassic occupation was also evident in some structures, though it is difficult to determine its continuity from the Terminal Classic. This occupation is not exclusive to the central plazas, being present in residential areas as well. Ceramics in some middens indicate an occupation related to other zones in the Belize Valley and the southern extreme of the Maya Mountains (Laporte and Quezada 1998). This occupation demonstrates the continuous use of residences and the persistence of ritual and possibly administrative activity in the site core.

El Chilonche in the Salsipuedes River Valley

The Salsipuedes River is the main tributary in the middle Mopan Valley, covering an extensive portion of the wet savannas of northern Dolores (Figure 10.1; Chocón et al. 1999). As one of the most representative settlements, El Chilonche is extensive, with eight plazas forming the central area and forty-four residential

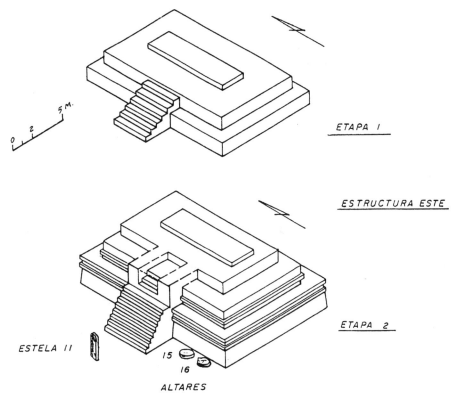

10.7 Sacul Group C, east structure: Phase 1 from the Late Classic and Phase 2 from the Terminal Classic.

groups. The site core consists of an Acropolis and a Public Ritual complex, separated by 1.7 kilometer. This pattern represents a notable change in settlement because, unlike the other southeastern Petén centers, this type of complex seems to have lost its role as the main nucleus of the site. This situation is not unique to El Chilonche, however, being shared by other near centers like El Muxanal and El Chal.

Although Late Preclassic constructions exist in the Public Ritual Complex, most buildings in the central plazas and residential groups date to the Late Classic. The Acropolis consists of six structures located on a high artificial platform, arranged in a closed plaza. The tunnels made by looters in different parts of the North and West Structures left eight chambers uncovered, four still showing remains of paint in the interior walls.

During the Terminal Classic, the shape of the Acropolis was deeply altered by formal changes. The exposed rooms were sealed in order to build a new temple, now destroyed. In addition, a water reservoir or *bukte* was built in a sector of the patio during the Late Classic and covered with stucco in the Terminal Classic. The structures in this period reached their maximum height and the access to the plaza through the South Structure was sealed. Finally, some Postclassic materials were detected only in the Acropolis and other nearby groups, though in a minor scale.

El Chal in the Upper San Juan Valley

Although El Chal does not lie in the Mopan Valley, it was an important site for the entire region and reflects the role of other neighboring centers like El Muxanal, La Puente, Copoja, and so on. Excavations and ceramic materials recovered in El Chal indicate that during the Late and Terminal Classic, its habitants had a strong building program, demonstrated by the construction volume represented in the structures and plaza levelings at the ceremonial center and residential groups (Morales 1995a, 1995b). The ceremonial center is defined by an acropolis and three ceremonial plazas, where the majority of carved monuments were located. Of a total of nineteen registered monuments, however, only five stelae and three altars are carved. The inscriptions, though very eroded, indicate that two monuments bore an Emblem Glyph during the Late Classic (Escobedo 1994a). The monuments have stylistic similarities with monuments from Naranjo, Ucanal, and Sacul, which is not surprising considering the relative proximity of these centers, and that all dates correspond to the eighth century.

During the Terminal Classic, the Northeast Plaza consisted of four structures defining a closed space, accessed from the northeast corner (Figure 10.8). The structures are rectangular stepped platforms, built with well-cut and polished limestone blocks. On the high platform, some remains of rooms with different accesses were noted. Construction activities during the Late Classic included a cornice in the East Structure, decorated with carved stones showing a double trapeze design, though this element may correspond to a second leveling in the plaza area during the Terminal Classic. Abundant middens were found in the patio corners and the structures' rear sides.

Interestingly, the Public Ritual Complex in El Chal is located at a considerable distance northeast of the ceremonial center. This large complex could have been the ceremonial center during the Preclassic, as at El Chilonche, and this pattern could be typical of the major wet savanna sites during the end of the Late Classic.

The area occupied by residential groups in El Chal is extensive, and has been divided into sectors based on distances among the group cores: Central El Chal with twenty-five groups, Arrepentimiento with forty groups, Panorama with nineteen groups, and Municipal with eighteen groups. This distribution may represent different economic activities (Panorama has a chert working area) and chronologies (Municipal is associated with the Public Ritual Complex). Therefore, Central El Chal would be the more representative to define residential aspects for the Terminal Classic.

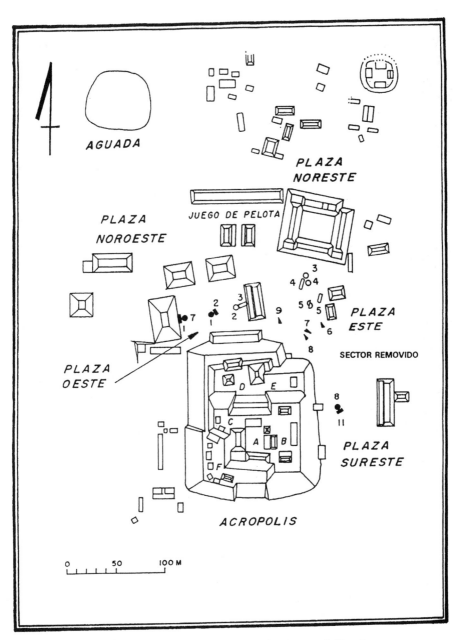

AGUADA

PLAZA
NORESTE

PLAZA
NOROESTE

JUEGO DE PELOTA

PLAZA
ESTE

SECTOR REMOVIDO

PLAZA
OESTE

D E

C

A B

F

PLAZA
SURESTE

ACROPOLIS

0   50   100 M

10.8 El Chal northeast group in the Terminal Classic.

TERMINAL CLASSIC CERAMICS IN THE MOPAN VALLEY

The Terminal Classic ceramic assemblage is the largest of any period in the Dolores region, as evident since the first analysis (Laporte et al. 1993), when the ceramic complexes of southeastern Petén were defined. In a later typological assessment (Laporte 1995), the Terminal Classic still incorporated more than 50 percent of the ceramic material recovered in the investigations of forty sites through 1998. These represent an extensive geographic expanse: the Dolores Plateau, the upper and middle Mopan Valley, the Salsipuedes Valley, the wet savannas related to the San Juan River, some caves, and other areas of the Poxte River and the Yaltutu sierra.

Terminal Classic material consists of 60,523 potsherds, part of a total sample of 135,383 sherds, which does not include the problematic Postclassic. The total is divided as follows:

Period	n	%
Middle Preclassic	1,503	1.1
Late Preclassic	8,959	6.6
Early Classic	5,916	4.4
Late Classic	58,482	43.2
Terminal Classic	60,523	44.7
Total	135,383	100

This sample includes six ceramic wares and eighteen groups that represent the inventory of ceramic artifacts used at that time. Because we are dealing here with a typological sequence that begins in the Late Classic, the changes are more of a quantitative nature, with some diagnostic additions. Some characteristics are extracted when considering ceramic wares, groups, and types, and the level of variety is discussed when needed. Observations pertain to the ceramic sherd collection, and not to the distribution obtained from the movement of complete vessels of ritual and funerary contexts.

Ixmabuy Complex—Terminal Classic
Uaxactun Unslipped Ware   n = 34,402   56.8 percent of the total (Table 10.2)

It is composed of only one ceramic group, Cambio. The majority type is not decorated (75.9 percent of the ware). A slight reduction in the use of decorative techniques exists in relation to the Late Classic, for ornamentation is used: incision, impression, striation, application, modeled, drawn work, coating, and polychromes. The striated decoration was more common than before (7.5 percent of the group), while impression declines precipitously (0.6 percent of the group). Chichicuil Slipped, whether cream or red, continues to be important, with 14.9 percent of the group. The wide distribution of utilitarian types impedes the identification of any production center. Nevertheless, several decorative techniques were focused mainly on the incense burner production (appliqués, mod-

Table 10.2

N = 34,402   56.8% of total

Cambio Group

Type	TC n=	% group	% total	t:v	LC n=	% group
Cambio Sin Engobe	26,114	75.9	43.2	5	24,774	67.6
ND/Inciso	416	1.2	0.7	4	202	0.6
Manteca Impreso	214	0.6	0.4	4	738	2.0
Encanto Estriado	2,584	7.5	4.3	10	1,343	3.7
Miseria Aplicado	172	0.5	0.3	3	1,028	2.8
Pedregal Modelado	163	0.5	0.3	8	2,197	6.0
ND/Calado	25	0.0	0.0	1	0	0.0
Chichicuil Con Baño	5,110	14.9	8.4	6	6,355	17.3
ND/Bicromo	1	0.0	0.0	1	0	0.0

TC = Terminal Classic   LC = Late Classic   t:v = varieties

eling, and drawn work). The censer fragments are ritual wares, and their quantity does not reflect their true importance when compared with the utilitarian material. However, their contextual presence is important for defining the Terminal Classic.

In addition, another ceramic ware was introduced into both Terminal Classic Ixmabuy and Postclassic Mopan complexes (Laporte and Quezada 1998), in order to categorize an easily eroded material with coarse finishing, abundant calcite temper, and thick paste. For this, the Temax Burdo ware was identified, and the Puluacax group previously defined for southern Belize (Hammond 1975) as well. This material was found in surface contexts and, though notably scarce (0.1 percent of the material), is a clear diagnostic. Its distribution is limited to the high mountain centers, especially Sacul, and the sites associated with the Chiquibul Valley across the Belize border. Conspicuously, it also exists at sites at the southern extreme of the Maya Mountains, such as Chinchila in the municipio of San Luis, probably reflecting its proximity to the production area in southern Belize.

Petén Gloss Ware   n=25,740   42.5 percent of the total (Table 10.3)

This ware contains eight ceramic groups formed by different slip colors and other traits. Two other groups are defined by the presence of painted decoration, whether on cream, buff, orange, or red background. Among these groups, only the red-slipped group reaches a high percentage (Tinaja, with 75.8 percent of the ware), as in the Late Classic. A middle range comprises 5 to 7 percent of the glossy material (Infierno, Zacatel-Joyac, and Palmar-Danta). A marked increase occurs in the painted ceramics, especially with cream or buff background (Zacatel-Joyac), which doubles in frequency. Orange and red backgrounds (Palmar-Danta) also increase, though to a lesser degree.

Table 10.3.

		N = 25,740	42.5% of total			
Group	TC n=	% class	% total	types	LC n=	% class
Harina	147	0.5	0.2	2	315	1.4
Azote	380	1.4	0.6	3	380	1.7
Tinaja	19,511	75.8	32.2	12	16,891	77.4
Hondo	73	0.3	0.1	1	—	—
Máquina	908	3.5	1.5	6	1,243	5.7
Infierno	1,345	5.2	2.2	10	1,292	5.9
Remate	4	0.1	0.0	1	—	—
Payaso	66	0.3	0.1	1	—	—
Zacatal-Joyac	1,620	6.3	2.7	7	653	3.0
Palmar-Danta	1,686	6.6	2.8	6	1,043	4.8

TC = Terminal Classic   LC = Late Classic

The remaining monochrome groups are found in lower frequencies. In relation to their presence in the Late Classic, a slight decline occurs with the cream and brown ceramic groups (Harina and Máquina), while the orange and black ones (Azote and Infierno) maintain the same frequency.

Tinaja Group

The distribution of the Tinaja Group in the sample is complex, because it includes thirteen ceramic types with twenty-seven varieties (Table 10.4). The majority type is Tinaja Red (68.6 percent of the group), being the main monochrome component, as it was in the Late Classic. Cameron Incised and Chaquiste Impressed show moderate increase, while Pantano Impressed is similarly represented as previously, though the presence of the sealed designs variety is more diagnostic. The remaining types are poorly represented. Unfortunately, the distribution of Tinaja Red is so extensive that it is impossible to designate production and distribution areas. Furthermore, it is also difficult at present to distinguish the gradual inclusion of calcite or ash temper, which needs to be done in the future.

Nevertheless, the distribution of Cameron, Chaquiste, and Pantano is similar throughout the region. Although it is found in all samples, its prominence in the Ixtonton collection is conspicuous, which supports consideration of that site as a probable ceramic production and distribution center. However, it is possible that other production centers existed, such as El Chal in the wet savannas of northern Dolores, as indicated by the importance of Pantano Impressed.

Although Cameron Incised includes material with abstract designs, plates with incision in the exterior rim are more common, usually in funerary and cave deposit contexts (like Aktun Ak'Ab). Some of these incised plates correspond to the Ceniza–Engobe Rojo (Ash–Red Slip) category (Belize Ceramic Group; Chase

Table 10.4.

		N = 34,402	56.8% of total			
Type	TC n=	% group	% total	t:v	LC n=	% group
Tinaja Rojo	17,678	68.6	29.2	5	15,776	72.3
Cameron Inciso	631	2.5	1.0	2	411	1.9
Tolla Acanalado	0	0	0	1	0	0
Chaquiste Impreso	804	3.1	1.3	4	247	1.1
Pantano Impreso	314	1.2	0.5	3	284	1.3
Chinja Impreso	17	0.1	0.0	1	13	0.1
ND/Estriado	26	0.1	0.1	1	130	0.6
ND/Aplicado	5	0.1	0.0	1	2	0.0
Rosa Punzonado	17	0.1	0.0	1	7	0.1
San Julio Modelado	9	0.1	0.0	1	2	0.0
Portia Gubiado-Inciso	9	0.1	0.0	5	19	0.1
ND/Calado	0	0.0	0.0	1	0	0.0
ND/Bicromo	1	0.0	0.0	1	2	0.0

TC = Terminal Classic   LC = Late Classic   t:v = varieties

1994; Foias 1996; LeCount 1994; López 1989). Its apparent functional restriction defines it as a diagnostic for Terminal Classic activities.

The presence of Subín Red, though less common in southeastern Petén, is important for its inter-regional connotation. Given that the difference between Tinaja and Subín is only in form, it is redefined as a Tinaja Red variety (Foias 1996: 479). While it has been reported in some sites, it usually comes from the Ixtonton collection, thus suggesting that it could be introduced from a production zone, possibly along the Pasión River, to this major center. However, its minor presence in the northern Dolores and Santa Ana samples (El Chal, El Chilonche, El Muxanal, Santa Ana-Zamir) may indicate different distribution dynamics.

Infierno Group

This is a large ceramic group formed by ten types and fourteen varieties (Table 10.5). Besides the nondecorated type, which is the major type in the Late and Terminal Classic, vessels decorated with incision (Carmelita) and impression (Ones) show a slight increase in the Terminal Classic, similar to that in the Tinaja Group. Toro Gouged-Incised maintains the same level of frequency, while Carro Modeled, though scarce, becomes a diagnostic.

Infierno Black appears in all collections of the region, making it impossible to determine any specific area of production. Minority types are conspicuously more common in Ixkun and Ixtonton (incised, impressed, and modeled), while Toro Gouged-Incised is exclusive to Sacul. Although it is not possible to suggest production centers, it is clear that the Infierno Group minority types are confined to

Table 10.5.

| | | N = 1345 | 2.2% of total | | | |
Type	TC n=	% group	% total	t:v	LC n=	% group
Infierno Negro	1,030	4.0	1.7	1	1,169	5.4
Carmelita Inciso	160	0.6	0.7	4	64	0.3
Chilar Acanalado	15	0.1	0.1	1	14	0.1
Ones Impreso	76	0.3	0.2	3	26	0.1
Tres Micos Impreso	5	0.1	0.0	1	—	—
ND/Impreso	12	0.1	0.1	1	—	—
Bambonal Plano-Relieve	—	—	—	—	6	0.0
Toro Gubiado-Inciso	12	0.1	0.1	1	13	0.1
Carro Modelado	30	0.1	0.1	1	—	—
ND/Bicromo	5	0.1	0.0	1	—	—
ND/Bicromo-Inciso	0	0.0	0.0	1	—	—

TC = Terminal Classic   LC = Late Classic   t:v = varieties

the upper Mopan River; their sporadic presence in site collections at other zones may indicate commercial activities.

Zacatel-Joyac and Palmar-Danta Groups

The Zacatel and Palmar groups are separated as an alternative to the usual lowland ceramic classification (Forsyth 1989), when considering the different techniques required by the main slip or base. The Zacatel-Joyac group has been integrated according to the bichrome and polychrome samples with a cream, buff, or gray slip background, considering that such colors may be the result of firing control. The group has seven types with twelve varieties (Table 10.6). Furthermore, the combined name for this ceramic group suggests the need to integrate a continuous evolution of its types, from Tepeu 2 toward the Tepeu 3 sphere.

Since the 1995 analysis, Zacatel-Joyac was found to be a significant painted group in Petén Gloss ware in southeastern Petén. Polychrome design was more important than bichrome. Although most types maintain the same frequencies from Late to Terminal Classic, a marked increment in the use of Zacatel Cream and Paixban Buff polychromes is evident, and in Juina Red/Buff bichrome as well.

Distribution of these types indicates a general presence in the various geographic zones, though they are usually more important in the Dolores Plateau sites, especially Ixtonton. It has been considered that this center could participate in the production and distribution control, given the variety of designs and general quality of the Ixtonton samples, and the use of vessels of this group in funerary offerings. However, the presence of Zacatel-Joyac group sherds at sites in the Dolores and Santa Ana wet savannas does not necessarily indicate an Ixtonton provenience.

Table 10.6.

		N = 1620	2.6% of total			
Type	TC n=	% group	% total	t:v	LC n=	% group
Naranjal Rojo/Crema	155	0.6	0.3	2	165	0.8
Chinos Negro/Crema	65	0.3	0.1	1	35	0.2
Zacatal Crema Policromo	630	2.5	1.1	3	199	0.9
Juinas Rojo/Ante	343	1.4	0.6	2	66	0.3
ND/Negro/Ante	43	0.2	0.1	2	—	—
Paixban Ante Policromo	384	1.5	0.6	1	183	0.8
Jato Negro/Gris	0	0	0	1	5	0.1

TC = Terminal Classic   LC = Late Classic   t:v = varieties

Table 10.7.

		N = 1686	2.8% of total			
Type	TC n=	% group	% total	t:v	LC n=	% group
Leona Rojo/Naranja	68	0.3	0.1	2	265	1.2
Chantuori Negro/Naranja	248	1.0	0.4	2	56	0.3
Saxche Naranja Policromo	0	0	0	—	26	0.1
Palmar Naranja Policromo	772	3.0	1.3	2	524	2.4
Yuhactal Negro/Rojo	562	2.2	0.9	1	172	0.1
Batcab Rojo Policromo	39	0.2	0.1	3	—	—
Central Farm Compuesto	0	0	0	1	—	—

TC = Terminal Classic   LC = Late Classic   t:v = varieties

In the case of the Palmar-Danta group, the use of a binomial name responds to the survival of its components until Tepeu 3. Although it was more important than Zacatel-Joyac during the Late Classic, both groups are equal in the Terminal Classic in southeastern Petén, each with a 6 percent increase of the total. In this period Palmar-Danta has six types and eleven varieties (Table 10.7). Polychrome designs over an orange background were important, like the main polychrome style during the Late Classic and even previous stages. Nevertheless, the simplicity of bichrome designs was common too.

Its distribution is very similar to the Zacatel-Joyac group, and seems to be more popular in Ixtonton than the rest of the sites. It was frequently used in burial offerings. However, it was not possible to define a continuity of design and other details, in order to assign its production to this site. Distribution seemed to be assured, at least, in the mountain zone in southeastern Petén. This ceramic group was less common in the sites located in the northern Dolores wet savannas than its upper Mopan counterpart.

Two considerations can be inferred from these painted ceramic groups. On the one hand, their social context differs in central and residential areas of sites, being more common in the latter. This suggests that an economic factor was not the only agent for explanation, and its social value was important (LeCount 1993: 239). On the other hand, Foias (1996: 572) has proposed the existence of an eastern sphere with polychromes on a cream base (central and northeastern Petén and part of Belize) and another western sphere that uses polychromes over orange background (Pasión River region toward Campeche). In southeastern Petén a combined use is observed, especially during the Terminal Classic.

Other Ceramic Classes in the Ixmabuy Complex Inventory

Other ceramic diagnostics appear when defining the Terminal Classic occupation, probably some ceramic classes different from Petén Gloss ware (like Pine Ridge Carbonate, Ceniza–Engobe Rojo (Ash–Red Slip), and other unusual groups related to this category. Therefore, though the distribution of the two groups in Pine Ridge Carbonate ware (or Red and Black Calcite classes according to LeCount [1994]: Dolphin Head [red] and Mount Maloney [black]) is not yet definitive, their affiliation with the Belize River Valley is clear (Gifford 1976). Both have specific slip traits and a distinctive form definition that falls between the tecomate and the open bowl with inflexed rim. This material is commonly associated with the wet savanna sites, the nearest area to the Belize River.

On the other hand, Fine Orange is the best diagnostic for the Terminal Classic. Even when the sample is small (n=234, 0.39 percent of the total), the classificatory diversity is noticeable by its three groups and eleven types (Table 10.8). This analysis considered these groups in a generic way, as has been established in the lowlands, maintaining the material with gray paste as Tres Naciones instead of using Chablekal, given the connotation that this would have with the Pasión River zone (Foias 1996: 703).

In southeastern Petén, Fine Orange ware has a distribution restricted to the polity cores, where these materials must have gone and from where they were redistributed to the other nearby centers. Three distribution centers are defined: Ixtonton in the upper Mopan, Calzada Mopan in the middle Mopan, and El Chal in the San Juan Valley. However, it is difficult to infer from which region this material comes without proper chemical analysis. Probable production areas are the Pasión River (Sabloff 1970), a Belize center, or a more distant zone in the Yucatán peninsula. In the mountain area, this peculiar ceramic class was found in a context that corresponds to residential zones, middens, funerary offerings, and deposits inside caves (Laporte 1994; Rodas and Laporte 1995).

Another diagnostic for the Terminal Classic is the incense burner. Although the presence of effigies stands out for this period, in the Terminal Classic the predominant censer form is a cylinder with wide lateral flanges with profuse appliquéd and incised decoration. The category of ceramic sub-complex was

Table 10.8.

N = 234   0.39% of total

Group	Type	n=	% class	% total
Altar	Altar Naranja	131	56.0	0.2
	Trapiche Inciso	3	1.7	0.0
	Cedro Acanalado	1	0.4	0.0
	Pabellón Moldeado-Tallado	36	15.4	0.1
	Tumba Negro/Naranja	29	12.4	0.1
	ND/Con Baño	4	1.7	0.0
	ND/Engobe Blanco Duro	1	0.4	0.0
Balancan	Provincia Plano-Relieve	2	0.9	0.0
Tres Naciones	Tres Naciones Gris	14	6.0	0.0
	Poite Inciso	9	3.8	0.0
	ND/Modelado-Tallado	3	1.3	0.0

used for their analysis, given the superficial contexts where they were found, and censers have an additional cultural meaning besides the chronological one (A. Chase and D. Chase 1987c: 48; Hermes 1993).

Ceramics in Ritual and Funerary Contexts

A total of sixty burials deposited during the Terminal Classic have been recovered. Because of the nature of the research, most of the burials come from Ixtonton (n=33), from both the central area and the residential zone. The remainder represent the high mountain (Sacul), the San Juan River Valley (La Lucha, El Ocote, El Chal), the Poxte River Valley (Ixtutz), the Salsipuedes River Valley (El Chilonche, Los Lagartos), and the Dolores Plateau itself (Ixcol, Ixkun, Curucuitz, Aktun Ak'Ab). This wide distribution predicts that more exploration in these and other zones will locate more Terminal Classic burials.

Of a total of 138 vessels that form the Terminal Classic collection, the most common context was burials (n=76), followed by caches and architectural offerings (n=30), caves (n=21), and middens (n=11).

In the burials, the following ceramic groups were preferred: Tinaja (n=22), especially the nondecorated and incised types; Zacatel-Joyac (n=17) and Palmar-Danta (n=16), both in their polychrome types; an intermediate range exists with Máquina (n=7) in its nondecorated type. The presence of Altar Group material (n=4) stands out, all coming from Ixtonton burials located in residential groups near the site core, a context similar to that of two samples of the Belize group (Figure 10.6). The remaining groups were minorities: Cambio, Harina, Azote, Hondo, Infierno, and Belize.

In architectural dedication activities, the use of Cambio group material was overwhelming (n=15), especially the nondecorated type, followed by the striated, and in less frequency, nondecorated Tinaja (n=6). Furthermore, in caches related to funerary ritual, the material used was mainly decorated with incising, impressions, or grooving of the Máquina, Infierno, and Zacatel-Joyac groups.

The material deposited inside caves was nondecorated or rim-incised material from the Tinaja group (n=10), but the use of Altar group vessels stands out too, with a similar frequency to the funerary offerings. In a minor way, some specimens from the Cambio, Zacatal-Joyac, Máquina, Payaso, and Belize groups were included. Some of these vessels could be local copies of the Altar group.

Against any expectation, instead of utilitarian types, complete slipped vessels were commonly found in middens: Zacatel-Joyac and Palmar-Danta were the more common ones, followed by Infierno, Máquina, Tinaja, and Harina. However, their inclusion could be of a more casual nature.

Generalizations on the Ceramic Sequence and Production

In sum, Terminal Classic ceramics in southeastern Petén are represented by the Ixmabuy Complex, which belongs to the Tepeu horizon, phase Tepeu 3. This complex represents continuity from the Late Classic, with changes in quantitative aspects, as well the addition of new diagnostic materials that indicate specific interregional relations. The increment in forms also increases, like the piriform vase and the inflexed or incurved tripod plate. Despite its correspondence with Tepeu 3, a considerable degree of variability exists at a regional scale, thus indicating different spheres of interaction and participation in regional exchange (Culbert 1973c; P. Rice 1986): Pasión River mouth, Eznab in northeastern Petén, Romero of Macanche, and Tolojobo at Yaxha. These are joined by Ixmabuy of southeastern Petén.

This phenomenon indicates a separation from the dynamic tie between the southeast and other Petén zones. The changes during the Terminal Classic indicate both greater regionalization and an economic reorganization process that began in the Late Classic and strengthened the rural or peripheral areas, at the expense of the usual economic cores of previous periods (P. Rice 1986: 281; Sharer and Chase 1976: 288). New ceramic modes develop in even more circumscribed areas, although some already established production and exchange networks continue. This situation created an unequal Terminal Classic time span: unlike its short duration in northeastern Petén and the Pasión River area, it maintained a continuous development.

This situation could also be caused by heterogeneous populations. Dunham and Prufer (1998) consider the possibility that the Maya Mountains sustained a complex ethnicity. Its broken topography may have isolated the original habitants, inducing a different identity and the creation of mixed communities. Under this view, the Terminal Classic apogee has been considered as related to a higher demand for Maya Mountains resources and a demographic increase coming from adjacent areas, where powerful centers were declining. However, this position does not explain the extreme Terminal Classic duration in the wet savannas zone, which lacked, at least, the mountains' mineral resources.

At the least, ceramic production could have been restricted to certain centers that, as a result of expansive and nucleating processes, turned out to be entities along the lines of the unitary state model. Although more craft specialization causing more differences between productive zones would be expected as a consequence of this rising complexity and nucleation, the wide margin of similarities shows characteristics of a decentralized system of ceramic producers (Lucero 1992; P. Rice 1989). This system, which seems to contradict the proposed political system, may be the result of access to clay and temper sources. The only evidence of any site specialization is the production of polychrome material with cream background in Ixtonton and some Pantano Impressed ollas from El Chal.

POLITICAL CHANGES DURING THE TERMINAL CLASSIC: EXPANSIONISM OR NUCLEATION

In southeastern Petén, after a long development, the Late Classic shows an area divided into more than twenty-six polities, whose cores promoted the rise of new centers, some as part of their dominions and others as rival polities (Figure 10.2). During the Terminal Classic all the centers were occupied and regional residential concentration is evident, thus indicating complex relations of political and ceremonial conduct, as well as the control of exchange networks.

At the same time, many centers seem to have declined in importance, despite having some occupation, especially in comparison with the high concentrations in Ixtonton, Sacul, Calzada Mopan, Ucanal, El Chal, and El Chilonche. At these latter sites, ritual activity is widespread, as indicated by the presence of incense burners in most buildings and near monuments, as well as intense activity near the structures, given the abundant ceramic and lithic materials recovered. Some sites still erected monuments as a way to continue the ancient practice initiated in the Late Classic. New architecture at Ixtonton and Calzada Mopan is decorated with masks and friezes that show a mosaic technique previously unknown in the zone.

The political processes occurring during the Terminal Classic in the Mopan River region can be presented based on the interaction between the mentioned centers, given their presence in the intra-regional affairs among the different geographic sectors for more than a millennium. For this, the historical records mentioned on monuments of the region will be presented, along with other considerations obtained directly from the settlement.

Historic Aspects of the Late and Terminal Classic

Monuments at sites in the northeastern Maya Mountains have been subject to epigraphic and iconographic analysis in order to obtain information about the inter-relations between the different polities (Escobedo 1991, 1993). These references are grouped in a time span not longer than sixty-four years, from A.D. 761 to 825. On these monuments, local Emblem Glyphs appear (only in Sacul, Ixtutz and Ucanal), as do references to rulers, records of royal visits, alliances, wars, and pilgrimages to sacred places, as in the case of the Naj Tunich caves. However, many monuments were looted before they could be recorded, especially at Ixtonton and Calzada Mopan, thus creating a strong bias toward those sites with inscriptions.

The only Ixtonton monument with inscriptions (Stela 1) indicates that its dedication could have been in A.D. 825 (Escobedo and Laporte 1994). Houston (personal communication, 1990) has indicated stylistic similarities between some monuments from Chichén Itzá and this stela, which is considered the latest in the zone. (Note that the presence of mosaic architectural sculpture at Ixtonton also bespeaks possible affiliations with the northern Maya area.)

The interactions between southeastern Petén centers is summarized in the historic links between Ixkun and Sacul. Ixkun Stela 2 records two wars against Sacul and Ucanal (Escobedo 1993; I. Graham 1980): the first occurred in 9.17.9.0.13 (December 21, A.D. 779) and the second in 9.17.9.7.17 (May 10, A.D. 780). In both cases only the toponyms of the rival sites are presented. Ixkun seems to be victorious in both conflicts given that the inscriptions of both rival sites fail to register any of these events.

In addition, several sites display captives on the monuments, including El Chal, Ixkun, Ucanal, Hatzcab Ceel, Caracol, and Ixtutz. As an example, the altar of Stela 3 at El Chal shows the captives as the main figures, and the captive is the only main figure of Altar 1, while on Stela 4 the main figure rests on the captive (Dillon 1982; Morales 1995a). This could be a new form of recording events in an iconographic way.

As an example of visits and alliances, both Ixkun Stela 1 and Sacul Stela 2 record Sacul ruler Ch'iyel's visit to Rabbit God K of Ixkun in 9.18.0.0.0 (October 11, A.D. 790; Escobedo 1993). This indicates that the earlier rivalry between both centers did not last for more than ten years. Both rulers appear on these two stelae, and it seems that they participated together in a war campaign against an unidentified center—could it be Ixtonton? As former enemies, this indicates the dynamism in the relations among the polities of the region. The wars between Ixkun, Sacul, and Ucanal constitute evidence that the mountain and savanna polities competed against each other at the end of the Late Classic.

Wars and Alliances: The Silent Terminal Classic Winners

At the end of the period when these stone monuments were erected, a fundamental change occurred in the regional political organization. Many centers lost the main role held in the Late Classic, when they were absorbed by other centers promoting an expansionism not seen before. While agglutinating other polities' cores and their derived sites, the segmentary process that earlier characterized them was abandoned, and the unitary concept predominated (Table 10.9). Some examples exemplify this process: 1) the subjugation of the Dolores Plateau polities by Ixtonton; 2) the persistence of Sacul as a high mountain polity; 3) the primary role maintained by El Chal and El Chilonche in the San Juan and Salsipuedes Valleys; 4) the predominant relationship between Ucanal and Calzada Mopan in the middle Mopan Valley.

In the Dolores Plateau during the Terminal Classic, the different polities (Ixkun, Curucuitz, Ixcol, Ixek, and Ixtutz) reduced their dynamism substantially. In contrast, Ixtonton embarked upon frenetic construction activity and massive residential concentration and increase. Ixkun also evidences this process and provides more tangible evidence of it.

Ixkun showed a stable construction process and occupation during the Late Classic, as indicated by the different stages in the central area enlargement, as well as the erection of monuments and increase in residential zones (Laporte et al. 1994). This dynamic includes the rise of secondary centers and the control of an extensive territory. This period of florescence is reached in A.D. 790, at least, as indicated by the dedication of Stela 1. Toward A.D. 800, the last carved monument in Ixkun, Stela 5, was erected, and the ruler Rabbit God K contemplated new construction. The labor force in his service piled stones to build new structures in the central plazas, including the acropolis; however, these remained unfinished when the parameters for the exterior sections were not set.

What could cause this? A circumstantial option might be the sudden disappearance of the ruler and abandonment of the site, according to the collapse model of the northeastern Petén centers. Nevertheless, the activity that continued in the residential sectors during the Terminal Classic indicates that some other important locality attracted and relocated the labor force. Besides Ixkun's traditional rival, Sacul, the only polity that had a continuous development during the Terminal Classic was Ixtonton, the major center of the upper Mopan River, located only 7.5 kilometers south of Ixkun. It appears that Ixkun's power was eclipsed and only a few people resided and produced in the ancient center, now dependent on Ixtonton. The other sites in the Dolores Plateau, even closer to the new and sole polity center, experienced the same end.

The fate of Sacul is distinct from that of Ixkun. What sites might have been absorbed by Sacul in the nucleation process occurring in the Terminal Classic? Undoubtedly, they were the nearest polities, like Caxeba in the Xaan River and El Mozote in the upper Chiquibul Valley, as indicated by their apparent lack of occupation in this period. During the Late Classic, Sacul participated in both regional exchange networks and a local ceramic production system; during the Terminal Classic the use of pastes with local characteristics increased. Utilitarian potsherds also reflect relations with the Maya Mountains to the south, as indicated by the Puluacax and Remate ceramic groups (Hammond 1975), and less related to other zones, as suggested by the scarcity of Fine Orange materials. The latter may indicate a separation from Ixtonton, if it is assumed that this site was the distributor of such exotic materials, then an isolationist attitude resulted from the rivalry

Table 10.9. Río Mopán region entities in the Terminal Classic and their Late Classic predecessors.

Site #	Site Name	Polity	Rank Size		Site #	Site Name	Polity	Rank Size
1	El Achiotal	El Achiotal	1		44	Sabaneta	Ix'On	3
2	Puente Machaquila	El Achiotal	3		45	La Union 2	Ix'On	3
3	Ixtutuz	Ixtutuz	1		46	Santa Rosita, 3	Ix'On	3
4	Poxte 2	Ixtutuz	2		47	El Nahual *	Pueblito	1
5	San Luis Pueblito	Pueblito	1		48	Santa Rosita, 4	Ix'On	3
6	Machaca 2	Pueblito	3		49	San Valentin Norte	Pueblito	3
7	Ixtonton	Ixtonton	1		50	Rio Grande	Pueblito	3
8	Moquena	Ixtonton	2		51	Santa Rosita, 2	Pueblito	3
9	Ixac	Ixtonton	2		52	El Rosario I	El Rosario	1
10	Mopan 2-Oeste	Ixtonton	3		53	El Rosario 4	El Rosario	2
11	Ixkun	Ixkun	1		54	El Rosario 2	El Rosario	2
12	Mopan 3-Este	Ixkun	2		55	El Rosario 3	El Rosario	2
13	El Tzic	Ixkun	2		56	Calzada Mopan	Calzada Mopan	1
14	Mopan 3-Sureste	Ixkun	3					
15	Mopan 3-Oeste	Ixkun	3		57	Agua, Blanca	Calzada Mopan	2
16	Nacimiento, Moquena	Ixkun	3		58	La Trinidad	Calzada Mopan	2
17	La Jutera	Ixkun	3		59	La Gloria 1	Calzada Mopan	2
18	Xaan Abajo	Ixkun	3					
19	Ixcol	Ixcol	1		60	El Limón	Calzada Mopan	2
20	Sukche	Ixcol	2					
21	Uitzil'Ox	Ixcol	3		61	Miguelón	Calzada Mopan	3
22	Ixcheu	Ixcol	3					
23	Curucuitz	Curucuitz	1		62	Las Delicias	Calzada Mopan	3
24	Poxte I	Curucuitz	2					
25	Tesik	Curucuitz	2		63	El Cabro	Calzada Mopan	3
26	Ixcoxol I	Curucuitz	3					
27	Ixcoxol 2	Curucuitz	3		64	El Calabazal 1	El Calabazal	1
28	Ixcoxol 3	Curucuitz	3		65	El Calabazal 2	El Calabazal	2
28A	Nocsos	Curucuitz	3		66	El Bombillo 1	El Calabazal	2
29	Sacul 1	Sacul	1		67	El Calabazal 3	El Calabazal	3
30	Sacul 4	Sacul	3		68	El Bombillo 2	El Calabazal	3
31	Sacul 3	Sacul	3		69	El Camalote	El Camalote	1
32	Sacul 2	Sacul	3		70	La Esperanza	El Camalote	2
33	Limones	Sacul	3		71	La Gloria 2	El Camalote	3
34	El Jutalito	Sacul	3		72	Canija	El Camalote	3
35	Caxeba	Caxeba	1		73	La Puente	La Puente	1
36	Xaan Arriba	Caxeba	2		74	Santo Domingo	La Puente	2
37	Canahui	Caxeba	2		75	Santo Toribio I	La Puente	3
38	Ixek	Ixek	1		76	Santa Cruz 2	La Puente	3
39	El Chapayal	Ixek			77	Santo Toribio 2	La Puente	3
40	Yaltutu	Ixek	2		78	Santa Cruz 1	La Puente	3
41	Ix'On	Ix'On	1		79	Copoja 1	Copoja	1
42	La Union 1	Ix'On	2		80	Copoja 2	Copoja	3
43	Ixjuju	Ix'On	3					

continued on next page

Site #	Site Name	Polity	Rank Size
81	El Ocote 1	El Ocote	1
82	El Ocote 4	El Ocote	
83	El Ocote 3	El Ocote	
84	El Ocote 2	El Ocote	3
85	San Miguel	El Ocote	3
86	El Muxanal	El Muxanal	I
87	El Chal	El Chal	1
88	El Quetzal	El Chal	2
89	Santa Rosita, I	Ix'On	2
89A	Colpetén	El Chal	2
90	El Chilonche	El Chilonche	
91	La Amapola	La Amapola	
92	El Aguacate	El Aguacate	
93	Los Lagartos	Los Lagartos	
94	Ucanal	Ucanal	
95	Monte Rico		
96	El Edén 1	El Tigrillo	
97	Nuevas Delicias 1		
98	Nuevas Delicias 2		
99	Nobel		3
100	Canchacan		
101	Ixbobo		
102	Xutilha		1
103	El Tigrillo	El Tigrillo	1
104	La Blanca		
105	El Chilar 2		
106	El Corozal		
107	Cueva San Miguel		
108	Chinchila		
109	Cansis		
110	Pusila Arriba		
111	Nuevas Delicias 3	Pueblito	
112	El Edén 2	El Edén	1
113	La Lucha	Pueblito	3
114	El Charcalito	El Tigrillo	3
115	Las Flores *	El Tigrillo	1
116	La Pimienta		
117	Poptun		
118	Santa Cruz		
119	Buen Retiro *		1
120	Bejucal		
121	El Mozote		1

Site #	Site Name	Polity	Rank Size
122	Itzpone **		
123	Sajalal/El Tambo		
124	El Cartucho		
125	Grano de Oro		
126	Chiquibul 1		2
127	El Pedregal 1		
128	El Pedregal 2		
129	El Pedregal 3		
130	El Pedregal 4		
131	Zamir		
132	El Rosario 5		
133	El Llanto		
134	El Muerto		
135	El Triunfo		
136	Cueva El Convento		
137	Cueva Las Brisas		
138	Sacul 5		
139	Las Flores Chiquibul		
140	Maringa 1		
141	Maringa 2		
142	La Vertiente		
143	La Rejoya		
144	La Cebada		
145	El Pital		3
146	El Naranjal		1
147	Chiquibul 2		2
148	Palestina		2
149	El Mamey		1
150	Jinaya		
151	La Güajra		
152	La Pepesca		3
153	Los Encuentros		3
154	La Providencia		1
155	Yok'ol Wits		1
156	El Camalote/Melchor		1
157	Buenos Aires		1
158	La Pacayera		
159	El Bucute		
160	El Juleque		
161	La Gloria-Sacul		
162	La Ponderosa		
163	Dos Hermanas		

* Preclassic site
** Historical site

that lasted from the Late Classic conflicts. In the Postclassic, Sacul again participated in the regional exchange networks. The cosmopolitan nature of Sacul defines it as a vital center that survived the decline of its old rivals and allies in the northwestern Maya Mountains.

The primary role maintained by El Chal in the San Juan River Valley is clear from the renewal of the massive structures in the central section of the site and the erection of monuments accompanying those of the Late Classic. With the nucleation process taken by El Chal, many sites were eclipsed, as in the case of the El Tigrillo and El Edén polities to the west and El Ocote, Copoja, and La Puente to the southeast. The later presence of Postclassic populations is evident by the presence of dated materials.

Furthermore, the same nucleation process occurs in the Salsipuedes River Valley, surrounding the massive center of El Chilonche, through new construction stages that demonstrate its predominant role in political affairs during the Terminal Classic and the transition to the Postclassic. Several old polities grouped with El Chilonche, and only some small Terminal Classic populations were left in Los Lagartos, La Amapola, El Camalote, and El Muxanal.

In the middle Mopan River Valley, the Terminal Classic situation is difficult to discern, due to the presence of two neighboring major centers located on the west bank of the Mopan River: Ucanal and Calzada Mopan. Both survived until the Postclassic. It is clear that they must have attracted a dynamic population that established different polities associated with the Mopan and Chiquibul Rivers: El Rosario, El Calabazal, El Triunfo, and El Naranjal, among others. The Terminal Classic and Postclassic populations continued to occupy minor areas of those settlements, though political and economic power was concentrated in the river-plain centers.

Hence, the dilemma is to determine the kind of relationship that existed between Ucanal and Calzada Mopan, given that no information that may allow their comparison is available. On the one hand, the important monuments of Ucanal put the site in a central lowland cosmopolitan scene, although it has limited settlement and its role as a polity core is poorly defined (Corzo et al. 1998). At the same time, Calzada Mopan has more than 400 residential groups, a formal central zone with a Public Ritual Complex, a bigger acropolis, and four ballcourts. Terminal Classic activities were declining, at least in the Acropolis zone. However, it does not have monuments that would illuminate its role in Late Classic historic events, and it could have caused the true eclipse of Ucanal instead of another more distant rival, turning into some kind of silent fifth column. This anonymous role is reminiscent of what has been said for the mountainous area between Ixtonton and Ixkun.

What was Ucanal's main role? The dependency on inscriptions for explaining Ucanal's political position has been unfavorable. Besides references at Sacul, Ixkun, and El Chal, other explicit ones come from Naranjo and Caracol, with whom the contacts were unfriendly. Ucanal first conducted a military campaign against Naranjo between A.D. 693 and 695 and later in 800 with Caracol. Ucanal was defeated in both and it is assumed that the site was subjugated by its rivals (I. Graham 1980; Grube 1994a: 86; Houston 1983: 33; Schele and Freidel 1990: 186–195). The result of this interpretation is that, instead of situating Ucanal as a center of confluence and relations, it is reduced to a weak and unfortunate center in Maya history, only an object of fights and disputes, and not capable of recovering. This image does not fit with the structural complexity of Ucanal and its long evolutionary process, and the continuing changes in alliances, as indicated between Sacul and Ixkun, reflect its short time span as a subjugate.

Besides the role of Ucanal in a turbulent Classic period, its cosmopolitan aspect stands out when considering that a new motif seems to be introduced after A.D. 830 in Terminal Classic iconography: celestial figures represented in stelae. Ucanal Stela 4, dated around A.D. 849, shows one of these figures, carrying an atlatl and darts (Chase 1985b: 111). This motif is also observed in Jimbal and Ixlu, and possibly in Naranjo, Flores, and Seibal.

Based on these distinctive traits, especially Stela 4, Thompson (1975) argued that, along with Seibal, Ucanal was one of two Putun outposts in the Terminal Classic. However, the Stela 4 iconography suggests rather that Ucanal responded to influences coming from the peninsula's northern area (Chase 1985b: 111), forces that could penetrate Petén from the Belize Valley. This possibility is reinforced by the presence of sculptural elements associated with building construction in Ixtonton and, coincidentally, in Ucanal's powerful neighbor, Calzada Mopan. These included masks built with mosaic technique, and sculptures and flowery noses that must have belonged to facades and corners, some in the form of nested quarter drums. The same may be indicated by the abundance of Fine Orange ware recovered from Ixtonton and Calzada Mopan.

What does the introduction of traits from a remote region like the northern Maya area mean in southeastern Petén? When considering the population continuity in the Mopan River Valley centers since the Late Classic, it is clear that commercial reorganization occurred, based on the increase of intermediaries and merchants linked to the northern Maya area. These individuals sought mineral products from the Maya Mountains, the trade of which had been suspended since the collapse of the Petén major centers that previously monopolized their transactions. This effective commercial activity could also attract in-migration and mixing with the original population, and finally even replacing it, as indicated by the presence of the Mopan language, developed in southeastern Petén sometime during the Terminal Classic, according to Swadesh's (1961) considerations of its separation from the Yucatecan Maya. If the new role of the trade route is correct, besides Ucanal, Calzada Mopan, and Ixtonton in the middle and upper Mopan, another center must have existed in the lower Mopan, probably El Camalote-Melchor or Providencia, without diminishing the importance of Xunantunich or any other center in the Belize River Valley.

It is not possible to determine how long the Terminal Classic lasted, though it must have reached the ninth century or even the twelfth, that is, 250 years after the Late Classic ended (Adams 1971; Ball 1977; Foias 1996; Pendergast 1985; Sabloff 1970, 1975; Smith 1955; Smith et al. 1960; Willey 1986). As we have seen, Ixtonton, Calzada Mopan, Ucanal, Sacul, El Chal, and El Chilonche formed the select group that advanced the main role and unitary nature of Terminal Classic states created out of a centuries-old segmentary base as a way to perpetuate southeast Petén populations and their function in the central lowlands. Even though these populations overcame such crucial political change, in the beginnings of the Postclassic their activities diminished, and only some movement of carved monuments is seen, as well as life in old buildings, continuity in the production of chert artifacts, and ritual manifestations dedicated to the ancient temples and stelae.

11

DATING COPÁN CULTURE-HISTORY
IMPLICATIONS FOR THE TERMINAL CLASSIC AND THE COLLAPSE

David Webster, AnnCorinne Freter, and Rebecca Storey

INTRODUCTION

Accurately dating ancient events or processes is one of the most essential, yet difficult, tasks faced by archaeologists. Mayanists, fortunately, often can rely on calendar dates to establish chronological frameworks for many great Classic centers prior to the eighth–ninth centuries. When we venture into the Terminal Classic and Postclassic periods and attempt to understand the Classic Maya "collapse," however, we leave behind the comfortable chronological anchorage of Long Count and period-ending dates.

Two decades ago Raymond Sidrys and Rainer Berger (1979) compared Long Count dates on Classic monuments with the then-available radiocarbon dates from both elite and commoner contexts. They concluded that these data sets together suggested the rapid demise of kings, a somewhat later disappearance of associated nobles, and a protracted survival of Maya commoners inconsistent with pervasive conceptions of an extremely catastrophic demographic collapse. But they noted that their radiocarbon sample from commoner contexts—thirty in all—was woefully small, and they urged "Maya archaeologists to obtain more commoner-associated ^{14}C dates, as these dates should eventually be of great value in resolving the depopulation issue and be more representative of the cultural situation as it really was" (Sidrys and Berger 1979: 274).

What must be dated if we are to understand "the cultural situation as it really was" is daunting. A few dates do little to resolve big issues such as how quickly political centralization unraveled, how rapidly populations declined after the disappearance of ruling dynasties, and how (or if) ceramic traditions changed. Nor can we necessarily rely any longer on stratigraphic or other information from the great royal centers, which were often largely or wholly abandoned in Terminal Classic times. Archaeologists must instead recover, as Sidrys and Berger advised, many dates from good contexts in lesser places that might relate to what Bey, Hanson, and Ringle (1997) call "post-monumental" times.

The experiments reviewed here demonstrate that at Copán, Honduras, we have amassed a very large, representative, and reliable sample. The sixteen accelerator mass spectrometer (AMS) radiocarbon dates reported below from commoner contexts total more than half the number Sidrys and Berger found in the entire literature in 1979, and they are from clearer contexts and are technically more reliable. But we also have hundreds of obsidian hydration dates from commoner (and elite) households that make excellent sense when checked against these AMS dates and that, not coincidentally, yield basically the same culture-historical patterns that Sidrys and Berger detected.

This data array derives from an obsidian hydration dating project carried out in conjunction with our regional settlement surveys and excavations. Settlement, political, demographic, and land-use reconstructions derived partly from the obsidian dates have already been presented in considerable detail and are not repeated here (Freter 1988, 1992, 1994, 1996, 1997; Paine and Freter 1996; Paine, Freter, and Webster 1996; Gonlin 1993; Webster 1999; Webster and Gonlin 1988; Webster and Freter 1990b; Webster, Freter, and Gonlin 2000; Webster, Sanders, and Van Rossum, 1992; Wingard 1992, 1996). This paper instead reviews a recent set of concordance experiments carried out on materials from eleven sites in the Copán Valley (Figure 11.1) that independently test and strongly support the hydration chronology central to these reconstructions.

BACKGROUND

We incorporated obsidian hydration dating into our settlement research at Copán in 1984, by which time we had surveyed and test-pitted much of the outlying Copán Valley, supplementing earlier surveys by others (Fash and Long 1983; Fash 1983a). A particular concern was small residential sites, which most effectively inform us about settlement and demographic trends. We hoped that assemblages from such sites, which often represent short slices of time, would enable us to identify occupation spans shorter than the ceramic phase(s) to which such sites were conventionally assigned.

Such refinement proved more difficult than expected. Most outlying sites yielded only ceramics of the Late Classic Coner complex, then dated to A.D. 700–900, when the Copán polity reached its demographic and political maturity. Finer ceramic seriation proved impractical because sherd collections were small, typically heavily eroded, and included only small percentages of diagnostic local fine wares or imports. Freter (1996) also determined that outlying ceramic production

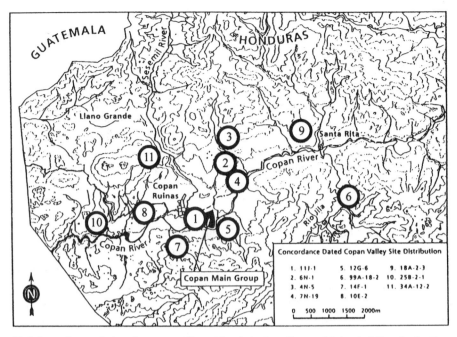

11.1 Locations of the eleven small residential sites from which obsidian hydration samples and AMS radiocarbon samples were obtained.

centers produced ceramics with different combinations of attributes from those recovered in or near the Copán's Main Group (the main basis for the existing ceramic sequence), and their behavioral and chronological implications were uncertain. Radiocarbon dating was not promising because existing dates often yielded anomalous results, and considerations of sampling and cost precluded its wide application.[1]

We turned to obsidian hydration dating in 1984 because the requisite obsidian was associated with sites of all scales, locations, and time ranges, and so could provide robust date arrays. Hydration dates were also cheap, so thousands of samples could be processed. The hydration dating method, however, was still inadequately tested under field conditions on the scale that we intended to apply it, so our research explored the efficacy of the method itself as much as its implications for Copán's culture history (Webster and Freter 1990b; Freter 1992, 1994).

IMPLICATIONS FOR THE COPÁN COLLAPSE

By 1990 Freter had processed for hydration 2,264 samples from 241 sites of all ranks (about 17 percent of all those then recorded). Initial dates agreed quite well with the established regional chronology for periods prior to the ninth century, suggesting that errors potentially affecting the hydration method were not serious or were canceling each other out. Only for the post–A.D. 900 intervals was there serious disagreement with the regional ceramic chronology. Our dates suggested continued elite activity long after the demise of Copán's royal dynasty around A.D. 810–822, a considerably protracted demographic decline, and that elements of the supposedly Late Classic Coner ceramic complex endured into Terminal Classic and Postclassic times. Independent supporting evidence came from two standard, uncalibrated radiocarbon dates from a sediment core reported by David Rue (1986, 1987). Rue's dates calibrate to one sigma(s) ranges of A.D. 1022–1177 and A.D. 1303–1413, suggesting much later forest clearing than originally envisioned.[2] Daniel Wolfman also obtained an archaeomagnetic date of A.D. 1100 from a burned floor in the Copán urban core.[3]

Standard Reconstruction of the Copán Collapse

Before chronometric dating methods were available, most scholars assumed that at Copán, as elsewhere in the Maya lowlands, the cessation of large-scale construction and erection of dated monuments signaled not only rapid political collapse but also the abandonment of the whole region. Some archaeologists, such as Longyear (1952) and Thompson (1940b) envisioned a more gradual demographic decline for Copán and other centers, but theirs was a distinctly minority opinion.

On the basis of research carried out since 1975, archaeologists now agree that Copán's royal dynasty lost power about A.D. 810–822. Major construction ended at the Copán Main Group at or shortly after that time and both the Main Group and the immediately adjacent royal domestic compound Group 10L-2 (Andrews and Fash 1992) were largely abandoned (the latter perhaps deliberately burned) before A.D. 900. When our own data and interpretations began to appear, some Mayanists (e.g., Braswell 1992) rejected a gradual political and demographic decline and the protracted use of Coner ceramic types, arguing that obsidian hydration was subject to so many potential errors that it was essentially useless. Many of these objections were easily dismissed (Webster, Freter, and Rue 1993). Whenever possible our samples were selected from contexts independently dated by other methods, a strategy that repeatedly showed good agreement (Freter 1992: Table 4). Dates generated for projects other than our own, such as the Tulane excavations in Group 10L-2 (Andrews and Falsh 1992), and Wendy Ashmore's (1991) investigations of elite residences to the northeast of the Main Group, produced excellent results (Webster, Freter, and Rue 1993).

Early on the then-new AMS (accelerator mass spectrometer) radiocarbon technique showed promising support for the hydration results. For example, Freter found charcoal in a hearth immediately adjacent to the exterior wall of a residential structure, and on the edge of the hearth was an unburned obsidian blade. She first dated the blade to A.D. 755±70.[4] A later AMS date on charcoal from the hearth was A.D. 740±90. The concordance experiments reviewed here are based on much more extensive correlations of obsidian hydration and AMS dates.

Ceramic Chronology and the Collapse

Prior to 1980, non-calendrical chronological reconstructions for Copán derived from stratigraphy, broad ceramic phasing, cross-dating, and a handful of standard radiocarbon dates, many of which appeared much too early for their contexts. Ceramic and architectural sequences were themselves strongly tied to monument dates and the associated dynastic sequence. Such dependence on calendrical dates obviously poses problems for detecting and dating post-monumental activity away from Copán's urban core.

Rene Viel has presented two successive ceramic sequences, as shown in Tables 11.1 and 11.2 (Viel 1983, 1993a, 1993b).[5] Note that the concept of a Terminal Classic period, central to this volume, is not formally used at Copán.

Our main concern is the Coner complex. Coner, most conspicuously signaled by the abundant use of Copador polychrome pottery, was thought in 1983 to begin around A.D. 700 and thereafter dominated the Copán Valley for 200 years, during which the population peaked and most sites were occupied (Fash 1983a). What we would call Terminal Classic in this scheme was the period from A.D. 800 to 900, roughly the interval between the royal dynastic collapse and the supposed depopulation of the valley, when some late variant of the Coner ceramic complex continued in use.

Viel identified a Postclassic Ejar complex that manifested itself as a fugitive set of offerings, especially of Tohil Plumbate vessels, deposited in and around the Main Group (Viel 1983: 538–539). He concluded that the Copán population disappeared from the valley shortly after the abandonment of the Main Group, or by about A.D. 850–900. Ejar was not a complete ceramic complex and Viel did not address the issue of what kinds of ceramic assemblages might have been used in Postclassic (i.e., post–A.D. 900) households in the Copán Valley because there presumably were no such households.

Viel's refined 1993 chronology began the Coner complex somewhat earlier, at A.D. 600–650, an adjustment that we had earlier suggested was more in line with the hydration dates (Webster and Freter 1990b). He additionally noted that "The fall of the centralized order does not necessarily mean the end of life at Copán. A progressive decline is a more likely model than a sudden death" (Viel 1993a: 17). This change indicates another step toward our own position. Accordingly he identified an Epiclassic facet of Coner in which Coner types were mixed with Fine Orange Ware (Pabellón Molded-Carved) ceramics during the period from A.D. 800 to about A.D. 950. This was followed by a Postclassic Ejar complex, defined by Fine Orange-Pabellón Molded Carved ceramics as well as by San Juan and Tohil Plumbate and other minority types. He describes Ejar as "a heterogeneous assemblage including *anything obviously post A.D. 800 and non-Coner*"

Table 11.1.

General Mesoamerican Periods	Copán Ceramic Complexes	Calendar Dates of Complexes
Postclassic	Ejar	after A.D. 900
Late Classic	Coner	A.D. 700–900
Middle Classic	Acbi	A.D. 400–700
Protoclassic/Early Classic	Bijac	A.D. 100–400
Late Preclassic	Chabij	400 B.C.–A.D. 100
Middle Preclassic	Uir (with Gordon funerary subcomplex)	900–400 B.C.

Table 11.2.

General Mesoamerican Periods	Copán Ceramic Complexes	Calendar Dates of Complexes
Postclassic	Ejar 2	A.D. 950–1000
Epiclassic	Coner/Ejar 1	A.D. 800–950
Late Classic/Epiclassic	Coner	A.D. 600–800
Middle Classic	Acbi	A.D. 400–600
Early Classic	Bijac	A.D. 100–400
Late Preclassic	Chabij	300 B.C.–A.D. 100
Middle Preclassic	Uir Phase (with Gordon funerary subcomplex)	900–300 B.C.
Early Preclassic	Rayo	1400–900 B.C.*

*After publication of his two 1993 articles Viel came to the conclusion that the Rayo complex began at least by 1400 B.C. (personal communication to Webster, 1997), so we use that date here.

(Viel 1993a: 17; emphasis ours). Ejar was defined on the basis of rare imported or rare types (number of sherds = 441; [Viel 1993b: 121]) that are not part of any larger Coner or Coner-like complex, although they might co-occur with Coner types before A.D. 950. There are no Coner ceramics after that date and the Plumbate (or Postclassic) facet of Ejar does not extend beyond A.D. 1000. Postclassic Ejar as envisioned by Viel in 1993 has no implications for whatever kind of household assemblages might have been in use. If such assemblages existed, they have no ceramic visibility in the 1993 scheme and by definition did not include Coner types. Although Viel does not say this in so many words, the implication of his 1993 sequence is that the Copán Valley was essentially depopulated by A.D. 950.

We note in passing that the post-dynastic ceramic patterns detected by Viel support our own demonstration that many elite-rank residences remained occupied long after the royal collapse. Continued deposition of imported ceramics and other valuable exotic objects in ritual contexts strongly suggests the presence of highly ranked individuals or groups who retained contacts with trading partners in distant regions and ancestral associations with the great monuments and buildings of dynastic times. We find this scenario much more convincing than one involving only "foreign" visitors to an otherwise empty valley.

Hydration Dating Chronology and Ceramic Issues

We originally accepted the 1983 standard version of the collapse and were surprised when our hydration dates suggested a more protracted process. Moreover, the problem could not be resolved by simply pushing back the whole relative hydration sequence so that its latest dates accorded with the conventional ending of Coner, because this would not shorten the inferred span of Coner or Coner-like ceramics and would do great violence to a comparatively secure benchmark in the Copán sequence—the Acbi-Coner transition. Two main culture-historical questions regarding the ceramic sequence are addressed by our experiments: (1) Do our radiocarbon and hydration dates, together or separately, support the timing of the Acbi-Coner transition, which was determined independently of them? (2) Do the radiocarbon and hydration dates, together and/or separately, confirm that sites associated entirely or overwhelmingly with Coner ceramics were occupied or even founded well after A.D. 950?

The inception of the Coner phase at A.D. 600–650 is now generally noncontroversial, so it can serve as a benchmark against which to test the obsidian hydration and radiocarbon dates generated by our project.[6] This issue is important here only because good agreement between the inception of Coner and the chronometric dates strengthens our confidence in the hydration dating method and its implications for the rest of the sequence.

Our position on the second and most contentious question should be made clear at the outset. We do not posit some set of Coner ceramic types that endured unchanged from ca. A.D. 600–650 until A.D. 1250 or later. Our point, rather, is that Coner or Coner-like types *as presently defined* persisted at least into the thirteenth or fourteenth centuries (see below for more details).

In summary, two very basic and conceptually separate questions are raised by critics of our hydration dating research: (1) whether obsidian hydration dating produces reasonably accurate results at Copán, and (2) whether some residential sites in the Copán Valley were occupied long after A.D. 850–950 by people using Coner-type ceramics. Although both questions were prompted by the obsidian hydration results, it is important to keep the accuracy issue separate from the culture-historical issue. Even if the hydration dates were shown to be highly unreliable, AMS dates might independently help resolve the second question.

A CONCORDANCE EXPERIMENT

One way to assess and refine the reliability of dating methods is to acquire a sophisticated grasp of their error factors and limitations, so that these can be effectively eliminated or systematically corrected. Alternatively, "There is no more practical way of testing any dating method than to compare it with another method, using the same or stratigraphically associated specimens. Concordant ages may indicate that both methods are correct; disparate ages demonstrate that at least one of the methods is incorrect" (Chappell et al. 1996: 543). This practical approach can reveal whether proposed error factors are operating at all, whether they seriously affect results, and what kind of methodological refinements might be necessary. We adopted an opportunistic concordance strategy at the inception of the obsidian hydration dating project, and later developed it more rigorously in the experiments reported here.

Research Goals of the Concordance Experiments

Our eleven concordance experiments were designed to answer the following questions:[7]

1. Can substantial relative and absolute agreement be demonstrated at Copán between two independent methods of dating site occupations?

2. Do radiocarbon dates independently corroborate the late presence of people and Coner ceramics in the Copán Valley (i.e., long after A.D. 850–950), as indicated by the hydration dates?

3. If radiocarbon dates suggest adjustments should be made to hydration spans, what sorts of adjustments are appropriate?

Research Design

A concordance experiment can either use independent methods to date the same object, or date different objects in close archaeological association. The first strategy is not feasible because the hydration and radiocarbon methods require different kinds of materials. The second is unfortunately limited because reliably close associations between obsidian and suitable radiocarbon samples are rare at Copán. We therefore devised a variation on the second strategy using the comparatively new method of AMS dating, which has been effective elsewhere in the Maya lowlands in evaluating chronological issues (Fedick and Taube 1992; Andrews and Hammond 1990). We compare hydration-derived occupation spans for eleven sites in the Copán Valley with sixteen AMS dates from burials at those same sites (see Table 11.3). We first did two pilot experiments using bone from intensively excavated sites, then ran the larger suite of dates with funding from the Foundation for the Advancement of Mesoamerican Studies, Inc. (FAMSI). Each set of compared dates constitutes a separate experiment identified by one or several letters of the alphabet, as shown in Table 11.3.

The experiments were set up as a blind test. All the hydration dates had previously been published (Freter 1988; Webster and Gonlin 1988; Gonlin 1993). In the case of two pilot radiocarbon submissions, the University of Arizona AMS laboratory was told only the site number for each sample, with no estimate of the date range. During the second phase of the project, hydration dates for each site

Table 11.3.

Experiment	Site	Altitude zone	Type of excavation	Number of radiocarbon samples	Number of hydration samples
A–D*	99A-18-2	700–749 m	intensive	5	27
E**	34A-12-2	850–899 m	intensive	2	19
F	10E-2	550–599 m	test pit	1	5
G	6N-1	550–599 m	test pit	1	22
H	25B-2-1	600–649 m	test pit	1	6
I	11J-1	550–599 m	test pit	1	6
J	4N-5	700–749 m	test pit	1	7
K	7N-19	600–649 m	test pit	1	4
L	12G-6	550–599 m	test pit	1	5
M	14F-1	550–599 m	test pit	1	14
N	18A-2-3	800–849 m	test pit	1	2

*Includes pilot date 2.
** Includes pilot date 1.

were submitted to FAMSI, and the radiocarbon samples were later sent to the AMS lab, each identified only by a letter.

Site Sampling and Chronological Assumptions

Small residential sites are central to our experiments. Two of those used here (11J-1 and 12G-6) are close to Copán's urban core. Nine others are in more rural locations, the most distant a four to five kilometer walk away from the Main Group (Figure 11.1). We chose small sites because they are likely to have shorter occupations and less contamination by extraneous materials than elite residences, they are easy to sample effectively, and they might have been occupied or even founded long after elite compounds were abandoned.

Hydration arrays from many such sites at Copán exhibit compact temporal spans, including some that are unexpectedly late (see Webster and Freter 1990b). Human burials or human bone fragments suitable for AMS samples were associated with the subset of small residential sites used here. Our assumptions are that (1) most obsidian and burials were deposited at a particular site during its occupation by the people who lived there, and (2) introduction of extraneous earlier or later materials has been minimal. All sites utilized in this set of experiments produced either pure Coner ceramics or predominantly Coner ceramics with traces of Acbi and earlier sherds. None produced any Ejar (Early Postclassic) sherds. Sites are located in all parts of the valley and are associated with many different slope exposures, soil types, and elevations, all of which are putative sources of serious errors in the hydration method.

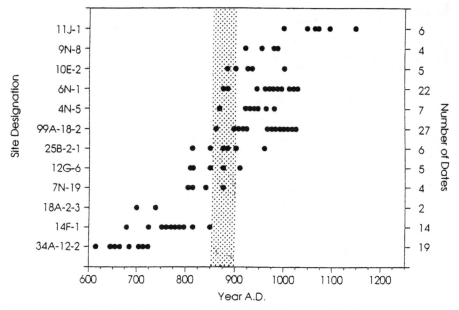

11.2 Distribution of the 121 obsidian hydration dates used in these experiments (there appear to be fewer dates because of the overlap among those very close in time). The gray bar indicates the period from A.D. 850 to 900, when according to the traditional reconstruction of Copán's culture-history the political and demographic collapse was supposed to have occurred. Note the large number of dates later than A.D. 900 in the sites chosen for this experiment.

Figure 11.2 shows the chronological distribution of the 120 hydration dates we use. Five sites have occupation spans that fall wholly, or mostly, before A.D. 900, the original (Viel 1983) estimate of the terminus of the Coner phase. The remainder all fall largely or entirely after that date. Collectively, this sample of sites can thus inform us about whether the hydration dating method is working both before and after A.D. 900–950.[8]

Dated Events and Occupation Spans

Each obsidian date derives from an event—exposure of a fresh obsidian surface—that presumably occurred at the site when it was occupied. Most events involved the production of a new prismatic blade rather than reuse of an old artifact. The interval between the earliest and latest events read by Freter for a site, expressed as calendar years A.D. (i.e., disregarding their error ranges), we define as the *minimum occupation span* as shown in Figure 11.2.

Each radiocarbon determination derives from an event (the death of an individual, or possibly bone formed shortly before death) at the site in question.

None of the obsidian samples was clearly a mortuary offering. Most come from general contexts in the excavations and represent discarded or lost implements, often from middens, although a few come from identified features or activity areas. A small number come from structure fill (i.e., from beneath pavements) and were selected only when obsidian samples from better contexts were very limited.

The Issue of Outliers

Displays of multiple chronometric dates of all kinds often show tight clusters with more distant outliers. Such outliers have very different implications depending upon what is being dated. Multiple radiocarbon dates run on a single sample have their own built-in imprecision due to uncontrolled errors. Outliers thus represent the quantitatively most extreme limits of imprecision in estimating the age of a single object. Assuming that these individual measurement errors are unbiased, they can be averaged to determine some more likely central date. The same logic does *not* apply to our hydration dates, nor to instances where we have multiple radiocarbon dates. Outliers in such arrays represent individual events in their own right, not extreme estimates of some central event (a point misunderstood by some critics [Cowgill and Kintigh 1997]). We can average multiple dates, but only for certain purposes. For example, averaging all the hydration or radiocarbon dates for one of our sites produces an estimate more likely to fall into the occupation interval than any individual date, but that mean date has no relevance for any particular event.

Bone Samples

Samples of human bone from each site were selected by Rebecca Storey, who had previously analyzed them. Bone collagen was extracted and dated at the University of Arizona AMS laboratory. All dates thus derive from the same kind of material, collagen, believed to be one of the most contamination-free sources of radiocarbon samples. Use of collagen negates the "old wood" error associated with many radiocarbon samples, and is more reliable than use of the apatite (mineral) bone component. Using bone from burials avoids errors resulting from agglutinating multiple charcoal fragments (often done in standard radiocarbon testing) and from using samples from different materials (as in the case of the charcoal, shell, and wood used in the Teotihuacan radiocarbon date array reported by Sugiyama [1998]).

Limitations of the Experiments

For our experiments we needed both obsidian and bone samples from the same site. Ideally, these sites should include those with the latest putative occupations (from the twelfth or thirteenth centuries), because these are most controversial.[9] Unfortunately, we have no burial samples from the latest sites, and in fact burials are rare at small Copán sites of any age. Because the latest date in any hydration array evaluated here is A.D. 1148, no conclusions about our reconstructions of Copán settlement history can logically be drawn from the lack of later radiocarbon dates. Good agreement between both dating methods for the sampled sites, however, increases our confidence that the whole hydration sequence is also reliable. Only if radiocarbon dating produced unanticipated late results (as we shall see it does) could our experiments directly confirm the extended occupations in the valley detected in our larger sample of sites.

Most of our experiments are not very useful in refining the durations of the occupation spans defined by obsidian hydration because single radiocarbon dates have no direct bearing on span lengths. If an individual radiocarbon date agrees well with an occupation span, it will not alter our conception of span length in any significant way. A single radiocarbon date that diverges significantly from its occupation span might suggest that one end of the span should be either earlier or later but has no implication concerning the opposite end. For example, a radiocarbon date that is a century too early might suggest an earlier occupation, but has no bearing on when occupation ceased. Divergence tells us that a span might be too short, but not how much too short. At least two radiocarbon dates are needed to assess span length, hence the importance of our two experiments (A-D, E) that do have multiple radiocarbon dates.

Some figures presented below juxtapose occupation spans and radiocarbon events, both represented as horizontal bars. Remember that the hydration arrays really do display estimated intervals of time because they represent more than one event, while each radiocarbon bar shows the error ranges of a single event, so the displays do not compare exactly the same kind of information.

SOURCES OF ERROR

Both the radiocarbon and obsidian hydration methods are subject to many sources of error. What we expect from them is not precision but reasonable accuracy in absolute terms and reasonable agreement in relative terms, given large samples and well-controlled contexts. Our research provides radiocarbon dates of requisite quality and quantity that supplement a much larger hydration sample. Results cannot simply be read, however, but rather must be interpreted with error factors in mind. We are not primarily concerned here with laboratory errors, nor with putative errors inherent in the obsidian hydration methodology (which after all are what are being explored) but rather with errors and uncertainties that derive from sampling, context, and probability ranges of specific dates.

Precision of Radiocarbon Dating

Radiocarbon dating is such a standard procedure that we tend to regard it, especially in its refined AMS form, as generally reliable and reasonably accurate. We make that assumption in the design of our experiments, but remind readers that radiocarbon dating has its own associated error and uncertainty factors. Radiocarbon arrays elsewhere sometimes diverge significantly from standard chronological sequences (e.g., Haas et al. 1987; Wenke 1991). Even where contexts are extremely good, multiple radiocarbon dates often produce surprisingly wide result ranges. A recent example is a suite of AMS dates run by multiple laboratories on materials submitted from the celebrated "Iceman" find made in the Italian Alps in 1991. Preservation of organic materials was excellent and context was about as well controlled and uncontaminated as any archaeologist could wish. Still, a large suite of dates on a range of human tissues and objects yielded 1 σ ranges of several centuries, and the eventual estimated age was determined by averaging many separate readings (Spindler 1994; Renfrew and Bahn 1996: 62; *Archaeometry* 1992: 346–347 [no author given]). Effective use of radiocarbon dating optimally requires such multiple dates to approximate a normal distribution around a central "event."

Our experiments can be envisioned as a version of the game "Battleship" in which the target is the minimum occupation span for a particular site, and each "shot" we fire is a radiocarbon date. In our game, however, misses or marginal hits that straddle the minimum occupation span within the associated error range are as important as direct hits in assessing agreement between the two dating methods. A weakness of most of our experiments is that we fire only single shots because only one radiocarbon sample is available. Most experiments are not, in a word, statistically robust and therefore are prone to disagreement because of small sample size. It is highly likely that some proportion of our single radiocarbon dates will suggest that estimated occupations should be longer, especially for sites with short hydration spans.

Too Much Agreement

Minimum occupation spans in Figure 11.2 range from 39 to 171 years. Most spans fall in the 100–171 year range, a reasonable duration for occupations at small residential sites. Taken together with the lack of extreme outliers, this pattern strongly suggests that spans are not too long. But the pattern raises a problem: with too much agreement between the radiocarbon dates, the occupation spans are bad. A little reflection shows the reason for this apparently counterintuitive assertion. If the hydration method were prone to serious errors it would yield some dates that are much too early or late for the sites in question, hence suggesting occupations that are much too long. Clearly accurate radiocarbon dates from such sites would have a greater chance of overlapping with an incorrectly determined long span than with a reasonably accurate shorter one.

Short span length produces another potential error. Because the confidence intervals of the radiocarbon determinations often approach the length of entire occupation spans, there will inevitably be a little overlap in some instances even though both methods of dating are working well. For both these reasons, if our short occupation spans are reasonably accurate some disagreement is a positive outcome, not a negative one.

Confidence Intervals

Each hydration date is expressed as a central tendency, with an associated 1σ confidence interval of ±70 years (see Freter 1992 for elaboration). For each hydration array there is a 33 percent chance that the beginning or end date could be deflected in either direction, up to the limits of its one σ error range. In a sample of eleven intervals there are twenty-two terminal dates, and on this basis alone we would expect about three to four spans to be longer than they actually are, even if we actually had managed to retrieve and date the earliest and latest obsidian. This error is compounded by the proximity of additional dates to the terminal dates defining the spans, which also complicates the effect.

Of course the radiocarbon dates are already expressed as 1σ or 2σ ranges. This means that roughly one out of every three radiocarbon dates that accurately capture some event will not overlap with that event at the 1σ range. Our experiments mainly compare single radiocarbon events with spans that include multiple hydration events, so the effects of this kind of error are reduced. Nevertheless, if we sampled burial events that occurred at the end or the beginning of the occupation span, we would expect that roughly one third of them would fail to incorporate the terminal obsidian event within their 1σ ranges even when both dating techniques were working well.

Contextual Errors and Contamination

Our basic assumption that each death event occurred within the span of a site occupation might be incorrect. Remains of individuals who died elsewhere before a site was occupied might have been moved to it later, or late intrusive burials might have been placed in an already abandoned site. Such "noise" poses particular problems because place of burial had important symbolic and social implications for the ancient Maya. Old burials of revered ancestors were sometimes introduced into newly established residences, and relics of long dead people were kept in houses or ritual buildings. Errors related to such activity are probably uncommon, but in a few cases lack of agreement between radiocarbon and obsidian dates might be a result of poor association. We think contamination by inappropriately old skeletal material is more likely than contamination by materials that are too young.

Extraneous obsidian might also make occupations seem longer than they were. Sites might have been established in locales where earlier obsidian had been discarded. Similarly, people probably often picked up old pieces of obsidian, brought them to their dwellings, then reused and discarded them at home. People might also have discarded tools at long-abandoned household sites. In all these cases the error would result in inappropriately long occupation spans. We do not believe this is a serious problem, although we cannot rule it out. Our occupation spans are convincingly short, none is plagued with any outlier that seems excessive, and we used no surface obsidian but only blades from clear excavation contexts.

We also anticipated that some individual radiocarbon dates might be wildly off, in the sense that they fail to conform not only to the hydration dates, but to chronological expectations derived from all other data concerning the site or context in question. As an example, if a burial from a site with only Coner-phase ceramics yielded a radiocarbon date in the A.D. 200 range, the date would have to be rejected. It might be a perfectly good date, but it would not constitute a fair test of the duration of the Coner phase, of the accuracy of the hydration method or, for that matter, of the radiocarbon method itself. When such suspect radiocarbon dates occur, they are identified and rejected for clearly stated reasons.

Sampling Errors

Another possible error is that the interval of time delimited by the hydration dates might be shorter than the actual occupation, causing some disagreement between the methods. For example, radiocarbon dates that seem too early might represent events that occurred in undetected early intervals of occupation. One aspect of this problem is the possible under-representation of pre-Coner obsidian. In some test pits no obsidian was found in the lower excavated levels, possibly because less obsidian was used in Acbi times, so these contexts could not be dated. We also know that in pre-Coner times obsidian from non-Ixtepeque sources, particularly El Chayal, was more commonly used. Chayal obsidian is visually distinctive and we did not date it in the interests of methodological consistency, thus further reducing the number of early samples.

We tried to sample obsidian from the earliest and latest excavated contexts at each site. Insofar as this strategy worked, larger samples would make no difference in the estimation of span length, which is determined only by two dates—the oldest and youngest. Remember, though, that our occupation spans are minimal ones. There are confidence intervals associated with the terminal dates of spans, as already discussed. More important, enlarging the number of dated obsidian samples and sampled contexts from individual sites increases the likelihood of inadvertently sampling the oldest and youngest obsidian present. Table 11.3 shows that occupation spans are defined by as many as twenty-seven hydration dates and by as few as two dates.[10] Underestimation of the original occupation span is most likely when hydration dates are few, so we expect more disagreement in this situation.

Obsidian and bone samples were taken from two extensively excavated rural sites, so control over both general contexts and burial contexts is excellent (see Experiments A-D and E, respectively). Elsewhere samples derive from test-pitting. Sometimes only parts of burials were recovered, often from midden or subfloor deposits, so we cannot always be sure how these relate to the main occupation of the site. We expect less agreement in the test-pitted sites.

We were not allowed to excavate architecture in test-pit operations, thus restricting our ability to determine architectural stratigraphy and make sure that the earliest contexts were sampled. Obsidian from late contexts was easier to sample than from early ones, and the dating project was especially concerned with site abandonment rather than site foundation. While we believe that the existing hydration arrays often reasonably capture both the founding and abandonment of residential sites, we would expect more disagreement between hydration and radiocarbon dates at the early ends of the spans rather than at the late ends.

Another sampling problem involves varying intensity of occupation, assuming that ancient per capita obsidian consumption was more or less constant. Imagine that a small household was initially founded by comparatively few people whose numbers increased as the household prospered, then dwindled again before final abandonment. Discarded obsidian would then disproportionately represent the middle range of occupation, and so might dominate our samples, resulting in an occupation span attenuated at each extreme. If large numbers of sites had such histories, then there would be a potential systematic bias toward unrealistically short spans. Other possibilities are equally likely. Sites might have been founded initially by large numbers of residents, or large numbers of people might abruptly have abandoned a site. In these cases, our chances of recovering early or late obsidian would be enhanced. We cannot know which of these patterns obtained, but each would have some deranging effect. Given our sampling strategies we are more likely to have recovered samples discarded by late occupants, whatever their numbers, than by small initial founding groups, so we expect that some spans began earlier.

Baseline Alignment

Both the radiocarbon and hydration methods require specific baseline dates for calibration equations, and disagreement will result unless calculations use the same one.[11] By convention, A.D. 1950 is used for radiocarbon determinations. Freter instead chose a 1985 baseline because she processed most hydration samples in 1984 and 1985, and her initial calculations suggested that a 1985 baseline gave a good fit with monument dates and the ceramic sequence. To properly compare the different kinds of dates, we must either shift the radiocarbon dates forward in time by thirty-five years, or the hydration dates backward by the same amount. We use the latter option, a choice that should be welcome to our critics who maintain that many of our dates are too late. In fact, we believe that the 1985 baseline gives better agreement than the 1950 one and we will continue to use it in future publications. We make the thirty-five-year shift here only to fairly assess relative overlap, and its absolute implications are not important. Because of this adjustment the experiments have no logical implications for occupation at Copán after A.D. 1113 (i.e., the latest hydration date of A.D. 1148 minus 35 years).

Table 11.4.

Experiment	Occupation Spans	AMS Radiocarbon Determinations
A-D/Pilot 2	A.D. 826–990; 1 σ range = A.D. 756–1060; 2 σ range = A.D. 686–1060. Mean date = A.D. 948.	SAMPLE A: Radiocarbon age = B.P 1115±60, or cal. 1 σ A.D. 883–997; 2 σ A.D. 778–1025. SAMPLE B: Radiocarbon age = B.P. 655±50, or cal. 1 σ 1288–1393; 2 σ A.D. 1278–1411. SAMPLE C: Radiocarbon age = B.P. 1345±60 or cal. 1 σ 646–768; 2 σ A.D. 603–856. SAMPLE D: Radiocarbon age = B.P. 1260±65, or cal. 1 σ A.D. 687–873; 2 σ A.D. 649–978. PILOT DATE 2: Radiocarbon age = B.P. 1030±50, or cal. 1 σ A.D. 985–1029; 2 σ A.D. 897–1154.
E	A.D. 579 to A.D. 688; 1 σ range = A.D. 509–758; 2 σ range = A.D. 439–828. Mean date = A.D. 645.	PILOT DATE 1: Radiocarbon age = B.P. 1375±50, or cal. 1 σ A.D. 642–689; 2 σ A.D. 600–772. SAMPLE E: Radiocarbon age = B.P. 1600±60, or cal. 1 σ A.D. 415–540; 2 σ A.D. 357–615.
F	A.D. 849–967; 1 σ range = A.D. 779–1037; 2 σ range = A.D. 709–1107. Mean date = A.D. 895.	Radiocarbon age = B.P. 1470±60, or cal. 1 σ A.D. 542–648; 2 σ A.D. 429–686.
G	A.D. 841–994; 1 σ range = A.D. 771–1064; 2 σ range = A.D. 701–1134. Mean date = A.D. 944.	Radiocarbon age = B.P. 1220±50, or cal. 1 σ A.D. 727–886; 2 σ A.D. 679–962.
H	A.D. 778–925; 1 σ range = A.D. 708–995; 2 σ range = A.D. 638–1065. Mean date = A.D. 845.	Radiocarbon age = B.P. 1200±50, or cal. 1 σ A.D. 776–942; 2 σ A.D. 689–983.
I	A.D. 965–1113; 1 σ range = A.D. 915–1183; 2 σ range = A.D. 845–1253. Mean date = A.D. 1036.	Radiocarbon age = B.P. 1125±60, or cal. 1 σ A.D. 784–994; 2 σ A.D. 776–1023.
J	A.D. 833–946;1 σ range = A.D. 763–1016; 2 σ range = A.D. 833–1086. Mean date = A.D. 903.	Radiocarbon age = B.P. 1685±30, or cal. 1 σ A.D. 264 (390) 418; 2 σ A.D. 260–427.
K	A.D. 769–840; 1 σ range = A.D. 699–910; 2 σ range = A.D 629–980. Mean date = A.D. 798.	Radiocarbon age = B.P. 1425±45, or cal. 1 σ A.D. 602–658; 2 σ A.D. 543–688.
L	A.D. 774–874; 1 σ range = A.D. 707–944; 2 σ range = A.D. 637–1014. Mean date = A.D. 816.	Radiocarbon age = B.P. 1335±50, or cal. 1 σ A.D. 653–768; 2 σ A.D. 610–800.
M	A.D. 643–814; 1 σ range = A.D. 573–884; 2 σ range = A.D. 503–954. Mean date = A.D. 740.	Radiocarbon age = B.P. 1270±50, or cal. 1 σ A.D. 687–858; 2 σ A.D. 656–938.
N	A.D. 664–703; 1 σ range = A.D. 594–773; 2 σ range = A.D. 524–843. Mean date = A.D. 684.	Radiocarbon age = B.P. 1605±65, or cal. 1 σ A.D. 407–541; 2 σ A.D. 262–622.

EVALUATION

Summary data for each of the experiments are summarized in Table 11.4.[12] Here we offer only the simplest descriptive evaluation of the results of our experiments, deferring more complex statistical and contextual analysis for future presentations.

Two radiocarbon dates agree if there is even minimal overlap between their 1σ or 2σ ranges. Although such fit might not seem as convincing as we would like, what is at issue here is reasonable agreement, not precision. We extend this logic to the error ranges of the hydration spans as well. We score the results of our experiments in the following manner:

Optimal fit: the 1σ range of the calibrated radiocarbon date overlaps with the associated minimum occupation span.

Excellent fit: the 1σ range error range of the calibrated radiocarbon date overlaps with the 1σ range of the minimum occupation span.

Acceptable fit: the 2σ range of the radiocarbon date overlaps with the 1σ or 2σ ranges of the minimum occupation span.

No fit: the 2σ calibrated radiocarbon error range does not overlap with the 2σ range of the minimum occupation span.

Not relevant: The radiocarbon date is rejected on contextual grounds and has no implications for the agreement of the two methods. There may also be radiocarbon outliers that cannot be logically rejected. These too have no implications for the agreement of the methods, although they might have contextual and chronological implications in their own right.

Applying this procedure to the data in Table 11.4 yields the outcomes listed in Table 11.5. According to extreme criticisms of the hydration method, no fit outcomes should dominate the results, with situational agreement occurring largely by chance. To the contrary, agreement is striking. Eleven of sixteen dates show excellent or optimal fits, and two others are acceptable fits within the 2σ ranges of both date sets. Only three outcomes are less than acceptable, and they require closer scrutiny to see if they are relevant to agreement.

Robust Experiment A-D

By far the best evidence comes from the robust Experiment A-D, which includes pilot date 2 (Figure 11.3). The average of the single or central intercepts of all five of the radiocarbon dates is A.D. 950, virtually a perfect match for the mean date from the hydration sequence, A.D. 943.[13] Reading the radiocarbon dates a bit more critically, one could conclude that the occupation probably fell within a range of about A.D. 646 to 1029, with some kind of extremely late outlier (B) after A.D. 1288. Let us look at the context of date B.

Site 99A-18-2 has two well-constructed stone house platforms (Gonlin 1993). Several burials were interred at shallow depths along the west wall of Structure 2.

Table 11.5.

Experiment	Optimal fit	Excellent fit	Acceptable fit	No fit	Not relevant
Pilot 2	X	—	—	—	—
Sample A	X	—	—	—	—
Sample B	—	—	—	—	X
Sample C	—	X	—	—	—
Sample D	X	—	—	—	—
Pilot 1	X	—	—	—	—
Sample E	—	X	—	—	—
Sample F	—	—	—	X	—
Sample G	X	—	—	—	—
Sample H	X	—	—	—	—
Sample I	X	—	—	—	—
Sample J	—	—	—	—	X
Sample K	—	—	X	—	—
Sample L	—	X	—	—	—
Sample M	X	—	—	—	—
Sample N	—	—	X	—	—

Burial 3, from which date B (1σ, A.D.1288–1393) derives, was the poorly preserved flexed burial of an infant or small child, placed in a shallow pit about thirty centimeters below the surface with only the broken fragment of a metate as an apparent mortuary offering. The burial was directly above the deeper burial of an adult and is clearly one of the latest ones interred. That it was intruded from above is obvious, but exactly when is not.

The site has features apart from its hydration dates that suggest late occupation. Its lithic assemblage yielded large retouched obsidian points, a rarity elsewhere, and it was one of the few rural sites we extensively excavated that showed a vertical sequence of rebuilding. While we cannot be certain how Burial 3 relates to the main occupation, we believe it to be a good date, indicative of human residence in the locale, if not at site 99A-18-2 itself. It shows no overlap even at the 1σ ranges with the occupation span, nor does it have direct contextual associations that closely support the date. We cannot simply reject date B as inconsistent with its context, however, because the association between late burials and Coner ceramics is one of the issues to be resolved. We have no independent information (hydration dates aside) on how late the occupation of this site, or some other sort of activity there, might have extended. We conclude that either date B captured a very late death event that occurred after the site was abandoned, or (more likely) that we failed to sample a late phase of occupation. In either case the death event is not relevant for assessing general agreement between the hydration and radiocarbon methods.

Removing date B from consideration, the other four radiocarbon dates collectively capture the occupation span, but suggest that it should begin a little earlier

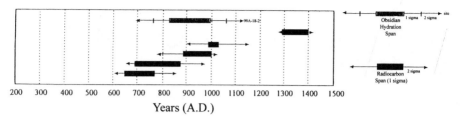

11.3 Experiment A–D (includes Pilot date 2).

unless the death event represented by date C is intrusive. There is an Acbi ceramic trace at this site so occupation (or other local activity) might well have begun in Acbi times, and radiocarbon date C is consistent with the Acbi/Coner transition.

Another way to evaluate this experiment is to imagine that it was done backwards, that is, that the radiocarbon dates were determined first and used to establish the occupation span. Seen from this perspective, we would have made twenty-seven solid hydration hits on the occupation range predicted by the radiocarbon dates.

Suppose that we could have afforded only one radiocarbon date (or alternatively found only one burial) at this site. Suppose further that the single date run was either B or C. Neither agrees particularly well with the predicted occupation span (although C is pretty close). If we had to judge by one of these dates alone, we would emphasize disagreement between the two dating methods. Yet the full suite of five dates convincingly argues for agreement. The lesson here is the deranging effect of small radiocarbon sample size, which characterizes most of our experiments. Had we multiple instead of single radiocarbon dates in Experiments K, L, and N, we might well see more pronounced overlap with the occupation spans.

Taken by themselves, the radiocarbon dates support the predicted late occupation and use of Coner-like ceramics in the valley. In fact date B is the latest date of any kind available, so far as we know, for the Copán region. It clearly suggests that at site 99A-18-2 at least one late death event, if not actual occupation, occurred between about A.D. 1288 and 1393. Ceramics from this site (Gonlin 1993: 357–363) are overwhelmingly Coner types. We recovered only the faintest trace of any Acbi material (two rim sherds), and no Ejar diagnostics. Unless one is willing to dismiss *both* radiocarbon and hydration dates, it is highly likely that 99A-18-2 was originally occupied *at least* by A.D. 700–800, and that occupation lasted, however intermittently, *at least* until the first quarter of the eleventh century, and possibly as late as the fourteenth century.

Experiment E

Experiment E (Figure 11.4) is instructive because it is the only other one for which we have multiple dates from both methods. If the two radiocarbon deter-

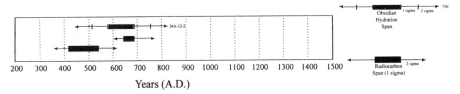

11.4 Experiment E (includes Pilot date 1).

minations had been made first, they would have suggested a maximum occupation span from the early fifth century to the late seventh century. Had the obsidian dates then been run, they would have been consistent with the latter part of this range. Site 34A-12-2 is the only one we extensively excavated whose ceramic assemblage substantially incorporates the Acbi-Coner transition (Gonlin 1993: 364–365). Both the hydration and radiocarbon dates are in excellent agreement with Viel's placement of this transition at A.D. 600–650, showing how well the hydration dates square with the absolute chronological implications of the regional ceramic sequence before A.D. 900.

Experiment E reveals that some Coner ceramic forms were certainly being used at least as early as A.D. 600. If we combine the information from Experiments A-D and E, both dating methods show that Coner-tradition ceramics were still being used at least as late as about A.D. 1025. Unless both dating methods are wrong, Coner or Coner-like ceramic forms persisted in the Copán Valley for at least 400 to 425 years.

Experiment J

A wide discrepancy exists in Experiment J. Site 4N-5 yielded a totally Coner ceramic assemblage, and its raw hydration-derived occupation span falls squarely into Viel's 1993 conception of Coner. The single radiocarbon date gives an Early Classic (Bijac complex) result, with its 1 σ range (A.D. 264–418) barely extending into Acbi times. Because the dating of Bijac is not controversial, this radiocarbon date is inconsistent with its general associations and is judged to be not relevant for our Coner concordance investigation.

Experiment F

This sample came from the poorly preserved burial of a one- to two-year-old infant at the base of a retaining wall. Hydration dates from above the burial (Unit 1, Level 1) are A.D. 901 and 926. Dates from midden material along the retaining wall beneath the burial (Unit 1, Level 3) are A.D. 884, 935, and 1002. The radiocarbon sample F is A.D. 542–648. The deposits around it contained only Coner ceramics. The radiocarbon date is thus too early for its ceramic associations. Some Acbi ceramics were encountered in small quantities elsewhere at the site,

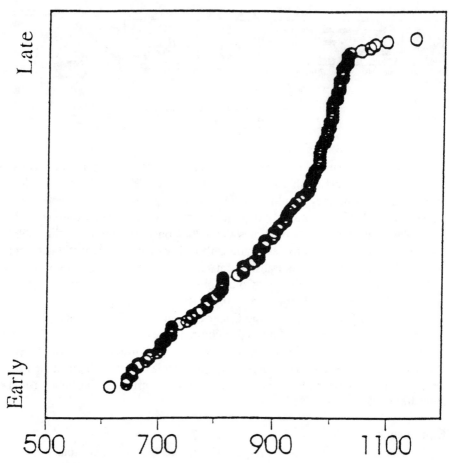

11.5 All 121 hydration dates listed in chronological order, without reference to site or context.

so the presence of an Acbi-phase burial is by itself not surprising; nevertheless, its stratigraphic position is anomalous. We cannot dismiss the date as not relevant, thus the no-fit classification.

Implications of the Separate Arrays

Figures 11.5 and 11.6 show all hydration and radiocarbon dates arranged in simple chronological order (omitting the rejected radiocarbon date J). Imagine that all we knew was that each set of dates came from sites dominated by Coner ceramics, some with slight Acbi admixture. What would we conclude? First, some sites were occupied at least until A.D. 1000–1025 as measured by both methods. Second, the radiocarbon array by itself suggests that occupation might

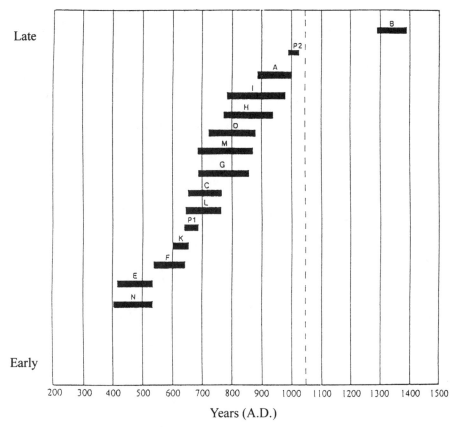

11.6 AMS dates arranged by chronological order (solid black bars show 1σ spans). No burials were available from sites hydration-dated later than the dashed line, so the display has no implications for later occupation except for the late date B.

have continued into the thirteenth to fourteenth centuries. Both arrays capture the expected Acbi/Coner transition at A.D. 600–650, and two radiocarbon dates suggest some sort of early-mid Acbi activity as well. The use of Coner or Coner-like assemblages extended for at least 400–450 years. The radiocarbon array independently indicates that such assemblages might have persisted well into the fourteenth century, for a maximum duration of 700–800 years.

SUMMARY AND CONCLUSIONS

We now return to the three basic questions addressed in our experiments.

  1. Can substantial relative and absolute agreement be demonstrated at
     Copán between two independent methods of dating site occupations?

The answer to this question is a resounding "yes." Thirteen of the fourteen relevant radiocarbon dates (93 percent of the cases) fit their associated occupation spans at an acceptable level or better. The strong inference is that the larger hydration array for Copán, which dates 230 additional sites (some with occupations later than those included here), is generally trustworthy. Disregarding the not relevant experiments, both methods retain independently the same general occupation order among sites, with Experiment F departing most from expectations. Taken as independent sets and as absolute dates, both methods yield similar conclusions.

2. Do radiocarbon dates independently corroborate the late presence of people and Coner or Coner-like ceramics in the Copán Valley (i.e., long after A.D. 850–950) as indicated by the hydration dates?

The radiocarbon dates in Experiment A-D by themselves demonstrate extended occupation of a site with an overwhelmingly Coner assemblage. The 1 range of pilot date 2 (A.D. 985–1029) falls entirely after A.D. 950, by which time, according to the revised ceramic sequence, no more Coner ceramics were used at Copán. Radiocarbon dates from Experiment E and their wider archaeological associations strongly support Viel's reconstruction of the Acbi/Coner transition at A.D. 600–650, and thus exhibit good absolute as well as relative implications. Radiocarbon dates from Experiment A-D show that it is highly likely that this Coner-phase site was occupied until at least A.D. 985–1029. A *minimal* duration of roughly 400 years for Coner-like ceramics is thus indicated independently by the radiocarbon dates at these two sites.

The late burial event at site 99A-18-2 (Experiment B) might indicate an even longer duration of Coner types. If it represents a late occupation undetected by our hydration dates, then Coner-like ceramics were still being used in the late thirteenth, or the fourteenth, century. If this burial was post-occupation, then people were probably living somewhere else in the valley, and as yet we have no indications of late, full household assemblages lacking Coner or Coner-like types. In either case the conclusion is the same—ceramic types and assemblages that would be labeled Coner, given current definitions of the phase, were probably still being used 600–700 years after the Acbi/Coner transition.

Disregarding any hydration dates at all, one could argue that the presence of a late and reasonably numerous agricultural population in the Copán Valley is independently indicated by the radiocarbon record. This conclusion also squares with the archaeomagnetic and palynological evidence cited earlier. In particular, the latest calibrated date from Rue's sediment sequence accords extremely well with Experiment B. The infant death event captured by this experiment might fall right into the 1 span (A.D. 1301–1413) of Rue's latest calibrated radiocarbon date, which suggests that significant numbers of farmers were still clearing land.

3. If radiocarbon dates suggest adjustments should be made to hydration spans, what sorts of adjustments are appropriate?

Divergence is shown at the early ends of occupation spans in Experiments N, K, F, L, G, and I (although both of the latter show overlap at the 1s level with their hydration spans and so are not very conclusive on this point). Experiments N, K, and L suggest that their occupation spans might begin somewhat earlier than predicted, or that extraneous old skeletal material was introduced. On the other hand, Experiments H and M show radiocarbon dates slightly later than the occupation spans. Given these findings, and the generally excellent agreement between the two dating methods, it does not appear that any adjustment to the hydration rate curve used for Copán is currently warranted.

Other Interpretations and Implications

As predicted, multiple radiocarbon samples from fully excavated sites produce the best results. We also detect no obvious distorting bias with altitude in our experiments. Both dating methods are in good agreement at sites that range in altitude from 550 to 900 meters. More specifically, both methods of dating agree very well in the sites at the highest elevations (Experiments A-D, E, and N). There is no obvious late bias associated with higher altitude sites as argued by Braswell (1992); two of these (34A-12-2 and 18A-2-3) in fact have early spans. Other suggested deranging effects such as soil pH, vegetation cover, or burning, are either nonexistent, minimal, or mutually cancel each other out.

Ceramic Implications

Joe Ball (1993b) observes that in the Maya lowlands the production and use of domestic pottery are essentially disconnected from the political fortunes of elite regal-ritual places. Our own work confirms and expands his conclusion, as well as that of Sidrys and Berger concerning the complexity of the collapse process. Only by gaining a comprehensive grasp of settlement and ceramic chronology can we make sense out of what happened beyond the penumbra of monument dates and massive architectural stratigraphy found at large centers, especially if post-monumental activity is reconstructed using ceramic complexes. Such reconstructions are only as reliable as our chronological control over the duration of those complexes provided by independent means.

Braswell (1996: 537) asserts that the lack of Postclassic ceramic assemblages at Copán has in part caused skepticism concerning our late hydration dates. This is a nonissue, based on the faulty logic that late dates associated with Coner ceramics cannot be correct because we have not identified any *other* Postclassic assemblages. Our dates show that Coner or Coner-like assemblages *are* Postclassic assemblages (although non-Coner ones might exist as well). Needless to say, our dates have no implications for the Ejar complex nor its chronology because they are not associated with Ejar sherds. Some of our late test-pitted sites might yield Ejar ceramics in burials or in caches if more intensively excavated. Far from compromising our dates, such finds would explicate the nature of late ceramic assemblages and help date the Ejar phenomenon.

If Coner or Coner-like ceramics persisted for centuries, traditional ceramic analysis alone (short of fine seriation) cannot determine when, after A.D. 600–650, sites yielding them were founded or abandoned. Nor could a limited sample of radiocarbon dates with certainty reveal the duration of Coner-like ceramic forms. Only the hydration date arrays reveal the great variation in occupational histories of hundreds of sites. Not surprisingly, some such occupations conform to standard chronological expectations, falling squarely into Coner as originally conceived (Webster and Freter 1990b: Figure 5).

Future ceramic research might divide the now-extended Coner ceramic phase into two or more new ones based on scrutiny of fine-grained changes. Rene Viel (personal communication to Webster, Feb. 1999) now believes that the co-existence of two distinct sets of ceramic assemblages after A.D. 900 is a distinct possibility. One such set would include Ejar types such as Tohil Plumbate, along with cruder, Coner-derived or related domestic wares. A second set of assemblages, mostly rural ones, would lack Ejar types, but otherwise have Coner-derived or related forms.

Freter herself detected new combinations of attributes in the collections from sites distant from Copán's urban core that appear to be time sensitive. Late Coner-like ceramics often are coarser, with larger temper and lower apparent firing temperatures than their earlier counterparts. Coner assemblages in which such forms are mixed with Ejar sherds, and in which imported polychromes from central Honduras are absent, could be defined as a new complex, a refinement of Viel's current identification of an Epiclassic facet that combines elements of both.[14] Similarly, late assemblages in which Coner types show subtle changes in their forms or shifts in frequency of diagnostics (e.g., absent or reduced Copador polychrome) could be used to define a new complex or facet. Our prediction is, however, that such newly defined ceramic complex(es), if they represent full household assemblages, will show strong developmental continuity out of Coner.

Intrusive people with complete "foreign" ceramic household assemblages (i.e., using no or very few Coner or Coner-like types and showing no appreciable continuity with Coner) might well have settled in the Copán Valley as the indigenous population declined. The latter possibility is not relevant to our argument because these would parallel, but not replace, the Coner or Coner-like assemblages in our own very large household sample. Residential sites might also be detected in which abundant Ejar fine paste wares are used in combination with Coner forms (quite possibly such sites exist).

One or another of these ceramic situations presumably characterizes the "small Postclassic village" recently located by William Fash and his students to the southwest of the Acropolis (Agurcia 1998: 354). We have seen only one brief report on this site (Manahan 2000), which apparently has an Ejar component in large, low platforms and associated burials and caches. Manahan concludes from several radiocarbon dates that the Ejar phase cannot extend beyond A.D. 1000, consistent with Viel's 1993 ceramic realignment. Whether there is a complete residential assemblage at this little community, and whether this assemblage is unrelated to Coner, are unclear to us. That some kind of Ejar presence at Copán extends to A.D. 1000 or later, especially around the Main Group, is not surprising.[15] Manahan's conclusion, however, seems to be that since his site and ceramic assemblage do not extend beyond A.D. 1000, neither can any others. On the contrary, discovery of sites or locales of this kind, whatever their age and whenever they were abandoned, has no direct bearing on our own results, although they certainly tell us something useful about settlement dynamics, ceramic variation, and movement of people in post-dynastic times at Copán. In some ways it even strengthens our own interpretations.[16] For example, if Ejar ends at A.D. 1000 as Manahan suggests, then the very late burial at site 19A-18-2 cannot be intrusive from some non-Coner, Ejar settlement elsewhere in the valley.

Each Maya polity and region is likely to exhibit a distinctive set of Terminal Classic/Postclassic transformations. For example, at La Milpa, Belize, both the monumental core and the surrounding residential sites seem to have been abruptly abandoned about A.D. 850 (Hammond et al. 1998; Hammond and Tourtellot, Chapter 13, this volume). To the extent that this conclusion is based on the presumed absence of Postclassic ceramics, it assumes that the chronological duration of the last major ceramic complex is well controlled. This assumption might be perfectly correct for La Milpa, but it was wrong at Copán.

In a recent article, Ridings (1996) asked rhetorically, "Where in the world does obsidian hydration dating work?" Our answer is that, recent criticisms (Antoviz et al. 1999) to the contrary, it works exceptionally well at Copán, where it has told us something unexpected, but also something very sensible, about the demise of a great Classic Maya polity.

NOTES

1. We recognize that proper terminology in radiocarbon and obsidian hydration conventions is *determinations* rather than *dates*. For the sake of brevity, we use the latter term.

2. Radiocarbon dates in this paper were calibrated using the 1993 Stuiver and Reimer Radiocarbon Calibration Computer Program—specifically the decadal tree ring option of that program. The calibration yields a 1σ confidence interval of 68.3 percent, and a 2σ interval of 95.4 percent. Radiocarbon spans are taken from the summary of minimum cal age ranges (cal ranges) and maximum cal age ranges as displayed on the calibration printouts for each sample. For conciseness the ranges are shown without the associated intercepts of the radiocarbon calibration curve. See Stuiver, M. and P. J. Reimer (1993) *Radiocarbon* 35: 215–230.

3. Wolfman's date is unpublished because of his sudden death, but nicely supplements Rue's findings. Braswell (1996: 537) is thus incorrect in asserting that there are no radiocarbon or archaeomagnetic dates from the Copán Valley later than A.D. 950 that suggest human presence in the valley after that time. (The radiocarbon dates were reported in Rue 1986, 1987; Webster, Freter, and Rue 1993; and other publications.)

4. Adjusted to the 1950 radiocarbon baseline; see discussion below.

5. Willey et al. (1994) have devised yet another version; it is very similar to Viel's 1993 scheme, but does admit the possibility of the late use of Coner or Coner-like ceramics.

6. The Acbi/Coner transition is most marked by the *obtrusive* occurrence of highly distinctive Copador polychrome pottery. We emphasize obtrusive because the Copador tradition appears older elsewhere on the southeast Maya periphery, most notably at Cerén, El Salvador (Webster, Gonlin, and Sheets 1997: 55–56). Copador certainly long predates A.D. 600 outside the Copán Valley and could be expected to occur in small amounts as early as the sixth century at Copán.

7. A twelfth experiment, not relevant to the issues discussed here, was also carried out. It attempted to correlate two single events at Copán urban core group 9N-8. The results of the radiocarbon date were rejected as inconsistent with the context.

8. When reporting or interpreting displays of dates, many archaeologists fail to report outliers or dates that otherwise seem unacceptable. We include and evaluate all dates here.

9. Our latest hydration date is A.D. 1235. If correct, this date indicates that at least a few people were still living in the Copán Valley as late as the early thirteenth century. Of course it is very unlikely that this date represents any kind of terminal occupation, and new hydration dates or radiocarbon dates might well indicate even later human presence.

10. We were allowed to take no more than half of the obsidian in each lot for dating. This sampling limit affects the estimated occupational spans because few dates could be run for sites where little obsidian was encountered in test excavations. More samples will generally indicate greater time spans, although there is probably a threshold of diminishing returns in this respect.

11. Specifically, the hydration equation is:

((micron reading 2 ÷ hydration rate) x 1000)-baseline date

or 1985.

12. Interested readers may obtain a complete list of all dates of both kinds, along with radiocarbon laboratory numbers and details of intercepts for the radiocarbon dates, from the senior author on request.

13. Because Experiment C has neither a single intercept nor a central intercept, we split the difference between its two recorded intercepts (A.D. 670 and 685) and used A.D. 677 in our calculation.

14. A clumsily worded statement of ours (Webster and Freter 1990b: 81) has been taken to mean that we found Ulua polychromes associated with contexts dated as late as the thirteenth century. We meant to imply only that such ceramics long outlasted the royal collapse. This confusion is our fault. We never believed that such pottery was used later than A.D. 950–1000, and we thank Rene Viel for bring the misstatement to our attention.

15. Interestingly, Wolfman's aforementioned archaeomagnetic date of A.D. 1100 comes from just such a large platform in the Las Sepulturas urban enclave. If this is an Ejar structure, it was used long after A.D. 1000.

16. Remember that the fact that most of the sites used in this experiment were not occupied much beyond A.D. 1000 is an artifact of our burial sampling, and so cannot be taken as support of Manahan's asserted terminus.

ACKNOWLEDGMENTS

We thank the National Science Foundation for generous funding provided for several field projects, and the Foundation for the Advancement of Mesoamerican Studies, Inc., for their support of the concordance experiment. Timothy Murtha assembled several of the data displays.

12

POLITICAL DECENTRALIZATION, DYNASTIC COLLAPSE, AND THE EARLY POSTCLASSIC IN THE URBAN CENTER OF COPÁN, HONDURAS

William L. Fash, E. Wyllys Andrews, and T. Kam Manahan

The demise of the Classic Maya tradition at the site of Copán, in western Honduras, has been the subject of a great deal of scientific and humanistic inquiry. It is doubtful if an entire book could do justice to the entirety of the data obtained in the scholarly efforts of dozens of researchers conducted over the course of the past century. The editors of the volume have chosen wisely in soliciting two papers on the subject: the present one, devoted to the center of the ancient kingdom, and the preceding chapter, which focuses on the outlying settlements in the valley. The two chapters also take different points of view with respect to the interpretation of the material record, particularly regarding the timing of events in the Copán Valley in the Terminal Classic and beyond.

Our subject is the decline of centralized political authority in the eighth century A.D., its subsequent dissolution, and the events that followed its apparently violent end ca. A.D. 822. While the Terminal Classic is traditionally defined as the period from 9.18.0.0.0 to 10.3.0.0.0 in the Long Count (A.D. 790–889, according to the GMT correlation), in the case of Copán the forces that set in motion the end of the Classic Maya order commenced slightly before that time. Here we briefly review the evidence for the decentralization of political power during the eighth century A.D. (Fash), before proceeding to a consideration of the lifeways and times of the final ruler, Yax Pasah (Andrews), and conclude with the striking new evidence for the reoccupation of the area just south of the Principal Group late in the tenth century A.D. (Manahan). This presentation is in keeping with the three-stage process for the "collapse" that was outlined nearly ten years ago (Fash and Sharer 1991), before some of the important new data presented here were available.

POLITICAL DECENTRALIZATION
IN THE TENTH-CENTURY COPÁN REALM

Early researchers quickly realized that one of the distinguishing features of the Classic Maya kingdom centered in the Copán Valley was the number and quality of inscribed monuments erected outside the Principal Group of ruins (Maudslay 1889–1902; Gordon 1896; Spinden 1912; Morley 1920). Figural and hieroglyphic stelae and altars were to be found in a number of different loci in the valley. However, when excavations of vaulted masonry buildings outside the site core began to uncover hieroglyphic benches, with accompanying pictorial imagery, scholars began to realize that new insights would be available on the structure of ancient society at this particular kingdom.

To date, hieroglyphic benches have been found inside elaborate edifices at four different elite residential compounds in the eastern half of the Copán pocket, the largest subdivision of the greater Copán Valley system, in the urban core of the kingdom. These inscribed benches or thrones all convey cosmological themes in their iconography (Baudez 1986, 1989), and three of the four also carry historical information in their hieroglyphic texts. When the fourth site (Group 8N-11) is more completely investigated, it is likely that historical texts will be found in one or more of the other large structures around the central plaza that remain to be excavated (Webster et al. 1998).

The number and diversity of these monuments, and the fact that all three of the historical inscriptions were dedicated during the reign of the sixteenth and final ruler, Yax Pasah, led one of us (Fash 1983a, 1986) to speculate that they were testimony to the waning power of the last king of Copán. Indeed, Fash even went so far as to suggest that rather than being the result of a peasant uprising, the collapse of divine rule at Copán may have been the result of a "nobles' revolt" (Fash 1983a, 1988, 1991). In this scenario, the noble families of the Copán Valley began to withhold the tribute that they had previously supplied to the royal line, resulting in economic disruptions and precipitating the end of the dynasty, and with it the Classic Maya tradition in the Copán Valley. The model was keyed into the increasingly abundant settlement and ecological data indicating that the population in the Copán pocket had exceeded the local carrying capacity, in large measure because the urban core completely covered the most fertile alluvial bottomlands in the region (Fash 1983b; Sanders 1989; Webster and Freter 1990b).

Over the past fifteen years, a broad array of new data and models have been produced that greatly enhance our understanding of these processes. There is now a considerably larger array of information regarding the causes, consequences, and timing of deforestation and erosion in the valley, as well as the regional settlement system through time and space (for useful reviews, see Webster n.d., 1999). A much more complete understanding of the site core and its historical record has been afforded by the intensive research of the archaeologists, epigraphers, and artists who participated in the Copán Acropolis Archaeological Project (e.g., Agurcia 1997; Andrews and Fash 1992; B. Fash 1992; B. Fash et al. 1992; Fash 1991, 1998; Freidel et al. 1993; Schele and Freidel 1990; Sharer et al. 1999; Stuart 1992, 1997). Of the explanatory models that have been elaborated recently, two are of particular interest for the present context.

The first model is that of William T. Sanders, elaborated in his important work on "Household, Lineage, and State at Eighth-Century Copán, Honduras" (Sanders 1989). Basing his analysis primarily upon settlement data and the excavations he directed at household units of the different social levels in the urban ward of Las Sepulturas, Sanders elucidated four major organizational tenets of Late Classic Copán society:

a. Extended family households varied considerably in social status, with polygyny closely related to this differentiation.

b. Households were incorporated into lineages of varying size and generational depth, closely integrated with a series of levels of ancestral cults.

c. The heads of maximal lineages formed a noble class and provided leadership in a number of separate but closely integrated spheres of activities—political, economic, and religious. The immediate supporting households of these nobles included close kin, distant relatives, and unrelated clients; internal rank distinctions were significant. Some members of these expanded lineages had economically specialized roles, but the majority were probably cultivators.

d. At the top of the hierarchy was the king and the royal lineage who may have had several thousand people as direct economic and political dependents.

(Sanders 1989: 102)

In looking at the specific example of the elaborate residential compound of Group 9N-8 and the "House of the Bacabs" (Webster 1989), Sanders concluded that the granting of titles to lineage heads, along with sculptural facades on their houses, could be seen as an expression of both the strengths and weaknesses of the Copán kingdom (Sanders 1989: 103). He felt this owed to the fact that the Copán state was only partially effective in monopolizing force, but that at the same time, the positions of the lineage heads were somewhat precarious because of the great power of the royal line. He argued that these features were in keeping with the political structure that Richard Fox (1977) defined as the segmentary state. Such a state is symbolically centralized, but the political position of the ruler is circumscribed by the power of a class of nobles with separate ascribed prerogatives and resources. Further, he suggested that the evidence at Copán accorded with the fact that segmentary states are characterized by "elaborate court protocol and ceremony, and there are almost innumerable titles—usually given to those men with independent power bases—that are largely ceremonial in nature" (Sanders 1989: 104). Further, Sanders made the particularly prescient observation that in Copán, "the power of the king is sharply circumscribed by councils of chiefs of local lineages" (Sanders 1989: 104).

The second model relevant to the present discussion is that presented by Joyce Marcus (1992) in her consideration of "Dynamic Models in Mesoamerican States." Marcus proposed that all Mesoamerican states went through similar stages, beginning with 1) a rapid growth and acquisition of territory following the formation of the state, followed by 2) a period of "filling in" of the territory and a growth in the size and power of secondary centers, which subsequently declare their independence from the old capital, leading to 3) the shrinking of its domain and its eventual collapse as a centralized authority structure. Marcus used the Copán case (among others) to illustrate her model, positing a very large Copán polity in the Early Classic, followed by the gradual shrinking of its territory following the achievement of independence by Quirigua (in A.D. 738), and thereafter the independence of other centers progressively closer to the capital, such as Los Higos, La Florida, and Río Amarillo. The withdrawal of the support of previously tributary centers came at precisely the time that demographic and political pressures within the Copán pocket made their contributions most necessary. Regarding the collapse, Marcus's "Dynamic Model" posits essentially the same political process that Fash (1983a, 1988, 1991) had posited earlier with the nobles' revolt, but on a regional scale, and including the heads of secondary centers in tribute-producing areas outside of the Copán pocket.

The political and economic consequences of the defeat (and apparently also the decapitation) of the thirteenth Copán king, Uaxaclahun Ubah K'awil (a.k.a. "18 Rabbit"), at the hands of the Quirigua dynast K'ak Tiliw (a.k.a. "Cauac Sky") have been much debated over the past couple of decades. All are in agreement that the results for Quirigua (where the event is recorded on five different monuments) were prestige-enhancing and that an explosion of monument erection occurred in the years following the beheading of the Copán sovereign. This is one case where "loser's history" is indeed recorded, since the Hieroglyphic Stairway at Copán cites the fateful date, and states that Ruler 13 died "with his flint, with his shield," that is, in battle (David Stuart, personal communications 1998). But what of the results of this humiliating and potentially disastrous event in the Copán kingdom? Archaeology, epigraphy, iconography, and ethnohistoric sources were all brought to bear to begin answering this question.

A previously little-understood structure on the Copán Acropolis turned out to have a very intriguing tale to tell about the response to the crisis generated by the violent end of Ruler 13's reign. The investigations of Structure 10L-22A were inspired by Barbara Fash's observation that the large sculpted mat designs which were still in place on the eastern facade of this structure might label the building as a mat house, or council house (Fash and Fash 1990; B. Fash et al. 1992). The investigations provided a variety of different kinds of evidence in support of this hypothesis, including many more of the large mat symbols, and roof ornaments labeling the building as a *nic te'il na* (flower house, also glossed as a council house in Colonial-period dictionaries). There were also nine toponymic glyphs on the facades of Structure 22A, thought to name specific places represented by the human figures that were placed above them in the building's entablature. A dance platform was found in front of the structure, in keeping with the descriptions of activities occurring at council houses in the ethnohistoric sources. Finally, the excavations documented the remains of a midden at the southwest corner of the building, interpreted as the residues of a feast that took place there toward the close of the Classic period (B. Fash et al. 1992; Fash and Fash 1996). A possible Long Count date for the dedication of the building, based on the large "9 Ahau" medallions that were repeated in pairs numerous times on all four facades of the structure, falls in A.D. 746 (9.15.15.0.0 9 Ahau 18 Xul), squarely in the reign of Ruler 14. Regardless of whether one accepts the "9 Ahau" glyphs as the dedicatory date of the building, the architectural stratigraphy of this structure and its neighbors (Structures 10L-22 and 10L-26) and their associated plaster floors place the construction of the final version of Structure 22A during the reign of Ruler 14 (Larios et al. 1994). Thus, this building represents the response of that king to the death of his distinguished and long-lived predecessor.

The imagery that adorned this building, with its explicit depiction of representatives of different wards (or lineages?) that comprised the seats of power of the kingdom, has been interpreted as the king's acknowledgment of the power of those secondary lords and their domains. Indeed, it has been suggested that their portrayal on the facades of this prominently placed structure (clearly visible from the Great Plaza, below) may have been a way of trying to invest the upper nobility in the success and the fate of the Copán kingdom. All of this, of course, is perfectly in keeping with the predictions made by Sanders (1989: 104) regarding the role of the noble lineage heads in circumscribing the power of the king, through their councils.

What remains to be done is to locate and identify the places represented by the toponyms, and their respective human figures, carved in stone on the facades of the council house. Andrews's research on the royal residential area (Andrews and Fash 1992) has provided what we hold to be a secure identification of one of the toponyms, that of *kanal*. Other likely candidates include the Type 4 sites located precisely one kilometer from the Principal Group, to the east (Group 8N-11), north (Group 8L-12), and west (Group 9J-5). Given the abundant iconographic and hieroglyphic sculptures known to have adorned the elite residential compounds in Late Classic Copán, it is likely simply a matter of time before they are uncovered.

For Ruler 15, we have the elegant testimony of the Hieroglyphic Stairway and Temple of Structure 10L-26, both of which bear his name and the information that he completed them. David Stuart (1997, n.d.) has proposed that Ruler 13 may have actually begun this grandiose encyclical and placed it on the west side of the penultimate pyramidal base of Structure 26 known as Esmeralda. It is abundantly clear from both the archaeology and the texts that Ruler 15 was the one to complete the final version of the temple pyramid, and the stairway and temple texts that adorned it. The stairway and the temple at its summit represent a retrospective history of the dynasty up to the date it was dedicated in A.D. 753, including the brief mention of the loss of Ruler 13. But the overarching message is that of the power and glory of the Copán kingdom, with portraits of the sovereigns and the citation of the most important events in their lives, including their birth, accession, monument dedications, and death. To bring home the point, the rulers are portrayed as warrior kings, bearing lance and shield and all the accoutrements of the supernatural patrons of war.

Barbara Fash (1992; Fash and Fash 1996) has emphasized the increasing use, explicitness, and sheer size of the depictions of martial themes in the Copán Acropolis sculpted building facades as the eighth century progressed. Clearly, there was the perception of a need to emphasize the military might of the dynasty, and various kinds of supernatural sanction for it, in the monuments of the last three kings of Copán. Indeed, when we look at the final building on the Copán Acropolis, identified as the funerary temple of Yax Pasah, we see portraits of the last ruler as a fearsome warrior, complete with shield, lance, shrunken trophy heads, and ropes for tying his captives subdued in battle. On an interior niche, Structure 18 bears the date 9.18.10.0.0, a mere ten years after the start of the Terminal Classic period, but already deep into the decline of the Copán state.

To place the message and size of Temple 18 in perspective, it is useful to look at the full array of monuments dedicated by Ruler 16. In so doing one sees that all of the grandiose building projects that Yax Pasah undertook were completed during the first thirteen years of his reign. He acceded to power in A.D. 763, dedicated Structure 21A in A.D. 771, Structure 11 in A.D. 773, and Structure 16 in A.D. 776. We know of not a single other building on the Acropolis that he constructed, until the comparatively very modest Temple 18 was dedicated in A.D. 800. During the last decades of his reign, Yax Pasah seems to have been content to let others dedicate monuments in their own honor in numerous elite residential compounds in the Copán Valley. The texts that have come to light thus far all say that they were commissioned under his authority, and one (inside Str. 9M-152) even says that he performed a period ending ceremony there. Yax Pasah's only other contribution was to commission a number of stone altars and small, portable objects to note his ritual observances of the passing of the anniversaries of his accession or period endings in the Principal Group, and in places of interest or import in the valley.

The ancient settlement that was nearly entirely destroyed by the establishment of the modern town of Copán Ruinas (Morley's Group 9) was also no doubt an important subcommunity in Late Classic Copán. A great number of inscribed hieroglyphic monuments were found there, including three (Stela 8, Altar T, Altar U) that were commissioned during the reign of Yax Pasah. A decade ago, it was suggested that this locus may have been the domain of an individual (dubbed "Personage A" by Stuart 1992, also known as Yahau Chan Ah Bac) that bore the Copán Emblem Glyph among his titles, and was thought to be the brother of Yax Pasah (Schele and Freidel 1990). Another possible sibling ("Personage B," whose name was glossed "Yax Kamlay"), was thought to have held sway over the royal residential area on the south edge of the Acropolis, Group 10L-2. These epigraphic interpretations were viewed as further evidence of the sharing of power by Yax Pasah (Schele and Freidel 1990; Bardsley 1996), in the final decades of his reign. However, David Stuart (personal communications 1997) has recently concluded that both of the names in question belong not to historical individuals, but rather to patron gods of the Copán kingdom. If sustained by future inquiry, this reading would disallow the interpretation of Group 9 as the private fiefdom of a brother of Yax Pasah, and would instead indicate that Yax Pasah was there, too, simply dedicating stone monuments to mark the passage of calendric anniversaries, as he recorded on small circular altars in the Acropolis and portable stone incensario lids found at caves in distinct locations in the Copán Valley.

This hardly seems to be the testimony of a powerful ruler, bolstered by tens of thousands of loyal subjects all obliged (let alone enthusiastic) to contribute their labor to impressive public works projects. Quite to the contrary, the lack of large-scale corporate labor projects, and the explicit depictions of him as a fearsome warrior on the panels of the diminutive Temple 18, would appear to indicate that Yax Pasah was experiencing considerable political difficulties in the last three decades of his reign.

Noble families residing outside the Copán pocket also signaled their importance by the use of hieratic monuments. In two cases, these monuments included inscriptions where the local lineage heads boast their own *ahaw* titles, to judge from Los Higos Stela 1 and Río Amarillo Altars 1 and 2. Marcus (1992) read these lordly titles as Emblem Glyphs proper and used that interpretation to posit that the satellite centers of Copán all broke away during the eighth century A.D. Again, the comparative anthropological data and evidence from other parts of Mesoamerica support the logic behind her conclusions. Neither of these sites' nobles, however, used the "Ch'ul" ("holy") title in these lordly appellatives.

The major structural problem that the burgeoning elite lineages posed for the Copán kingdom is one for which the Council House, alone, was not enough to solve. There were too many eligible adult males to fill the available political offices, and the jockeying for position among the elite lineages who aspired to greater glory is thought by many of us to have reached intolerable levels. This situation weakened the authority and power—to whatever degree perceived, or real—of the king himself. The sculptures and public seating accommodation in the residential compounds spanning the social spectrum from Types 2–4 in the Copán Valley show the importance that display and pageantry held in eighth century Copán, and very likely elsewhere. This elite competition made for chronic instability throughout the Maya area during the closing century of the Classic era, as is shown by the number of new regal-ritual centers formed by disgruntled members of the aristocracy of the old capitals, and the frequency and intensity of the wars that took place between all the major players, and even many of the minor ones.

The timing of and circumstances surrounding the end of the reign of the sixteenth Copán ruler have been the subjects of considerable scholarly debate and speculation. As noted, the Initial Series text inscribed in the west interior niche of Temple 18 records the date A.D. 800. Ten years later, he is cited as performing a "hand-scattering" ceremony in the inscription on Structure 1-B-1 in the Acropolis of Quirigua. The suggestion was made that Yax Pasah may have retreated from Copán to Quirigua, in keeping with the evidence for a rapprochement between the two centers in the final inscriptions of Quirigua. However, the discovery of some human skeletal material in the looted and ransacked tomb of Temple 18 suggested that Yax Pasah may in fact have been buried in the last building that he is known to have dedicated at Copán.

Further, Linda Schele believed that the "6 Ahau" reference on the text of Copán Stela 11 dates its erection to A.D. 820, and shows Yax Pasah in the maw of the Underworld, as an apotheosized ruler (Schele and Mathews 1998). This would place the date of death of Yax Pasah between A.D. 810 (Quirigua Str. 1-B-1) and 820 (Stela 11). Nikolai Grube and Schele (1987) also believe Copán Altar L to be the accession monument of a successor to Yax Pasah, whose name they decipher as U Kit Tok, in A.D. 822. David Stuart (1992) is unconvinced by either the placement of the Calendar Round date inscribed on the altar's south face (it could as well be fifty-two years earlier, in A.D. 770), or that the office into which this individual acceded was that of the high king. W. Fash (1991 and elsewhere) agrees with the placement of the Calendar Round date in A.D. 822, but is unable to bring himself to recognize U Kit Tok as a high king, both because of the lack of that designation on the altar text and the fact that its carving was never completed. This may well have been a pretender to the throne in the chaotic years following the death of Ruler 16, but if so his power base was so limited that the words that would have declared him king were never carved.

THE ROYAL RESIDENCE IN THE LATE AND TERMINAL CLASSIC

Yax Pasah and his predecessors lived and acted in two connected worlds, one a larger stage that included the city, the valley, and the entire Copán realm, and the second a much smaller place where he was surrounded by kinsmen and other families with whom he had grown up—his own residential neighborhood. These neighborhoods, scattered around the Copán pocket and probably beyond it, may have been the homes of extended noble and royal lineages that provided the inherited status and power that enabled ranking members of these residential groups to claim the throne for one of their own (Viel 1999). For the Maya of Copán, this world would all have been one, with its widening levels of participation and influence blending naturally. The archaeologist, however, sees distinct architectural groups representing each level of interaction. The larger stage within Copán is the Acropolis and the adjoining great plazas, with public buildings and monuments. For Yax Pasah, if not yet for earlier rulers, we have now identified the smaller stage where he grew up and built his home.

Immediately to the south of the Acropolis lies Group 10L-2, a group of three courtyards and several other buildings and platforms (Figure 12.1). Altogether the group contains about thirty structures, including several large vaulted buildings with elaborate sculptured facades, smaller residential structures with masonry vaults or perishable roofs, and simple platforms, some with perishable structures. The Copán River, when cutting into the east side of the Acropolis in the early twentieth century, also gouged deep into Group 10L-2, probably washing away another courtyard with ten or so buildings around it.

All of the structures on the surface of Group 10L-2 investigated from 1990 to 1994 by the Middle American Research Institute at Tulane University were built during or just before the Late Classic Coner phase, between about A.D. 600 and perhaps 770 or 780 (Andrews and Fash 1992; Andrews and Bill n.d.; Bill 1997; Doonan 1996). Evidence of earlier habitation just south of the Acropolis is widespread, although flooding of the Copán River before the Late Classic removed most of these remains. Excavations to sterile river sand and gravels indicate an occupation going back into the Late Preclassic and Protoclassic in this part of the site, and thick buried middens in several areas date to the second half of the Early Classic period (late Acbi phase). These, and one burial accompanied by several magnificent ceramic vases with elaborate resist painting, testify to a substantial population in Group 10L-2 between about A.D. 500 and 600. Large masonry buildings of this period, however, if there are any in 10L-2, have not been found. The earliest small group of vaulted rooms and platforms with vaulted tombs, next to the base of the Acropolis, was constructed during the transition between the Acbi and Coner phases, about A.D. 600–650.

With this possible early exception, all of the architecture visible in Group 10L-2 was constructed during the reigns of the last five kings of the Copán dynasty, beginning with Ruler 12 (Smoke Imix), who sat on the throne from A.D. 628 to 695. Each courtyard contains evidence of three major construction phases, although this is a simplification of reality. Not all buildings show all three phases, and some structures and areas were enlarged and altered more than three times.

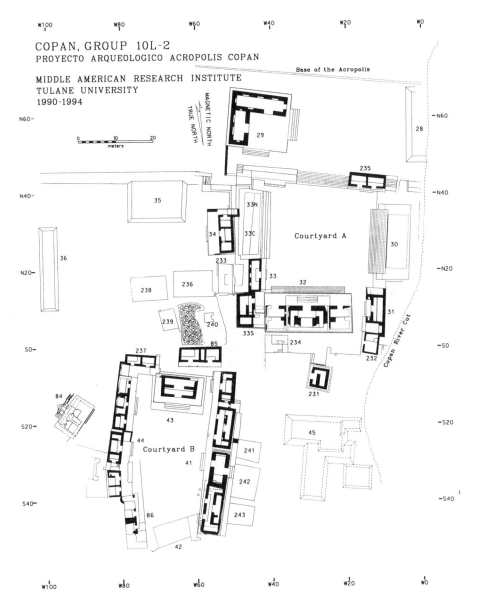

COPAN, GROUP 10L-2
PROYECTO ARQUEOLOGICO ACROPOLIS COPAN

Base of the Acropolis

MIDDLE AMERICAN RESEARCH INSTITUTE
TULANE UNIVERSITY
1990-1994

MAGNETIC NORTH
TRUE NORTH

0   10   20
meters

N60—

—N60

N40—

—N40

N20—

—N20

S0—

—S0

S20—

—S20

S40—

—S40

Courtyard A

Courtyard B

Copan River Cut

29   28

235

35   33N

34   33C   30

36   233

238   236   33   32   31

239   240   33S   234   232

85   237

84   43   231

44   45

41   241

86   242

42   243

W100   W80   W60   W40   W20   W0

*12.1 The residential compound of Yax Pasah, the sixteenth and last ruler in the
Copán dynasty, in Group 10L-2. Yax Pasah built his own house, 10L-32-1st, shortly
after taking the throne in A.D. 763. He also built 10L-30, a high ceremonial platform,
and 10L-41A, a smaller residence for a relative, at the northeast corner of Courtyard
B. The other structures are earlier, although all date to the Late Classic Coner phase.
At the north end of the group lies Structure 10L-29, a* waybil, *where the lineage
ancestors sleep.*

The courtyards were planned and the buildings around them started at one time, almost certainly in the reign of Ruler 12, and the final great construction took place during the early years of Yax Pasah's rule. There is limited evidence from sculpture to suggest the second general construction phase dates to the reign of Ruler 14 (Smoke Monkey) (A.D. 738–749) or slightly earlier, but between the first and last episode there were probably many renovations and enlargements in different parts of Group 10L-2.

The core of Group 10L-2 today consists of Courtyard A, at the base of the Acropolis, and Courtyard B, at the southwest corner of A. Courtyard C, about thirty meters west of Courtyard B, is slightly smaller and less regular, and it has not been excavated. Courtyard A, one side of which is formed by a four-meter-high stair rising to a broad terrace that runs along the south side of the Acropolis, is broader than Courtyard B and is surrounded by vaulted buildings and large stepped, flat-topped platforms for ritual, dance, and other public events. At the south end of the courtyard is Structure 10L-32, the largest edifice in Group 10L-2, which inscriptions identify as the house of Yax Pasah, the final ruler in the Copán dynasty. 10L-32-1st consists of a two-stage platform supporting a large central building with a throne and side screens, flanked by two smaller vaulted buildings standing on the lower level of the platform. The identical side buildings each have front rooms and central doors to raised back chambers, which were probably sleeping quarters. This double arrangement is somewhat similar to rooms flanking the central chamber of 9N-82 in Las Sepulturas, where Sanders (1989: 96) suggested the lineage head may have domiciled more than one wife. All three structures bore life-sized carved figures of a young man in regal garb, wearing a water lily headdress and seated on a water lily monster mask, who must be the youthful Yax Pasah at the time he built his house, shortly after his accession in A.D. 763. To raise the new structure, Yax Pasah dismantled most of an earlier building, 10L-32-2nd, except for a vaulted tomb under its central stair, which probably contained the remains of his father, who although unidentified was definitely not Ruler 15 (Smoke Shell), the previous ruler.

Yax Pasah also built a large, flat-topped ritual platform on the east side of Courtyard A, covering a similar structure that had been commissioned by one of his lineage predecessors. The rest of the buildings around Courtyard A are smaller and earlier. To the left of Yax Pasah's house is Structure 10L-33, built in the years of Ruler 12, containing one vaulted room with niches, a C-shaped bench, and a facade with sculpture that proclaimed the descent of its builders from Yax K'uk Mo', the founder of the dynasty. Just above Courtyard A, on the wide terrace at the base of the Acropolis, rests the large, L-shaped Structure 10L-29, also built early in the Courtyard A sequence. Its two long rooms contained eight or nine huge wall niches for offerings, but no benches. The upper facades bore ten human heads with markings that identify them as monkey or scribal deities, perhaps the patrons of the Group 10L-2 lineage, with ancestor or serpent cartouches above each head. We believe this building was a *waybil*, a shrine where offerings were made to invoke the spirits of the ancestors and the power of their supernatural guardians (Freidel et al. 1993: 189–190). The remaining buildings around Courtyard A include houses and ceremonial constructions, all predating Yax Pasah. Some buildings bear sculpture with central Mexican Tlaloc and year sign motifs, which are linked at Copán to the founder of the dynasty.

Courtyard B, nearly touching the southwest corner of A, is also a mixture of domestic, ritual, and administrative architecture. Structure 10L-41, running the full east side of the courtyard, included four vaulted buildings on a single low platform, each strikingly different from the others in internal arrangement (Andrews et al. 1999). The final addition, at the north end, was a set of three domestic rooms built by Yax Pasah, possibly for a relative, about the time he commissioned his own structures on Courtyard A. The other three were probably for ritual and administration. They show similarities to long structures at Utatlán that are probably the lineage administrative buildings described in ethnohistorical sources (Carmack 1981: 287–290, 385). All of the other structures around Courtyard B appear to have been domiciles, except for a two-room vaulted shrine at the north end of the courtyard. The others ranged from a three-room vaulted structure at the center of Structure 10L-44, on the west side of the courtyard, to small, pole-and-thatch rooms on low platforms on the south. The mixing of expensive and simple residential structures around one enclosed courtyard and even on one platform suggests a group of related individuals of different statuses, possibly with retainers. The composition of this residential unit would have been similar to that suggested by Sanders (1989: 102) for wards in the Las Sepulturas zone of Copán.

Yax Pasah's structures on Courtyard A are the largest in Group 10L-2, but, as on the Acropolis, his buildings and monuments seem to have been erected early in his reign (Andrews 1995). His dwelling (10L-32-1st), his ceremonial platform (10L-30-1st), and the smaller house on Courtyard B that he had built for a relative (10L-41A-1st) used identical masonry and construction techniques, different from those employed earlier in Group 10L-2, and were therefore probably raised at the same time. All three are stratigraphically the latest structures around their courtyards. His portraits on 10L-32 show that he was young when it was built, probably not long after his accession in A.D. 763. This pattern is similar to his construction record on the more public space of the Acropolis, where, as noted above, his most important buildings except 10L-18, his tomb, were dedicated within twelve years of his accession. Most of his carved monuments on the Acropolis also date early in his reign.

Yax Pasah is linked to Group 10L-2 by three carved monuments that bear his name and refer to events during the first half of his reign. These are Altars F?, G? and an altar that appears to have been pushed off the northwest corner of Structure 10L-30. No other person is mentioned on the inscribed monuments from Group 10L-2. The three monuments refer to events in Yax Pasah's life that occurred between A.D. 775 and 788, in the first twenty-five years of his reign. Two or three additional small, round altars associated with 10L-2 buildings commemorate the katun ending at A.D. 790, but no inscriptions are known in Group 10L-2 during the final thirty years of Yax Pasah's kingship.

Yax Pasah's death about A.D. 820, therefore, appears to have followed years of waning royal power (Schele and Freidel 1990: 341). The architectural and sculptural record of the final decades of the Copán dynasty in Group 10L-2, as on the Acropolis, suggests that the king's ability to command labor, skilled or unskilled, had declined. Trash began to accumulate in areas that were formerly swept clean. Middens containing Coner ceramics formed behind Structure 10L-32, Yax Pasah's house, behind 10L-33, and in corners at the base of the 10L-29 platform. Some of these trash piles were deep and some shallow, but all of them formed before the buildings near them were vandalized, indicating that they date to the final years of the Copán dynasty, rather than later. Four radiocarbon dates come from charcoal in these middens (Table 12.1). Two indicate a Terminal Classic date but two are earlier, and these raise the possibility that some of the floor middens around Courtyard A began to pile up early in Yax Pasah's reign, or even earlier.

Two buildings in Courtyard A provided evidence of violent destruction at the end of the Classic period. At least one lintel over a long niche deep inside Structure 10L-29, the temple of the lineage ancestors, was intentionally exposed to fire until the burning hardwood beams could no longer support the weight of the wall and vault above it. It fell, bringing down the entire structure. Burn marks on the floor indicate that the lintel above the door was also burned, probably at the same time. Structure 10L-33, another old house of the lineage claiming kinship to the founder of the dynasty, was similarly destroyed by burning the lintel over the wide central doorway. Structure 10L-41, the four-building lineage house in Courtyard B, showed large burn marks on the terrace outside at least one doorway, perhaps too large to result from burned offerings, but as this part of the structure was cleared in the late nineteenth century, we cannot be sure the building was burned or destroyed. Yax Pasah's house was also cleared in the early 1890s, but it collapsed on top of the Coner middens that had accumulated behind it during the last years of the king's life. We think Structure 10L-32, as the most visible and important building in Group 10L-2, suffered the same violent end at the same time as the vaulted buildings in Group 10L-2 that we excavated one hundred years later. A broad area behind 10L-32 shows extensive burning, with mixed charcoal and burned red earth, covered by the wall and vault fall off the back of Yax Pasah's house. The one large vaulted structure on the surface of the Acropolis that has been excavated in recent years, Structure 10L-22A (B. Fash et al. 1992), was also destroyed by burning (Fash 1991: 132), and we suspect that other royal buildings that were cleared out a century ago suffered similar fates.

Table 12.1.

Conventional ^{14}C Age B.P., Calibrated Dates A.D., Laboratory Number	Structure or Midden Location (Operation/Suboperation/Lot), Archaeological Context of the Charcoal, Ceramic Phase, and Comments
1220 ± 50 750 (820) 890 1σ 680 (820) 940 2σ Beta-54851	10L-29 (48/8/190), from one of two burned wooden beams found beside each other on the floor of the north room, just below a collapsed wall niche, sealed beneath the wall and vault collapse. Since the sample probably includes charcoal from the xylem to the interior of the beam, it should predate the death of the tree and the construction of 10L-29. Coner phase, probably between A.D. 700 and 763, the date of Yax Pasah's accession.
1730 ± 100 200 (330) 450 1σ 100 (330) 550 2σ Beta-40313	10L-31(48/4/68), from a possible midden in 2 cm of red, sandy soil on outside plaster floor that turns up to east wall of Room 1. Wall collapse lay immediately above this thin layer. Late Coner phase. The entire 2-sigma range falls before the expected A.D. 775–850 date of this lens, and it is likely that this was not a late midden.
1470 ± 100 500 (600) 650 1σ 400 (600) 750 2σ Beta-40305	10L-32/10L-234 (48/1/77). A thin, dark sheet midden on the cobble and flagstone floor of the patio south of 10L-32, 10B20 cm south of the steps to the tiny 10L-234. The charcoal was covered by a large Coner jar neck fragment immediately below thick layers of wall and vault fall from 10L-32. Late Coner phase. The sample contained only .25 gram of carbon and was given extended counting. The 2-sigma range precedes the expected A.D. 775–850 date of this midden.
1370 ± 80 620 (650) 720 1σ 560 (650) 830 2σ Beta-40307	10L-32/10L-231 (48/1/322). A deep, localized midden just above the cobble and flagstone floor of the patio behind 10L-32 and just west of 10L-231, below the wall and vault fall of 10L-32. This rich midden may have been trash from 10L-231. Late Coner phase. The 2-sigma range overlaps the expected A.D. 775–850 date of this midden, although the intercept is 125 years earlier.
1180 ± 50 810 (870) 930 1σ 740 (870) 980 2σ Beta-40306	10L-32 (48/1/298). An extensive 3-cm-thick midden on the plaster floor, 50–100 cm south of (behind) 10L-32, below a huge, sloping pile of wall and vault fall. The charcoal was mixed with burned red earth, indicating that the burning occurred on the floor, possibly at the time 10L-32 collapsed or was destroyed. Late Coner phase, expected date A.D. 775–850.
1160 ± 80 810 (910) 970 1σ 690 (910) 1010 2σ Beta-64091	10L-233 (48/6/93). A diffuse midden, 5B10 cm thick, on the plaster floor in front of 10L-233, behind 10L-33. The midden extends north between the backs of 10L-33-Center and 10L-34. Probably trash from 10L-233, a low, crudely built domestic platform probably occupied by junior relatives, servants or other clients of the royal family in Courtyard A. The midden was covered by the deep wall and vault fall of 10L-33 and 10L-34. The sample contained only .5 gram of carbon and was given extended counting. Late Coner phase, expected date A.D. 775–850.

Note: Radiocarbon ages were calibrated using the University of Washington Quaternary Isotope Lab Radiocarbon Calibration Program Rev. 3.0.3 (Stuiver and Reimer 1993). Calibrated dates have been rounded to the nearest decade. 1σ indicates 68% probability, and 2σ indicates 95% probability.

Neither hieroglyphic inscriptions nor archaeological evidence is available to help us identify the attackers of central Copán (Fash 1991: 173–177). Limited, internal conflict (Webster 1999: 40–41; Webster et al. 2000: 208–209), perhaps led by nobles who had belonged to the Copán polity, is one possibility; an attack on an already greatly weakened Copán by a distant enemy, such as Quirigua, is another. Neither scenario has direct evidence to support it. Sporadic, internal conflict seems an unlikely explanation for the events in Group 10L-2, because, we believe, there was a political and demographic collapse throughout the Copán Valley at about this time. The process and concomitants of cultural decline in the Copán Valley seem similar to what would happen throughout the Maya lowlands in the coming decades. Widespread and persistent conflict of the kind recently documented at the end of the Classic period in the Petexbatun region (Demarest 1997; Demarest et al. 1997) seems a more relevant model for the collapse of the Copán kingdom than either of the two extremes mentioned above.

The burning and destruction of some buildings in the royal compound is likely, for several reasons, to have happened not long after Yax Pasah's death about A.D. 820. One is that the collapsed walls and vaults fell onto middens containing ceramics that are fully in the Coner tradition. Second, the building and platform floors onto which the walls fell were immaculately clean until the building collapse, suggesting that they were still maintained by the families that lived there at the time of Yax Pasah's death. And finally, a few other middens, studied recently by Cassandra R. Bill (1997, personal communications 1997–2000), appear to have accumulated in Group 10L-2 after the buildings collapsed, and the ceramics in them, although still in the Coner tradition, are different from earlier Coner assemblages.

One of these middens, an extensive and deep trash dump, lies at the northwest corner of Structure 10L-30, where it eventually covered both Yax Pasah's Structure 30 altar, which had been thrown off this high platform and damaged, and the adjacent steps to the Structure 10L-29 terrace just to the north of 10L-30. This deposit must be the remains of trash swept off the 10L-29 terrace by a small group living in perishable houses. The latest-looking midden encountered in Group 10L-2 is a deep deposit of soil, ash, bones, pottery, and other artifacts in the patio outside the doorway to Structure 10L-33-South (C. R. Bill, personal communication 2000). The late Coner ceramics in these trash deposits provide evidence for an occupation of Group 10L-2 after the fall of the dynasty and the destruction of its most important buildings. The Structure 10L-33-South patio midden was eventually sealed by collapse debris from 10L-33-South, following which there is no evidence for any occupation of Group 10L-2. The midden around the 10L-30 altar was also finally sealed by the collapse of the 10L-30 platform, so it is clear that structures continued to decay. Not all of the eventual deterioration of buildings in this group can be attributed, therefore, to violent political events that occurred at the end of the dynasty.

The span represented by these few late middens around Courtyard A would not have been long. An occupation by a few families lasting fifty years beyond Yax Pasah's death seems consistent with the few middens and their impoverished content, but this final domestic use of the royal residence might have lasted closer to a century. We do not know who these individuals were, but they were living in a courtyard already mostly in ruins, and their numbers, possessions, and lifestyle did not match those of the previous noble inhabitants. There is, in other words, no evidence for continued elite activity in Group 10L-2, or on the Acropolis, after the political collapse and probable destruction of central Copán at the end of the Late Classic period.

Radiocarbon dates from Group 10L-2 suggest final abandonment dates before A.D. 900, coinciding with the disappearance of the late Coner ceramic complex at Copán, represented in Group 10L-2 by the latest middens. The center of the site appears then to have been unoccupied for fifty or a hundred years, until the arrival about A.D. 975 or 1000 of the small group of Early Postclassic Ejarphase settlers whose remains and activities are described below.

Archaeologists of the Pennsylvania State University project (PAC II) at Copán have argued that the Coner population in the Copán Valley remained at its peak of about 26,600 until A.D. 900 and that half this population was lost in the next seventy-five years. Thirty percent of the population was still left from A.D. 1000 to 1050, they believe, and the decline continued until near total abandonment of the valley by A.D. 1250 (Webster 1999: 38–41, 2000: 198–211; Webster et al. 1992). This interpretation of Copán population dynamics, which posits a declining number of inhabitants in the valley for about 350 years beyond the traditional end of the Coner phase at A.D. 900, is based on a large number of obsidian hydration measurements from many sites of all sizes all over the valley.

The argument for an extended Copán decline maintains that the Coner phase, with Coner ceramics, continued for about 400 years after the collapse of the dynasty, until A.D. 1250 (Freter 1992: 119; Webster and Freter 1990b). Since the Coner phase began by A.D. 650 (Bill 1997; Viel 1993a), the extended chronology would require this ceramic complex to last 600 years with relatively little change, a duration probably unequaled by any other ceramic complex in the Classic or Postclassic period in the Maya area or the rest of Mesoamerica.

We are unwilling to accept the extension of the Coner ceramic complex for three and a half centuries past the end of the Late Classic period. Our reluctance stems not only from the presence of a small but clearly defined Early Postclassic settlement at the site, with pottery unlike that of the Coner phase, but also from our belief that obsidian hydration dating is not yet accurate enough to serve well the chronological purposes for which it has been employed at Copán (Braswell 1992; Braswell et al. 1996a; Freter 1992; Webster et al. 1992; Webster et al. 1993). The 1σ standard deviation of the Copán obsidian hydration dates is argued to be ± 70 years, but we believe that this number underestimates the probable range of error.

We think that nearly all the obsidian from Copán dated in recent years between A.D. 950 and 1250 was used and discarded during the Late Classic period, before A.D. 950.

THE EARLY POSTCLASSIC OCCUPATION

Although ample data point to a rapid and violent demise of the Copán dynasty, evidence testifying to subsequent activities has been extremely limited. Traditional Early Postclassic (A.D. 1000–1200) ceramic markers such as Tohil Plumbate (Shepard 1948) and Las Vegas Polychrome, a type from central Honduras with clear ties to the white-slipped vessels of the Nicoya region such as Papagayo Polychrome (Abel-Vidor et al. 1987; Lothrop 1926), have been rare. Likewise, green obsidian from central Mexico, imported strictly in blade form with ground platforms during the Early Postclassic period, is scarce. Reported evidence of Postclassic activity at Copán was limited to several intrusive burials, either cut into the plaza floor or interred within abandoned rooms of several structures in the Main Group, with most activity concentrated in the East Court (Longyear 1952: 75). Additionally, several sheet middens indicate Early Postclassic reuse of previously abandoned ceremonial structures within the Main Group and the surrounding area, including Ballcourt B (Fash and Lane 1983). The most striking evidence previously known came from Temple 18, mentioned above, which was sacked and looted during the Early Postclassic. The lack of any identifiable Early Postclassic domestic component, however, had until recently necessitated the attribution of these limited activities to passing pilgrimages through the otherwise abandoned Main Group (Fash and Sharer 1991; Longyear 1952).

Sylvanus Morley (1920: 430), using the latest known dates recorded upon the stelae and hieroglyphic altars of Copán, first postulated that the abandonment of Copán was sudden and rapid, resulting in virtual complete depopulation within a matter of decades after dynastic collapse. The limited Postclassic activity discovered by the Peabody and subsequent Carnegie expeditions allowed John Longyear (1952: 71) to confirm Morley's theory while refining it slightly with his ceramic sequence. This model gained further corroboration through Rene Viel's (1983: 533–539) ceramic seriation, which dated the Late Classic Coner ceramic phase from about A.D. 650 to 850, and which initially placed the local Early Postclassic Ejar ceramic phase from A.D. 900 to 1200 based upon the presence of imported fine-paste ceramics that, although rare at Copán, are ubiquitous throughout Mesoamerica during that time. Viel (1993b: 143) later constricted the range of the Ejar phase to span only A.D. 950 to 1000, as almost no new Ejar material had been discovered in the wake of the previous decade of intensive excavation and no evidence for a local population had been found.

An examination of the previous Ejar finds helps to contextualize this poorly understood period of Copán's history within the broader sociopolitical history of the polity. First, the discoveries made by the Peabody and Carnegie projects as reported by Longyear (1952) were extremely rare, limited to four burials in the Main Group primarily within the East Court, and an additional two interments from the surrounding area. The first was located about one kilometer to the northwest of the Main Group, and the other, the remarkable Tomb 10 (Longyear 1952: 43), was located about 100 meters south of the Acropolis in an area that has since been eroded by the river in the years following its discovery by the Peabody project. Second, the burials were intrusive to the structures in which they were found; in more than one instance they consisted of nothing more than placing the body near floor level of an abandoned room and filling in the chamber with rubble. The probable exception is Tomb 10, a fairly elaborate crypt that held a lone child. Although the excavators recorded no structure associated with the feature, it now seems probable that the burial was placed within a simple platform that escaped detection. Third, the interments typically contained at least one piece of reused carved stone, taken from the facades of structures at the center of the site, most often from Temple 18, suggesting that these modest burials were placed well after the Main Group fell into disarray.

As a final point, the associated grave furniture, vessels of Tohil Plumbate (N=5), Las Vegas Polychrome (N=3), an undetermined variety of Fine Orange (N=1) and ladle-handle censers (N=3), were all found without a single Coner vessel, utilitarian or otherwise. Although Fine Orange Wares are traditionally associated with the Terminal Classic, their appearance at Copán seems to be especially late. Limited numbers of Fine Orange sherds, perhaps a handful in all (Viel [1993b: 122] reports fifteen sherds), along with several whole vessels, have been reported from terminal occupations in outlying elite residential compounds, but the presence of the ware is almost surely contemporaneous with, or slightly later than, dynastic collapse. In the Ejar ceramic complex, Fine Orange plays a more prominent role, although it is still rare. This imported trade ware is the only ceramic type that can be found in both Terminal Classic and Early Postclassic deposits. The fact that the ware is found in both contexts does not, however, indicate continuity between the two ceramic phases. To the contrary, we argue that the Ejar phase represented a greatly reduced, almost ephemeral occupation that shared no clear evidence for continuity with the preceding Coner phase.

In an effort to locate more such elusive Early Postclassic evidence, Manahan initiated the Copán Postclassic Archaeological Project (CPAP) in 1995, focusing upon the dense residential zone to the south of the Main Group known locally as the Bosque area, in particular the settlement south of Ballcourt B, Copán's second ballcourt (Figure 12.2). Ballcourt B presented the best starting point, as it was the only locus that had yielded significant quantities of Early Postclassic markers (Fash and Lane 1983: 539–540). These artifacts were also found in association with portable stone incense burners and several pieces of sculpture taken from the jambs of Structure 10L-18, creating the first link between the deliberate destruction of the tomb within Temple 18 and Early Postclassic activity near Ballcourt

B. CPAP investigation of Structure 11L-77, located on the southeast edge of Ballcourt B, quickly yielded quantities of Early Postclassic markers on the long, low platform, establishing that the building contained an extensive Ejar component. Further excavations confirmed that the entire construction dated to the Early Postclassic, making it the first reported Ejar-phase residence at Copán (Manahan 1995).

Subsequent CPAP research expanded the search for Ejar first to the entire Bosque area and later to a larger portion of the Copán Valley, with intriguing results, summarized below. The nature of the Ejar settlement itself explains in part why no Early Postclassic structures had been previously identified. While Ejar structures may be twenty meters long, none stand more than a meter above the modern ground surface, and the structures do not form the discrete patio groups seen in earlier periods. In the five-tiered site settlement hierarchy established by Willey and Leventhal (1979), Ejar structures are categorized as either the lowest tier, Type 1, or merely as isolated mounds. The low Ejar platforms, their lack of formal arrangements, and research projects that have focused upon monu-

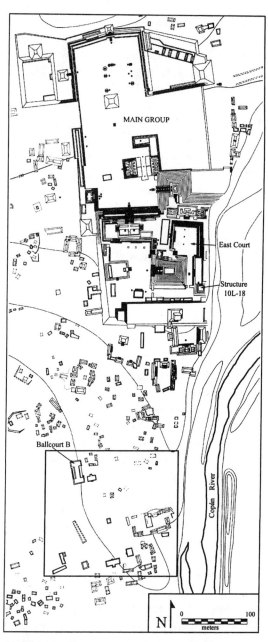

12.2 The Main Group and the southeastern part of the El Bosque zone at Copán. The box delimits the principal Copán Postclassic Archaeological Project (CPAP) study area, enlarged in Figure 12.3 (adapted from Fash and Long 1983).

mental architecture and larger domestic buildings have together ensured that the elusive Ejar phase remained obscured from investigation until recently.

Findings from ongoing CPAP investigations are beginning to illustrate lifeways for the Ejar-phase inhabitants of Copán that are distinct from what has been documented for even the latest Terminal Classic inhabitants. Data derived from the archaeologically visible aspects of Ejar life—settlement patterns, architectural features, burial practices, and ceramic and chipped stone technologies—all show that the Ejar-phase residents practiced a way of life unknown to Copanecos in dynastic times.

Ejar-phase constructions are a drop in the sea of visible architecture, almost all of which bears a substantial Coner-phase component. Building from the identification of Structure 11L-77, CPAP investigated more than fifty structures in the Bosque area. These were selected by several criteria. As additional Ejar structures surfaced in the Bosque, a clearer picture of Ejar settlement emerged. To date, CPAP has identified eight Ejar-phase structures, concentrated in the southeast corner of the Bosque area, and within close proximity to the Río Copán (Figure 12.3). The structures, all large, low, flat platforms of varying dimensions, are located near an impressive Type 3 Classic period elite residence, which undoubtedly served as bountiful quarry for the Ejar residents. The Ejar buildings cluster around an area free of other structures to form a large, irregular courtyard-like area toward which all excavated structures face, creating a settlement pattern that is unique at Copán. Furthermore, the Ejar-phase inhabitants chose to construct their buildings from scratch rather than reoccupying or modifying the extensive surrounding domestic architecture. A second phase of investigation expanded the search to a large segment of the surrounding valley. More than ninety structures were selected from the site map (Fash and Long 1983) for investigation. In contrast to the results within the Bosque, CPAP failed to identify a single Ejar structure from the sample outside of the Bosque settlement. Additional small clusters of Ejar settlement may exist, but they have escaped detection, and there cannot be many of them.

Although the Ejar buildings vary in proportions and size, they share several stylistic architectural features and construction techniques. The exteriors of all substructures were constructed from cut and sometimes dressed blocks of stone that were probably quarried from nearby abandoned Late Classic structures. The walls were constructed without lime plaster, the stones being set in adobe mortar. The platforms varied in height between one to almost two meters above the ancient ground surface. Construction fills of all structures were a mix of dirt, large and small unmodified river cobbles, and cut stones. The fill of several platforms also included discarded whole and broken pieces of sculpted stones from earlier Coner structures.

In contrast to the more substantial substructures, the Ejar superstructures were constructed primarily of perishable materials. The floors of all structures

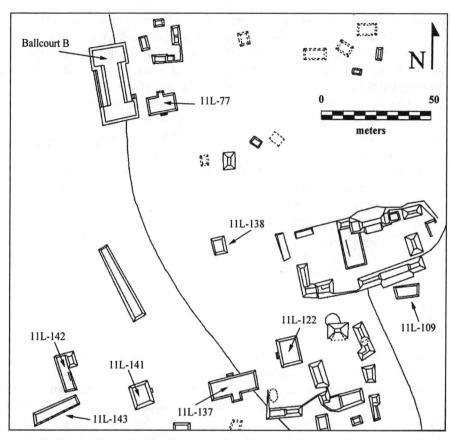

12.3 The principal Copán Postclassic Archaeological Project (CPAP) study area in the southeastern part of El Bosque. Ballcourt B is 200 m south of the Acropolis and 200 m west of the Río Copán. Structure numbers denote Ejar-phase buildings identified to date (adapted from Fash and Long 1983).

were of tamped earth that preserved poorly. All of the investigated structures yielded copious quantities of daub, fired sufficiently when the structures burned to preserve impressions of the wattle, and two structures also contained the remains of cut stone rear walls that may have risen 1.5 meters above the substructure floor. With these exceptions, all walls of the excavated superstructures were built of wattle and daub and would have supported a perishable roof.

Several archaeological features offer powerful testimony to both the uniqueness and the late date of the structures in comparison to Coner buildings. Perhaps the most unusual feature was a cache of six recycled pieces of sculpture encountered in the construction fill just inside the rear wall of Structure 11L-77 on the central longitudinal axis. Of the six carved stones, one portrayed the head of a zoomorphic figure, four were feathers, and the sixth showed feathers on one side and a hand clutching the hair of a human head on the other. This last piece of sculpture has been refitted to the northwest jamb of Structure 10L-18 in the Main Group, and the other pieces show motifs, style, and depth of relief that are also consistent with the sculptural program of Temple 18.

Reused Classic-period sculpture also appears frequently in association with Early Postclassic burials, a fact first noted by Longyear (1952: 47) in his report of Ejar-phase interments uncovered by the Peabody project. This pattern held true for the two burials encountered during the course of excavation. The two burials, one a cist from Structure 11L-77, and the other a crypt from Structure 11L-137, each contained a single block of sculpture reused as a wall stone in the burial chamber. The piece of sculpture from 11L-77 came from Structure 10L-18, while the sculpture from the 11L-137 crypt originally formed part of the niche motif from nearby Structure 10L-41, a building in Yax Pasah's residential compound (Group 10L-2). Classic-period sculpture has also been recovered from the walls of Ejar structures. Carved stones from the facades of Structures 10L-18, 10L-41, and 10L-32, all buildings closely associated with Yax Pasah, were reused as Ejar wall stones.

One particular piece of reused sculpture set into the rear platform facing of Structure 11L-137, a fish, almost certainly from the fill or the collapsed fill of Structure 10L-32-1st, raises questions about how much the late inhabitants of the site knew of the earlier Classic inhabitants, their rulers, and the iconography of their monuments. The facade of the house of Yax Pasah's immediate lineage predecessor in Group 10L-2, Structure 10L-32-2nd, was adorned with carved fish. Structure 10L-31, at the east side of 10L-32, also bore a fish. A similar fish was one of the place glyphs on Structure 10L-22A, the council house on the Acropolis (B. Fash 1992, B. Fash et al. 1992). This fish, set into the facade above the central entrance, faced south toward Structure 10L-32, leading to the hypothesis that Group 10L-2 was, as suggested above, one of the nine seats of noble power represented in the council house—the fish place, or *kanal*. When Yax Pasah built his house, he cached a fish from the earlier structure under the center of his throne, and others were placed in and below the bench. The fish motif remained important to him, as it had been to his predecessor, even though he did not place fish on his own facade.

The vaulted tomb of Yax Pasah's ancestor in Structure 10L-32-2nd, under the stair of the final platform, was looted in antiquity, and we think that this desecration may be attributed to the Ejar settlers, who lived approximately two hundred meters to the south, although it could have been entered at the time the vaults were torn down and the building was burned. The Ejar people may have encountered the fish in the fill of Structure 10L-32-1st in the process of looting the tomb. The carved stones they collected indicate that they probably also looted Yax Pasah's tomb in 10L-18 and removed sculpture from Structure 10L-16 and Structures 10L-30 and 10L-41 in Group 10L-2. Their looting seems to have been focused, rather than random, and their interest in the fish could suggest that they knew of its importance to Late Classic Copanecos.

The two Ejar burials contain utilitarian and trade vessels that date to the Early Postclassic period. The cist in Structure 11L-77 held a single adult and a vessel of Tohil Plumbate near the individual's head. The crypt in Structure 11L-137 contained the crushed and poorly preserved remains of at least three individuals: two females, one child of approximately two years, and possibly an infant. The individuals were found interred with the remains of at least thirteen vessels, of which nine were completely or partially reconstructible. The vessels included both utilitarian and fine-paste imported wares but lacked any diagnostic Coner ceramics. The utilitarian vessels include two globular unslipped incised jars similar to Tamoa Buff Incised at Cihuatán (Fowler 1981: 206), two ladle censers that are identical to Tamoa Red-on-buff (Fowler 1981: 209), a large fillet-rim incensario, and an unslipped jar of the Ejar utilitarian type Kan Burnished. Imported trade wares included an olive-green Tohil Plumbate jar, a Las Vegas Polychrome effigy jar, and two Las Vegas Polychrome deep-rimmed tripod plates.

Ejar utilitarian and fine-paste ceramics were present on the surface of the platforms, in construction fill, and in midden deposits typically encountered along the rear or sides of the structures. Fine-paste pottery types such as Tohil Plumbate, Las Vegas Polychrome, and Fine Orange ware together include between 0.5 and 1.8 percent of the total overall material recovered, and from 2 to 6.5 percent of Ejar assemblages. Although the full range of utilitarian types is still being established, the Ejar utilitarian assemblage represents a significant reduction in number of types and the nadir of quality in the long ceramic history of Copán. Utilitarian Ejar ceramics are distinguished in general by their crude, often chunky pastes and wide range of variation within forms that, coupled with an expedient execution style, makes them highly distinctive from their Coner counterparts. No Coner types have been found to continue into the Ejar phase, and no evolution of forms can be traced from one phase to the next.

Ejar chipped stone assemblages bespeak a similar break from earlier established patterns. The local production of prismatic blades, a technology that dominated Coner household assemblages and constituted almost all of the lithic material, is seemingly absent during the Ejar phase. Instead, Ejar residents chose to scavenge and recycle local discarded blades and to import blades with ground platforms as finished objects. Blades were imported from more diverse sources: Pachuca and Ucareo obsidian from Mexico and La Esperanza blades from central Honduras formed a much greater proportion of the assemblage than in Coner. Ejar chipped stone technology diverges perhaps most dramatically from earlier assemblages in terms of percussion technology, particularly with the biface industry. Whereas bifacial tools are very rare in Coner assemblages, crude projectile points made of obsidian or chert are common in Ejar. Excavations from Structure 11L-77 alone produced more than 100 projectile points. The increase in projectile points is diagnostic of the Early Postclassic period, but the lack of locally manufactured blades in the Copán assemblage shows greater affinity to assemblages from southern Mesoamerica outside the Maya area than to those from other southern Maya lowland sites.

Believing that the Tohil Plumbate from Tomb 10 signaled what he termed a "Toltec horizon," Viel (1993b: 143) dated the Early Postclassic Ejar phase from A.D. 950 to 1000, a short span suggested by the ephemeral occupation. This interval corresponds well to the height of distribution of Tohil Plumbate, the wane of Fine Orange wares, and the spread of Las Vegas Polychrome, as seen in the Río Blanco phase at Los Naranjos (Baudez and Becquelin 1973).

Although regional comparative dating places the Ejar ceramic complex squarely within the Early Postclassic phase, radiometric dating was required to produce chronometric dates for the Ejar occupation. Carbonized pieces of the wattle and daub walls of Structures 11L-77 and 11L-141, as well as bones from the crypt of 11L-137, were selected for dating. Three samples were run from each structure, and AMS was used for all but two of the samples (Table 12.2). The results of the ^{14}C assays correspond well to the dates derived from ceramic comparisons, as calibrated intercept dates range from A.D. 970 to A.D. 1085, with one outlier of A.D. 1260. Most intercepts fall between A.D. 990 and 1020. These chronometric dates confirm Viel's view of an early, short-lived Early Postclassic period at Copán.

We see complete temporal and cultural disjunctions between the end of the Classic period and the final habitation of the site. Ejar lifeways illustrate patterns that are much more indicative of Early Postclassic Central America rather than of the Terminal Classic southern Maya lowlands. Ejar settlement pattern, settlement density, architectural style, and material culture show trends that are remarkably divergent from those seen in the Classic period. While the presence of Plumbate and Fine Orange shows trade ties to piedmont Guatemala and the greater Usumacinta drainage, other components of the assemblage, such as Las Vegas Polychrome, show contact with central Honduras and influence from lower Central America that is absent at other southern Maya lowland sites during this turbulent time period.

The Ejar inhabitants' penchant for mining Coner architecture for building materials and architectural adornments, coupled with the relatively late chronometric dates obtained from their residences, strongly suggest to us a reoccupation of the site following a period of complete abandonment. This interpretation is further strengthened by the fact that the Ejar-phase residents built their structures from scavenged materials rather than reusing or modifying the extensive surrounding architecture. The difference becomes starker when one contrasts this break from tradition to the rich architectural histories of residential compounds, such as that of Group 9N-8, which extended from the Terminal Classic back for

Table 12.2.

Laboratory Number and Conventional ^{14}C Age B.P.	Calibrated Date A.D. (± 1-sigma error)	Structure	Material Dated
Beta-91486 1060 ± 60	900 (990) 1020	11L-77	Wood charcoal from carbonized wattle of superstructure
Beta-91487 1100 ± 80	885 (905, 910, 975) 1015	11L-77	Wood charcoal from carbonized wattle of superstructure
Beta-91488 1010 ± 50	990 (1020) 1035	11L-77	Wood charcoal from carbonized wattle of superstructure
Beta-139612 920 ± 40	1035 (1055, 1085, 1150) 1175	11L-137	Human bone from Burial 58/3/1
Beta-139613 780 ± 40	1225 (1260) 1275	11L-137	Human bone from Burial 58/3/1
Beta-139614 1070 ± 40	965 (990) 1005	11L-137	Human bone from Burial 58/3/1
Beta-139615 1030 ± 40	990 (1005) 1025	11L-141	Wood charcoal from carbonized wattle of superstructure
Beta-139616 1100 ± 40	895 (970) 995	11L-141	Wood charcoal from carbonized wattle of superstructure
Beta-139617 980 ± 40	1010 (1025) 1040	11L-141	Carbonized cotton seeds recovered from floor.

Note: Radiocarbon ages were calibrated using the INTCAL98 database (Stuiver et al. 1998).

centuries to the earliest occupation of Copán. Whether these ultimate residents were descendants of the original inhabitants of the valley or settlers from central Honduras or the El Salvador highlands is unknown. The radical changes in Ejar lifeways show that this late population drew inspiration from very different sources than their predecessors. While we do not wish to oversimplify the issue of reconstructing ethnic identity, we also feel that this final occupation was most likely by non-Maya peoples. Wherever they may have originated, the ultimate inhabitants, faced with their own set of problems, were neither able to survive for long nor to make much of a lasting contribution to the crowded landscape of abandoned residential architecture.

CONCLUSIONS

We have approached the end of Classic Copán from three perspectives. Fash discusses the evidence for weakness and instability during the reign of the last kings, especially of Yax Pasah, the final king in the dynasty. He finds that the fortunes of the city correspond well to the model proposed by Marcus (1992) for the growth and decline of other powerful Mesoamerican cities. The peak of power and external influence at Copán had been reached by the beginning of the Late Classic, after which began a slow decline that may have started with the capture and sacrifice of Ruler 13 (18 Rabbit) and ended with the collapse of the Copán dynasty about A.D. 820. His successor, Ruler 14 (Smoke Monkey), built a large council house with prominent sculptures of nine lords, each seated over the name of the place each represented, acknowledging thereby that his rule relied upon other nobles and their supporters, both within Copán and in more distant communities. With views akin to those of Sanders (1989), who argues for a noble class of lineage heads who usually supported but could also oppose the ruler and his lineage, Fash postulates that the main structural problem at Copán, and elsewhere in the Late Classic Maya lowlands, was competition for a limited number of political offices by a growing number of eligible adult males, against a backdrop of population increase and nutritional stress. The result was endemic competition and warfare.

Andrews looks at the Late and Terminal Classic and the collapse at Copán from a narrower perspective, the residential neighborhood of Yax Pasah, the final king in the dynasty, who reigned from A.D. 763 to about 820. Several of Yax Pasah's hieroglyphic monuments in Group 10L-2 tell about rituals he conducted and allow the identification of his house, which contained the tomb of the lineage head who preceded him. None of his monuments contains a reference to a date later than A.D. 788. As on the Acropolis, just above Group 10L-2, Yax Pasah's buildings in this complex date to early in his years as king. Middens with Coner ceramics began to form in previously clean areas near residential structures toward the end of the Late Classic. About the time of Yax Pasah's death, the lintels of several buildings in Group 10L-2 appear to have been burned, with the goal of bringing down the walls and vaults. We think that this violent event signals the end of the Copán dynasty and royal power, and the beginning of the demographic decline. A few middens with terminal Coner pottery piled up in the royal residence, almost certainly after this destruction, but these contain no post-Coner ceramics, indicating abandonment of the royal residence and probably the Acropolis by A.D. 900.

We believe that the Copán Valley was also abandoned during the Terminal Classic period, that no significant occupation remained after about A.D. 900, and that a gap of several generations separated the end of the Classic period from the appearance of the Early Postclassic Ejar settlement a few hundred meters south of the Acropolis. Elsewhere, throughout the Copán Valley, the latest pottery found in excavations or on the surface belongs to the Late Classic Coner ceramic complex, as in Group 10L-2 and on the Acropolis. Although many obsidian hydration dates from the Copán Valley indicate that the Coner ceramic complex lasted 600 or 650 years, until about A.D. 1250, we believe that this dating method is not reliable. The documentation of an Early Postclassic settlement at Copán requires an end to the Coner complex before A.D. 950.

Manahan describes his recent investigations of the small Early Postclassic Ejar population, which seems limited to a settlement at the southeast corner of El Bosque, south of the Acropolis, near Ballcourt B and the Copán River. The eight known platforms are less than a meter high, but some are long enough to have supported more than one perishable dwelling with tamped earth floors. The cut stones of the platform facings, set without lime mortar or plaster, were usually robbed from nearby Coner buildings but included some sculpted stones from Structure 10L-18, Yax Pasah's tomb on the Acropolis, and from 10L-32 and 10L-41, two of the most important buildings in Yax Pasah's residence. Yax Pasah's tomb and the tomb of his ancestor in 10L-32 were robbed in antiquity, and we think the Ejar settlers are the likely malefactors, since there is no evidence of anyone at the site after this small Ejar group disappeared. All the ceramics associated with this occupation are Early Postclassic, including exotic Fine Orange, Tohil Plumbate, Las Vegas Polychrome, and a local unslipped incised pottery similar to the Early Postclassic Tamoa Red-on-buff at Cihuatán, 100 kilometers south of Copán. The lithic industry also shows a complete break with the Late Classic, having no locally produced prismatic blades but an abundance of bifacial projectile points. A series of radiocarbon dates from three Ejar structures indicates a short occupation, from about A.D. 950 to 1050.

The Terminal Classic, corresponding roughly to the ninth century, was a time of decline and collapse at Copán, as it was throughout the Maya lowlands. It brought to an end several centuries of increasing population, deforestation, hillside erosion, nutritional stress, competition among elites for limited labor, land, and power, and almost certainly—toward the end—conflict and warfare. Rapid population growth has been documented at site after site, culminating about A.D. 800. Late Classic Copán rulers suffered military setbacks at the hands of distant enemies, came to rely increasingly upon their noble supporters, and eventually lost power. Yax Pasah, the last king, built several major structures on the Acropolis and three in Group 10L-2, but all except his tomb were dedicated within fifteen years of his accession to the throne. Thereafter he seems to have lacked the power and resources to undertake public or private architecture of consequence. Eventually, trash piled up around his house and those of his relatives and it was never removed. Yax Pasah's death and the burning of the royal compound, perhaps at the hands of neighboring communities once subservient to the expanding Copán state, occurred early in the Terminal Classic, and about A.D. 900 the city of Copán and its hinterlands were abandoned.

Several generations later a small group of farmers settled among the decaying buildings a few hundred meters south of the Acropolis, bringing with them diagnostic Early Postclassic pottery and artifact traditions of southeastern Mesoamerica.

They looted tombs and carried off pieces of sculpture to set in their own simple platforms, and within a few generations they, too, had gone, leaving to the forest the thousand empty buildings of a once-powerful city.

13

OUT WITH A WHIMPER
LA MILPA IN THE TERMINAL CLASSIC

Norman Hammond and Gair Tourtellot

t all depends, as President Clinton might have said, on precisely what you mean by "Terminal Classic": Sabloff (1975: Fig 4) follows Smith (1955: Table 8) in assigning a span beginning at 10.0.0.0.0 (A.D. 830), but subsequently (1990: 18, 130) runs it from A.D. 800 to 1000, as do Hammond (1982: Fig. 4.1) and Sharer (Morley, Brainerd, and Sharer 1983: Table 1; Sharer 1994: Table 2.1). Foias and Bishop (1997: Fig. 1) revert to the A.D. 830 beginning, correlated with the Bayal/Sepens phases in the Pasión region, and end the Terminal Classic in A.D. 950; Tourtellot and González (Chapter 4, this volume) use a span of A.D. 830–1000, but Bey et al. (1997: Table 1) propose a span of A.D. 900–1100 in Yucatán. Smith (1955: 3–4) has Tepeu 3 at Uaxactún ending "sometime after 10.3.0.0.0 (A.D. 889)," while Sabloff (1975: Fig. 4) gives it a firm ending at 10.3.0.0.0 (A.D. 889), while continuing Bayal at Seibal through 10.5.0.0.0 (A.D. 928). A number of major cities have no dated monuments in the ninth century, and thus do not have a Terminal Classic, however defined; others, including Piedras Negras, Yaxchilan, Calakmul, and Copán, dedicate their last monuments some years before A.D. 830. Bey et al. (1997: 249) suggest that "Terminal Classic is a term best used to define the final post-monumental Classic occupation of Maya centers, rather than as a single pan-lowland time period."

A beginning for the Terminal Classic that marks the initial decline in overall monument dedications after the high point of 9.18.0.0.0 (A.D. 790: Morley 1937–38, IV: Figs. 148–149), that is, at A.D. 800, makes more general sense than one contingent upon the anomalous florescence of Seibal and the possible millennial associations of the *baktun*-ending in A.D. 830. The timing of the end is evanescent: people on the brink of abandoning their cities tend not to spend their time carving and dating monuments. The latest known Initial Series of 10.4.0.0.0 is on Toniná Monument 101, the same *katun*-ending date is recorded on a jade from Tzibanché, and San Lorenzo (Campeche) Stela 1 may possibly date to 10.5.0.0.0, suggesting an end to Classic history by A.D. 930. Although the superstructure of Late Classic elite culture, with its public buildings and patronage art, thus collapsed, this may simply push the rest of society below the level of datable archaeological visibility. People may stay around for some time after the last effort at maintaining royal rituals, perhaps, as claimed at Copán on the basis of obsidian hydration dates, for several centuries, or as at Lamanai, indefinitely.

All this goes to show that the Terminal Classic is rather difficult to pin down in archaeological reality; although only one generation or so, less than two *katunob*, separates the earliest from the latest proposed beginning and ending dates (except in Yucatán), there is a paucity of precisely dated events outside a handful of sites. At La Milpa this has serious repercussions; we do not know whether we have a Terminal Classic or not. If the period is held to begin in A.D. 800, we probably do; if in A.D. 830, possibly not. The one sherd of Pabellon Molded-carved fine paste pottery, a type formally introduced in the Pasión at the latter date, from a topsoil context does not suggest an occupation long thereafter. So at La Milpa the schematics of chronology count.

The site itself lies in the northwest of Belize, close to the frontiers with Mexico and Guatemala. Roughly equidistant from the very large cities of Tikal and Calakmul, some ninety kilometers to the southwest and northwest respectively, about twenty kilometers east from the major center of Río Azul in northeastern Guatemala, and forty kilometers west of Lamanai, on New River Lagoon in the coastal plain of Belize (see Tourtellot et al. 1993: Fig 1), the La Milpa community covers an estimated seventy-eight square kilometers. Discovered by J. Eric S. Thompson (1938), the site lacked buildings and monuments sufficiently impressive or well preserved to attract further exploration until the late 1980s (Hammond 1991b). The La Milpa Archaeological Project (LaMAP) of Boston University and the National Geographic Society carried out initial evaluation in 1990 and began full-scale research in 1992. The research design embraced a set of complementary mapping, excavation, and environmental studies. Mapping began with a complete contour survey of the central square kilometer, with the ceremonial precinct at its core, for which a new and accurate site plan was produced. Transects were cut and mapped north, south, and east from the central area (independent research to the west along the boundary of Programme for Belize land by Hubert Robichaux [1995] and ongoing research into water management by Vernon Scarborough and colleagues [1995] have together approximated a western transect), that to the south nearly reaching, and that to the east extending beyond, the city limits at five kilometers from the center. The transects were intended to provide continuous samples of topography, settlement, and landscape engineering (terraces, berms, etc.). A stratified sample of fifteen randomly positioned survey blocks was mapped in detail and subjected to intensive surface collection and test excavation by John Rose (Tourtellot et al. 1994), as a statistically robust complement. As we became aware of the idiosyncrasies of La Milpa's urban layout, we added targeted objectives, such as the successful location of northern and western minor centers 3.5 kilometers from the site core, predicted to exist on the basis of a proposed cosmological model (Tourtellot et al. 2000).

Mapping was subject to constraints imposed by the biotope status of the Programme for Belize lands; only underbrush could be cleared without specific per-tree permission for cutting larger growth. The same limitation was imposed on excavations, precluding large area coverage. In the survey blocks and transects, sampling of households (in separate programs by Gloria Everson, Jason González, and John Rose) was not impeded by this condition, nor was the program of targeted test-pitting in the ceremonial precinct. One tree was removed from the top of Structure 5 in the course of total excavation preceding anticipated restoration, but on larger structures our policy of avoiding major architectural exposure in the absence of assured future maintenance was in accord with the landowners' objective of environmental preservation.

The site-core excavation program included a set of plaza test pits to determine the stratigraphic history of La Milpa, which demonstrated pre-Late Classic occupation only below the Great Plaza area (see below); stela-setting excavations to determine which monuments were in situ and which reset (Hammond and Bobo 1994), one of which (Op. B11) was enlarged and shifted in focus when it encountered an Early Classic royal tomb; and the cleaning, recording, and in a few cases lateral or vertical extension, of the numerous looters' trenches that penetrate almost every major building. In some cases, looters' trenches were also then backfilled to stabilize structures in danger of collapse, notably Structure 5. With the exception of that building, intended for restoration, all excavations at La Milpa through the 2000 season have been completely backfilled and are in most cases already undetectable.

The site core lies 190 meters above sea level on a limestone ridge dissected by ravines, at 17°50'06"N, 89°03'06"W (UTM 16Q BQ 2-82-637E, 19-72-929N). Monumental architecture, with buildings up to twenty-four meters high and ninety meters long, covers some 650 by 400 meters (twenty-six hectares) in two areas linked by a *sacbe* causeway spanning the narrow neck of land between the eastern and western drainages (Figure 13.1). Seasonal runoff from these may have been managed for water-supply and agricultural purposes (Scarborough et al. 1995).

The northern sector includes the Great Plaza (Plaza A), bordered by three major temple-pyramids, Structures 1–3, and enclosing a fourth, Str. 10, together with two ballcourts, Strs. 6–7 and 11–12, aligned on opposite axes (Schultz et al. 1994). Str. 10 faces south and is axially aligned on the ninety-meter-long "palace,"

13.1 Plan of the ceremonial core of La Milpa (by G. Tourtellot, inked by H. A. Shelley).

Str. 8; their construction as an ensemble seems to have occurred late in the history of the Great Plaza, partly blocking Str. 3 and the stair to the raised court behind Str. 9; whether either, or both, covers a smaller precursor is not known. Strs. 9 and 2 are also aligned; both pairs, like most other structures on the plaza, date in final form to the Late/Terminal Classic period (we use this designation because of the present difficulty in separating them [Kosakowsky et al. 1998; Sagebiel 1999]). The lack of substantial buildings on the north and northwest sides of the plaza suggests that the final redevelopment remained incomplete when La Milpa was abandoned.

The southern area is reached from the Great Plaza by a sacbe sloping down between Structures 3 and 8 and then cutting southeast to enter Plaza B at its northwest corner. It comprises the large Plazas B and C, linked only circuitously through Court D to the southeast, with a small totally enclosed court between them (reached presumably through a portal vault in one of the surrounding range structures), and the Southern Acropolis, with its enclosing arc of large courtyard groups. Apart from the plain Stela 14 beside the sacbe, there are no monuments in this area except for a plain altar, possibly moved from the Great Plaza, in the Platform 135 Group courtyard. Most of the buildings are range structures, apart from Structure 21, the fifth of La Milpa's large pyramids. This lacks a front stair, masonry facing, and a superstructure, and contrary to previous opinions appears to have been abandoned unfinished (Hammond et al. 1998). The surface of Plaza B is a sloping natural land surface lacking floor construction, and it seems likely that here too only the enclosing range structures had been completed.

Buried construction in the Platform 61 Group, off the southeast corner of the plaza complex, suggests expansion of public space into a zone previously occupied by residential compounds; a quarry still containing stockpiles of limestone rubble blocks among the modest buildings northwest of Plaza B indicates interrupted construction activity in the area toward Plaza A. This zone was very lightly occupied, as though the Great Plaza and Acropolis groups were initially firmly separated, while the lack of a western parapet to the sacbe in its northern portion, and an eastern parapet in the southern part, suggests that the linking causeway itself may also never have been completed.

In the Great Plaza itself, looters' trenches show a complex, though modest, antecedent construction history in the Early Classic period (A.D. 250–600), with occupation deposits and plaster floors of the Late Preclassic (400 B.C.–A.D. 250) in almost every excavation to bedrock (Hammond et al. 1996). The visible surface architecture, however, dates entirely to the Late/Terminal Classic, although Str. 1 also exhibits multiple phases of construction (again visible in looters' sections) within that period (as well as earlier, inner phases), and its featureless flat top also suggests an incomplete final phase.

Cut limestone blocks were used for construction fill in the Early Classic, but by the late eighth century there was a shift to using large, rough chert nodules and massive lumps of limestone, loosely packed although surprisingly stable. The shift can be seen in the last two phases of Structure 1, while on Structure 5 the rubble-cored later phase is dated precisely to A.D. 780; the plaster floor sealing the ruler Ukay's Stela 7 of 9.17.10.0.0. (Grube 1994) into its socket is continuous with the stair plaster of the small pyramid. Since the Stela 7 text does not imply that this is the final monument of Ukay's reign, he may well have been responsible for some, or much, of the major construction program utilizing chert/rubble cores.

Use of Structure 5 at the end of the eighth century and perhaps into the ninth is indicated by the subsequent modification of the stair block with the addition of an extended low front platform over the plaster floor of A.D. 780, flanked by battered-front outsets in the angles between the side walls of the stair and the front wall of the lowest pyramid tier. These are similar in design to those at Lubaantun in southern Belize (Hammond 1975: 65, 186–193), dated there firmly to the mid-ninth century after 10.0.0.0.0 by the presence of Fine Orange sherds sealed into Phase V construction fill.

No such precision is possible in the southern part of the site core. There are only sparse sherds of Late Preclassic and Early Classic pottery from this area, indicating that it did not form part of the nucleated earlier settlement under Plaza A, and all ceramics associated with architecture fall into the Late/Terminal Classic period after A.D. 700. The "Ukay" horizon of loose-fill construction, consistent on other architectural criteria also, includes many structures in this sector of the ceremonial precinct and suggests a major and rapid expansion.

The most complex architectural stratigraphy is found in the northern courtyards of the Southern Acropolis, between Structures 32 and 38 (Hammond et al. 1998), and in Structure 69, part of the Platform 135 Group immediately to the west (Hammond et al. 1996). On the acropolis, excavations in 1998 showed three major phases of development, the earliest comprising substantial stone-faced terraces creating an expanded level ridgetop and the latest including a well-built drain, allowing rainfall into the Platform 115 courtyard to pass to the outside.

On the south side of the courtyard, Structure 38 contained a throne room with three successive seats, the latter two polychrome benches with relief decoration; the room had then been infilled to the accompaniment of termination rituals including the burning of *pom* incense and pinewood. The latter yielded an AMS radiocarbon date (OxA–8079: 1220±35 bp) calibrated at A.D. 770–880, with two probability peaks at A.D. 790 (the higher) and A.D. 850, indicating the likelihood of ninth-century activity (Figure 13.2). The infilling was accompanied by a reversal of Structure 38's orientation to face south, onto the Platform 120 court at a lower level than Platform 115. This court has only one phase of construction, arguably correlated with the third phase of the northern court; on its southern side is Structure 39, approached by an impressive set of broad stairs and terraces. Excavation in 1998 showed that the superstructure doorway had been

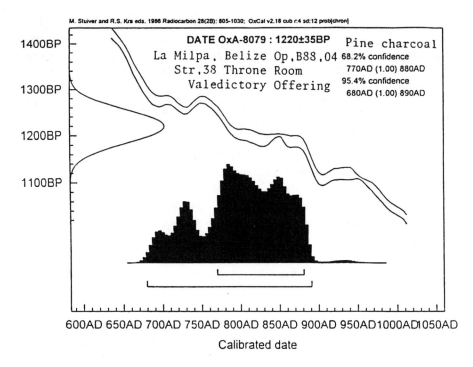

13.2 AMS radiocarbon dating of the termination of the Str. 38 throne room, prior to reorientation of Str. 38 on to the new throne room in Str. 39 on the court to the south: the probability curve indicates a late-eighth/mid-ninth-century event.

blocked, and this building also reversed to face south onto yet another new court; within the south-facing room was a specular-hematite painted bench 7.4 meters long, possibly a throne although lacking the upstanding balusters and frontal relief decoration of the more elaborate examples in Strs. 38, 65, and 69.

The new court was never completed and the different degrees of incompletion document the planned construction program. While Platform 123 had been faced with masonry, and already supported two small substructures at its eastern end, Platform 131 immediately downslope had only its rubble core in position, and on Platform 130 even this was not quite finished; at its southeast corner part of the underlying massive boulder support projected. The intended limits of the development were marked by long rubble banks that on the south incorporating the demolished remains of Structure 44, but immediately within them Areas 127, 128, and 129 were still natural hillslope, the first with several lines of boulders laid out for future terrace construction. A small quarry at the south end of Area 127 had steep, toolmarked walls, and had been partly infilled with trash. The pottery from this includes types of Tepeu 3 rather than Tepeu 2 affiliation, supporting the notion of at least an early-ninth-century date for this grandiose southernmost expansion of La Milpa's civic core. Since the Southern Acropolis seems to have been a seat of royal power, with its successive thrones, the development was arguably under the highest elite control, and its abandonment a potent demonstration of how suddenly that control ceased.

MONUMENTS

La Milpa was first explored, and named, by J. Eric S. Thompson (1938; Hammond 1991b) in March 1938. He spent only two days at the site, but mapped Plaza A in his notebook and documented Stelae 1–12 along the east side of the plaza. Although many stelae were carved, most were badly eroded, and only Stela 7 yielded a legible date. This was 9.17.10.0.0 12 Ahau 8 Pax (November 30, A.D. 780, G-M-T correlation at 584285). Stelae 13–19 were discovered in the 1990s: Stela 14 in situ and Stela 15 unerected south of the plaza (Guderjan 1991), Stelae 16 and 17 displaced and fragmentary in it, and the butt only of Stela 18 set into the base of Structure 9's stair. The plain Stela 19, the first to be found outside the site core, was discovered in situ at the La Milpa East minor center, 3.5 kilometers from the Great Plaza, by Gloria Everson in 1998 (see below).

Study of the carved monuments by Nikolai Grube (1994; Grube and Hammond 1998) has shown that at least Stelae 1, 6, 15, and 16 are of Early Classic date, although none is in situ and all except Stela 15 are fragments. Stela 10, although plain, stands in situ and can be assigned to the beginning of the Early Classic on the basis of the vessels in its dedicatory cache (Hammond and Bobo 1994: 23). Stela 12 may be stylistically dated as early as 9.12.0.0.0 (A.D. 672), although this raises a problem in that La Milpa has virtually no documented occupation in the seventh century; it was still standing as recently as the early nineteenth century (Hammond and Bobo 1994: 30). The plain Stelae 11 and 14 (in situ) and fragmentary Stela 9 (recycled as an altar for Stela 10 many centuries after the latter was erected, and when it was partly buried by topsoil accumulation) seem to be Late Classic on the basis of location (Stelae 11 and 14), thick cross-sections, and raw material; the Early Classic monuments are generally of a much finer limestone. Stelae 4 and 8 appear to be late eighth century from their similarity of carving style to Stela 7. La Milpa thus has one very early stela (10), together with seven (7, 8, 11, 12, 14, 18, 19) of late date, still in their original locations.

The remaining ten stelae are displaced. Of these, Stelae 3 and 6 are fragments re-erected in front of Structure 1 long after its abandonment. Their broken bases are set in shallow pits cut into topsoil and erosion deposits from the pyramid. Stelae 1 and 2, although recumbent, are aligned with them, while Stelae 4 and 5 lie a few meters forward in front of Structure 1, and the plain fragment of Stela 17 was laid flat into the plaza floor where the line between Stelae 3 and 6 crosses one drawn orthogonally equidistant from Stelae 4 and 5. This complex episode of resetting, apparently never completed, has been interpreted by Hammond and

Bobo (1994: 30–32) as part of a revitalization movement, arguably (but not provably) dated to the Contact period.

Stelae 13 and 16 were found lying on the surface of the Great Plaza, Stela 13 close to the east end and Stela 16 (together with a fragment from a larger, plain stela, possibly Stela 9 or 18) near the west end of the north ballcourt, Structure 11–12. Stela 15 lay west of the small Structure 54, midway between the two main groups of the site core. Heavy looting, perhaps occasioned by the stela's presence, made assessment of context difficult, but excavation showed no socket into which the stela might formerly have been set at this locus (Hammond and Bobo 1994: 24).

Stela 20, discovered as four fragments (comprising the upper portion of a figure) under looters' backdirt in front of their trench into the center of Structure 1, is a special case: it lay on the pre-looter (i.e., pre-1979) ground surface, but was not there when Thompson explored the site in 1938. The carved surface, found upmost, is crisp and uneroded, the other surfaces too clean to have been weathered for centuries. Stela 20 was clearly buried until the looters found it. The most likely locale, given the stratigraphic relationship with the looters' backdirt, is inside the tandem building (Str. 199) butted onto the front of Structure 1. This was penetrated by the looters' trench, which then continued east as a tunnel into the pyramid, the marl fill from which was found covering the stela fragments. The fact that they were found together suggests that a hitherto entire, but cracked, upper half fell apart when moved and was dumped as unsaleable. The absence of the lower half lacks explanation, since it may have been present when the looters came, but broken and unnoticed (and could still lie in the unremoved portion of their backdirt—one uncarved fragment, of the right thickness to be part of the butt, was recovered in 2000). Alternatively, the upper portion of Stela 20 could have been moved to the Structure 1 locale from elsewhere, as seems to have been the case with other fragmentary monuments (Hammond and Bobo 1994); but whether, given its condition and apparent absence from the surface in 1938, this was at the same putatively Protohistoric date seems doubtful. If it was indeed rehoused in the tandem structure, a Terminal Classic date for this would be feasible and paralleled by similar enshrining actions at Xunantunich.

Any Terminal Classic (taken as post-800) association for the La Milpa monuments is thus limited to possible initial dedication of carved Stelae 4 and 8 (if they postdate the similar Stela 7), and plain Stelae 9, 11, 14, 18, and 19. In addition, a Terminal Classic date for the resetting of Stelae 1–6 in front of Structure 1 is possible but unlikely for the reasons given by Hammond and Bobo (1994: 30). For Stela 20 it is possible, but remains moot.

CERAMICS

A substantial quantity of pottery has been recovered from stratified contexts in all parts of the site core, and also from housemound excavations on the East Transect

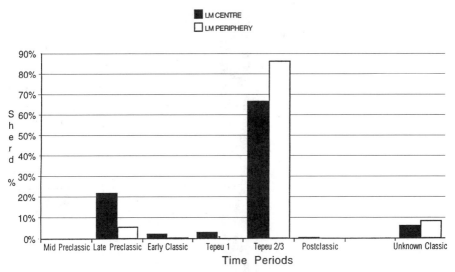

13.3 *Dating of La Milpa ceramics.*

and from landscape engineering features in Survey Blocks 1–15. This has been analyzed by Kerry Sagebiel and Laura J. Kosakowsky (1997; see also Kosakowsky et al. 1998; Sagebiel 1999), who note the presence of small amounts (< 4 percent each of total sherd counts) of Early Classic and Tepeu 1 material in the site core (and almost none in the periphery: Figure 13.3). Late/Terminal Classic (Tepeu 2/3) pottery is about 66 percent of the core total and 87 percent of the periphery total. (The core also has about 21 percent Late Preclassic versus the periphery's 5 percent.) Postclassic pottery, consisting of effigy and spiked censer sherds (Hammond and Bobo 1994: Fig. 2, Plates 3–7) from around the stelae, is less than 1 percent in the core and absent from the periphery. Of the 77 peripheral loci analyzed in 1996, 8 had Late Preclassic occupation, 2 Early Classic, 0 Tepeu 1, and 71 Tepeu 2/3 (Figure 13.4). The picture is equally clear in terms of raw sherd counts: of a periphery total of 13,000 identified by 1997, more than 12,000 were Tepeu 2/3 and less than 1,000 Late Preclassic; in the core just over 2,000 of the 10,000 sherds were Late Preclassic and more than 6,500 Tepeu 2/3, with Early Classic and Tepeu 1 together amassing a few hundred (Figure 13.5).

Unfortunately, from the point of view of this paper, that overwhelming majority of Tepeu 2/3 sherds cannot be reliably separated into the two Uaxactún complexes, even though La Milpa's affiliation is more with northeastern Petén than with either the Belize valley or northern Belize. Clear Terminal Classic markers such as Plumbate and Fine Orange are totally or almost absent: a few sherds of nonspecific fine paste ware were found around Stela 11, and a thumbnail-sized

LM PERIPHERY: OCCUPIED PLACES IN EACH PERIOD

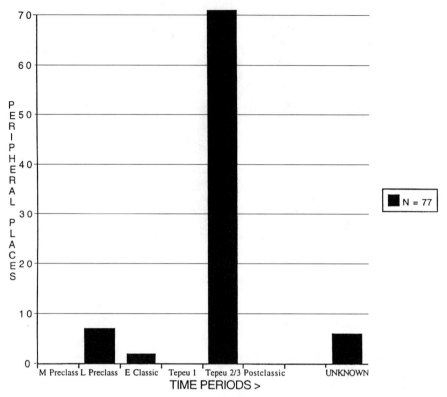

13.4 Dating of occupied peripheral loci at La Milpa.

sherd of Pabellon Molded-carved was recovered from topsoil on Structure 69. It might be argued that La Milpa was off the distribution routes for fine paste, since Tikal to the southwest—closer to the sources of production on the Pasión—had only small amounts in the epigonal Eznab complex (T. Patrick Culbert, personal communication, 1998). However, Río Azul, located much closer, yielded both Fine Paste (Fine Orange and Fine Gray) and Plumbate wares (Adams 1999: 72), showing that the trade routes were still running through northeasternmost Petén in the ninth century. Lamanai, east of La Milpa, yielded only one Pabellon Molded-carved vessel and a few sherds, but Altun Ha farther to the east produced an "appreciable quantity in a limited number of final-use or surface-scatter situations, largely very near the central precinct" (David M. Pendergast, personal communication, 1998). Had La Milpa been functioning long after A.D. 830, a similar

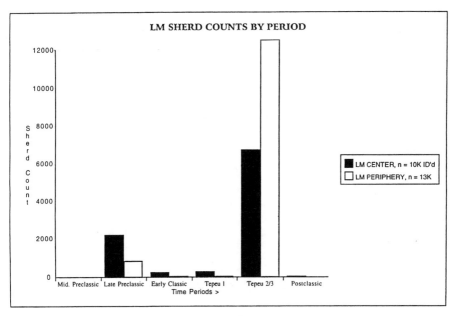

13.5 Sherd counts for the La Milpa sequence (through 1996).

situation to those at Río Azul and Altun Ha might have been expected, given its large size and the dynamic construction program in operation immediately prior to abandonment.

COLLAPSE

Dating of that abandonment to around 10.0.0.0.0–10.1.0.0.0 (when Caracol, Ucanal, Nakum, and Xunantunich in the region to the south all dedicated their last monuments) does nothing to provide an explanation; the Tikal-Calakmul conflict was long over, its resolution having preceded La Milpa's Late Classic renaissance (Martin and Grube 1995). Tikal itself was still functioning, although La Milpa's late ceramics do not suggest close ties. The decay of Tikal's regional power may have had repercussions, although the lack of defenses and of evidence for conflict at La Milpa suggest that they were not military ones. The strong northern impact seen in the Tecep-phase architecture and ceramics of Nohmul, downstream on the Río Hondo (Hammond et al. 1988), and at Río Azul (Adams 1999) is absent and likely to have come when La Milpa was already in desuetude. La Milpa lacked positive attractions, such as good chert supplies, a nearby river for water and transportation, or abundant and well-watered good agricultural land.

Its spectacular Late/Terminal Classic development, overall high population size (estimated at 46,000 within a five-kilometer radius), and density show that in the short term, at least, the land around La Milpa could support a substantial community (as it did throughout the surrounding upland region). An episode of Late Classic soil erosion was noted in local *bajo* cores (N. Dunning, personal communication, 2000) but was far less intense than a Late Preclassic episode engendered by apparently much smaller and more scattered communities. Terracing and berms suggest attempts to maximize production and minimize soil loss (though probably less desperately than we have surmised in previous papers), and the onset of drought, or a disjunction between rainfall and the growing season, would have had serious long-term consequences in an area dependent on rainfall agriculture. The evidence from La Milpa where it exists is, however, of response to a short-term, perhaps very short-term, problem.

We are left with a conundrum: occupation at La Milpa ceased unexpectedly, in the middle of a burst of centrally directed public works aggrandizing the already impressive ceremonial precinct. Elite residences, religious structures, and administrative infrastructure were all undergoing expansion and refurbishment when the end came. Whether events such as the deliberate demolition and careful infilling of Structures 65 and 69 presaged this, or form part of an earlier, unrelated, and incomplete cycle of redevelopment, we do not know. The large number of buildings that may have been simultaneously under construction at the time of abandonment (including major structures in both portions of the ceremonial precinct, the sacbe linking them, and construction outside the center such as the La Milpa West minor center 3.5 kilometers away), their wide distribution, and the large quantities of material, transport, and labor thus implied, might plausibly have strained the local labor supply. This in turn could have put agricultural productivity under stress, and even resulted in the sort of disquiet that leads to revolt or emigration.

Abrams (1994: 106), however, has emphasized that labor requirements for Maya structures were often low, and La Milpa would seem to have had some 20,000 able adults at its rulers' disposal. We could be seeing the incomplete state of construction at the end of one in an intended succession of building campaigns at a more modest and sustainable rate, a plan interrupted before work could be resumed. One problem is that we have little idea of the "normal" pace of such efforts, and whether multiple projects involving different kinds of buildings would have been simultaneously pursued, as they seem on the evidence to have been at La Milpa.

Epigonal occupation of the "squatter" type is striking by its absence. The construction of Str. 86 in the Great Plaza and the possible associated rubble "altar" inside Structure 5, just over 100 meters to the northeast, are the only evidence so far of people staying around La Milpa; the substantial, dense population documented throughout the settlement area seems to have melted away. Yet there is absolutely no sign of violence or wanton destruction, such as marked the collapse of some of the Petexbatun sites. In some ways it is tempting to say that La

Milpa went out with a bang, on a cultural high in the midst of its prosperity, but that would perhaps create the wrong impression. La Milpa went out with a whimper—not a long, drawn-out howl of slow decline but a short, almost silent sigh, leaving unanswerable, perhaps unaskable, questions hanging in the air.

ACKNOWLEDGMENTS

Research at La Milpa was funded by grants from the National Geographic Society, generous gifts from Raymond and Beverly Sackler, Mary Ann Harrell, and an anonymous donor through Boston University, and in both financial and practical ways by Boston University. Work was carried out under a permit from the Belize Department of Archaeology, where we appreciate the cooperation of the late Harriot W. Topsey, Allan Moore, John Morris, and Brian Woodye. The landowner, Programme for Belize, afforded us every facility: we are grateful to Joy Grant, to Ramón Pacheco and his precursors as managers of the La Milpa Research Station, and to John Masson. Our colleagues in other projects working in and around La Milpa have been most collegial: we thank Nicholas Dunning, Vernon Scarborough, and Fred Valdez Jr. Lastly, we thank our own colleagues in LaMAP, whose efforts made this paper possible.

14

COMMONER SENSE
LATE AND TERMINAL CLASSIC SOCIAL STRATEGIES IN THE XUNANTUNICH AREA

Wendy Ashmore, Jason Yaeger, and Cynthia Robin

W‌hatever happened in the Maya lowlands at the end of the Classic period, the events and processes involved were surely complex, and must have varied markedly across the social and political landscape. In this essay, we illustrate some of that complexity and variability on at least two social scales. First, our focus on the lives of people in farmsteads and communities beyond the monumental civic centers helps complement the more intense attention customarily paid to elites and royals living in the hearts of those centers. Not only were our ancient informants subject in different ways than their overlords to the upheavals of Late and Terminal Classic times, they also responded with a somewhat different repertoire of tactics, in part because of their distinct social, political, and economic standing. And that brings us to the second kind of complexity and variation: by looking more closely at a relatively small area and populace, we recognize that, even at this scale, fortunes and strategies could be quite diverse, depending on local circumstances and specific histories. "Commoners" certainly did not have all social or other characteristics "in common" with one another, and we gain in understanding the complexity of this class—and their contemporaries—by identifying more fully the varied ways in which all people lived through the events of this period.

Specifically, in this paper we describe social integration, differentiation, and change in Late and Terminal Classic times within two commoner settlements near the civic center of Xunantunich, Belize. One of these, San Lorenzo, experienced a discontinuous history of occupation beginning in Middle Preclassic times, the best documented portion of which pertains to the Late and Terminal Classic periods. The other, Chan Nòohol, was a sector of a larger settlement we call Chan, the latter with roots likewise in the Middle Preclassic, but within which the Chan Nòohol area evinced a virtual boom-bust sequence late in the Late Classic period. The seeming abruptness of this demographic expansion and collapse is likely somewhat deceptive, in part an artifact of imprecision in dating (e.g., Smith 1992). Nevertheless, the contrasts between periods are dramatic. And for each settlement, the archaeological record attests to varying sorts of self-sufficiency and dependency of its residents relative to larger economic, ritual, and political spheres. In neither case are the reasons for ultimate "collapse" fully clear, but by examining both of these places in some detail, along with other instances of local settlement considered in passing here, we can clarify some of the mosaic of prosperity, decline, rallying, contraction, and abandonment in this part of the Belize Valley. Our analysis complements and our findings broadly parallel those provided elsewhere (Ashmore 1998; LeCount et al. 2002; Leventhal and Ashmore 1999) concerning royal strategies within the Xunantunich civic core.

Highlighting the final integrative and differentiating behaviors for which we have evidence allows us to infer the social strategies of local residents in their responses, successful or otherwise, to this time of flux. Although the majority of our data pertain to the Late Classic period, we contend that understanding local manifestations of Terminal Classic society and the "Maya collapse" is possible only through detailed reference to and comparison with antecedent social forms and strategies.

By way of background, we first describe Xunantunich and the areas near it that we examined, outlining briefly the recent program of settlement research on which the paper builds. Because the Xunantunich Archaeological Project (XAP) and its Settlement Survey (XSS) were framed specifically to address issues of social change in Late and Terminal Classic times, we couch discussion in terms of cumulative earlier findings in the larger region and of the evolving interpretive models shaping our research. We then introduce briefly our project's definitions of the Late and Terminal Classic periods. These and other time spans recognized by XAP derive principally from the ceramic chronology developed by Lisa LeCount, an analysis described more fully elsewhere (LeCount 1992, 1996; LeCount et al. 2002). Following a condensed account of XSS findings, we proceed to the San Lorenzo and Chan Nòohol case studies, and then to concluding discussion about the end of the Classic in the Xunantunich area.

XUNANTUNICH AND ANCIENT MAYA SETTLEMENT

The site of Xunantunich, once known as Benque Viejo, is a compact civic center perched dramatically on a ridge overlooking the Mopán River Valley, southwest of the Mopán-Macal confluence forming the Belize River (Figures 14.1 and 14.2). Other publications (e.g., Ashmore 1998; LeCount 1999; LeCount et al. 2002;

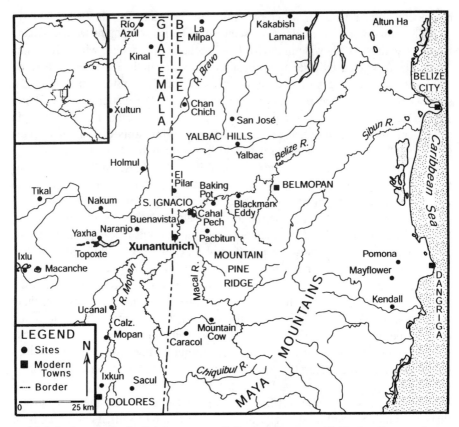

14.1 Archaeological sites in western Belize and eastern El Petén, Guatemala.

Leventhal and Ashmore 1999) describe the site and summarize the genesis of the
Xunantunich Archaeological Project (XAP, 1991–1997). For purposes of this
chapter, the two most important points are that, from the outset, we believed the
civic center could be understood only in a larger settlement context, and that we
knew our proposed Xunantunich Settlement Survey (XSS) and associated excavations would benefit enormously from the recent spate of related inquiry in
adjoining areas.

From the earliest incidental examinations a century or more past, through the
pathbreaking work of Gordon Willey and his colleagues (1965) at and around
Barton Ramie, to the burgeoning wealth of studies of the last two decades, that
broad swath of varied topography straddling the middle and upper Belize River
Valley has become one of the most attentively examined stretches of terrain and
ancient settlement in all of the Maya lowlands. Taken together, these investiga-

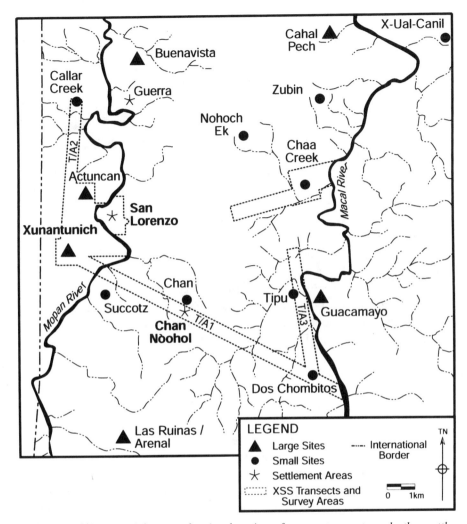

14.2 Map of Xunantunich area, showing location of survey transects and other settlement areas.

tions document an agrarian landscape, first settled in Early Preclassic times (e.g., Awe 1992), widely occupied by the Middle Preclassic, and marked by autochthonous emergence of numerous, relatively small civic centers beginning in the Middle to Late Preclassic. Such centers were probably most frequently competitive peers, although they may have been organized hierarchically at other times, and were likely collectively subordinate to political authority farther west a good bit of the time, especially to Naranjo in the Late Classic (e.g., Ball 1993b; Ball and Taschek

1991; Houston, Stuart, and Taube 1992; Reents-Budet 1994; Taschek and Ball 1992). Among these jockeying local centers, Xunantunich was founded remarkably late, intrusive to a well-developed social landscape, and, notably, seems to have thrived when polities and networks farther west were crumbling (e.g., Ashmore 1998; Ashmore and Leventhal 1993; LeCount et al. 2002; Leventhal and Ashmore 1999). Much less clear, however, were the practical effects on farmers of centuries of competition among local lords, and then of the abrupt founding of Xunantunich. Who, if anyone, controlled the farmers' hearts, minds, or produce? And to what extent?

Throughout the occupation record, settlement density in the region varied locally with proximity to rivers (e.g., Ford 1990; Willey et al. 1965), soil quality (e.g., Fedick 1989; Ford and Fedick 1992), localized political histories (e.g., Ehret 1995; Yaeger 2000b), and other factors (e.g., Neff 1998). Diverse models have been proposed to describe political, economic, and ritual integration of local and regionwide society (e.g., Ball and Taschek 1991; Garber 1994; Willey et al. 1965). In formulating XSS research, our questions reduced to the following related pair: How did the localization and growth history of agrarian settlement relate to the founding and decline of Xunantunich? And what roles did farmers play in the larger events and developments of the Late and Terminal Classic?

Existing models (e.g., Ball 1987; de Montmollin 1989; Ford 1990; Fry 1990; Marcus 1993; D. Rice 1986; Tourtellot 1993) had led us to expect that, collectively, the farmers around Xunantunich would have been long established on the land, with their lives probably tied relatively loosely to the fortunes or mandates of any of the multiple small civic centers in the vicinity (see again Figure 14.2). More specifically, in formulating the research design, review of the literature led to two broad hypotheses concerning the agrarian populace in the Xunantunich area (Ashmore 1993): that the cumulative effect of centuries of apparent competition or succession among rulers of small-scale and probably weak local polities should have left farmers linked more strongly to the land than to their overlords, and that the kind of Terminal Classic social and demographic resilience evident in other parts of Belize should have pertained in the Xunantunich area as well. Even in the lakes region of central Petén, Don Rice (1986: 337–339) had described post–Late Classic settlement history as marked by "continuity with change" rather than collapse. Closer to the Xunantunich case, multiple analysts had argued that the location of Belizean sites, on the periphery of core lowland polities, should have contributed to such resilience (e.g., Culbert 1988: 88; Fry 1990: 295, 296; Hammond 1981: 163, 171). The index of such resilience was persistence of occupation into Postclassic times and, in the extreme case of Lamanai, extended to a whole city's "missing" the "collapse" altogether (e.g., Pendergast 1986).

To address the fit between models and local data, XSS sampled settlement traces via three 400-meter-wide survey transects shown on Figure 14.2 (Ashmore et al. 1994; Neff et al. 1995; Yaeger and Connell 1993), plus systematic coverage in opportunistically selected intervening areas, including Actuncán, San Lorenzo, and Chaa Creek (e.g., Connell 1993; McGovern 1993; VandenBosch 1992; Yaeger 1992). On the transects, initial shovel tests were augmented by a formal test-pitting program sampling a stratified cross-section of mapped sites (Ehret 1995). And several programs examined selected areas more intensively with particular research issues in mind (e.g., Connell 1998; Ehret 1998; McGovern 1994; Neff 1998; Robin 1996b; VandenBosch 1993, 1995; Yaeger 1995a). San Lorenzo and Chan Nòohol were two of these areas.

Together, this diverse set of inquiries documented a settlement record broadly paralleling those elsewhere in the region, but with localized variation in the histories of individual settlements. Some flux can be linked tentatively to larger political and economic developments, such as the drop in late-seventh-century occupation around Callar Creek, near the larger center of Buenavista del Cayo, possibly attendant on competition between the latter and the newly ascendant Xunantunich (e.g., Ashmore and Leventhal 1993; Ball 1993b; Ball and Taschek 1991; Ehret 1995, 1998; Reents-Budet 1994: 294–305; Taschek and Ball 1992: 492–493). We were particularly impressed, however, by the general concordance between local commoner settlement history and that of Xunantunich, and even more strongly so by the pervasiveness of decline and abandonment throughout the study area by the close of the Terminal Classic.[1]

How do some of the more common explanations for decline and abandonment fare in light of XAP settlement data? Although L. Theodore Neff's (1998) and Cynthia Robin's studies suggest, respectively, that the Late Classic was a time of marked agricultural intensification in the area (i.e., via terracing, both near and away from domestic sites), and that some families were expanding into arguably more marginal lands (see Chan Nòohol, below), there is no overt sign of environmental degradation like that found in the Petén lakes district (Deevey et al. 1979) or the Copán Valley (Fash 1991). Demographic reconstructions from XSS data are still in progress, but preliminary estimates suggest Late Classic population densities of ca. 452 per square kilometer (Neff 1998; Neff et al. 1995), densities that are high (e.g., Culbert 1988: 86) but surely coincide with elaboration of the cited terracing.[2] Nor is there direct, tangible evidence of disease. Sustained or heightened violence may be implied by a mass secondary burial at a Chaa Creek site (CC5, Plantain Group; Connell 1995: 207), but it could represent simply sequential interments; XAP encountered no comparable examples elsewhere (LeCount et al. 1998). And the defensible siting for Xunantunich could as easily—or simultaneously—represent appropriation of prominent sacred space (Ashmore 1998), while military dress of figures on the three Xunantunich carved stelae are part of widespread, well-established royal iconography.

Absent dramatically pervasive new local tolls on the populace, and reasoning from the integrative models we had thought most plausible, we had expected that the overall quality of land and riverine resources should have allowed farmers to continue well beyond the eclipse of rule by overlords in Xunantunich and other nearby centers. Particularly suggestive to us had been the potentially extended post-dynastic occupation at Copán (e.g., Fash and Sharer 1991; Freter 1994; Gonlin 1994; Webster and Freter 1990c); the substantial Postclassic presence at Barton Ramie/Baking Pot (Fry 1990; Willey et al. 1965); the proximity of Tipú, occupied well into Colonial times (e.g., Graham 1991; Graham et al. 1985; Jones 1989); and models of enduring community life in Colonial Yucatán despite flux in political organization (e.g., Farriss 1984; Marcus 1993; Roys 1957).[3] But with the exception of Nohoch Ek (Ball 1987: 13), Tipú (Graham et al. 1985; Neff et al. 1995), and sparse finds suggesting pilgrims' visits at an otherwise-abandoned Xunantunich (Schmidt 1978: 106), none of the sites shown in Figure 14.2 have yielded ceramic or other stylistically diagnostic evidence of Postclassic occupation for which reports are available to us.

Settlement contraction in this area was thus severe and virtually permanent, at or preceding the onset of the Postclassic. Population declined from the cited peak of ca. 452 per square kilometer in the Late Classic to essentially nil in the Postclassic, although Tipú may have been quite large, a riparian refuge from that period through Colonial times. The larger pattern manifests a climax-crash sequence seen frequently elsewhere in the Maya lowlands (e.g., de Montmollin 1995), but its timing and severity were stunningly pronounced in the Xunantunich area, where prevailing general models implied that a relative autonomy and rich agrarian resources could have reduced commoners' vulnerability to the riptides that sank their overlords. This dissonance between expectations and evidence led us to look again at the models. Just how much autonomy did they have? How was it exercised and to what effect? How did commoners' behavior relate to the collapse?

Before turning more directly to the social strategies of San Lorenzo and Chan Nòohol farmers, we need to consider briefly two matters: chronology and initial interpretive models for local settlement.

XAP chronology is based on ceramic analysis and radiocarbon age assessments (LeCount 1992, 1996; LeCount et al. 1998, 2002). LeCount's relative ceramic sequencing derives from stylistic, seriational, and stratigraphic analysis of pottery excavated in XAP operations, drawing as well on comparison with earlier studies at Xunantunich (i.e., Thompson 1940a) and cross-ties with established sequences from nearby sites (especially Gifford 1976). The absolute chronology linked to this relative sequence relies principally on a series of radiocarbon assessments (LeCount et al. 1998, 2002). The ceramic phases most pertinent to our discussion are the Samal (A.D. 600–670) and Hats' Chaak (A.D. 670–780), broadly spanning the Late Classic period, and the Tsak' (A.D. 780–890), the local ceramic manifestation of Terminal Classic times.

Turning to interpretive social models, both Jason Yaeger (e.g., 1995a) and Cynthia Robin (e.g., in Neff et al. 1995) initially invoked variants of a household *developmental cycle* (Fortes 1958; Goody 1958) to help account for the forms of their settlement data. Building most directly from Gair Tourtellot's (1988a) and William Haviland's (1988) applications, associating ancient Maya domestic group morphology and palimpsest changes in family composition, they provisionally interpreted mounds found in isolation as remains of developmentally young, nuclear-family households, and larger, multi-mound groups as developmentally older house-holds with extended or more heterogeneous family groupings (compare McAnany 1993). A parallel model may be extended, with due interpretive caution and ap-propriate adjustments, to lineage and community growth. However, both Yaeger and Robin have recognized the effects of economic and ritual practices as even more potent in accounting for not only house and household forms, but also means of integrating the disparate units (e.g., Hilton 1985).

Our focus in the rest of the paper is, then, on life in selected local commoner contexts during the final period before catastrophic settlement collapse. Different expressions of and responses to Late Classic prosperity and stress were followed by varied manifestations of decline, rallying, and social and demographic dissolu-tion. In our concluding discussion, we suggest some of what may have gone wrong, and draw together some evidential lines for a picture of strategies invoked by ancient Maya farmers, successfully or otherwise, for weathering the vicissi-tudes of Late and Terminal Classic times. We acknowledge that these suggestions are far from demonstrated explanations. Together with depiction of royal strate-gies within the civic core, however (Ashmore 1998; LeCount et al. 2002; Leventhal and LeCount 1997), these working inferences offer prospective insights on how local people across the social spectrum responded to stressful developments pro-voked largely at some distance from them.

SAN LORENZO

San Lorenzo is a small, rural settlement cluster consisting of seventeen residential groups, a chert quarry, and several other cultural features sitting on a ridge of ancient alluvial terraces overlooking the fertile floodplain of the Mopán River (Fig-ures 14.2 and 14.3). The site's domestic groups are either isolated structures (n=9) or patio groups (n=7), with the exception of SL34, a group of two struc-tures lacking a patio. XAP began work at San Lorenzo in 1992, when Yaeger (1992; also VandenBosch 1992) mapped the site and Sabrina M. Chase (1992, 1993) began excavating SL22. Yaeger (1994, 1995b, 1996, 2000a) expanded the excavation program in order to evaluate a model of community growth related to the domes-tic developmental cycle (Haviland 1988; Tourtellot 1988a; Yaeger 1995a; Yaeger and LeCount 1995). The resulting research design stipulated testing every domestic group possible, with extensive excavation of five groups and SL13, a special-function complex located just beyond the edge of the settlement (see Figure 14.3).

The results of these excavations indicate that San Lorenzo was established perhaps as early as the Early Classic Ak'ab phase (A.D. 300–600) and grew

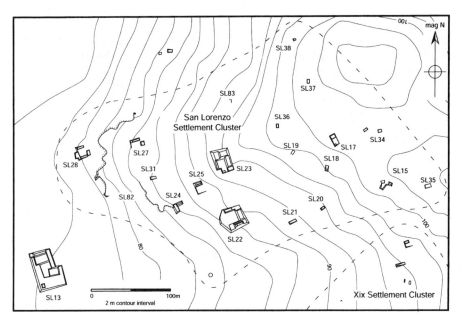

14.3 The San Lorenzo settlement cluster.

rapidly in the Samal phase, reaching its maximum size during the Hats' Chaak phase, when all seventeen domestic groups were occupied. The settlement then shrank markedly, however, as its inhabitants abandoned two-thirds of the settlement's domestic groups by the Tsak' phase, the last period of occupation at the site.

There is a striking parallel between the San Lorenzo and Xunantunich trajectories of Samal-phase growth, Hats' Chaak expansion, and Tsak' contraction and abandonment, a parallel that suggests that San Lorenzo was linked relatively tightly to Xunantunich. The Chan Nòohol data discussed below show a similar pattern. This should not have surprised us; the founding of the Xunantunich center and the ambitious Hats' Chaak building program there would have required new levels of corvée labor and tribute from the local population. These changes created a dynamic social milieu that provided residents of rural settlements like San Lorenzo with opportunities to negotiate and redefine their places within local communities and the polity by creating and stressing affiliations with other groups outside their settlements, notably the polity's ruling elite. For their part, the rulers of Xunantunich had to accommodate their strategies to the social and political structures presented by established settlements like San Lorenzo (LeCount et al. 2002; also Schortman, Urban, and Ausec 1997).

Hats' Chaak–Phase Strategies of Affiliation

Most definitions of *community* posit that community members share under-standings created and recreated in daily pursuits and interactions (e.g., Murdock 1949; Redfield 1955; Watanabe 1992), and Yaeger (2000b) has argued that this was true at ancient San Lorenzo. Another central aspect of the community, how-ever, is an explicit, socially constituted identity created by focusing on shared characteristics and highlighting differences between the community members and outsiders (e.g., Anderson 1987; Cohen 1985). Excavation data presented below show that San Lorenzo was a socially and economically heterogeneous settlement. In the face of these inequalities, feasts forged intra-settlement bonds and made a local identity more explicit, while they simultaneously defined and reinforced the social relationships of inequality that characterized the settlement.

One obvious local inequality was the amount of labor invested in domestic architecture. All of the isolated structures that we tested, save one (SL25), and two of the seven patio groups (SL17, SL28) consisted of low house platforms faced almost entirely with cobblestones and topped by perishable, wattle-and-daub buildings. Two other patio groups (SL15, SL27) were similar in size and construction materials, but included at least one platform faced with limestone blocks. The remaining four groups (SL22, SL23, SL24, SL25) were quite dis-tinct, marked by much larger substructure platforms faced with limestone blocks, many of which supported buildings with masonry walls. The construction of these latter houses required a significant amount of labor and probably required the work of specialized masons in some cases, suggesting that these four house-holds could mobilize extra-household labor (see also Abrams 1994). The prod-ucts of this significant difference, the houses, remained durable testaments to underlying social inequalities that made this labor appropriation possible (e.g., McGuire and Schiffer 1983).

It is notable that the only three households with evidence of feasting were among those that built the most labor-intensive homes. Excavations at most do-mestic groups at San Lorenzo yielded little faunal material, but we found signifi-cant quantities of animal bones only in association with three of the largest patio groups (SL22, SL23, SL24). This might seem to indicate that few San Lorenzo residents consumed meat, but bone chemistry studies show that all people at nearby Barton Ramie ate roughly similar amounts of meat in the Late Classic period (Gerry 1993). If this were true at ancient San Lorenzo, then the restricted distribution of faunal remains plausibly reflects where meat was consumed, and higher frequencies of ceremonial items like *incensarios* and serving vessels in these groups suggest that ritual feasts provided one context for meat consump-tion (see also Houston, Stuart, and Taube 1989; LeCount 1996; McAnany 1995). Spatial and ceramic analyses suggest that San Lorenzo feasts in Hats' Chaak times were inclusive in LeCount's (1996) terms, except perhaps at SL13 (see below).

Why did only three households host feasts, and why were those same households able to requisition the labor of others to help build their homes? Patricia McAnany (1995: 96–97) has argued that the initial settlers at Maya sites often controlled the best local resources through the "principle of first occupancy." Given that two of the hosting groups (SL22, SL23) were also among the first to have been established at San Lorenzo, it seems possible that precedence of occupation gave the Hats' Chaak–phase members of these households privileged claims to land and other resources through their ancestors, whose veneration was perhaps a focus of some Hats' Chaak rituals and feasts (McAnany 1995; Tozzer 1941: 92). We would argue that through feasting, the San Lorenzo residents came together to celebrate important occasions and share food and gifts, thus cementing their bonds of commonality. But in doing so, they also acknowledged that the economic and political resources needed to host these feasts—whether access to meat or access to the oldest and/or most powerful ancestors—were not evenly distributed throughout the community.

These kinds of local social differences presumably always existed at San Lorenzo and similar settlements, but the rapid growth of Xunantunich and its rulers' polity-building strategies provided new symbolic and material resources for strategies by which San Lorenzo residents sought to reinforce local inequalities, such as the use of material symbols connected to the polity elite. For example, not everyone in Hats' Chaak San Lorenzo wore ornaments of exotic materials, like marine shell pendants, and only those families living in the largest houses possessed greenstone beads. Many scholars have argued that ancient Mesoamerican elites gave exotic items as gifts in order to maintain their political positions (Hirth 1992; Rice 1987b). Assuming this was true at Xunantunich, San Lorenzo residents who wore exotic items did so most likely because of the cosmological significance of the raw material and because possession of these goods demonstrated a social connection to the rulers of the polity. Similarly, in designing their homes, a few families—the same ones who wore greenstone beads, lived in the largest houses, and hosted feasts—chose to use basal moldings and high interior benches that mimicked elite architecture of the region, the nearest examples of which were at Xunantunich. By using these features, limestone block masonry, and finished plaster patio surfaces in their homes, these households created domestic settings that were visually more akin to ceremonial plazas and elite residential compounds at Xunantunich than to the wattle-and-daub huts of their neighbors.

Another venue for creating and reinforcing extra-community affiliations was SL13, located just west of San Lorenzo (see Figure 14.3). This complex was built early in the Hats' Chaak phase, and this timing, the group's location between distinct settlements, and the amount of labor required to build it suggest that the lords of Xunantunich coordinated its construction. Unique architecture; high frequencies of incensarios, serving vessels, and ornaments; the quantity of faunal remains; and a bone flute all suggest that SL13 was a venue for ritual celebrations (Yaeger 2000a). Although the data do not allow us to discriminate the many ritual activities that presumably took place in SL13, the spatial distinction between an exterior plastered space and an interior patio area suggests that many rituals divided participants into those who could enter the patio and those who could not (e.g., Rapaport 1990), using criteria that probably varied contextually. It is likely that some rituals brought people from several settlements together, and that in some of these, intra-settlement status differences determined access to the inner patio. In such cases, the ritual practices reflected and reproduced vertical social distinctions internal to the settlements, while creating horizontal affiliations among those people included and among those excluded from the inner sanctum, forming identities that crosscut local settlements and potentially competed with local loyalties.

The data from San Lorenzo suggest that the settlement's Hats' Chaak residents shared a community identity that was made explicit in practices like ritual feasts. But these feasts and other common events like house construction both required and reproduced inequalities within the community. It seems likely that the hosting families sought to maintain or increase their privileged status through these practices and by representing connections, whether real or not, to the elite of Xunantunich (see also Schortman and Nakamura 1991). For their part, the residents of the simpler houses at San Lorenzo must have had their own reasons for participating in these practices that legitimated local inequalities, whether it was to ensure access to land or chert resources, to improve the community's connections to the polity elite, or to satisfy familial obligations. These diverse strategies generated new patterns of local social organization that we suggest necessarily involved a tension between local affiliations and extra-settlement affiliations (Yaeger 2000b; also McAnany 1993; Schortman, Urban, and Ausec 1997). The resulting organization, however, apparently could not endure the weakening and eventual dissolution of regional political authority in subsequent times, and indeed may have contributed to this process.

Tsak'-Phase Changes

Only five domestic groups (SL21, SL22, SL23, SL24, SL31) at San Lorenzo show strong evidence of Tsak'-phase occupation, as does SL13. It was primarily the once-powerful families who remained at San Lorenzo, but the social and political context in which they lived was very different from that of the preceding phase, and their social strategies had changed concomitantly. Xunantunich underwent a significant transformation beginning in the early part of the Tsak' phase. While the polity's rulers commissioned their most explicit statements of political authority on three carved stelae, large and important sections of their capital were abandoned (LeCount 1999; LeCount et al. 2002; Leventhal and LeCount 1997), and the polity as a whole suffered a marked population decline (Ehret 1995; Neff 1998; Neff et al. 1995).

There were some continuities in practice at San Lorenzo. For example, rituals involving the creation of ancestors by burying deceased relatives continued, and an empty Tsak'-phase burial chamber in SL22 Str. 3 suggests that at least one once-powerful family took one of its ancestors when leaving San Lorenzo. But those Tsak'-phase practices that we can identify in San Lorenzo clearly lack the differentiating quality of the Hats' Chaak–phase practices from which they evolved. Building practices clearly demonstrate these changing strategies. San Lorenzo residents built no new houses in the Tsak' phase, restricting their efforts to minor additions and modifications to existing structures. Moreover, they faced these constructions with pieces of limestone whose rough shaping required minimal labor, suggesting that house building had become a family affair that no longer drew on whatever intra-community inequalities remained. Furthermore, these modifications did not mimic elite architecture: no Tsak' construction employed basal moldings or benches, and remodeling in one building (SL22 Str. 3) actually eliminated an existing interior bench. The families in the larger house groups no longer tried to differentiate themselves through their architecture, perhaps in part because the Xunantunich elite were no longer a source of legitimating symbols or perhaps because the smaller Tsak'-phase community lacked enough residents from whom they wanted to distinguish themselves or whose labor they wanted or had rights to claim. The disappearance of polychrome vessels from the regional ceramic assemblage at this time suggests that this de-emphasis of differentiating displays was widespread (Yaeger and LeCount 1995; also see LeCount 1996, 1999 for a broader discussion).

At the same time that San Lorenzo residents no longer referred to Xunantunich in their buildings, the strategies by which the polity's rulers maintained their ties to their hinterland changed. Within Tsak' times, the SL13 complex ceased to function as a ritual complex. The collapse of buildings facing the internal patio and the exterior plastered area early in the Tsak' phase scattered construction materials and other debris over the two main venues for celebrations that had helped reproduce and strengthen differences within San Lorenzo and had likely fostered affiliations with the polity's rulers. Despite later use of the complex, this debris was never removed, and portions of these once-important activity areas remained unused. The timing of this shift parallels increasingly exclusionist practices within the Xunantunich core (LeCount 1999; LeCount et al. 2002).

Eventually both San Lorenzo and Xunantunich were abandoned, probably by the early eleventh century. One key to understanding the processes of abandonment lies, in Yaeger's view, in the changing social and political relationships created and maintained through local practices. It seems plausible that demographic decline was facilitated by a weakening of community identity, caused perhaps in part by Hats' Chaak–phase practices that created an ever-widening rift between local leaders and the rest of the community's residents, an identity that was never successfully replaced by a polity-level identity.

CHAN NÒOHOL

Chan Nòohol, part of the larger Chan settlement, is a cluster of seven small domestic units (CN1–7), each consisting of one or two mounds (Figure 14.4). Robin undertook excavations at Chan Nòohol in 1996 and 1997 to examine the marked expansion and contraction of settlement in the Xunantunich area in relation to larger social, economic, and political developments of Late and Terminal Classic times (Robin 1996a, 1996b, 1997, 1999, 2001). Investigations combined excavation in mounds and in the areas around them to examine archaeological and chemical evidence of activities across the settlement (e.g., J. Braswell 1998; Dunning 1989, 1992; Robin 2000; Smyth and Dore 1992; Smyth, Dore, and Dunning 1995).

Inquiry had been instigated specifically by Robin's initial analysis of transect survey data, indicating that one- or two-mound settlement units comprised more than half (61 percent) of the 280 documented groups, and that size related strongly to longevity. Whereas most one- and two-mound units were occupied solely in Late Classic times, the local settlement peak, groups of five or more mounds evinced both earlier founding and later persistence.[4] This numerical preponderance of small groups at a Late Classic settlement peak resembles patterns elsewhere in the Belize River area (e.g., Ford 1990: 173, 175), but contrasts with situations in other parts of the southern lowlands, where more complex, multimound domestic groups predominate at the settlement apogee (e.g., Haviland 1988; McAnany 1993; Rice 1988; Sanders 1981; Tourtellot 1988a; Willey 1981). In social terms, the Late Classic settlement pattern in the Xunantunich area, where the majority of surveyed mound groups have only one or two mounds, suggests widespread expansion and then truncation of domestic development, or perhaps a change in preferred residence-group composition, from extended to other family forms (see also Ford 1990; Rice 1988; Yaeger 1995a; compare Tourtellot's [1988a: 118] comments on Dzibilchaltun).

Extending the developmental-cycle model, a community also grows as new families choose to move into or near existing family compounds. These new families may be descendants of established residents, or they may be newcomers, related to local households as distant or fictive kin, or through economic ties. Accordingly, in longer-lived settlements, growth reflects some combination of longer individual household histories plus the influx of new families. These settlements should be represented archaeologically as morphologically complex mound clusters, their constituent units ranging from isolated mounds to multiple-mound groups, as at San Lorenzo (Figure 14.3; see also Yaeger 1995a). At the other end of the spectrum are settlements of families moving into previously uninhabited spaces. In cases where further growth did not occur, these new settlements enter the archaeological record as morphologically simple mound clusters whose constituent units contain only one or two mounds, as at Chan Nòohol (Figure 14.4). With their shorter occupation histories, these simpler clusters are characterized by an apparent burst and brevity of occupation.

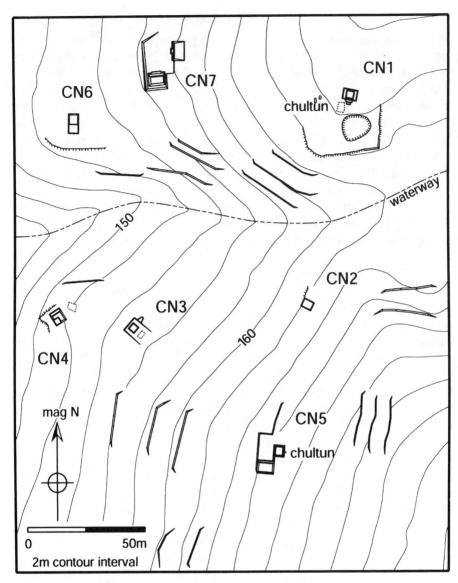

14.4 The Chan Nòohol settlement cluster. Dotted-line entities are non-mound cobble features.

Longer-lived settlement clusters in the Xunantunich sample are generally found near permanent waterways, alluvial floodplains, or on hilltops, plausibly because of economic or ritual advantages. In contrast, simpler, demonstrably shorter-lived settlements—such as Chan Nòohol—are often situated beside streams now running only intermittently, their water supply augmented by artificial reservoirs (waterholes or *aguadas*), and the households linked to terraces that would have enhanced agricultural production (e.g., Dunning and Beach 1994; Fedick 1994; Neff 1998; Neff et al. 1995; Turner 1983). The implied ranking in locational preferences and their relative benefits suggest that the Late Classic settlement expansion is similar to broadly contemporary colonization of less desirable land documented elsewhere (e.g., Ford and Fedick 1992). Socially, the simpler settlement clusters may be comparable to what are called *kahtaló'ob,* newly inhabited farming areas, in Yucatec ethnographic literature (Hanks 1990; Kray 1997; Redfield and Villa Rojas 1934).

Hats' Chaak–Phase Strategies of Affiliation

Based on ceramic chronologies, the emergence of new Late Classic settlement clusters in the survey area corresponds roughly with Xunantunich's rise to political and economic power, paralleling the first part of the trajectory described earlier for San Lorenzo. At Chan Nòohol specifically, however, ceramics excavated from fill, occupation, and refuse contexts together suggest that this cluster of households was occupied wholly within the Hats' Chaak phase.[5] Adjoining a larger established community, Chan Nòohol fits the profile of the simpler settlements filling in arguably less-desirable land.

Chan Nòohol's seven small domestic units are located on flat to gently sloping terrain adjacent to a currently intermittent stream (Figure 14.4). Two units (CN1, CN5) are associated with *chultuns,* and one (CN1) is next to a waterhole. Although modern agricultural potentials are not a direct proxy for ancient soil fertility, we note that those of the Vaca suite Cuxu subsuite soils of Chan Nòohol are considered "limited" under mechanized farming practices (King et al. 1992). Whatever the ancient productivity quotients, however, Chan Nòohol residents enhanced local capacities with terracing. Household units were associated with one to three terraces apiece, excavation of which recovered maize glumes and other macrobotanical remains that suggest a range of crops that likely grew on the terraces.

Moreover, each of the seven household units yielded a range of artifacts, ecofacts, soil chemistry signatures, and architectural remains indicating the same set of basic domestic and agricultural activities. High frequencies of artifacts and activity areas associated with food-production processes, from sowing to serving, coupled with low frequencies of artifacts associated with other activities, indicate that food production was the primary activity for Chan Nòohol residents, and agricultural produce most likely the only item—beyond labor itself—exported from the settlement.

Despite the simple and seemingly homogeneous nature of the mounds before excavation and the overall redundancy of activities and materials in Chan Nòohol daily life, there was—as in San Lorenzo—clear variability in architecture and in the quantity and quality of the artifacts families used. Beyond the inference that all residential substructures supported perishable buildings, and only perishable ones, architectural diversity was evident, especially in comparisons between one- and two-mound domestic units. Dwelling substructures at single-mound units (CN1, CN2, CN3, CN4, CN6) were smaller and less elaborate in construction, although four of the five units had cut-block limestone on one facade, inferred on other grounds to be the front. Three had low benches (CN1, CN2, CN4), and two had a formal front step (CN1, CN3). Dwelling substructures in two-mound units (CN5, CN7) had cut-block limestone on all facades. Two dwellings had low benches (Str. 2 at CN5, Str. 1 at CN7) and two had a front step (both at CN7). Although none of the Chan Nòohol dwellings need have required extra-household help in construction, the variation in their outward appearance could well have reflected and fostered a degree of social distinction.

Local differences in architecture roughly parallel relative access to material items (compare Smith 1987). Residents of two-mound units (CN5, CN7) were, perhaps not surprisingly, the only residents of Chan Nòohol who possessed nonlocal, possibly luxury items, such as objects made of greenstone and marine shell, mostly *Strombus* sp. Although quantities of the foregoing were small, the same two households also yielded higher percentages of ash-ware serving vessels, and CN7 had specialized ritual objects, such as incensarios.

As interesting in social terms, however, was an apparent exception to the correlation between investment or display in architecture and those in portable goods. This was the observation that residents of the unassuming single-mound unit CN1, associated with the aguada, had higher percentages of ash-ware serving vessels and the only deposits of animal bone. Proximity to the artificial waterhole may be a key here. As LeCount notes (1996: Chapter 7), Xunantunich-area ash-ware serving vessels are formally reminiscent of small-scale ritual feasting vessels shown in Classic art (Chase 1985b; Coe 1978; Houston, Stuart, and Taube 1989; Taube 1989) and known from ethnographically recorded small-scale feasts (Bunzel 1952; Hanks 1990; Redfield and Villa Rojas 1934; Wisdom 1940). In contemporary Maya communities, waterholes often serve as focal points for integrating distinct social groups (Vogt 1969, 1976). If the ceramics and faunal remains do represent expanded feasting activities undertaken at the household nearest the aguada, this waterhole may have been important, not only economically, as a store of water in an area distant from a permanent source, but also as a focus for inclusive rituals reinforcing group identity. Other observable commonalities, such as a restricted range of orientations for all Chan Nòohol buildings and the construction of all groups except CN7 to face the intermittent stream, may be further expressions of group identity and a focus on water.

Supporting evidence for the special role of CN1 comes from the unusually large extent of its houselot's cleared outdoor "work area," a functional designation derived from distinctive combinations of artifact and soil-chemistry signatures (Robin 1999, 2000). Robin's ethnoarchaeological study in a modern village near Valladolid, Yucatán, suggests that the size of cleared exterior work space in houselots correlates directly with the frequency with which households host communal feasts (ibid.). Thus, although the CN1 household unit remained architecturally unimposing, it seems to have played an important role relative to integrating the larger settlement, and specifically in association with what may have been a communal waterhole.

Although all Chan Nòohol households seem to have hosted some rituals involving one or a combination of ash-ware serving vessels, incensarios, drums, caching, and burials, integration of local residents into larger social spheres involved mechanisms similar to those at San Lorenzo, but smaller in scale or simpler in expression. Not surprisingly, all people of Chan Nòohol, including residents of CN5 and CN7, had less access to nonlocal luxury items such as greenstone than did families with deeper genealogical ties to the land, including some at San Lorenzo as well as elsewhere in the Xunantunich area (J. Braswell 1998; Connell 1997; LeCount 1996). This plausibly reflects more attenuated links to elite-controlled distribution, here filtered through Chan community leaders as well (e.g., Ehret 1998). And not surprisingly, Chan Nòohol yielded quantitatively less evidence for larger-scale feasting activities than did longer-lived households in the area (see San Lorenzo above; also J. Braswell 1998; Connell 1997; LeCount 1996).

It is also worth noting that, despite an excavation strategy that explored probable burial locations (e.g., Welsh 1988), only one interment was encountered, at CN5. It would seem that some aspects of ancestor veneration may have been largely absent from Chan Nòohol. Perhaps the rituals associated with these, and surely with other integrative gatherings, were conducted at households of more-established families in the larger Chan settlement (compare Robin 1989; Wilk and Wilhite 1991). If members of Chan Nòohol were, indeed, collectively burying their dead elsewhere and participating in larger-scale feasts at longer-standing households in Chan and occasionally at Xunantunich, the links would have enhanced solidarity within the larger social entities.

Tsak'-Phase Changes

With Tsak'-phase demographic decline and social change, the Chan Nòohol case marks the local extreme, the settlement having been effectively abandoned by that time.[6] Inasmuch as Chan Nòohol farmers occupied arguably less desirable land, and had limited material wealth and social status, these residents of the Xunantunich area likely responded more readily to Tsak'-phase pulls on the social, economic, and political fabric. As important, however, survey and test-pitting yielded almost no evidence of Tsak'-phase occupation elsewhere at Chan (Ehret in Ashmore et al. 1994; Ehret 1995), and none at all in the plausible center of the settlement, site O/A1-005 (Ehret 1995).

DISCUSSION

It is important to note that XAP and XSS data analyses remain ongoing, and other lines of inquiry relevant to local social and demographic collapse are still in progress, by ourselves and several project colleagues. Among these is critical study of agricultural productivity that will help link the subsistence and larger economies in which local commoners participated (e.g., Neff 1999). Nevertheless, we offer the following provisional thoughts on developments at San Lorenzo and Chan Nòohol and on the collapse of local society before the end of the Tsak' phase.

Both San Lorenzo and Chan Nòohol exemplify aspects of larger patterns plausibly widespread in the Xunantunich area, but the detailed information from extensive excavations in these two settlements allows finer discrimination of strategies for integration and survival. The data evince variation between agrarian settlements and among the farmers resident there. We reiterate that "commoners" certainly did not have all social or other characteristics "in common" with one another, and that we gain in understanding the complexity of this class—and their contemporaries—by identifying more fully the varied ways in which all people lived through the events of this period.

In both San Lorenzo and Chan Nòohol, domestic architecture and ritual performance helped bind social groups together, even as they often distinguished neighbor from neighbor. Sheer proximity, shared labor in construction, shared expressive styles, and shared ritual reinforced community identity (e.g., Blanton 1994). Differentially elaborate (or simple) material display and differential relations with prestigious outsiders created distinctions among households and, perhaps in some cases, tensions in the social order. The more established, arguably more advantageously situated San Lorenzo also survived longer than did the smaller, and perhaps more marginally grounded settlement we call Chan Nòohol. But both invoked similar strategies for social differentiation and integration, if with variable levels of investment.

Although differences in environmental resources were doubtless important in underwriting localized prosperity, growth, and social cohesion, we would not ascribe all inter-settlement contrasts reductively to environmental variability. We believe the data highlight as well the effects of differential social embeddedness and interdependence, established within individual household, lineage, and community histories, by means of the economic and ritual practices cited earlier. The strategies used across these settlements were broadly the same and evidently quite effective for a time. But in both cases, they ultimately failed. What happened? And to what degree and for whom is "failure" the appropriate term?

Lacking clear evidence for environmental degradation, significantly expanded violence, or heightened disease in this period, we offer, briefly, one possible social and economic scenario for the demise of a populace that otherwise, on aforementioned theoretical grounds, should not have disappeared when it did. It prospectively accounts not only for collapse here, but also for the antecedent

Hats' Chaak–phase boom. And although necessarily remaining somewhat speculative, this scenario provides a broader context for potentially situating events documented at the two commoner settlements examined here.

If, indeed, the enhanced productivity of the area's terraced fields proves to have been as effective as we posit, we suggest that economic and demographic growth and then collapse in this part of the Belize River Valley may relate to escalating and ultimately catastrophic economic and demographic stress farther west. More specifically, we recall Culbert's (1988: 92ff) model of potential subsistence catchments of 50- or 100-kilometer radius for Late Classic Tikal—radii embracing the Xunantunich area—and the text-based political models of alliances and war involving Naranjo (e.g., Martin and Grube 2000; Reents-Budet 1994; Schele and Freidel 1990). We suggest that, as militarism among the larger polities grew during the Late Classic, and as demand increased for foodstuffs to feed their beleaguered populations, the natural attractions of this part of the Belize River Valley area likewise rose. Within what had always been an important corridor and, in some stretches, a breadbasket (e.g., Fedick and Ford 1990; Willey et al. 1965), control of the area's productive resources was increasingly coveted. Terraces were built to expand productivity for subsistence and surplus demands, toward enhancing both staple and wealth finance (D'Altroy and Earle 1985). In this light, Naranjo's oft-cited seventh-century alliance with (or patronage of) Buenavista del Cayo may be plausibly interpreted, in part, as a move to bolster the latter's claim against upstart Xunantunich for control of local produce and populace. The lords at Xunantunich ultimately prevailed in this competition, and both the kind of demographic expansion seen at Chan Nòohol and the apparently relatively close involvement of Xunantunich lords in affairs at San Lorenzo may reflect different responses to heightened economic opportunity associated with the rising polity, its capital, and rulers.

But the center, and the commoners attached to it, could not hold. As polities in the Petén heartland collapsed, from the late eighth century on, Xunantunich's external links declined along with the sources of demand that had underwritten its prosperity. Before the end of the ninth century, within the span of the Tsak' ceramic phase, both local people and foreign visitors were emphatically excluded from previously open central precincts and the rituals held there (LeCount 1999; LeCount et al. 2002; Leventhal and LeCount 1997). As a consequence of changes for the ruling class, the earlier economic and political opportunities and inducements to farmers to settle locally dissolved as well, and weakened rulers in the center could no longer induce or entice people to stay. There is no evidence of mass death; people probably simply moved on, perhaps to join distant kin or follow more potent leaders elsewhere (compare D. Rice [1986] and Culbert [1988: 75] concerning possibly analogous demographic shifts in Petén). Longer-established, arguably more prosperous families stayed on longer, albeit in reduced circumstances, as at San Lorenzo, while farmers on the newer fringes of old settlements disappeared earliest, and seemingly most abruptly. Collective abandonment of farmsteads and communities was likely gradual, however, despite boom-bust appearances partly induced, as noted earlier, by imprecision inherent in ceramic dating. Defection of farming families to other polities would have exacerbated the decline at Xunantunich by reducing production. Farther downstream, Baking Pot–Barton Ramie survived, as did settlements in the uplands north of the valley, both areas presumably able to draw more effectively on growing political and economic networks linked to the Caribbean coast. Xunantunich may have been on the periphery, but it was still too close to and too closely involved with the Petén core to be buffered from collapse.

Although we certainly cannot consider commoners' actions in the Xunantunich area as wholly independent of elite behavior, the richly textured evidence of strategies for social differentiation and integration at San Lorenzo and Chan Nòohol argues eloquently for varied individual-, household-, and settlement-level decision making. In both the Hats' Chaak–phase florescence and subsequent Tsak'-phase collapse, commoners' practices fomented community solidarity, structured social order, and left material legacies of complex and varied lives.

NOTES

1. By the time we formulated XSS research, we were aware that Joseph Ball (1987) had remarked already on the paucity of Terminal Classic/Early Postclassic ceramics he had encountered in the vicinity, and on the marked contrast with adjoining areas in this regard. We certainly had no reason to doubt him, but as Ball noted in the same paper, the situation merited closer examination. Because we were uncertain of the range of places Ball had examined (Ashmore 1993: 11), because there were other hints of scattered late occupation in the area (besides Tipú; see below), and—most of all—because we, too, wanted to examine the larger, derived models further, we thought it worth looking directly at the local situation ourselves.

2. The Late Classic population density figure cited here derives from Neff's (1998) preliminary demographic analyses for T/A1 and T/A2, and represents a combined average for the two in Hats' Chaak times. ("Hats' Chaak" is a Late Classic ceramic phase defined later in the text.)

3. Although the area now occupied by the Negroman-Tipú site was first settled by 300 B.C., it is best known for its Colonial occupation. Just across the Macal River, the site of Guacamayo may have been part of a continuous settlement with what is now considered Tipú. Although Guacamayo has yet to be surveyed (Neff et al. 1995: 145–146), it is said to have at least four major architectural groups, the largest of which included several structures estimated at 15–20 meters high. This may well have been the civic center for that portion of the Macal River Valley in Classic times.

4. XSS ceramic samples from surface collections and shovel-testpits were usually small in number and poor in physical preservation. Consequently, availability of temporal diagnostics often permitted distinctions only to the more general LC designation, not finer Samal or Hats' Chaak discriminations (Ehret in Ashmore et al. 1994; Robin in Neff et al. 1995).

5. Two episodes of Preclassic activity in the Chan Nòohol area lack continuity with the Hats' Chaak–phase settlement (Robin 1999).

6. Tsak' occupation originally reported from test-pitting at CN7 (site T/A1-069; Ehret 1995: 174) was based on a rim sherd of Mount Maloney Black (lot 183M/2; Ehret n.d.), a pottery type whose lip form has proven unusually sensitive as a temporal diagnostic (LeCount 1992, 1996: 146–150). Robin's excavations recovered a few additional Tsak' diagnostics, but the collection was insufficient in size and too superficial in context to attest to continued occupation.

ACKNOWLEDGMENTS

We gratefully acknowledge the strong support the Belize Department of Archaeology has given since the outset of the Xunantunich Archaeological Project in 1991. We value particularly the encouragement of Commissioner of Archaeology John Morris, and of his predecessors, Allan Moore and the late Harriot Topsey. We also thank all our XAP colleagues, especially Richard M. Leventhal, Lisa LeCount, XAP foreman Florentin Penados, XSS foreman/*capitán* Lucrecio Chan, and the many crew members from San José Succotz and Benque Viejo del Carmen whose hard and careful work provided the empirical foundation upon which we have built the arguments presented in this paper. Mssrs. Rudy Juan, Dorrell Biddle, Mel Xix, David Magaña, and Amalio Matus kindly granted permission for our investigations on their property. And numerous scholars working elsewhere in the Belize Valley have generously shared invaluable insights as well as data. We are grateful to Lisa LeCount, Tom Patterson, Gordon Willey, and the volume's editors for comments on earlier drafts of this paper.

Funding for our work came principally from the National Science Foundation (SBR9321503, SBR9530949, SBR9618540), the University of Pennsylvania Museum, and Penn's Department of Anthropology and School of Arts and Sciences. Yaeger and Robin were awarded Fulbright/II-E and Sigma Xi grants, as well as Dissertation Grants from the University of Pennsylvania Graduate School of Arts and Sciences. Yaeger also held the Lisa Lynn Brodey-Foley Memorial Grant of the Department of Anthropology and a junior fellowship in pre-Columbian studies at Dumbarton Oaks. We thank them all for their generous support of our work.

15

TRANSFORMATIONS, PERIODICITY, AND URBAN DEVELOPMENT IN THE THREE RIVERS REGION

R.E.W. Adams, H. R. Robichaux, Fred Valdez Jr.,
Brett A. Houk, and Ruth Mathews

INTRODUCTION
Geography and Research History

The region under study, designated as the Three Rivers region, is approximately two thousand square kilometers in area and trapezoidal in shape. The sites of La Honradez, Aguada Cancuen, Blue Creek, and San José are near the corners of the trapezoid (Figures 15.1 and 15.2). This region has been subdivided into western (Guatemala) and eastern (Belize) zones for analytical purposes. The largest western zone sites are Río Azul, Kinal, and La Honradez. La Milpa is the largest eastern center. Currently, Emblem Glyphs are known for Río Azul (Stuart 1986; Houston 1986) and La Milpa (Grube 1994c), and a possible Dos Hombres (eastern zone) Emblem Glyph has been found on a polychrome plate fragment from that site.

Three rivers, the Río Azul (Blue Creek in Belize), the Río Bravo, and Booth's, three escarpments in the eastern zone, and the Bajo de Azucar and the Río Azul floodplain form the major topographic features of the region (Figure 15.2). More than eighty sites have been found in the region to date. These sites range in size from single house mounds and single groups of house mounds to a twenty-five-courtyard-sized eastern site (La Milpa) and Río Azul, at thirty-nine courtyards in the west.

Research in the area prior to 1992 includes: Adams and Gatling 1964; Adams and Jones 1981; the Río Azul Project, Adams 1990a; and Guderjan's surveys in the eastern zone (1991). Research actually began in 1959 with the Sun Oil survey

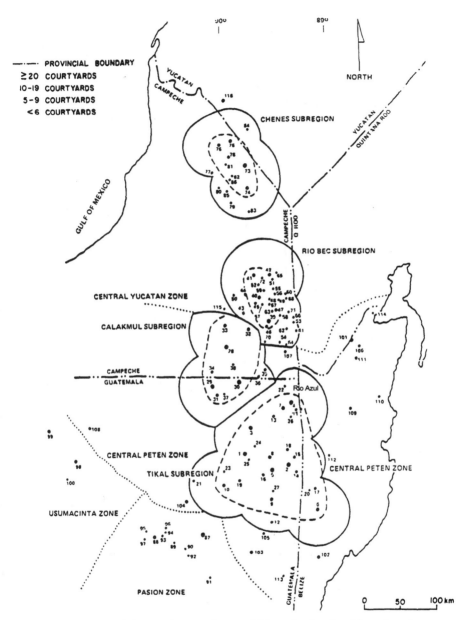

15.1 *General map of the southern and central Maya lowlands with major sites mentioned in the text noted. The outlines are those delimiting the hypothetical Classic regional states of Calakmul, Tikal, and the Chenes. Some centers of Río Bec Region are now thought to have been incorporated into the Calakmul Regional State, while other centers may have formed independent city-states. (After Adams and Jones, 1981.)*

Figure 2. Map of the Three Rivers Region (after H. R. Robichaux, 1995)

15.2 Map of the Three Rivers region with major sites and settlement pattern transect survey lines noted. (After Robichaux, 1995.)

in which the gravity and seismic survey teams were instructed by John Gatling, resident geologist, to record all archaeological sites encountered. The survey lines were cut on a one-kilometer grid for a zone of about 300 square kilometers. Two major sites, Río Azul and Kinal, were reported, as well as twenty-seven other sites.

The Río Azul Project was a site-specific project that had as its general focus the reconstruction of the functional structure of the city partly by means of being able to assign each of the 729 buildings a function. Changes through time were also a concern. The Río Azul Project completed five field seasons between 1983 and 1987.

From 1990 to 1991, work in the western sector was pursued by the Ixcanrio Regional Project. The objectives of this project were to reconstruct the economic, social, and political infrastructures supporting Río Azul and Kinal. After 1991 the security problems of working in that part of Guatemala became too great, and we took advantage of an opportunity to move into the adjacent part of Belize. We based our initial five years of work on a detailed twenty-year plan

(Adams 1990b) designed to study the regional aspects of Maya culture in our area. It now appears that the long-range plan will be fulfilled certainly in the Belize zone and perhaps in the Guatemalan zone in the future.

The major western sites of La Honradez and Xultun (just beyond the boundaries of our region) have only been mapped (von Euw 1978; von Euw and Graham 1984). What is known of their culture history is derived from dates and texts on their stelae.

Present research includes and is partly summarized by Houk (1996), Houk and Robichaux (1996), Robichaux (1995), Scarborough (1994), Tourtellot and Rose (1993), Tourtellot et al. (1993), and Valdez et al. (1997). Results of the NASA-JPL Airborne Synthetic Aperture Radar Survey (AIRSAR) of 1990 have also been utilized. Our work in Belize is in a zone of about 600 square kilometers but takes account of work going on outside the boundaries of our permit zone. The Programme for Belize Archaeological Project includes several investigations: regional survey, intensive settlement pattern survey transects (Hubert Robichaux, Paul Hughbanks, Jon Lohse, Jon Hageman), water management studies (Vernon Scarborough), and soil studies (Nicholas Dunning). This study also considers work at three large sites by colleagues Norman Hammond and Gair Tourtellot (La Milpa), Thomas Guderjan (Blue Creek), and Brett Houk and Hubert Robichaux (Chan Chich). Other work by collaborating scholars has been taken into account. Dr. Richardson B. Gill improved our population history charts immeasurably by logarithmic presentation. The National Geographic Society, National Endowment for the Humanities, The Friends of Río Azul, The National Science Foundation, The University of Texas at Austin, The University of Texas at San Antonio, and other entities and private individuals have supported our work. We thank them all.

ASSUMPTIONS AND THEORETICAL BIASES

1. That the basic structures of civilizations are hierarchically organized major cultural institutions; e.g., in politics, the state.

2. That cities are at the apices of the community patterns in such complex cultures; assume special functions in administration, economics, and religion at the minimum together with the correlated developments in those institutions; e.g., craft specialization aggregates.

3. That the assumption in the research plans for the Río Azul Project and the Programme for Belize Archaeological Project (1983–1998) are also correct and are that:
    a. the major premises of anthropology have been demonstrated; culture as patterned behavior traditional to a social group and transmitted through time.
    b. that one analytical approach to the study of culture (of several possible), that of cultural institutions, is viable.

c. that archaeology can detect patterned behavior from past cultures in patterned data from fieldwork.

d. that major cultural institutions are best reflected in their secondary characteristics; e.g., the economic sector in market and other exchange variants.

e. that archaeology has developed an array of fieldwork techniques that will elicit data on most major cultural institutions (except, perhaps, legal systems and the like).

FIELD AND ANALYTICAL METHODOLOGY

In both field and analytical work the distinction is drawn between land suitable for residence, land suitable for cultivation, and land unsuitable for either purpose. This is based on Brokaw and Mallory's vegetation surveys in the eastern zone (1993), and the regional and Río Azul projects' work in the western zone. Twenty-three percent is unsuitable for habitation in the eastern zone, a figure increasing to about 35 percent in the western zone. The average used is 30 percent for the entire zone, leaving a net of 1400 square kilometers estimated as habitable. Based on our surveys we split the 1400 square kilometers into a 240-square-kilometer maximum urban area and a 1160-square-kilometer residual rural area. The total areas were used only in the period of maximum population, Late Classic 2, which is also used as the benchmark period. We used only half the rural area (580 square kilometers) when calculating the rural populations of Early Classic 2–3, Late Classic 1, Late Classic 3, and Early Postclassic when the western zone shows practically no rural people. We used one-fourth of the rural area, 290 square kilometers, in the Middle and Late Preclassic of the region when settlement appears to be tightly tied to the major rivers. Early Classic 1, a period of population depression, was also calculated as one-fourth of the rural area. Urban populations were calculated as nil for the first two periods, Middle and Late Preclassic, and one-fourth area (60 square kilometers) for Early Classic 1, and Late Classic 1. One-half of the urban area (120 square kilometers) was used as a calculation base for Early Classic 2–3, Late Classic 3, and Early Postclassic. This is explained in more detail in the appendix.

Careful and high-intensity survey and sample excavations in survey transects located to the west of Dos Hombres and La Milpa in the eastern zone were used as the basis for extrapolation to general rural populations in both zones of the region. Late Classic 2–period population was used as the baseline and as 100 percent. All other period populations are calculated as percentages of the base figures. Table 15.1 presents most of the relevant data. Conversations and data exchange with Hammond and Tourtellot of the La Milpa Project after both projects had done substantial settlement work indicate that our population estimates are nearly identical. Further, work from 1970 to 1973 in the Río Bec area, about 100 kilometers to the northwest, also shows general similarities in population estimates and fluctuations.

Table 15.1.

Periods	Approximate dates	Percentage of LC 2 pop	Possible Pop/km²	Urban/Rural populations*	Total Pop/ 2000 km²
Early Postclassic	A.D. 900?–1250	10%	urb: 92 rur: 18	1/2 total area urb: 11,040 rur: 10,440	21,480
Late Classic 3	A.D. 810–850	94%	urb: 869 rur: 167	1/2 total area urb: 104,272 rur: 96,693	200,965
Late Classic 2	A.D. 680–810	100%	urb: 924.4 rur: 177.5	1/2 total area urb: 221,860 rur: 205,900	427,760
Late Classic 1	A.D. 550–680	22%	urb: 203 rur: 39	1/4 urb: 12,180 1/2 rur: 22,581	34,761
Early Classic 2–3	A.D. 400–550	61%	urb: 564 rur: 108	1/2 total area urb: 67,680 rur: 62,640	130,320
Early Classic 1	A.D. 250–400	5%	urb: 46 rur: 9	1/4 total area urb: 2,760 rur: 2,610	5,370
Late Preclassic	400 B.C.–A.D. 250	33%	rur: 60	1/4 rur. area 17,400	17,400
Mid. Preclassic	800–400 B.C.	8%	rur: 14	1/4 rur. area 4,060	4,060

* 30% of 2000 km² =1400, which is separated into 240 km² urban and 1160 km² rural for the period of maximum population, Late Classic 2.

THE ESTIMATION OF URBAN POPULATIONS

Ancient Maya urban communities are assumed to consist of two principal components: a central precinct and a surrounding supportive area associated with the nucleated zone. The latter is sometimes referred to as the community's "sustaining area" (e.g., Satterthwaite 1951; Haviland 1970: 28; Willey 1981: 402), and is here designated as "interactive rural area," but neither phrase fully expresses the nature of these areas. Beyond these lie what can be designated "true rural" areas, which are lower in population density and more disengaged from the nucleated centers in daily life.

The *central precinct* would be the extensive plaster floored area where the community's elite resided and principally where political, economic, religious, and administrative activities took place. The *interactive rural area* would have a population density several times that of true rural areas, and would be principally where food and economic production activities in service to the communities took place. This area would also provide the labor force for public construction and be the source for conscripted soldiers in the event of need.

The data generated by settlement pattern studies at Tikal (Carr and Hazard 1961; Puleston 1973, 1983) were used as a benchmark from which to estimate the size of the interactive rural areas for communities in the Three Rivers region. The central precinct of Tikal has been estimated to be of eighty-five-courtyard size (Adams 1981: 240), and the total Tikal community (including the sustaining area) has been estimated to extend outward to about a six-kilometer radius, giving the community of Tikal a total area of ca. 120 square kilometers.

We assume that there is a direct correlation between the size of the central precinct of a community and the total area of the community. That is, it appears that the larger the courtyard count, the larger the community as a whole. We compared the courtyard counts of the central precincts of centers in the Three Rivers region with the benchmark count of Tikal (85) as a way of estimating community sizes for those of the Three Rivers region. If, for example, a Three Rivers region center had a courtyard count that was one-fourth that of Tikal, we estimated that the former would have had a total community area one-fourth that of Tikal, or about thirty square kilometers. This method will not provide perfectly correct estimations, but we believe that they will generally be within a reasonable range of the true figures. Where we had specific data on the size of the interactive rural areas of Three Rivers region communities based upon actual survey and excavation data, we used those figures rather than those from the foregoing system of estimation.

For estimating population densities present within Three Rivers region communities, we used data derived from a survey in the interactive rural area of La Milpa (ca. 900 persons per square kilometer) as representative of other large sites in the region. A downward adjustment was made for smaller communities based upon their relative sizes.

Additionally, it should be noted that the areas of the central precincts of Three Rivers region communities are generally very small in comparison to the sizes of the communities as wholes. For example, the mapped central precinct of La Milpa (Tourtellot and Rose 1993: site map) upon which the site's twenty-five-courtyard count is based, has a total area of less than one square kilometer. Thus, for the survey-generated total community size of ca. fifty-nine square kilometers of inhabitable land (Table 15.2), the central precinct accounts for less than 1.7 percent of the total, with the remaining 98.3 percent of the community being the interactive rural area. In order to simplify the population estimation process, we have assumed that the survey-generated population density of the interactive rural area (ca. 900 persons per square kilometer) is also applicable to the central precinct. While the actual population density figure for the central precinct may be higher or lower, the error generated by making this assumption will not be large. For example, if the population density of the central precinct is actually three

Table 15.2.

Courtyard Counts on 3 Rivers sites of 5 or more	Estimated community size (km²)	Estimated habitable portions (courtyard totals) (km²)		Estimated population density (per km²)	Est. urban population communities this size	Number of communities this size	Est. total pop. for communities this size
25	72	59	(50)	900	53,100	2	60,600
20	28.2	19.7	(59)	900	17,730	3	53,190
14–15	20.4	14.3	(29)	900	12,870	2	25,740
11–12	16.2	11.4	(50)	900	10,260	5	51,300
7–8	10.6	7.4	(30)	800	5,920	4	23,680
5	7.0	4.9	(15)	500	2,450	3	7,350
						Total:	221,860

times higher (2,700 persons per square kilometer), the population error for the total community will be only ca. 3 percent.

SUMMARY AND COMMENTARY

As is always the case with archaeological reconstructions, the data are uneven in reliability, sparse in other parts, and lacking for still other segments of culture history. This is in spite of our fifteen years of site-specific and intensive rural countryside work in the region. We have taken our best data from several parts of the region and extrapolated and adjusted it. The work continuing in the Programme for Belize Archaeological Project under the direction of Dr. Fred Valdez Jr., will undoubtedly improve the quality of the data and allow more accurate and sophisticated analyses.

Population History (Table 15.1; Figure 15.3)

Patterns of rural population growth show a long buildup in the Preclassic to about 5 percent of the maximum eventually reached. This growth takes about 850 years to accomplish and is likely the result of natural increase. An apparent drop of about 69 percent takes place at the end of the Late Preclassic but a strong recovery follows in Early Classic 2–3, building to a new high of about 130,320 people. This is the first population surge in the region and represents about a 2,300 percent increase in a period of about 150 years. A combination of immigration into the region and natural increase are suggested as the cause of this first surge. A second population drop takes place at the end of the Early Classic during the Hiatus, a diminution of about 73 percent in a period of about 100 years.

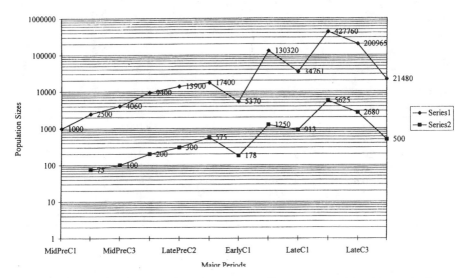

15.3 Population chart for the Three Rivers region based on data in Table 1. The lower line specifies the elite class fraction, while the upper line is inclusive and indicates the total population. The display is logarithmic.

Thereafter comes the second population surge, which builds to a maximum of about 427,760 within 125 years, a gain of about 1,100 percent. This rise is almost certainly a result of immigration from outside the region, but what fraction is to be allocated to that factor and how much to natural increase can only be estimated with present data. A decline in the Terminal Classic (Late Classic 3) period is on the order of 53 percent for about 100 years, and the decline in rural population continues thereafter without recovery to less than the 11 percent level by A.D. 1250.

Urbanization and Political History (Tables 15.2, 15.3; Figure 15.4)

In terms of urbanization of the region, we analyzed the patterns by means of the rank-order nearest neighbor method and the rank-size rule (Adams and Jones 1981). Based on these results and comparisons with artifact, iconographic, and epigraphic material, we reached the following tentative conclusions. The small and large centers along the Río Azul are the earliest known for the region, and Río Azul is only exceeded or matched in age and size in the southern lowlands by Nakbe, which dates to ca. 620 B.C. (Hansen 1991). Small religious and administrative centers proliferated during the Late Preclassic and form a generally pluralistic pattern, likely reflecting a diffused pattern of political authority. This pattern apparently continues through Early Classic 1 with a mosaic of small principalities

Table 15.3. Number of sites according to period; note that not all sites are dated by excavated materials or monuments.

No. of sites according to rank; ?; group; group; (no. refers to courtyards)	Middle Preclassic	Late Preclassic	Early Classic	Early Classic II–III	Late Classic I	Late Classic II	Late Classic III/ Early Postclassic
1: 1; (39)	—	—	—	1	1?	—	—
2: 4; (19–25)	—	—	—	2	2?	5	4
3: 7; (11–14)	—	—	—	—	—	6	3?
4: 13; (3–8)	1	5	3?	5?	5?	9?	6?
5: 14+; (2)	3?	5	6?	2	3?	5??	5
6: 34+; (1)	—	3	3	4	—	34??	1

building up around the many centers. This pattern changes drastically in the west during Early Classic 2–3 with the establishment and construction of the city of Río Azul. Adams (1990a) has interpreted this as being a result of the conquest and political integration of the Río Azul zone by the Tikal regional state. At this time the log normal relationship between La Milpa and Río Azul perhaps reflects a subordinate position for the former. However, in the larger picture, Tikal almost certainly had a primate relationship with most of its subordinate cities at this time with an estimated size of fifty courtyards. Río Azul and perhaps La Milpa were its subordinates.

The Hiatus and the putative civil wars of that period are reflected in abandonment, destruction of centers, monument breakage, and in other ways. Rural population appears to have dropped drastically in the western part of our region, but how this relates to other regional population histories is unclear.

Late Classic 1 is a period of recovery and political decentralization. Río Azul's ruler of A.D. 690 put up a monument in front of a major temple structure, but this is the only one from the Late Classic at the site. La Milpa and other eastern centers show a stronger recovery and apparent political independence in their building programs both then and later.

Late Classic 2 is a period of maximum construction, except at Río Azul. The Kinal fortress is built from scratch, perhaps motivated by the military disaster that had overtaken Río Azul at the end of the Early Classic. La Honradez, La Milpa, and all the other smaller centers of the region flourished in their context of vast supporting populations. However, all of this apparent prosperity ultimately led to disaster and collapse.

Looking at urban population histories (summarized in Table 15.3, Figures 15.4, and 15.5), it is clear that residents within the courtyard complexes and

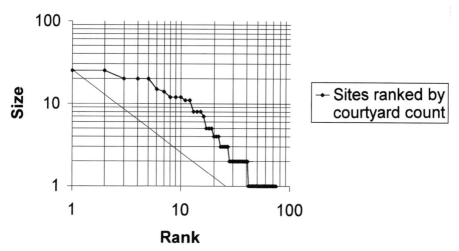

15.4 *Rank-size analysis of Three Rivers Region sites. The sample size is 75 sites and the period is Late Classic 2.*

living in the paved zones of the centers were always a small fraction of total regional population. We have distinguished these people from those judged to be interactive with a center but living outside of it. The limits to the interactive rural residential areas have been defined as those zones within which population density is several orders of magnitude greater than that found beyond their boundaries. Beyond these boundaries, population densities dropped to an average of 177.5 per square kilometer in Late Classic 2 (see Table 15.1; Robichaux 1995). The average core urban population is about 10 percent of the total regional population for the entire Classic period (A.D. 250 to 850), but is 18.4 percent in Late Classic 2. The total interactive population in Early Classic 2–3 period is an astounding 60 percent. This is the period of the establishment of Río Azul and may represent a relatively brief episode of political and military instability in the region. The consequence would have been concentration within the western urban zones for security reasons. The persuasiveness of this explanation depends on how much credence one gives to the interpretation advanced by Adams, which is to the effect that Río Azul became a part of the Tikal regional state at this time. After the long interval of the Hiatus and its population drop, the Late Classic 2 demographic maximum again produces a 50 percent fraction of the total population as interactive with centers. Another notable pattern in the data and analyzed estimates is that of increasing numbers of urban zones through the Classic, culminating in Late Classic 2 with twelve urban centers of medium to large size compared with only five of those sizes in Early Classic 2–3.

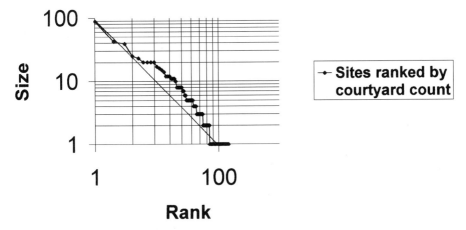

15.5 Rank-Size analysis of Tikal region sites, including those of the Three Rivers region. The sample size is 146 and the period is Late Classic 2.

EVOLUTIONARY PERSPECTIVE AND EXPLANATORY MODELS

In terms of evolutionary perspective, the rank-order and rank-size patterns combined with construction and population histories seem to show several interesting features. First the regional urban centers show chrysalis growth patterns rather than transformational change. That is, growth patterns produce not much qualitative change in the nature of the centers before they reach a threshold of twenty-five courtyards or more. As suggested by our geographer colleague, Richard Jones (Adams and Jones 1981: 318), this threshold excludes those sites that were not either capitals of regional states or administrative capitals of districts. Río Azul shows a transformational growth, but also an extraordinarily rapid growth, and apparently this was a result of the influx of outside population as well as incorporation into the Tikal regional state.

La Milpa shows a periodic growth pattern, one enlargement in the Early Classic and one in Late Classic 2 (Tourtellot et al. 1993). According to the rank-size analysis it may well have been a part of the Tikal regional state in Early Classic times. However, its suite of carved monuments may imply that it was more a client state than a subordinate unit in the larger Tikal state. La Milpa reached its threshold size in the later period and possibly became a regional capital in its own right in Late Classic 2, according to the above analysis. Indeed, Robichaux has recently deciphered a clause on Río Azul Stela 2, which alludes to a visit to Río Azul from an important personage from La Milpa (Robichaux, personal communication, 1997). Río Azul at this time was long past its prime; it was being reconstructed somewhat, but added only the equivalent of four courtyards of architecture during the Late Classic.

Secondly, the feudal model (analogy) proposed by Adams and Smith (1981) best fits the Late Classic 2 period. Criticism of the model has partly been on the basis of its lack of fit to the processual circumstances of the Late Roman Empire, which produced Europe's feudal societies. The latter were partly the result of political and economic decentralization; disintegration is probably a more accurate term. Our proposed feudal model is not only structurally similar to Late Classic 2 society, but now also has processual similarities.

In the Three Rivers regional version of Late Classic 2, ontogeny possibly recapitulates phylogeny. This is a processual analogy to paleontology and means that the embryonic development of the individual summarily recapitulates the evolutionary history of its species. The great number of new centers that were established in the Three Rivers region in Late Classic 2 may recapitulate some of the Late Preclassic developmental history in the sense of population buildup, reorganization of the population, and development of administrative structures.

Commentary on periodicity is always intriguing, can generate endless controversy, and perhaps is misleading in any theoretical way. However, one should at least make a trial examination of the culture and population histories of the Three Rivers region in this way.

In terms of population history, there are three population buildups, as can be seen by referring to Figure 15.3. There are four cultural florescences as measured by transformations, major building episodes, and inferred political events. The beginnings of these florescences are three to four hundred years apart and the episodes have durations of from 150 to 200 years. Finally, there are at least three disasters in the record as measured by population decline, cessation of construction, and inferred political events. The greatest disaster is that of the collapse of ca. A.D. 850. Another occurred ca. A.D. 530, which is the Hiatus. Both catastrophes are pretty clearly triggered by long-term droughts and associated ecological problems. The earliest disaster is more problematic and was less traumatic. It seems to have occurred about A.D. 150 about the end of the Late Preclassic and perhaps is associated with a drought episode as measured by the drying up of the major shallow lakes in northwestern Petén, specifically those at Nakbe and later at El Mirador (Hansen 1990; Gill 1999). Braudel (1984: 71–85) discerned the operation of natural cycles of this sort in his longest historical periods ("conjunctures"), and perhaps we have that kind of phenomenon here.

THE REGIONAL TERMINAL CLASSIC OF THREE RIVERS

A chronological gap between the Terminal Classic and Postclassic periods exists at most sites in northern Belize. Using Colha as a baseline, it was first believed that an interface might be defined between the end of the Classic and the "new" occupants defining Postclassic life. However, the site of Lamanai provided evidence for a phase at this interface that demonstrated some combined features or attributes, particularly as observed in the ceramics.

That "interface" complex was absent at Colha and at most sites in northern Belize (and generally at most sites in the central lowland area that present a Postclassic occupation-reoccupation). With an interface complex identified, it is clear that there exists a gap in occupational sequence at most sites. This gap in habitation is estimated to range from fifty to 100 years. The reason for the age estimate is based on the length of time required for forest rejuvenation. It has been argued (John Masson, personal communication 1994) that it takes only fifty years or so for a deforested area to return to a climax forest. While trees of 150 or 300 years of age will not be present, all species of the forest will be present and secondary growth will be subdued.

The ceramics, tools, and so forth brought in and used by the Postclassic Maya are distinctly different from those identified for the Late Classic period. There are two significant reasons that may account for the differences. First, there are cultural preferences and/or influences from the north (Yucatán). It is believed that the new Postclassic occupants may be from the northern areas, moving into abandoned locations that were nonetheless resource-rich (e.g., chert at Colha). The second factor in material culture change is that quite a different environment existed in the Early Postclassic from what was available in the Late Classic. The forest reclaimed many locations, new creatures inhabited the returned forest, and, therefore, a different inventory of tools was required for a fuller exploitation of the available resources. Hunting, processing, and collecting tools, as well as meal preparation items (stone tools, pottery, etc.), vary from their Terminal Classic counterparts.

Therefore, the Terminal Classic at most locations represents a complete end of a particular lifeway. The transition to a new "system" is clear at Lamanai and a distinctive Postclassic adaptation is noticeable at many sites. The Postclassic reoccupation of many abandoned locations is an adaptation to an environment that was unknown to the Terminal Classic Maya.

TERMINAL CLASSIC DEPOSITS IN THE EASTERN ZONE

Although the mechanisms that triggered the collapse of Late Classic Maya culture in the Three Rivers region are imprecisely understood, recent excavations at Chan Chich (Houk et al. 1999) and Dos Hombres (Houk 1996) have encountered problematic deposits that may bear on the nature and timing of the process. Superficially, these features resemble middens in terms of their composition, but ritual termination deposits in terms of their contexts. At both sites, large quantities of broken ceramics and other artifacts were found on elite residential courtyard floors or steps to buildings. In each case, time-sensitive ceramics place the formation of the deposits in the Terminal Classic (ca. A.D. 850).

At Dos Hombres, a midden-like deposit was encountered in a test pit in a small, elite courtyard at the entrance to the elevated acropolis at the site. Approximately 4.3 cubic meters were excavated in this thick (approximately 40–50 centimeter) layer of material, deposited on the floor of the courtyard. Some of the most exotic artifacts at the site, including numerous large fragments of vessels, an eccentric biface of imported chert, a roller stamp, a figurine head with an elaborate bird headdress, a ceramic animal face, a drilled jaguar tooth, an obsidian biface, numerous obsidian blade fragments, and an anthropomorphic whistle, were recovered from this deposit. Although most of the ceramics were utilitarian (striated or unslipped), exotic ceramics, including a Cubeta Incised sherd with hieroglyphs, Daylight Orange plate fragments, and Palmar Orange Polychrome vessels sherds, were also recovered. A total of 6,731 sherds were recovered, exclusive of very small fragments. Assuming that the feature extends across the entire courtyard, this sample would represent approximately 6.5 percent of the total, estimated to be 104,000 sherds. Conservatively, this projected sherd count total would represent at least 1,000 complete vessels (Houk 1996).

The dating of the deposit at Dos Hombres is tied to Daylight Orange and Dolphin Head Red sherds that appear during the Tepeu 3–sphere phase in the region. Although the deposit is midden-like, it lacks substantial amounts of faunal material and includes numerous large vessel fragments that may have been broken in place.

At Chan Chich, similar deposits were encountered on the steps of two palace structures. Large fragments of vessels, exotic artifacts, and human skeletal material were concentrated on the lower three steps of Structures C-2 and C-6. A partially reconstructible Pabellon Modeled Carved (Fine Orange) vessel dates these features to the Terminal Classic. In both cases, faunal remains were absent or only present in small samples.

The significance of these features lies in their contexts. Although they resemble middens, the deposit locations in elite courtyards or on palace steps argue against this interpretation. Other have interpreted similar deposits as middens of Terminal Classic squatters (e.g., Culbert 1993b; Guderjan 1995), but Houk et al. (1999) argue that the context and composition of these features as defined herein more closely resemble a ritual termination deposit. For example, in the same courtyard at Dos Hombres where the Terminal Classic feature was found, a sealed deposit of smashed polychromes and stuccoed ceramics and obsidian fragments in a pink-colored marl matrix marked the apparent termination of an earlier (Tepeu 2–3) construction phase (Houk 1996). This event was followed by a large-scale renovation of the courtyard (Houk 1996).

Contextually, the later Terminal Classic event at Dos Hombres is comparable to the earlier ritual, and strong similarities exist between the Tepeu 2 event and the Terminal Classic event at Chan Chich. The scope and finality of the two Terminal Classic events, however, are important. They may represent more secular events mimicking the earlier rituals but directed at terminating not a structure or courtyard but the elite inhabitants. At Dos Hombres, the problematic deposit physically blocked the entrance to the Acropolis with nearly fifty centimeters of smashed ceramics. At Chan Chich, smashed artifacts were found on palace steps but not at the base of an adjacent courtyard wall, suggesting that the focus of the event was the elite residence.

The deposits under discussion, therefore, may reflect crucial elements in the "Great Collapse" in the region. Similar deposits have been excavated at Blue Creek (Guderjan 1995; Hanratty 1998) and are suspected to exist at Punta de Cacao, an eastern zone site (Guderjan et al. 1991). Their widespread occurrence argues for a pan-regional, calamitous event that marked the destruction of southern elite culture in a short period of time. At Río Azul, the then-ancient Stela 1 had been enclosed in a protective shrine, but this was half filled with the smashed remains of Tepeu 3–sphere polychrome pottery. Adams (1999) has suggested that Río Azul Stela 4, erected ca. A.D. 840, marks an incursion of Puuc Maya into the region. This interpretation is bolstered by the Terminal Classic appearance at Río Azul of trickle ware and slate ware potteries. Colha, about thirty kilometers to the southeast, also has strong evidence of northern Maya intrusion, and a military one at that (Eaton 1980). Whatever the case, however, these termination ritual features represent the abandonment of the urban centers in the region and precede or accompany a massive depopulation of the countryside.

APPENDIX: DERIVATION OF POPULATION ESTIMATES FOR THE THREE RIVERS REGION IN BELIZE AND GUATEMLALA

Population estimations for the Three Rivers region were principally based upon the data from Robichaux's surveys and excavations within and near the ancient communities of La Milpa and Dos Hombres in northwestern Belize. The empirically determined period of maximum population, Late Classic 2, was used as a baseline from which we extrapolated population estimates for the other temporal periods.

The number of possible residences per square kilometer was derived by the use of Robichaux's Tables 11 and 12 (1995: 181, 186). In Table 12, Robichaux used a 32 percent reduction factor. We elected to use Culbert's 21.5 percent reduction factor (Culbert et al. 1990: 115), as we thought this number best represented the Three Rivers region's demography. Because of this change, column B in Table 12 is multiplied by .785 instead of .68. The resulting average number of residences per square kilometer in the Late Classic 2 period is 102 instead of 96. Robichaux's Table 11 presents the number of test pits that contained ceramics from the different temporal periods. This table was used along with the possible 102 residences to determine the percentage of Late Classic 2 population applicable to periods other than the Late Classic 2. A conservative estimate of five people per household was used in computing populations. The total area within the Three Rivers region was reduced by 30 percent to account for uninhabitable terrain (bajos and floodplains).

We used the Tikal courtyard estimate of eighty-five courtyards and total community size of 120 square kilometers as a benchmark from which to estimate the size of urban zones within the Three Rivers region. By way of example, a community having a courtyard count one-half that of Tikal's was estimated to have a total community area (central precinct plus interactive rural area) of sixty square kilometers.[2] The one exception to the use of this methodology was for La Milpa. For that site we used actual data collected from Robichaux's survey that indicated that the La Milpa community had a radius of 4.8 kilometers. This radius generates a total community size of 72.3 square kilometers (4.8^2 x 3.14 = 72.3 km^2) for La Milpa.

The total Three Rivers urban area equals 342.4 square kilometers. This was reduced by 30 percent (uninhabitable land) to 240 square kilometers. The total rural area was estimated at 1160 square kilometers (1400–240). Based upon survey data, the population density for the largest urban areas was estimated at ca. 900 persons per square kilometer, and for rural areas at ca. 177 persons per square kilometer.

The total estimated Late Classic 2 population is 427,760, of which 221,860 lived within large- and medium-sized communities, and 205,900 in rural areas. The Preclassic periods were calculated for rural areas only, as no urban population has been perceived during this period.

The figures in Table 1 were computed as follows:

EARLY POSTCLASSIC:
Urban–10% of $924p/km^2$ = $92p/km^2$; 92 X 120 km^2 = 11,040 persons
Rural–10% $177p/km^2$ = $18p/km^2$; 18 X 120 km^2 = 10,440 persons

LATE CLASSIC 3:
Urban–94% of $924p/km^2$ = $869p/km^2$; 869 X 120 km^2 = 104,272 persons
Rural–94% of $177p/km^2$ = $167p/km^2$; 167 X 120 km^2 = 96,693 persons

LATE CLASSIC 1:
Urban–22% of $924p/km^2$ = $203p/km^2$; 203 X 60 km^2 = 12,180 persons
Rural–22% of $177p/km^2$ = $39p/km^2$; 39 X 580 km^2 = 22,581 persons

EARLY CLASSIC 2–3:
Urban–61% of $924p/km^2$ = $564p/km^2$; 564 X 120 km^2 = 67,680 persons
Rural–61% of $177p/km^2$ = $108p/km^2$; 108 X 580 km^2 = 62,640 persons

EARLY CLASSIC 1:
Urban–5% of $924p/km^2$ = $46p/km^2$; 46 X 60 km^2 = 2,760 persons
Rural–5% of $177p/km^2$ = $9p/km^2$; 9 X 290 km^2 = 2,610 persons

Late Preclassic:
Urban-None
Rural–33% of 177p/km^2=60p/km^2; 60 X 290 km^2 = 17,400 persons

Middle Preclassic:
Urban-None
Rural–8% of 177p/km^2=14p/km^2; 14 X 290 km^2 = 4,060 persons

16

TERMINAL CLASSIC STATUS-LINKED CERAMICS AND THE MAYA "COLLAPSE"
DE FACTO REFUSE AT CARACOL, BELIZE

Arlen F. Chase and Diane Z. Chase

t the heart of considerations of the Classic Maya "collapse" is the identification of any and all activities that took place at the end of the Classic period during the ninth century A.D. However, it often has proved difficult to isolate the latest activities within sites in the southern lowlands. In northern Belize, ceramic blending and continuities make it difficult to know where the Classic period ends and the Postclassic begins (D. Chase and A. Chase 1982, 1988; Graham 1987b; Pendergast 1967, 1986a). Farther south and west in the southern lowlands, clear distinctions existed between Classic and Postclassic–period traditions (Bullard 1973; A. Chase and D. Chase 1983, 1985; Sharer and Chase 1976). However, here it often proves difficult to demarcate the line between the Late and Terminal Classic periods.

Post–A.D. 790, Terminal Classic Caracol, in contrast to some southern lowland Maya sites, had a vibrant and expansive population. There was substantial occupation within Caracol's surrounding settlement area, and monumental architecture (presumably indicative of mobilized labor) continued to be constructed within the site epicenter after A.D. 800. Stone monuments inscribed with hieroglyphs continued to be erected in the central plazas of Caracol until at least A.D. 859. Terminal Classic special deposits—both caches and burials—were made within established ritual traditions. Isotopic analysis also shows a continuation of the distinctive elite diet that is characteristic of the individuals in Caracol's Classic-era epicentral tombs (A. Chase and D. Chase in press; D. Chase et al. 1998). Thus, the latest occupants to live in Caracol's epicentral palaces were a functioning elite, and not merely squatters. They appear to have maintained their material well-being and long-distance trade contacts until approximately A.D. 895.

Archaeologically, the Terminal Classic is often identified by specific ceramic traits and markers—in some cases categorized as complete fine paste complexes, such as Boca, Jimba, and/or Bayal (Adams 1973b; Sabloff 1973), and in other cases recognized through particular forms or decorative modes, such as modeled-carved scenes or banded "dress-shirt" designs (Smith 1955; Culbert 1973c). Contextual analysis of material found on the latest floors of Caracol's buildings, however, indicates that most commonly used and easily recognizable Terminal Classic ceramic identifiers have a fairly restricted distribution at the site and, in fact, formed a distinct ceramic serving ware subcomplex. At Caracol, easily recognizable Terminal Classic material is strongly associated with epicentral palaces, only rarely being encountered in the residential groups that comprise the site core (in spite of extensive testing). Thus, the latest Caracol elite appear to have utilized ceramic serving vessels that were, for the most part, not widely available to the site's general populace. However, on-floor remains from Caracol's palaces contain a great variety of vessels and include non-fineware, plainware forms that are also found in situ within the site's general settlement. Thus, if solely traditional fineware markers were employed as identifiers for the Terminal Classic, population outside the Caracol epicenter could inappropriately be dismissed or be considered absent. But the combined archaeological information from Caracol suggests the opposite.

Research at Caracol is significant to a broader understanding of the "Classic Maya collapse" in that it provides a variable view of Terminal Classic activities. The city of Caracol maintained much of its previous activities and vibrancy. Nevertheless, final activities do suggest significant variances with Late Classic patterns, and it is in these differences that some clues may be found as to what caused the ultimate abandonment of the site. Furthermore, the differential distribution of Terminal Classic ceramics at Caracol may have methodological implications for the identification of Terminal Classic activities at other southern lowland sites.

CERAMIC IDENTIFICATION OF THE TERMINAL CLASSIC

Until recently much of what we thought we knew about the Maya collapse was based upon limited data that were difficult to interpret. Stone monuments, with their easily readable dates, provided one clue as to how late a given site was occupied. Certain ceramic types were found in the latest occupation levels at many Classic-period sites and, thus, came to be associated with the collapse. In particular, Fine Orange paste wares and modeled-carved vessels—ceramics that were easily recognized, and at the same time infrequently found, in the southern lowlands—came to play a defining role; the even rarer Plumbate was viewed as being even later, a true "Postclassic" ceramic vessel form. Thus, along with stone monuments, certain ceramics became defining artifacts for the latest Classic Maya.

With the exception of the easily identified finewares, it can prove extremely difficult to distinguish materials related to the "collapse" era from those dating to the Late Classic height of Maya civilization. The problems are perhaps best illustrated at Uaxactun, Guatemala, where the final ceramic phase, Tepeu 3, "was determined by subtracting all recognized earlier types from the vast surface accumulations" (Smith 1955: 13). Sabloff (1973: 114, 121) pointed to similar analytical problems in phasing late ceramics at both Seibal and Altar de Sacrificios. He indicates that "it is virtually impossible to point to a definitely pure Bayal deposit at Seibal" or "to isolate a pure Jimba deposit" at Altar de Sacrificios. At Tikal, however, Culbert (1973c: 69) noted that the "Eznab Complex [Terminal Classic] shows a clear continuity with Imix [Late Classic] but fortunately includes a number of common and distinctive markers that make identification easy." More interesting from the standpoint of this paper, both he (1973: 69–70) and Fry (1969: 166) generally found the relatively rare Eznab materials in and among stone-constructed range structures or "palaces," commenting that the "total avoidance of small structures for residence is surprising, even for a period with such light occupation."

Part of the inability to identify and interpret abandonment materials at the central Petén sites excavated in the 1960s and earlier may be attributed to methodological considerations, such as excavation strategies that did not overly focus on horizontal context and analytical difficulties in dealing with surface materials and large "sherd scatters." However, problems in identifying late use-related deposits may also be related to the history of Maya archaeology. For instance, we surmise that, at the time that many central Petén sites were dug, a general belief existed that in situ living floors—akin to those found in the American Southwest—likely would not be encountered in Maya palaces or range buildings because of a widespread perception that these buildings were not really lived in. Even though early Mayanists, such as Maler, camped out in these palaces, all noted the dampness of the buildings, the hard bench surfaces, and their general unsuitability for long-term occupation. Following up on these earlier observations and looking at their architectural plans, George Andrews (1975: 43) specifically suggested that these "spaces are not really suited to living purposes." To some degree the idea that Maya stone palaces were nonresidential may have been a holdover of the "vacant ceremonial center" model that dominated Maya archaeological thought in the 1950s and 1960s (Bullard 1960, 1964; Vogt 1961, 1964; Willey 1956). This view of Maya palaces began to change through the work of Harrison (1969, 1999), who ascribed a habitation function to some of the palace buildings at Tikal's Central Acropolis, and Adams (1974), who explicitly correlated Uaxactun's palace benches with sleeping space.

The latest materials found within and about epicentral buildings at many Maya sites generally were not believed to have resulted from the intended use of these structures. Instead, these remains were ascribed to the sporadic activities of population remnants who were camping out in largely deserted centers. At Tikal (Harrison 1999: 48) and Altun Ha (Pendergast 1990a), rooms that were full of Terminal Classic refuse were initially interpreted as confirming such a disjunctive situation. For various reasons, then, the latest materials at many southern lowland sites were deemed to be "worthless" for meaningful interpretation (Adams 1971: 8) and often were interpreted simply as the incomplete remains of squatters from the "commoner" sector of Classic Maya society (Culbert 1988: 74). Within this context, then, any southern lowland Maya site with substantial, use-related Terminal Classic occupation is likely to provide an elaborated, if not an alternative, view of the events leading up to the "collapse."

TERMINAL CLASSIC CARACOL

Evidence for Terminal Classic occupation at Caracol comes from varying kinds of data. Numerous carved stone monuments with hieroglyphic texts date to this time horizon. Caracol's monuments continued to be erected until 10.1.10.0.0 (A.D. 859; Stela 10 [Houston 1987c: fig. 71b])—much later than at some sites, such as Dos Pilas—but ended slightly earlier than at others, such as Tikal. These stone monuments have varied content. Some, such as Stelae 11 (A.D. 800; 9.18.10.0.0 [Houston 1987c: fig. 71a]) and 19 (A.D. 820; 9.19.10.0.0 [Grube 1994: fig. 9.6]), are relatively traditional in portraying single rulers in standard pose. Others are less continuous with earlier traditions—showing portraits of two individuals and portraying captives or themes of alliance (A.D. 800 to A.D. 849; Stela 17 and Altars 10, 12, 13, 22, and 23 [Chase, Grube, and Chase 1991; Grube 1994: fig. 9.4, n.d.]). Some are composed only of incised texts (A.D. 798 and A.D. 859; Ballcourt Marker 3 [Chase, Grube, and Chase 1991] and Stela 10). One monument dating to A.D. 810 (9.19.0.0.0; Stela 18 [A. Chase and D. Chase 1987b]) portrays a huge upreared snake or vision serpent above a bound captive. Terminal Classic monuments are erected outside (Stela 17; Altars 10 and 22) the epicenter as well as within it. The hieroglyphic texts at Caracol contain some of the latest warfare events in the southern lowlands. Altar 12, dating to 9.19.10.0.0 (A.D. 820), records a warfare event that may reference the decapitation of a Tikal lord in the context of a shared ceremony between Ucanal, Naranjo, and Caracol (Grube 1994: 97). The very latest Caracol monuments have iconographic themes—captives and alliance—suggestive of warfare, but no specific textual references to war.

There is evidence for significant construction activity in the epicenter of Caracol during the Terminal Classic period. The final renovation of Caana (Figure 16.1), the tallest and most massive palace construction at Caracol (A. Chase and D. Chase in press) was undertaken after A.D. 800 and likely required the mobilization of considerable labor. The latest phase of this construction entailed raising the summit floor approximately 4 meters as well as substantial palace-room construction. Late construction activity in the form of finished architecture was also

16.1 View of Caana, Caracol's largest architectural complex, from the summit of Structure B5. The range buildings that are visible were all constructed during the Terminal Classic period.

undertaken in the C Group and the elite residential area called "Barrio" located east of Caana. Unused building materials were also stored adjacent to Structure A7. Interrupted construction efforts are in evidence immediately south of the epicenter; excavations during the 2000 field season in the vicinity of Caracol Structure B71 proved that its underlying platform was a massive repository of Terminal Classic trash—presumably a huge unfinished fill block that was to have supported a raised complex like the Central Acropolis. Building efforts outside of the site epicenter are less easy to document, partially due to a research sampling strategy that resulted in very limited architectural penetration and areal clearing operations within the residential core of the site—as opposed to the more substantial penetration and clearing that was done in Caracol's epicenter. However, late building efforts are also more difficult to isolate in the site's non-palace residential groups because of the relative lack of fineware markers. That occupation continued in this area is evident, however, as discussed below.

The identification of special deposits—burials and caches—that are purely Terminal Classic in date is also a problem because the vessels accompanying these deposits largely continued within the already established Late Classic ce-

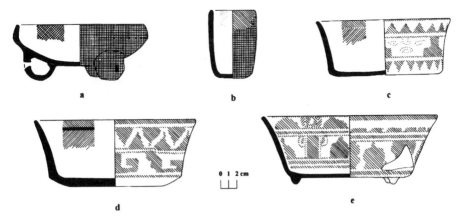

16.2 Vessels from an unsealed cache intruded through the latest summit floor of Structure B19: (a) burned Tinaja Red; (b) burned Tinaja Red; (c), (d), and (e) Danta Orange-polychrome.

ramic traditions. However, there are several burials within the epicenter that can be clearly associated with the Terminal Classic because of both their decorative modes (on fineware offerings) and their stratigraphic associations. These include interments in Structures B5, B34, and the C Group. Stable isotope analysis was undertaken on bone from one of these individuals, the person buried in a crypt in Structure B5 (part of a palace compound); significantly, that analysis indicates that the individual ate the same diet as other Late Classic individuals living in the epicentral palaces, suggesting a continuity of the Late Classic palace diet into the Terminal Classic (A. Chase and D. Chase in press). Identification of Terminal Classic special deposits outside the Caracol epicenter is exceedingly difficult, as residential interments generally do not contain ceramics that match those in the epicentral on-floor palace deposits. However, there are several interments with vessels that are stylistically Terminal Classic in that they include "coffee-bean eye" applique bowls (Caro Incised) and footed vases with ridged decorative panels.

Like the burials, Terminal Classic caches are also difficult to identify, with the exception of clearly late and unsealed deposits in Structures A6 and B19 (Figure 16.2). It is likely that some Terminal Classic caches are undifferentiated from earlier versions. However, the latest caches in the core residential area are not typical Late Classic–period face caches (barrel-like vessels with crude faces on their exterior [A. Chase 1994: fig. 13.7]) or finger bowls (small lip-to-lip dishes literally containing fingers [D. Chase and A. Chase 1998: fig. 4]), but rather crude undecorated barrels and cups. Thus, caching vessels and, by extension, practices, may be slightly discontinuous in the Terminal Classic.

16.3 In situ vessels from the floor of the rear room of Structure B4.

Perhaps the most abundant Terminal Classic database at Caracol exists in the on-floor debris associated with the epicentral stone architecture (Figure 16.3). This debris includes bone (animal and human, worked and unworked), artifacts (including jadeite and marine shell), and pottery (in many cases whole, or almost

Table 16.1.

Building	Lot	Lab #	Date	Corrected	one-sigma	two-sigma
Str. A6	C8N/2	Beta-43518	880 ± 60	cal A.D. 1166	1039–1225	1020–1270
Str. A6	C8S/4	Beta-61211	1140 ± 50	cal A.D. 893	880–979	781–1012
Barrio	C76N/6	Beta-61790	1150 ± 70	cal A.D. 890	789–984	709–1020
Str. B6	C18B/19-5	Beta-18065	1160 ± 70	cal A.D. 886	780–969	680–1010
Caana sum.	C4B/26-15	Beta-18053	830 ± 120	cal A.D. 1221	1030–1280	980–1392
Caana mid	C17K/9	Beta-43524	1170 ± 50	cal A.D. 883	785–941	714–980
Caana r. 1	C16I/16&17	Beta-43520	1230 ± 50	cal A.D. 781	689–881	670–890
Caana red	C16L/12	Beta-43522	1320 ± 80	cal A.D. 673	647–777	590–890
Caana r. 2	C17G/4	Beta-43523	1640 ± 100	cal A.D. 411	257–540	140–620

whole, vessels). On-floor palace materials indicate continued access to trade items and faunal remains that suggest a healthy variability in diet (Teeter 1997). By far the most abundant on-floor materials consist of smashed pottery vessels. Although each location has some different items, there is tremendous continuity in the forms that occur from one palace context to the next (Table 16.2). These ceramics are perhaps the best data source for discussions about Terminal Classic Caracol.

The abandonment of epicentral Caracol appears to have happened suddenly. Many of the epicentral palaces are associated with provisional trash (Schiffer 1987: 65) in exterior areas and had crushed, but complete, serving, storage, and fineware pottery on their interior floors. Importantly, an unburied child was found in an interior doorway of one of Caracol's palaces (A. Chase and D. Chase 1994a: 5) and a burning appears on the floors of many of the central palaces (A. Chase and D. Chase 1987a: 35–36). Dates for the burning on the floors of Caracol's palaces cluster shortly before A.D. 900 (Table 16.1) and, in conjunction with the unburied child and use-related (non-ritual) pottery and trash, are suggestive of the sudden abandonment of the epicentral buildings (D. Chase and A. Chase 2002). The discovery of incomplete, but in-progress, building modifications (in the vicinity of Structures A7 and B71) also supports this interpretation. Thus, the archaeological situation at Caracol apparently differs from that at sites like Tikal (Harrison 1999) and Altun Ha (Pendergast 1990a), where entire rooms were piled full of secondarily deposited trash. At Caracol, in contrast, the latest palace deposits are seemingly de facto refuse—items and garbage caught in a hurried or unplanned exit.

The latest epicentral Caracol ceramics can be dated via a series of associated radiocarbon dates to between A.D. 800 and 1100 (Table 16.1). Nine samples have been run from floor contexts in the epicenter of Caracol. Three of these dates are early; either they are out-of-context, represent the burning of earlier materials, or correlate with previous ritual activities that took place in certain palace rooms in Caana; possibly all three explanations are pertinent. Four dates from four different

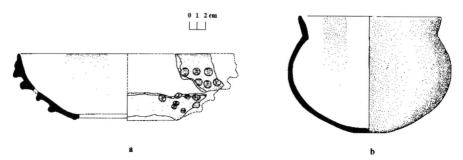

16.4 Late vessels from Structures A2 and A6: (a) Miseria Appliqued; (b) Nohpek Unslipped.

epicentral locales (Structures A6, B6, B14 [Caana], B23 [Barrio]) all cluster about a ten-year time period dating from A.D. 883 to A.D. 893. In combination with the unburied child in the summit Caana palace, these four contexts may represent the final palace activity at Caracol and could conceivably be correlated with a single violent episode and abandonment. However, two other dates—both associated with temples (one from the floor of Structure A6 and one from near Structure B19 on the summit of Caana, which date to A.D. 1166 and 1221, respectively)— suggest a later occupation or at least visitation of the site. The dates and recovered ceramic data from Structure A6 (specifically a Nohpek Unslipped vessel [Figure 16.4b]) could be used to argue for lingering populations at Caracol well past A.D. 1000 that may have continued to use the abandoned epicentral temples for ritual purposes.

ON-FLOOR DEPOSITS AT CARACOL

From the beginning of the Caracol project in 1985 we have been concerned with the identification of in situ floor deposits and what they could reveal about the Maya collapse (A. Chase 1994). At Caracol a number of latest-use in-situ deposits were recovered on the floors of specific buildings. With the exception of the temple buildings Structures A6 and B19, most multiple-vessel on-floor contexts from Caracol were found in the site's epicentral palaces (Structures B4 and B6 from the south side of the B Plaza; Structure B64 in the "C Group," Structure B24 in "Barrio," Structure A39 in the "Central Acropolis," and the various palace buildings of "Caana"), architectural descriptions of which have been presented in detail elsewhere (A. Chase and D. Chase in press). The recovered vessels are found both within and immediately outside these palace buildings. Besides sharing general ceramic forms (Table 16.2), most of these palaces are also associated with a similar set of faunal remains (Teeter 1997).

Thus far some eleven discrete on-floor contexts, exclusive of Caana (Caracol's massive central building complex), have yielded vessel sets within Caracol's epi-

Table 16.2.

| | A39 | B4f | B4r | B6 | B24 | B64 | A8 | D16 | Cedro | Sam | Bayal | Tabanos | Caana | | A3 | A2 | A6 | Zero | Rooster |
													palaces	B19					
footed vases	1	1	—	—	2	—	—	1	—	—	—	—	2	—	1	—	—	—	—
pedestaled vases	1	—	—	—	1	1	—	—	—	—	—	—	1	—	—	—	—	—	—
flat vase	—	—	—	—	—	1	—	—	—	—	—	—	1	—	—	—	1	—	—
footed plates	1	1	—	—	1	1	—	—	—	—	—	—	15	—	—	3	(6)	—	—
footed bowls	1	2	—	—	3	4	—	—	—	—	—	—	1	2	—	—	—	—	—
pedestaled dish	—	—	—	—	—	—	—	—	—	—	—	—	—	—	—	1	1	—	—
molcajete	1	—	1	—	—	1	1	—	—	—	—	—	—	—	—	—	1	—	—
deep bowls	—	1	—	—	—	—	—	—	—	—	—	—	5	—	—	—	—	—	—
spouted bowls	2	1	1	—	—	—	—	—	—	—	—	—	1	1	—	—	—	—	—
other small bowls	—	—	1	—	—	2	—	—	—	—	—	—	1	2	—	—	1	—	—
collared bowl	—	—	1	—	—	2	—	—	—	—	—	—	1	—	—	1	—	—	—
large bowls	—	1	—	—	—	—	—	—	—	—	—	1	—	3	—	—	4	—	—
cups	2	—	—	—	—	—	—	—	—	—	—	—	—	1	—	—	—	—	—
large platters	2	—	—	—	—	—	—	—	1	—	1	—	1	—	—	2	—	—	—
plainware ollas	—	2	—	—	—	—	—	—	—	—	—	—	1	—	—	—	23	—	—
cooking bowls	—	—	—	—	—	—	—	—	—	—	—	—	—	—	—	—	2	—	—
candelario	—	1	—	—	—	—	—	—	—	—	—	1	—	—	—	—	—	—	—
small jar	—	—	—	—	—	1	—	—	—	—	—	—	1	—	—	—	1	—	—
punctated jar	—	2	—	—	—	—	—	—	—	—	—	—	1	—	—	1	—	—	—
plain jar (monkey spouts)	—	1	(1)	(1)	(2)	1(1)	—	—	—	—	—	—	2	—	—	—	—	—	—
barrels	—	—	2	—	—	—	—	—	—	—	—	—	2	—	—	—	—	—	—
miniatures	—	—	—	2	—	—	—	—	—	—	—	—	—	—	—	1	3	—	—
drum	1	—	—	—	—	—	—	—	—	—	—	—	—	—	—	—	—	—	—
3-prong burner	1	—	—	—	—	—	—	—	—	—	—	—	—	—	—	—	—	—	—
effigy lid	—	—	—	—	—	—	—	—	—	—	—	—	1	—	—	—	1	—	—
scored platter-like censers	—	—	—	—	—	2	—	—	—	—	—	—	—	—	—	—	—	—	—
pedestaled barrel censer & lid	—	—	—	—	—	—	—	—	—	—	—	—	1	—	—	—	—	—	—
pedestaled large brazier	—	—	—	—	—	—	—	—	—	—	—	—	—	—	1	—	—	—	—
spiked censers	—	—	—	—	—	—	—	—	—	—	—	—	—	—	1	2	2	—	—
effigy censers	—	—	—	—	—	—	—	—	—	—	—	—	—	1	1	1	2	1	1

center; all have a bearing on the interpretation of the latest use or abandonment of the site's buildings and architectural complexes. Six test excavations from the outlying settlement have also yielded at least one reconstructible vessel associated with the latest building floor or stairs. Twelve more discrete contexts have been identified in and around the buildings of Caana, for a total of twenty-nine relevant contexts that have provided associated sets of on-floor reconstructible vessels. These materials may be integrated with a tightly dated set of vessels that come from more than 220 burials and over 150 caches excavated at Caracol. Few equivalent comparative on-floor materials have been derived from excavations at other sites of the southern lowlands; one exception is Aguateca (Inomata 1997; Inomata and Triadan 2000).

Approximately 140 whole or largely reconstructible vessels are represented in these "abandonment" deposits. Contextually, these deposits and vessels can be separated into "ritual" or "domestic" deposits, although some contexts exhibit both ritual and domestic aspects. Latest-use ritual deposits include: (1) unsealed caches of pottery vessels intruded through earlier floors, as occurred in Structures B19 (Figure 16.2) and A6; (2) censerware positioned either at the base of or within "temples," as occurred in epicentral Structures A3 (A. Chase and D. Chase 1987a: fig. 9), A6, and B19 (A. Chase and D. Chase 1987a: fig. 19) as well as in residential groups "Zero" and "Rooster" (Figure 16.5); and, in the outlying Caracol region, (3) the deposition of pottery in caves (Pendergast 1969, 1971; Helmke n.d.). Latest use-related domestic materials include: (4) in situ ceramics and artifacts within palace buildings, such as occurred in Structures B4, B6, B24, A39, and in many of the rooms on Caana; and (5) the dumping of garbage outside formal buildings, presumably for collection and movement elsewhere (Schiffer's [1987: 65] "provisional trash"), such as is associated with epicentral Structures A39, B4, and B64 and with outlying "core" residential groups "Tabanos," "Bayal," "Sam," and "Cedro" (Figure 16.6). More problematic contexts combining ritual and domestic items are also seen in (6) the deposition of vessels and skeletal remains on the floors of certain "temple" buildings, such as Structures A6 and B19. Importantly, the Maya practice of dumping large quantities of refuse into abandoned rooms has not been encountered at Caracol, presumably indicating that the site's garbage removal system was still functioning at the time of epicentral abandonment (and possibly also that portions of Caracol's terraces were still being built and used [A. Chase and D. Chase 1998b]).

There do appear to be differences between the ritual and domestic Terminal Classic vessel sets. In particular, effigy censers occur in ritual contexts both within and without the epicenter; they are located in epicentral temples and are also found in outlying residential groups (Figure 16.5) on the basal stairs of eastern buildings that once functioned as shrines or mausoleums (A. Chase and D. Chase 1994b). The only polychrome Terminal Classic vessels derive from an unsealed cache through the summit floor of an epicentral temple (Figure 16.2).

0 1 2 cm

a

b

16.5 Incensarios from core settlement: (a) and (b), Pedregal Modeled.

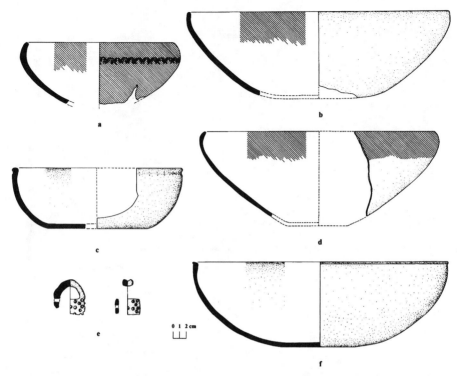

16.6 On-floor vessels from core settlement: (a) Pantano Impressed; (b) and (d), possibly Tinaja Red; (c) and (f), possibly Valentin Unslipped; (e) Chaquistero Composite.

Of even more interest, the only clearly identifiable cooking vessels in the site epicenter occur on the floor of Structure A6, a ritual building with the greatest longevity of use at Caracol (approximately one thousand years). Because cooking vessels are not associated with Caracol's palaces (presumably because elite food was brought from a communal kitchen located outside the palace itself [A. Chase and D. Chase in press]), then their presence in the Structure A6 temple requires some explanation. The Postclassic cooking vessels (Figure 16.4b) may represent the desecration of an important ritual building, perhaps by individuals other than native Caracoleños. Alternatively, these vessels may represent late food offerings left in place by Postclassic peoples, similar to the situation known for Late Postclassic Santa Rita Corozal (Structure 81; D. Chase and A. Chase 1988, 2002).

Following extended analysis and vessel reconstruction, however, the Caracol deposits form recognizable ceramic groupings (Table 16.2) that are distinct from the ceramics known from Late Classic contexts (as represented by the finewares, plainwares, and censerware from the site's burials and tombs). Thus, unlike the situations reported for Altar de Sacrificios, Seibal, and Tikal, the Caracol materials can be sequenced into an identifiable entity or phase. This diverse ceramic corpus exhibits ties to Terminal Classic materials found at other sites. Ceramically, the Caracol refuse deposits are characterized by:

1. Tinaja Red footed bowls (some decorated) with incurving rims (Figures 16.7a, 16.7b);

2. flaring-walled deep bowls (some can be called "cups") that can be plain or associated with ridging and/or incision (Figures 16.7c, 16.7e);

3. footed cylinders with diagonal incision and/or fluting framed with raised ridges (Figures 16.7d, 16.7g);

4. flat-based, rounded-rim plates with oven-shaped tripod feet and occasional basal flanges and incision, both black-and red-slipped (Figures 16.7f, 16.7h; see also A. Chase 1994: fig. 13.11b, c, e, o);

5. incurved-rim *molcajetes* or grater bowls, some Fine Orange (Figure 16.7i);

6. large ridged barrels (Figure 16.7j);

7. collared bowls, both incised (Figure 16.7k) and Fine Orange (Figure 16.7q);

8. Fine Orange vessels or copies that exhibit modeled-carving and a variety of forms (low dish, pedestaled barrel, footed cylinder, collared bowl) of both Belizean (Figure 16.7l; see also Graham, McNatt, and Gutchen 1980) and central Petén extraction (Figure 16.7n; see also Sabloff 1975);

9. special forms, both small—such as *candeleros* (Figure 16.7o), some with handles (Figure 16.6e)—and large—such as drums (Figure 16.7v);

10. jars with minimal impressed shoulder decoration (Figure 16.7m);

11. large incurved bowls, both plain and decorated on their shoulders with stamping, impressing, punctated designs, or rocker incision (Figure 16.7r);

12. non-striated plainware ollas, some fairly wide-mouthed (Figure 16.7p; see also A. Chase 1994: fig. 13.11.k)

13. large, usually interior-slipped, platters (Figure 16.7s); and

14. a great diversity in censers (Figures 16.7t and 16.7u; see also A. Chase and D. Chase 1987a: figs. 9 and 19), possibly including portable burners (Figure 16.7w).

Importantly, many types believed to be diagnostic of a Terminal Classic date in Petén (A. Chase and D. Chase 1983; Culbert 1993a, n.d.) and Pasión regions (Sabloff 1975), such as Encanto Striated, Chaquiste Impressed, Subin Red, and Cameron Incised, either do not occur or are extremely rare in the Caracol sample. And elaborately stamped Pantano Impressed jars (Sabloff 1975)—dated to the

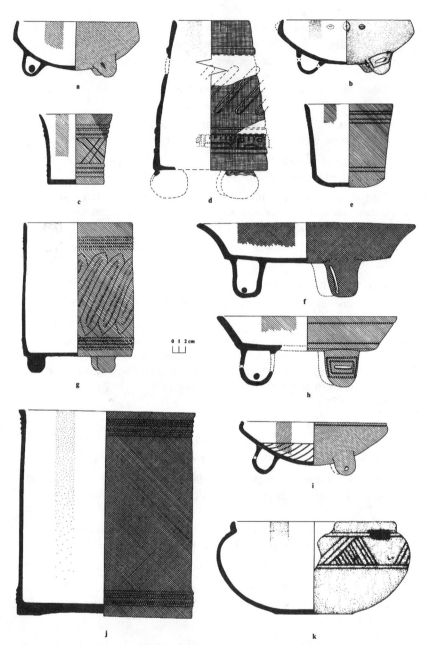

16.7a. On-floor vessels from epicentral Caracol: (a) Tinaja Red; (b) eroded San Julio Modeled; (c) Cohune Composite; (d) possibly Holtun Gouged-incised; (e) Cameron Incised (variety unspecified); (f) Infierno Black; (g) Cohune Composite; (h) Platon Punctated-incised (variety unspecified); (i) Trapiche Incised; (j) possibly Bambonal Plano-relief; (k) Conchita Incised.

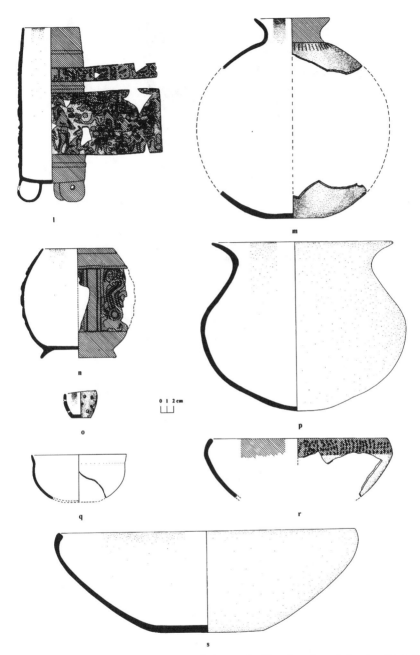

16.7b. On-floor vessels from epicentral Caracol: (l) related to Sahcaba Modeled-carved (see Graham et al. 1980); (m) and (r), possibly Pantano Impressed; (n) Pabellon Modeled-carved; (o) Chaquistero Composite; (p) Valentin Unslipped; (q) Altar Orange; (s) possibly Valentin Unslipped.

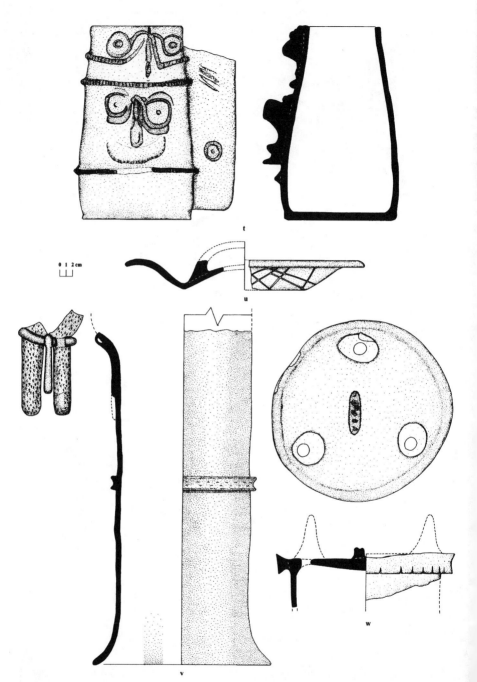

16.7c. On-floor vessels from epicentral Caracol: (t) possibly Pedregal Modeled; (u) unnamed incised; (v) and (w), Cohune Composite.

Terminal Classic elsewhere (Culbert 1973c)—appear to be stratigraphically earlier at Caracol.

LIMITED DISTRIBUTION STATUS-LINKED CERAMICS

The traditional ceramic markers of the Terminal Classic—fineware pottery and decorative modes—are well represented in the Caracol on-floor sample (Table 16.2, Figure 16.7). These materials largely come from the site's epicentral masonry buildings but are generally not in evidence in the outlying settlement. In fact, these ceramic markers were recovered in only a very limited way in the settlement area. Nor are any of the traditional markers, such as Fine Orange, noted from burials, although some interments can be ascribed to this late era based on stratigraphic position and/or on the possession of other ceramic traits. While this could be the result of sampling problems, we feel that the widespread absence of these materials in the core test units is significant (D. Chase and A. Chase n.d.).

Although an epicentral palace fineware subcomplex is fairly well documented at Caracol, such a subcomplex is not well represented in the surrounding residential group excavations. Part of the reason for this may be the different excavation methodologies that were employed. While the central palaces were areally stripped, thereby leading to the recovery of vessel sets, most of the outlying residential groups were only tested by smaller excavations. However, more than 100 outlying residential groups were tested through more than 300 excavations. In four residential groups (Cedro, Sam, Bayal, and Tabanos), almost completely reconstructible non-ritual utilitarian vessels were recovered in small test excavations. These vessels are generally large platters or bowls that are similar in form to some of those found on the floors of the epicentral palaces (Table 16.2; Figure 16.6). Nearly whole examples of some of the censer types found in association with the epicentral buildings have also been recovered in primary contexts in small test excavations in outlying residential groups (Rooster, Zero), again implying contemporaneity in occupation. However, no complete "Terminal Classic" ceramic subcomplexes were recovered in the outlying settlement and, even more telling, traditional Terminal Classic fineware markers were extremely rare.

The Caracol Terminal Classic ceramic situation, with its strong correlation of clearly identifiable late fineware ceramics with the epicentral masonry buildings (as opposed to the outlying settlement), is by no means unique in the southern lowlands. In fact, a similar dichotomy is in evidence at Tikal (Culbert 1973c: 69–70; Fry 1969: 166) and Altar de Sacrificios (Adams 1973b: 148). At Seibal, Terminal Classic ceramics were so distinctive that Sabloff (1973: 122) argued that "it would appear that there was a replacement of one group of pottery with a special function—serving vessels—by another group with a similar function." Contrary to the Caracol, Tikal, and Altar de Sacrificios situations, Sabloff (1975: 110, 238) indicated that Terminal Classic ceramics were common in small structure units at

Seibal. More recently, however, Tourtellot (1988b: 405–406, 1990) revised the Seibal picture by noting that only those Seibal house mounds in or close to that site's epicenter yielded Terminal Classic Bayal deposits. He has further argued that the Bayal ceramic materials might not indicate the complete temporal replacement of earlier Tepejilote pottery at Seibal; instead, as a ceramic subcomplex, Bayal pottery could be representative of an intrusive population that grafted their pottery styles onto a continuing Late Classic Tepejilote ceramic tradition (Tourtellot 1988b, 1990).

Thus, southern lowland Terminal Classic ceramic materials at large centers generally correlate with epicentral (or major architecture) distributions associated with the latest use of masonry constructions (Culbert 1973c: 67–68; Adams 1973b: 148) and also appear to be additive to pre-existing Late Classic complexes. In general, contexts outside of site epicenters that contain Terminal Classic ceramic markers are rare (caves are one exception [Pendergast 1971; Helmke 1999]).

Burial associations are also informative. At Seibal, many burials with Terminal Classic ceramic markers occur in special "residential units" (in which a small low shrine is located in the middle of the group's residential plaza) located relatively close to that site's epicenter (Tourtellot 1990: 140). However, Terminal Classic burials with definable ceramic markers and the special residential groupings seen at Seibal are barely represented at other sites. Only two possible examples of Seibal-like residential units are noted at Tikal (Becker 1982, Plaza Plan 4) and only two potential examples have been noted at Caracol thus far. At Uaxactun, two architecturally sealed burials, both in epicentral monumental architecture, yielded easily identifiable Terminal Classic ceramic markers. At Tikal, very few burials are correlated with the site's latest occupation and most Terminal Classic Eznab ceramics occur only in the site's epicenter. At Caracol, none of the site's burials contain traditional Terminal Classic ceramic markers (D. Chase 1994), although some of these markers do occur in burials found in southeastern Petén (Laporte 1994), which was part of Caracol's wider political domain (A. Chase and D. Chase 1996c: 808).

Overarching ceramic similarities appear to have existed on the elite level for many southern lowland sites during the Terminal Classic, even though "regionalized" Late Classic ceramic complexes often continued into the Terminal Classic at such sites. Terminal Classic ceramics at Caracol, Tikal, Seibal, Altar de Sacrificios, and Uaxactun are closely linked through the sharing of several identical shapes, finewares, and even decorative scenes. Specifically, the basic fineware tripod bowls at all sites are almost identical, showing great standardization within a broad geographical range. Molded-carved finewares bearing similar iconographic scenes are also shared. Finally, a broad range of fine paste wares, known to be of external origin, also occurs at all these central lowland sites. At Seibal such Terminal Classic materials can be associated with the uppermost population stratum iconographically and contextually. At Caracol, not only is this material explicitly correlated with the continued use of palace locales, but rooms were also not filled with refuse as occurs at some sites, suggesting a functioning garbage recycling system. The wealth of artifactual materials—jadeite, carved shell, and carved bone—found in the latest provisional and de facto refuse at Caracol is typically associated only with the Maya "elite." Rather than being impoverished and disorganized "commoners," the final occupants of the epicentral stone palaces probably represent the final Maya elite at Caracol.

But how are these latest materials—and the inferred elite—related to the rest of a site's population? Various contradictory scenarios have been offered. Tourtellot (1988b: 404–405) questioned whether there was a depopulation of the outlying areas at Seibal or whether the use of the latest finewares was linked to status. He was at an impasse over whether or not the Seibal archaeological situation represented a foreign elite concentrated in that site's epicenter "surrounded by a sea of native commoners" (Tourtellot 1988b: 405) or whether it represented "a highly stressed and greatly diminished population living in a relatively nucleated settlement" (Tourtellot 1990: 140). The Tikal situation was similarly nebulous. Ford (1986: 62, 65) argued that Terminal Classic outlying occupation in the area intermediate to Yaxhá and Tikal was only slightly decreased from that of the Late Classic era; however, Culbert and his colleagues (1990: 119) suggested that there was a significantly reduced population within greater Tikal. At Caracol Terminal Classic finewares were concentrated in the epicenter, but the distribution of Terminal Classic censerware and certain utilitarian plainwares indicated that both the epicenter and the urban core were still occupied.

The latest deposits of on-floor de facto refuse at Caracol reveal a multiplicity of censer types in use during the Terminal Classic: platform-prong incensarios (burners; Figures 16.7w and 16.8), broad scored incensarios (sometimes with handles; Figure 16.7u), spiked bowls (Figure 16.4a), and flanged and modeled cylinders (Figure 16.7t). With the exception of the spiked bowl censers, which have been found only in Caracol's A Group and may represent a very late ritual use of this plaza area, the other three kinds of censers have been found liberally scattered throughout the more than 300 test excavations carried out in residential groups in the Caracol core (Figures 16.5 and 16.8). The late ceramic associations of the various epicentral censers are contextually clear (and earlier censer forms can also be securely placed in stratigraphic contexts [e.g., D. Chase and A. Chase 1998: 305]). In the settlement core of Caracol, censer materials that are similar to those in the epicenter are always stratigraphically late, with pieces of these censers occurring in both surface deposits and, more rarely, in upper building and plaza fills. Thus, the censer distribution and deposition at Caracol supports coeval occupation of both the residential core and site epicenter immediately prior to final abandonment. The distribution of certain late plainware and other domestic forms (ollas, jars, bowls, and platters; Figures 16.6b, 16.6c, 16.6d, 16.6f, 16.7m, 16.7p, and 16.7s) also supports such an interpretation.

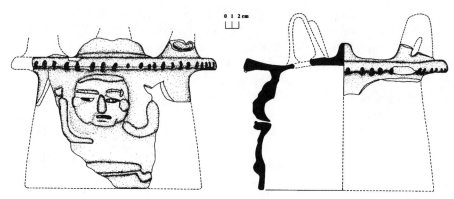

16.8 Effigy three-prong burner (Cohune Composite) associated with a burial in the outlying core settlement.

We would suggest that these distributions point to two things: first, dating terminal Maya archaeological remains based solely on the presence of distinctive finewares is problematic because they may have had only limited distributions; and, second, there is a strong probability that the limited distribution of Terminal Classic finewares is due to a "status-linked" ceramic subcomplex. These conclusions have important implications for interpreting the Terminal Classic period. It makes it a difficult time period to recognize in other than elite- or upper-status contexts, meaning that inferences of population decline based solely on the lack of standard Terminal Classic "type-fossils" in settlement test-pit and sherd data are likely not valid. The lack of these presumed "status-linked" ceramics in the majority of excavated contexts at Caracol is in striking contrast to the homogeneity seen in the distribution of earlier Late Classic ceramics (and serving wares) at the site and may be a factor in the site's demise. Nevertheless, the uniformity of fineware Terminal Classic forms and vessels found both at Caracol and across sites throughout the southern lowlands suggests increased contact between the elites at these sites (especially as indicated in physical trade items). Both the disjunctive ceramic distributions within sites and the similarities in fineware ceramic distributions (and types) between sites should be considered in Terminal Classic "collapse" scenarios.

The magnitude of contact between elites in the Terminal Classic—as represented in physically shared ceramic types over a broad area—is strikingly different from the smaller-scale regionalization that characterizes the Late Classic period. The sharing of Terminal Classic ceramic forms and types by the latest elites across the southern lowlands may have been indicative of an attempted incorporation of many of the late elites of the southern lowlands into an extremely large political unit—perhaps along the lines of elite incorporation into the Inca empire in

South America (Bauer 1987, 1992; Malpass 1993a). There, distinctive Inca ceramics are found only among the elite stratum of conquered groups, grafted onto already existing independent local ceramic traditions. Thus, on the basis of an interpretation of Caracol's on-floor contexts and a re-evaluation of materials at other southern lowland sites, the Terminal Classic period may be framed as an era that manifested a greater differentiation of elites from the rest of the population— the potential incorporation of many diverse Maya elites into one (or more) large-scale political system(s).

CONCLUSIONS

Regardless of the length of the Terminal Classic era, the latest de facto on-floor deposits at Caracol indicate that the final abandonment of the epicentral buildings was sudden and relatively rapid. In several cases a series of complete vessels and other artifacts (including chipped stone from weapons and iconography on ceramics related to warfare) are found crushed in situ on floors. In other cases, sheet deposits of reconstructible ceramics are found exterior to residential palace structures and are considered to be "provisional refuse" (Schiffer 1987); materials in such deposits range from complete to partial ceramic specimens to sherds and are indicative of either partial or interrupted collection procedures for garbage removal. Judging from content and contextual considerations at Caracol, these deposits do not appear to be related to termination rituals (e.g., Mock 1998d).

The occurrence of easily recognizable late fineware materials in surface and collapse levels of epicentral stone buildings across the southern lowlands and their general absence in residential units has been used to argue for a rapid population breakdown at the end of the Late Classic period, a breakdown associated with an epicentral coalescence of disorganized commoners in a situation of "cultural impoverishment" following the disappearance of the traditional Classic elites (Culbert 1973c: 65, 1988: 74). However, the archaeological data from Caracol appear to be indicative of a different scenario.

Caracol evinced significant late epicentral monumental construction activity and appears to have maintained continuity in elite diet (D. Chase et al. 1998). Caracol Terminal Classic fineware deposits are epicentrally concentrated and unevenly distributed throughout the site. As at Tikal, they correlate with vaulted architecture and palaces. However, censerware and plainware ceramic materials that co-occur with such finewares in the epicenter are found throughout the outlying residential settlement, usually in association with eastern buildings that functioned as mausoleums (A. Chase and D. Chase 1994b). These deposits suggest that there was occupation and construction at Caracol in the epicenter for at least forty years after the site's last dated monument (Stela 10—A.D. 859 or 10.1.10.0.0) and that the surrounding core probably continued to be occupied even later. A depleted population does not appear to have hurriedly migrated into the site center as part of a "last gasp" of Classic Maya civilization.

The Terminal Classic situation indicated by ceramic distributions contrasts greatly with that seen during the preceding Late Classic period, when access to almost all material items appears to have been widespread at Caracol. It has been suggested instead that "status-linked" ceramics were in use during the Terminal Classic era by those individuals occupying the site's epicentral palaces. And, it is suspected that the breakdown in uniform ceramic subcomplex usage correlates with a breakdown in the shared identity that was a unifying factor at Caracol through the eighth century. Evidence instead suggests the implementation of a more strict two-part structuring of Terminal Classic Caracol society into "elite" and "other" individuals, potentially mirroring earlier (i.e., Early Classic) more restrictive social orders.

The probability that "status-linked" ceramics existed during the Terminal Classic period has other potential implications for the Maya collapse. Besides sharing similar forms, many of these ceramics also exhibit almost identical iconography and decorative scenes. Many of the fineware vessels also were tradewares into the sites in which they occur. The use of these ceramics appears to have been restricted to the latest elites. It is this elite association that we find so informative, for it would appear to mirror both Aztec (Brumfiel 1987a, 1987b) and Inca (Malpass 1993b: 10–12; 1993c: 237; Murra 1980) patterns of elite incorporation through the presentation of foreign goods. We take the widespread distribution of these ceramic markers in the southern Maya lowlands (in conjunction with changes in iconographic themes, particularly seen on stone monuments) to indicate that the last elites at a great many sites were bound together in some way—potentially as part of a broader political (or minimally ideological) system, even as they were segregating themselves from the rest of their own societies.

Although both occupation and construction continued at Caracol during the Terminal Classic period, there are apparent discontinuities. Not only do certain ceramics not continue to be widely shared and distributed at Caracol, but the predominant Late Classic ritual patterns begin to break down. There appears to be a lessened focus on the highly standardized Late Classic Caracol pattern of veneration of the dead (A. Chase and D. Chase 1994b; D. Chase and A. Chase 1998) that is correlated with burials and caches in eastern buildings in residential groups. These important eastern buildings, however, still continued to be associated with ritual, as can be seen by the incense burners deposited on their steps in several excavated groups. Caracol stone monument erection enjoys a brief flourish at the onset of the Terminal Classic period (Chase, Grube, and Chase 1991), but the carved stones embrace new iconographic themes (A. Chase 1985) and are also more widely distributed at the site than at any other time. There is also a general reduction of rulers' portraits and textual foci on rulers' life histories on these final stelae and altars. And, no monuments appear to have been erected during the final forty years of elite dominance. The lack of focus on rulers' portraits and texts, the dichotomy in the final material culture remains at the site, and the unity of elite ceramic types and iconographic themes with other Maya sites of Terminal Classic date suggest to us that the carefully established Caracol-specific identity of the Late Classic period (A. Chase and D. Chase 1996b) was supplanted by a more pan-Maya elite identity at Caracol in the Terminal Classic period. We argue that the archaeological materials found on the floors of Caracol's epicentral palaces do not represent a group of disorganized peasant squatters, who were the survivors of some unknown calamity, but rather an organized group of people who were tied into a much broader non-local frame and perhaps linked to a new ideological reality (A. Chase 1985; Ringle et al. 1998). The recovered deposits from the site's epicentral buildings represent the material remains of its final elite—an elite who witnessed, if not directed, this changed ideological order.

Caracol and other sites (particularly the excavations at Dos Pilas that demonstrate Maya defensive posture [Demarest 1993; Demarest et al. 1997]) do show substantial evidence for increased warfare toward the end of the Classic period and at the beginning of the Terminal Classic era (A. Chase and D. Chase 1992; Chase, Grube, and Chase 1991). At Caracol, captives are depicted on Terminal Classic monuments and pottery; conquests and captives are also noted in late inscriptions. In fact, Caracol records the latest war events known in the southern lowlands, but within a framework of increased iconographic portrayal of alliances between former enemies (Grube n.d.). Weapons are frequently found within Caracol's floor refuse, as is human bone. And, the extensive burning found in many buildings, especially when combined with the remains of an unburied child on the floor of one of Caracol's palaces, could be viewed as evidence of a site-wide final calamity caused by war. Warfare clearly continued into and through the Terminal Classic era. But warfare for what goal and what reason?

Contrary to the traditional paradigm (in which small-scale, site-specific political systems abruptly fragment, with ensuing rapid depopulation during the late eighth and early ninth centuries), the archaeological evidence for heightened warfare, shifting identities, changes in monument erection, and the shared distributions of status-linked ceramics across sites, may be interpreted alternatively as representing the integration of the latest Maya elites of the southern lowlands into larger, but highly competitive, political units as the Terminal Classic period progressed toward the tenth century. Sites such as Caracol may have been aspiring to create their own Terminal Classic expansionist polities or "empires." Ceramic similarities among sites and the replacement of past site—or even region-specific—patterns (such as those correlated with the veneration of the dead at Caracol) may be seen as reflective of greater cohesion among the elites of what had been a more regionalized mosaic of polities earlier in the Late Classic period. Some of the latest monuments in the southern lowlands depict local rulers whose changing style of dress suggests that they may have joined this new order; this is particularly seen iconographically on the monuments at Machaquilá (A. Chase 1985b). The termination of a site's carved stone monument record during the Terminal

Classic period might, in fact, reflect the final incorporation of previously independent elites into a higher-order expansionist polity. Whether centered on Seibal, on
Chichen-Itza, or on one or more other unknown centers, the widespread distribution of uniform elite finewares throughout the southern lowlands is archaeologically
undeniable.

In comparing the Maya "collapse" to the trajectories of other early state societies, Lowe (1985: 160) noted that "most state systems have ended in a universal
empire" and that the current scenarios of the Maya collapse make the Classic
Maya a "glaring exception" to this generalized pattern. However, it seems to us
that the Maya case may not be as unique as previously implied. Thus, whether
imposed from without, simply emulated by an indigenous elite, or resulting from
a combination of processes, the similarity of materials, archaeological distributions, iconography, and, potentially, processes across Terminal Classic sites of
the southern lowlands can be viewed as reflecting the existence of one or more
attempted expansionist polities that ultimately fell apart and, in so doing, completely ruptured Maya society in the southern lowlands.

ACKNOWLEDGMENTS

The Caracol Project has been supported by the University of Central Florida, the Government of Belize (especially the Department of Archaeology), the United States Agency
for International Development, the Harry Frank Guggenheim Foundation, the National
Science Foundation (Grants BNS-8619996, SBR-9311773, and SBR-9708637), the Miami
Institute of Maya Studies, the Dart Foundation, the Foundation for the Advancement
of Mesoamerican Studies, Inc., the Stans Foundation, the Ahau Foundation, the J. I.
Kislak Foundation, and private donations. Earlier versions of this paper were presented at the 93rd Annual Meetings of the American Anthropological Association in
Atlanta, Georgia, in 1994 and at the UCLA Maya weekend in 1995; however, this paper
is substantially revised from these previous presentations. We would like to thank
both Joyce Marcus for her comments on an early version of this paper and Prudence
Rice for forcing us to more tightly focus our arguments in an intermediate version.
Arthur Demarest and Don Rice provided additional comments that called for further
clarification. All have helped us strengthen this current work.

17

CERAMICS AND SETTLEMENT PATTERNS AT TERMINAL CLASSIC–PERIOD LAGOON SITES IN NORTHEASTERN BELIZE

Marilyn A. Masson and Shirley Boteler Mock

he archaeological settlement patterns of northeastern Belize during the Terminal Classic period reveal that coastal or interior wetland locations were attractive places for community establishment or continued occupation. While some upland inland sites in this region were abandoned at this time, other previously established upland and aquatic-oriented communities continued to be occupied throughout the Terminal Classic and into the Postclassic period. Coastal and inland communities grew affluent through participation in maritime exchange along the Caribbean coast that created new opportunities for entrepreneurial growth in the centuries following the collapse of interior Classic-period political centers. Belize communities extracted the region's rich natural resources and manufactured products from them that were destined for exchange in a burgeoning network of circum-peninsular maritime trade that formed around Yucatán (Sabloff and Rathje 1975a; Andrews et al. 2000). This trade was stimulated by the expansionist military and economic efforts of the core city of Chichen Itza during Terminal Classic/Early Postclassic times (Kepecs et al. 1994). Smaller communities in northeastern Belize (towns, villages, and hamlets) directly participated in this maritime exchange through regional markets or through direct exchange with coastal merchants, and we feel that this pattern directly undermined the economic foundations of older, inland regional capitals in the Belize subregion. This process culminated in the social transformations of the Terminal Classic period and the emergence of loosely centralized provinces that may have been conducive to the amplification of commercial exchange.

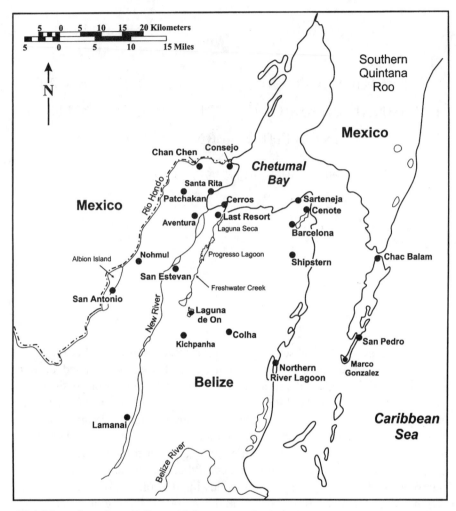

17.1 Map of northern Belize with locations of selected sites mentioned in the text.

This chapter examines the socioeconomic transition of the Terminal Classic from the perspective of a set of sites located at coastal and inland lagoon locations of northeastern Belize (Figures 17.1, 17.2, 17.3). The coastal site of Northern River Lagoon (Figures 17.2, 17.4) is primarily a Late to Terminal Classic site that was abandoned and not substantially reoccupied after the ninth century A.D. In contrast, the coastal site of Saktunja (Figure 17.5) continued to be occupied after the Terminal Classic period (Mock 1994a, 1999) until Spanish contact. At Progresso Lagoon, located along the inland waterway of Freshwater Creek that connects interior sites to the Caribbean Sea (Figures 17.1, 17.2), continuity in site

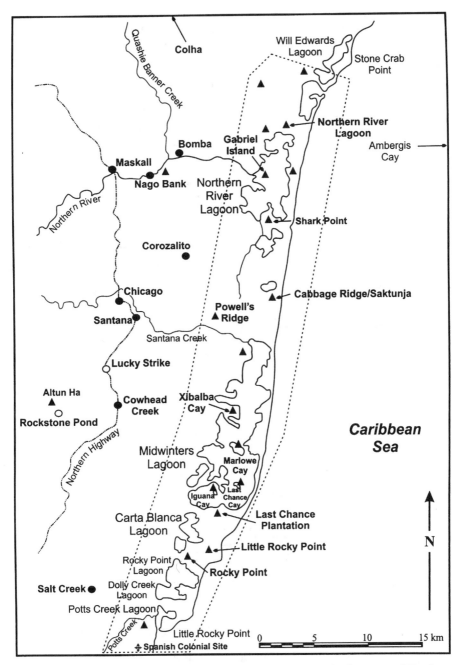

17.2 Map of Northern Belize Coastal Project sites, showing the location of Northern River Lagoon and Saktunja.

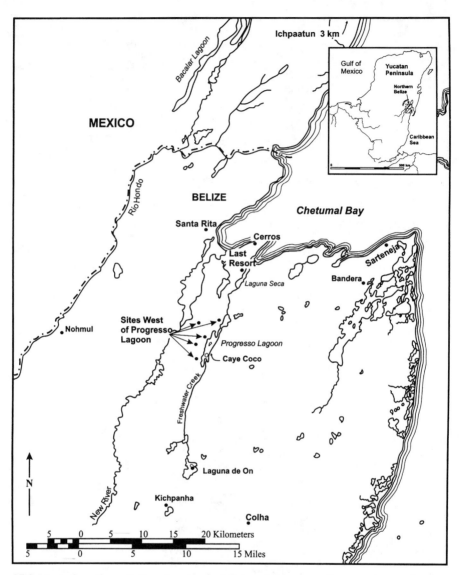

17.3 Map of northern Belize showing locations of Progresso Lagoon sites and others along the Freshwater Creek drainage.

occupation is also observed from the Terminal Classic to contact. The island site of Caye Coco (Figure 17.6) was founded in the Terminal Classic as one of several elite shrine centers at Progresso Lagoon and later formed the Postclassic political nucleus of communities scattered around the shores. We outline diachronic patterns in settlement and ceramic production found at each of these sites. Our data

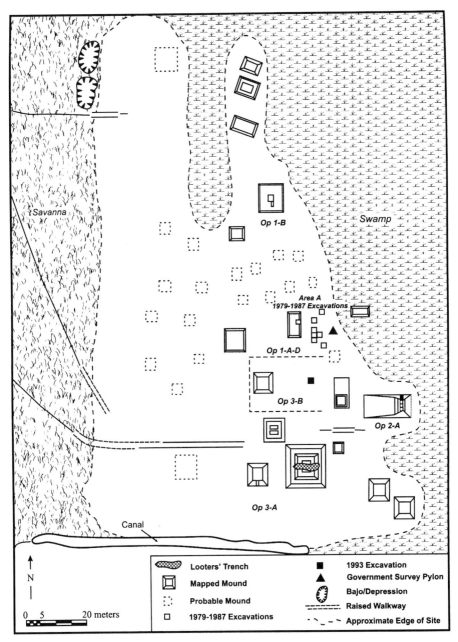

Op 1-B

Savanna

Swamp

Area A
1979-1987 Excavations

Op 1-A-D

Op 3-B

Op 2-A

Op 3-A

Canal

N

0   5   20 meters

	Looters' Trench		1993 Excavation
	Mapped Mound		Government Survey Pylon
	Probable Mound		Bajo/Depression
	1979-1987 Excavations		Raised Walkway
			Approximate Edge of Site

17.4 Map of the site of Northern River Lagoon.

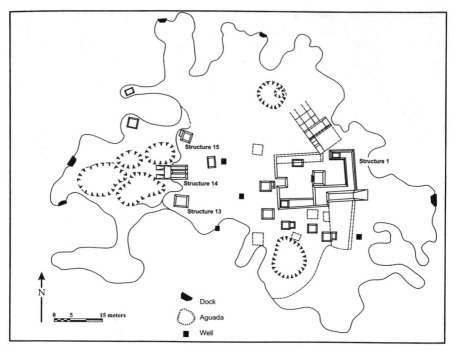

17.5 Map of the site of Saktunja.

suggest that northeastern Belize was an advantageous setting for Maya entrepreneurial communities during the Late to Terminal Classic periods. In contrast to other subregions of the southern lowlands, this area maintained substantial population levels throughout the collapse of Classic-period political hierarchies, and it did so primarily through engaging in maritime trade networks driven by the distant but powerful economic interests of the northern center of Chichen Itza (A.D. 800–1000 or 1100, Andrews et al. 2000). A similar strategy may have aided the political center of Lamanai (Pendergast 1986a), one of the few Classic-period centers in northern Belize that never collapsed. Occupational continuity from the Terminal Classic to later periods is variable at the sites where we have worked.

Ceramic data from the coastal sites of Northern River Lagoon (NRL) and Saktunja reveal that inhabitants during the Late to Terminal Classic periods (A.D. 750–1000) were engaged in the production of salt and preservation of salted marine fish. These resources were probably destined for inland consumer sites in northern Belize and other areas reached by coastal canoe trade. NRL probably also served as a coastal trading port for exchange of products obtained from trading canoes to the interior, and delivering interior products to coastal merchants. The highly diverse assemblage of elite and utility pottery types at NRL

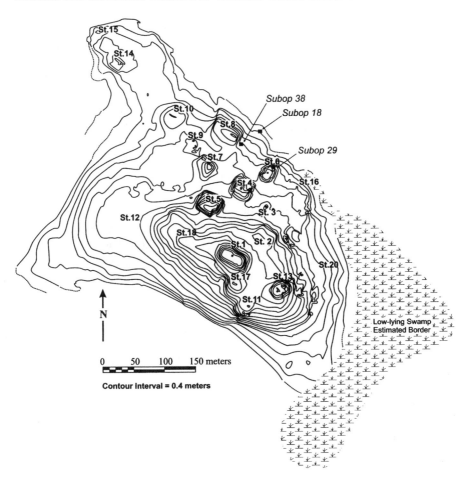

17.6 Map of Caye Coco showing the location of all structures, including Structures 1 and 13 that were initially constructed during the Terminal Classic period (all others were completely built during Postclassic), and the location of Terminal Classic middens and features at Suboperations 18, 26, and 38.

indicates the extent of far-ranging northern and southern lowlands networks to which this northern Belize coastal community was tied through trade. These diverse types include those local to northern Belize, other locally made vessels that exhibit stylistic emulation of decorations and forms popular in northern Yucatán and the Petén interior, and a variety of unique vessels that are either imported or represent local experimentation with new combinations of decorative attributes.

At Progresso Lagoon, Terminal Classic settlement (A.D. 750–950) is dispersed along the west bank of this eight-kilometer-long semi-saline lagoon (Figure 17.3). Two small clusters of elite architecture are found among kilometers of dispersed, low house mounds. Maya settlement at the island of Caye Coco began in the Terminal Classic. At least two structures were built at the top of a hill at the center of the island, and domestic platforms and middens are also present (Rosenswig 1999; Rosenswig and Masson 2001). Ceramics at Progresso Lagoon sites bear close resemblances to types defined at Santa Rita, Cerros, and Nohmul (D. Chase 1982b; Walker 1990). It is not known to what degree pottery was produced locally at Progresso or was obtained in markets of the northeastern Belize area. The technological quality of the majority of utilitarian types is poor, and a diverse array of paste groups implies that ceramics were obtained from a large number of producers. The presence of diverse ceramic forms and paste groups at Terminal Classic households at this lagoon implies that the circulation systems for ceramic products made at different communities were well developed, and marketplaces may have facilitated such exchange. Influence from northern Yucatán is observed in some common types present among Terminal Classic assemblages at Caye Coco.

Northeastern Belize was a hub of Terminal Classic settlement and economic activity. Ceramic production patterns were strongly rooted in eastern southern lowland traditions, although they also incorporated stylistic and technological attributes from the northern sphere of Chichen Itza into their changing pottery traditions, and some vessels may have been imported. The exact origins of the slate ware pastes at Caye Coco await sourcing studies planned for the future.

Local economic industries of the Terminal Classic period at Progresso Lagoon were diverse. The lagoon has marine shell resources (conch are still obtained locally), coarse-grained chert resources, forest and aquatic game (and fish), and kilometers of fertile agricultural land. Progresso is located along the Freshwater Creek drainage, one of three inland waterways that link the interior of northern Belize to the Caribbean Sea (Figures 17.1, 17.3). This waterway provided easy access to coastal trading ports such as Cerros, within a day's journey by canoe. Settlements along the western shore of Progresso Lagoon extend from its bank almost to the margins of the New River, a major parallel aquatic vein located 4.5 kilometers to the west. In addition to extracting local resources, Progresso Lagoon settlements were located between two primary waterways and may have profited from riverine transport of products made at southern interior sites to coastal ports of the Caribbean Sea.

By ca. A.D. 1000–1100, Late Classic and Terminal Classic ceramic types represented at NRL and Saktunja disappeared from local assemblages, and types that are diagnostic to the Postclassic period had replaced earlier traditions by this time. Middens at the island of Caye Coco at Progresso Lagoon provide data on the transition between Terminal Classic and Late Postclassic assemblages. Ceramics in these middens suggest that by A.D. 1000, occupants of Caye Coco ceased to manufacture types that resemble those of the Terminal Classic period. We have identified an Early Postclassic (ca. A.D. 900–1050) assemblage at this site, represented by two primary ceramic type groups: Zakpah Orange Red and

Tsabak Unslipped-Striated, following Walker's work at Cerros (1990). Zakpah Orange Red is rare at Saktunja and is absent at NRL. The distribution of this pottery type is not well understood. By A.D. 1100, forms and surface decoration of Late Postclassic Payil Red and Santa Unslipped ceramic forms and pastes were established, as the numbers of Zakpah Orange Red and Tsabak Unslipped diminish.

Important differences between Terminal Classic and Early Postclassic–period pottery assemblages likely reflect changes in the organization of regional economies over time. Most notably, the brief cessation of use of pottery similar to that of northern Yucatán implies a breakdown in distant networks prior to the rise of Mayapán to power and the onset of the Late Postclassic. In this chapter we describe variation in ceramic assemblages at two coastal sites (NRL and Saktunja) and two inland lagoon sites (Laguna de On and Caye Coco), shown in Figure 17.1. Patterns at these sites are considered in the context of the history of research on Terminal Classic economic and social organization in northeastern Belize, including problems faced in placing this period within a tight cultural historical framework.

POLITICAL DYNAMICS AND ECONOMIC SYSTEMS OF THE NORTHERN BELIZE TERMINAL CLASSIC

The Terminal Classic period has been identified archaeologically through various types of evidence. Changes in ceramic production hail this transition, as reflected by the identification of new ceramic types for each period in northern Belize (D. Chase 1982b; Graham 1987b; Valdez 1987, 1994; Walker 1990). Lithic-type changes also have been used to identify this period (Hester 1985; Hester and Shafer 1991b; Roemer 1984; Michaels 1987, 1994; Michaels and Shafer 1994; Shafer and Hester 1983, 1988). Studies from Colha, Belize, document an increase in blade production and distribution during the Terminal Classic period that may correlate with an increase in warfare (Masson 1989, 2001; Roemer 1984). The relationship of these changes in economic production to political changes is poorly understood for the northern Belize subregion.

In the Petexbatun area, ceramic trends documented by Foias and Bishop (1997) indicate that political collapse profoundly disrupted elite gift exchange networks initially, and eventually, localized utilitarian production. Such impacts varied across the southern lowlands landscape (Chase and Rice 1985; Freidel 1986d; Sabloff and Andrews 1986b; Sabloff and Henderson 1993b). More data are needed to identify subregional variation in adaptations to political and economic changes of the Terminal Classic period. Rice (1987a) has characterized this period as one of regionalism in ceramic traditions. For this reason, societal changes of this period should be examined first on a local basis, as patterns varied greatly from coastal zones to the Petén interior (Culbert 1988). To what extent did political collapse affect local economies? Some scholars cite evidence suggesting that community production economies were fairly autonomous even during the height of Classic-period political hierarchies (Hester and Shafer 1994; King and Potter 1994; McAnany 1989, 1993; Potter and King 1995; Rice 1987a; Fedick 1991), and utilitarian production was not tightly centralized through political institutions.

Finely crafted items were reserved for the elite class (Ball 1993b; Rathje 1973: 440) and their production and distribution were quite different from that observed for utilitarian items, although utility vessels such as jars may have been used to transport elite goods (Mock 1994a, 1999). Prestige products, such as finely made polychrome vases (Reents-Budet 1994) or eccentric flints (Gibson 1986; Hester and Shafer 1994), have been identified as part of a low-volume system of production for limited, exclusive distribution separate from that of utilitarian production and exchange spheres (Ball 1993b; Gibson 1986; Hester and Shafer 1994). Some rare trade pottery found at coastal sites in Belize may represent more highly valued items. It is not known, however, whether the rarity of these items is due to their lack of significance or their high value in coastal trading networks. Studies thus far have not identified a prestigious pottery gift exchange network for the Terminal Classic in northeastern Belize. In fact, similar studies of the Petexbatun (Foias and Bishop 1997) and sites near Xunantunich (LeCount 1999) indicate that inter-elite gift exchange was on the decline during the Terminal Classic period. This chapter focuses primarily on common, utilitarian pottery types, although the presence of exotic trade vessels or well-made, idiosyncratic vessels local to northeastern Belize is discussed for the coastal sites.

Production of utilitarian goods occurred primarily at the community level during the Late Classic, Terminal Classic, and Postclassic periods (Rands and Bishop 1980; Rice 1987a). Little is known about specific communities where production may have taken place, with a few exceptions. Graham traces the development of possible community pottery forms made at Lamanai (1987b), and the analysis of distributions of Late Classic polychrome pottery helps narrow down the location of production sites for these ceramics (Mock 1994a, 1997b). Pottery firing hearths may have been identified at the Postclassic settlement of Laguna de On (Masson 2000). Communities specialized to varying degrees in particular items for regional exchange or trade (Hester and Shafer 1994; McKillop 1989, 1996; Mock 1994a, 1999; Rands and Bishop 1980; Rice 1987a; Shafer and Hester 1983). Intercommunity exchange seems to have been commonplace either directly or through regional markets (Freidel 1986d; McAnany 1991; Masson and Freidel 2002; West 2002).

Some scholars note the appearance of new artifacts or architectural attributes suggesting the intrusion of foreigners in Belize and other areas of the lowlands including Petén, Pasión, and northwestern Yucatán subregions (Andrews and Robles 1986; D. Chase and A. Chase 1982; A. Chase 1983, 1986; Fox 1987; Rice and Rice 1985; D. Rice 1986: 317–321; Sabloff and Willey 1967; Thompson 1970: 42; Tourtellot et al. 1992: 91–92; Valdez and Adams 1982; Valdez 1987; Mock

1994b; Hester 1985; Michaels 1987; Willey and Shimkin 1973). Recent examinations have questioned the foreign identity of glyphs and images at sites such as Seibal, however (Stuart 1993: 338–339; Tourtellot and González, Chapter 4, this volume). Archaeological evidence has also negated the intrusion hypothesis in the Petexbatun region (Demarest 1997; Foias and Bishop 1997; Wright 1997a). Changing ceramic styles from the Late to Terminal Classic periods, or from the Terminal Classic to Postclassic periods, are often used to identify a break in ethnic continuity. These changes are not consistent from community to community.

The establishment of distant trading ties could also contribute to changes in ceramic styles. Studies of fine-grained changes from quality stratigraphic contexts are needed to answer these questions in the southern lowlands. Ringle et al. (1998) discuss a pan-Mesoamerican stylistic interaction sphere among elites participating in feathered serpent cult symbolism and ritual. This international ideological emulation accompanied the development of extensive trading ties throughout Epiclassic (Terminal Classic) Mesoamerica. Such well-documented elite interaction could also have ushered in changes in ceramic styles. Later in this chapter, the participation of Caye Coco in this pan-Mesoamerican sphere of ideological interaction is described.

CHRONOLOGY

To fully examine the links between political dynamics and ceramic production, distribution, and utilization, the establishment of chronology is critical. It has been recently suggested that attributes of ceramic types linger for a considerable period of time following political transformations for the Terminal Classic period at Copán (Webster and Gonlin 1988; Webster and Freter 1990a, 1990b), and for the Late Preclassic period within the Maya area (Sullivan and Valdez n.d.). In regions beyond Mesoamerica such as Harappa, ceramic stylistic types continued to be produced after the collapse of political centralization, a pattern that Wright (1991) attributes to the control of production among kin-based elements of society that were not immediately affected by political change. This phenomenon suggests that the full economic ramifications of events such as political centralization and decentralization are not immediately apparent, and this observation appears to hold true for most major Maya chronological transformations. Production organized by community or family groups may have been maintained for several generations without complex political hierarchies.

At Copán this pattern has been identified in the endurance of the Late Classic/ Early Postclassic Coner-phase and agrarian populations in the Copán pocket for 200 years after signs of kingship are no longer observed at this polity (Webster and Gonlin 1988; Webster and Freter 1990a: Figure 2.1, 1990b). Tourtellot (1993: 225–226) notes "we should be more suspicious of early abandonment dates in general," in referring to the problem of enduring patterns of ceramic type production for a considerable period after political collapse at Copán. The Copán argument for enduring Classic-period assemblages has been recently challenged (Fash et al., Chapter 12, this volume) and the debate continues (Webster et al., Chapter 11, this volume), but the point is well taken and such issues should be considered in interpretations of collapse chronology.

Similar arguments have been presented for the archaeological record of Belize. These are reflected in various interpretations of site chronologies. The literature is divided over whether a single Terminal Classic/Early Postclassic period is represented (Ball 1983a; D. Chase 1982b: 5, 554; A. Chase 1983: 1214–1215; D. Chase and A. Chase 1988; Graham 1985, 1987b; Walker 1990) or whether two periods are observed, a Terminal Classic and an Early Postclassic (Mock 1994a, n.d.a, n.d.b; Valdez 1987, 1994). Scholars divide Late Classic and Terminal Classic components at various intervals that fall between A.D. 650 and A.D. 1000. Terminal Classic/Early Postclassic components are placed between A.D. 800 and 1100. Similar problems are noted for the Late Postclassic period (D. Chase 1982b; D. Chase and A. Chase 1988; Walker 1990; Masson 2000; Valdez 1987; Graham 1987b).

These chronological disparities are partly due to the stratigraphic context. Terminal Classic ceramics are in some cases, as at Saktunja and NRL, lying on top of or intrude into earlier deposits. This stratigraphy suggests to Mock that they represent different cultural units that reflect the abandonment and reoccupation of certain areas or structures on the site, although Masson (1995, 1997) has argued that similar evidence at other sites may also represent continuities. Mock (n.d.a, n.d.b, 1999) also suggests that functional or status differences that affect distributions of ceramic types within sites or between sites may account for the differences between contemporary Terminal Classic ceramic assemblages, and Masson (2000) has suggested this pattern for Postclassic period functionally and spatially distinct assemblages that are contemporary.

Many sites in northern Belize have ninth-century occupations. Some sites may have been abandoned temporarily after A.D. 900, as argued for Colha (Hester 1985; Michaels 1987; Valdez and Adams 1982; Valdez 1987, 1994). Others appear to have been occupied throughout the Terminal Classic/Postclassic transition for two additional centuries (A.D. 900–1000/1100) or longer, into the Late Postclassic period (A.D. 1100–1500) as observed at Laguna de On (Valdez et al. 1992; Valdez 1993; Masson 1995, 1999), Santa Rita (D. Chase 1982b), Cerros (Walker 1990), Lamanai (Graham 1987b), Barton Ramie (Willey et al. 1965), and Saktunja (Mock n.d.a). These distinctions are not always easy to make without good stratified deposits (Graham 1985, 1987b; Lincoln 1986; Masson 1995). Suitable contexts for samples for absolute dating tend to be sealed, buried deposits that are not located toward the site's disturbed surface zones. Later dates for terminal occupations might thus be difficult to obtain (Masson 2000). As Willey (1986: 21) notes, these issues greatly affect interpretations of the dynamics of the Petén Classic-period political collapse.

TERMINAL CLASSIC CERAMICS AND SETTLEMENT IN COASTAL BELIZE

The Northern Belize Coastal Project (NBCP, Figure 17.2) has documented a hierarchy of trading sites present during the Late to Terminal Classic transition and into the Postclassic period (Mock 1994a, 1999, n.d.b). The endurance of some of these sites over the transition indicates the significance of maritime trade during these late periods for the Belize region (Andrews and Vail 1990; Guderjan and Garber 1995; McKillop 1989; McKillop and Healy 1989; Mock n.d.a, n.d.b). Moreover, salt production was an impetus for trade during the Late to Terminal Classic periods (Mock 1994a, n.d.a).

The NRL site (Figure 17.4), located on the Northern River Lagoon (Figure 17.2), served as a trans-shipment port to inland sites such as Colha and Kichpanha during the Late to Terminal Classic transition (A.D. 680–900). Its location adjacent to the perennial Northern River facilitated the movement of goods presumably received from exchange with smaller coastal sites such as Saktunja, sites in the Belize interior, and materials obtained from maritime merchants (Mock 1994a, 1997b, n.d.a). Mock bases this interpretation of a socioeconomic relationship on the recovery of numerous ceramic types identical to Colha in addition to NRL's obvious role as a consumer of Colha-manufactured stone tools. Specialized ceramics attest to a flourishing salt-making industry (*sal cocida*) at this time and to NRL's role as a probable producer and distributor of this resource to interior sites such as Colha (Mock 1994a, 1997b, 1999, n.d.a).

The presence of substantial quantities of utilized stemmed and unstemmed chert blades provides additional support for a Late to Terminal Classic transition date for NRL (Graham 1987b: 75–76; Shafer and Hester 1983, 1988). Radiocarbon dates also indicate occupation of the site from the late seventh century to early tenth century (Mock 1994a, 1999). Polychrome ceramics linger at the smaller site of Saktunja, overlapping with transitional red-slipped types until around A.D. 1000 (Figure 17.7a-e). This pottery is intermingled with Postclassic materials in some areas of the site, in contrast to NRL. Whether the site of NRL was wholly or partially abandoned after the Terminal Classic is unclear at this point. Postclassic Palmul Incised and Navula Unslipped vessels were found in one surface context directly on top of Terminal Classic ceramics, indicating a later but more limited occupation than Saktunja (Mock 1994a). As at other sites in northern Belize, the presence of these ceramics may indicate post-abandonment ritual activities. It is also possible that limited site sampling has affected the quantification and these interpretations of Postclassic materials at these sites.

Great variety is a characteristic of the Late to Terminal Classic–period jar and *olla* types at Saktunja and NRL, such as the different neck and rim treatments on what are variously called Cayo and Alexander's Unslipped and TuTu Camp Striated. At Saktunja, Terminal Classic unslipped jars have short necks and single or double rolled, padded, or thickened rims (Figure 17.8a-i) that differ from those reported at other sites, where tall, outcurving necks and sharply everted rims are more

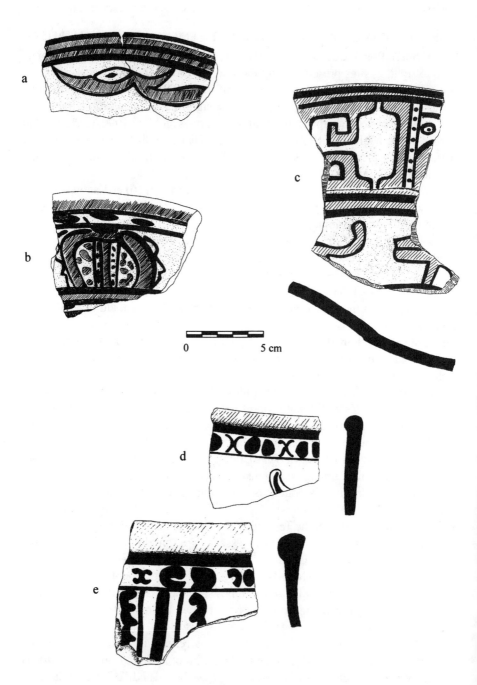

0   5 cm

17.7 Polychromes from NRL and Saktunja.

common. Striations are present but the vessel surfaces resemble the later (unstriated) Postclassic Navula Unslipped (or Santa Unslipped) type in their brushed or smoothed treatments. Body sherds can thus be difficult to type or place chronologically. Navula-like or Santa-like unslipped folded olla rims are also present in Terminal Classic levels at Caye Coco, and these rims also share a chunky calcite or grit temper with the Santa Unslipped wares. However, these earlier attributes do not numerically dominate the unslipped assemblage, as is the case for Postclassic levels.

Both NRL and Saktunja, along with other coastal communities, were initially settled in the Late Classic period as specialized localities engaged in production of salt by the sal cocida (boiling sea water) method. This activity is identified from the dense deposits of ceramic debris associated with this process. These small communities also extracted and processed marine resources, such as salted fish and marine shell raw materials or artifacts (Mock 1994a, 1997a, 1999, n.d.b; Masson n.d.). The archaeological contexts of salt-making and specialized ceramic products indicate that the sal cocida method was practiced during the Late to Terminal Classic and that this was discontinued by A.D. 1100 at NRL and Saktunja, probably due to the grander scale and superior quality of northern Yucatecan salt-making facilities (Andrews and Mock 2002).

The term "transition" used to characterize this period in the title of this volume reflects the fact that the definition of the Terminal Classic period as a transitional era carries an expectation that deposits of this date will have mixed chronological indicators. Transitional ceramics do not fit easily into a uniform regional and chronological type:variety classification. As mentioned previously, some scholars interpret a conjoined Terminal Classic and Early Postclassic in Belize as a transitional phase (D. Chase 1982b; Graham 1985, 1987b; Walker 1990; see also Rice 1987a for Petén). The NRL ceramic assemblage, in light of the site's role as a trading node, provides an example of the wide range of ceramics being produced or obtained from a variety of sources at this time.

Ceramics are well preserved at both Saktunja and NRL, but the latter site is distinguished by deep lenses of well-preserved Late to Terminal Classic sherds, suggesting either a dense occupation at this coastal community or the presence of stockpiled nonlocal ceramics stored for exchange (Mock 1994a; see also Reents-Budet 1994). This is particularly true of the Terminal Classic, as assemblages of this date exhibit a profusion of elaborate decorative elements such as dichrome, resist painting, vertical fluting, modeled-carving, and punctations combined with new composite types. These trends suggest an acceleration of complex levels of information exchange and stylistic expression. The representation of a wide variety of status-related ceramics at NRL and the recovery of a functionally complete complex is in marked contrast to other salt-making sites on the coast of Belize (Graham and Pendergast 1989; MacKinnon and Kepecs 1989; McKillop 1994; Valdez and Mock 1991). Some of this decorative experimentation within certain

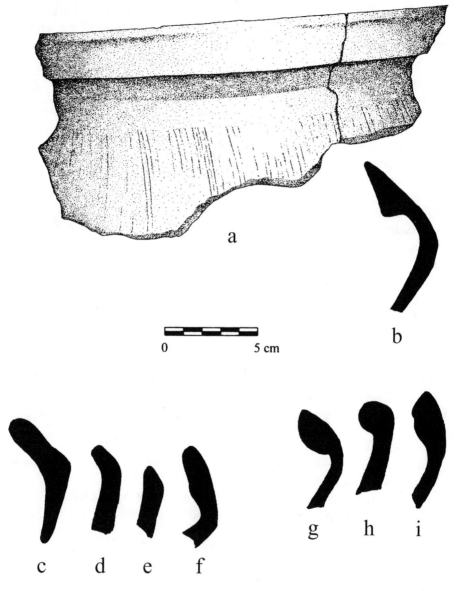

0   5 cm

17.8 Unslipped vessel forms from Saktunja.

types laid the foundations for preferred, more standardized Postclassic traditions that followed. For example, Miseria Applique censer types and annular-based vessels display attributes that were later incorporated into the Postclassic unslipped spiked censer tradition (Mock 1994a).

The pattern of retrospective borrowing of technological attributes and stylistic conventions is especially apparent within the black-slipped types of the Achote Black group. Of all the groups, this one displays the greatest number of decorative techniques and slip crossovers, including applique, impression, stamping, incision (deep and shallow), and modeling. It also has the greatest number of forms, including vases, cylinders, bowls, and platters. No black-slipped jars were recovered at Saktunja or NRL. Attributes such as the subtractive treatment of slip in the Toro Gouged-Incised and Cubeta Incised varieties persist into the Postclassic in thicker-walled, red slipped types such as Carved Red Ware, Zakpah Orange Red, and slate ware paste pottery (Mock 1994b, n.d.b). Transitional Achote Black paste becomes more yellow and sandy with coarse inclusions in the coastal Belize assemblages. Slip color varieties include a fire-dull black, a glossy black, and a golden brown differentially fired slip, making many sherds difficult to classify (Rice 1987a), though these are often subsumed under the type name of Achote Black.

Achote Black and its varieties are common in Petén (Ball 1977; Gifford 1976; Rice 1987a; Sabloff 1975) and among other Late to Terminal Classic assemblages in Belize such as Colha (Valdez 1987), Santa Rita (D. Chase 1982b), Cerros (Walker 1990), and sites surveyed in the NBCP Project such as Gabriel's Island, Shark's Point, Rocky Point, Pott's Creek Lagoon, and sites at Midwinter's Lagoon (Figure 17.2). Ball (1977: 135) associates Achote varieties with Tinaja Red and northern types, while Valdez (1987) proposes that it is of northern Belize origin. Mock (1994a) also argues for the existence of at least one northern Belize production center, based on the frequency and considerable variety found in this area. Achote Black's incorporation of decorative attributes with slate wares from the north is discussed below, and this is particularly observed in ceramic bowls from NRL (Mock 1994a). Decorative modes are also shared with locally produced ceramics of the Daylight Orange group at Saktunja and NRL, suggesting a close relationship in the manufacturing locales and techniques of these two types. Experimentation with resist and differential firing on the Daylight Orange type is illustrated on sherds from NRL (Figures 17.9a-c). A composite vessel from NRL (Figure 17.10a) shows a combination of decorative techniques on a single pot.

Connections with northern Yucatán at NRL are indicated by the presence of Cehpech-related slate wares such as Chumayel Red-on-slate, Sacalum Black-on-slate, and Pixtun Trickle-on-gray that were probably obtained through trade (Ball 1977; Mock 1994a; Smith 1971; Valdez 1987; Walker 1990). Forms include restricted-mouth jars with rolled or straight rims and occasional strap handles. These jars probably were used to ship products from the north and were subsequently reused by the local inhabitants (Mock n.d.a). Bowls with rounded sides and flat bottoms and small basal break tripod bowls with vertical or slightly out-flared walls and oven-shaped supports are also characteristic. Other Terminal Classic sites in northern Belize and Quintana Roo such as Nohmul (D. Chase 1982b: 502–

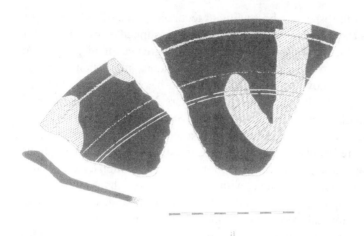

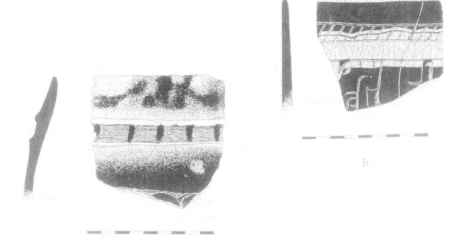

17.9 Transitional resist techniques on Terminal Classic ceramics from NRL.

503), Cerros (Walker 1990), Becan (Ball 1977), and Colha (Valdez 1987) also have revealed small quantities of slate wares thought to be indicative of exchange or communication with the northern lowlands. This is curious considering the local production of salt at coastal sites during the Late to Terminal Classic using labor-intensive processes when salt was also available in northern Yucatán. Per-

17.10 Sherds from NRL, including, a) a composite ceramic bowl, b) Tunich Red-on-orange, c) Zacatel cream bowl.

haps other commodities were important for exchange with the north through coastal trading sites on the Belize coast, such as NRL. Although slate ware sherds are common in Terminal Classic deposits at NRL, they are less common at Saktunja, perhaps due to this smaller site's subordinate relationship to the larger site of NRL.

Ties to Petén, the Belize Valley, and the southern Belize coast are demon-strated in the NRL assemblage by the presence of unit-stamped and punctated jars (Adams 1971; Hammond 1975; Sabloff 1975) and ash-tempered wares such as Puhui-zibal Composite (Gifford 1976; Thompson 1939; Willey et al. 1965). Other ties to ceramic traditions of Petén are observed in the frequency of Subin Red bowls with incurved walls and slightly restricted orifices (Adams 1971; Sabloff 1975; Valdez 1987). In the Terminal Classic, however, the vessel body and cir-cumferential ridge become thicker and cruder and the slip becomes more orange and streaky. Tinaja Red slipped, straight-necked, and outcurved-neck water jars and thin-walled bowls (Adams 1971: 235; Ball 1977; Sabloff 1975; Valdez 1987; Valdez et al. 1995) are common at NRL and Saktunja, but in Terminal Classic depos-its there was experimentation in forms and slips. For instance, the vertical-necked jars at Saktunja in the Terminal Classic deposits have the darker red slip characteristic of Payil Red. As alluded to previously, large jars with everted rims become less common in the subsequent Postclassic in favor of small rolled-rim vessels, and the deep red-slipped Payil Red dish at Saktunja evolves into a thin-walled vessel with a simple pointed or rounded lip. One unusual bowl has an exterior padded rim that is sharply beveled on the vessel interior (Mock n.d.b). Paste studies are needed to determine the developmental links between Tinaja Red and Payil Red.

Both Saktunja and NRL are characterized by the presence of ceramics in the Palmar group such as Tunich-Red-on-Orange plates (see also Sabloff 1975: 126, 127; Mock n.d.b) and Yucatal Black-on-Red bowls in addition to the ubiquitous Palmar Orange polychromes characterized by in-beveled or rounded rims (Figure 17.10b). The rarer Zacatel Cream (Figure 17.10c) polychrome bowls and an unnamed black and red on cream polychrome type of the Palmar Group are recovered at NRL in Terminal Classic deposits, but not at Saktunja. The presence of the Palmar Orange polychrome plates with beveled or round rims (Figure 17.7a-e) is curious because polychromes generally diminish or disappear at other Terminal Classic sites in Belize and Petén (Adams 1971; Rice 1987a). Coinciden-tally, identical polychrome sherds also have been recovered on Gabriel's Island in Northern River Lagoon and at the interior sites of Kichpanha and Colha. The latter site may have been the locus of production for these types (Mock 1998c). The ubiquitous presence of these polychromes in Late to Terminal Classic deposits at all four sites suggests that the plates, unlike the status-laden fine polychromes described by Reents-Budet (1994), were produced for more general, non-elite consumption (Mock 1994a, 1997b, n.d.b; Valdez 1987). However, they are not noted in NBCP surveys at other coastal sites.

Zacatel Cream bowls (Figure 17.10c) also represent the Palmar Group at NRL, although they are not recovered at Saktunja. They occur at NRL in smaller bowl forms that may be related to drinking activities or rituals. The slip of this type changes over time in a manner similar to that of Achote Black, as the black-on-cream slip becomes golden brown with streaked brown interiors. In some cases, the cream slip is barely discernible in otherwise well-preserved ceramics (Mock 1999, n.d.b).

A new type defined at NRL is Fat Polychrome (Figure 17.7d, 17.7e), occurring in large, thick basins with bolstered rims, obviously influenced by northern slate ware forms. This distinctive, very late type also is found at Saktunja and the Salt Creek site directly south on Midwinter's Lagoon, but it is not found at Colha or Kichpanha, suggesting yet another spatially uneven distribution pattern.

The Late to Terminal Classic ceramic inventory of the Pibil Luum complex of NRL is composed primarily of Tepeu 3 types with some overlap of Tepeu 2 types as defined at Uaxactun. This complex is very similar to the Masson complex as defined by Valdez (1987) at Colha, except for the greater numbers of types and varieties at NRL, which might be expected of a trading station. Ceramics of the Pibil Luum complex exhibit the variability characteristic of northern Belize assemblages during this time period (A. Chase and D. Chase 1987a; Graham 1987b: 78). The following description of NRL ceramics focuses primarily on types that represent the Terminal Classic period and may continue from the Late Classic. These types also include those that are new to the Classic period inventory at this site and that are not traditionally defined within Late Classic Tepeu 2 and 3 spheres.

Evidence of Late Classic to Terminal Classic transitional occupation at both sites is signaled by subtle changes in diagnostic ceramic attributes, paralleling Graham's (1987b: 79) analysis of ceramics from Lamanai. For example, Graham observes an evolution of Early Postclassic large pedestal-based bowls from antecedent Late Classic Roaring Creek Red and Daylight Orange types. These types anticipate Buk-phase Postclassic chalices characteristic of Lamanai. Similar Late Classic large basal-break bowls with ring bases noted in the NRL ceramic assemblage are placed in the Kik Red group, a Terminal Classic type (D. Chase 1982b) common to northeastern Belize. This type closely resembles the Daylight Orange group in form, and it may replace this group in northern Belize. Daylight Orange: Darknight Variety occurs at NRL in a large outcurved bowl form with thickened or beveled rim, a smaller bowl with out-flared walls, and a round-sided bowl with flat bottom (Figure 17.9a). Another type, Daylight Orange: Dark Night Composite, was established at NRL (Figure 17.10a). The Daylight group, according to Ball (1983a), reflects connections to other central Belize sites, although the Daylight Orange: Variety Unspecified has been difficult to recognize in the archaeological assemblages.

Kik Red exemplifies the reiteration of earlier ceramic complexes in forms and surface treatment, especially in its characteristics of differentially fired slip color and waxy surface finish. These characteristics recall attributes of Late Preclassic–period types, including San Antonio Golden Brown and Sierra Red. This retrospective trend continues during the Postclassic period (Willey et al. 1965; Masson 2000). Willey et al. explained this phenomenon as a lack of Postclassic creativity that led to emulation of earlier pottery attributes. Postclassic construction efforts often disturbed deposits of earlier age, and thus occupants of Postclassic communities would have been familiar with prior pottery traditions. Emulation and creative recombination of earlier attributes may have been symbolically significant in expressing links to past occupants, and this strategy in inventing new Postclassic forms with retrospective decorative attributes can alternatively be viewed as a highly creative process.

Included in the eclectic assemblage at NRL are unslipped miniature vessels, possibly used as paint pots (Mock 1994a; Smith and Gifford 1966). Portions of ceramic drums (including one anthropomorphic example) are present in Late to Terminal Classic assemblages at NRL (Mock 1994a) and continue into the Postclassic period at Saktunja. Lubaantun-style mold-made figurines and whistles known from Seibal (Willey 1978), Altar de Sacrificios (Willey 1972), and southern Belize (McKillop 1989; Thompson 1939: 156, Figure 92i-j, Plate 22: 1, 3; Willey et al. 1965: 398, Figure 257j; Willey 1972: 14–74) are mixed in with transitional types but date to the early part of the transition.

Coastal sites such as NRL or Saktunja are unlikely locales for surplus ceramic production geared toward exchange because of the environmental conditions, such as humidity, wind, rainfall, and lack of suitable potting clays (Mock 1999). Decorated utility as well as elite-status types recovered at NRL were thus presumably produced by outside potters. They represent a vast network of dynamically changing social and economic relationships and a consumer demand for fine pottery during the Late to Terminal Classic transition.

The sites of NRL and Saktunja may represent cadet settlements, founded perhaps by kin groups around the eighth century A.D. at a time when population movements and settlement shifts were common (Culbert 1988; Mock 1994a). These population shifts, also reflected in the abandonment of some inland sites, may have been triggered by pressures from burgeoning populations on resources at inland locations (Culbert 1977: 525–528, 1988; Dahlin 1976; D. Rice 1993a: 31; Thompson 1954; Webb 1964; Valdez 1987; Willey and Shimkin 1973: 491). Political factors also contributed to the decline of certain areas, as indicated by the acceleration of warfare documented among Petén and Petexbatun polities (Demarest and Houston 1990; Demarest 1997; Demarest et al. 1997; Foias and Bishop 1997; Wright 1997a; Schele and Miller 1986: 28–29; Webster 1977).

The magnitude or direction of population movements during this time period is difficult to assess. Even low numbers of elites, whether settlers or visitors, could stimulate important changes in ceramic inventories through processes of stimulus diffusion (Clark and Gosser 1995) or through the establishment of new networks of exchange and emulation. Schele's (1995) analysis of epigraphic and ethnohistoric records (following Barrera Vásquez and Morley 1949) suggests that migrations out of Petén accompanied the decline of Classic-period centers, and that such migrations followed a route that passed through Belize and eastern

Quintana Roo toward northern Yucatán. Archaeologists have suggested similar scenarios (A. Chase 1986; Pendergast 1985; Ball and Taschek 1989). Coastal sites such as NRL and Saktunja would have been a logical place for settlement in this diaspora. The diversity of artifacts may reflect settlement of this area by different cultural groups.

TERMINAL CLASSIC PATTERNS AT INLAND LAGOONS IN NORTHEASTERN BELIZE

Terminal Classic–period settlement has been detected at Laguna de On (Honey Camp Lagoon) and Progresso Lagoon (Figure 17.3). At the former site, this occupation is found in artifact scatters around the shores of the lagoon (which has been heavily impacted by development) and in the final phases of residential platform groups identified at the southwest shore of Laguna de On (Masson 1997). At Progresso Lagoon, Terminal Classic domestic occupation is found in dispersed residential mounds and middens that sprawl intermittently for eight kilometers along the lagoon's west shore and extend at least two kilometers into modern cane fields along a bluff to the west of the shoreline (Figure 17.3). At least two small clusters of elite platform groups indicate central foci for upper-status ritual and domestic activities along the shore, and the larger center of Rancho Corozal to the north of Progresso may have been an administrative node with influence over the lagoon sites. The two elite platform groups to the west of Progresso have structures of modest height (four to five meters).

The island site of Caye Coco (Figure 17.6) was also first settled by Maya populations during the Terminal Classic period, although Preceramic (Late Archaic) deposits are also found on the island. Terminal Classic settlement is reflected in basal deposits of house mounds and middens (Sastry 2001) found in several locations at Caye Coco and in two structures that were initially constructed at this time (Rosenswig 1999; Digrius and Masson 2001). These structures rise three to four meters above surrounding terrain and were capped by later Postclassic construction activities. Fifteen other mounds at this site (ranging from one to four meters in height) fully date to the Late Postclassic period (Rosenswig 1999). The presence of Terminal Classic mounded architecture, house structures, and middens across the site suggest that the island formed a third focus of elite activity, along with the two large platform groups identified along the west shore and Rancho Corozal to the north. At both Laguna de On and Caye Coco, Terminal Classic settlement and the presence of modest ritual architecture suggest that multiple, affluent petty elites occupied these lagoons, accompanied by a population of dispersed agrarian households. These families showed little concern for organizing their communities in a nucleated or centralized fashion. A desire for lagoon shore access may have contributed to the linear dispersion of house mounds along these waterways, although the platform groups are two kilometers to the west of the lagoon, midway between Progresso Lagoon and the New River in a rich agricultural zone. The platform groups may have been constructed in more central places, enabling them to access resources of the watersheds of both the New River and Progresso Lagoon/Freshwater Creek.

TERMINAL CLASSIC ARCHITECTURE AT CAYE COCO

Of the two mounded structures of Terminal Classic date at Caye Coco, Structure 1 reveals evidence of elite activity at this site. Structure 13 has been heavily looted, and little information is available regarding the function of this mound. We have only had the opportunity to document its construction profile and chronology through cleaning and mapping a looter's trench and taking ceramic samples from the fill (Rosenswig 1999). In contrast, Structure 1 has been subjected to intensive investigation. This mound was built over a natural limestone hill at the central, highest point on the island (Figure 17.6). It rises ten meters above the water level of the lagoon, but this is largely due to natural topography. Construction materials above the natural bedrock hill consist of 1.8–2 meters of fill and earlier floors and structures (West 1999: Figure 8.7, 8.8). The first construction phase is of Terminal Classic date. At least two wall alignments of buildings of this period have been detected in the fill of Structure 1. Of these alignments, only one has been partially exposed and allows preliminary interpretations (Digrius and Masson 2001). This alignment represents a circular platform, marked by a three-course retaining wall and an interior core of rubble fill. Approximately one-fourth of this platform was exposed during the 2000 season. Terminal Classic ceramics were lying on its surface and within the top stones of the rubble core (Figure 17.11). Based on rim form and paste characteristics described in D. Chase (1982) and Walker (1990), these ceramics include: Chambel or Buyuk Striated (D. Chase 1982b: 510, Figure 3-6c, 3-6d; Walker 1990: 73, Figure 2.4, 2.5a), Campbells Red (D. Chase 1982b: 497–498, Figure 3-6l), Tinaja Red (or a local variant, Kik Red, D. Chase 1982b: 496, Figure 3-6k), Achote Black (D. Chase 1982b: 506), and Cubeta Incised (D. Chase 1982b: 507). This assemblage clearly resembles those of the Terminal Classic period reported from Nohmul and Cerros by Chase and Walker.

Penetrating excavations within this structure have not been conducted, and interpretations of its function are preliminary. One skull was encountered that was protruding from the structure's surface, presenting a possible burial or cranium interred within it (Digrius and Masson 2001). This round structure resembles a Terminal Classic/Early Postclassic platform (Structure 9) excavated at Nohmul (D. Chase and A. Chase 1982). This structure and its artifact assemblage led Chase and Chase to infer that an invasion by northern Itza groups had occurred at Nohmul. A recent publication by Ringle and colleagues (1998) documents the economic and ideological interaction of elites at a number of core Mesoamerican Epiclassic centers, including Chichen Itza, which they chronologically place at A.D. 800–1000 based on new radiocarbon dates from terminal construction phases

17.11 Terminal Classic round structure from Structure 1, Caye Coco.

at this site, though the site is thought to have been politically significant for at least a century longer (Bey et al. 1997; Andrews et al. 2000). An important component of this network of trading is the participation of elites at core Mesoamerican centers in a cult of the feathered serpent, which used shared symbolic elements and mythology and formed a symbolic language that was conducive to distant commerce. Round structures have a long history and probably variable religious meaning in northern Belize (Sidrys 1983; Aimers et al. 2000), but they are associated with feathered serpent symbolism during the Epiclassic (Ringle et al. 1998: 219, 221–222) and Postclassic periods (Pollock 1936: 160; Fox 1987: 60). The round structure at Caye Coco may provide evidence of the participation of local founding elites in this Mesoamerican interaction sphere. The presence of this ritual platform probably also indicates the importance of the Chichen Itza maritime trade network to the Terminal Classic production economy of Progresso Lagoon, located only twelve kilometers from the coast.

The second building episode of Structure 1, also of Terminal Classic date, was constructed to a height of sixty centimeters above the round structure. It has been detected in the form of a plaster floor that extends over the round structure and beyond it to the north by at least three meters. This floor overlies ca. fifty-five centimeters of construction-fill rubble that contains Terminal Classic ceramic sherds. Intruding into this floor, at least seven burial pits have been detected. These burials are incomplete, and represent secondary interments. Terminal Classic sherds, including Achote Black, have been recovered with the only excavated interment in this floor (Digrius and Masson 2001). This floor and its burial intrusions represent a structure of mortuary function, perhaps where important members of elite family groups of the Caye Coco community were interred. The final construction phase of Structure 1 is of Late Postclassic date, represented by sixty centimeters of large limestone rubble fill that is capped by a limestone rubble surface (West 1999). This construction phase gives Structure 1 its final shape, a rectangular Late Postclassic long structure that is thought to represent a council house or meeting hall of public function for island residents. In contrast to other Postclassic mounded architecture at the site, its artifact assemblage indicates it was not used as a residence, because domestic features are absent and domestic artifacts are scarce (Masson 1999).

TERMINAL CLASSIC CERAMICS AT LAGUNA DE ON AND CAYE COCO

Ceramics identified from the Terminal Classic period at Laguna de On identified by Fred Valdez (1993) include Alexander's Unslipped jars, Tutu Camp Striated (Encanto) jars, Tinaja Red jars, Subin Red bowls and basins, Achote Black bowls and plates, Tunich Red-on-orange plates, Yuhactal Black on Red plates, Daylight Orange: Darknight Variety plates and bowls, Palmar Orange Polychrome plates and cylinders, and Zacatel Cream Polychrome plates and cylinders (Valdez 1993). These types were found in surface occupations of three house mounds situated atop an elevated (1–1.5 meter) platform on the lagoon's southwest shore (Masson 1997). These types are also found in pottery described above for coastal sites Mock examined.

Basal levels of seventy-centimeter-deep middens along the north shore of Caye Coco also yielded Terminal Classic pottery. Deep midden deposits have been detected along much of the north shore of the island along the waterline and they extend into currently submerged deposits. It is not known whether water levels were lower in the past and these middens represent shoreline activities or dumping, or whether midden trash was dumped into the water during Maya occupations. The water levels rise and recede at least two meters within any given summer, depending on the amount of rain. Midden soil consists of a mixture of clay, decomposed limestone, and lagoon sand. Testing of midden deposits along the shoreline suggests that they accumulated at varying temporal intervals between the eighth and fifteenth centuries. Materials described here are from Suboperation 18, which has Terminal Classic period (ca. A.D. 750–1000) and Late Postclassic period (A.D. 1100–1500) deposits, based on the results of AMS dating.

Of specific relevance to this chapter, faunal bone from Level 6 (fifty centimeters below surface) of these deposits has been AMS-dated to a calibrated range of A.D. 720–990 (1160+/–50 B.P., Stafford Research Lab #SR-5440). This midden lacks a component bridging the eleventh-century temporal gap between

Terminal Classic (eighth to tenth century) and Late Postclassic (twelfth to fifteenth century) occupations. Deposits farther upslope, including Suboperations 29 and 38, have materials that date to between A.D. 860 and 1040 (calibrated date of 1070+/–50 B.P., Stafford Research Lab #SR-5519), based on an AMS date of a carbonized log at the base of a large fire pit (two meters in diameter, one meter deep) in Level 8 of Suboperation 29. This fire pit was full of burned charcoal and logs, ash, *Pomacea* shell, and Zakpah Orange Red and Tsabak Unslipped sandy paste ceramics. An identical assemblage primarily comprising these types was found in lower levels of a midden at Suboperation 38, which is thus probably contemporary with Suboperation 29. We believe that this assemblage represents an Early Postclassic component in the brief interval falling between A.D. 900 and 1050/1100 when diverse Terminal Classic–period types disappeared from local assemblages and the tradition of calcite-tempered Payil Red and Santa Unslipped Late Postclassic types had not yet emerged.

Unfortunately, these waterlogged Terminal Classic deposits of Suboperation 18 have eroded much of the surface finish off the abundant sherds recovered from this context, inhibiting their type:variety identifications. Paste and rim characteristics provide some clues to their typology. The eroded slip sherds exhibit a variety of sand-tempered pastes as well as calcite-tempered and possible ash-tempered pastes. These paste characteristics resemble those that have been described for Kik Red, Campbells Red, Achote Black, Savinal Cream, and Metzabok Slate (D. Chase 1982b: 495–512). Rim forms from Suboperation 18 (midden) and Structure 1 (round structure) Terminal Classic deposits include some that match published type descriptions and others that do not, as shown in Figure 17.12. Sandy paste, eroded-slip sherds that resemble descriptions by Chase (1982: 511) and Walker (1990: 70) of Terminal Classic Taak Orange and later Early Postclassic Zakpah Orange Red (Walker 1990: 80) are present as well (Figure 17.12b). Slate ware, cream, or ash-tempered paste sherds are common in the Terminal Classic Levels 5 and 6 of the Suboperation 18 midden (Figure 17.13). Other brown sandy and calcite-tempered paste-eroded slip sherds are also common.

In general, Terminal Classic midden deposits underlying Postclassic levels at Caye Coco are recognized by their great variety of paste characteristics and the presence of numerous, poorly fired sand-tempered sherds in a range of orange, buff, and brown colors. Slips, where preserved, are waxy or glossy and of an olive, buff, or black color, and resemble characteristics described for Savinal Cream or Metzabok Slate (D. Chase 1982b: 502, 506). Chase believes that these types are related to northern Yucatán wares, including Peto Cream ware and Puuc Slate ware, respectively. In some cases, black slipped sherds seem to erode to reveal an olive or buff underslip. These are most likely fragments of the Achote Black type group, which has variable slip characteristics (D. Chase 1982b: 507).

Vessel forms identified for eroded-slip rim sherds in these deposits include ring-based *comals,* collared neck, rolled rim, and thickened rim small ollas, large and small incurving-rim bowls, inward beveled incurving-rim bowls, incised slate ware body sherds (fine paste, soapy-smooth slip, sherds shown in Figure 17.13a) dishes, folded rim (squared lip) restricted orifice bowls (*tecomates*), out-flaring wall jars (perhaps Chambel Striated), strap handle vessels, direct rim dishes (perhaps Kik Red), ring-based or flanged shallow bowls or plates (Kik Red and Taak Orange Red), direct rim plates, and an incised, flanged, miniature sag-bottom bowl with a pointed, vented foot (slate ware paste, Figure 17.13b). Incised and gouged sherds are also present among slate or cream ware sherds (perhaps Yantho Incised or Usukum Gouged-Incised cream wares as defined by D. Chase 1982b: 503–504) and buff sandy eroded slip sherds (perhaps Tzibana Gouged Incised as defined by D. Chase 1982b: 499). The presence of numerous slate or cream ware body sherds in these midden levels suggests influence from Yucatán, as at Nohmul (D. Chase 1982b).

The presence of Achote Black, Kik Red, Taak Orange Red, and a variety of other less common eroded slipped sherds in this assemblage also ties it to other southern lowland sites in the northeast corner of Belize, including Cerros, NRL, and Saktunja. Achote Black and Kik Red in particular share some important similarities in form with other wares in the interior of Belize, referred to as either the same type (Achote Black) or other types (Tinaja Red), as discussed in considerable detail in the previous section of this chapter. If the Suboperation 18 ceramics of the basal levels were more complete or had better-preserved slips, better typological comparisons would be possible.

An abundance of sand-tempered, eroded-slip types is observed in the Terminal Classic assemblage of Caye Coco (Figure 17.12b), which contrasts with most paste types described from Nohmul and Cerros that have predominantly calcite tempers. A type described at Nohmul (D. Chase 1982b: 512) and Cerros (Walker 1990: 70), Taak Orange Red, matches the buff sandy paste characteristics of a major ceramic type in the Terminal Classic levels of Caye Coco in its inclusion of sand grains, eroded slip, slip color, and incompletely fired cores. At Caye Coco, a paste group with the same characteristics continues into the Early Postclassic and is identified in these levels as Zakpah Orange Red, as defined at Cerros (Walker 1990: 80). More types of vessels are made from this paste group in the Early Postclassic than in the Terminal Classic at Caye Coco, but we see a continuity in paste and slip technology between these two types. As at Cerros, Early Postclassic Zakpah Orange Red at Caye Coco is associated with beveled-rim bowls, flanged dishes, and chalices. These forms are associated with Kik Red in the Terminal Classic period at Nohmul (D. Chase 1982b: 496) but appear to be made of different, sandy paste later at Caye Coco.

Unslipped sherds in the Terminal Classic levels of the Suboperation 18 midden exhibit a variety of sand-tempered and fine calcite-tempered pastes. These often have incompletely fired cores. Buff sandy pastes are common, though brown and orange sandy pastes also occur. A red or gray sandy paste type identified as

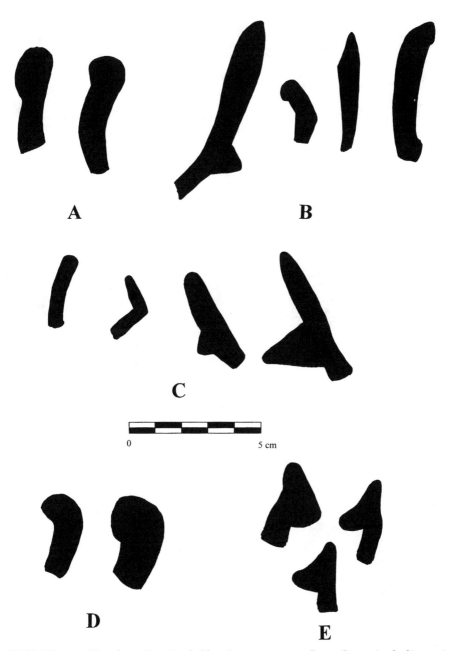

A

B

C

D

E

0   5 cm

17.12 Rim profiles from Terminal Classic contexts at Caye Coco, including: a) Campbells Red (from Structure 1, round structure); b) Taak Orange Red, Zakpah Orange Red or other buff sandy eroded slipped type (from Suboperation 18, example on the left has a slate-like eroded slip); c) Red slipped sherds, Tinaja Red or Kik Red (from Structure 1, round structure); d and e) possible Chambel and Buyuk Striated.

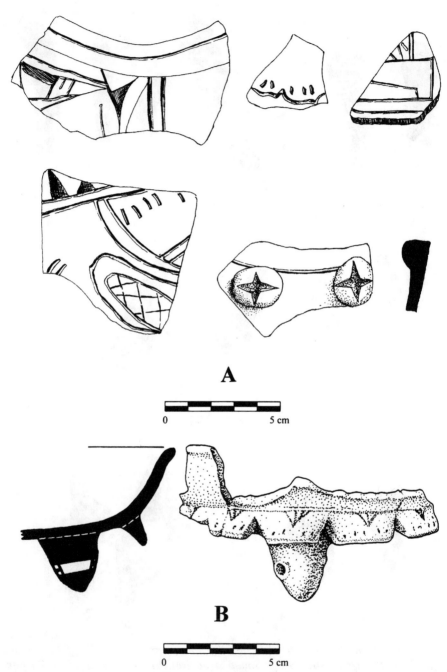

A

0   5 cm

B

0   5 cm

17.13 Slate ware sherds from Suboperation 18, Caye Coco, including: a) body sherds (actual size) with gouged-incised decoration or applique (bottom right example), and b) eroded slipped slate ware incised, flanged, vented foot dish.

Tsabak Unslipped (Walker 1990: 91, Figure 2.8a)—a large, thick, outflaring or direct-rim neck olla form—is observed in Terminal Classic levels of Suboperation 18 at Caye Coco (Figure 17.14). Vessels with Tsabak Unslipped-like pastes endure in these middens, in various forms, through the Postclassic period. Their identification in the Terminal Classic at Caye Coco conflicts with evidence from Cerros, where they were associated with the earlier half of the Postclassic period. No types resembling Tsabak Unslipped are described in the Terminal Classic ceramic assemblages from Nohmul (D. Chase 1982b) or Cerros (Walker 1990). However, descriptions of Cerros' Early Facet Kanan–phase Tsabak Unslipped acutely characterize the Caye Coco sherds, as does the illustration of the outflaring and direct rims associated with this type (Walker 1990: Figure 2.8a). We submit that at Caye Coco, Tsabak Unslipped originates earlier, in the Terminal Classic period, where it is one of several types of unslipped ollas used at this time. The outflaring or direct-rim Tsabak Unslipped olla continues through the Early Postclassic at Caye Coco (when this type dominates unslipped assemblages), and in the Late Postclassic; sherds with Tsabak-paste characteristics are more commonly associated with censer pedestals.

Forms reflected in unslipped rim sherds from Terminal Classic deposits at Caye Coco include thickened, rolled, everted, outbeveled-grooved, folded rim vessels, direct rim bowls, comals, and the Tsabak ollas. These rim forms are identified with Terminal Classic vessel types at Nohmul and Cerros, including Chambel Striated and Buyuk Striated (Figure 17.12d-e). In both these types, striation is not commonly observed above the juncture of the jar body and neck, and most thickened, rolled, everted, and folded rim sherds that may belong to these types at Caye Coco do not exhibit striations either, as would be expected if they belonged to these types. Numerous thin striated body sherds are also present in these midden levels that probably reflect these types as well. At Progresso shore sites and at Structure 1 of Caye Coco, the most common striated type is quite similar in form to Piste Striated ollas of northern Yucatán (Smith 1971). Comals are not reported in the types described from Nohmul (D. Chase 1982b) and Cerros (Walker 1990), and this may reflect an important difference with Caye Coco, where they are common in Terminal Classic levels. The wide range of paste types observed in the unslipped sherds suggests that numerous forms and types of vessels are represented in these Terminal Classic deposits, perhaps due to the multiplicity of production locales and the widespread exchange in northeastern Belize and beyond referred to in the discussion of coastal sites above.

ARTIFACTS INDICATING
TERMINAL CLASSIC ECONOMIC ACTIVITY AT CAYE COCO

Other artifacts (besides ceramic vessel sherds) present in Terminal Classic levels of Caye Coco middens include chert and chalcedony tool fragments and flakes, obsidian blades, marine shell, spindle whorls, net weights, and ground stone. The

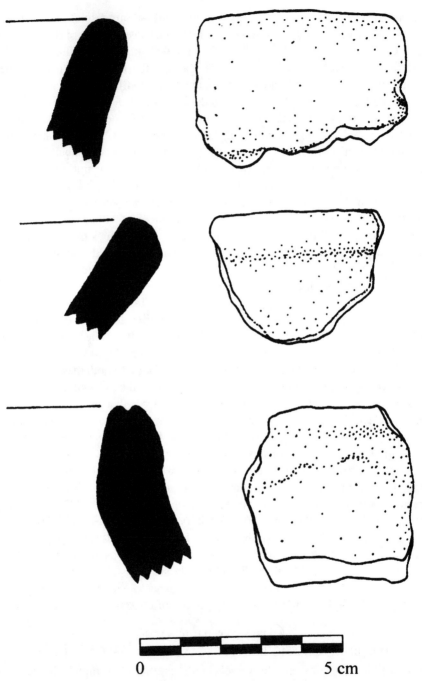

0   5 cm

17.14 Unslipped sherds from Caye Coco, including Tsabak Unslipped, a sandy paste type found in Terminal Classic and Early Postclassic deposits.

raw material types of lithic tools and flakes indicate that residents of this site were actively engaged in exchange with the site of Colha for formal lithic tools, and they also produced expedient biface and uniface tools made of coarse cherts available at Progresso Lagoon for their own use (Oland 1999, 2000).

The presence of obsidian blades in Caye Coco Terminal Classic middens is indicated by a ratio of 0.18 obsidian blades per chert or chalcedony tool at the site. Terminal Classic–period deposits on the shore of Laguna de On have a similar obsidian to chert or chalcedony tool ratio of 0.13. Higher ratios of obsidian to non-obsidian lithic tools are documented for the Postclassic period (Masson and Chaya 2000). The Terminal Classic ratios indicate that distant trade connections were important to daily economies. Obsidian trade was also probably accompanied by the exchange of many other perishable goods. Although obsidian was common, it was not as important or more important than local lithic resources as it was during the Postclassic period (Masson and Chaya 2000). In the Terminal Classic patterns at Progresso, the roots of this long-term, long-distance utilitarian dependency of the Postclassic were anticipated (also noted for the Petén lakes, Rice 1987a).

Patterns of shell-working at Caye Coco follow a trend similar to that of obsidian. This industry is present during the Terminal Classic and represents a small-scale craft industry that transformed a local resource into a valuable commodity. The scale of shell-working at Caye Coco is amplified during the Postclassic period, with some contexts of this period exhibiting from four to forty times the amount of marine shell debris than is found in Terminal Classic contexts at the site. Spindle whorls likewise link textile industries of the Terminal Classic period with those of the Postclassic period, although these durable artifacts are in low frequencies in both sets of deposits. Fishing and turtling were equally important in both periods as indicated by quantities of net weights.

The trends observed in non-ceramic artifacts reflect the exploitation of local resources at Progresso used to make products for local or regional exchange in northeastern Belize. Forest products, honey, and cacao were also important commodities from northern Belize at the time of Spanish contact (Piña Chan 1978), although these are more difficult to detect archaeologically. Terminal Classic populations of these inland lagoons probably used many diverse local resources. The ceramic attributes suggest some emulation of northern wares alongside the production of distinctively local traditions, and they imply that the Terminal Classic economy was dually rooted in intercommunity exchange within northeastern Belize as well as the broader Caribbean coastal network linked to the northern Yucatecan sphere, highland Guatemala, and other areas.

SUMMARY

Settlement and ceramic data from the northeastern Belize zone of coastlines, lagoons, swamps, rivers, and fertile agricultural lands indicate that occupants of this region thrived during the Terminal Classic. Their economy and political ideology were oriented toward local and maritime interaction. The geographically intermediate position of the northeastern area of Belize between the southern interior and northern Yucatán placed its inhabitants in an advantageous position to capitalize on Caribbean trading initiated by Chichen Itza's empire. Settlements here experienced a dynamic transition and likely found advantages in the collapse of interior core centers and their affiliated Late Classic polities in northeastern Belize.

Survey data suggest that population levels at A.D. 800 exceed those documented for earlier times in some areas of the southern lowlands, followed shortly by a precipitous fall at some inland sites that were densely settled in the Classic period (Rice and Culbert 1990: 24; Fry 1990: Figure 14.2; Turner II 1990: Figure 15.1; Santley 1990: Figures 16.2, 16.3). Collapsing inland Classic-period settlements were most affected by their ties to Petén core political economies. Occupants of these settlements may have migrated to coastal or riverine locations, along with other refugees from urban centers in the interior core. Terminal Classic settlement in rural portions of Petén (A. Chase 1979; Willey 1986: 21) and in Belize at sites like Pulltrouser Swamp and Barton Ramie does not appear as severely impacted by the Petén collapse, and this suggests to Fry (1990: 295) that the economy of Belize was not as intimately tied to Petén by this period. Our research supports this interpretation and that of David Pendergast (1986a), who suggests that the Classic-period center of Lamanai thrived into the Postclassic period through reorienting its political and economic affiliations toward northern Yucatán. Northeastern Belize communities that we have investigated seem to have embraced this strategy. These Terminal Classic adaptations set the stage for burgeoning Postclassic populations at inland lagoon sites like Laguna de On and Caye Coco that were linked to a continued flourishing maritime mercantile economy. Some disjuncture is observed on the Belize coast, in which settlement during the Postclassic period is diminished at sites like NRL.

The Belize zone has been characterized as the periphery or "buffer zone" by Rathje (1971, 1972, 1973) during the Formative and Classic periods. This characterization is based on the relatively reduced scale of its architectural monuments, the comparatively low number of hieroglyphic texts, and the possession of lesser quantities of elite craft items compared to the Petén core of southern lowlands Maya society. Buffer zone advantages included the rich resources and proximity to coastal networks of exchange. During the Terminal Classic period, this relative core-periphery relationship broke down. The eastern riverine and coastal lowlands of Belize and southern Quintana Roo became a hub for settlement and trade, and this area was the home of thriving local populations as well as probable migrants.

While few centralizing political activities are evident in northeastern Belize during the Terminal Classic, the dispersed, decentralized, and semiautonomous communities of this region were contemporary with the powerful core city of Chichen Itza (Kepecs et al. 1994), and the effects of this primate city on the Terminal Classic Maya world have been partly considered in this chapter. Settlement data indicate the presence of many affluent hamlets and villages and relatively small-scale political centers in northeastern Belize during the Terminal Classic period (Pendergast 1985; Sidrys 1983; Walker 1990). Producers at these communities flourished under these conditions, and a diverse range of products from northeastern Belize were probably destined for local as well as far-flung exchange spheres around the Yucatán peninsula. A long-term amplification of these patterns is observed at Postclassic sites of this area that likely derives from the outward-looking exchange networks established during the Terminal Classic period by innovators and opportunists who occupied sites like NRL, Saktunja, Laguna de On, and Progresso Lagoon. These Terminal Classic populations seem to have managed, at some sites, to turn the Classic-period collapse into an opportunity to build a new Maya world.

ACKNOWLEDGMENTS

Research at NRL has been supported by grants awarded to Thomas Hester and Harry Shafer for the Colha Regional Project by the Centro de Estudi Ricerche Ligabue, the National Science Foundation, the National Geographic Society, and the National Endowment for the Humanities. Further fieldwork has been possible through a National Science Foundation Dissertation Improvement Grant and Foundation for the Advancement of Mesoamerican Studies, Inc. (to Shirley Mock), along with field support from Mr. Hilly Martinez of Belize City. Research at Caye Coco was conducted with the aid of the National Science Foundation, the Foundation for the Advancement of Mesoamerican Studies, Inc., the Center for Field Research: Earthwatch, and the Department of Anthropology at the University at Albany–SUNY. The authors are exceedingly grateful to the Department of Archaeology, Belmopan, Belize, for providing research permits to perform this work. We also thank Thomas Hester, Harry Shafer, and Fred Valdez for years of support and opportunities leading to these projects, and we are grateful to Robert Rosenswig and Lauren Sullivan for reading and commenting on early versions of this manuscript.

18

OUT OF SIGHT
THE POSTCLASSIC AND EARLY COLONIAL PERIODS
AT CHAU HIIX, BELIZE

Christopher R. Andres and K. Anne Pyburn

his paper examines evidence from the ancient Maya community of Chau Hiix, Belize, dating to the Terminal Classic through the Postclassic period (A.D. 900–1525) and the early years of Spanish influence (post–A.D. 1525) in Central America. While many lines of evidence are contributing to our emerging understanding of Chau Hiix, this paper remains a preliminary analysis focusing on three categories of data we see as basic to assessing early Colonial-period occupation of the site. These bodies of information include the community's physical setting, the Postclassic ceramic assemblage, and post–A.D. 900 architecture and architectural modifications. These data are comparable to data from contemporary communities in Belize and allow us to begin considering the extent to which the community's inhabitants were affected by European presence in the southern lowlands. The Chau Hiix data are relevant to the ongoing reconstruction of the political and economic relationships that existed between indigenous communities in Belize and Petén at the time of Spanish contact and before.

AN ISLAND IN THE JUNGLE

After ten years of research we have drawn a number of conclusions about the ancient community that left us the archaeological site of Chau Hiix, but sometimes it takes a while for the obvious to sink in. Although the site's physical location has clear implications for trade and subsistence (Pyburn n.d.), Chau Hiix's setting was probably also important for protection during the Postclassic and Colonial periods (Andres and Pyburn 1999). Settlement pattern work in Petén has demonstrated populations shifted from mainland to island and peninsular locations at the end of the Classic period (Rice 1986: 339, 1988: 236; Rice and Rice 1990). Although the precise reason(s) for these movements is uncertain, shifting settlement probably reflects increasing use of waterways and aquatic resources but may also reflect a need for defense (Rice 1986: 236). Although not located on an Island, Chau Hiix's setting is extremely defensible, as discussed below.

Postclassic settlement patterns in other parts of Belize often mirror lacustrine defensibility noted in Petén. Although associated with a somewhat wider range of environments than Guatemalan centers, Postclassic communities in Belize are similarly closely associated with major bodies of water: Lamanai is found at the head of the New River Lagoon (Pendergast 1986a: 245), Santa Rita Corozal lies on Chetumal Bay (D. Chase 1990: 199), Marco González is at the southern tip of Ambergris Caye (Graham and Pendergast 1989), and Cerros (which was reoccupied during the Postclassic period) is situated on Lowry's Bight in Chetumal Bay (Freidel 1986c: xiii). Chau Hiix lies on Western Lagoon near its outlet into Spanish Creek, which in turn flows into Black Creek. The site is accessible by water year-round and a mere two-kilometer portage from Dawson's Creek allows canoe access to Lamanai on the New River (Figure 18.1). During the rainy season, backed up floodwater in the Belize River results in a reversal of current that allows canoes to float down the Belize River from Petén and then up Black Creek to Chau Hiix (Pyburn n.d.).

Both Chau Hiix's location and Classic-period trade goods ranging from hematite and jade to saltwater pearls, *Spondylus* shells, and obsidian indicate the residents were active members of an extensive network during the Classic period. Particularly distinctive trade items recovered linking Chau Hiix with Classic-period centers in Petén and beyond include an inscribed bone hairpin mentioning a site in the Petexbatun (Rosemary Joyce, personal communication) and a lidded, stuccoed cylinder tripod from Teotihuacan (Robert Fry, personal communication). As discussed below, excavation results at Chau Hiix indicate the center was far from isolated during the Postclassic, although the size of Chau Hiix's interaction sphere most likely contracted as population levels dropped off at the site in the Late Postclassic or Early Colonial period.

Chau Hiix's defensible riparian setting gives the site more in common with Petén sites than initially might meet the eye. Presently, Chau Hiix sits beside a savanna in the dry season that becomes a lagoon in the wet season. Water level in the lagoon is unpredictable and we never know when the water will go up or down and strand us in the mud. Despite spending much of our time and resources coping with the logistics of mud, we were slow to realize that the Maya residents would have had to cope with similar circumstances if they wanted to leave or if they wanted to participate in a trade network. After talking with the people who currently live in the area, it is clear that the unpredictable rainfall

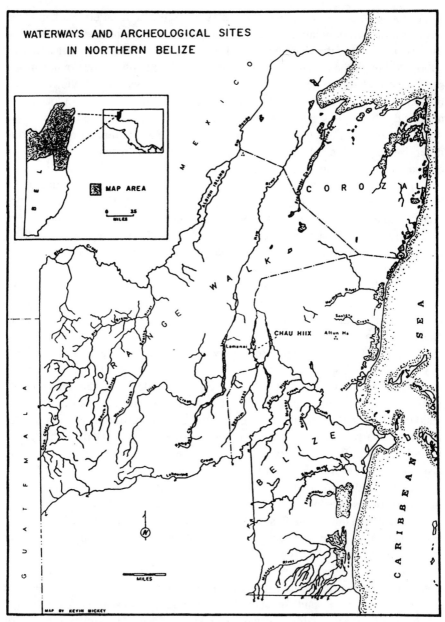

18.1 Selected archaeological sites and waterways in northern Belize.

makes a wretched situation for farmers, a situation that would have been as difficult one thousand years ago as it is today. What emerges from this picture is that while Chau Hiix is not situated on an actual island, it often might as well be. Located close to Spanish Creek and literally bounded by expanses of water (or mud) six months of the year, Chau Hiix's physical setting is similar to that of contemporary Petén Postclassic communities such as Nojpeten (Jones 1998). As considered below, Chau Hiix's island-like qualities may have been a significant factor that minimized (or prevented) contact between the site's Maya residents and members of Spanish expeditions that began making forays into the region in the 1550s (Pendergast 1991).

CONSIDERING SPANISH-MAYA CONTACT AT CHAU HIIX

Despite Postclassic and probable early Colonial-period occupation of Chau Hiix, little evidence of Spanish contact has been encountered at the site. Typical markers of Spanish presence in Maya communities include olive jars and Majolica wares, glass beads, and a range of copper, brass, silver, and iron objects (often needles, rings, locks, earrings, bells, and coffin nails) (Graham 1991: 324–328, 1998: 51–52; Pendergast 1991: 347, 1993). Despite numerous surface collections on the main platform and partial excavation of all buildings bordering it, no readily identifiable early Colonial-period artifacts had been identified. Two badly decomposed fragments of copper accompanying two Late Postclassic/Early Colonial–period burials may represent Spanish contact. The burials appear to be the most recent found at the site to date; both were supine with hands crossed over the pelvis. Both had copper stains and adhering fragments of copper on the left ring finger. Otherwise, European artifacts at the site reflect nineteenth-century use of the area by residents of nearby Crooked Tree village and by logwood cutters.

While signs of Spanish presence are lacking at Chau Hiix, it is important to keep in mind that such evidence is likely to be ephemeral at many sites, even those where the Spanish are known to have been present. Inventories of Spanish-made artifacts recovered at Lamanai, for example, are surprisingly small, with only 487 olive jar sherds recovered from church cemetery and lagoon-side middens (Pendergast 1991: 347). Such low artifact densities indicate long-term use of a limited number of vessels and suggest that Spanish control of Belize was poorly established in the early years following incorporation of the region into the Spanish *encomienda* system in 1544 (Graham 1991; Jones 1984).

Similarly, Graham (1991: 323–324) concludes that intermittent Spanish presence had very little effect on local ceramic and lithic production at Tipu. As indicated by the frequent recovery of stone tools in surface contexts, locally available chert clearly continued to be the most important raw material at Chau Hiix, as it was at Tipu (ibid.), following European contact. The evidence at hand suggests Chau Hiix was inaccessible enough to avoid Spanish visits and that activity at the site was little affected by Spanish presence in the region. If the copper fragments, which are unique at Chau Hiix, had a European origin, they could have been traded between Maya trade partners without direct Spanish contact at Chau Hiix. The slightly unusual positioning of the bodies, though not unique, could reflect the Christianizing influence noted in mortuary patterns at both Lamanai (Graham 1991; Pendergast 1986b: 4) and Tipu (Cohen et al. 1997: 80; Graham 1991: 331).

POSTCLASSIC AND COLONIAL–PERIOD CONSTRUCTION AT CHAU HIIX

Lamanai could scarcely have remained a viable community in a vacuum, created by collapse of political and social organization at neighboring Lowland centers and with the accompanying dissolution of intersite networks: it is therefore likely that the path of events at the site was repeated, at least in its main aspects, elsewhere in the area. (Pendergast 1986a: 226).

While Spanish presence is archaeologically invisible or lacking at Chau Hiix, there is abundant evidence of Maya occupation during the time of Spanish contact at Lamanai in the second half of the fifteenth century. Despite a reduction in the overall level of cultural activity at Chau Hiix between the Classic and Postclassic periods, ceramic and architectural data indicate substantial ceremonial and possible residential use of the main platform during the Postclassic period (A.D. 900 through ca. A.D. 1500). Evidence of continuous use of the site-center architecture is intriguing because it is both variable and has proved archaeologically unpredictable.

Many of the larger structures in the site center show signs of only intermittent use between the end of the Classic period and initial Spanish contact in 1544. The construction of a Postclassic stairway on top of ten centimeters of humus and collapse debris at the base of Structure 1, for example, indicates the structure was not continuously maintained throughout the pre-contact period (Andres 2000). Structure 3, a modest temple structure southwest of Structure 1, demonstrates even less use between its probable Classic-period abandonment and activities that left deposits of Late Postclassic Mayapán-style effigy *incensarios* on its summit (Figure 18.2) (Cook and Pyburn 1995).

Furthermore, excavation of a significant portion of a modest residential structure (Structure 14) on the southern edge of the main platform yielded ceramic debris in fill layers dating no later than the Terminal Classic Period. This evidence, combined with a complete absence of Postclassic material from the surfaces of other structures on the main platform, indicates the main group did not experience the same overall level of maintenance and use during the Postclassic as it did during the Classic period. Instead, certain Classic-period structures became the focus of intermittent Postclassic activities, which in some cases diverged significantly from the buildings' Classic-period functions.

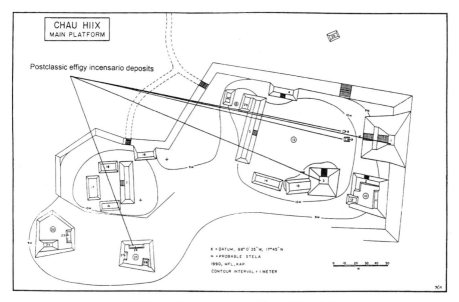

18.2 The main platform at Chau Hiix, Belize.

Structure 1

Structure 1, the primary civic-ceremonial structure located on the eastern edge of the main platform, was a focus of both construction and ceremonial activity during the Postclassic period. Apparently established in the Late Preclassic (ca. 300 B.C. to A.D. 200), the building grew incrementally through a series of construction campaigns mounted primarily during the Classic period. Like the easternmost structures at many Maya sites (Chase and Chase 1994b: 53), Structure 1 apparently served as an elite funerary monument. Three elaborate tombs, one dating to the Terminal Preclassic (though altered in the Early Classic) and two dating to the Late/Terminal Classic period, have been discovered in the structure (Andres 1998; Pyburn 1998: 279; Wrobel et al. 1997). Areal excavation and trenching of Structure 1 suggests that the facade increasingly came to resemble that of Structure B-6 at Altun Ha, with a vaulted gallery built across the outset axial stairway during the Late or Terminal Classic period (e.g., Pendergast 1982: 53, fig. 30). Poor preservation of what appears to be Postclassic remodeling of the building's facade limits our understanding of the final portion of the construction sequence. Architectural modification thought to postdate A.D. 900, however, takes several forms.

Clearing along Structure 1's western base during the 1998 and 1999 field seasons revealed the addition of an axial stairway to the front of the building. Although poorly preserved, the stairway consists of at least eight broad steps constructed from double courses of rough-cut limestone blocks (Figure 18.3). The quality of the construction is lower than that of underlying Classic-period staircases, with most steps formed from multiple irregular limestone fragments rather than the carefully cut blocks of earlier construction phases. Traces of plaster remaining on several risers suggest the quality of the masonry was concealed beneath a thick plaster coating. Excavation indicates the stairs were outset from the building's facade and measured more than five meters in width. Although additional excavation is necessary to further explore the function and extent of the addition, the stairs apparently extended from the most recent plaza floor (Plaza Floor 1) to a badly eroded platform surface located approximately three meters up the western facade. The presence of Postclassic incised redware sherds (similar to those reported from Lamanai [Pendergast 1981a]) on the stairs and in the construction fill suggests an Early to Middle Postclassic–period date. The overall pattern of Postclassic maintenance and renewal of earlier ceremonial architecture strongly parallels Postclassic activities focused on Structure N 10-9 at neighboring Lamanai (Pendergast 1986a: 241).

Six or seven courses of dressed stone protruding through the humus near Structure 1's summit suggest late construction was not limited to the western stair-base. The proximity of these features to the surface and their association with Mayapán-style effigy censer sherds suggest this construction also dates to the Postclassic period, though further investigation is necessary before this can be conclusively established. If contemporary with the plaza-level construction, these features would point to large-scale Postclassic modification of Structure 1's facade.

Postclassic modification of Classic-period ceremonial structures has received little regional treatment. Such construction is not, however, limited to Chau Hiix. Construction focused on Structure 1 at Chau Hiix closely parallels Postclassic refurbishment of larger Classic-period ceremonial structures at Cerros and Lamanai. While the back and sides of Temple Structure N 10-9 at Lamanai were allowed to decay following the structure's abandonment at the end of the Classic period, lower portions of the facade and the central stairway were rebuilt during the Postclassic and stair-side outsets were added in the twelfth or thirteenth centuries (Pendergast 1986a: 241). Classic-period temple structures at Cerros were also the focus of late construction activities as indicated by Middle Postclassic (A.D. 1150–1300) renewal of the Late Preclassic stairway and superstructure of Structure 4B, and the addition of a Late Postclassic superstructure on the summit of Structure 29 (Freidel 1986c: 9, 11; Walker 1990: 317–318). Freidel's (1986c: 9) description of the "rough slab stairway" leading from Structure 4A to the Postclassic superstructure atop Structure 4B closely corresponds with the construction activity documented at Chau Hiix. Fragments of Xakbeeb Incised vessels (similar to Middle Postclassic redware "chalices" from Lamanai) were associated with Postclassic architectural renewal at Cerros (Walker 1990: 317), as they are at

18.3 Postclassic renewal of axial stairway, Structure 1, Chau Hiix.

Chau Hiix. Taken together, these architectural data suggest portions of northern Belizean ceremonial structures continued to be used at centers that sustained Postclassic populations. Related patterns of ceremonial behavior may be reflected

in the performance of Postclassic ceremonial activities on Classic-period platforms in other parts of the southern lowlands (e.g., Fry 1985: 132).

Structures 8 and 9

Another late addition to the central platform, Structure 9, was added no earlier than the Terminal Classic and possibly significantly later (David Pendergast,
personal communication). Although seriously disturbed by plant and animal activity, this small structure appears to have been conceived as an altar, placed
immediately in front of Structure 1. The structure consisted of a pile of poorly
aligned cut stones that were probably originally part of Structure 1's facade.

Drainage created by the addition of Structure 9 to the central platform encouraged the growth of cohune palms, which pull lower deposits up into more
recent layers of strata as they grow. Structure 9 was situated over a Terminal
Classic burial, but the original deposition of the burial may predate the construction of the altar, since similarly positioned platform burials are known from other
Belizean sites (McAnany 1995). When the site was discovered, Structure 9 was
littered with Late Postclassic offerings, including incensarios, jade beads, animal
teeth, a tapir skull, and shell fragments (Cook 1996: 8–9; Cook and Pyburn 1995: 5).

Structure 8, which in reality consists of a square alignment of a single course
of cut stones without foundations and associated debris, is located immediately
north of Structure 9 on the central platform. In the absence of associated materials, the significance of the alignment is unknown; nevertheless, the construction
appears to be deliberate and encloses an area sufficient for a small dwelling.
Whatever its purpose, this feature was clearly constructed after Structure 1 ceased
to be maintained, since it is unevenly aligned with other central platform structures and would have blocked access to the central stairway. In fact, like Structure 9, it seems probable that the stones used to create Structure 8's wall alignments were robbed from Structure 1, though whether they were ripped from an
extant facade or simply pulled from structural tumble is unknown. Also like Structure 9, Structure 8 was associated with smashed effigy incensarios deposited
after some period of abandonment in the most recent layer of humus (Cook and
Pyburn 1995: 5).

Both the form and placement of Chau Hiix Structures 8 and 9 call to mind
structures reported at other locations in northern Belize. Like the Chau Hiix structures, Lamanai structure N9-59 is a low masonry platform constructed at plaza
level on the primary axis west of Classic-period Temple Structure N9-56 during
the Postclassic period (Pendergast 1981a: 51, 1986a: 242). Two small masonry
platforms were also constructed west of Plaza N 10/3 at Lamanai during the
fifteenth or sixteenth century (Pendergast 1986a: 241). The Lamanai platforms
differ somewhat from those at Chau Hiix in that they supported repositioned
Classic-period stelae.[1] David Pendergast's (1981a: 51) observation that "the core
of the [N9-59] platform yielded . . . an offering of two vessels accompanied by

jade and shell beads" and several Postclassic censers (Pendergast 1985: 100, fig. 4) indicates that the Lamanai and Chau Hiix structures were the focus of similar offertory activities, including the burning of incense.

Looking beyond Chau Hiix, Structures 8 and 9 fall into a surprisingly wide-spread class of Postclassic architecture. Described as "altars" in Diane Chase's (1985b) examination of Postclassic ritual, low freestanding square or rectangular platforms showing no evidence of superimposed structures have been identified in Classic-period ceremonial contexts at a variety of locations in northern Belize, including Santa Rita Corozal (Chase 1985b: 115), Lamanai (Pendergast 1986a: 241), Cerros (Scarborough and Freidel, personal communication 2000), and Chan Chen (Sidrys 1983: 103, 117), as well as farther afield at Cozumel (Rathje and Sabloff 1975). Poorly preserved but possibly related Postclassic features additionally were constructed on the summits of Classic-period temple structures at Altun Ha (Pendergast 1982: 139–140; 1986a: 234) and Cerros (Freidel 1986c: 9, 11; Scarborough 1991a: 52; Walker 1990: 273, 319), and formally similar structures (described as "shrines" by some authors—e.g., Potter 1982) have been reported abutting Classic-period ceremonial structures at Lamanai (Pendergast 1988: 6–7) and Colhá (Potter 1982: 103–104). As in the case of the fully detached platforms at Chau Hiix, a variety of ceremonial deposits including censers (Pendergast 1985: 100, fig. 4 d, f, h; Walker 1990: 269), obsidian blades (Sidrys 1983: 122; Walker 1990: 273), ceremonial ceramics (Pendergast 1982: 140), shell and jadeite ornaments (Pendergast 1981a: 51), and human burials (Chase 1985b: 116) have been recovered in association with these Postclassic platforms.

Structure 2

Structure 2 is believed to have been an elite residential compound during most of the occupation of Chau Hiix. At the time of discovery it contained no standing architecture and clearly had been burned and shallowly plowed to be planted in corn at some recent period. In addition to the agricultural disturbance, animal burrowing and regrowth of the cohune palm forest over the structure have destroyed the upper twenty to fifty centimeters of stratigraphy. The stratigraphy destroyed, however, was not that of architectural construction but of the interment of at least seventy individuals in the building, both during and subsequent to its use as a residence. Some of the burials were interred under living floors, but these were disturbed by later interments that cut through and disturbed earlier layers (Andres and Wrobel 2000; Wrobel 1999; Wrobel et al. 2000). Because the burials associated with floors would have been covered with plaster, and because the ultimate layers of architecture are missing (from plowing and erosion), burials recovered from Structure 2 within five centimeters of the modern ground surface were not the most recent. The latest burials, which were excavated from the ground surface of the abandoned building after significant deterioration had occurred, are considerably deeper and penetrate the Terminal

Classic material nearest the surface. The copper-associated Postclassic burials described above are more deeply buried below modern ground surface than most of the earlier burials, a stratigraphic anomaly that proved somewhat challenging in the context of extreme bioturbation. Nevertheless, ceramic associations with these interments correspond exactly to the Terminal through Late Postclassic types described by Graham (1987b) at Lamanai, with few exceptions.

POSTCLASSIC AND COLONIAL–PERIOD CERAMICS AT CHAU HIIX

The majority of the late ceramics from the main platform have been recovered from caches, burials, and surface deposits associated with Structures 1, 2, 3, 8, and 9 in the site center. The recovery of Terminal Classic through Late Postclassic ceramics from Structures 1 and 2, as well as from surface contexts in many surrounding residential groups (Cook and Pyburn 1995; Fry 1997), indicates that Chau Hiix continued to be occupied long after many neighboring Maya centers were abandoned early in the tenth century A.D. (e.g., Pendergast 1992: 71–72). Excavations of Structures 1 and 2 also indicate that Early Postclassic material is frequently mixed with Terminal Classic diagnostic pottery, or with Middle Postclassic wares with few breaks in the stratigraphy—a fact that suggests populations of the Late and Terminal Classic were the ancestors of at least some of the site's Postclassic residents. Chau Hiix's late ceramic assemblages furthermore point to significant contact between Lamanai and Chau Hiix extending through at least the Late Postclassic period.

While analysis of the Chau Hiix ceramic assemblage is ongoing, the site's Postclassic ceramics closely resemble those described for Lamanai (Robert Fry and David Pendergast, personal communication). Here, we provide a preliminary description of the most distinctive Terminal through Late Postclassic vessels recovered at Chau Hiix, focusing on the inclusion of Postclassic redwares and censerwares in ceremonial deposits, the distribution of these vessels in the site center, and the extent to which the formal and decorative features of post–A.D. 900 Chau Hiix ceramics point to Lamanai as their probable point of origin.

Types of Postclassic Deposits: Caches, Burials, and "Smash and Scatter"

Two caches with pottery have been recovered from Structure 1. While this number is small compared to that at Lamanai (Pendergast 1998), the deposits are revealing, for they suggest both continuity and discontinuity in the building's use between the Classic and Postclassic periods. Excavated by Ingrid Webber during the 1996 field season, Caches 1 and 2 were intruded into rubble midway up Structure 1's western face. Both axial offerings were placed considerably above the Postclassic construction at Structure 1's base and do not appear to have been directly related to other recognizable Postclassic construction activities.

Cache 1 (Context CHE 50-3-4-96) consists of the pedestal base and several body sherds from a Lamanai-style redware urn that was encountered about forty centimeters below modern ground surface. Although the uppermost layers of soil on the structure have been subject to significant root disturbance, this appears to be a secondary deposit of a previously broken vessel. (This interpretation is based on the fact that a significant number of sherds were never recovered despite screening of the surrounding soil.) The post-slip incised panels of the pedestal base depict serpent and reptile eye motifs (Prudence Rice, personal communication 1997) similar to those reported on vessels at Lamanai, Marco González, and in central Petén (Graham and Pendergast 1989: 9; Pendergast 1982: 51; P. Rice 1983a, 1983b, 1989).

A second cache (Cache 2/Context CHE 50-3-39-96) was recovered several meters away from Cache 1 at approximately the same depth. This offering consisted of two complete vessels placed in a typical lip-to-lip arrangement. The uppermost vessel has been identified as a Terminal Classic San José V–type redware bowl that was inverted over a probable Early to Middle Postclassic polychrome bowl (Robert Fry, personal communication). The orange and red bowl has three black concentric bands below the rim and an unidentifiable central figure.

Placement of similar Postclassic deposits in the collapse debris of monumental structures at Lamanai and Altun Ha (Pendergast 1998: 59, fig. 6.6; 1982: 39–42) demonstrates that caching was characteristic of Postclassic ceremonialism in northern Belize. It is noteworthy that earlier temple structures continued to be receptacles for caches during the Postclassic period (Andres 2000), but caching practices do seem to have shifted at these sites, since offerings are often intruded into crumbling buildings rather than incorporated into new construction (see Pendergast 1981b: 4, however, for an exception to this pattern). Although resulting in similar deposits, continuity in Classic to Postclassic caching activity was probably motivated by different concerns at different locations. In the case of abandoned centers, caching practices reflect periodic visits by residents of other communities, and cache placement may have been determined by practical considerations such as structure size and accessibility. At centers such as Lamanai and Chau Hiix, people may actually have remembered the locations used by their forebears. Offerings may therefore reflect revitalization activities (see Fry 1985) perhaps intended to reinvigorate entirely abandoned communities (Hammond and Bobo 1994) or rededications of dilapidated structures at still-populated centers (Pendergast 1998: 59; Walker 1990). Despite the lack of maintenance of the monuments, people may still have made offerings to signify attachment to place.

In addition to three Classic-period tomb burials, two Postclassic burials have been excavated in the rubble overlying Structure 1. One of these was placed inside an enormous Postclassic vessel. Encountered in Operation 50-6 during the 1996 field season, Burial 45 was placed midway up Structure 1's western facade on the building's primary axis. Like most urn burials, the skeletal elements had been displaced within the vessel as decomposition took place, but positioning allowed recognition of the burial as a primary interment (Della Cook, personal communication).

The most outstanding feature of this burial was the elaborate vessel placed over the individual. Made to contain an adult male, the vessel is truly massive, measuring between 75 and 100 centimeters in height, with an orifice diameter of approximately 50 centimeters. The vessel's overall proportions, incised decoration, pedestal-base, and segmented flange so closely resemble features of Middle Postclassic "Buk"-phase (A.D. 1100–1350) urns reported from Lamanai that the vessel was almost certainly manufactured at the neighboring center (Andres and Fry 1997). Furthermore, the context in which the vessel was recovered and its function at Chau Hiix link it to Lamanai, where nearly identical vessels were included as offerings in opulent burials and also served as Postclassic burial containers (Pendergast 1981a: 47).

Structure 2, immediately south of Structure 1, almost certainly served as the major elite residence during occupation of the site. Although relatively unprepossessing, consisting of small platforms arranged around the edges of a large platform, its location at the entrance to the central platform and its very lengthy occupation argue for its elite significance. In fact, despite extensive excavation of the structure, including meticulous attention to stratigraphy, little is known about the Classic-period form of the structure other than that it was enlarged several times, because standing walls were apparently razed in the Terminal Classic or later, and subsequent floors were obliterated when the structure became a necropolis in the Postclassic (Wrobel 1999).

Analysis of the burial data from Structure 2, which include both complete and partial primary and secondary inhumations, indicates that a minimum number of seventy individuals is represented. The skeletal information is still under investigation, but ceramic associations make it clear that the vast majority of the interments occurred in the Early to Middle Postclassic. Although whole at the time of burial, most burial vessels have been broken and disturbed both by the bioturbation typical of the site and the repeated reuse of the structure for additional burials. In many cases it has been impossible to distinguish the mortuary furniture of one interment from that of a later intrusive interment, especially because the Maya excavators were apparently willing to place pieces of earlier burials they encountered, including both grave goods and disturbed skeletal bits, into the new grave they were digging. Although this makes for a stratigraphic and chronological nightmare, it provides some very important insight into the significance of burial in the structure, which in the Postclassic was quite popular, but not because of a promise of "perpetual care" or multigenerational reverence. The vessels collected from Structure 2 (and some of them are from caches laid down during construction episodes) are overwhelmingly creamy orange chalices and redware bowls identified by Graham as Terminal Classic to Early and Middle Postclassic (illustrated in Figures 18.4 and 18.5). A complete analysis of these vessels is pending.

The final types of deposits, including large numbers of Postclassic ceramics, are composed of vessels smashed or placed on several of the structures bordering the main plaza. Dubbed "smash and scatter" deposits by David Pendergast (1998: 59) at Lamanai, these deposits generally consist of two distinct wares at Chau Hiix: unslipped Mayapán-style (Chen Mul Modeled) censerwares and fragments of a variety of Postclassic redware vessel forms (Graham 1987b; Graham and Pendergast 1989; Pendergast 1981a). Although deposits of these two wares are not entirely discrete, they probably represent surface deposits from different time periods that became mixed in the humus.

On some outlying structures at Chau Hiix, complete or nearly complete shallow Postclassic bowls appear to have been placed or even stacked on top of the larger structures in the largest plazuela groups. In at least three cases, complete unslipped or redware bowls were encountered within the humus layer or even the leaf litter above abandoned residences. These deposits originally suggested continuous occupation of these structures, because they are not clearly ceremonial in character. Subsequent excavations suggest that these superficial deposits were made after a period of abandonment and probably do represent offerings rather than domestic debris.

Types of Postclassic Pottery: Incised Redwares and Modeled Incensarios

Numerous fragments of elaborate incised redware vessels similar to those reported from "Buk"-phase (ca. A.D. 1100–1350) contexts at Lamanai (Graham 1987b: 81–88) have been recovered from humus and collapse debris overlying Structure 1 and in the vicinity of Structure 2 at Chau Hiix. Although deposits are common in the site center, they have generally proved challenging to excavate, define, and classify (Andres 2000).

The layers of fill and construction material eroding from abandoned Maya monumental structures at a steep angle do not move downward at the same rate. Layers closer to the surface move faster than deeper layers that only gradually become unstable as exterior erosion removes ever deeper layers. Consequently, surface deposits are difficult to recover from Structure 1 in their entirety since they tend to be distributed through downwardly mobile humus and collapse debris at a 45-degree angle; concentrations of sherds are exposed, defined, and removed only to have additional sherds (often from the same vessels) appear well downslope from initial sherd concentrations. This pattern is characteristic of a number of deposits encountered during excavation of Structure 1, with the uppermost fragments at times separated from the most deeply buried sherds by as much as seventy centimeters of disturbed and collapsing fill. Often, neither the higher nor the lower portions are in situ. Despite this complication, both the censer forms and the evidence of burning associated with them and surrounding (if somewhat displaced) soil suggest that the concentrations accompanied offertory incense burning. These deposits include substantial portions of at least a

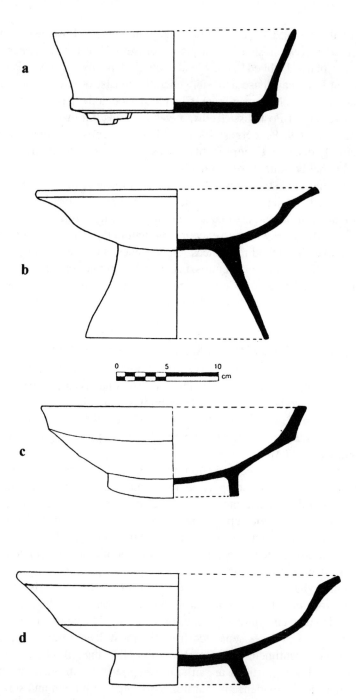

18.4 Terminal and Postclassic–period ceramics from Chau Hiix: (a) ?, (b) "chalice," (c) San José V-type bowl (?), (d) San José V-type bowl.

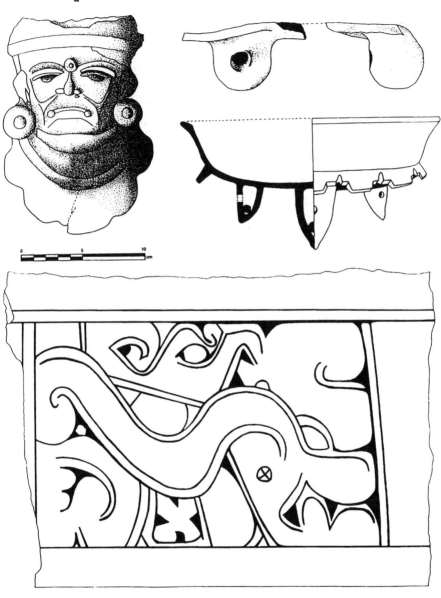

18.5 Postclassic-period ceramics from Chau Hiix: (a) Mayapán-style effigy incensario, (b) vented vessel foot, (c) tripod bowl from Structure 2, (d) incised panel from Postclassic "censer."

dozen Postclassic vessels, including Lamanai-style "chalices" and post-slip incised redware bowls.

The numbers of fragments from single vessels clearly distinguish these offertory deposits from random sherds eroded from building fill. As some of the vessels were found in the humus, we initially viewed all such deposits as offerings intruded into the surface of abandoned portions of monumental buildings. However, subsequent excavations failed to demonstrate that each vessel was actually a "cache" in the formal sense of the term since some were probably simply placed on the surface of the abandoned building (e.g., Coe 1959; Loten and Pendergast 1984: 5). Ultimately, extensive root disturbance and the instability of the surrounding matrix suggest the vessels were associated with post-abandonment surfaces, whether buried in them or placed upon them.

Mayapán-style effigy censerwares occur in "smash and scatter" deposits on several structures in and around the main plaza (Figures 18.2 and 18.5a). A concentration of at least a half dozen smashed effigy censers was initially discovered together with the handle of a Postclassic ladle censer on the surface of Structure 9. Additional censer sherds were also found in surface contexts in the main plaza on Structure 8 and on Structure 26, the northernmost structure in a residential group southwest of the site center (Cook 1996: 8–9; Cook and Pyburn 1995: 5).

The greatest concentration of effigy censer sherds is on Structure 1, which had sherds recovered on its summit and eastern and western slopes. Censer fragments and the handle of a second ladle censer were found in the humus during trenching of the structure's centerline between 1995 and 1999. The presence of reduced quantities of censer sherds toward the structure's base suggests that the ceramics eroded from deposits on the building's summit (an interesting consequence of surficial ceramic deposition also noted at Cerros; Walker 1990: 269).

Formal Features of Late Ceramics at Chau Hiix

Although ceramics recovered from late deposits at Chau Hiix share certain formal and decorative features with vessels from several locations in Belize, they most closely resemble vessels reported at Lamanai. San José V–type pedestal base redware bowls are particularly common in Terminal Classic–Early Postclassic–period ceremonial deposits at Chau Hiix, having been recovered mainly from Structure 1 and from several burials in Structure 2, but also from a few locations outside the site center (Figures 18.4c and 18.4d). Characterized by sharp medial angles, flaring rims, low pedestal bases, and orange slips, this form is identified by Graham (1987b: 78) as a marker of the Terminal Classic throughout Belize, occurring in a number of types, including Roaring Creek Red and Daylight Orange (Gifford 1976), and at a number of locations ranging from San José (Thompson 1939) to T'au Witz in the Stann Creek District (Graham 1985: 220, fig. 6b) and Lamanai (Graham 1987b: 76d) to Altun Ha (Pendergast 1982: 163; fig. 93c).

While the range of "Buk"-phase (A.D. 1050–1350) forms is less extensive at Chau Hiix than at Lamanai, the Chau Hiix assemblage includes examples of the Lamanai "chalice" and "censer" forms as well as many comparable bowl forms. As at Lamanai (e.g., Graham 1987b: 84, fig. 5d and e; Pendergast 1981a: 45, fig. 15), Chau Hiix chalices are characterized by low basins set atop high pedestal bases (Figure 18.4b). Slips are bright orange and some pedestal bases display elaborate incised decoration (often complex geometric designs). Contexts of chalice recovery are also similar at Lamanai and Chau Hiix, with chalices found on the stairs of Classic-period ceremonial structures at N10-9 Lamanai (Pendergast 1981a: 51) and Structure 1 at Chau Hiix.

The distinctive "Buk"-phase "censers" originally reported by Pendergast (1981a) are also present at Chau Hiix. As at Lamanai, these ceremonial vessels are defined by their massive proportions, orange slips, pedestal bases, segmented flanges, and bands of post-slip incised decoration around their pedestal bases and rims (Figures 18.5d and 18.6e) (Andres and Fry 1997). Resemblances between the vessels at Lamanai and Chau Hiix extend to the urns' decoration, which often includes stylized serpent and reptilian motifs (Graham and Pendergast 1989: 11; Pendergast 1981a: 48, 47, fig. 20) (Figure 18.5d). The enormous burial urn from Structure 1 is a "Buk" urn, as is the pedestal base of the similar smaller vessel included in a nearby offering. Fragments of other formally similar urns are periodically encountered in humus contexts on the centerline of Structure 1.

The final group of "Buk"-phase vessels present at Chau Hiix consists of several redware bowls recovered from surface contexts on Structure 1 and accompanying Postclassic burials in Structure 2. Included among these are shallow, footless bowls with exterior bands of naturalistic and geometric incised decoration (Figure 18.6a-d, f) (similar to those illustrated by Pendergast 1981a: 50, fig. 26b and Graham 1987b: 84, fig. 5j and k) and tripod bowls with segmented flanges, hollow vented feet, and post-slip incised decoration (Figure 18.5c) (also see Pendergast 1981a: 50, fig. 26k, m-o). As noted, simple red or unslipped bowls occur at some outlying structures at the site.

Although the quantity of "Buk"-phase ceramics recovered from the main platform at Chau Hiix is the third largest in Belize, there is currently no convincing evidence (e.g., no kilns, unfired lumps of clay, concentrations of waste sherds, and few obvious tools such as burnishing stones from Postclassic contexts) that the vessels were actually produced at the site. Looking beyond Chau Hiix, several locations initially appear to be possible points of origin for the site's Postclassic redwares. As discussed by Liz Graham (1987b: 86), Middle Postclassic "Buk"-phase ceramics are currently known from several Belizean sites, having been recovered at Altun Ha (Pendergast 1982: 140), Mayflower (Graham 1985: 222), and Negroman-Tipu (Graham 1987b: 86). More recently, similar incised redwares and vessel forms parallel to those at Lamanai (chalices in particular) have been reported at Laguna de On (Mock 1998a: 193–194). Because limited numbers of

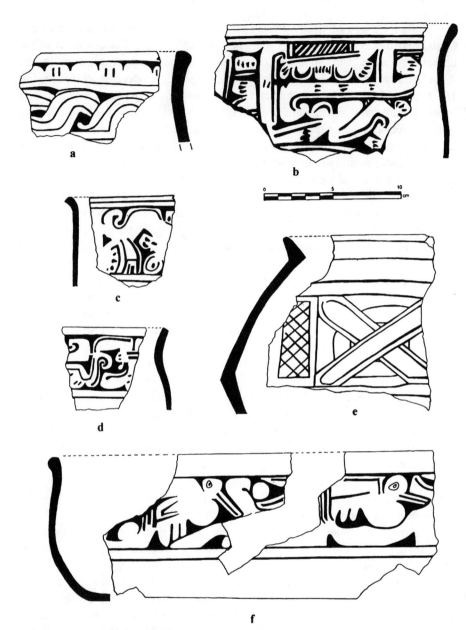

18.6 Postclassic-period ceramics from Chau Hiix: (a-d, f) post-slip incised redware bowls, (e) "censer" fragment.

"Buk"-like sherds have been found at these locations, it is reasonably safe to rule out these communities as sources for the Chau Hiix vessels. Large quantities of "Buk" "censers" comparable to those at Chau Hiix have been reported from roughly contemporary deposits (A.D. 1130–1300) at Marco González on Ambergris Cay (Graham and Pendergast 1989: 9, fig 7a-f), however, the vessels' diminutive size (particularly that of the urns) and yellower slips distinguish them from those at both Lamanai (ibid.: 8, 11) and Chau Hiix. The massive size, lustrous orange slip, and incision of the Chau Hiix vessels bear a much closer resemblance to the Postclassic Lamanai assemblage than to that of Marco González. Similarities between the Lamanai and Chau Hiix vessels are so striking, in fact, that Robert Fry believes the "Buk"-phase ceramics recovered at Chau Hiix were manufactured at the larger center and brought to Chau Hiix (Andres and Fry 1997), though the unwieldy size suggests that the potter may have traveled rather than the pot.

The Late Postclassic ceramic assemblage at Chau Hiix is smaller than that of Middle Postclassic (A.D. 1050–1350) times, indicating decreased use of the site's ceremonial precinct. The large numbers of Mayapán-style effigy censers recovered on the main platform and the presence of post-slip incised "sag-bottom" redware bowls with hollow cylindrical feet (markers of "Cib"-phase [A.D. 1350–1450] deposits at Lamanai—Graham 1987b: 88–91) indicate continued ceremonial use of the main group after the Middle Postclassic (Figure 18.5b). As discussed by Elizabeth Graham (ibid.), large Mayapán-style effigy censers like those at Chau Hiix appear during the fourteenth century at Lamanai and persist into the subsequent "Yglesias" phase (A.D. 1450–1700). Ultimately, strong formal and decorative similarities between these vessels at Lamanai and Chau Hiix and the anchoring of the Lamanai ceramic assemblage with C-14 dates point to continuous activity on the main platform at Chau Hiix up to the time of Spanish contact.

DISTINCTIVE ARCHAEOLOGICAL PATTERNS AT CHAU HIIX

While there are numerous ceramic and architectural similarities between Lamanai and Chau Hiix, there are interesting differences between the two centers besides the latter's much more modest proportions and lack of Spanish artifacts. Postclassic people at Chau Hiix were inclined to build their shrines and even possibly their houses with cut stone ripped from monumental architecture. Final occupations of Structure 2 and reuse of Structure 6 resemble "squatter residences" reported at some sites, although the lack of standing architecture makes comparison difficult. In some areas of the site, modest constructions are built over earlier more prepossessing buildings after a period of abandonment and decay. Five small Late Postclassic houses were, for example, built immediately adjacent to the north edge of the central platform at Chau Hiix, some of these making use of suspiciously well-dressed stones.

As noted, several structures at Chau Hiix, including the main "palace" group, were used as necropoli during the Postclassic, and similar patterns have been noted in the upper layers of several palaces situated near the site center. In contrast to this practice, late burials at Lamanai—or Indian Church, as the Maya site became known in the time of the Spanish—were placed in a Christian-style cemetery (Graham 1991).

SUMMARY AND CONCLUSIONS

In conclusion, we think it is fair to speculate that Chau Hiix was one of the Maya communities that "had no permanent Spanish residents" but was "a major attraction for native refugees fleeing the north" (Jones 1998: 40). We base this interpretation on the abundance of Postclassic evidence from the site, including the production of locally familiar stone tools, the reconstruction of new houses and addition of new elements of ceremonial structures, and the continued association of ceremonial ceramics with the Classic-period ceremonial architecture. This is not to suggest, however, that cultural discontinuities do not exist across the Classic-Postclassic divide and that local differences do not distinguish Chau Hiix from other Postclassic centers. Postclassic practices at Chau Hiix are, for example, set apart from those at neighboring Lamanai by the destruction of some earlier architecture and the increased use of palaces for burial of elite dead. A possible explanation is that, though many of the original residents remained at Chau Hiix, new people with slightly different customs and perhaps disproportionately higher status joined the community, because it was often the elites who were most threatened by the Spanish or were better able to flee them. This may account for the overcrowding of the elite burial area in Structure 2.

Jones (1998: 40) also notes that "[t]he townspeople engaged in a lively underground trade in cacao, forest products, metal tools, and cotton cloth that bypassed Spanish controls but required contact with the Itzas and other regional groups." Chau Hiix is actually situated on a trade route between Lamanai and Tipu, and Tipu was itself on the route that led to the Itza capital of Tayasal. The fact that both Lamanai and Tipu reverted to certain aboriginal practices after flirtations with conversion to Christianity (Graham 1991: 330–331; Jones 1998; Pendergast 1986b: 1, 5) presents the possibility that residents of Chau Hiix were equally unreceptive to Spanish economic and religious practices. Furthermore, the fact that Chau Hiix was remote yet connected to other Postclassic centers via Classic-period trade routes would have placed Chau Hiix in an excellent position to engage in illicit trade. As suggested by the site's probable nonlocal Postclassic ceremonial ceramics, connections clearly existed with settlements such as Lamanai during the Postclassic. Differences in burial patterns in Structure 2 suggest Chau Hiix may even have been a destination for residents of Lamanai or other towns who fled to more remote communities to avoid the demands of Spanish *encomienda*.

Returning to the logistical difficulties mentioned at the beginning of this paper, we suspect that the extensive system of canals and dams surrounding Chau Hiix was no longer in use during the Postclassic. Without maintenance of these features, access to the site would have been difficult, as it is today. The site is not easily accessible to strangers during high water, because the entrance from Spanish Creek is through one canal that could easily be concealed with a small amount of displaced vegetation. In the dry season, when it is possible to walk the one-kilometer distance from the permanent watercourse of Spanish Creek and across the base of the dry lagoon directly to the site, visitors would have to pass across a large area of open ground, where they could be easily spotted and routed or picked off by archers (D. Rice 1988: 243). (Small quantities of projectile points have been recovered from superficial deposits at Chau Hiix.) In sum, Chau Hiix's favorable combination of lagoon resources, access to trade routes, and easy concealment and defensibility are factors that probably contributed to the site's residential and ceremonial significance between the years of the "collapse" and the arrival of Europeans in Belize. It seems likely that the residents of Chau Hiix had exactly as much contact with the Spanish as they wished and no more, due to the community's ancient and strategic location.

NOTE

1. This assumes that the Chau Hiix platforms did not support repositioned stelae that were subsequently looted. Monuments do appear to have been removed from other areas of the main platform as well as from smaller ceremonial groups surrounding the site center (Pyburn 1991). The burial in Structure 9 was encountered when a disturbed area on the eastern side of the structure was investigated. Whether the disturbance to the casually constructed building was caused by the removal of a stela or by hunters dislodging an animal from its burrow, some sort of human activity is indicated. Crooked Tree residents describe the removal and destruction of at least one monument from the vicinity of Chau Hiix during the past thirty years.

ACKNOWLEDGMENTS

During the ten-year span of the Chau Hiix Archaeological Project our work has been permitted by the Department of Archaeology of the government of Belize. Mr. Harriot Topsey, Mr. John Morris, Mr. Alan Moore, Mr. Brian Woodeye, Ms. Teresa Batty, and Mr. George Thompson have all provided us with information, guidance, and encouragement. Investigations at Chau Hiix have been funded by National Science Foundation Grant #9507204, Indiana University, the Glenn A. Black Laboratory of Archaeology, as well as by the generous contributions of the Raymond Foundation. Numerous scholars, graduate students, and field school students have contributed to our understanding of Chau Hiix through their participation in mapping and excavation projects and the analysis of archaeological materials. We are particularly grateful to Dr. Robert E. Fry for his ceramic evaluations and to Michael F. Lane for generating the map of the site center included in this paper. We would also like to acknowledge Mr. Rudolph Crawford, his family, and the residents of Crooked Tree Village, Belize, without whose efforts and sustained interest investigations at Chau Hiix would be impossible.

19

HIGH TIMES IN THE HILL COUNTRY
A PERSPECTIVE FROM THE TERMINAL CLASSIC PUUC REGION

Kelli Carmean, Nicholas Dunning, and Jeff Karl Kowalski

ere we present our current understanding of Puuc archaeology as part of a broader effort to assemble comparative regional material for the Terminal Classic Maya lowlands. In working toward this goal, we first review recent archaeological projects in the Puuc region, presenting a summary of new architectural, ceramic, settlement pattern, iconographic, and epigraphic evidence and interpretations, emphasizing the Terminal Classic period. This summary is meant to present a sample of recent work, rather than an exhaustive review. We then present our vision of the sociopolitical dynamics of the Puuc polities during the Terminal Classic. Finally, we close this chapter by identifying future directions in which fruitful new work in Puuc archaeology could be directed.

We define the Terminal Classic as that period between A.D. 770 and 950 (see Pollock 1980 for traditional Terminal Classic dates of A.D. 800 to 1000). These were high times in the hill country of Yucatán and Campeche: the major Puuc cities were at their height, their inhabitants constructing architecture in Classic Puuc styles (see Pollock [1980] and Andrews [1995] for discussion of the evolution of Puuc architectural styles) and making and using western Cehpech ceramics. This ceramic tradition stretches back at least into the Late Classic period in association with Early Puuc–style architecture, with some Cehpech ceramics extending even earlier in association with Proto-Puuc and Early Oxkintok architecture (Boucher 1990; Rivera Dorado 1996; Smyth 1998)—a situation that has been a chronological headache for archaeologists working in the northern lowlands. Bey et al. (1997) have suggested a terminological revision for the Epiclassic northern lowlands, naming it the Late Classic, with dates of A.D. 600 to 925. Although we acknowledge the reasoning behind Bey et al.'s argument, we prefer to revise the calendrical dates and retain the Terminal Classic nomenclature so that Puuc chronology remains terminologically comparable with the rest of the Maya lowlands. Furthermore, we point out the obvious correlation between such Terminal Classic hallmarks as the Seibal stelae in the southern lowlands and the eastern Puuc florescence. It is also clear that the appearance of Sotuta-related materials in the Puuc marks a notable regional decline and a significant break with the Terminal Classic Puuc florescence.

The rulers of the Terminal Classic Puuc cities were clearly utilizing southern lowland Classic Maya concepts of kingship, as well as experimenting with variations of shared rulership and integrating "Mexican" elements into their sculpture and architecture (Kowalski 1987; Grube 1994b; Kowalski and Dunning 1999). This blending suggests significant external cultural contacts overlying a basic Maya origin and heritage, mixed with local innovations. Within this varied cultural framework, the Puuc rulers and nobility were able to establish small-scale states that held dominion first over their own hill region and eventually possibly expanding out into limited areas of the northern peninsula. Faced with environmental challenges from an increasingly overpopulated homeland, and military challenges due to the increasing stature of Chichen Itza, many Puuc centers appear to have largely ceased monumental construction by around A.D. 950, with abandonment following either rapidly or slowly thereafter. However, a few Puuc centers were not abandoned in the Terminal Classic and continued to be occupied and construct monumental architecture into the Postclassic.

RECENT ARCHAEOLOGICAL RESEARCH IN THE PUUC REGION

Dunning (1992) suggested that the Terminal Classic settlement system of the Puuc region contained at least seven identifiable hierarchical levels. Communities within the region ranged in size and importance from the giant first-rank sites of Uxmal and Oxkintok (and possibly Yaxhom) to diminutive seventh-rank, seasonally occupied hamlets (Figure 19.1). Archaeological work in the Puuc over the past fifteen years has focused largely on major (Rank 1–3) and large minor (Rank 4–5) sites, a fact that may bias our understanding of regional settlement dynamics. However, some survey work surrounding and between centers has provided data on smaller sites and rural settlement.

Oxkintok

The site of Oxkintok is located at the northwestern tip of the Puuc range, strategically positioned to control the passage of trade between the Campeche coast and the northern plains (Rivera Dorado 1991: 10). Substantial Middle Classic (A.D. 400 to 550) monumental construction appears to have occurred at this

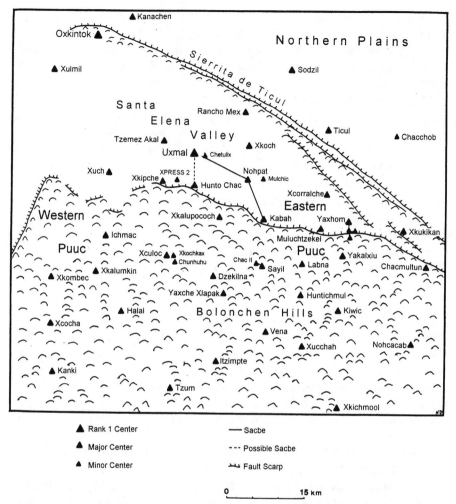

19.1 Map of the Puuc region showing most major sites and minor sites mentioned in the text.

sprawling site, evident in Early Oxkintok–style architecture, architectural inscriptions with Long Count dates, and ceramics with earlier and less substantial construction in the Late Formative and Early Classic (Rivera Dorado 1994, 1996). Middle Classic Oxkintok and other sites in the western Puuc were clearly influenced by Teotihuacan-related material culture and symbolism, a pattern pervasive in other parts of the Maya lowlands at this time (Dunning and Andrews 1994). After A.D. 550, construction in the Proto-Puuc style becomes even more robust, but curiously hieroglyphic texts are no longer evident (García Campillo 1991: 63, 74).

Beginning in A.D. 751, when Stela 20 was erected, a greater number of sculptural and hieroglyphic texts began to reappear at Oxkintok. These monuments feature northern variants of the "Classic Motif," a prominent standing individual, richly dressed, and apparently representing a series of "portraits" of historical rulers and other members of the elite. According to García Campillo (1991: 65) these monuments are typically associated with architecture in the Early Puuc style and were carved between the mid-eighth and the beginning of the ninth century. They feature the "names and portraits of the elite personages of the city" and are characterized by a Classic style of stone carving, which relates the school of Oxkintok to contemporary workshops in the Usumacinta River region and in Palenque.

The last years of the eighth and first years of the ninth century are associated with a diminished number of texts in the central zone of Oxkintok, accompanied by an increase in inscriptions and sculpture in architectural groups located at greater distances from the center. These monuments appear to depict a series of "dignitaries or important local personages who occupied the decorated structures," date to no later than about A.D. 820, and may reflect an "atomization" of political power at Oxkintok prior to a brief hiatus in the inscriptional record between about A.D. 820 and 850 (García Campillo 1991: 70–75).

The Terminal Classic period at Oxkintok is known as the Nak phase (A.D. 850–1000), which witnessed "the triumph of the Puuc subculture or tradition" at the site (Rivera Dorado 1991: 47). Terminal Classic monuments at Oxkintok mark a dramatic shift from the earlier "Classic" stela style at the site, and probably are the products of an influx of new peoples as well as simply new ideas. At least thirteen new monuments (the largest number in the site's history) were erected during this time, located chiefly among the central architectural groups of the city. These new monuments display changes in style and iconography that demonstrate "strong foreign" (probably "Mexican") influences and multifigured and narrative "panel style" compositions (del Mar de Pablo Aguilera 1991: 90). The subject matter of the narrative scenes include audiences in palaces, warriors standing alone or taking captives, or scenes of deity impersonators involved in dance and ritual. One of the earliest of these new monuments is Stela 3 (Figure 19.2), dated to A.D. 849 (10.1.0.0.0 5 Ahaw 2 Kayab) (García Campillo 1991: 70). The display of several figures and what may be two "ruler" figures seated on a bench on the same monument leads us to ask whether the site was governed at this time by a single paramount king or by some sort of council. On the side of the monument is a large warrior figure standing in profile. He holds what may be an atlatl and apparently has a tubular nose-bar. His outsize scale suggests that the power of the elite figures shown on the front of the stela may have depended heavily on the support of such non-Classic-looking fighters. Based on style and known dates, however, it appears that the Terminal Classic monuments were not carved later than the middle of the tenth century.

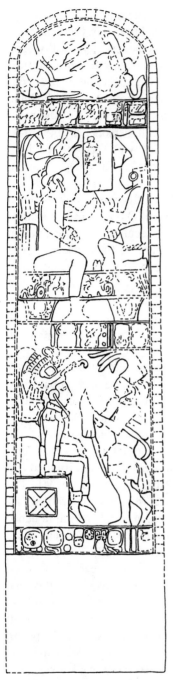

19.2 *Stela 3 from Oxkintok (after Pollock 1980, fig. 544b).*

Partly on the basis of its monumental output, Rivera Dorado (1991: 47) has suggested that Oxkintok became part of a "great political entity or territory" during the Terminal Classic period. However, the site does not seem to have experienced the same type of architectural "boom" that marked the same period at eastern Puuc centers such as Uxmal, Kabah, or Sayil. Indeed, Rivera Dorado (1991: 47) notes that few imposing Classic Puuc–style structures have been discovered at Oxkintok, although late veneers were added to some major structures and small, late structures abound in the site's residential areas. For this reason, Rivera Dorado suggests that Oxkintok lost power during the Terminal Classic, as the political, economic, and military power of Uxmal and other eastern Puuc centers increased. Intriguingly, the city reached its greatest areal extent and probable population apogee between A.D. 850 and 950 (López de la Rosa and Velázquez Morlet 1992), suggesting that it continued to flourish as an important urban and economic center even as its political status was waning. García Campillo (1991: 75) notes that the "mini-hiatus" between the Late Classic and Terminal Classic monumental traditions may reflect an "important political crisis" that involved violent episodes connected with the purposeful destruction of some of the site's earlier monuments and the militaristic emphasis in the iconography of the Terminal Classic sculptures. It seems possible that the replacement of the more Classic sculptural tradition at the site by the more non-Classic monuments signals the dissolution of an earlier dynasty and powerful local lineages and their replacement (probably by force) by new leadership with strong ties to Uxmal and/ or other eastern Puuc cities. Unfortunately, there is a paucity of settlement data for the area between Oxkintok and Uxmal that might shed light on the relationship between these two important centers.

Excavations in the ballcourt revealed the intentional destruction and burial of the ring stones toward the end of the Terminal Classic. This pattern is also seen at Uxmal and Edzná (Rivera Dorado 1994: 56–57) and may suggest the ceremonial as well as literal ending of significant occupation of the site. Residential occupation at Oxkintok dropped dramatically after A.D. 950, but residual, localized occupation continued in some parts of the site until sometime between A.D. 1000 and 1050 (López de la Rosa and Velázquez Morlet 1992).

Uxmal

Although Late Preclassic ceramics have been found in non-architectural contexts at Uxmal, the principal occupation of this large site clearly dates to the Late and Terminal Classic periods (Barrera Rubio 1987; Brainerd 1958; Smith 1971). A few Middle Classic, Proto-Puuc–style buildings have been identified at Uxmal, but the first significant surge in construction appears to coincide with the Early Puuc architectural style beginning around A.D. 700 (Andrews 1995). Interpretations of the post-conquest Books of Chilam Balam place the "founding" of Uxmal by the Tutul Xiw lineage in the mid-eighth century A.D., perhaps coming to the Puuc from Tikal (Schele, Grube, and Boot 1998; Schele and Mathews 1998: 259). Indeed, the majority of Uxmal's construction probably dates to the Classic Puuc (A.D. 770 to 950), with much of the major construction occurring late in that period (Andrews 1995; Kowalski 1987).

Uxmal's architecture, art, iconography, and epigraphy indicate that it probably had a political organization based on the principle of "divine kingship" during the Terminal Classic. At Uxmal most stelae were erected on a specialized Stela Platform, a pattern common in major eastern Puuc sites (e.g., Sayil, Itzimpte, Yaxche Xlapak, and Yaxhom). These monuments display different figural compositions and formats and, like stelae and other monumental art at various northern Maya sites, they feature a blend of traditional stylistic and iconographic features that relate them to the earlier Classic monuments of the southern lowlands. However, the stelae also incorporate non-Classic, localized, and/or possibly foreign stylistic and iconographic features. These indicate they were carved during a period of dramatic change in the Maya world, including the expansion of inter-regional exchange networks that linked northern Maya centers with other Mesoamerican capitals and ports-of-trade. Despite innovative and localized stylistic and iconographic features, the composition of most of Uxmal's stelae continue to concentrate attention on a principal figure, who was likely the divine king (K'ul Ahaw) of Uxmal (e.g., Stelae 1, 2, 3, 4, 5, 6, 11, 12, 14, and 15; see photos and drawings in Graham 1992). Stela 2, perhaps carved about A.D. 810 to 830 (Proskouriakoff 1950: 163–164), is typical of the "Classic Motif" monuments at Uxmal, depicting a single principal figure holding a circular shield and manikin scepter, standing above a basal captive panel and beneath three small winged flying figures (Figure 19.3). The accompanying short glyphic texts are too badly

eroded to read but probably named the ruler and perhaps referred to the event depicted, as well as naming the bound captive in the lower panel. Most
stelae at other major eastern Puuc sites (e.g.,
Xcorralche, Muluchtzekel, Sayil, Yaxche
Xlapak, Itzimpte, and Tzum) also employ
the Classic Motif, with short inscriptions
naming the pictured *ahaw* (Dunning
1992; Proskouriakoff 1950; Von Euw
1977).

Two other Uxmal monuments,
however, Stelae 7 and 13, feature a
different compositional format, the
so-called "panel style" arrangement in
which two (or more) figures of comparable size and visual importance are
placed in upper and lower sculptured
panels that are often separated by glyph
bands (Proskouriakoff 1950). As at
Oxkintok, these monuments may represent some form of political power-
sharing. At Uxmal, as in other Classic
Maya polities, the king's authority depended on the support of other
high-ranking lineages (McAnany 1995).
Another source of evidence regarding
the king's relationship to others in the
community is the columnar monument
known as Altar 10 (Graham 1992: 115).
This altar may originally have been located in an outlying group southeast of
the Uxmal site center, apparently a residential palace compound with a substantial pyramid temple structure on the west
side of the largest courtyard. In addition
to mentioning Lord Chaak, the reigning
K'ul Ahaw of Uxmal, this altar also mentions four other individuals, most prominently an individual named "E-Wits-Ahaw,"
who is named as a *y-itah* (companion) of
Lord Chaak and as a *chok* ("sprout" or
royal offspring) (Grube 1994b: 323–324).

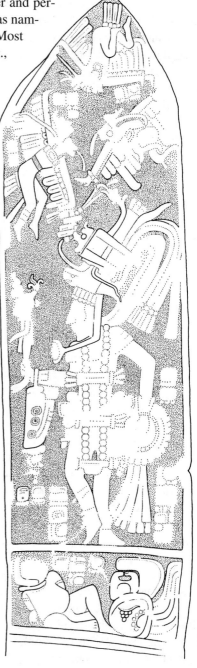

19.3 Stela 2 from Uxmal (after Gra-
ham 1992, p. 87).

The placement of Altar 10 in front of the probable residence of E-Wits-Ahaw publicly displayed his ancestry and his close ties to Lord Chaak.

Lord Chaak (or "*Chan-Chak-K'ak'nal-Ahaw*" [Schele and Mathews 1998]) has been specifically linked to the construction of some of the most spectacular buildings at Uxmal: the House of the Governor, the Nunnery Quadrangle, and Ballcourt 1, all built between A.D. 890 and 915 (Kowalski 1987, 1994; Dunning and Kowalski 1994; Kowalski and Dunning 1999). The Nunnery Quadrangle is a potent symbol of Lord Chaak's political power, in essence forming a huge, elaborate cosmogram placing the king's throne at the center of the Maya universe (Kowalski 1994; Dunning and Kowalski 1994; Kowalski and Dunning 1999; Schele and Mathews 1998). Another testament to this ruler's clout is the House of the Governor, which may have combined aspects of a royal residence with those of a *Popol Na*–type council hall (Kowalski and Dunning 1999), the massive supporting platform of which required a huge labor investment for its construction (Kowalski 1987). As such, Uxmal appears to have represented itself as the symbolic epicenter of the Puuc region.

In the late 1980s Barrera Rubio and Huchím Herrera (1990) conducted architectural restorations of the Great Platform underlying the House of the Governor. Through this work they identified two building stages for the Great Platform; the earliest saw construction underlying the area where the House of the Governor would later be built, and the second saw the enlargement of the Platform's eastern flank (with a stylistic change from squared to rounded corners) and major stairway additions and changes. Ceramic remains are primarily Cehpech, with very minimal amounts of Sotuta mixed with Cehpech in the later construction phase. As such, Barrera and Huchím accept a partial overlap of Uxmal with Chichen Itza and suggest quite late dates for both the Great Platform (late 900s to early 1000s) and the House of the Governor (from A.D. 1000 to 1050). However, these late dates are based in part on the assumption of a late Terminal Classic/Early Postclassic date for Chichen Itza and associated Sotuta ceramics. If Chichen Itza was principally a Terminal Classic site (see Robles, Chapter 21, this volume), or had substantial Terminal Classic occupation and construction episodes, then these dates would be at least a century earlier. Using architectural, iconographic, and epigraphic evidence, other studies of the House of the Governor (Kowalski 1987; Kowalski and Dunning 1999) place its construction much earlier—to A.D. 900 to 915, late in Uxmal's sequence—under the direction of Lord Chaak, whose portrait appears above the main doorway.

Lord Chaak is also depicted on Stela 14, a monument using a variation of the Classic motif but with numerous non-Classic elements, many of which relate iconographically to Chichen Itza (Graham 1992: 108; Kowalski 1987, 1994, 1998). Many other lines of evidence point to a significant relationship, most likely an alliance of some kind, between Uxmal and Chichen Itza around A.D. 900: shared feathered serpent iconography at the Nunnery Quadrangle and Ballcourt 1, the presence of prominent round buildings, and the identification of named Chichen Itza personages in Uxmal's inscriptions (Kowalski 1994, 1998; Kowalski et al. 1993; Dunning and Kowalski 1994; Kowalski and Dunning 1998; Schele and Mathews 1998). It is possible that such an alliance was instrumental in the militaristic expansion of Uxmal during the reign of Lord Chaak (Dunning and Kowalski 1994; Kowalski and Dunning 1999). Battles dating to this period of conquest warfare may be depicted in the murals of Mulchic, a small site near Uxmal (Walters and Kowalski 2000), and in the Upper Temple of the Jaguars at Chichen Itza (Schele and Mathews 1998: 234–235). Whether in alliance with Chichen Itza or purely through its own resources, Uxmal clearly became the paramount city in at least the northern portion of the Puuc in the period around A.D. 900 (Dunning 1992; Dunning and Kowalski 1994). In addition to the construction of huge monumental architecture in the site center at that time, the residential area of the city sprawled to perhaps twenty square kilometers, and the site was linked by *sacbeob* to the neighboring major centers of Nohpat, Kabah, and possibly Hunto Chac (Carrasco 1993; Dunning 1992, 2002). Nevertheless, by no later than A.D. 950 all monumental construction at Uxmal appears to have ceased and a remnant population occupied formerly sacred places in the site center. Any alliance Uxmal may have enjoyed with Chichen Itza was also a thing of the past.

Barrera and Huchím (1990) report a small "Postclassic" (Sotuta ceramic–related) occupation of the site, in the form of two residential "C-shaped" structures on top of the Great Platform of the House of the Governor. Additional "C-shaped" structures were found in the Nunnery Quadrangle, in the area south of the House of the Birds quadrangle (Huchim Herrera and Toscano H. 1999), and in association with a round temple (Kowalski et al. 1993). With architectural links to Itza-inspired buildings, the Uxmal Round Structure contained Cehpech ceramic offerings at its initial late Terminal Classic construction, and Tohil Plumbate ceramic offerings in the building's post-abandonment debris. As such, there appears to have been a small, late Terminal Classic/Early Postclassic occupation at Uxmal by individuals with strong links to the now clearly dominant Chichen Itza.

Kabah

Excavation of the eastern half of the famous Codz Pop palace revealed a facade ornamented with gigantic stone warrior sculptures (Carrasco and Pérez 1993), which together with previously known sculptured door jambs (Pollock 1980, figs. 372, 373) reveal this building as a monument to military conquest. Epigraphic and iconographic work at Kabah, principally on a lintel from the Manos Rojas building and the Codz Pop jambs, has identified four rulers. Carrasco and Pérez (1993) suggest dates associated with these rulers of A.D. 890, 950, 987, and one that may roughly correspond to the same time period as Ballcourt 1 at Tula, Hidalgo. However, Grube and Schele (1995: 196, 203) suggest earlier dates of A.D. 876 (10.2.7.0.0) and A.D. 883 (10.2.13.15.11) for the Manos Rojas lintel and Codz Pop jambs, respectively. Nevertheless, ceramic evidence suggests that occupation continued much later at Kabah than at Uxmal: an assemblage of 27.2 percent Sotuta and 3.7 percent Hocaba from the Manos Rojas building. A supporting radiocarbon date—A.D. 1210 ± 40—also suggests a very late use of at least some portions of the site. Carrasco and Pérez suggest that even after the abandonment of Uxmal, the rulers of Kabah continued to "cooperate" with the rulers of Chichen Itza—apparently after battles that damaged many of the central buildings—adopting not only ceramic but foreign architectural traditions as well as the Postclassic reuse of carved stones, until the final abandonment of the site sometime during Hocaba times. We suggest that the evidence indicates that at least a portion of Kabah's elite survived the collapse of Uxmal and continued to occupy limited portions of the site center. However, by Hocaba times, this occupation appears to have reduced to little more than "squatting" in a few buildings.

Settlement survey along the Kabah-Nohpat-Uxmal sacbé has revealed a number of interesting results (Carrasco 1993). Roughly continuous habitation—both platforms with small-scale foundation braces as well as those with vaulted architecture—exists between Kabah and Nohpat, but not between Nohpat and Uxmal. Instead, formal entryways (*pilonos*) existed on the sacbé at the entrance/exit to both Nohpat and Uxmal, but not at the entrance/exit to Kabah and Nohpat. Carrasco interprets these findings as suggesting peaceful, nonformalized interaction between Kabah and Nohpat, whereas Nohpat and Uxmal may have been more interested in clearly defining their respective territorial limits and tributary populations, as independent *kuuchkabaloob* (polity controlled by a ruling lineage or lineages, generally including a council of powerful members, *batabob*). As such, the assumption of a special, "allied" relationship among Kabah, Nohpat, and Uxmal, due to the interlinking sacbé system, may not be as straightforward as has been assumed. It also appears that the apparent dominance of Uxmal in this triad was probably a late and fairly short-lived phenomenon (Dunning and Kowalski 1994).

Xkipché

A University of Bonn project spent several years working at Xkipché, a large minor (Rank 4) site located nine kilometers south-southwest of Uxmal (Prem 1991). The palace at Xkipché appears to have witnessed numerous building phases. Ephemeral buried deposits begin in the Middle Preclassic (500 B.C.) with occupation continuing through the Postclassic (chronometric dates at the site came from thermoluminesence dating, which the excavator reports as being somewhat problematic [Reindel 1997]). Principal construction and occupation of the palace date to the Late and Terminal Classic periods. After a number of building phases and additions spanning several hundred years, the then-current palace remodification was left unfinished, and probably shortly thereafter the site was abandoned. A small Sotuta-using occupation of the site occurred, resulting in the building of simple and poorly constructed residential structures near the palace (similar to those at Uxmal noted above). In addition, a number of Plumbate offerings, as well as censer fragments (Chen Mul Modeled) similar to those found at Mayapán, were placed within the fallen debris of monumental architecture. The research at Xkipché also suggests that Cehpech ceramics have a firm beginning in the Classic period and should not be viewed as corresponding solely to the Terminal Classic.

Settlement survey in the peripheral areas of Xkipché and nearby smaller sites indicates that the residential zone of the site was expanding outward through time and that some expansions of residential architecture were abandoned before completion (Dunning 2000). Portions of the urban zone also appear to have been formally demarcated by special features, a pattern first noted at Sayil (Tourtellot et al. 1988).

Sayil

The large (Rank 2) site of Sayil occupies the northern end of a large valley in the Bolonchen Hills. The ceramic assemblage from Sayil consists almost entirely (98 percent) of Cehpech ceramics (Tourtellot and Sabloff 1994), with minimal traces of earlier and later ceramics found in non-stratigraphic contexts. Andrews's (1985) survey of Sayil's architecture found that the site contains a relatively low percentage (5.6 percent, compared to 26 percent at other Puuc sites) of the Classic Mosaic style (defined by Andrews as the latest architectural style at most Puuc sites). As such, the primary period of construction of monumental and vaulted architecture at Sayil may have occurred somewhat earlier than other Puuc sites. Several radiocarbon as well as obsidian hydration dates also confirm Sayil's placement relatively early in the Terminal Classic period. Sayil's obsidian derives from Guatemalan sources (almost exclusively from El Chayal), suggesting that earlier, Classic-period trade routes were dominant, rather than the even earlier Teotihuacan, or the later Toltec/Chontal Maya routes out of Central Mexico (Tourtellot and Sabloff 1994).

Excavations in the first and second story of Sayil's Great Palace have also shed light on Sayil's origin (Carrasco and Boucher 1990). The first and second story both contain substructures that were demolished to build the present three-story palace, all in a relatively brief burst of construction during the Terminal Classic. The first story contains a substructure from the Late Classic, with ceramic materials from early Cehpech times as well as the local Late Classic Motul ceramics and Petén-originating polychromes (Saxché Naranja) suggesting some kind of Puuc-Petén trade interaction during the Late Classic. Ceramic materials from the second story's substructure can also be identified as coming from early Cehpech times: the appearance of Thin Slate, a high percentage of "*chorreada*" (drip) motifs, the presence of slate wares with partially vitrified finishes, and chultun jars with interior rim handles. Late Classic Motul ceramics were absent. Later Cehpech characteristics include more incised and impressed designs. Through excavations such as those in Sayil's Great Palace, it may be possible to quantitatively distinguish early from late Cehpech ceramic types. Clearly, more excavations and quantitative data presentations may be able to refine what appears now as a very long use of Cehpech ceramics. In addition to the chronological refinement, this new information identifies Sayil's origins in the Late Classic, and confirms that it was Sayil's Terminal Classic era that saw the period of most rapid growth.

The core area of Sayil consists of a series of sacbeob linking major architectural complexes, including the Great Palace and Stelae Platform. Sayil's stelae employ the Classic Motif, depicting prominent individual lords who were probably site rulers. However, archaeological evidence suggests that these lords ruled at least in part by *sharing* political and religious power with other lineages (Carmean 1998). Specialized pyramidal features were used to demarcate at least some boundaries of the urban area (Tourtellot et al. 1988).

The residential area of Sayil is estimated at approximately 4.5 square kilometers (Dunning 1989, 1992; Tourtellot and Sabloff 1994) but may have been larger, particularly if the nearby center of Chac II is included as part of greater Sayil (Smyth et al. 1998). A large portion of Sayil's population was engaged in agriculture, cultivating house-lot gardens, infields, and probably outfields in adjacent valleys (Killion et al. 1989; Dunning 1989, 1992; Smyth, Dore, and Dunning 1995). Wealth among Sayil's lineages was at least partly based in the control of prime agricultural land (Carmean 1991; Dunning 1992; Smyth, Dore, and Dunning 1995). Agricultural products were probably also supplied to the city by nearby subsidiary minor centers. By using traditional room-count methods, scholars have estimated the Terminal Classic urban population of Sayil to number approximately 10,000 to 11,000 (Tourtellot, Sabloff, and Smyth 1990). A closely matched population figure was also derived by estimating the holding capacity of Sayil's water-storage *chultuns* (cisterns), but only by using a very low minimum per-person water requirement (McAnany 1990). Likewise, only by pushing estimates of agricultural productivity beyond their likely sustainable limits could the carrying capacity of Sayil's probable "catchment area" be made to accommodate this large population (Dunning 1992). Becquelin and Michelet (1994) have questioned the reality of the large population figures for Sayil, an important issue that will be addressed further below.

The "C-shaped" structures found at the Mirador Flats area of Sayil (Tourtellot et al. 1992) and on the Great Palace terrace (Ruppert and Smith 1957) attest to some kind of continued occupation after the abandonment of the monumental architecture of the central core. The discovery of a reused cornice stone in a foundation brace-room addition in the Miguel T hectare (Tourtellot and Sabloff 1994) also points to a short span of continued occupation, even of the residential area of the site. As such, Sayil's primary occupation appears to have spanned the period from A.D. 800 to 950, with some post-abandonment reoccupation.

Chac II

The site of Chac II is situated in the northwest corner of the Sayil Valley less than two kilometers from the Great Palace. Mapping at Chac II and Sayil suggests that this smaller "center" was a part of the Sayil urban system in the Terminal Classic (Smyth et al. 1998). However, much of the monumental construction and a significant amount of residential occupation at Chac II predate the Terminal Classic (Smyth 1998). Radiocarbon dates and architectural, ceramic (a mixture of Cehpech and earlier Motul ceramics), and obsidian hydration evidence indicate that Chac II was a thriving community in Early and Middle Classic times, participating in Teotihuacan-linked trade systems similar to Oxkintok's. Chac II's prominence within the Sayil Valley was probably not usurped by Sayil proper until relatively late in the Late Classic period. It is also possible that the Chac II elite were the founders of Sayil and that the larger site was, in essence, a massive extension of Chac II.

Labná

Research conducted at Labná has centered on stratigraphic and restoration work in the central area, as well as settlement pattern survey in the area surrounding the site (Gallareta Negrón et al. 1994, 1995). Although habitation continued away from the site in all directions, much of the available land apparently went unused for residential construction, as suggested by limestone outcrops that were not utilized for basal platforms or as stone quarries. The southwestern border of the Labná Valley is demarcated by hilltop masonry residences (including "Las Gemelas," which was unfinished before abandonment), apparently taking advantage of a natural rainfall catchment area. Settlement generally stops at the rough line of hills that defines the Labná Valley.

Excavations in Labná's internal sacbe have revealed two construction stages: the earlier is associated with Early Puuc (and perhaps Proto-Puuc) architecture, and the latter is associated with the Puuc Mosaic style. The early sacbe construction probably utilized fill from even earlier buildings that had fallen into disuse and/ or were in the process of being demolished prior to subsequent remodeling and enlargement in the newer Classic Puuc style. Evidence of Late Preclassic/Early Classic structures consists of foundation walls of structures covered by later, Terminal Classic construction. Ceramics associated with these early periods include Late Chicanel and Chakán materials. To date, Middle and Late Classic materials have not been found at the site.

The recent work at Labná confirms that the platform and east wing of the palace were not finished, as was noted by Pollock and by Edward Thompson. Gallareta et al. (1994: 43) suggest the work may never have been completed due to structural flaws in the architectural design itself, flaws that may have been due to the hasty construction by its economically strapped patrons. No Sotuta materials or post-occupational reuse have thus far been reported for Labná, suggesting the somewhat quick abandonment of this Rank 3 center.

Xcalumkín and the Xculoc Area

Mapping and excavations at Xculoc and nearby sites and ethnoarchaeological investigations in the modern village of Xculoc led Becquelin and Michelet (1994) to question whether population estimates made for Terminal Classic Sayil and other Maya sites might not be unrealistically high. Using floor space averages (versus room counts) and ethnographically based water use figures (versus absolute minimal water consumption figures), Becquelin and Michelet suggest that the Sayil estimates (see above) should be revised downward by 30 to 50 percent. Notably, a reduction of 30 percent would put Sayil and other peak Puuc population estimates in line with reasonable, sustainable, carrying capacity estimates. Nevertheless, even despite this 30 percent reduction, it is likely that regional populations in the Puuc were precariously high, that is, high enough to make them vulnerable to any significant perturbations in the food production and distribution system (Dunning 1992).

Archaeological work at and between Xculoc and nearby sites (Xcochkax, Chunhuhub, and Xpostanil) in the western part of the Puuc suggests that no clearly dominant center existed in this area, a markedly different regional organization than that found in the eastern Puuc (Becquelin 1994; Michelet, Becquelin, and Arnauld 2000). This work also revealed a possible division of Cehpech into early, middle, and late phases (Becquelin 1994: 69). Early Cehpech includes a high percentage of Sacalum Black-on-Slate and members of the Teabo group. Middle Cehpech includes a lessening of Sacalum in favor of Holactun Black-on-Cream, the persistence of Teabo, and the appearance of the Ticul group. Late Cehpech includes a strong percentage of Holactun, which is substituted for Sacalum, a lessening of Ticul and Teabo groups, and the appearance of fine paste groups.

On the basis of epigraphic, iconographic, and archaeological evidence it can be suggested that the site of Xcalumkín may have had some kind of joint government similar to a *multepal* as known from Mayapán, and as suspected for Chichen Itza, rather than the regal-centric organization much more common for the Classic Maya (Grube 1994b; Grube and Schele 1995; Michelet 1998). The site center lacks any truly monumental architecture generally suggestive of divine kingship—rather, it possesses numerous midsized compounds. Several of these compounds are replete with lengthy glyphic inscriptions, none of which mention an ahaw but many of which refer to concurrent *sahalob,* a title used for subordinate "deputies" of the king in the Usumacinta region. At Xkalumkin, the *sahal* title seems to refer to officials of equal rank within a type of collective government (Grube 1994b). More limited epigraphic evidence from several other western Puuc sites (Xkombec, Xcocha, and Ichmac) also suggests conciliar governance may have been more widespread in the region. Perhaps even another variant political organization occurred at Halal, where the site center consists of a single, massive acropolis complex connected to outlying groups by sacbeob (Pollock 1980: 546–553). These findings indicate that more than one type of political organization existed in the Puuc region during this time period. While multepal political organization differs significantly from the Classic-period regal-centric pattern seen at eastern Puuc centers such as Uxmal and Sayil, a multepal organization may simply represent an extreme version of decentralized governance, based on the political importance of powerful lineages, embedded in the traditional Classic pattern (Carmean 1998; Carmean and Sabloff 1996; McAnany 1995). We will elaborate further on these ideas in the concluding sections.

Ah Canul Province

At the time of Spanish contact, the western Puuc region and northwesternmost Yucatán were under the domain of the Ah Canul kuuchkabal, a council government dominated in part by the Canul lineage (Okoshi Harada 1992). Ethnohistoric and archaeological work in parts of the western Puuc have demonstrated a continuity of occupation at some sites from Classic through Postclassic and into Colonial times (Williams-Beck and Okoshi Harada 1998). The site of Xuch, for example, appears to have been an important Late Classic through Postclassic center. In addition to Xkalumkin, other sites in the western Puuc (e.g., Xkombec, Xcocha, and Ichmac) exhibit epigraphic and architectural evidence of decentralized governance (Nikolai Grube, personal communication 1999; Williams-Beck 1997). Sites in this area also have a notable absence of dynastic stelae. It is possible that the shared governance system that appears to have developed in the western Puuc during the Late Classic may have persisted into the Postclassic in this region (Williams-Beck and Okoshi Harada 1998). Notably, many sites in the western Puuc that show continuity into the Postclassic appear to be associated with significant water sources.

URBAN AND RURAL SETTLEMENT
AND DEMOGRAPHY OF THE PUUC REGION

As one moves south and east into the heart of the Puuc region, depth to permanent groundwater increases and becomes progressively less accessible (Dunning 1992). Thus, in most of the eastern Puuc, accessible permanent groundwater is virtually nonexistent. As such, pre-Columbian populations in much of the Puuc were utterly dependent on capturing and storing rainwater for their survival (Kurjack, Garza, and Lucas 1979; McAnany 1995; Zapata Peraza 1986). Rain catchment surfaces and water-storage chultuns are a ubiquitous feature of domestic architecture in Puuc sites because these features were absolutely necessary for survival (see, for example, Figure 19.4). A fascinating aspect of ancient settlement in the Puuc is the virtual absence of chultuns in "rural" settlement groups—the domestic architecture located beyond the evident margins of minor and major centers (Dunning 1989, 1992, 1999, 2002; Graff 1991). Such rural settlement clusters range in size from modest "hamlets" with five or six foundation braces and a variety of other features to groups of a few amorphous *chich*

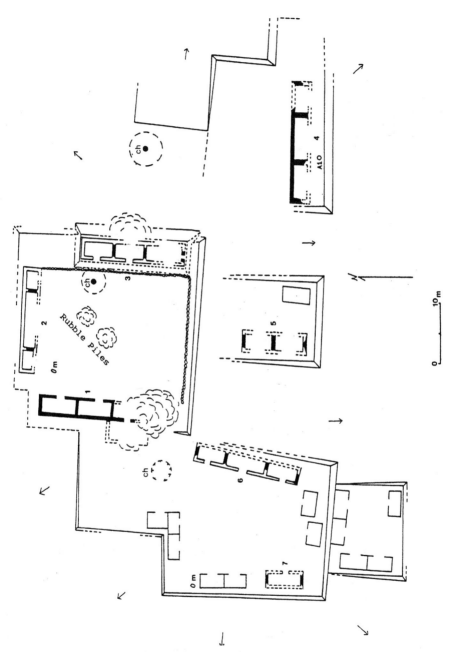

19.4 Map of the central group of XPRESS2 (after Dunning, n.d., fig. A3–6); ch = chultun, m = metate, A = altar. Vaulted structures indicated by double lines. Foundation braces indicated by single lines.

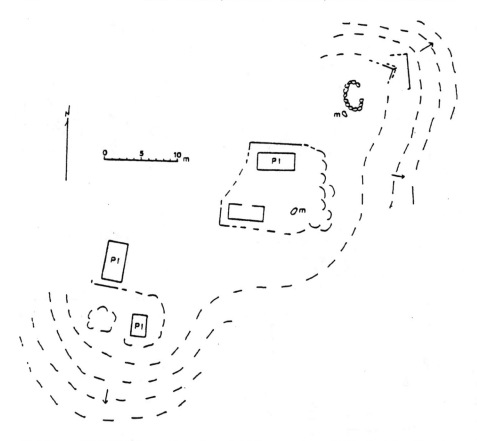

19.5 Map of XPRESS Group C-3, about 1.5 kilometer west of Xkipche (after Dunning n.d., fig. A2–6). This group (without chultuns) is typical of rural "hamlets" in the Puuc. Pl = platform; m = metate.

mounds or crude rubble platforms (Figure 19.5). These clusters never bear evidence of vaulted architecture and more than 95 percent of them completely lack chultuns despite the availability of rock outcrops suitable for their construction. Given the lack of alternative water sources in the Puuc, we can only assume that these settlements were not occupied during the long dry season and represent seasonally occupied farmsteads.

As discussed in the section on Sayil above, the nature of Puuc settlement can be aptly described as "nucleated dispersion": while large tracts of good soil were kept open within the urban area—probably for intensive garden and infield cultivation—settlement did not simply continue to disperse across the landscape but was reined in at demarcated limits. If, as we believe, large urban infields were indeed under the jurisdiction of prominent elite groups, both the nucleated nature of urban settlement and the lack of a year-round, dispersed rural population may reflect the means by which elite control was extended into the countryside— namely by preventing the farming population from dispersing permanently into surrounding areas. Instead, small, nucleated outlying centers (with chultuns indicating their permanent occupation; Figure 19.4) emerged, quite possibly under the control of the same elite groups who enjoyed prominence within the large centers. Indeed, the regional settlement of the Terminal Classic eastern Puuc included a blossoming of numerous small, late sites around and between older, larger centers, probably representing the need to expand agricultural production onto virtually all available land. Even with intensive urban gardening and infield production, it is clear that major Puuc centers could not have produced enough food without also expanding their control over surrounding land and minor centers (Dunning 1989, 1992). As discussed earlier, even if demographic figures for Sayil and other Puuc centers are revised downward, it is likely that by the tenth century A.D., population in many parts of the Puuc would have been precariously close to carrying capacity.

Dunning (1992) proposed that drought was the environmental perturbation most likely to have resulted in the depopulation of the Puuc region in the tenth century because of the inherently variable nature of rainfall in the Puuc, the general lack of accessible surface or groundwater in most of the region, and the complete dependence of local populations on rainwater both for agriculture and domestic consumption. Paleoenvironmental studies at several lakes in Quintana Roo have now analyzed the oxygen isotopes and geochemistry of sediment cores to show a long period of aridity in the Yucatán peninsula around A.D. 200 to 1300 that intensified during the Maya collapse about A.D. 700 to 900 (Curtis, Hodell, and Brenner 1996; Gill 2000; Hodell, Curtis, and Brenner 1995; Leyden, Brenner, and Dahlin 1998). We do not yet know how extensive or intensive this drought was, because evidence thus far is conflicting. For example, in the paleoenvironmental study nearest to the Puuc, Leyden et al. (1996) could find no evidence for it in the dry, northwestern Yucatán. Hodell et al. (1995) have suggested that the drought periods in the Maya lowlands relate to pan-Caribbean climatic cycles, but it is also likely that human modifications of the environment also would have contributed to regional drought problems, particularly the effects of prolonged deforestation on local soil water balances and transpiration rates (see Dunning 1992; Leyden et al. 1998). It is also problematic that the peak of population growth in the Puuc region, which was utterly dependent on rainfall, occurred precisely when drought was supposed to be triggering catastrophic population decline in other parts of the Maya lowlands. Part of this conundrum may simply be a product of inadequate temporal and spatial resolution in the paleoecological data at present, as well as the continued difficulty in distinguishing human and natural environmental disturbances (Dunning and Beach 2000). Nevertheless, we still view drought as the most logical environmental trigger factor for depopulation in the Puuc, but more evidence is needed before this can be effectively demonstrated.

A CURRENT MODEL OF PUUC
SOCIOPOLITICAL ORGANIZATION AND CHRONOLOGY

Given the possible Preclassic dates for Xkipché's initial founding, and the evidence for strong Early Classic–period occupation at Oxkintok, Chac II, and a few other sites, it appears that what was to become the Terminal Classic Puuc Florescence—the high times in the hill country—has strong local roots in the region. We envision a scattered Preclassic occupation that became gradually more substantial in the Classic period, and more populous still, perhaps dangerously so, by the Terminal Classic. Late Classic population growth may have included elite immigrant groups coming from the southern lowlands (Schele and Mathews 1998: 258–260; Nikolai Grube, personal communication 1999). As the florescence in the Terminal Classic clearly points toward a southern lowland Classic Maya cultural orientation, this southern elite arrival may have helped spur this development. With time—and technological innovations regarding dry season survival (chultuns)—the inhabitants were able to capitalize on the pockets of relatively rich Puuc soils, and expand into the full height of the Terminal Classic Puuc Florescence. This expansion appears to have taken numerous forms: 1) population growth, 2) population dispersal into new areas both within and beyond the Puuc region, 3) architectural and sculptural elaboration, 4) increase in social inequality and political centralization, 5) contact and perhaps initial alliance-building with other politically centralizing groups, specifically Chichen Itza (Kowalski et al. 1993; Kowalski and Dunning 1999), and 6) perhaps some kind of increased scale of economic specialization and trade (Smyth et al. 1995; see also Rivera 1994).

The internal organization and centralization of the Puuc polities, however, probably never quite reached the degree attained in the southern Maya centers, or certainly in highland Mexico. During their short Terminal Classic (A.D. 770 to 925) apogee, Puuc rulers may simply never have had the time to establish firm, religiously legitimized, politically stable dynasties that were able to rule their subjects relatively unquestioned. However, if we extend Puuc society back into the Classic and even the Preclassic periods—as can be suggested from recent research—the existence of long and vital potential "proto-dynasties" could be argued. Nevertheless, even given this greater time depth, many of the Puuc centers appear to have remained hovering around the edges of that fragile cusp of politically centralized statehood. Uxmal, at least under the reign of Lord Chaak, appears to have temporarily reached this status, as elaborated below. We envision a series of independent, small-scale, regal-ritual, dynastically focused kingdoms in the eastern Puuc—relatively newly centralized with the beginning of the Terminal Classic—jockeying for power and status among themselves, while seeking to maintain their centralized status within their own communities in the face of the centrifugal forces of the still-strong lineage heads (see Carmean 1998; Carmean and Sabloff 1996; Dunning 1992; Kurjack 1994). That some centers were unable to maintain this delicate balance is certain, and the slightly earlier (before the very end of the Terminal Classic) abandonment of Sayil may be one such example.

However, in the western Puuc even less centralization is evident. In the Middle and Late Classic a small regional state may have been centered at Oxkintok, but its power was significantly dissipated by the onset of the Terminal Classic (Rivera Dorado 1996). Data from the Xculoc region suggest myriad independent, very small-scale polities (Becquelin 1994). It is noteworthy that with the exception of Oxkintok, western Puuc sites are virtually devoid of the dynastic stelae found at many major eastern Puuc sites (Dunning 1992). Evidence from Xkalumkin and nearby sites suggests that the Maya there may have begun experimenting with a form of conciliar government (Grube 1994b; Michelet 1998). It is also possible that some variant of this shared governance model survived into the Postclassic Ah Canul province (Williams-Beck and Okoshi Harada 1998). Clearly there seems to have been a variety of community leadership forms, perhaps forming a continuum from relatively centralized kingdoms to communities in which governance was shared more equally among a number of prominent lineages.

Perhaps one of the most important questions that is just beginning to be asked is the role of Uxmal in the late Terminal Classic Puuc. What was the extent and depth of Uxmal's control of the region? To what extent was the apparently unfettered reign of Lord Chaak an anomaly in the Puuc? We hypothesize that Uxmal may have added a degree of internal instability to the region by mounting an attempt to establish political and military sovereignty over her nearby Puuc neighbors. Evidence for this attempt comes in the form of an apparent decline in the construction of new (post–A.D. 850) monumental architecture chiefly in those sites closest to Uxmal (e.g., Xkipche and Xkoch), while construction continued at sites clearly tied to Uxmal's ascendancy (e.g., Nohpat and Kabah). As such, the nearer to Uxmal (and Nohpat and Kabah) one comes, the less post–A.D. 850 monumental construction one sees, as if construction labor were being siphoned off and put to work at Uxmal itself. This phenomenon of labor monopolization has parallels in other early societies where rulers and polities were competing for control of a finite labor pool (e.g., Kaufman 1988; Renfrew 1983; Renfrew and Level 1979). As noted above in the discussion of Kabah, while there is an apparent abundance of settlement features along the sacbe connecting Kabah and Nohpat, such features appear to be absent along much of the Nohpat-Uxmal sacbe. We think it is possible that Uxmal seized control of an already existing Nohpat/Kabah polity late in the ninth century, subsequently making itself a late addition to the sacbe system (Dunning 1992; Kowalski and Dunning 1999). However, the exact relationship between these three major centers remains unknown.

Kurjack has (1994) suggested that the palaces—residences of elite extended families—also served as "garrisons" for the leaders of military expeditions, placing even secondary centers in a position to defend themselves. Whether Uxmal expanded its political and economic grasp through military means has yet to be firmly established. The militarism evident in the late monumental art of Uxmal, Kabah, and Oxkintok, and the possible commemoration of an Uxmal military victory at Mulchic all point toward increased militarism around A.D. 900 and after. As in other parts of the Maya lowlands, the introduction of conquest warfare may well have jeopardized the stability of food production (see, for example, Demarest 1996). The late fortification of the Uxmal site center also points to increasingly dramatic militarism in the tenth century (Barrera Rubio 1990; Kurjack, Garza, and Lucas 1979). On the northern plains, several other sites appear to have been fortified around this time (Webster 1978). The site of Chacchob is of particular interest, resembling a fortified outpost on the frontier between Uxmal and Chichen Itza.

Additional lines of evidence indicate that Uxmal rose to regional dominance during the Terminal Classic. The construction of monumental architecture during the reign of Lord Chaak around A.D. 900 was on a scale unprecedented in the history of both the site and region, signaling the builders' intention to create a suitable capital for the emerging state (Dunning and Kowalski 1994; Kowalski 1987). The Nunnery Quadrangle in particular was clearly a monument erected to proclaim the paramount importance of Lord Chaak in the local Maya world (Kowalski 1994; Kowalski and Dunning 1999; Schele and Mathews 1998). The references to Chichen Itza within Uxmal's inscriptions and iconography indicate a relationship with that emerging Terminal Classic center not enjoyed by other Puuc communities. Finally, the persistence of Uxmal as an important place in the minds of the Yucatec Maya long after its abandonment (as recorded in various post-conquest ethnohistoric sources) suggests that this city had played an unusually important role in the history of the northern lowlands (Kowalski 1987).

Conversely, there is other evidence suggesting that the Uxmal regional state was short-lived and may have controlled only a limited area of the Puuc. Thus far, all evidence for Uxmal as a regional capital is tied to a single ruler, Lord Chaak, suggesting that the site's pre-eminence may have lasted only twenty to forty years. With the possible exception of Mulchic, there are no known references to Lord Chaak or other Uxmal rulers outside of Uxmal, suggesting that the regional state either controlled a fairly limited area or was only in power for a very short period. Limited archaeological data currently suggest that the territory controlled by the Uxmal state may have been no larger than about a thirty-kilometer radius around the site proper. Nevertheless, that area included a sizeable number of major sites and probably the entire Santa Elena Valley, the area within the Puuc most prized for its extensive zones of prime agricultural lands (Dunning 1992). Conversely, the interactions between Uxmal and Chichen Itza suggest that Uxmal may have expanded its political influence onto the northern plains. Clearly, the extent of Uxmal's power remains an issue open for debate and in need of further investigation.

We propose the following hypothesis that we would like to see tested against future archaeological work: with or without her direct Puuc "allies" (e.g., Kabah and Nohpat), Uxmal may have made a bid for broader regional power by enlisting the aide of non-Puuc allies, that is, Chichen Itza. Along with—and indeed perhaps spurred on by—an increasingly precarious population-to-cultivable-land ratio, Uxmal's precipitous political move may have thrown the entire region into a tailspin from which it never recovered, and made it particularly vulnerable to Chichen Itza's growing power. Numerous examples of unfinished monumental works (at Xkipché, Oxkintok, Labná, Uxmal, Yaxché Xlapak, and at Chunhuhub, among others [Reindel 1997: 247]) may indicate a sudden, unforeseen end to a culture in the midst of its glory. The intentional destruction and burial of ballcourt ring stones at Oxkintok, Uxmal, and Edzná in the Terminal Classic (see Rivera Dorado 1994) may relate to the symbolic as well as literal end of autonomy for these sites. Additionally, the murals in the Upper Temple of the Jaguars at Chichen Itza depict successful battles in a red, hilly region, perhaps providing pictorial representation of the fate of the Puuc centers (Andrews V and Sabloff 1986; Schele and Mathews 1998).

As Uxmal's power declined and that center was itself subdued by Chichen Itza, some centers in the eastern Puuc, such as Kabah, apparently were able to continue their existence for a short while, even within the new, undoubtedly chaotic, political situation. In the early Postclassic (post–A.D. 950), the clear but comparatively modest presence in some Puuc sites of Sotuta-using peoples suggests either remnants of Puuc peoples, or newcomers from Chichen Itza, or Chichen Itza–related peoples, or perhaps a combination of the above possibilities. Periodic religious worship appears to be one of the major activities of these later occupations. The nature and the dating of this post-abandonment reuse is of considerable importance for understanding the Terminal Classic to Postclassic transition. As suggested by Bey et al. (1997), we agree that the siting of the "C-shaped" structures suggests a relatively short-lived attempt to maintain the centralized political control, however truncated, of the earlier era. Differing with Bey et al., however, we envision the presence of non-Puuc peoples (probably related to the Sotuta-using Itza sphere) while agreeing that Cehpech ceramic continuity also points to the cultural and economic continuity of the local population. Specifically, we hypothesize a Pure Florescent elite and nobility, now fallen on hard times, allying themselves with more powerful Sotuta-using peoples expanding from Chichen Itza, who together try to reassert political control in the remaining Puuc communities. It is also possible that the apparent Itza presence in the Puuc marked a period in which the remaining population was made subject to the Chichen Itza state. Schele and Freidel (1990: 374) have suggested that some of the rulers subjugated by the Itza may have resided at Chichen Itza and administered their territories through intermediaries, as did members of the later multepal government at Mayapán. Although the post-florescent populations in the Puuc may have attempted to regain/retain political authority in the region, the scale of local population as well as social and political disruption may have been too great, and the remnant/immigrant population was simply able to live for a while in the slowly crumbling cities, and to make offerings in the rubble of the most important buildings.

Intriguingly, at least a few western Puuc centers (e.g., Xuch) appear to have more successfully weathered the Terminal Classic to Postclassic transition (Williams-Beck and Okoshi Harada 1998). These sites are currently undergoing further investigation that we hope will shed more light on the nature of this transition. Whether the relative success of these centers had an environmental (e.g., more permanent water sources closer to the western coastal plain), sociopolitical (e.g., more adaptive shared governance structure), or economic (e.g., ties to emerging Postclassic economic networks) basis remains to be determined.

IMPLICATIONS FOR THE CLASSIC COLLAPSE

Clearly, the mid-tenth-century decline of the Puuc centers and the depopulation of the region was not as sudden, uniform, or complete as we once believed (e.g., Dunning 1992; Tourtellot and Sabloff 1994). For example, we see a lack of congruence between the change in monumental architecture and ceramic changes (see Andrews V and Sabloff 1986: 450), in that monumental architecture is abandoned, while ceramic traditions continue. This fact may point to at least two nonexclusive conclusions: 1) that, much like work at Copán has demonstrated, the decline of the Puuc centers was initially an elite collapse that did not have immediate or major impacts on the larger population, and 2) that the elite were not involved in ceramic production, at least not for the majority of the Cehpech wares. In short, the nature and timing of the depopulation of the Puuc is far from clear. Some communities appear to have been abandoned fairly suddenly, others to have significantly lingered, and a few (along the western and northern margins of the region) to have transformed into Postclassic centers.

In an effort to remain true to the goal of providing a chapter that is regionally comparable regarding the causes of the Maya collapse, we now turn to a brief summary using "prime mover"–type terminology. Based on recent archaeological, demographic, and iconographic research, it appears that a general assessment of the Terminal Classic Puuc region can be offered. As with other views of the southern lowlands Classic collapse, the Puuc evidence suggests multicausal factors. One clear factor in the decline of the Puuc region in the Terminal Classic is population growth, which caused significant agricultural stress. Climatic change in the form of drought may have been a further causal factor, particularly given the utter dependence of the Puuc's population on rainfall. However, our present understanding of Puuc cultural history does not accord well with apparent paleoenvironmental trends suggesting that the Maya lowlands was experiencing peak aridity during the time that regional population was growing rapidly.

An additional stress on the Terminal Classic Puuc region appears to have been endemic political competition and warfare, both within and from outside the Puuc region. We know that Chichen Itza experienced a rapid political ascent during the late period at Uxmal and gained large-scale dominance after the fall of that site; indeed, the rise of the former may have a direct link to the decline of the latter. Moreover, it appears that at least in some cases the initial collapse of the Terminal Classic Puuc centers may have primarily been an elite collapse, as the Puuc royal rulers lost status and divine legitimization through their inability to control ecological or political events occurring around them, much as their Classic period, southern lowland counterparts did approximately a century earlier.

With regard to the question of which of the forces and factors discussed above had primacy in the collapse of Classic Maya society in the Puuc, further speculation is premature. Our understanding of both the internal chronology of the Puuc as well as the precise meshing of this culture history with that of other parts of the northern lowlands is too coarse to allow for a clear determination of event sequences. Furthermore, the lack of adequate paleoenvironmental data from the Puuc itself severely hampers our ability to assess the role of ecological factors in the collapse. Because of these data deficiencies, we conclude by outlining ways in which we see these inadequacies best being addressed.

FUTURE DIRECTIONS IN PUUC ARCHAEOLOGY

On the basis of the previous brief review of recent work in the Puuc, a number of new—or better, continuing—directions present themselves (we also refer the reader to Ball's [1994] excellent summary chapter on northern Maya archaeology). Any future-directions section would not be complete without yet another plea for more and better chronological information. The Puuc ceramic sequence, not only for the Terminal Classic but for both earlier and later periods as well, remains vague and imprecise. Clearly, as at Sayil, stratigraphy is not always readily available, nor are radiocarbon, thermoluminescence, and obsidian hydration dates without their attendant possibilities for error, misinterpretation, and idiosyncratic interpretation. However, some promising first efforts have been made at Sayil, Chac II, Xkipché, and in the Xculoc region, efforts that need to be expanded to other sites and regions. Despite such stratigraphic and absolute dating challenges, any model of Puuc society, such as that presented above, still must be reconciled against chronological and archaeological reality.

The resolution of the overlap issue, of central importance for northern Yucatán prehistory, remains controversial, and although most scholars now accept at least a partial overlap, the areal and temporal extent of the overlap is still hotly debated (see Cobos Palma, Chapter 22, this volume). We favor a partial overlap that begins in the mid–Terminal Classic period (mid-ninth century), but with Chichen Itza continuing to thrive for some time after the fall of Uxmal. Another issue presents itself through the presentation of the foregoing model: if Uxmal *did* try to assert itself as a regional capital, what archaeological evidence would we need to see to validate this hypothesis? Future examination of critical areas of the hypothesized Uxmal state, such as that between Uxmal and Oxkintok, could prove enlightening. We hypothesize a Chichen Itza military presence in the Puuc, but clear, *unambiguous* indicators of that presence still elude us. What exactly does the presence of late, round temples in the Puuc mean? What does the presence of "non-Puuc"–style architecture and sculpture mean? What does the presence of non-Cehpech ceramics mean? A number of possibilities, apart from military conquest by Chichen Itza, present themselves. For example, such remains may be indicators of an attempt by Puuc elite to voluntarily co-opt the symbols, both religious and political, of a successful neighbor. This emulation may or may not have been related to Uxmal's need—perceived or otherwise—to buttress her own power. Such archaeological patterning may also suggest intermarriage or elite alliance formation. As Ringle, Gallareta Negron, and Bey (1998) have suggested, the appearance of such nonlocal traits may also indicate the spread of a broader, "pan-Mesoamerica" cult that had little specific relationship with Chichen Itza as a conquering military power.

Clearly, we need to utilize broader anthropological understanding and ethnoarchaeology to systematically illuminate the sociopolitical implications behind changing artistic styles, particularly when such change occurs shortly before the settlement's abandonment. The results of such endeavors must then be combined with the formulation of archaeologically testable hypotheses. Even more clearly, we have much "dirt archaeology" still to do before the culture history and sociopolitical dynamics of the Puuc region are understood.

Our review has also pointed out that our understanding of the internal organization of Puuc communities and polities is improving but far from adequate. That varying degrees of shared governance characterized different Puuc communities at times during the Late and Terminal Classic periods is clear. What is much less clear are the bases for and nature of such governance systems. Even in the Uxmal regional state under the reign of the seemingly omnipotent Lord Chaak, shared governance seems to have played a role. A program of research combining archaeological and epigraphic investigations, similar to that done in the Copán Valley, could help clarify the nature of rulership and governance at various centers.

The Puuc region also presents a unique opportunity to investigate the nature of rural settlement. Because of the dependence of Classic populations on chultuns to meet their domestic water needs, the identification of apparently seasonally occupied "hamlets" and farmsteads may be possible. Do these rural settlements have other indications of seasonal occupation? Can we identify a unique artifactual signature of seasonal occupation that can be transferred to other regions? If so, the implications for our understanding of ancient Maya settlement systems and demography are enormous.

We have suggested that drought may have been a significant factor in the depopulation of the Puuc region. Unfortunately, that suggestion is made without the benefit of much paleoenvironmental data from the Puuc region itself. Paleo-ecological data from the Puuc is sorely needed to compare with the growing body of information from other regions. Ideally, a program targeting the retrieval of a suite of paleoenvironmental and paleodietary data in combination with settlement studies, such as has been done in the Copán Valley and Petexbatun regions, can be accomplished in the Puuc. Until such data and analyses are forthcoming, arguments about the degree to which drought or other environmental perturbations may have influenced cultural history and the extent to which agricultural failure may have driven regional depopulation must remain speculative.

Finally, our review has noted that there is growing evidence that the depopulation of the Puuc was a more gradual process than once believed, with some sites showing evidence of small lingering populations, while a few others continued to be occupied well into the Postclassic. If we are to understand the nature of the Terminal Classic in the Puuc and elsewhere in the northern lowlands, then we must also further examine both communities that were abandoned and those that carried on. Only then can we truly understand the high times in the hill country.

20

THE RISE AND FALL OF TERMINAL CLASSIC YAXUNA, YUCATÁN, MEXICO

Charles Suhler, Traci Ardren, David Freidel, and Dave Johnstone

SOME OPENING THOUGHTS

From the days of the Carnegie project, when intrepid archaeologists came down to Yaxuna from Chichen Itza on muleback to survey and test-excavate the mounds there, the relationship between the mighty Itza capital and its smaller neighbor to the south has been a matter of interest and conjecture. The great causeway linking Yaxuna to Coba in the northeast was cause to hope that Yaxuna might provide something of a developmental and chronological stepping-stone between the cities of the southern lowland tradition, with their carved stone stelae and towering pyramids, and Chichen Itza with its equally magnificent but quite different high culture.

The relationship between the catastrophic fall of the southern lowland cities and the equally remarkable rise of Chichen Itza was, and remains, an intriguing and productive puzzle. Yaxuna was indeed a piece of that puzzle. It was, we think, something of a salient society of the great southern lowland tradition as originally suspected by the Carnegie archaeologists (Brainerd 1958; Freidel 1986d). At the same time, it was clearly a local power in a prosperous and well-populated part of the north for much of its history. The rise and fall of Yaxuna during the Terminal Classic period bears on these two distinct sources for government and large-scale community in the central northern lowlands, and reflects also on the rise and fall of Chichen Itza, its great neighbor to the north.

The Terminal Classic in northern Yucatán was a time of great activity and movement among the political and economic entities that made up competing

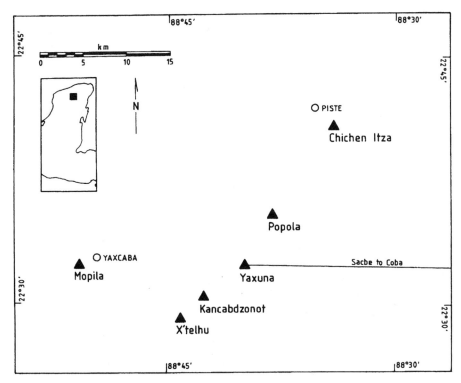

20.1   Location of Yaxuna on Peninsula.

polities on the peninsula. Our ten years of research at the site of Yaxuna (Figures 20.1, 20.2) provide a useful vantage point for a consideration of Terminal Classic archaeology in the northern middle of the peninsula.

One original impetus for the Selz Foundation Yaxuna Archaeological Project was the investigation of Terminal Classic interaction between Yaxuna, Coba, and Chichen Itza (Freidel 1987). In the beginning, members of the project believed that Yaxuna, after its Late Preclassic and Early Classic–period heyday (Brainerd 1958), was primarily a Terminal Classic community, as evinced by the 100 km sacbe between Yaxuna and the eastern center of Coba. Hypothetically, the causeway represented a counter to the expansionist pursuits of Chichen Itza in that period. Once excavation began, a singular Terminal Classic florescence proved simplistic as an understanding of the site. We discovered that Yaxuna had a long and continuous occupational history beginning in the frontier of the Middle and Late Formative, or ca. 400 B.C. (Suhler et al. 1998).

Indeed, one discovery from our research at Yaxuna is that there were no remarkable hiatus events in site occupation throughout the pre-Columbian period (Figure 20.3). The only one of which we are certain began during the War of the

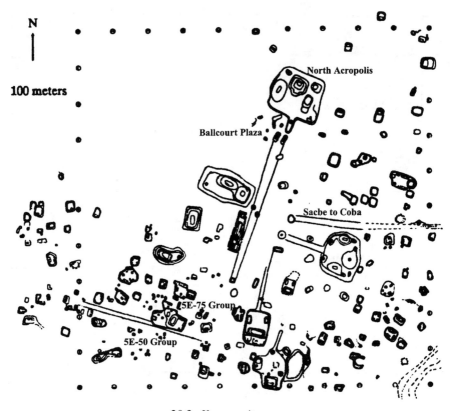

20.2   Yaxuna   site   map.

Castes and ended in the early 1930s with the founding of the modern pueblo, situated approximately 1.5 kilometers to the west of the monumental precinct of archaeological Yaxuna. Present-day Yaxuna is home to over 500 traditional Maya— some of the best archaeological excavators and stonemasons on the peninsula. However, they represent but the latest Maya occupation at Yaxuna.

As we now see it, long-term prehistoric settlement continuity resulted from the central geographical placement of Yaxuna in the path of both east-west and north-south communication and trade routes. Control of Yaxuna (and its surrounding environs) was desirable (and perhaps necessary) to control east-west movement across the peninsula and southern access into the Chenes region and Petén. Locally at least three large cenotes, or freshwater holes, are clustered within the center of Yaxuna, and this no doubt provided another strategic reason for enduring settlement.

Despite the demotion of the Terminal Classic to one of a long series of major occupations, earlier ideas about the participation of Yaxuna in Terminal Classic

AD	Uxmal	Oxkintok	Mayapan	Dzibilchaltun	Chichen Itza	Yaxuna	Ek Balam	Coba
1600			Colonial				Cizin	
1550							Colonial	
1500								
1450					Small Postclassic Occupation	Yaxuna V Postclassic	Xtbay Postclassic	Seco Postclassic
1400	Hocaba Postclassic	Hocaba Postclassic	Hocaba-Tases Postclassic	Chechem Postclassic				
1350								
1300					Conquest by Mayapan			
1250								
1200								
1150	Sotuta Sotuta	Sotuta Sotuta	Sotuta Sotuta	Zipche Sotuta	Itza Empire on Yucatan Peninsula	Yaxuna IVb Sotuta Minor Occ.		
1100								
1050								
1000							Late Yumcab	Oro
950	Cehpech Cehpech	Cehpech Cehpech	Cehpech Cehpech	Copo 2 Cehpech	Itza Expansion	Yaxuna IVa Cehpech	Cehpech with some Sotuta presence	Cehpech with Sotuta presence
900								
850					Sotuta Development			
800						Early/Late Facets		
750	Motul Cehpech-Late Classic mix	Motul Cehpech-Late Classic mix	Motul Cehpech-Late Classic mix	Copo 1 Late Classic w/some Cehpech	Cehpech Dedications			
700								
650						Yaxuna III Late Classic		Palmas Late Classic
600							Early Yumcab Late Classic	
550								
500								

Benavides 1988   Varela 1990   Smith 1971   Andrews V, 1981   Suhler et al. this volume   Suhler, Ardren, Johnstone 1998   Bey, et al, 1998   Robles 1990

20.3 Yaxuna/Regional ceramic chronology.

wars between Chichen Itza and Coba continue to inform our current understanding. Much recent research has noted the pervasive role of warfare in the Maya world at various times, and the role of war in the rise of Chichen Itza remains a productive theme archaeologically and iconographically. Our research at Yaxuna suggests a Terminal Classic period characterized by widespread conflict, political changes, and population movements. These changes do not seem to imply a "collapse" as known in the southern lowlands, but instead are characteristic of the cultural reformation that northern lowland polities underwent at this time.

A TERMINAL CLASSIC MODEL

Chichen Itza is clearly a remarkable and distinctive historical development in the Terminal Classic period of the north. In our current perspective, the cultural changes at Yaxuna during the Terminal Classic are due in large part to the growing domination of the Itza, extending out from their capital in the center of the peninsula. Ultimately, an Itza incursion and occupation marks the end of the Terminal Classic at Yaxuna. Nevertheless, we have identified an earlier component of the Terminal Classic that is just as important at Yaxuna, one that is quite distinctive from what follows. Following close on the heels of Coba's occupation of Yaxuna in the Late Classic (Ardren et al. 1998), this early Terminal Classic period is distinguished by a variant of the Cehpech ceramic complex at Yaxuna.

We believe Cehpech (predominantly slate ware) ceramics developed into a fully functional complex in the Puuc hills. From there their makers and purveyors began an inexorable eastward march across the peninsula sometime in the early A.D. 700s. A developmental slate ware sequence is indicated by rudimentary slate wares from Early Classic contexts at Yaxuna (representing 3.3 percent of sealed Early Classic lots, about the same as many other imports), Ek Balam (Bey et al.

1998), and Coba (Robles 1990). Nevertheless, it is not until the end of the Terminal Classic that they represent a homogenous ceramic assemblage at these respective central, northeastern, and eastern sites.

Therefore, while the rise of Chichen Itza helps define the history of the northern Terminal Classic regionally, the appearance of Cehpech ceramics is likewise an indicator of Terminal Classic peoples there. Prior to the articulation of chronological and ceramic sphere "overlap" models in the northern lowlands (Andrews and Sabloff 1986; Lincoln 1986), archaeologists tended to treat Cehpech pottery-making people as chronologically earlier than the heyday at Chichen Itza: Cehpech ceramics dated to the Terminal Classic and Itza history was a product of a Mexicanized Early Postclassic (R. Smith 1971; Brainerd 1958; Tozzer 1957; Andrews IV 1965). Continuing research in the northern peninsula has now demonstrated considerable temporal overlap between Chichen Itza and the Cehpech-using sites.

The ceramic types (Fine Orange, Plumbate) that played a major role in defining a distinctively foreign Early Postclassic Chichen Itza are found in small quantities and usually in specialized deposits. These features are quite often outside the routine construction and midden contexts where the majority of Sotuta wares have been found (Lincoln 1986; Suhler and Freidel 1995; Cobos Palma, Chapter 22, this volume). Likewise, the foreign elements in the iconography of Chichen Itza notwithstanding (Taube 1994), there is a core iconographic program that remained mainstream Maya in both content and meaning throughout the late florescence of the city (Kurjack, Maldonado, and Robertson 1991; Schele and Freidel 1990; Krochock 1998). Even the architecture developed out of and was built using earlier extant peninsular forms (Winemiller and Cobos 1999; Pollock 1980: 587). We think there was a close relationship between the Puuc cities and Chichen Itza and between Cehpech and Sotuta ceramic spheres. In our view the majority of Chichen Itza Sotuta ceramics were slate wares, a variant of the Cehpech ceramic wares that were popular throughout the northern peninsula during the Terminal Classic.

The mechanisms by which Cehpech ceramics and technology spread across the northern peninsula as coherent complexes, completely replacing previous ceramic complexes, are not yet fully understood. We have developed the following Terminal Classic processual model to provide a framing context to complement our discussion of Terminal Classic Yaxuna. For purposes of explanation, orientation, and cross-reference with other peninsular sites, we have divided the northern Terminal Classic into four stages. The time periods provided should be taken more as placeholders than hard boundaries and will surely shift as we (and others) further develop this model.

1. Slate Ware Expansion and Conquest (A.D. 700–800)

At the end of the Late Classic, Puuc groups emerging from sites such as Oxkintok, Sayil, and Uxmal began campaigns of eastward movement and territorial expansion. This period sees the Puuc-Cehpech absorption or conquest of sites such as Yaxuna, Coba, and Tancah, as well as the Puuc founding of Chichen Itza. At Terminal Classic Yaxuna, Cehpech slate wares appear as a functional complex, in concert with core-veneer architecture, a change in burial patterns, and evidence of new rulership at the site. Historically, the *Chilam Balam of Chumayel* records that those who would eventually be known as the Itza entered the peninsula during Katun 8 at the end of the seventh century (Roys 1967: 70– 72).

As we (and others) have noted, the first Terminal Classic structures built at Chichen Itza, for example, the Caracol, were dedicated with early Cehpceh ceramics (Lincoln 1986; Suhler and Freidel 1995). Additionally, we would assign to this same period at Chichen Itza traditional Maya accession architecture, for example, Monjas East Wing with its tripartite depiction of the cosmos and the ruler seated in the heavens. One of the early Terminal Classic buildings at Yaxuna, Structure 6F-68, discussed in more detail below, was built as a popol na, or council house, a structure type first recognized at Late Classic Copán. These factors lead us to believe that competing regional polities that practiced the Maya concept of kingship first mark the northern lowland Terminal Classic. The recent discovery of a named king at Ek Balam (Vargas and Castillo 2001) serves to further reinforce this idea. These polities sent out populations, technologies, and even perhaps ruling families in order to make territorial claims at geographically strategic cities like Yaxuna, Coba, Ek Balam, and Chichen Itza.

2. In Situ Evolution and Balkanization (A.D. 800–900)

This period follows the conquest and/or economic envelopment of the peninsula by Cehpech-using peoples. In our opinion, this interval witnessed the separation between eastern and western Cehpech ceramic spheres (at least at the level of vessel form/shape [Robles and Andrews 1986]), as well as the development of the Sotuta complex at Chichen Itza and its associated satellites. Further supporting this perspective, and arguing for extensive regional diversity, Fernando Robles has identified at least six separate Terminal Classic Cehpech complexes on the peninsula (Robles n.d.).

Interestingly, it is during this time at Chichen Itza that we see the first dedications of what were considered Toltec buildings, diagnostic of the Early Postclassic, or Mexican period, at the site. Krochock (1998) places the earliest hieroglyphic Chichen Itza date at A.D. 832 and the last at 894, information fitting well within our proposed scenario. At this point in time we are inclined to view these phenomena as the beginning of Itza identity. In all probability, this period saw the introduction of the people who have been identified as Toltec or Mexican. While we might not agree with this geographical determination, we do recognize the potential for a population influx and the associated evolving syncretism characterized by this period at Chichen.

In our opinion, this syncretism presents an explanatory avenue for Sotuta ceramic complex development (including the "foreign" ceramic types [Fine Orange wares, Plumbates] and the appearance of what has been labeled "Mexican" architecture [patio quads, large colonnades, etc.]). This in situ Sotuta development accompanied the diminishing importance of public hieroglyphic inscriptions directed at the individual level. Organizationally, we think this influx of new population was a catalyst in the Itza's move away from individual rulership and toward the institution of multepal.

Others before us (Andrews IV 1970; Brainerd 1958; Smith 1971; Lincoln 1986) have argued for early and late Sotuta phases. Winemiller and Cobos (1999) go even further, suggesting an early period of A.D. 750–900. We agree with the latter's dating and also believe that structures such as the Akab' Dzib, Monjas, Sub-Castillo, Monjas Complex, Temple of the Chac Mool, and the High Priest's grave, to name but a few, were erected during this early period (Suhler and Freidel 1995; Ardren and Suhler 1999). In a small point of deviation, we would posit an initial Cehpech phase developing into Sotuta complex at Chichen Itza.

3. Rise of Chichen Itza Empire and Peninsular Conquest (A.D. 900–1000)

In an earlier paper, we noted buried destruction episodes at Chichen Itza, especially in the Temple of the Chac Mool (Suhler and Freidel 1995). We think this may have been related to a period of internal realignment at the site, with a portion of the population departing for unknown places, perhaps also suggested in the *Chilam Balam of Chumayel,* where there are references to unrest at Chichen Itza and new government (Roys 1967: 75–78). If we are correct, this episode of internal strife solved the Itzas' complexities of cultural integration under the principles of multepal. As we have already noted (Suhler and Freidel 1995), the eventual return of these exiles' descendants had grave consequences for Chichen Itza.

Itza territory at this time was marked on the northwest by the trading port of Isla Cerritos, extending along the coast for ca. sixty kilometers to the east (Gallareta and Andrews 1988; Andrews et al. 1988; Kepecs et al. 1994). On the eastern interior, the boundary seems to have been in the vicinity of Ichmul de Morley (Smith et al. 1998), while the western boundary was probably somewhere east of Izamal (a somewhat tenuous proposition, given that data from this area are somewhat scanty). The initial southern Itza boundary was some unknown distance to the north of Yaxuna, perhaps somewhere near the modern village of Popola, ten kilometers away (Krochock 1990). With their internal social integration complete and their core polity secure, the Itza set forth on the road to conquest and empire.

We think Yaxuna was probably one of the first sites to fall and that the *Chilam Balam of Chumayel* chronicled this event in the context of a Yaxuna–Chichen Itza standoff (Roys 1933: 72–75). Strategically, such a move would have closed off Coba's access to the center of the peninsula, isolating them on the eastern edge of the peninsula. Archaeologically, we base our argument on ceramic data;

Yaxuna has no presence of the Piza complex, identified by Robles (1990) as Sotuta materials at Coba and dated to A.D. 1100–1200. Its presence in what we consider specialized proveniences at Coba (deposited with Stela B-1 and below the floor of Structure 1's temple [Robles 1990: 239]—both in apparently dedicatory deposits) leads us to identify Piza as a dedicatory complex, marking Itza presence (perhaps conquest) at Coba. Piza complex materials' absence at Yaxuna informs us that Yaxuna fell prior to Coba, and as the following paragraph explains, also before the fall of the peninsula's western cities.

With the potential Coba invasion route down the sacbe sealed by the conquest of Yaxuna, the Itza were free to concentrate on the western polities. As Stanton (1999) points out, Uxmal also seems to have fallen victim to Chichen Itza at the beginning of the tenth century. The Itza may have placed Lord Chak on the Uxmal throne and also absorbed Kabah into their hegemony. At Dzibilchaltun, the Zipche 1 ceramic complex containing Sotuta-phase deposits bracketed by earlier Cehpech and later Hocaba-Tases complexes has been identified (Bey et al. 1997: 116). In studying the Dzibilchaltun material, we have noted several features that bear some resemblance to the types of destruction features we have identified at Yaxuna and other sites. These include Structures 95, 95A, and 96 (all of which contained "floor middens"—subtext in many cases for termination deposits [Andrews IV and Andrews V 1980: 207–232]) dating to the end of Copo. In this case they would have been terminated by Zipche 1 materials and would fit with our model of Itza peninsular conquest.

Once the western portion of the peninsula was under Itza rule, we think they turned their attention toward Coba. Ironically, here they may have used Coba's own sacbe against them, using it as an assault avenue to quickly move troops and supplies east. During his survey, Villa Rojas (1934) noted earthen ramparts constructed across the sacbe, perhaps constructed by the forces of Yaxuna as they retreated east early in this period or by the forces of Coba as they attempted to stem the advancing Itza tide at the end of this period.

We agree with Stanton (1999) that prior to their actual occupation and/or conquest of Coba, the Itza had already surrounded and pressed upon the polity from the north, west, and probably south, while committing an end run in the trade war with their occupation of Cozumel. This provided them with a Caribbean base of operations. With the west under their control and access to east coast markets gained, Chichen Itza was now free to absorb or conquer the last impediment on the peninsula: the Coba polity. As noted above, we believe the Sotuta-Piza complex marks the Itza presence at, if not conquest and occupation of, Coba ca. A.D. 1100.

We think the consolidation of empire on the peninsula was commemorated by many of the Gran Nivelación construction projects at Chichen Itza, including the Great Ballcourt, construction of El Castillo over the Sub-Castillo, as well as renovations to the Caracol, to name but a few (Suhler and Freidel 1995). The rows of individual Maya supporting the roof of the Court of a Thousand Columns vividly demonstrate the primacy of a new form of government on the peninsula. Nonetheless, as Freidel et al. (1993: 383–385) demonstrate, even the Great Ballcourt at Chichen Itza portrays an essential Mayaness.

4. Rule of Peninsula by Itza (A.D. 1000–1250)

We view this time as the golden period of Itza empire. In this vein we must disagree with others who posit a ca. A.D. 1000 downfall for Chichen Itza (Cobos, Chapter 22, this volume; Ringle et al. 1991; Bey et al. 1997). We believe the Itza empire during this period ruled over a large portion of the Yucatán peninsula, campaigned as far as Petén and northern Belize, and had coastal trade contacts as far south as Ambergis and Marco Gonzalez Keys in Belize and Lamanai on the riverine interior (Cobos 1989; Guderjan et al. 1989; Pendergast 1990b).

For the end of the Itza, we accept the historically chronicled date of A.D. 1250 and believe they were brought down by the forces centered on Mayapán but from as far away as the eastern coast. We believe these final conquering forces were made up of those Itza who had been exiled at the end of our postulated Terminal Classic phase three or the beginning of phase four, two and a half centuries earlier. There is a pattern of Mayapán-style (Postclassic) materials associated with final terminations at the Caracol, Temple of the Warriors, and High Priest's Grave, to name but a few (Suhler and Freidel 1995). Additionally, Mayapán also utilized rule by multepal, first begun at Chichen Itza (Schele and Freidel 1990) and apparently still practiced by those who went into exile in the tenth century and returned to conquer Chichen Itza in the middle of the thirteenth.

While there may have been some post-termination occupation at Chichen Itza (we find the Casa Redonda a possible candidate), after A.D. 1250 the empire was broken and control of the peninsula passed on to the people of Mayapán.

We hope this model helps explain our orientation in the following description of what we believe to have been Yaxuna's role in the Terminal Classic history of the northern Yucatán peninsula. We will now move to a consideration of that history from the vantage point of Yaxuna.

LATE CLASSIC YAXUNA ANTECEDENTS

In considering Yaxuna and its Terminal Classic history, we find that no period exists in a vacuum. Therefore, a consideration of Terminal Classic Yaxuna must take into account the preceding history of the site (and peninsula) because the political landscape of the Terminal Classic evolved from a markedly different Late Classic.

Late Classic Yaxuna (Yaxuna III [ca. 600–730]) was a dynamic time, a recovery from a late Early Classic denouement that severed most ties with the southern lowlands (Ardren, Suhler, and Johnstone 1998). This resurgence at Yaxuna paralleled events in the rest of the north, where the Late Classic marks a separation from the southern lowlands and development of northern peninsula-oriented interaction areas (Robles and Andrews 1986; Andrews and Robles 1985).

Ceramically, the Late Classic period at Yaxuna is now discernible and provides clear evidence of a substantial, if specialized, population. The Arena Rojo type as defined by Robles (1990) and known as Corona Red at Tancah on the east coast (Ball 1982) dominates the Late Classic Yaxuna III ceramic assemblage. This red-slipped, sherd-tempered type comprises 45 percent of the Late Classic Yaxuna ceramics (Johnstone 1998). While present at other northern sites, Arena Rojo at Yaxuna occurs in much greater frequency and in more forms than elsewhere. We think it entirely possible that Yaxuna and its surrounding area was the center of production, distribution, and consumption for the Arena Rojo ceramic complex.

In terms of comparative ceramic assemblages, the closest documented fit occurs between Yaxuna and the site of Pixoy, located approximately thirty kilometers northeast of Yaxuna (Johnstone 1998). Ek Balam does not seem to exhibit the high frequencies of Arena seen at Yaxuna and Pixoy, suggesting a boundary somewhere between Pixoy and Ek Balam, forty kilometers to the northeast. Whatever the boundaries may eventually prove to be, it appears that Late Classic economic polity zones were much reduced from their Early Classic predecessors. In Early Classic times, an almost homogenous ceramic horizon, dominated by Xanaba group ceramic assemblages, exists from Xelha on the east coast, west to Yaxuna, and then northwest to Komchen on the northern plains (Johnstone 1998).

Excavations at the terminus of the Yaxuna-Coba sacbe indicate it was built during Late Classic Yaxuna III and not during the Terminal Classic Yaxuna IVa (Ardren et al. 1998), as had been previously assumed. Clearly, Coba claimed a large part of the peninsula during the Late Classic and Yaxuna represented the westernmost outpost of its polity (Ardren 1997). The impetus for the eastern peninsula Coba-to-Yaxuna causeway salient may actually be found in the history of the western part of the peninsula. As covered in our above model, we believe that during the Late Classic various Puuc groups centered at western capitals such as Oxkintok, Sayil, Uxmal, and Dzibilchaltun were conducting campaigns of territorial expansion and consolidation in the western regions of the peninsula. Archaeological investigations document some evidence of struggles for control between Puuc interlopers and local northwest coast peoples at cities like Dzibilchaltun (Andrews IV and Andrews V 1980). Once their home polities were secure, we believe the Puuc polities began to push their territorial desires eastward into the central northern lowlands, thus initiating Phase 1 of the above Terminal Classic model.

In spite of the physical sacbe connection, Yaxuna Arena Rojo ceramics were not arriving at Coba in large quantities, and there was a corresponding lack of Coba Late Classic types at Yaxuna. This indicates that intersite commerce in domestic ceramics was not a factor in the Late Classic Yaxuna-Coba relationship.

Evidently, the white road was being used to transport other materials, perhaps troops (Hassig 1992), and foodstuffs to support the outpost. Additionally, relatively high percentages of Puuc-originating slate wares (24 percent) in the Late Classic deposits at Yaxuna indicate some kind of economic and political interaction with western Late Classic Puuc polities prior to their Terminal Classic expropriation of the peninsula. Yaxuna was like many border communities, profiting by the presence of a tense, if open, border between territorial rivals.

Architecture is another means of monitoring these regional relationships in the central northern lowlands. Late Classic Yaxuna III standing masonry buildings were characterized by load-bearing walls topped with corbel vaults constructed of tabular slabs, typical features of what E. Wyllys Andrews IV (1965) termed the Florescent, now the Late Classic, in the northern lowlands. However, we unearthed very few new Yaxuna III–period constructions in our limited horizontal excavations in major architectural complexes outside the North Acropolis. On the other hand, excavations at the North Acropolis (Figure 20.4, our biggest sample of monumental architecture) did show that most buildings exhibited Yaxuna III modifications.

The settlement zone also presents evidence of Yaxuna III occupation. Structure 5E-75 group excavations (Figure 20.5) documented the deliberate termination of an Early Classic platform toward the end of Yaxuna IIb phase, probably by people using east coast ceramic types (Freidel et al. 1992; Stanton 1998). Following this razing, the 5E-75 platform was reoriented to the north, with a new stairway on the northern side. The platform was then capped by a foundation brace for a substantial three-roomed superstructure with load-bearing masonry walls. A round column in the central room's doorway faced north across a raised plaza surface on the platform. This overall plan is commensurate with a ritual and public function for the building. An example of this plan was described by R. M. Leventhal as a shrine in an elaborate Late Classic household at Copan in Honduras (Leventhal 1983). Closer to home, A. L. Smith found examples of this floorplan at Uxmal in the Puuc region (A. L. Smith 1962) and generally noted that such tandem plan designs seemed to predate the characteristic patio quad signature design of Chichen Itza's settlement (see Cobos Palma, Chapter 22, this volume).

This construction was undertaken during Yaxuna III times. Given the probable public and ritual function of this superstructure as a temple or shrine, its clear orientation to the massive ancient acropolis directly to the north, and the superficial modification of structures in that acropolis, we discern continuation of inexpensive community refurbishment documented in the North Acropolis during the Late Classic at Yaxuna.

Mortuary patterns also differed from the Terminal Classic Yaxuna IVb. Two residential burials were found associated with Arena Rojo platters, dating them to Late Classic Yaxuna III. Both burials lacked a stone-lined and capped crypt and represent a very unusual departure from earlier and later burial patterns at Yaxuna,

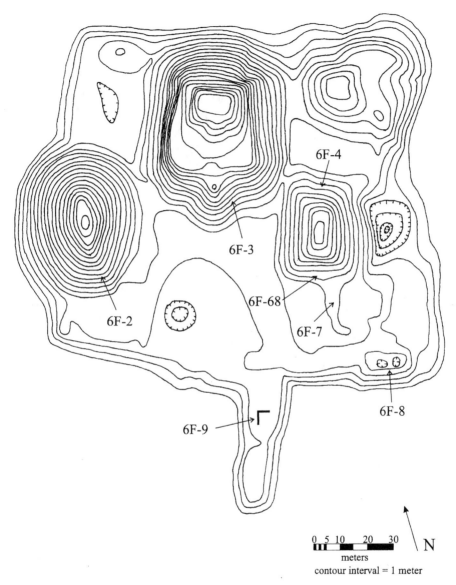

20.4 *Map of North Acropolis.*

yet one consistent with the small sample from Late Classic Palmas–period Coba (Bennett 1993; Ardren 1998; Shaw 1998). Each burial was accompanied by carved jade and bone ornaments, a marked contrast to later Terminal Classic Yaxuna IVa mortuary assemblages from residential contexts.

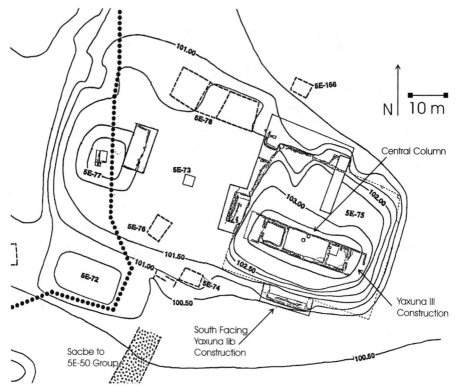

20.5 Map of 5E-75 area.

Late Classic Yaxuna III can be discerned as a relatively populous community based on the settlement-wide distribution of the period's diagnostic ceramics. The two burials alluded to above suggest that some people were prosperous enough to be accompanied by wealth in death. The architecture suggests cheap refurbishment of extant public buildings and evinces broad Late Classic masonry techniques and designs. We see Yaxuna in this period functioning as a western garrison for the Coba polity, to which it was connected by a broad and militarily expeditious roadway (Shaw 1998). Ceramically, the differences between Yaxuna and the Puuc sites in this period are enough to suggest that commerce in this material, gift exchange of fancy vessels, or diplomatic feasting involving imported signature ceramics were infrequent at best.

THE TERMINAL CLASSIC

We divide the Yaxuna Terminal Classic into two phases, Yaxuna IVa (A.D. 730–900) and IVb (A.D. 900–1250; see Suhler, Ardren, and Johnstone 1998; Suhler 1996). The difference between the two lies in the political affiliation and ceramic assemblage of each phase: Yaxuna IVa is the Puuc/Coba/Cehpech occupation while IVb is the Chichen Itza/Sotuta occupation. Yaxuna IVa represents the best-documented occupational phase at the site, with some evidence in almost every excavation undertaken. In addition to reutilized mound groups and structures, there are also new Yaxuna IVa constructions that span the structural range: single-room, ground surface foundation braces; multistructure residential groups; multiroom, multistory palaces; and defensive works. Additionally, Yaxuna IVa architecture is the first to exhibit clearly Puuc characteristics: core-veneer masonry, decorative columns, decorated moldings, specialized "boot-shaped" stones for vaulting, modular cornices, mosaic stonework, as well as extensive use of flagstone flooring (Pollock 1980). To date we have mapped over 600 structures at the site. Analysis of surface ceramics collected during the course of our investigations shows that perhaps as many as 75 percent of the mapped structures had Yaxuna IVa occupations. Because the great majority of these structures are now rubble piles marked by wall lines, excavation is required to posit anything more than a rough chronological assessment that may or may not prove correct.

As previously mentioned, slate ware finishes and forms are known from at least the late Early Classic at Yaxuna and Ek Balam. It is not until Yaxuna IVa, however, that we see a quantitative and qualitative shift in the occurrence. The mechanisms for the en masse arrival of this new ceramic technology are not fully understood. However, we do know that our most robust samples of these earliest Yaxuna IVa types are found at North Acropolis Structure 6F-68 and Structure 6F-8. Here they are marked by western peninsula forms and surface finishes, exhibiting such early and western hallmarks as slippered, hollow feet and distinctive forms such as those illustrated in Robles and Andrews (1986: Figure 3.5). As time passed, these western traits began to drop out of the Yaxuna IVa inventory as the ceramics became more and more like those of Coba, eventually arriving at the point where large portions of the two sites' inventories are virtually the same.

The transition from Late Classic Yaxuna III to Terminal Classic Yaxuna IVa was not peaceful and the violent disjunction between the two periods is apparent in the archaeological record. This is especially true in the North Acropolis, where our excavations have revealed hostile Yaxuna IVa activity centered on Yaxuna III monumental architecture. We now review the evidence for this transition, beginning with the buildings of the North Acropolis.

THE YAXUNA IVA TERMINAL CLASSIC
The North Acropolis

We have not found evidence of a Yaxuna IVa–sponsored destruction event at Structure 6F-3/2nd at the end of Yaxuna III, even though we know the building continued to be used during the Yaxuna IVa occupation phase. We can only surmise that a fourteen-meter-tall building with a centuries-long tradition of political accessions (Suhler 1996) at the apical point of the monumental center continued to prove useful for such purposes. We surmise that the Yaxuna IVa lords would have crafted any destruction or ritual desecration at this locale with an eye toward transfer of power and continued use of the building. This is in marked contrast to the substantial destruction and desecration carried out at immediately adjacent and contemporary Structure 6F-4/2nd. There are several possible reasons for this differential treatment. Perhaps the small stone building constituting Structure 6F-4/2nd was elite residential, rather than ritual, space and was connected to the particular people who were being conquered in this event. Alternatively, the locus of 6F-4/2nd had been previously subjected to severe destruction when the gallery there had been trenched along the centerline. Thus, the people burning the small building may have wanted that side of 6F-4 to remain utterly ruined and abandoned because they were connected to the people who had carried out the original trenching. We return to 6F-4 below. Yaxuna IVa construction at Structure 6F-3 was limited to the building of a staircase (A) over the Yaxuna III Stair B (Structure 6F-3/1st). The Stair A side walls were formed of square (ca. 30-meter), well shaped, and pecked Puuc-style veneer facing stones, tying this construction to other Terminal Classic (Yaxuna IVa) building activity in the North Acropolis. Additionally, the ceramics from the Stair A fill were primarily Terminal Classic Coba types, again assigning construction of Stair A to this period. This staircase was never finished, leading us to believe it was begun late in the Yaxuna IVa phase.

At structure 6F-4, as noted above, we found extensive evidence for hostile treatment of the building at the hands of the arriving Yaxuna IVa inhabitants. Like other violent times (Suhler 1996) in the history of antecedent Structure 6F-4 construction episodes, the Yaxuna IVa–sponsored destruction began by negating the existence and power of the previous structure.

The northern and western sides of Structure 6F-4 were subjected to a variety of terminating activities. In the Yaxuna III masonry room improvised from the western end of the late Early Classic vaulted gallery (Figure 20.6), the desecrators dug holes into the floors and burned fires inside. The intense heat blackened, spalled, cracked, and discolored the floors and subfloor fill and blew out large portions of wall stones, creating an oval, concave area .90 meter wide, 1.4 meters high, and .20 meter deep at its center. Following this burning, the vault was intentionally collapsed into the room.

The final construction atop Structure 6F-4 proper was a Yaxuna IVa masonry altar built against the southeast exterior corner of the Structure 6F-4/2nd Yaxuna III upper terrace bench and room. The construction technique was pure Puuc—the walls were two courses of Puuc-style veneer masonry blocks (Figure 20.7). The polished plaster surface had been blackened by repeated exposure to heat. Within the box we found a concentrated matrix of organic material, charcoal, small rocks, and sherds, all extensively burned. The construction material surrounding this burned matrix did not, however, exhibit any evidence of the discoloration or spalling associated with burning. Therefore, some object com-

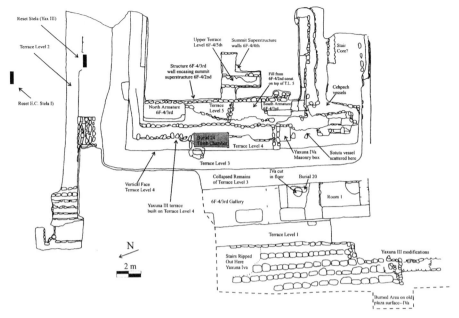

20.6   Yaxuna IVa destruction at 6F-4.

posed of organic material, possibly in a ceramic container, was burned at an
unknown location, placed in the box, covered with unburned stones and smaller
rocks and gravel to the top of the box, and capped by packed marl and polished
plaster. This masonry box is a dedicatory feature, an altar built at the beginning of
Yaxuna IVa to terminate the Yaxuna III occupation of the North Acropolis while
heralding Yaxuna IVa.

The people of Yaxuna IVa also terminated the Yaxuna III Structure 6F-8,
located a little over thirty meters to the south of Structure 6F-4. Our relatively
small area of investigation revealed a hole dug through the floor on the building's
southern exposed wall prior to the collapsing of the vaults (Figure 20.8). We
believe that evidence from Yaxuna and other Maya sites shows the cutting of
floors to represent a desecratory act along the continuum of Maya ritual practice. To
the almost immediate north of this hole, the Yaxuna IVa Maya left more concrete
evidence of termination activity. A ten-centimeter-deep by eighty-centimeter-
wide ash deposit was laid against the interior northern wall. A tightly concentrated assemblage also lay against the wall: Artifacts included ceramic vessels
(whole and fragments), faunal remains, obsidian blades, and a chert biface, all
badly burned (Figure 20.9). In fact, the heat in the burned area was so intense
that it discolored the ten-centimeter plaster floor from top to bottom, much like
the terminations in Room 1 of Structure 6F-4.

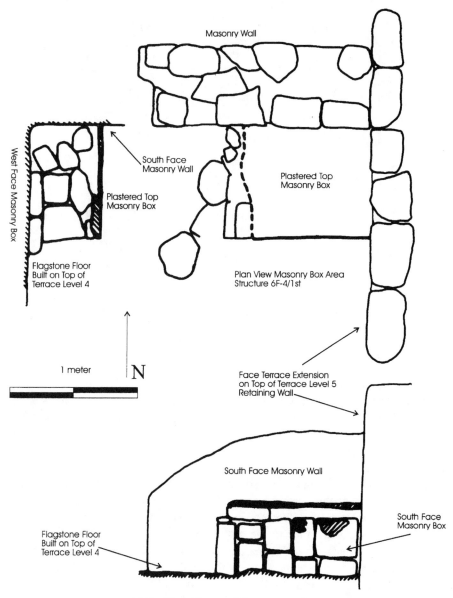

20.7 6F-4, Yaxuna IVa masonry box.

Believed coeval with the construction of the Yaxuna IVa Structure 6F-4 altar mentioned previously was Terminal Classic Structure 6F-68, built onto the southern end of Structure 6F-4. Excavations below and behind Structure 6F-68 revealed cut floors, truncated vertical surfaces, and then naked dry core fill, all

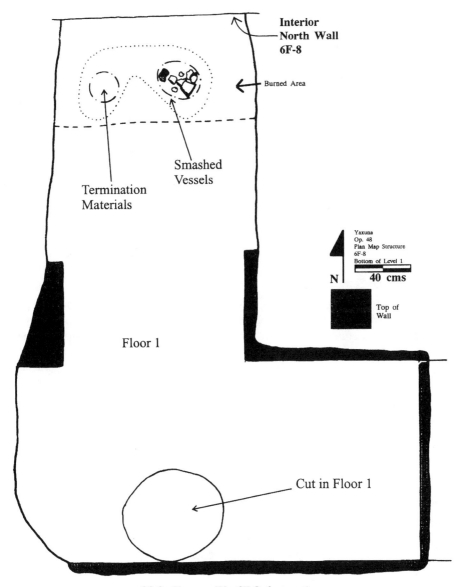

20.8 Yaxuna IVa 6F-8 destruction.

indicating the removal of extant architecture prior to construction of the Terminal Classic building. The building is a three-room vaulted structure built using a mixture of Yaxuna III cut stone, load-bearing interior masonry walls, and Yaxuna IVa Puuc-veneer construction on the exterior facade and interior vault. The superstructure itself sat atop a thirty-centimeter-high decorated building platform, or

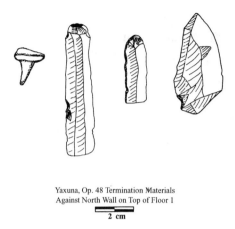

Yaxuna, Op. 48 Termination Materials
Against North Wall on Top of Floor 1

2 cm

20.9   6F-8 termination deposit materials.

plinth. The decorations on this plinth indicate that it was a lineage house, or "popol na" (Suhler 1996), first defined at Copán (Fash et al. 1992).

Structure 6F-68 contained the great majority of our most truly western Puuc Cehpech ceramic types. That fact, along with the mixed architecture, suggests it is one of the earlier Yaxuna IVa buildings, built in the early to middle eighth century. It also shows that when the Puuc contingent arrived at Yaxuna, it comprised an organized presence, complete with the organs of council and rule.

Ballcourt Plaza Construction

Also built during Yaxuna IVa was a ballcourt complex, located fifty meters south of the southern edge of the acropolis and consisting of the ballcourt ranges themselves (Structures 6F-15, 16). We found neither standing architecture nor decorated elements associated with the ballcourt. It appears to have been built rapidly using expedient construction materials and techniques (Johnstone 1994: 68), a pattern reminiscent of Stair A at Structure 6F-3, some 150 meters to the north. Ballcourts are not unknown in the north (n=25) and the dimensions and layout of the Yaxuna example show it to be rather typical of those described in Kurjack et al. (1991).

A semi-subterranean sweatbath (Structure 6F-12) was built fifteen meters to the north of the ballcourt ranges. The sweatbath's dedicatory cache comprised burned and broken ceramics and human bone, suggesting venerated use of desecrated material, a pattern already noted in the altar on the southern terrace of Structure 6F-4 during this same period.

The placement of the ballcourt complex changed public space into a more restricted and semiprivate ceremonial space (Johnstone 1994: 68). Again the architecture makes extensive use of core-veneer masonry and flagstone flooring. Ballcourts are powerful locales, used for creation and sacrifice, inextricably tied to conflict, and certainly used during times of war (Scarborough and Wilcox 1991). We think the construction of the Yaxuna Ballcourt is a direct reflection of the armed and competing camps that vied for control of the peninsula during the Terminal Classic.

Terminal Classic Mortuary Sample

The Terminal Classic at Yaxuna has yielded a large mortuary sample (n=24) from both residential and elite contexts (Bennett 1993). Analysis of these interments has provided a glimpse of Yaxuna IVa Maya burial patterns. Individuals of all economic levels were usually buried in household crypts placed beneath the plaster floors of living areas. Only three Terminal Classic burials were not placed in crypts—these all show signs of having been sacrificial victims. Household crypts were constructed of large thin rocks placed on edge to demarcate the burial space (Bennett 1993). Arms were often hanging loose and under the body or crossed over the pelvis. All primary burials were extended and supine, but orientation was variable. After the items needed in the Underworld had been placed in the crypt, large capstones were put over the top and the floor replaced. Often these crypts were reused several times and later burials caused disturbance to the lower/earlier individuals. In these cases the orientation of the second burial was reversed from the first. Men, women, and children have been found together in the same crypt, indicating some crypts were perhaps created for domestic groups, such as lineages, as opposed to specific individuals.

Ten of the twenty-four individuals had mortuary ceramic vessels associated with their interment. Because some of the Yaxuna IVa burials were clearly disturbed by Sotuta peoples during Yaxuna IVb, it is likely that an even higher number of burials originally contained ceramic offerings. The most common placement was over the skull, but vessels were also placed over the chest and pelvis. The burial goods of women (n=15) were much more consistent than those of men (n=7); in nearly all female interments a shell pendant was found in the pelvic region, and bone from the tibia of the white-tailed deer was found along the lower half of the body. These pendants are trapezoidal with two holes at the narrow end for suspension and are made of *Spondylus americanus* shell. Landa describes that young girls wore these pendants below the waist and that they were removed at marriage (Tozzer 1941). Men were buried with a greater diversity of grave items that often reflected their occupation as warriors, shamans, or healers. Obsidian bladelets were common in male burials, as were unique items such as poison bottles, star-shaped jewelry, and small *sastuns,* or divining stones.

Like most ancient populations in Mesoamerica, females were smaller in stature and suffered more malnutrition, as evidenced in a higher percentage of gumline caries and macrohypoplasia (Bennett 1994: 105). The entire population appears to have had a diet based on carbohydrates, which caused a high percentage of adult gumline caries, although the incidence of childhood malnutrition seems fairly low (Bennett 1994: 105). This suggests that nursing children received sufficient calories but that the overall diet of the adult population was low in protein and high in corn or other starches. Life expectancy was shorter for women than for men, and we have no evidence of a woman living beyond thirty-five years, although all appear to have died of natural causes. A number of men seem to have lived to be more than forty-five years of age. Both men and women practiced culturally specific cranial deformation, with no discernible differences in style, and both men and women modified their teeth with filing, although only men had hematite inlays.

Regional Dynamics

In addition to the ceramic and architectural evidence from the main site of Yaxuna, other data from outlying sites in the Yaxuna area suggest that these satellites were also brought into the Coba/Cehpech hegemony (Freidel 1987). Robertson (1986) proposed that iconographic differences between sculpture from the Yaxuna region (and, in particular, from Xtelhu to the southwest and Popola to the north of Yaxuna) and sculpture from Chichen Itza were significant enough to represent separate chronological periods—the Yaxcaba (Yaxuna) style being Late Classic while the Chichen Itza style was Terminal Classic to Postclassic. As Freidel (1987) noted, Robertson's iconographic temporal assignments mirrored the ceramic arguments of the time: Cehpech was generally regarded as earlier than Sotuta on the peninsula. Now the consensus is that for a period of time Cehpech and Sotuta were coeval, registering different polity affiliations. This shift strengthens the case for the alternative hypothesis that stylistic and iconographic differences between the adjacent Chichen Itza and Yaxuna regions register different political and military affiliations in Terminal Classic times. The iconographic programs of Chichen Itza and the Yaxuna area do, however, share some ritual themes, like processions and militaristic themes (Schele and Freidel 1990; Freidel 1992). This common focus on captives and warriors is further indication that strife and conflict were an integral part of life during the Terminal Classic on the northern peninsula, as is evidently the case elsewhere in the Maya world.

Epigraphically, the title of "*sahal,*" marking a second-level lord in the western part of the southern lowlands, appears on an accession panel from the small site of Mopila, twelve kilometers to the west of Yaxuna (Freidel 1990: 77; Schele and Freidel 1990). The title is unknown at Chichen Itza. At the site of Xkalumkin in Campeche, an individual acceded to the position of sahal in A.D. 733 (the beginning of our Yaxuna IVa phase). Schele and Grube (1995: 92) and Nikolai Grube (1994b) have determined that cadres of such sahalob ruled this capital in the absence of kings or ahawob during the eighth century. Beyond these occurrences, the title is exclusively found in southern lowland centers along the Usumacinta and within the western rivers district (Stuart 1984; Grube 1994b; Schele and Freidel 1990: 58). When added to the fine-ware ceramics produced in this area (Sabloff 1975) and present in Campeche and the northern plains, the distribution of sahal titles presents a case for very direct and reasonably early contacts between the people of the western southern lowlands and those of Campeche and the northern peninsula. Such connections may mark population movements that played a role in the growth and eastern movement of the groups from the Puuc cities.

END OF THE YAXUNA IVA TERMINAL CLASSIC

Violence and termination also characterize the transition from a Puuc/Cehpech-influenced Yaxuna IVa to the Chichen/Sotuta-dominated Yaxuna IVb. We believe forces allied with or from Chichen Itza conquered Yaxuna sometime ca. 900, perhaps making Yaxuna one of the first casualties of the developing Itza empire. For at least the later part of the Terminal Classic period, Yaxuna's people had been living with the presence of war and were engaged in activities to protect and defend the territory claimed by the local and/or distant lords of the city. Eventually, their sphere of power imploded and forced them to fortify areas of the site itself.

Defensive Works

We have identified defensive works dating to the end of Yaxuna IVa. At least a portion of the Yaxuna population enclosed themselves within the North Acropolis and the satellite site of Xkanha, located 1.75 kilometers north. We have also noted analogous surface features at the East Acropolis, located just south of the last one-half kilometer of the Yaxuna-Coba sacbe. Thus it is entirely possible that at the end of the Yaxuna IVa period occupation consisted of fortified acropoli, each defending itself against attacking forces.

The North Acropolis pyramids and superstructures were arranged on a raised platform roughly 100 by 100 meters and some eight meters high at the highest point. It was ringed in antiquity on the summit by 330 meters of crudely constructed walls and palisade foundation braces (Figure 20.10 [Ambrosino et al. 2001]). When existing structures and the established edge of the platform are included, the total defensive circumference can be calculated at 465 meters. The walls vary in thickness from .60 to three meters and are rarely over a meter tall; they are most likely the basal remains of a wooden or thorny palisade, such as proposed for the Petexbatun region (Demarest et al. 1997) and as known in the ethnohistorical literature on the Maya (Pagden 1971). In several places the walls run over earlier structures, as in the case of Structure 6F-88 on the southern perimeter of the North Acropolis wall system. This was a small, rectangular platform exhibiting the same type of Puuc veneer stone as seen at Structure 6F-68 and had been dismantled to facilitate placement of the wall, its stones built into the wall. This association dates the wall to the end of Yaxuna IVa. When combined with platform edge placement at the top of a steep slope two to four meters above the surrounding ground surface, a one-meter-high stone wall augmented with wooden palisades would present a formidable obstacle.

Although apparently built in haste (Ambrosino et al. 2001), the wall system nonetheless demonstrates application of a defensive theory and strategy. Access into the North Acropolis was controlled through four entranceways. In some cases the entrances are associated with small guard stations, low platforms of rough rock that could have served to support pole scaffolds and platforms as portrayed in Maya mural art and graffiti. This would have served to elevate and extend line of sight from each post. In other locations the entrances are baffled and thus further restricted. The plaza on the North Acropolis was partitioned by a number of internal walls, further augmenting the defensive measures provided by the perimeter walls. This partitioning of space on the acropolis allowed for separate defense of individual enclosed areas and provided the defenders with pull-back zones if the invaders were to breach the outer barriers in large numbers.

Fortifications at Xkanha

The outpost of Xkanha, 1.75 kilometers north from the center of Yaxuna, is situated on a natural bedrock outcropping adjacent to a freshwater cenote (Figure 20.11 [Ardren 1997]). It has a commanding view of the northern frontier of Yaxuna territory that was the most likely avenue of approach from Chichen Itza. During earlier periods, the Xkanha Acropolis was an elite palace. However, during the Terminal Classic period the structures were renovated to serve as a garrison or staging area for military action on the outskirts of Yaxuna.

Key defensive elements were the modification of a small entrance area into a platform 2.5 meters above the earlier acropolis floor. This tower was located on the northeastern corner of the acropolis, the only position in which both the main entrance and interior plaza could be seen. All the doorways into structures on the Xkanha Acropolis were narrowed with crude reused stone and a massive twenty-meter-long wall was erected over the only stairway leading into the acropolis. This wall was three to five meters high and built of large boulders set between well-shaped wall stones. Like some other defensive walls in the northern lowlands (Webster 1979), the Xkanha wall was built quickly, without the usual consideration for permanence and quality construction that characterizes most formal Maya architecture.

Both strongholds were unable to withstand attack from Chichen Itza for an extended time and each was overrun and destroyed as actual and symbolic seats of power. The invading forces did not intend to occupy the fortified strongholds themselves. The real battle was over the surrounding territorial holdings. The fortified acropolis groups were conquered, terminated, and left in a state of ruin, insuring that neither they nor their vanquished patrons could be used in further action against the new rule imposed by Chichen Itza.

THE YAXUNA IVA–IVB TRANSITION

North Acropolis

As in the case of the Yaxuna III–IVa transition, we found no termination activities marking the Yaxuna IVb arrival at Structure 6F-3. However, the Yaxuna IVa Stair A may provide some detail on the end of the Puuc-allied occupation at Yaxuna. Even among other Yaxuna IVa constructions, Stair A represents atypical construction techniques and materials: unworked stones in a matrix of loose, dark soil. This is the only place at Yaxuna where we encountered this type of fill. Normal fill for Yaxuna IVa was a mix of dry core fill underlying a concrete core with veneer exterior. The overall inferior nature of Stair A implies hurried con-

20.10   North Acropolis with wall.

struction. Additionally, the staircase was never completed, ending some six meters below the top of the vaulted passage. The use of atypical construction techniques and low-grade materials suggest to us that the staircase was built in a time of stress, when the authorities were impaired. Its unfinished state points to Stair A as one of the last Yaxuna IVa monumental constructions at Yaxuna, its completion interrupted by the siege and fall of the city.

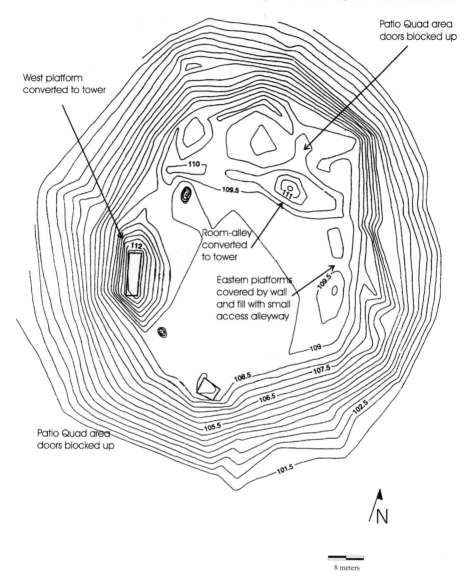

Patio Quad area
doors blocked up

West platform
converted to tower

110

109.5

111

Room-alley
converted
to tower

112

Eastern platforms
covered by wall
and fill with small
access alleyway

109.5

0

109

108.5

107.5

106.5

102.5

Patio Quad area
doors blocked up

105.5

101.5

N

8 meters

20.11   Xkanha and wall.

In the case of Structure 6F-68, the Puuc-style council house along the south-ern edge of Structure 6F-4, a termination carried out at this building was deliber-ate, focused, and extensive enough to require construction of support structures appended to the building (Figure 20.12). Large amounts of culinary wares around the base of the low, rectangular Structure 6F-7 platform are remains of Itza-led feasts celebrating Structure 6F-68's desecration. A Sotuta tripod grater bowl fragment from the central floor cut in Room 2 fit another from the northwestern side of Structure 6F-7. This artifactual relationship ties the two deposits together and establishes that feasting began while the Structure 6F-68 vaults were intact. Additionally, the presence of Sotuta ceramics interspersed with the Yaxuna IVa Cehpech materials represents what we call "signature materials." Such artifacts occur in contexts that demonstrate the dominance of their makers while ritually overpowering an enemy place. They might have been smashed during feasting, or deposited whole with the burned and smashed materials of the enemy.

Contextually, the destruction visited upon Structure 6F-68 manifests many of the hallmarks we have come to associate with termination events: large holes were dug through each of the three-room floors, intense fires were burned within each room, whole ceramic vessels, fragments, and large amounts of elite material culture were smashed and scattered throughout the rooms and in a roughly five-meter-wide strip along the face of the building (Ambrosino 1998.) Particularly hard hit was the westernmost room. Burial 25, a stone-lined crypt intrusive to the original structure, had been re-entered, an attempt was made to remove all grave goods, and the skeletal material accessible to the desecrating ritualists (from the pelvis up [Figure 20.13]) had been scrambled (Ambrosino 1997). Examination of the pelvis indicated a female occupant and the few artifacts from the disturbed deposit included mosaic jade elements and the backing for a mirror. The presence of a royal female in a lineage house suggests that the occupying Puuc forces used females as a means of cementing relationships between the new rulers and any extant leaders of the previous regime at Yaxuna. This type of behavior is known from other Maya sites and time periods. Consider the case at Naranjo in the late seventh century when a daughter of the Calakmul king was sent to the site to rehabilitate a disgraced and punished dynasty (Schele and Freidel 1990).

After the Burial 25 desecration, intense fires were burned in both the crypt and the room. The doorway to this room was filled with a fifty-centimeter-high deposit of white marl interspersed with horizontally bedded sherd layers. In front of the room we found a stone stool, painted in red and black, and several smashed but whole ceramic vessels, some in early western Cehpech style. We believe several of these vessels may have originally come from Burial 25. Additional material in front of the building included fragments of *manos, metates,* projectile points, jade implements, shell, human bone, animal bone, and so forth. Finally, the jambs and lintels were pulled and the entire building was collapsed into itself and to the south, where it covered and preserved the stratigraphic record of termination.

Ballcourt Plaza

The ballcourt itself had several areas of white marl deposits with bedded sherd layers, much like the ones found at Structure 6F-68. Ceramic analysis of

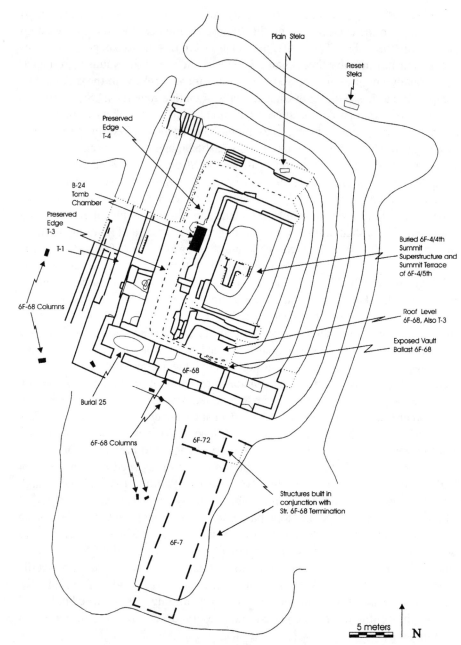

Plain Stela

Reset Stela

Preserved Edge T-4

B-24 Tomb Chamber

Preserved Edge T-3

T-1

6F-68 Columns

Buried 6F-4/4th Summit Superstructure and Summit Terrace of 6F-4/5th

Roof Level 6F-68, Also T-3

Exposed Vault Ballast 6F-68

6F-68

Burial 25

6F-68 Columns

6F-72

Structures built in conjunction with Str. 6F-68 Termination

6F-7

5 meters

N

20.12 6F-68 area at time of Yaxuna IVb termination.

these layers indicates the presence of Yaxuna IVb ceramics among the predominant Yaxuna IVa types. We again view this as a situation representing the use of signature artifacts, as discussed previously. The associated steam bath was also purposefully filled in. This fill comprised earth, ceramic fragments, and an almost life-size, sitting stone sculpture of a female torso. Prior to being dumped upside down into the steam bath, the statue was decapitated and the legs had been cut off. Such behavior does not fall within the range of venerating burial practices.

YAXUNA IVB OCCUPATION

The Sotuta occupation of Yaxuna is a drastic reduction from the Yaxuna IVa period. We have found no evidence of occupation or construction in the settlement zone or at the Xkanha satellite site. Our only traces of Yaxuna IVb occupation are found in a very restricted locale on Structure 6F-3 of the North Acropolis and in the area of the Ballcourt Plaza. In the North Acropolis, Structure 6F-3 shows some evidence of Yaxuna IVb occupation. However, this assessment is based on stratigraphy associated with the end of Yaxuna IVb and is discussed in the section that follows. Suffice it to say here that in Structure 6F-3, accession architecture was utilized during Yaxuna IVb times. Access to the under-stair corridor and the chamber was possible from the topmost part of the uncompleted Stair A, which remained uncompleted afterward. This suggests that while the building was used the new rulers did not undertake improvements.

Yaxuna IVb occupation was, in the areas we were able to discern it, rather ephemeral compared to earlier occupations of the settlement. Evidence from the North Acropolis provides for only a single Yaxuna IVb construction. This is Structure 6F-9, a single-room, free-standing vaulted building constructed on a finger of land extending out from the southern center of the North Acropolis. While we extracted very little information from this building, its dedicatory cache included a Sotuta *incensario* fragment (Figure 20.14). Architecturally, it exhibited the most traditionally Puuc-style elements, including true boot-shaped vault stones and false soffits (Figure 20.15), suggesting that it was raised as tribute by the conquered.

Beyond our work, there has been significant reconstruction activity undertaken since 1996 in other ballcourt plaza structures by Lic. Lourdes Toscano and the CRY-INAH. Based on our observations of the reconstructed buildings, the entire ballcourt plaza may have been a small locus of Yaxuna IVb Sotuta occupation. As such, it is quite different in both size and scope than the Yaxuna IVa occupation it replaced. In fact, it may represent no more than a caretaker population, placed at the site to monitor Sotuta interests in the area and to keep open the lines of commerce to both the east coast and the southern regions of the peninsula. As we have already discussed, such an occupation is in marked contrast to the extensive construction and population numbers that characterized Yaxuna IVa.

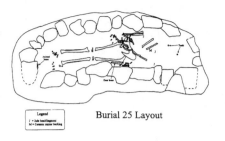

Burial 25 Layout

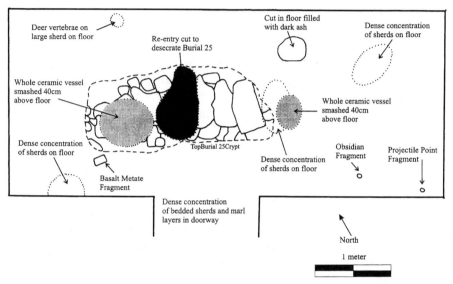

20.13 Burial 25.

In another work (Suhler and Freidel 1995), we stated our belief that an alliance of forces led by Mayapán conquered Chichen Itza sometime around A.D. 1250. Evidence from Yaxuna indicates that forces using Mayapán ceramics also brought about the end of Yaxuna IVb and its modest settlement in the monumental center of the site. Interestingly enough, the Chichen-related Structure 6F-9 was not deliberately collapsed at the end of Yaxuna IVb. Rather, the people of Yaxuna recall that this building was standing until sometime in the 1940s or 1950s, when a large tree that had taken root in the roof fell to the east, carrying with it a large portion of the building. This information was borne out during excavation when we encountered the burial of a youth believed killed by a lead ball sometime during the Colonial (Republican?) period. Little of the fine veneer stones of this shrine's exterior were observable when we were working at Yaxuna. Subsequent work by the CRY-INAH revealed the existence of these veneer stones along the base of the building. It is possible that its termination after A.D. 1250 involved stripping a

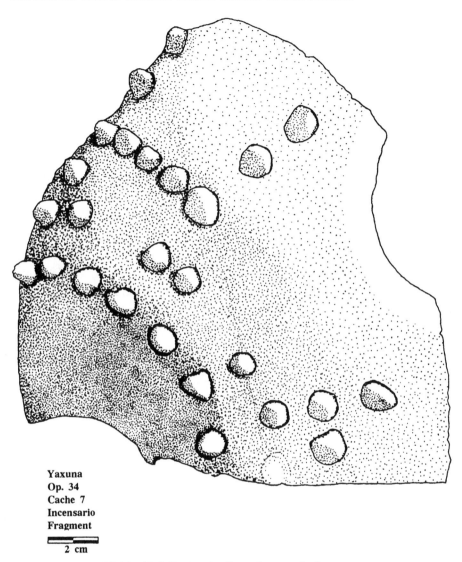

Yaxuna
Op. 34
Cache 7
Incensario
Fragment

2 cm

20.14 6F-9 Espita Applique incensario fragment.

decorated exterior and leaving the concrete wall core exposed, thereby leaving the building standing but "flayed," lacking meaning or publicly accessible statement of its purpose. In the northeastern settlement zone, Ardren (1997) excavated a Postclassic shrine with recycled decorated veneer stones along its base wall.

On the North Acropolis proper and at Structure 6F-3, we have some evidence for the types of stratigraphic deposits associated with architectural terminations.

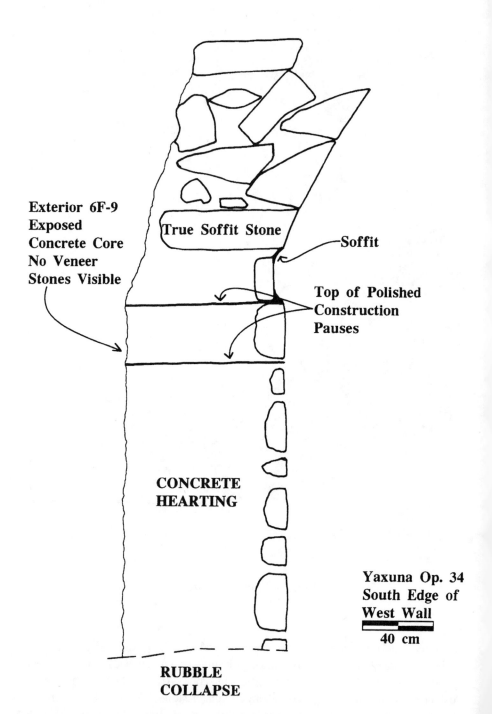

Exterior 6F-9
Exposed
Concrete Core
No Veneer
Stones Visible

True Soffit Stone

Soffit

Top of Polished
Construction
Pauses

CONCRETE
HEARTING

Yaxuna Op. 34
South Edge of
West Wall

40 cm

RUBBLE
COLLAPSE

20.15 6F-9 architectural details.

Burial 19 was placed into an oval pit cut through the floor of the east-west corridor that ran under the staircase, directly in front of the chamber doorway (Figure 20.16). Osteological analysis of what may represent one of the last pre-Columbian Maya to inhabit the site center of Yaxuna reveals a robust male twenty-five to thirty years of age. All of the teeth, including the articulating surfaces, were, however, covered with a thin layer of dental calculus, indicating his diet for some time prior to his death consisted of nonsolid food, most likely corn gruel or pozole, perhaps a product of captivity or siege. Position of the body suggests he was placed bound, face-down on his knees, with his arms bent at the elbows, and his hands tight together under the chin (probably tied). Cranial preservation was poor; the skull appears to have been crushed by two deliberately placed stones prior to the catastrophic and deliberate collapse of the corridor's vault (Bennett 1994). Dispatch by stoning (whether murder or sacrifice is a culturally relative issue) has been documented from both the Mul Chic murals and Caste War history (Barrera Rubio 1980; Reed 1964).

The only associated artifact was a portion of a Chen Mul (Postclassic, Yaxuna V) incensario, another occurrence of a signature vessel. It was accompanied by a veritable menagerie of faunal material that trailed from the pit and into the southwest corner of the chamber. Species represented in the pit included two deer skulls with horns, a bird skeleton, a small rodent skeleton, and portions of a snake. Faunal scatter included the bones of fetal and adult deer, rabbit, birds, lizards, and snakes. Just underneath the doorway of the chamber we found a Chen Mul incensario face and arm (Figure 20.17).

We think Burial 19 was a Sotuta occupant of Yaxuna sacrificed by the forces of Mayapán—and a miserable one in life as well as death (Bennett [1994] found that, in addition to the extended gruel diet, he had the heavy neck muscles of a tump-line porter). Shortly after deposition of the individual and associated material, the roofs of the chamber and corridor were collapsed, ending the 900-year use-span of Structure 6F-3.

Following the end of Yaxuna IVb there was some sort of activity at the site during the Postclassic (Yaxuna V). We have excavated examples of Postclassic altars and shrines in the site center and at Xkanha (Ardren 1997). However, we have recovered no evidence of occupation: no mound groups, no house mounds, no ceremonial structure larger than a small shrine or altar on a pre-existing structure. Given the fact that there exists ceremonial or ritual architecture, we feel there should also be domestic architecture for the populations that built the shrines and altars. However, we find it likely that Postclassic Yaxuna V settlement lies outside the site center. Such a settlement pattern would mark a disjunction from the previous 1,700 years of occupation at the site. If this is the case, the reasons for such a change must remain opaque pending further and more extensive exploration of the Postclassic period at Yaxuna.

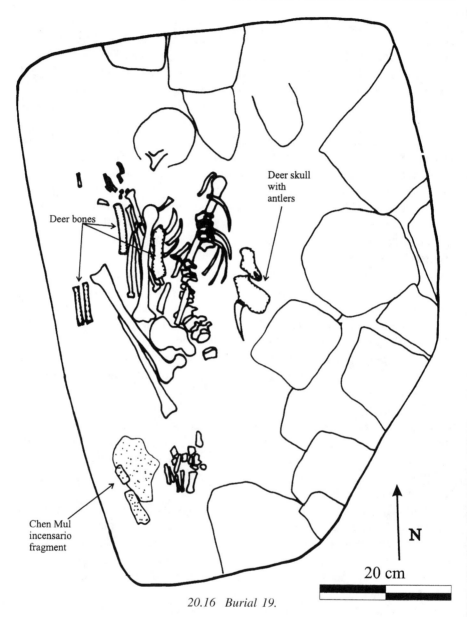

Deer skull
with
antlers

Deer bones

Chen Mul
incensario
fragment

N

20 cm

20.16   Burial 19.

CONCLUDING THOUGHTS

The inhabitants of Yaxuna, over the long-term, reaped the benefits of living in a strategic locale relative to trade routes crossing the interior of the northern lowlands. Some 100 kilometers south of the nearest salt beds on the northern coast,

Yaxuna traders may well have moved that precious condiment overland into towns and cities of the central lowlands beginning in Preclassic times. (The public buildings are massive and there are links in both ceramics and architecture to the south.) In the Early Classic period, Yaxuna had rulers who were clearly mainstream in their access to exotic wealth and craft objects (Suhler and Freidel 1998; Freidel and Suhler 1998). Again, our data register a prosperous community with far-flung trading ties. In the Late Classic, Yaxuna was quite clearly part of a larger, regional network, as manifested in the longest intersite stone road in the Maya world tying it to Coba, the largest city in the northeastern lowlands. The Terminal Classic witnessed the construction of two elaborate Puuc-style palaces at Yaxuna, only one of which was investigated by our project (the other, a two-story palace, is in the Southeastern Acropolis.) Again, outside alliances are strong in this period. Through all these periods, we have data from the settlement zone to show the existence of sizable residential populations, populations no doubt attracted by the prospects of profitable work.

But clearly there was a price to be paid for living in a community, whether independent capital or vassal to outsiders, that was strategic in the commercial and political interests of regional powers. Violence marked the succession of periods we so dispassionately correlate with ceramic spheres and architectural styles, and we predict that future settlement archaeology at Yaxuna will further document its impact on the lives of ordinary residents. One can get a glimpse of northern lowland urban warfare in the Terminal Classic victory murals painted in the Upper Temple of the Jaguars and the Monjas at Chichen Itza. Nevertheless, the objective of conquest or takeover at Yaxuna must have been generally aimed at capitalizing on the presence of the community (as the populations remain high across the transitions), so, the majority of the time, the dangers to citizenry must have been offset by the advantages. Such equations, however, fatally changed with the advent of the Terminal Classic period. Chichen Itza, located only twenty kilometers north of Yaxuna, needed no additional strategic commercial entrepôt or military garrison town in the central northern lowlands. It could provide those functions perfectly well. The goal of Chichen Itza's war against Yaxuna must have been apparent to the people there as well as to their rulers. The desperation evinced in the rapidly thrown up fortifications around their high places is clear enough: none of these places had a chance to withstand any lengthy siege. Visual inspection of the recent CRY-INAH work to the south of the North Acropolis and to the west of the ballcourt group shows a broad, roughly oval plaza area demarcated by small, masonry range structures on low platforms. It would be reasonable to speculate that this was Chichen Itza's little market town at Yaxuna after thorough destruction of the Puuc-style palaces and other more ambitious facilities of the previous Yaxuna IVa phase. We have in hand clear data that the Northern Acropolis was neglected in this phase. The demotion of Yaxuna from a town to a village under the Itza is pretty decisive.

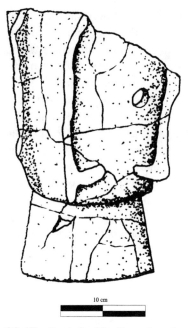

10 cm

20.17 Burial 19 Postclassic incensario fragments.

The fall of Yaxuna in the Terminal Classic seems tied, then, to the rise of Chichen Itza in a purely local geographical sense in that they were natural competitors for regional trade passing through the north-central interior. Commensurate with this notion of a trade node in the area, we see glimpses throughout Yaxuna's history of strangers and struggles involving alliance to polities outside the area. But why, then, did Yaxuna not recover when Chichen Itza's own people finally fell back on their last redoubts and were slaughtered by their enemies? The Postclassic population at Yaxuna was small and ephemeral at best.

However, someone remembered the glory of the white road that stretched eastward from Yaxuna to Coba like the legendary white umbilicus still recounted today in some villages as linking Chichen Itza to the east coast. They built a small Postclassic shrine on the platform at the terminus of the causeway and placed a few precious items in it. Perhaps with the fall of Chichen Itza the main trade routes really had shifted decisively to the coast in the Postclassic period, as Rathje and Sabloff (1973) proposed in anticipation of their work on Cozumel Island. Conversely, perhaps the rise of Chichen Itza in the first place was motivated by the presence of high-volume trade routes in the northern interior (Krochock 1998), along with rich chocolate-growing lands in the many earth-filled sinkholes of that area. Such scenarios imply that the eighth century north of the eighteenth latitude was still a time of prosperity and large farming populations capable of sustaining such trade (and not a time of catastrophic drought and famine). Such speculations are not without potential for testing, but they point to the need for more systematic excavation in interior sites of the northern lowlands.

21

THE DECLINE OF THE EAST
THE CLASSIC TO POSTCLASSIC TRANSITION AT EK BALAM, YUCATÁN

*William M. Ringle, George J. Bey III, Tara Bond Freeman, Craig A. Hanson,
Charles W. Houck, and J. Gregory Smith*

It is a measure of progress that this volume includes four case studies of the Terminal Classic from northern Yucatán, rather than the single synthetic article of its predecessor (Andrews IV 1973). Although one might still second Andrews IV's (1965) complaint that the northern lowlands remain a "world apart" to many Maya archaeologists, the pace of fieldwork there has expanded enormously, much of it still unpublished. We remain far from an understanding of the Terminal Classic interchange between north and south, but internal events in the north are beginning to emerge in a somewhat more comprehensible light.

One thread linking developments in northern Maya archaeology over the past twenty-five years has been the recognition of the importance of regional diversity. This theme was first sounded by E. Wyllys Andrews IV (1960, 1965, 1973) in a series of papers on Dzibilchaltún, including his summary article on the northern "collapse." In these, Andrews attempted to decouple what would now be referred to as the Terminal Classic chronologies of the northern and southern lowlands, arguing that the two areas underwent quite different trajectories. Far from paralleling the decline in the south, the ninth century in the north was a period of great cultural vigor characterized by the Puuc architectural style and tenth *baktun* hieroglyphic dates. The divergence was such that Andrews believed that the span from A.D. 800 to 1200 warranted an altogether different terminology, which he preferred to designate as the Florescent Period.[1]

Somewhat later, Ball argued that heterogeneity at the site level must also be recognized and that one need not suppose that sites rose or fell in unison. Ball

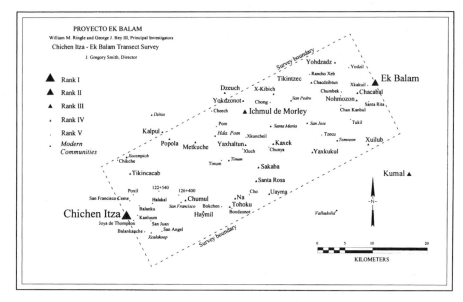

21.1 Map of the Ek Balam-Chichén Itzá transect.

(1979: 19) emphasized that caution must be exerted when making cross-peninsular arguments:

> There is no reason whatsoever why the sequences of development or temporal relationships at Becan, Edzná, or Dzibilchaltún should replicate the sequences of development or temporal relationships of Uxmal, Chichén Itzá, and Mayapán. Rather, I would suggest that Mayanists could well profit from development of an appreciation for the extent of diversity present within the archaeological record, . . . and a new emphasis on illuminating rather than homogenizing such diversity where it occurs.

In this paper, we present a striking example of such regional diversity, the case of Ek Balam, Yucatán, a large center about twenty-five kilometers north of ancient Sací, modern Valladolid (Figure 21.1). The importance of this site is borne out in the meager historical record. In the words of an important sixteenth-century *Relación,* it was one of the *"principales cabeceras de esta provincia"* under the leadership of the founding ruler Ek Balam and his successor, He Blai Chac, who supposedly arrived from the east (de la Garza et al. 1983: II: 138–139). During this initial heroic age, Ek Balam and his four "captains" were each said to have been responsible for the construction of one of the buildings surrounding the main plaza. Some indication of the territorial ambitions of the city comes from mentions of conflict with neighboring Yalcoba and a statement in the *Relación de Nabalam* indicating that it and Tahcoba were at one time tributaries of a later king of Ek Balam, Namom Cupul (de la Garza et al. 1983: II: 186). In addition to providing tribute, the latter towns also worshiped an "idol" located in Ek Balam. Whether or not these stories have any truth to them, Ek Balam reached its considerable apex during the Late Terminal Classic period. (Both archaeology and ethnohistory indicate that the site was also important during the Late Postclassic, after which it became a colonial reduction community with a small *ramada* chapel.) The stone "idol" mentioned previously may be a reference to one of the two finished stelae now in the main plaza of Ek Balam, one of which, Stela 1, bears an Emblem Glyph (Figure 21.5c). This supports the *Relación*'s contention that Ek Balam was a significant regional political center, since Emblem Glyphs are extremely rare in northern Yucatán (Ringle, Bey, and Peraza 1991).

This prima facie evidence for political autonomy would be unremarkable were it not for the wider culture-historical context within which the site evolved. A fragmentary Long Count date on Stela 1 places it sometime within the first few decades of baktun 10, or after A.D. 830. This agrees well with a radiocarbon date taken on a wooden lintel from a passageway in a secondary pyramid atop the main acropolis (Str. GT-1), giving a 1σ calibrated date of A.D. 783 (881) 940.[2] These dates indicate that Stela 1 was contemporary with most of the other hieroglyphic dates from northern Yucatán (see Grube 1994b for a compendium), as well as indicating a relatively late date for continued architectural activity on the acropolis.

The contemporaries most important to understanding Ek Balam's political trajectory are Chichén Itzá, some fifty-one kilometers to the west-southwest, and Cobá, about sixty kilometers to the southeast, both within two days' walk. While discussions of the northern Terminal Classic have usually emphasized the relationship between Chichén Itzá and sites in the Puuc and on the northwest plains, demonstration of the immense size and northern ceramic affiliations of Late Classic Cobá (Folan, Kintz, and Fletcher 1983; Garduño 1979; Benavides 1981a, 1981b; Robles 1990; Gallareta 1984) caused many Mayanists to rethink prior emphases. Consequently, several recent models have explored the implications of a possible Chichén Itza–Cobá confrontation during the period (Andrews and Robles 1985; Robles and Andrews 1986; Schele and Freidel 1990: 352–354). In these scenarios, as in earlier western-oriented discussions, Chichén eventually emerged as the winner and gradually was able to exercise dominion over virtually the entire peninsula. It was this contrast between hypothesized large-scale peninsular "empires" with apparent evidence for political independence at the very interface between these macrostates that drew us to Ek Balam. Could evidence for regional dominion by one or the other of these centers be established or, failing that, must our conception of the hegemonic extent of these states be modified?

THE EK BALAM PROJECT

To address these questions we initiated detailed survey of Ek Balam itself. During five field seasons we systematically mapped about 3.3 square kilometers of an

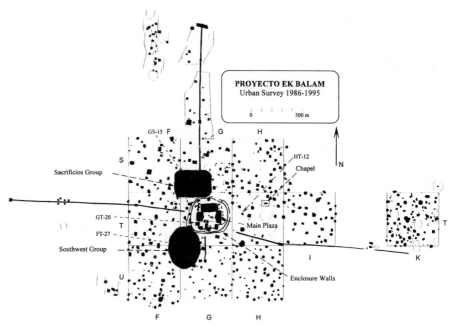

21.2 Map of the Ek Balam urban survey.

estimated 12–15 square kilometers of continuous urban settlement, clearly demonstrating the site's importance as a major urban center and demographic focus (Figure 21.2). Our survey included the central 2.25 square kilometers of the site, two additional 500-meter-square blocks extending eastward, exploration along the three longest causeways (including several cleared milpas), and several milpas far to the north and south. These indicate that settlement continues at least two kilometers from the site center; Quadrat KT indicates that in some cases occupation continued to be quite dense even at this distance. Our areal estimate is therefore a conservative one. Nearly 700 structures lie within the survey boundaries.

Because the study of large urban centers could not alone provide answers to the research questions we were addressing, we extended our settlement study to include both the immediate hinterlands (referred to as the "rural survey," directed by Charles Houck) and survey of settlement between Ek Balam and Chichén Itzá (referred to as the "intersite survey," directed by J. Gregory Smith). Our rural survey, examining the lands presumed to be under direct control of Ek Balam, is defined as that area within a radius of fifteen kilometers from Ek Balam's center. Its purpose was to assess population density and organization, as well as the disposition of natural features such as water sources, in relation to the urban core. Initially sites were selected on an ad hoc basis, but during the 1994–1995

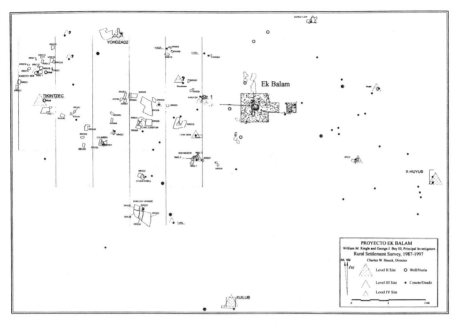

21.3 Map of the Ek Balam rural survey.

seasons Houck concentrated on sampling an 8X10-kilometer block to the west of Ek Balam, providing a link between the site center and the intersite survey. The rural survey has examined sites ranging from "vacant" milpas to presumed second-tier administrative centers, including a thirty-hectare settlement sample of one of the most important of these, Xuilub. In all, 4.11 square kilometers were surveyed (Houck 1996, 1998; Figure 21.3).

The concerns of the intersite survey were determination of the economic, cultural, and political boundaries between Ek Balam and Chichén Itzá. A related concern was to better define the stratigraphic relationship between the Late Terminal Classic ceramic units of these two sites in hopes of resolving the overlap question (e.g., essays in Sabloff and Andrews V 1986). The survey sampling universe was defined as a twenty-kilometer-wide swath between the two sites (Figure 21.1). Ichmul de Morley received particular attention since it is almost certainly the largest site between Ek Balam and Chichén and is approximately a day's walk from each (24.6 kilometers from Ek Balam, 28.5 kilometers from Chichén Itzá). Here we mapped, surface collected, and test-pitted a comparable thirty-hectare settlement sample (Ringle and Smith 1998). During 1998 and 1999, Smith returned to conduct a more extensive survey within the transect, in the process locating several new sites, including one with a ballcourt (Smith 1999; Ringle, Bey, and Smith 2000). The boundary between Ek Balam and Cobá was not an explicit goal of the project, but in 1999 we were able to survey seventy hectares of the large site of Kumal about seventeen kilometers to the southwest of Ek Balam and in the general direction of Cobá (Ringle, Bey, et al. 2000).

At Ek Balam, excavations were placed primarily within clusters of elite architecture. They include several structures in the Sacrificios Group, just northwest of the enclosure walls, in the Grupo Suroeste, to the southwest of the enclosure walls, and finally limited excavations within the main group, particularly Structure GT-20.[3] Hanson also recovered important stratigraphic information while exploring the Postclassic/Colonial community located just east of the enclosure walls. Excavation information was supplemented by surface collections from the vast majority of the structures surveyed, including several cases in which we surface-collected entire platforms. In the rural survey, Houck excavated fifty-eight tests pits in addition to approximately 200 surface collections. At Ichmul, most of the structures were surface-collected and Smith excavated test pits in twenty-two of the sixty-seven structures, as well as limited testing at four other sites.

Challenging field conditions in all three of these subprojects has meant that our total sample is but a small fraction of the total universe at each survey level. Nevertheless, comparable data are otherwise unavailable for the northern plains.[4] In addition to Ek Balam, we now have information on approximately fifty-nine rural loci, including nine sites with elite architecture, four of which have civic structures over seven meters in height. A total of forty-three sites have been identified in the intersite transect (Garza T. and Kurjack 1980; Andrews, Gallareta, and Cobos 1989; Ringle and Smith 1998; Smith 1998b), twenty-nine of which have been visited.

Ceramic Chronology

Excavations and survey have documented a reasonably continuous occupation from the Middle Formative through the sixteenth century A.D. (Bey et al. 1998).[5] Altogether our ceramic assemblage totals over 275,000 sherds divided into six ceramic phases, although further subphases may eventually be defined. Ceramic evidence indicates that Late Terminal Classic ceramic production far exceeded that of any other period. At present, a single ceramic complex, the Late Yumcab, spans the period from about A.D. 700 to 1050. This pattern is typical of most other Cehpech-sphere complexes in the north but unfortunately prevents an easy distinction between the Late and Terminal Classic deposits, especially since certain late diagnostics, such as Fine Orange and Plumbate, are notorious for their scarcity.

Ek Balam participated in the general homogenization of ceramic production across the northern peninsula during this span. The spread of the Cehpech ceramic sphere at the expense of southern connections has been noted at northern sites such as Cobá (Robles 1990: 259), and like these, polychromes are absent at

Late Classic Ek Balam. The Late Yumcab ceramic complex is a typical representative of the Cehpech sphere in having a predominance of the Muna Slipped and Chum/Encanto Unslipped groups, which together comprise 69 percent of all identified pottery recovered by the Ek Balam project between 1987 and 1996.

A distinction based on the paste color of Muna Slate has been used to differentiate Eastern and Western subspheres of the Cehpech sphere (Robles and Andrews 1986: 77–78). This distinction has not proved useful at Ek Balam, where a wide range of paste color from pink to gray is common (Bey et al. 1992) and may be due to differences in firing techniques and/or local clay varieties. Nevertheless, several regional variations suggestive of local production and distribution occur within the Cehpech sphere. The unslipped wares from Ek Balam most resemble those from the Puuc region and northwestern plains in favoring Chum Unslipped/Yokat Striated rather than Vista Alegre Striated, which is characteristic of Cobá and the east coast (Robles 1990: 179). *Tecomates* are a typical form of Vista Alegre, but one that is fairly rare at Ek Balam. However, Cehpech lots we recently recovered from the Puuc site of Kiuic demonstrate several strong contrasts with Ek Balam. Thin slates and Teabo Red are common at Kiuic but rare at Ek Balam, as are appliqué types. A basic difference in serving wares is also apparent, in that annular base bowls are preferred at Kiuic, while tripodal *cajetes* are by far more common at Ek Balam.

Another characteristic of the Yumcab complex is the virtual absence of fine paste wares. The Fine Gray Chablekal group is relatively common at Dzibilchaltún in Copo II contexts (Andrews 1981: 334) and in low quantities at many other sites.[6] Our failure to recover fine paste wares may be in part the result of sampling bias, since the 1995 excavations of GT-20, our first excavation of a building within the walled site center, produced a modest amount of both Fine Orange and Fine Gray pottery (n=121, or .41 percent of the building assemblage). In contrast, a very large midden sample from Structure FT-27, a large platform complex just 200 meters outside the walled center, produced about a tenth as many fine paste sherds, suggesting fine paste ceramics may be highly localized in their distribution, even among elite assemblages.

Based on ceramics and associated architecture, the Late Yumcab complex is roughly coeval with the Oro complex at Cobá (A.D. 730–1100), the Chacpel complex at Isla Cerritos (A.D. 700–900), and the Copo II complex at Dzibilchaltún (A.D. 800–1000). We tentatively date the Late Yumcab phase to A.D. 700–1050 but stress we have no absolute dates to define its boundaries. Our estimate for the conclusion of the Yumcab phase is based primarily on the absence of a well-defined Early Postclassic complex. Late Yumcab seems to give way directly to our Tases-sphere Xtabay complex, the types of which are usually identified as Mid-Late Postclassic in date.

Our late date for the conclusion of the Yumcab phase raises the question of its articulation with the Sotuta sphere of Chichén Itzá, previously placed in the

Early Postclassic but increasingly viewed as Terminal Classic in date (Sanders 1960; Ball 1979; Lincoln 1986; Robles 1990). It might be argued that the absence of Sotuta sherds, coupled with the scarcity of fine paste wares, Plumbate, and Hocaba types, indicate Ek Balam was abandoned at the conclusion of the Late Classic period. We have discussed this question at length in previous studies (Bey et al. 1998; Ringle, Bey, and Peraza L. 1991; Ringle, Gallareta, and Bey 1998). To summarize, we support the assignment of the Sotuta sphere to the Terminal Classic period. With the additional ceramic data now available from across the peninsula, it seems clear that the Sotuta complex was a rather restricted regional variant, but because sites probably did not rise or fall in unison, the question of whether overlap of the Sotuta and Cehpech complexes were partial or total is moot. Since both Sotuta types at Chichén and Cehpech types at Ek Balam (and elsewhere) are associated with tenth-cycle Long Count dates, it is highly likely that both polities were contemporaries.

This is supported by the distribution of ceramics in our rural and intersite surveys. Like Ek Balam, Houck's rural hinterland lots lacked any evidence of Sotuta presence and were dominated by Yumcab types. At Ichmul de Morley, midway between its two far larger neighbors, Sotuta-sphere sherds represented 8.79 percent of all identified sherds by count and 12.56 percent by weight. Fine paste ceramics were a negligible presence, under 0.5 percent, only a single sherd of which was clearly Silho (X) Fine Orange. In contrast, Late Yumcab Cehpech-affiliated ceramics constituted 53.49 percent and 44.25 percent by count and weight, respectively.[7] Intersite transect sites also show similar low percentages of Sotuta types, partially correlating with their distance to Chichén but also with site size. (Ichmul, in fact, has the highest percentage of Sotuta.) In contrast, recent excavations at Chichén (Lincoln 1990; Cobos 1995; Schmidt, personal communication 1995; Pérez de H. 1998) have recovered almost pure Sotuta deposits. The nearby outlier Yulá (Anderson 1998) is likewise an almost pure Sotuta site.

Since technologically Sotuta is clearly related to the far more widespread Cehpech complex, the latter most likely antedates the former. This position finds some support in our intersite survey excavations. Test pits in the large elite platform N0000E0350, just north of the main plaza, show a priority of Yumcab over Sotuta types (Figure 21.4). It should be noted that Cehpech-related types continue alongside those of the Sotuta sphere, becoming popular only as Sotuta types appeared. Ichmul being a relatively minor site, the advent of Sotuta ceramics there may lag well behind its origins at Chichén. However, the low frequency of Cehpech slateware in earlier levels, mixed with Early Classic types that disappear as Sotuta arrives, argues for the priority of Cehpech production.

The Postclassic Xtabay phase is a Tases affiliate and is characterized by types such as Navula Unslipped, Mama Red, and Chen Mul Modeled. Types characteristic of the post-Sotuta Hocaba complex are essentially absent. The relatively seamless transition from Late Yumcab to Postclassic Xtabay lots throughout the

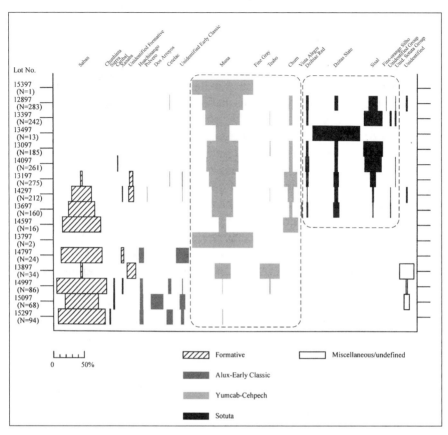

21.4 "Battleship" ceramic frequency curve, Str. N0000E0350, Op. 2, Pit 1, Ichmul de Morley.

Ek Balam urban and rural hinterland areas argues for the absence of a locally distinct Early Postclassic complex. Although conceivably the absence of a local Early Postclassic complex may have resulted from the destruction and temporary abandonment of Ek Balam, the fact that this same transition is visible throughout the rural area and at other sites such as Cobá (Robles 1990) argues against an occupation hiatus. The boundaries of this transition are as yet largely guesswork but would seem to undermine the equation between the end of the Cehpech tradition and the close of the Terminal Classic.

Demography

The distribution of urban settlement, as far as our sample permits us to judge, is generally concentric with respect to distance to the site center and does not cluster appreciably around elite buildings. Occupations are assigned primarily on the basis of surface collections. We placed from one to four 2x2-meter squares on all structures surveyed since 1992. These squares were then intensively checked for surface artifacts. Although surface collections in general match sub-surface deposits fairly well in cases where both are available, surface collection totals may be biased in favor of later phases. Since, however, Late Classic Yumcab types form the vast majority of sherds, that factor can be discounted with respect to the topic under consideration.

The impression of settlement density must be tempered by the fact that many structures yielded few or no sherds, even when as a last resort we conducted grab samples. This suggests a significant number were not residences, but special-purpose structures or outbuildings of one sort or another. Even where ceramics are present, assignment of occupations is problematic, primarily because of erosion and consequent small sample sizes. For the purposes of this paper, we rely upon a subsample of 306 structures beyond the site nucleus that had a total of ten or more identified sherds. Structures were chosen from all of the survey quadrats except for the central GT. We experimented with two definitions of an occupation, one in which at least 5 percent of all identified sherds came from a given phase, and another where a 10 percent cutoff was used.

By either criterion, occupation was overwhelmingly Late Terminal Classic Yumcab, with more than 90 percent of the sample structures being occupied, even at the higher cutoff level. Occupation was also uniformly distributed, with only squares HU and FU reporting lesser Yumcab ceramic percentages because of high Early Classic occupancy. Most of the identifiable domestic architecture is also from this period.

Postclassic occupation estimates vary from 19 to 28 percent of the sample, depending upon the cutoff used, but the majority of these reflect very light artifact deposition. Overall, Postclassic ceramics formed less than 6 percent of the total from Ek Balam, or less than one-tenth of the number of Yumcab-phase sherds. Postclassic (Xtabay-phase) buildings are clustered in the squares adjacent to a sixteenth-century ramada chapel (quadrats HT, HS, IT, and probably IS), although none were found in HU to its south. Limited architectural evidence also supports this clustering. A Postclassic mound type identified by Hanson consists of a single line of stones delimiting a low terrace along the west edge of a mound; all examples of this type cluster in the above quadrats. The only sign of Postclassic architectural activity within the enclosure walls is a small one-room east coast–style "temple" atop the Early Yumcab platform GT-10 and possibly small one-room shrines on earlier pyramids. Surface offerings of Chen Mul *incensario* fragments were also noted on several of the major Late Classic structures. Because identifying the Postclassic occupation was a specific concern of the project, and we therefore made an effort to weight coverage to the east side of the site where Postclassic settlement was known, the conclusion seems inescapable that there was a major loss of population in the urban zone.[8]

Rural survey results indicate that forty-three loci (73 percent) possessed Yumcab ceramics, while only twenty-three (39 percent) had Xtabay types, but this again obscures the true disparity between the two. A total of 11,811 Yumcab-phase sherds weighing 90.99 kilograms were recovered from rural sites compared with just 702 (or 7.68 kilograms) from the following Xtabay phase. This ratio, better than 10:1, was present at all of the major second- and third-tier sites with the exception of X-Huyub, which apparently was temporarily abandoned during the Yumcab phase. Sotuta and Hocaba ceramics were almost nonexistent in the rural zone.

Turning to the intersite survey, about 75 percent of structures at Ichmul de Morley had some Sotuta ceramics, but only 15 percent had enough to suggest occupation. Cehpech-sphere ceramics were evenly and heavily distributed across the site, while Sotuta ceramics were widely scattered but at much lower frequencies. In all cases, Yumcab sherds were many times the number of Sotuta sherds. Interestingly, Sotuta sherds were not well represented in our site-center sample but were present in low numbers on a number of larger platforms of clearly elite status in the outlying settlement sample. The minor role of Sotuta ceramics must be tempered by two observations. First, several examples of Cehpech types with Sotuta forms and modes were noted, including a number of *molcajete* fragments made with Muna Slate ware paste and slip. Second, our limited obsidian collection from Ichmul suggests it enjoyed much greater access to the green obsidian distributed by Chichén than did Ek Balam.

The Postclassic decline at Ichmul was severe: only 122 (0.75 percent) Xtabay-phase sherds were collected from the entire site. These were scattered across the site in numbers too low to indicate occupations, except for one very small sample whose high Postclassic frequency can be attributed to sampling error. Only a single Postclassic sherd was collected from the site center. Like the rural survey sample, there were no Hocaba-related ceramics.

There can be little doubt from our data that the Postclassic decline of the Ek Balam region was severe and involved more than just the cessation of monumental construction or the redistribution of population. The center of Ek Balam was abandoned, with only the occasional visitor stopping to leave modest offerings of effigy censers among the decaying grandeur of the main plaza. Outside the walls, some minor building additions were made, as for instance to Structure GS-12, but most of our occupation evidence comes from the area east of the site center in squares HS, HT, and IS. Rural communities and those between Chichén and Ek Balam alike were abandoned. Whether the little evidence we have for Postclassic occupation was continuous or not remains unclear.

The two centuries between A.D. 1000 and 1200 remain an enigmatic gap in the northern Maya archaeological record, with little supporting evidence of how this transition was effected. As noted above, in areas not under Itzá dominance the major Classic-Postclassic ceramic transition was between the Cehpech and

Tases complexes, with no clear-cut Early Postclassic complex intervening (Bey et al. 1998; Ringle, Gallareta, and Bey 1998). This pattern is evident at both Ek Balam and at Cobá, although in each case Postclassic settlement was clearly substantially reduced. Beginning around A.D. 1000–1050, sites with a strong Sotuta presence were marked by a gradually increasing admixture of Hocaba types (Brainerd's "coarse slateware," especially Black-on-cream) followed by a replacement of Sotuta by Tases types, but still accompanied by residual Hocaba production. The earliest Mayapán deposits, dating to around A.D. 1200, belong to this latter transition, while those of late Chichén, Zipche II at Dzibilchaltún, late Uxmal, and elsewhere, to the first.

At Ichmul de Morley and Yulá (Anderson 1998; personal communication 1999), the absence of Hocaba and Tases sherds indicates these towns probably were largely abandoned by A.D. 1000 and that any remaining inhabitants no longer participated in the Itzá production-distribution network. Hocaba ceramics are also absent from nearby Yaxuna (Brainerd 1958; Suhler et al. 1998), despite some evidence of intrusive Sotuta deposits. Although Hocaba ceramics continued to be produced in quantity at Chichén and in the Chikinchel region (Kepecs 1998), at the former these were in apparently post-monumental contexts. The absence of Hocaba ceramics at nearby sites such as Ichmul, Yaxuna, and Yulá further supports the contention that the retrenchment of the Itzá production-distribution sphere occurred at the end of the Terminal Classic, and probably did not appreciably outlast the florescence of its neighbors.

Late Classic Ek Balam

At Ek Balam, the Late Classic demographic peak was accompanied by increased investment in monumental architecture. The buildings around the main plaza are some of the most impressive in northern Yucatán, although our work and the work of I.N.A.H. demonstrate that elite architecture was being erected from at least the Early Classic period onward. Abundant Formative material from test pits further belies the story that Lord Ek Balam was somehow responsible for the founding of the city, although the story may reflect the advent of a new dynastic line during the Late Classic.

The monumental core of Ek Balam consists of three enormous platforms (GT-1, 2, 3) delimiting three sides of the main plaza. The southern end is enclosed by another large platform (GT-10) and two "temple assemblages," an architectural grouping consisting of a pyramid at right angles to a long, multiroom or hall-like structure (Strs. GT-15, 16 and GT-19, 20).[9] A number of lesser structures are found within and without this complex, including a ballcourt (GT-8) and several shrines and altars, for lack of better terms. The whole is surrounded by double enclosure walls, apparently first identified by Eric von Euw in the 1970s. Such walls are common at a number of northern sites, such as Cuca, Chacchob, Muna, Uxmal, and others (Kurjack and Andrews 1976; Webster 1978; Kurjack and Garza T. 1981: 303–304) and are discussed below. A series of long narrow platforms between the buildings around the main plaza create a third, innermost enclosure wall. The "civic" armature of the site is completed by five *sacbeob* that radiate from the monumental core. Four of these run generally in the cardinal directions, forming a cruciform pattern suggestive of Landa's description of Postclassic towns and Uayeb rituals (Bey and Ringle 1989; Ringle and Bey 1992). These causeways generally terminate in smaller complexes of elite architecture, frequently consisting of temple assemblages.

Temple assemblages appear to be one key to understanding Late Classic settlement over much of the northern plains, as they are farther afield (Fox 1989). Temple assemblages form the nuclei of smaller sites, where they are the principal monumental architecture, and of elite clusters at larger sites such as Ek Balam and Chichén Itzá. We have suggested this may reflect a segmentary form of organization, perhaps of important noble families and their retainers, with the longer building perhaps being identifiable as a *popol na*.[10] This pattern may have its roots in the Late Formative period, at sites such as Mirador (Andrews IV and Andrews V 1980: 21–41; Ringle 1999), but by far the majority date to the Late Terminal Classic period. At larger sites of this period, several such units were often integrated into a single whole, resembling quite closely the *cuchcabal* form of political organization described for the Late Postclassic in ethnohistorical sources.

At least three elite architectural styles span the Late Terminal Classic apogee of Ek Balam. The latest is a simplified version of the Pure Florescent style, which clearly had an enormous influence on local architects. Structure GT-2, for instance, is a sixteen-meter-high basal platform supporting a classic Puuc-range structure along its rear (west) edge, reminiscent of the House of the Deer at Chichén or the House of the Governors at Uxmal. Unlike Puuc structures farther west, however, mosaic facade sculpture is much reduced for the site as a whole. Although we have found a few "Chac" noses, corresponding facial sections of such masks are unknown. (The few masks we have found are carved from single blocks of stone.) Upper wall zones were instead plain or decorated with simple geometric motifs, such as mat designs. Typical Puuc ornaments such as banded colonettes, drum altars, and three-part moldings are also not uncommon. Structure GT-8, which we had identified as a ballcourt on the basis of limited trenching, proved to be a Pure Florescent add-on to an earlier structure when further excavated by Vargas. A fragmentary ballcourt ring bearing only "9 baktun" indicates the style arrived relatively early at Ek Balam compared to other dated examples.

Much of the architecture of the site center structures predates the Pure Florescent style. Exposed facades of GT-8, GT-15, and GT-1, among others, show the use of less finely cut and more irregularly coursed stone covered with thick coats of stucco, sometimes modeled. This masonry closely resembles some of the structures from Cobá. Also typical is the use of stucco-covered *tableros* in the upper wall zone, sometimes in association with stone armatures that once supported stucco sculptures (e.g., GT-15). Finally, several platforms, including GT-8 and GT-1, bear an unusual facade of multiple aprons. Vault stones are often well dressed but are quite long in profile, acting as integral parts of the wall rather than as decorative veneer. Recent discovery of elaborately modeled three-dimensional stucco sculpture on the upper facades of GT-1 are without precedent in the north and suggest prototypes to the south or possibly southeast.

Structures GT-10, GT-16, and GT-20, in contrast, are even earlier, but still within the Yumcab complex. Megalithic blocks were used for the retaining walls and foundations of GT-10 and GT-16. GT-20 is distinguished by irregularly coursed walls covered with thick coats of modeled stucco, but most notably by vaults of thin, roughly fashioned slabs. Although perhaps several centuries old by the onset of the Pure Florescent period, ceramic deposits and architectural renovations indicate that these buildings continued to be used and remodeled throughout the Late Classic. For instance, excavation of a small shrine atop GT-20 demonstrated it was a Chenes-style addition. Somewhat later several of the doorways of the main hall were walled up. Whether this was due to a change in building function or for defensive purposes is unclear.

This eclecticism is reflected in the layout of the site center. Structures GT-1, GT-2, and GT-3 and the lesser pyramids GT-16 and GT-18 created an enclosed central space surrounded by massive architecture. This is unlike most northern site centers, where the emphasis is on horizontal, rather than vertical, masses, and where central spaces are often more accessible. The net result is a type of main plaza reminiscent of more southerly centers. On the other hand, the enclosure walls are wholly within the northern tradition.

Ek Balam's distinctive blend of southern and western influences is also reflected in its sculpture. The main example of the former is Ek Balam Stela 1 (Figure 21.5b), a badly fractured monument apparently from the site center. As reconstructed by Graham, the monument depicts a standing figure holding a God K "manikin scepter." Below the figure is a zone with a bound captive facing right; most probably a companion once faced left. Above the central figure is an "ancestor cartouche" similar to that of Yaxchilán Stela 4.

Several aspects of the stela are noteworthy. First, its Long Count date is a rarity in northern Yucatán. The only other surviving tenth baktun Long Count date in the north comes from the Temple of the Initial Series at Chichén about forty years later, though several "short count" dates from Chichén and other sites are contemporary. Although late, the iconography is quite traditional, harking back to motifs characteristic of Cobá stelae 50–200 years earlier, such as the basal zone of captive figures and the long pendant necklace extending almost to the figure's knees.[11] These motifs are ubiquitous at Cobá, being found on Stelae 1, 2, 3, 5, 6, 20, and 21, and probably others were they not so eroded (Thompson, Pollock, and Charlot 1932; Graham and von Euw 1997).

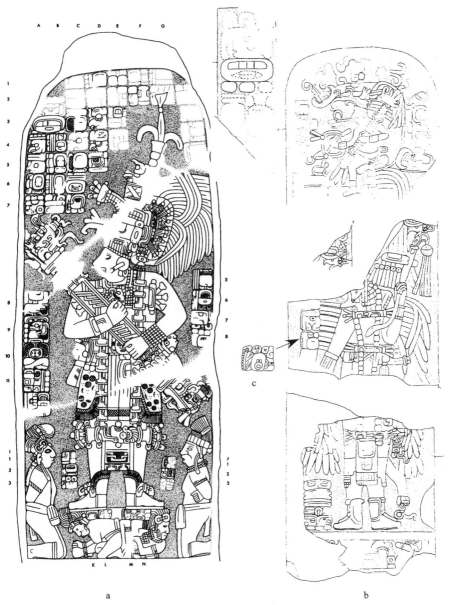

a   b

21.5 a. Cobá Stela 20 (Graham and von Euw 1997); b. Ek Balam Stela 1 (preliminary drawing courtesy Ian Graham); c. Ek Balam Emblem Glyph from GT-1 balustrade (author drawing).

These similarities, however, are probably retentions from a general pre-Florescent sculptural tradition across the northern plains. Similar necklaces may be seen at Oxkintok on lintels from 3C7 and 3C10 (Pollock 1980: 523a, 536) and on Uxmal Stelae 2 and 3, for instance. The Cobá and Oxkintok versions differ in having a single shin-high crosspiece rather than the three present on the Ek Balam and Uxmal stelae. Ek Balam also differs from the Cobá stelae in that the emblem of authority is the God K scepter, whereas nearly all figures at Cobá hold serpent bars. God K scepters are known from Edzná, Uxmal (St. 2 and 6), Dzibilchaltún (St. 9 and 19), Oxkintok, and Sayil (St. 5), among others. Finally, Ek Balam's Stela 1 diverges from Cobá in its emphasis on ancestors (the figures of the cartouche above the main figure and probably the two eroded figures on each side of the monument). No ancestor cartouches are present at Cobá, nor were flanking figures carved on its stelae. Here more southerly prototypes are suggested.

Another sculpture in the more naturalistic Late Classic style is a reclining bench figure depicting either a captive or a *bacab* from the GT-20 shrine. Two ballcourt panels from Ichmul de Morley (Proskouriakoff 1950: Figure 82a,b) also show poses typical of ballplayer panels from the southern lowlands, especially those from "Site Q" and Yaxchilán, although the workmanship of the Ichmul panels is inferior. Fragments of modeled stucco from GT-1 and GT-20 are also excellent examples of this tradition, as are painted capstones recently reported by Vargas et al. (1999).

In contrast, other pieces reflect the cruder style of Puuc sculpture. In 1987 we found two seated figures that may originally have been affixed to a building facade (Figure 21.6). Similar patterns of facial tattooing are present on heads from the Puuc zone, including Maxcanu (Pollock 1980: Figure 576e), Kabah (Pollock 1980: Figure 377c,d), and the "Queen of Uxmal." These may be from the same workshop as two warrior torsos found in the main plaza. One headless warrior carries several darts; the other is a captive with his hands bound behind his back. Less easily classified are several miscellaneous sculptures of composite "monsters" that probably also decorated architectural facades. While it is tempting to see a chronological progression from "naturalistic" to Puuc styles, Stela 1 and the stucco facades of GT-1, as well as the Puuc-like architecture of GT-7, are apparently the work of a single ruler, U Kit Kan Lek.

Post-Florescent Classic-Period Activity

At some point, construction activity in and perhaps use of the site center seems to have waned, and new types of elite architecture appear.[12] The timing of this transition is difficult to pinpoint. Lacadena's (in Vargas et al. 1999; Vargas and Castillo 1999a, 1999b) discussion of hieroglyphic dates associated with a ruler possibly named U Kit Kan Lek indicates dedication of buildings on the GT-1 acropolis and the GT-7/8 ballcourt between A. D. 830 and 841 or so. Voss and

21.6 Two Puuc-style architectural sculptures from Ek Balam (drawings by Gabriel Euan C.)

Eberl (1999) have also noted the appearance of the Ek Balam Emblem Glyph on the Halakal lintel (10.2.0.7.9, A.D. 870), suggesting that Hun Pik Tok, one of the figures on the panel, is a later ruler of Ek Balam. They also believe this same person may appear in the inscriptions of Chichén.[13] This ruler is not yet attested on texts from Ek Balam itself, although he may appear in eroded sections of Stela 1. Nevertheless, the construction stage that buried the stucco facade of GT-1 is probably attributable to a later ruler and minimally indicates significant construction activity there until at least A.D. 870–900. Our radiocarbon date could pertain to either of these stages.

Evidence for the succeeding period is architectural, the majority of it from the Sacrificios Group. As detailed elsewhere (Bey, Hanson, and Ringle 1997), Str. GS-12 shows the clear superimposition of a large basal platform bearing a C-shaped structure (GS-12-1) above a razed building faced with high-quality Florescent masonry (GS-12-sub). The superstructure of GS-12-1 rests on a low terrace and consists of a twenty-eight-meter-long masonry rear wall and two end walls. The rear wall was at least a meter high and perhaps significantly more and was fronted by a low bench or step. The building was open at the front (there were no columns) and undoubtedly had a perishable roof. What is particularly noteworthy is that the ceramics from the construction fill of both construction stages belonged to the Yumcab phase, although small additions to the final platform were made during the Postclassic. Surface collections from two other C-shaped structures (Structures FT-24 and FT-45) were also overwhelmingly Yumcab in date, as were those from a single test pit into FT-45.

We believe the introduction of C-shaped structures parallels their introduction at places such as Uxmal, where they appear to be post-monumental as well, including structures on the House of the Governors, in the center of the Monjas quadrangle, and near Ballcourt 1 (Ruz L. 1953; Bey, Hanson, and Ringle 1997). The incorporation of feathered serpent segments from the main ballcourt in some of the Uxmal C-shaped structures strongly supports their late date, as does recovery of Silho, Plumbate, and Hocaba sherds in excavations. Since the rings date the court to ca. A.D. 905, the C-shaped structures must be minimally mid-tenth century in date.

The importance of the Sacrificios Group prior to the construction of GS-12-1 is evident from the use of Florescent masonry in several other structures, including GS-14 and GS-15, large residential platforms; GS-50, a small keyhole-shaped building, perhaps a sweat bath; and probably the vaulted buildings GS-25, GS-4, GS-8, and GT-50. Cut stones were also discovered on the surface of the highest mound, GS-10. Post-Florescent architecture contemporary with GS-12-1 has been identified primarily on the basis of the poor quality of construction. Probably the best evidence comes from modifications to GS-15, in which sections of the earlier veneer masonry were left as facades to renovations that were otherwise crudely done. Other structures lacked cut stone altogether, such as Structure GS-11, a long low platform with evidence for a single, long rear wall reminiscent of GS-12 but without any evidence of a bench or plaster floors.

We differ somewhat on our interpretation of the significance of these developments. Bey prefers to see the Sacrificios Group as a new focus of power during the post-monumental period, perhaps inhabited by a new group of elites. In support he points to modifications to elite houses GS-14 and GS-15, the mound GS-10, and the presence of a ballcourt, GS-7. Ballcourts are rare in Yucatán and were probably markers of significant prestige. While ceramic lots clearly placed it in the Yumcab phase, limited excavations of its alley failed to uncover much cut stone, suggesting it may have been late. In his view, GS-12 is an integral part of the group, perhaps its lineage house. Ringle, however, sees GS-12 as a later imposition on a Florescent-period civic complex. He points to the vaulted architecture and its association with the sacbe, and notes that Late Classic ballcourts are typically located at sacbe termini in northern Yucatán. The form and orientation of the court also appear to be typical of northern Yucatecan courts such as those of Cobá in having sloping benches and no defined endzones. He thus believes the ballcourt and most other structures are Florescent in date or earlier. Furthermore, the other two C-shaped buildings are not associated with civic architectural groups but are instead isolated.

Whatever the internal history of the group, social turmoil is indicated by unfinished platform additions to several buildings in the vicinity, including Structures GS-4, GS-14, and GS-39. That these were unfinished is clear from the lack of any subfloor fill on their surfaces; all are today exposed heavy rubble. Only the extension to GS-14 has been excavated; no sherds in its fill postdate the Yumcab phase. Although these abandoned additions most likely date to the end of the Yumcab phase, we cannot rule out the possibility that they instead mark the demise of Florescent-style construction.

Because of our inability to consistently distinguish Yumcab facets, understanding of the demographics of this transition is poor, but it is likely that the declining political fortunes of the site were accompanied by some population loss. This transition, however, is not marked by any clear-cut evidence for military defeat or occupation, nor loss of political independence. In some contexts Sotuta ceramics do appear, primarily in surface deposits, as for example a few vessels found around the base of Str. GT-15 (Carlos Peraza, personal communication 1997). We have found others in our own excavations here and there, but the quantities so far uncovered are modest and do not bespeak long-term occupation by or strong economic ties with outsiders.

EXPLAINING THE COLLAPSE

Cowgill (1988) has cautioned that civilizational collapse is a concept fraught with imprecision. It is necessary, he argues, to distinguish between the level at which "collapse" is operating (state, society, or civilizational), whether decline involves wholesale social collapse or merely political fragmentation, and whether decline is rapid or gradual, complete or partial. We would add that arguments should distinguish locally contingent events from broader processual or systemic trends, although the distinction between the two is not always clear-cut.

With respect to the lowland Maya case, one of the difficulties is a terminological one: the Terminal Classic (and increasingly the Early Postclassic) has simply meant too many things to too many people. Even its initial formulations demonstrated an uneasy balance between developmental and chronological senses. In an early definition of the term, the Terminal Classic was

> the period during which the processes of the downfall worked out their course. There are some difficulties in choosing a period term by which to designate the Tepeu 3 horizon. Traditionally, there has been a tendency to include the horizon as the last part of the Late Classic Period because of clear ceramic continuities with earlier horizons. On the other hand, most of the patterns that gave rise to the idea of Classicism had ceased by this time. We have, therefore, adopted the designation "Terminal Classic" in this volume with the hope that it will connote both the continuity and the destruction of previous patterns demonstrated in the archaeological record. (Culbert 1973b: 16–17)

"Terminal Classic" was thus utilized as the Tepeu 3 period designator (thus privileging ceramic data, more specifically the ceramic sequence of the central southern lowlands) and as the period of the "Maya collapse." The two senses were made compatible by the assumption that it represented a "horizon," briefly but widely experienced throughout the lowlands. Containment of the events during this time span within a single ceramic period, reinforced by the relatively short span over which hieroglyphic dates ceased to be erected, encouraged their treatment as part of a single, relatively brief process. (Note "downfall" in the singular in the passage above, although Culbert recognized the challenge the Dzibilchaltún data potentially presented.) Culbert's (1988) more recent consideration is very much in this vein, with virtually no consideration of the northern lowlands.

Data collected over the past twenty-five years suggest the collapse was a protracted and far from monolithic process. Demarest and colleagues argue for the abandonment of the Petexbatun area well before the dates traditionally assigned to the Terminal Classic, while Chichén, Kabah, and perhaps Uxmal seem to have hung on until A.D. 1000–1050, thus opening up nearly three centuries for the "collapse." Other sites, such as Lamanai, seem to have weathered whatever crises occurred elsewhere. We must therefore be wary of assuming that the failure of particular polities was the result of general systemic processes, rather than of restricted, contingent factors, such as military defeat or local environmental degradation.

Another problem with the concept of the Terminal Classic has been our choice of chronological markers. In many cases, late occupations are defined on the basis of markers of limited areal distribution, even within particular sites, including fine paste wares, particularly Silho (X) Fine Orange and Tohil Plumbate, or in northern Yucatán, Sotuta slate wares. These markers were either imports or produced in limited regions, and were hence dependent upon particular distribution networks. In addition to status and ethnicity, ideology may also have affected the composition of such networks. We have argued, for instance, that Plumbates and fine paste imports, particularly Silho Fine Orange, were distributed chiefly by sites participating in the cult of Quetzalcoatl (Ringle, Gallareta, and Bey 1998: 216–218) and may have been involved in related ritual, feasting, or pilgrimage activities. As such, they may well have been excluded from other markets because of ideological differences. Whether or not this eventually proves true, the restrictions on the distribution of these ceramics render them of limited value in dating individual structures, particularly of the humbler sort. This has resulted in the separation of what were actually contemporaneous deposits, producing rather dramatic changes between Late and Terminal Classic settlement patterns (or Pure and Modified Florescent in the north), whereas in reality the transition may have been much more gradual.

Cobos (Chapter 22, this volume; Winemiller and Cobos 1999) has recently argued for a subdivision in the Sotuta complex. Developing observations by Lincoln (1990), he argues that Silho Fine Orange and Thin Slate are characteristic of the earlier facet and Plumbate of the later, and that sites such as Ek Balam, Dzibilchaltún, and Cobá were contemporaneous only with the earlier facet. During the later period, A.D. 900–1050, Chichén, Uxmal, and perhaps Tihó rose to regional prominence. This framework has much merit, since it is supported also by architectural superimpositions and style changes at Chichén itself and is close to our own thinking about when Ek Balam declined. But again the diagnostic ceramics are specialty wares of limited distribution whose absence can be attributed to a variety of explanations besides chronology. Thus, the absence of Plumbate at Ek Balam is not necessarily confirmatory, since the earlier diagnostics, Fine Orange and Thin Slate, are also in short supply there.

Climatic Change

Environmental crisis and warfare continue to be two of the major systemic explanations for the "Maya collapse." However, environmental crisis theories emphasizing overpopulation, pressure on agricultural resources, and consequent ecosystem degradation may be faulted for ignoring what would seem to be the far more fragile northern lowlands. Northern Yucatán receives less rainfall and has thinner soils, yet on present evidence seems to have been more densely settled than most areas of the south during the Late Terminal Classic and persisted for an addition 100 to 200 years. One alternative to local overexploitation models has been to identify factors that disrupted otherwise relatively balanced adaptations over wide areas. Several authors (e.g., Folan, Gunn, et al. 1983; Dahlin 1983) have noted the correlation of the end of the Classic period with the onset of the Medieval Climatic Optimum (A.D. 900–1200/1300). Over the past decade additional studies have attempted to verify the relevance of global climatic change using data specific to Yucatán. Most publicized are the results from Lake Chichancanab, southeast of Ek Balam (Hodell, Curtis, and Brenner 1995). Particularly dry conditions were noted in a core at a position judged to date to ca. 1140 B.P., suggesting a dry period lasting from A.D. 800 to 1000 with peak aridity ca. A.D. 922 that the authors cautiously note correlates with the end of the Terminal Classic period.

These authors and their colleagues have also conducted similar but less publicized studies at Lakes Cobá, San José Chulchaca, and Sayaucil, in effect providing a transect across the peninsula (Whitmore et al. 1996; Leyden et al. 1994, 1998). These sediment cores do not reflect a similar severe period of desiccation, though human influence is evident, as are what may have been more extreme east-west differences in precipitation. The lack of drought "spikes" are perhaps attributable in part to poor resolution in the upper sections of the cores, but it is also interesting to note that these lakes reflect much less colluvium resulting from agricultural erosion than do sites in the south, such as Lake Petén Itzá. On the other hand, data from Punta Laguna, located not far north of Lake Cobá, do indicate dry conditions for an extended period, from 1785 to 943 B.P. (Curtis, Hodell, and Brenner 1996), with an end to drought conditions ca. 930 B.P. (ca. A.D. 1100). Peaks were registered at A.D. 862 and 986. Note, however, that this core indicates that dry conditions lasted for most of the Classic period, indicating they must somehow have been generally favorable for social expansion.

All in all, drought seems unlikely to have been the proximate cause of cultural disruption at Ek Balam, which occupies what would seem to be a well-buffered section of the peninsula. The area around Valladolid has a relatively high level of rainfall and some of the highest average maize yields in Yucatán (Duch Gary 1988: 227–228; Ringle 1985: Figure 6.1). Furthermore, rainfall is better distributed throughout the year than in areas farther east. The potable water supply was also well protected, being derived almost exclusively from the water table. Locally this is approximately twenty meters below the surface and can be reached via the numerous *cenotes* that dot the region (Figure 21.3). Efforts by Houck and project member John McCall located fifty cenotes in the greater Ek Balam region, and more undoubtedly exist. The floors of the deeper sinkholes (*rejolladas*) that pepper the landscape could also be quarried for a few meters until the water table was reached. Twenty-six *dzadzes* (partially or seasonally inundated rejolladas) and five wells in sinkholes were found in our mapping. These sinks were almost certainly used agriculturally as well, providing somewhat more humid soil for specialty crops. Such groundwater-based resources might be expected to be more resilient than rainfall or runoff-based systems.

Most crops were dependent on rainfall, however, and so may have felt the effects of increasing aridity while drinking water remained available. Considerable evidence exists for global climatic changes during the Medieval Climatic Optimum. High-resolution data from Quelccaya, Peru, glacier cores (Thompson et al. 1985; Kolata 1993: 284–291) and from Lake Marcacocha, Peru (Chepstow-Lusty et al. 1996), reflect warm, dry conditions after A.D. 1000/1050 to 1400, the Quelccaya data suggesting such activity may have begun as early as A.D. 920–950. Comparable evidence exists for California (Stine 1994) and Europe. The tenth-century drought spikes in the studies above may be a local manifestation of these trends. If so, this would suggest climatic factors were most important about a century after many northern centers began to unravel, and may have provided a final blow to remaining population concentrations. Nevertheless, the Yucatán cores suggest that the severity of climatic deterioration may have differed significantly from region to region.

Conflict

An increased incidence of warfare has been the chief competing explanation for the abandonment of northern centers. Certainly conflict is a common theme of Florescent-period iconography. Mention has already been made of captive and warrior sculptures in the main plaza. Militaristic themes are also evident in two recently exposed "shrines" flanking the main stairway of GT-1. Each has before it a large stucco mask from which issues a long serpent tongue bearing a text. This mask appears to be a crudely executed human face (perhaps originally modeled in stucco) wearing the war serpent headdress. The texts commemorate the dedication of the stairs, or perhaps the masks themselves, by U Kit Kan Lek, indicating that the central part of this acropolis may have been a war memorial.

Given the propensities of societies to remove, bury, or rebuild in the aftermath of conflicts, actual evidence of battles and skirmishes is extremely scarce in the north. Instead, recourse is usually made to permanent facilities interpreted as having played a defensive role, particularly enclosure walls (Kurjack and Andrews 1976; Webster 1978, 1980). Since Ek Balam is one such site, a brief review of the evidence is warranted.

Mural scenes from two buildings at Chichén Itzá support a defensive function for Terminal Classic walls. The southwest panel of the Upper Temple of the Jaguars (Miller 1977: Figure 7; Coggins and Shane 1984: Figure 19) and the mural in Room 22 of Las Monjas (Bolles 1977: 198–209, *passim*) clearly depict attacks on enclosure walls by Itzá soldiers. Furthermore, the south panel of the Upper Temple of the Jaguars shows a siege tower near what might be the profile of a defensive wall abutting the pyramid under attack (Miller 1977: Figure 3; Coggins and Shane 1984: Figure 20).

The Monjas mural is interesting in depicting dual enclosure walls. Although plain in design, the stonework of the outer wall is of well-coursed rectangular blocks. The inner wall, though its image is less well preserved, is more elaborate, with serrated *almenas* (merlons) along its top, and surrounds two temple-platforms. Since blocks are not indicated, this wall may have been stuccoed. Interestingly, none of the murals indicate that the walls supported perishable superstructures, either wooden palisades or thorn bushes, such as the conquistadors encountered. It is also by no means clear that the Chichén murals refer to local events, since their backdrops include hills, vegetation, and bodies of water not characteristic of the northern plains.[14]

Archaeological evidence for walls is relatively abundant at both Late Classic and Late Postclassic sites (Kurjack and Garza T. 1981: 303–304). During the Postclassic, there seems little doubt that the walls of Mayapán and Tulum were defensive, given their parapets, tunnel-like entrances, and corner redoubts. A similar wall isolates and protects a peninsula forming part of the site of Xelhá (Lothrop 1924: 134). The most detailed study of Classic-period enclosure walls was carried out by Webster (1978, 1980) at the sites of Chacchob, Cuca, and Dzonot Aké. Additional walled sites from the period include Chichén Itzá, Chunchucmil, Muna, Aké, Uxmal, Yaxuna, and Ek Balam.

Farther afield, the Petexbatun project has recently gathered considerable evidence linking eighth-century warfare and the construction of wall systems. Like the Ek Balam walls, the walls of the Petexbatun region often consist of concentric pairs of enclosures and employ baffled entrances (Demarest et al. 1997). Unlike the Ek Balam walls, however, the Petexbatun walls were for the most part hurriedly built of dry-laid masonry, in some cases "running right over existing buildings and often poorly placed in relation to the local topography" (Demarest et al. 1997: 231). Existing buildings were frequently dismantled for the necessary building material, and there seems little effort at architectural elaboration. Some sites, such as Dos Pilas, had more than one wall system, each protecting a specific civic group. Many of the smaller secondary and tertiary Petexbatun sites were also well defended, in some cases by excavated ditches.

The paired concentric walls of Ek Balam are clearly within the northern Yucatán tradition in terms of construction techniques (well-built masonry walls), scale (wall profiles are significantly smaller than Postclassic examples), and layout (paired concentric walls are also known from Cuca, Chacchob, and Muna). During 1987 we exposed three sections of the Ek Balam walls. Trenches 2-87 and 3-87 crossed the inner and outer walls respectively in the northwest section of the site, while Trench 1-87 explored a section of the outer wall associated with Str. GT-22 to the southwest. Trench 2-87 revealed that the inner wall, about 2.7 meters thick at that point, still stood to a height of about one meter and had been faced with Florescent cut stone. A substantial amount of cut stone lay on the surface and within the debris talus on either side. On the exterior (west) side, approximately four courses of the wall were still in situ. On the interior side, stones were also faced, but were larger and less regularly coursed. In addition, several extant patches indicated the walls had been covered with red-painted stucco.[15] Using the area of the cut stone in the debris, Chris von Nagy estimated that the walls originally stood to a height of at least 2.1 meters.

Stucco floors extended from the base of both walls; in fact the stucco lapped up from the floor onto the front of the inner enclosure, indicating wall and floor were finished or refinished contemporaneously. We recovered 101 sherds in two lots from below these floors. All belonged to the Cehpech sphere except a single Dzibiac Red sherd, a member of the Sotuta sphere. Both the stonework and the ceramics support a Florescent-period construction date. The single Sotuta sherd indicates that these ceramics were already being imported in small quantities, an additional small piece of evidence for chronological overlap. A few additional Sotuta-sphere sherds were found in unsealed lots above the floors as well. Although limitations of time, resources, and permission prevented us from actually cutting into the walls, we did clear the upper surface and found no traces of previous construction phases.

The debris associated with the exterior wall was generally less than that associated with the inner wall, suggesting it was somewhat smaller. Trench 3-87 demonstrated it was about 2.6 meters in width at that point. The wall debris here stood to a height of about .6 meter at its highest and contrasted with the inner wall in several respects. It was faced with roughly faced blocks rather than the Florescent stones used on the inner wall, and we found no trace of any stucco covering. Traces of plaster floor were again found on either side of the wall, but closer examination demonstrated that this plaster floor ran underneath the wall. (Again, we did not excavate within the wall, but the floor was probably continuous.) The small sample of sealed ceramics from below this floor was wholly Cehpech; a very few Sotuta sherds were found in the debris above the floor.

The walls present some puzzling defensive considerations. Very little of the site would have been protected by the walls, and certain impressive elite groups would have been left defenseless. There was no permanent water supply within the walls to sustain defenders.[16] Our mapping located only five *chultuns* within the walls, the majority of which were extremely modest in size. Two shallow depressions along the eastern edge of the main plaza may have been pools or reservoirs of some sort, but it seems unlikely that a large defensive force could have resisted siege for very long. While it may be objected that defenses were against raids rather than sieges, the siege towers depicted at Chichén argue for more elaborate campaigns.

Another consideration is that certain sections of the walls appear difficult to defend. Some sections were apparently missing. Whether they were never constructed or scavenged for later construction is unknown, but certainly the entire northern section is relatively unimpressive. Another factor is that the walls were built in close proximity to or even abutting substantial buildings outside their bounds. For instance, in excavating the exterior wall we found the edge of a buried platform (GT-27) only 1.5 meters outside the exterior wall. The retaining wall of this platform rested on a plaster floor also extending underneath the enclosure wall, although the outer wall was apparently not stuccoed. The fact that the enclosure wall collapsed directly onto this stucco floor indicates that it was being kept clear, and that therefore the platform and the wall were in contemporary use, although the enclosure wall was probably built later. The platform would thus have provided an elevated position from which to attack and breach the enclosure wall. Similar arguments may be advanced for several other substantial platforms adjacent to or abutting the enclosure walls, although they are unexcavated (e.g., GT-22, -24, -25, -26, and -28). It would be difficult to argue that such structures were built after defensive walls were built, because this would imply either the builders knowingly imperiled their defenses or that the threat was no longer significant.

The site center was further enclosed by what amounted to a third wall, a series of narrow platforms that linked the major structures surrounding the main plaza. In some cases such walls were only a few meters in length, such as those between Strs. GT-1, -2, and -3, while others are tens of meters in length. Sections of this wall were subsequently cleared by I.N.A.H. archaeologists, but their date is unclear. Like the inner enclosure wall, this wall exhibited formal Florescent period cut-stone facing, including stairways, and were not ramparts hurriedly thrown up for defense purposes. Structure GT-18, a formal entryway to the south sacbe, also articulated with this inner wall on its east and west sides, suggesting the wall was meant to limit access to and visibility of the site center.

Beyond the urban limits, our rural and intersite surveys have yet to locate a single enclosure wall. This is particularly striking in the case of Ichmul de Morley, whose apparent wealth would seem to have been an inviting target for its far larger neighbors. Several other secondary centers between Ek Balam and Chichén have been surveyed in sufficient detail to state unequivocally that no enclosure walls were employed. Our seventy-hectare sample of Kumal likewise failed to locate enclosure walls.

Late Classic walls are in fact usually confined to certain of the largest sites of the Late Terminal Classic, although Cuca and Chacchob may be exceptions. Entire regions lack enclosure walls, such as the Puuc zone apart from Uxmal and northern Quintana Roo. While many of these sites have not been fully surveyed, sufficient settlement work has been done at Cobá, Kabah, Labna, Sayil, Oxkintok, and others to be quite sure they never had enclosure walls.

A more nuanced interpretation of northern enclosure walls suggests they were in equal measure marks of civic prestige, intended to segregate and restrict access to that space associated with the highest administrative and ritual activities, as they did in centers throughout Mesoamerica.[17] The walls of Chichén, for example, were surmounted by sculpture and extended some distance along the sacbe to the Sacred Cenote, and probably prefigure later *coatepantli*. As such, enclosure walls were part of a general construction trend formalizing the relationship between center and periphery, which also included the building of sacbes and formally arranged clusters of civic architecture. This may reflect the growing importance of lesser nobility, as has been suggested at southern lowland sites such as Yaxchilán (Schele and Freidel 1990) and Copán. The walls may therefore have been designed to present the *image* of a powerful center, a type of construction permitted only the most powerful of regional centers.[18] Another resonance was that of the roughly circular sacred center isolated from domestic space by these same barriers. Traffic inward was carefully shuttled along the sacbes through gateways and formal entry structures (GT-18, GT-50, GT-26), which obscured the impressive expanse of the main plaza until passage of the final barrier.

This is not to deny that the walls, particularly in their final form, were designed as defensive fortifications. In fact, they provide strong evidence of the sophistication of defensive architecture in the northern Maya lowlands. As we have discussed, however, they seem to be flawed in ways similar to the Aguateca and Chunchucmil defensive systems. Although they would have served as defenses in armed conflicts, as seen in the depiction of walls in Chichén murals, it remains an open question whether the first wall was initially built for this purpose. It is also possible that the evolution of the wall system represents a shift in function over time. The limited evidence for a later date for the outermost wall, of poorer construction than the inner, may reflect increased military pressure result-ing in strengthened defenses and the construction of a "killing alley." Like the walls at Dos Pilas, the outer wall at Ek Balam was built close to existing struc-tures, which, as pointed out, may have negated defensive capabilities of the wall system. The builders would have, we think, been aware of that, and it may repre-sent a compromise between defensive pressure and the limitations imposed by existing architecture. If they were overly concerned about this problem they could have created a vacant zone around the outer wall, which they did not. The wall-ing-up of GT-20 and the construction of other walls within the two enclosure walls may also be part of a late expression of defensive construction, although the dating of these is as yet unclear.

The ultimate failure of this wall system may be reflected in the possible con-struction of a fourth wall that has been identified as having run across the main plaza east/west, cutting off the southern buildings and forming a demarcated area consisting of the wall, GT-1, GT-2, and GT-3. It is poorly constructed and not dated. In fact, it may be a later wall built to make the plaza into a cattle corral. If, however, the wall turns out to be Late or Terminal Classic in date, it would sug-gest that at one point Ek Balam was under a siege, and a hastily built wall was thrown up across the plaza in a final effort at defense.

CONCLUSION

If material culture is at all a trustworthy guide to past demography, we must acknowledge a very significant regional Postclassic population decline in east-central Yucatán. This reflects not only abandonment of construction and civic architecture, but also a major decline in residential occupation. Furthermore, this decline cannot be attributed simply to the fall of the urban center, because it is mirrored at every level in our rural and intersite surveys.

Evidence for late-ninth or early-tenth-century monumental construction on GT-1 is within a few years of the latest hieroglyphic dates anywhere on the peninsula, with the possible exception of the High Priest's grave, making it un-likely that K'ak' u Pakal and his associates were able to overcome Ek Balam. The fact that GS-12 could be built, occupied, and enlarged during the post-monumental period and into the Xtabay phase, yet without Plumbate or Hocaba sherds, also indicates that old barriers to distribution and production were still being main-tained well into the tenth century. Evidence from the rural and intersite surveys indicates that Sotuta and Hocaba producers were unable to make inroads into these zones as well.

Thus, at present we lack evidence for attributing Ek Balam's collapse to militarism, although further large-scale excavations may provide this. It seems that whatever territorial expansion was accomplished by Chichén did not move in the direction of Ek Balam. The stronger presence in the Chikinchel region to the north (Kepecs 1998) may indicate a flanking movement designed to cut off Ek

Balam from the coast, but even so it remains unclear how that would have resulted in the observed population collapse.

While warfare was likely a significant factor in Terminal Classic disruptions, it seems insufficient as the sole basis of social collapse. There is first the question of whether the type of warfare practiced by pre-Columbian societies could have resulted in the degree of depopulation apparent in the archaeological record. Warfare was typically practiced to get slaves and booty, but more importantly to gain tribute and tributaries. While there are accounts of cities being razed to the ground, such incidents are unusual and were typically the result of particularly bitter circumstances. More often the intent of conquest was simply to divert the flow of tribute and to appropriate labor. It seems doubtful whether any one city would have been either capable or desirous of ravaging the entire northern plains.

Troubling too is the lack of evidence. Iconography often depicts acts of subjection by local warriors, but it is usually impossible to determine who the victims were and the scale at which such wars were fought. Surely the Itzás cannot be held responsible for every conflict of the Late Classic period, but there has been little effort to examine other potential rivalries. Itzá conquest has usually been identified on the basis of pottery. The quantities in question are usually small, however, and may have arrived for a number of other reasons, such as trade or presentations. Sotuta presence has sometimes been claimed on the basis of foreign imports such as Fine Orange and Plumbate, which again may have arrived for other reasons and by other distribution networks. The disjunction between pottery distribution and that of other classes of evidence (e.g., art and architectural styles) makes it incumbent that we develop stronger models linking ethnicity and ceramic spheres if we wish to continue using the latter in political arguments.

Trial models often become reified in the literature on northern warfare, a good case being that of the hypothesized conflict between Cobá and Chichén. Most Cobá monuments cluster in the seventh century (Thompson et al. 1932: 183). The latest, Stela 20 at A.D. 780, is about fifty years later than the penultimate stela, and about the same amount earlier than the earliest of the Chichén hieroglyphic dates. The most important class of public political monuments thus shows no evidence of chronological overlap. The Cobá architectural sequence is as yet also poorly understood. As noted above, the Puuc style evidently made no inroads into Cobá. Although clearly there are late structures at Cobá, such as the Pinturas group and various east coast–style rooms built on some of the Late Classic pyramids, the great majority of its architecture would appear to also be seventh to eighth century, including the Nohoch Mul. Ceramically, only trace amounts of Sotuta pottery were found at Cobá (Robles 1990), while Fine Orange and Plumbate are virtually absent, leading Robles and Andrews (1986) to conclude that Chichén never made any inroads into the immediate sphere around Cobá, contra Suhler et al. (1998: 178), who argue for outright conquest. At base the claim for a ninth-century confrontation between Chichén and Cobá is really a statement of what may have happened. While quite possibly true—indeed it would be strange had the two centers never come into conflict—it is well to remember the types of evidence upon which claims of warfare are based, and at Cobá particularly, the lack of supporting dates for the period in question.

While predatory states may have existed, the Florescent-period cities of the northern plains were able to grow and prosper alongside each other for at least 150 years. During this period, increasing population may have favored the emergence of ever-larger regional centers whose basic wealth was probably measured in human capital. A chief concern must therefore have been the recruitment and retention of subject populations. Militarism may have been one factor encouraging population aggregations, but competitive monumental architectural projects may have been another means whereby elites funneled labor, and hence wealth, into their cities. The original pyramid schemes, such centers thrived as long as such projects could be sustained or enlarged.

As many have noted (e.g., Andrews 1990), the great achievement of Chichén Itzá was to break free of these limitations by incorporating itself into pan-Mesoamerican trade networks, providing quantities of new preciosities such as turquoise, gold, and green obsidian, as well as increasing the flow of jade and cacao. The combination of these with new ideological claims may have provided a powerful incentive to elite lines elsewhere to reconsider their political allegiances. Thus, rather than military attack, neighboring polities may have been undermined from within as component segments were seduced by richer alternatives.

But it would be wrong to view the new order as simply a shift of elites to another, richer site. Chichén seems to present a new type of center. Unlike typical northern centers whose power rested upon regional control of a series of towns, content to worship the traditional deities with perhaps the addition of a local ancestor or two, Chichén asserted itself as a transcendent spiritual center. We have elsewhere detailed our reasons for believing Chichén was a major cult center related to Epiclassic centers elsewhere in Mesoamerica (Ringle, Gallareta, and Bey 1998). It is perhaps instructive to examine how another such center, Cholula, functioned, although at a later date. Although the area directly administered by Cholula was relatively small, elites came from a much wider area to be confirmed in office and to pay homage to the Quetzalcoatl priests who functioned as the main political leaders. The reference to Cholula as the Rome of the New World by early observers was thus perhaps more acute than generally credited, because like the Holy Roman Empire, whatever political influence Cholula wielded was based upon its far greater spiritual prestige.

Such ideological authority is one way in which claims of Itzá dominion in Yucatán may be understood, as exerting not direct political control but rather conveying legitimacy and, not incidentally, access to the riches confirming authority. Chichén's increasing success as the fount of legitimacy directly challenged the basis for monumental architecture elsewhere, and one by one these buildings were abandoned. Henceforth, the history of large centers in Yucatán was arguably related to Feathered Serpent worship and to the establishment of new centers of religious legitimacy, such as Mayapán.

Ek Balam appears to have been one of the last surviving traditional kingdoms of the northern plains, able to renew itself during the Florescent building boom while retaining certain traditional emblems of authority. Wealthy and large enough to compete with Chichén for many years, eventually its power base eroded and became insufficient to maintain its monumental core. Political fragmentation was followed at some later date by apparent demographic collapse, but the linkage between the two remains obscure.

To return to the point made at the outset, the factors affecting Ek Balam's decline, while widespread, were by no means universal. Furthermore, across the peninsula the reactions of different centers to these new historical circumstances varied considerably, both chronologically and qualitatively. Some chose resistance, as Ek Balam apparently did, others were conquered outright, while others willingly accepted the new order. Others may even have tried to co-opt it, as Uxmal possibly did. The Chichén arrangement itself fell apart rapidly not much later, perhaps because of disruptions to other cult centers such as Tajin and Cholula between A.D. 1000 and 1100, or perhaps to legendary incursions by peoples from the east. Environmental deterioration may also have varied considerably in its impact. Sites dependent on water storage may have been particularly vulnerable, while sites able to tap the water table, such as Ek Balam, would be better buffered. But certainly enough questions remain that we may expect another "collapse" volume twenty-five years hence.

NOTES

1. The term is actually Brainerd's (1958), who defined it as the chronological phase during which Cehpech slate wares were produced. At Dzibilchaltún, however, it was used to designate the period during which concrete-and-veneer masonry was being erected, and hence was primarily an architectural rather than a ceramic phase. The Pure Florescent (A.D. 800–1000) corresponded to the Puuc style and the Modified Florescent to the late buildings of Chichén Itzá. Cehpech ceramics both preceded and outlasted the Pure Florescent (Andrews V 1981: Figure 11.1).

2. Teledyne Isotope sample I-15,102; uncorrected date of 1180 B.P. ±8. Although the calibrated age is A.D. 880 using the CALIB3.03c computer program (Stuiver and Reimer 1993) and the decadal tree ring calibration dataset, there are actually intercepts between A.D. 783–787, 811–820, 830–840, 868–893, and 929–940. The probability distribution shows that the span A.D. 811–843 contains over half of the 1σ curve area, and is probably closest to the true date. The computer-generated 2σ range and midpoint are A.D. 781 (880) 976.

3. Arqlga. Leticia Vargas and co-workers have extensively restored several of the monumental structures around the main plaza.

4. Dunning's (1992) work in the Sayil vicinity is the nearest comparable study, although his work focused on sites with elite architecture.

5. This article does not include the data from Ichmul de Morley, the other sites in the intersite transect, or from Kumal.

6. Contrary to recent assertions (Suhler, Ardren, and Johnstone 1998: 178), Fine Gray is scarce at Puuc centers and can hardly be termed a "trademark ware." Its absence at Yaxuna is characteristic of the Cehpech sphere generally. Robles (1990: 155–160) found only 132 in the Cobá collection of 41,000 sherds (.32 percent).

7. The Late Yumcab numbers are probably inflated, because they include all sherds identified as "eroded slate ware," some percentage of which are probably Sotuta affiliates. However, 3,938 sherds could be positively placed in the Muna Slate group, but only 625 sherds belonged to the corresponding (Sotuta) Dzitas Slate group. With regard to unslipped sherds, 2,272 belonged to the Chum group versus 553 of the Sisal group. There is thus a fairly consistent four- to sixfold predominance of Cehpech versus Sotuta types.

8. The extremely modest Postclassic occupation, and the even rarer traces of Colonial occupation, are at variance with ethnohistorical sources. The *Relaciones* of Ek Balam and of Nabalam, Tahcab, and Cozumel (de la Garza et al. 1983: II: 135–140, 185–190) indicate Ek Balam was the head of a *cuchcabal*. During the following Colonial period Ek Balam was a chapel town containing the population of four other reduced villages. Although its substantial tribute indicates a significant population, our data suggest relatively sparse local occupation. Perhaps a further cluster may yet be found elsewhere in the site, but that seems unlikely.

9. As defined by Proskouriakoff (1962: 91), "In the typical temple assemblage [at Mayapán], a pyramid temple with serpent columns . . . stands at right angles to the colonnaded hall, and the shrine, which remains roughly centered on the hall, is turned to face the temple." She contrasted it with the basic ceremonial group, in which "the colonnaded hall is combined with a raised shrine and an oratory" (Proskouriakoff 1962: 90). In our view both are variants of a single architectural complex, at Mayapán the contrast perhaps being attributable to ethnic differences. Earlier, during the Late Classic, a similar complex is ubiquitous in eastern Yucatán and elsewhere, although at this horizon a long open hall, a perishable *palapa,* or a line of vaulted rooms anticipate the colonnaded hall and a pyramidal mound presages the serpent temple and the raised shrine. The exception is Chíchen Itzá, where both were already present. The similar placement of both forms at the center of sites, often in association with ballcourts and *sacbeob,* argue for their essential identity.

10. Although in 1989 we suggested each might belong to a corporate patronymic lineage, we have more recently suggested that each might be better considered as a more restricted elite family or lineage, or perhaps a noble "house" (Ringle and Bey 2001).

11. The latest Cobá stela with these motifs is Stela 20, dated to 9.17.0.0.0 (A.D. 780), or about fifty years before Ek Balam Stela 1.

12. In our view, in the north the term "Terminal Classic" is best reserved for this post-monumental period, although it would therefore postdate the southern Terminal Classic.

13. This depends upon a reading of Ek Balam's Emblem Glyph as *tal,* which they relate to a phonetic *ah-ta-la* at Chichén. Ek Balam's Emblem Glyph has as its main sign T580, possibly /lo/, which they believe functioned simply to indicate the final conso-

nant of the root *tal*. This interpretation seems unlikely, both because the expected sign would be /la/ rather than /lo/ and because most main signs do not function only as final syllables. We suggest its name may be based upon a root *loh*, "to save, redeem, free" or perhaps *ol*, "heart." The prefix may be a locative or a local variant of T36.

14. Miller (1977: 212–213) suggested the scrub vegetation indicated a highland location possibly in Oaxaca. Others have suggested a reference to the Puuc hills, but none of the sites located in the hill country are fortified. We (Ringle, Gallareta N., Bey 1998) have tentatively suggested that these murals may represent the history of a pan-Mesoamerican cult of Quetzalcoatl, significant episodes of which concern Epiclassic highland sites.

15. Excavation of the southern *sacbe* entrance in 1994 by I.N.A.H. archaeologists Leticia Vargas de la Peña, Thelma Sierra Sosa, and Carlos Peraza Lope has demonstrated similar construction there as well. The walls at Chacchob were of rough or uncut stone. Although Webster found no traces of stucco plaza floors at Chacchob, plaster traces suggest the "wall was surfaced completely with plaster, in striking contrast to the lack of surfacing in plaza areas in the interior of the site" (Webster 1978: 380).

16. This is true also for Chacchob, which has no permanent sources within the confines of the wall, the main sources apparently being a roofed *cenote* at the nearby *rancho* (Webster 1978; Pollock and Stromsvik 1953).

17. This was probably true for Postclassic systems as well. Lothrop (1924: 67, 89–91) noted an "Inner Enclosure" at Tulum, several structures connected by a wall seemingly intended to limit access to the main plaza:

> The massive bulk of the Great Wall proclaims that its function was largely military. The Inner Inclosure [sic], however, appears to have been a religious compound, for the character of the buildings which form it is apparently religious and the nature of the walls is such that they would not well serve for defense. It is to be noted, however, that the walls are heavier on the north, where they overlook a small beach and cove, offering admirable protection for repelling a landing force. (Lothrop 1924: 67)

Similarly, Landa mentions two walls at Mayapán. The inner, said to have been about one-eighth of a league in extent, had only two narrow gates, and "in the centre of this enclosure they built their temples. . . . In this enclosure they built houses for the lords only" (Landa/Tozzer 1941: 24–25). This wall has not in fact been attested archaeologically.

18. Dark (1995: 107–108) touches upon the problematics associated with a straightforward functional interpretation of "military" artifacts. He notes that Bodiam Castle, Sussex, may well have been "an old soldier's dream house" instead of a functioning sanctuary.

22

CHICHÉN ITZÁ
SETTLEMENT AND HEGEMONY
DURING THE TERMINAL CLASSIC PERIOD

Rafael Cobos Palma

he "linear succession model" (Tozzer 1957) depicts Chichén Itzá as an isolated site that flourished during the Early Postclassic period after the collapse of settlements such as Uxmal. However, this model belongs to the past. Much of the criticism of the "linear succession model" is substantiated by results obtained from ceramic and settlement studies conducted at the local and regional levels since the 1970s in western, central, and eastern Yucatán (Figure 22.1).

The results of archaeological investigations realized to this date in the northern Maya lowlands show that emphasis has been given to the chronology of the Late Classic and Terminal Classic periods. Moreover, several of these chronological studies are either directly or indirectly associated with Chichén Itzá and its Sotuta ceramic complex in a framework advanced by Ball (1979a: 32–34, Figure 17) twenty years ago. In brief, Ball's reconstruction of the archaeological sequence in the northern lowlands is explained by the linear succession or traditional model, the nonlinear partial overlap model (Hypothesis A), and the nonlinear total overlap model (Hypothesis B). For the cultural historical reconstruction of northern Yucatán, Chichén Itzá might have been partially or totally contemporaneous to other Maya settlements.

The nonlinear partial overlap model, or Hypothesis A, states that Cehpech ceramics predate Sotuta ceramics and were partially contemporaneous during the end of the Classic period. Sotuta materials dominated the ceramic inventory of the northern Maya lowlands after Cehpech ceramics ceased to be used. In the

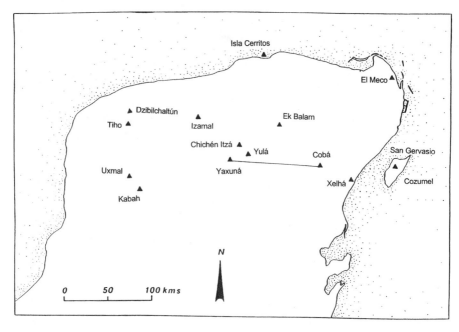

22.1 Location of Chichén Itzá and other northern Maya lowland sites mentioned in the text.

cultural-historic reconstruction of northern Yucatán, Hypothesis A implies that the great Maya sites with their Cehpech ceramic component coexisted for a short period with Chichén Itzá and its Sotuta ceramics (Ball 1979a; Lincoln 1986). The nonlinear total overlap model, or Hypothesis B, maintains that Cehpech and Sotuta ceramics were completely contemporaneous at the end of the Classic period. Hypothesis B implies that Classic Maya sites with their Cehpech ceramics totally coexisted with Chichén Itzá and its Sotuta component (Ball 1979a; Lincoln 1986).

Considering the few ceramic studies conducted at the site level late in the 1970s, Hypothesis A and Hypothesis B could have been interpreted as two mutually exclusive alternatives (see Ball 1979a: 34), either partial or total overlap but not both. However, Andrews V and Sabloff (1986: 447; see also Robles and Andrews 1986: 67) added a spatial dimension to the overlap due to the fact that some regions of northern Yucatán showed a partial overlap, whereas in other zones the overlap "was total." For instance, Andrews and Sabloff (1986: 447) acknowledged that Cehpech ceramics continued to be used. However, Cehpech ceramics mixed with Sotuta ceramics and, eventually, the Sotuta ceramics of Chichén Itzá "definitely continued past the end of Cehpech ceramics." Other settlements show a Cehpech component mixed with a small amount of Sotuta ceramics and both ceramics continued into Hocaba times of the Postclassic period. There are other regions where Cehpech or Sotuta materials were used after A.D. 900 and, in each case, these ceramics also continued into Hocaba times.

Using data from Dzibilchaltún and Isla Cerritos to reconstruct cultural-historical events dating between A.D. 700/800 and 1000/1100 in the northern Maya lowlands, the partial overlap reconstruction is favored (Hypothesis A). In fact, Andrews (1990), Andrews and Robles (1985), Andrews IV and Andrews V (1980), Andrews V (1979, 1981), and Robles and Andrews (1986) argue that the partial overlap between Cehpech and Sotuta ceramics lasted some 150 or 200 years between A.D. 850/900 and 1000/1100. After this partial overlap, Chichén Itzá flourished 100 to 200 years after the Cehpech ceramics disappeared.

In other regions Cehpech ceramics (see Bey et al. 1992 for the similarities and differences between the Cehpech ceramics of eastern and western Yucatán) and Sotuta ceramics were totally contemporaneous between A.D. 750/800 and 1050, and they continued into Hocaba times. It is noteworthy to mention some regional variants, however. For instance, at Yaxuná (Suhler et al. 1998), El Meco (Robles 1986), Xelhá (Canché 1992), and San Gervasio in Cozumel (Peraza 1993), Cehpech and Sotuta ceramics were associated with and continued into Hocaba. At settlements such as Ek' Balam (Bey et al. 1998) and Cobá (Robles 1990) with Cehpech ceramics, and Chichén Itzá (Lincoln 1990) and the Chikinchel region of northeastern Yucatán (Kepecs 1998) with Sotuta ceramics, Hocaba ceramics also continued. Furthermore, Chichén Itzá and settlements located in the western portion of the Chikinchel region do not have a Cehpech component.

At Uxmal Kowalski (1998: 416; see also Dunning and Kowalski 1994: 80–90; Kowalski et al. 1996: 289–291) suggested that the chronological overlap between Uxmal and Chichén Itzá was partial, and that around the middle of the tenth century A.D., Uxmal local elite "may have lost their ability to govern." However, a more detailed ceramic analysis than Robert Smith's study of the Cehpech ceramics is needed at Uxmal, and this analysis may corroborate Kowalski's affirmation or reveal that Cehpech and Sotuta ceramics totally overlapped at the site.

Therefore, as Andrews V and Sabloff (1986: 447) indicated, depending on the region or site in northern Yucatán where archaeological work is conducted, one should expect to find evidence to support partial or total overlap. Neither of these overlaps excludes one from the other. They seem to have coexisted regionally during the three or four centuries in which Cehpech ceramics existed (Bey et al. 1998: 114–116; Kepecs 1998: 125–129; Robles 1990: 177–217; Smith 1971: 134; Suhler et al. 1998: 177–179), and during the two or two and a half centuries in which Sotuta ceramics existed (Anderson 1998: 152; Smith 1971: 134). A careful review of the ceramic evidence uncovered in several settlements of northern Yucatán reveals that, at a regional level, a total overlap occurred when slate, unslipped, and red ceramic wares of Cehpech and Sotuta were in use during the eighth century A.D. Sometime between A.D. 700 and 800, the Yucatán settlements cut their ceramic ties with the southern Maya lowlands, the regional differentiation between eastern and western Cehpech began, and Sotuta materials were being used in central Yucatán.

Dating the Sotuta ceramic complex between A.D. 750/800 and 1050 went from the "realm of personal impressions and guesswork" (Ball 1979a: 33) to a proposal substantiated by stratigraphic contexts, ceramic analyses, and radiocarbon-14 dates. For instance, Ball (1979a: 33) suggested that archaeologists might "extend the tenure of Sotuta back some 50 to 100 years rather than to lengthen that of Cehpech." A decade later, Ball and Taschek (1989: 192) acknowledged that the political, economic, and social apogee of Chichén Itzá occurred between A.D. 700 and 1200, although they also felt "reasonably safe in further narrowing this interval by some fifty to a hundred years at each end."

Bey et al. (1997), Cobos (1998b), Lincoln (1986), and Ringle et al. (1991, 1998) date the apogee of Chichén Itzá between A.D. 750/800 and 1000/1050. Placing the peak of Chichén Itzá 150 years earlier than it is traditionally suggested is based upon the following: ceramic analyses conducted in several northern Maya sites, recalibrated radiocarbon dates, regional distribution patterns of archaeological materials such as obsidian, turquoise, gold, tumbaga, and the presence of the Quetzalcoatl/Kukulkan cult in the Maya area. Moving back 150 years the dating of Chichén Itzá places Sotuta ceramics within the chronological framework of the beginning and differentiation of the northern Maya lowlands ceramic traditions dating to the Late Classic and Terminal Classic periods.

If Cehpech and Sotuta began their contemporaneity as early as the eighth century A.D., when did Cehpech and Sotuta initiate their partial overlap at Dzibilchaltún and Isla Cerritos? Why did Yaxuná, El Meco, Xelhá, and San Gervasio in Cozumel, with a predominant Cehpech ceramic component, coexist with the minority presence of Sotuta ceramics? Why did both ceramic complexes continue into Hocaba? Why did Ek' Balam and Cobá, whose Cehpech ceramics continued into Hocaba, preserve their ceramic components without mixing with Sotuta ceramics while they were contemporaneous to Chichén Itzá? The answers to each one of these questions are directly related to two events that took place in central Yucatán late in the Late Classic period and during the Terminal Classic period, between A.D. 750/800 and 1050. These events include: (1) the establishment of Chichén Itzá as an important settlement and its transformation into a regional state and the rise of Sotuta ceramics, and (2) the chronological contemporaneity of Chichén Itzá and its northern Yucatecan neighbors during the early and late phases of the Sotuta ceramic complex.

This paper has two aims: first, to use ceramic and settlement-pattern data to show how Chichén Itzá rose as an important settlement and political entity between A.D. 750/800 and 1050; second, to demonstrate that the degree of chronological contemporaneity of Chichén Itzá and other northern Yucatán settlements changed throughout time. In other words, the end of the Late Classic period and the beginning of the Terminal Classic period in the northern Maya lowlands can be characterized by a total overlap. However, by the end of the Terminal Classic period, some sites' ceramic complexes overlapped only partially while other settlements continued with a total overlap.

THE SOTUTA CERAMIC COMPLEX: EARLY AND LATE PHASES

Andrews IV (1970), Brainerd (1958), Lincoln (1990), and Smith (1971) recognized a distinction between the early and late phases of occupation at Chichén Itzá as evident in ceramics. I use settlement patterns and ceramic data to distinguish between an "Old" and "New" Chichén Itzá, which has no relationship with the "Old" and "New" Chichén Itzá defined by ethnicity, iconography, or art history studies (see for example Tozzer 1957).

The difference between early and late settlements at Chichén Itzá becomes evident when ceramics are considered, specifically forms and ceramic types associated either with early or late phases of the Sotuta ceramic complex. The main wares of the Sotuta ceramic complex include Chichen Unslipped, Chichen Slate, Chichen Red, Fine Orange, Plumbate, and Fine Buff (see Lincoln 1986; Smith 1971: 134–135). The majority wares such as Chichen Unslipped, Chichen Slate, and Chichen Red had their origins in the ceramic traditions of central and western Yucatán and southern Campeche. For instance, Dzitas and Sisal ceramic groups developed in northern Yucatán during the Late Classic period in the area located between Izamal, Isla Cerritos, and Chichén Itzá (see Robles 1988: 67–68; Robles 1990: 211–214; Robles and Andrews 1986: 87, 89). According to Brainerd (1958: 55; see also Bey et al. 1992; Boucher 1992; Robles 1990: 177–217), Chichén Itzá slate ware ceramics "stem from that of the Florescent Medium Slateware which seems to have been used throughout the Northern Yucatán Peninsula," although it was also influenced by ceramics from the Río Bec area in southern Campeche.

Chichen Red ware is also "grounded in Florescent tradition, the Thin Redware of the Puuc sites. Slip and paste of the two wares show marked similarity. However, the shape and decoration of Mexican Medium Redware show more influence from X Fine Orange ware [and the] forms seem to be X [Silho] Fine Orange copies" (Brainerd 1958: 56). According to Kepecs (1998: 126), the geographical distribution of Dzibiac Red ceramic type is limited to Chichén Itzá, sites located between Chichén Itzá and the northern coast of Yucatán (Cupul and Chikinchel regions), Isla Cerritos, and Mayapán.

Fine Orange and Plumbate wares are two important components of the Chichén Itzá Sotuta ceramic complex, and their origins of manufacture are located in the lower Usumacinta (southwestern Campeche, eastern Tabasco, northeastern Chiapas) and the western portion of the Guatemala highlands, respectively (for Fine Orange see Bishop 1994; Foias and Bishop 1994; for Plumbate see Dutton and Hobbs 1943; Neff 1984; Neff and Bishop 1988; Shepard 1948).

The Fine Orange collection of Chichén Itzá contains "nothing but fine-orange Silho group sherds" (Smith 1971: 184) and the presence of Silho Orange in the northern lowlands dates to the ninth century (see Ball 1978: 102–103; Gallareta et al. 1989: 321, Figure 6; Robles 1988: 67–68). Tohil Plumbate originated at Tajumulco, Guatemala, either late in the ninth century or early in the tenth century, and its arrival at sites such as Becan, Ambergris Caye, Uxmal, Isla Cerritos, Yulá, and Chichén Itzá dates between A.D. 850/900 and 1100 (Anderson 1998, Table 1; Andrews et al. 1988; Ball 1977: 47, 135–136, 164; Kowalski et al. 1996; Lincoln 1990: 297–301; Shepard 1948: 130–131; Smith 1971: 185; Valdez et al. 1995).

The distinctive ceramic forms of Chichen Unslipped include jars, bowl censers, hourglass censers, ladle censers, tripod censers, bowls, and griddles (Brainerd 1958: 54–55; Smith 1971: 170–173). Forms associated with both early and late phases of Sotuta ceramics include jars with "medium-high outcurving to vertical neck" (Smith 1971: 173; see also 171–172), and bowl and ladle censers (Andrews IV 1970: 19, Figures 15, 53f; Brainerd 1958: 94–95, Figures 69–70, 104; Smith 1971: 171, Figure 12a-e). Tall biconical or hourglass censers appeared only in the late phase of the Sotuta complex and are absent in subsequent Postclassic ceramic complexes of Chichén Itzá (Andrews IV 1970: 56, Figure 16; see also Brainerd 1958: 94–95, Figures 68f, 75e, and 104c; Smith 1971: 172). According to Smith (1971: 173), griddles "are either of the Tases Phase (Postclassic period, after A.D. 1300), perhaps even more recent manufacture, or were made in Sotuta Phase times and are precursors of the more recent griddle."

Characteristic ceramic forms of Chichen Slate include jars, dishes, and bowls without supports and bottoms that are either flattened or rounded (Brainerd 1958: 55; Smith 1971: 174–178). The jars have high vertical or "slightly outcurving" necks and everted rims (Smith 1971: 177). Dishes with rounded sides are shallow and wide and do not have supports, however other dishes "are more flaring and round to a slightly convex base supported by hollow bulbous feet" (Smith 1971: 177). These bulbous feet are similar to the Silho Orange pyriform vessels.

It is noteworthy that in Brainerd's (1958: 53, 116, Figures 4p, 50n) ceramic analysis he identified Chichén Itzá Thin Slate ware and dated this ware to the Florescent period. Following a typological criterion, Thin Slate ware was included in the Cehpech ceramic complex and it is "easily differentiated from Puuc Slate" (Smith 1971: 156). However, Andrews IV (1970: 40), Brainerd (1958: 53), Lincoln (1990: 302), and Smith (1971: 29–30) recognized that Thin Slate is closely associated with Dzitas Slate type of Chichen Slate ware and Muna Slate type of Puuc Slate ware. The distinctive forms of Thin Slate include jars, tripod dishes, cylindrical vases, and hemispherical and deep bowls (Andrews IV 1970: 40, 59, Figures 34a, b, c, d, 35a, b: Brainerd 1958: 53, Figures 4p, 10h, 15ls, 18j, 21d, 32d, e, 35e, 50n, 51a, c, 61b, e, f, j, l; Smith 1971: 29–30, 134, 154–156, 163, Figures 7a, h, o, r).

Forms characteristic of Chichen Red ware include jars like those described in Chichen Slate ware, dishes with rounded sides, tripod dishes and dishes with flaring sides, cylindrical vases, and bowls without supports and flattened bottoms (Brainerd 1958: 55–56, Figures 84–88; Smith 1971: 178–181; see also Andrews IV 1970: 58). According to Brainerd (1958: 56), the ceramic forms of his Mexican Medium Redware (Chichen Red ware) "seem to be X Fine Orange copies."

On the basis of the ceramic information, archaeologists have suggested early and late phases of occupation at Chichén Itzá. For instance, Brainerd's (1958: 34–35) materials pertaining to the Florescent Stage and Early Mexican substage, which correspond to Ticul Thin ware of the Cehpech ceramic complex and Sotuta ceramics (see Smith 1971: 15–16, 29–30, 134–135, 162–163, 170–192), are associated with structures and architectural groups dating to the early phase. According to Brainerd (1958: 36, 38–40, 42–44), excavations conducted by members of the Carnegie Institution of Washington at the Akab'dzib Cenote, the Southwest Group, the Temples of the Three and Four Lintels, the Initial Series Group, and the Monjas Complex uncovered Medium Slateware (or Chichen Slate ware of Smith 1971: 16), Medium Redware (or Chichen Red ware of Smith 1971: 15–16), and Thin Slateware (Thin Slate ware of Smith 1971: 29–30). The ceramics at both the Akab'dzib Cenote and architectural groups were found in "several seemingly pure deposits, many deposits showing varying degrees of Middle Mexican or Florescent mixture, but no Pure Florescent deposits" (Brainerd 1958: 94, see also pages 36 and 43).

Excavations at El Mercado (3D11), the Southeast Colonnade (3D10), and the Northeast Colonnade (2D10) at the Great Terrace uncovered only Sotuta ceramics, and no Chichén Itzá Thin Slate or Puuc Slate wares were found (see Brainerd 1958: 36–38, 40). However, excavations conducted in the foundations of the West Colonnade (3D1) by Peña et al. (1991: 90–95) revealed the overwhelming presence of Sotuta ceramics mixed with a small number of Cehpech materials including Muna Slate, Akil Impressed (Puuc Slate ware), and Ticul Thin Slate (Thin Slate ware). The findings of Sotuta and Cehpech ceramics in the foundations of Structure 3D1 seem to be stratigraphically associated with the substructures of El Castillo (2D5) and the Temple of the Warriors (Temple of the Chacmool).

In 1954 Smith (1971: 162, 168, 171, 190, 259–260) found seventy-five Cehpech sherds underlying Sotuta ceramics in the lowest levels of Cut 1 (levels G46 to G48, Temples of the Three and Four Lintels), Cut 2 (levels G2 and G3, Temples of the Three and Four Lintels), and Cut 5 (the Initial Series Group). Smith also reported the presence of Cehpech ceramics associated with Sotuta materials in the upper levels of Cut 2 (Temples of the Three and Four Lintels), in three levels of Cut 8 and two levels of Cut 9 (the Southwest Group), and the surface level of Cut 15 (the High Priest's Grave Group). With the exception of Cut 17, where Smith (1971: 260) found one Cehpech sherd, all of the ceramic materials found in Cut 17 and Cuts 13, 14, 16, 18, and 19 revealed a majority presence of Sotuta ceramics. Smith excavated Cuts 13, 14, 16, 17, 18, and 19 at different points of the Great Terrace.

The Cehpech ceramic types found in Cuts 1, 2, 5, 8, and 9 by Smith (1971: 162–163) include: Yokat Striated jars (Puuc Unslipped ware), Muna Slate with gray slip and Sacalum Black-on-slate basins; Muna Slate with gray slip, Tekit Incised, and Akil Impressed tripod dishes with basal break; Tekit Incised jars (Puuc Slate ware), Teabo Red jars (Puuc Red ware), and Ticul Thin Slate hemispherical bowls, tripod dishes, and jars (Thin Slate ware). All of these types are closely related to western Cehpech ceramics (see comments by Bey et al. 1992; Robles 1990: 259–262; Smith 1971: 163), although the presence of Akil Impressed suggests contacts with eastern Yucatán (see Bey et al. 1992; Robles 1990: 199).

It is noteworthy that Smith (1971: 162, see also pages 171, 259–260) only used sherds from Cuts 1, 10, 14, 16, and 17 for "determining the component parts of the Sotuta Ceramic Complex," and did not use cuts in his ceramic analysis that revealed the presence of Cehpech materials associated with Sotuta ceramics. At Yulá, a small site located some five kilometers southeast of Chichén Itzá, Anderson (1998: 162, Table 1) reported that Sotuta ceramics occur "in all strata," and although Cehpech "is totally absent from the lowest levels of the two deepest test units," it is found mixed with Sotuta materials in upper levels. Therefore, and with the exception of levels G46 to G48 in Cut 1, levels G2 and G3 in Cut 2, and the lower levels in Cut 5, the findings of Smith and Anderson corroborate Brainerd's observations regarding the absence of contexts containing only Cehpech ceramics at Chichén Itzá (Brainerd 1958: 36, 43, 94).

Brainerd (1958: 35, Figures 104–109) and Smith (1971: 173, 177, 181) acknowledged that several ceramic forms appeared during the Modified Florescent Period at Chichén Itzá, and these forms were the hallmark of the Sotuta ceramic complex. Andrews IV (1970: 19–44, 56–61) used ceramic materials recovered from surface deposits at the Balankanche Cave to support Brainerd's and Smith's observations. Furthermore, Andrews IV (1970: 59, Figures 34a-c, f, 35a-b) found three cylindrical vases, one hemispherical bowl, and two bolster-rim basins whose forms "were common in the Pure Florescent overlapped with or continued on into the Modified phase." Andrews IV (1970: 59) recognized that these vessels were typologically similar to the vessels described by Brainerd (1958: 116) as "Chichén Itzá Thin Slate," and suggested assigning the Balankanche vessels to the Modified Florescent period, which is commonly associated with the apogee of Chichén Itzá.

One of Lincoln's (1990: 390) goals in his investigation during 1983 and 1985 at Chichén Itzá was "to dispel the notion that a meaningful contrast can be discerned between 'old' and 'new' components of the site." Lincoln (1990: 7, 210–211) indicated that the buildings of Chichén Itzá were built and modified in the same archaeological phase whose ceramic component is associated with the Sotuta ceramic complex, and "these episodes of construction apparently did not correlate with major changes in the fashion or inventory of material culture at the site." Using ceramics collected from his test excavations 1, 5, 6, 10, 11, 13, 17, and 18 and the results of ceramics analysis, Lincoln (1990: 212–214, 219–221) recognized an early phase and a late phase in his study area, which included the southern portion of Quadrant 5C, all of Quadrant 5D, and the northwestern corner of Quadrant 6E. This early phase of occupation is associated with Thin Slate ware and Holactun Cream of the Cehpech ceramic complex, and Chichen Slate ware, Chichen Red ware, Chichen Unslipped ware, and Fine Orange ware of the Sotuta ceramic complex. Platforms Ho'Che, Ek'Xux, Culub, Chac Bolay, Xkixpachoch, and Uayuc date to the early phase of occupation (Lincoln 1990: 301–313, 355–360).

Remains of a late phase of occupation found by Lincoln (1990: 355–356) included Sotuta ceramics without Thin Slate ware and Holactun Cream of the Cehpech ceramic complex. Ceramics collected mainly in test excavation 8 were used by Lincoln to recognize the late phase in his study area, although ceramics uncovered in test excavations 2, 5, 9, 10, and 11 "seem to hold an intermediate position" (Lincoln 1990: 359). Platforms Ho'Che, Cuuc, and Culub date to the late phase of occupation at the site.

I conducted excavations at the Group Sacbe 61 and termini groups located to the west, northwest, and east of the Great Terrace at Chichén Itzá (Cobos 1998a). The ceramic types found in the excavations include: Sisal Unslipped, Piste Striated, Espita Appliqué (Chichen Unslipped ware), Dzitas Slate, Balantun Black-on-slate (Chichen Slate ware), Dzibiac Red (Chichen Red ware), Silho Orange (Fine Orange ware). These ceramic types and their forms are similar to other Sotuta materials reported by Anderson (1998), Brainerd (1958), Lincoln (1990), Smith (1971), and Pérez de Heredia (1998).

To summarize, the presence of ceramic types pertaining to Cehpech and Sotuta ceramics can be used to differentiate between an early phase and a late phase of occupation at Chichén Itzá. Ceramics associated with the early phase include Thin Slate ware; jars, bowl censers, ladle censers, and tripod censers of Chichen Unslipped ware; vessels of Chichen Red ware; and Fine Orange ware. Ceramics associated with the late phase include hourglass censers and other vessels of Chichen Unslipped, Chichen Slate, Fine Orange, and Plumbate wares.

THE SETTLEMENT PATTERNS OF
CHICHÉN ITZÁ AND SOTUTA CERAMICS

Lincoln (1990: 307, see also 304) suggested that Thin Slate ware could be used as an indicator "of the barely perceptible break between early and later facets of the sequence within Chichén Itzá." I agree with Lincoln, and, as indicated previously, excavations by the Carnegie Institution of Washington at the Akab'dzib Cenote, the Southwest Group, the Temples of the Three and Four Lintels, the Initial

Series Group, the Monjas Complex, and the lowest levels of the West Colonnade revealed the presence of Thin Slate ware associated with Chichen Slate ware, and Chichen Red ware. Moreover, on the basis of his ceramic data, Lincoln (1990: 304) determined that Platforms Ho'Che (test excavations 10 and 11), Culub (test excavations 5 and 6), and Uayuc (test excavation 17) "were probably built during the early facet."

Test excavations 5 and 6 were conducted on the surface of Platform Culub (see Lincoln 1990: 305–306, 492–506, Map Sheet III). Test excavation 5 was placed at the center of a plaza surrounded by Structures 5D42 (temple), 5D43 (altar), 5D41 (range structure), and 5D40 (gallery-patio), whereas test excavation 6 was placed near the northwest corner of the platform. The ceramic evidence dates Platform Culub to the early phase of occupation, and this could be used to argue that Structures 5D42, 5D43, 5D40, and 5D41 are contemporaneous with the Initial Series Group and structures standing on Platform Ho'Che. Moreover, the presence of a grouping including temple, altar, range structure, and gallery-patio structure at Platform Culub, the Initial Series Group, and Platform Ho'Che are part of the early pattern of occupation at Chichén Itzá.

For instance, the Initial Series Group is formed by a temple (5C4), a range structure (5C14), a gallery-patio (5C11), an altar (5C17), and several other structures. The Long Count date 10.2.9.1.9 9 Muluk 7 Zac reported from building 5C4 dates the Initial Series Group to A.D. 878 (Grube 1994: 344; Krochock 1988: 26–27, 29). Ceramics associated with this group belong to the Sotuta complex, although an early test excavation placed near the east wall of 5C11 revealed a "fair collection of Cehpech Phase sherds in the lowest levels" (Smith 1971: 260).

A temple (5D1), an altar (5D23), a range structure (5D2), and gallery-patio (5D3) sit upon Platform Ho'Che (Lincoln 1990: 398-Note 4, 401–451, 492–497). Test excavations 10 and 11 were placed on the platform, and the ceramic evidence revealed the presence of Thin Slate ware in the deepest levels of the test units and its absence in the upper levels. Lincoln (1990: 304-note 40, 359) used these data to suggest that Platform Ho'Che was built during the early phase of occupation at Chichén Itzá.

According to Ruppert (1952: 134) several lintels of Structure 5D2 were used in the Casa Principal or main building of the Hacienda Chichén Itzá, so it may be possible that the Water Trough lintel belongs to 5D2. However, Lincoln (1990: 413-Note 12) believes that this lintel was from a different structure. Two Long Count dates associated with the Water Trough lintel date to the ninth century A.D. (10.1.17.5.13 11 Ben 11 Kumku, or 10.1.18.6.6 6 Chicchan 18 Kumku) (Grube 1994: 344).

The mapping of major architectural groups and minor structures associated with these groups, as well as the study of internal causeways, are two of the investigations I conducted as part of the Chichén Itzá Archaeological Project of INAH. During five field seasons, from 1993 to 1997, fieldwork was carried out in a transect 4 kilometers long and 1.2 kilometers wide. The transect extends 2.5 kilometers to the northwest and 1.5 kilometers to the southeast of structure 2D5 (El Castillo), and the surveyed area is as large as that surveyed by the Carnegie Institution of Washington (cf. Ruppert 1952, Figure 151).

During the fieldwork conducted at Chichén Itzá, it was confirmed that typical Late and Terminal Classic Maya elite residences include eight range structures or palace-type buildings located to the south and east of 2D5 (El Castillo). These range structures at Chichén Itzá include Structures 3C9 (Casa Colorada), 4C1 (the Monjas Complex), 4D1 (Akab'dzib), 5C14 (House of the Phalli), 5D2, 7B2, and 7B3 (Temple of the Three Lintels), and 3E24 (Bóvedas in the East Group) (Bolles 1977; Lincoln 1986: 155, 184–185; 1990: 605–607; Ruppert 1952: 3, 43, 130, 134, 145, 146, Figures 30–32, 60, 93, 96, 107–108).

Other interesting finds at Chichén Itzá include five new gallery-patio (2Z13, 3B23, 3F3, 3G2, 4F24) and five new patio (1A21, 2A17, 3B12, 4F49, 21Y23) structures. The Carnegie Institution of Washington reported and mapped eleven gallery-patio (2D6, 3B3, 3B8, 3D11, 4E3, 4F14, 5B17, 5B19, 5C11, 5D3, 6E3) and two patio (3C13, 5D7) structures (Ruppert 1943, 1950; Ruppert and Smith 1955), and Lincoln (1990: 459–460, 534–536) recorded two gallery-patios (5D13, 5D40) and one patio (5D70).

We know of nine gallery-patios (2D6, 3B23, 3F3, 3G2, 4F14, 5B17, 5B19, 5D13, 6E3) and three patios (1A21, 2A17, 21Y23) associated with temples and altars in ten architectural groups at Chichén Itzá. For instance, El Castillo, Venus Platform, and gallery-patio 2D6 illustrate the architectural pattern at the site. The presence of seven gallery-patios and three patios associated with an equal number of temples and altars is documented in ten architectural groups located 2.5 kilometers from Structure 2D5 (El Castillo). Gallery-patios or patios have not been found in areas or sites with Pure Florescent or Modified Florescent architecture located more than 2.5 km away from the site center (Anderson 1998; Andrews et al. 1989; Garza and Kurjack 1980; Love 1987; personal field observations 1993–1997).

In summary, the architectural pattern observed in several groups located in the southern part of Chichén Itzá corresponds to the tri-functional compound defined by Lincoln (1990: 398-Note 4, 401–451, 492–497), consisting of a temple, a gallery-patio, and a range structure. Lincoln noted three tri-functional compounds that include Structures 5C4, 5C11, and 5C14 in the Initial Series Group, Structures 5D1, 5D3, and 5D2 on Platform Ho'Che, and Structures 5D42, 5D40, and 5D41 on Platform Culub.

In 1992 Ringle and Bey (1992, Figures 8–10) used Ruppert (1952) and Lincoln (1990) survey data to suggest that a second architectural pattern exists at Chichén Itzá. This second architectural plan is designated by Ringle and Bey as the "temple assemblage" and is characterized by a temple, an altar, and a colonnaded hall. Ringle and Bey mentioned five examples, which include Structures

Table 22.1. Ceramic limits, architectural complexes, and causeways associated with the Early Sotuta (700/750–900) Ceramic Complex.

Ceramic Wares, Groups, and Types	Architectural Complexes	Causeway System
CHICHEN UNSLIPPED: Jars Ladle censers Tripod censers Bowls	Monjas Complex El Castillo-Substructure Temple of the Chac	Early causeway system associated either with two architectural groups linked by a causeway or Tamanché/Sayil pattern where architectural groups form a straight line
CHICHEN SLATE: Jars Dishes Bowls with supports Bowls with bottoms flattened or rounded	Mool Osario Group (Strs. 3C1,3C3) Xtoloc Group	Sacbe 4 Monjas Complex–Osario Group Sacbe 7 Monjas Complex–Three Lintels
	Casa Colorada	Sacbe 15
CHICHEN RED: Jars Dishes (rounded sides) Tripod dishes Cylindrical vases Bowls with flattened bottoms	Southwest Group Initial Series Group One, Three, and Four Lintels	Osario Group–Xtoloc Group Sacbe 16 Xtoloc Group–Casa Redonda Sacbe 7-25 Monjas Complex–Initial Series
FINE ORANGE WARE: Fine-orange Silho	Temple of the Hieroglyphic Jambs	Sacbe 32 El Castillo Substructure–Strs. 3E6 and 3E7
THIN SLATE WARE: Jars Tripod dishes Cylindrical vases Basins Bowls Slate Muna Group	Ho'Che Platform Casa Redonda	Sacbe 26 Initial Series–Ho'Che Platform Sacbe 7-33 Monjas Complex–Southwest Group

2B1 and unnamed mound, Structures 2C7 and 2C8, Structures 2D8 and 3D1, Structures 5B1 and 5A2, and Structures 5B16 and 5B13.

In this work it is suggested that gallery-patios such as structures 5B17 and 5B19 of the Southwest Group, 5C11 of the Initial Series Group, 5D3 on Platform Ho'Che, and 5D40 on Platform Culub are associated with temples, altars, range structures, and colonnaded halls in architectural groups located to the south, southwest, and southeast of the Monjas Complex during the early phase of occupation at Chichén Itzá. Ceramic materials associated with the early phase of occupation include Thin Slate ware; jars, ladle censers, and tripod censers of Chichen

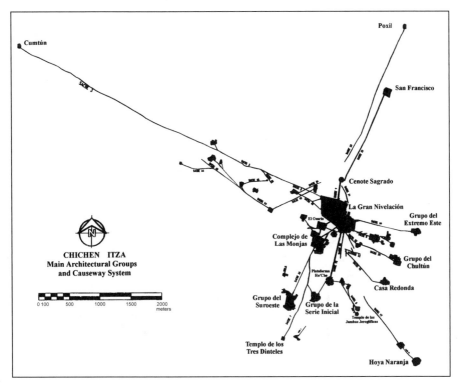

22.2 Chichén Itzá main architectural groups and causeway system.

Unslipped ware; and vessels of Chichen Slate ware, Chichen Red ware, and Fine Orange ware (Table 22.1). Furthermore, hieroglyphic texts dating to the ninth century are associated with the early phase of occupation at Chichén Itzá (Grube 1994).

When Chichén Itzá flourished during the late phase of occupation, the epicenter of the site was located at the Great Terrace, and gallery-patio structures associated with temples and altars were built at the site center as well as in peripheral groups. The architectural pattern consisting of a temple, altar, and gallery-patio is represented at the Great Terrace by structures 2D5 (El Castillo), 2D4 (Venus Platform), and 2D6 (gallery-patio), whereas in the periphery of the site some of the groups showing the same architectural pattern include the Far East Group (3G4, 3G6, 3G2), Plazas Group (3F1, 3F6, 3F3), Chultún Group (4F15, 4F13, 4F14), the southern portion of Platform Ek'Xux (5D12, unnumbered altar, 5D13), and Temple of the Hieroglyphic Jambs (6E1, 6E2, 6E3) (Figures 22.2, 22.3, 22.4, 22.5). Hourglass censers and other vessels of Chichen Unslipped, Chichen Slate, Chichen Red, Fine Orange, Plumbate, and Fine Buff

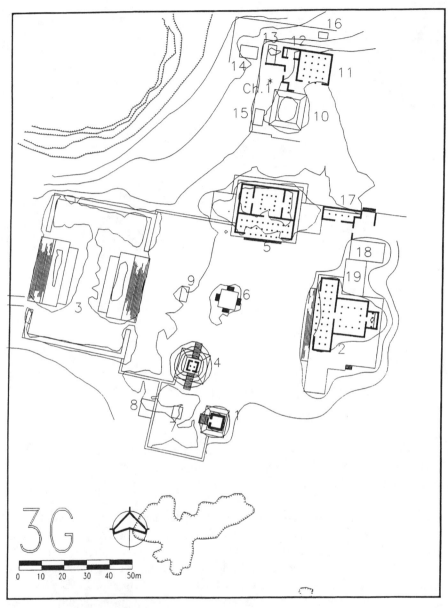

22.3 Detailed plan of the Grupo del Extremo Este.

are associated with the late phase of occupation (Table 22.2). Puuc Slate and Thin Slate wares as well as hieroglyphic texts are absent in the late phase of Chichén Itzá's occupation.

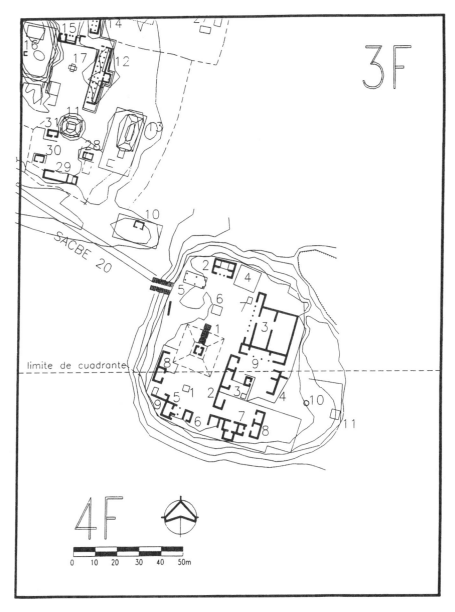

22.4 Detailed section of the Grupo de las Plazas.

After A.D. 900 Chichén Itzá acquired its final layout after having consolidated its internal structure during the early phase of the Sotuta ceramic complex, or between A.D. 750/800 and 900. Moreover, the tenth century A.D. marked the

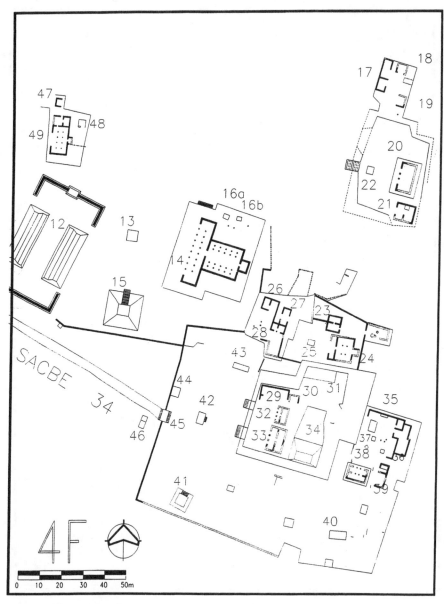

22.5 *Detailed section of the Grupo del Chultún.*

expansion of Chichén Itzá in northern Yucatán when it rose as a regional capital. This regional capital controlled small settlements located at its periphery, secured an area between the north coast and central Yucatán, established and controlled

Table 22.2. Ceramic limits, architectural complexes, and causeways associated with the Late Sotuta (900–1050) Ceramic Complex.

Ceramic Wares, Groups, and Types	Architectural Complexes	Causeway System
CHICHEN UNSLIPPED: Jars Hourglass censers Ladle censers Tripod censers Bowls Griddles	The Great Terrace and associated buildings El Caracol (Str. 3C15)	Late causeway system associated with the Great Terrace. Old and new causeways link the Great Terrace with peripheral groups in a dendritic pattern
	Wall Panels	Sacbe 1 Great Terrace–Sacred Cenote
CHICHEN SLATE: Jars Dishes Bowls with supports Bowls with bottoms flattened or rounded	(Str. 3C16) Far East Group Plazas Group Chultun Group	Sacbe 3 Great Terrace–Cumtún Sacbe 5 Great Terrace–El Caracol
CHICHEN RED: Jars Dishes (rounded sides) Tripod dishes Cylindrical vases Bowls with flattened bottoms	Temple of the Hieroglyphic Jambs Holtun Group Xtoloc Group	Sacbe 6 Great Terrace–East Group Sacbe 8 Ek'Xux Platform–Temple of the Hieroglyphic Jambs Sacbe 12 Great Terrace–Ho'Che Platform
FINE ORANGE WARE: Fine-orange Silho	Osario Group (Strs. 3C1-3C4)	Sacbe 19 Great Terrace–Far East Group
PLUMBATE WARE	Cumtún (site located	
FINE BUFF WARE	6 km to the northwest of El Castillo)	Sacbe 49 Great Terrace–Structure 2B2
		Sacbe 66 Ho'Che–Ek'Xux Platforms

its own trade port in the northern coast, and expanded its realm along the eastern and western coasts of the Yucatán peninsula.

CHICHÉN ITZÁ AND ITS NORTHERN NEIGHBORS: A.D. 750/800–900

The early phase of the Sotuta ceramic complex (A.D. 750/800–900) is associated with the Monjas Complex, the High Priest's Grave, the Southwest Group, the Initial Series Group, Temples of the Three and Four Lintels, the Temple of the Chacmool, and El Castillo-sub. Ceramics of the early Sotuta phase were used in a limited area located in central and north-central Yucatán, and this explains their

Table 22.3.

Dates A.D.	Chichén Itzá	Dzibil-chaltún	Isla Cerritos	Ek Balam	Yaxuná	Cobá	El Meco	Xelhá	San Gervasio
1200									
1150			Tomburro	Xtabay	Yaxuna V	Seco			
1100	Hocaba	Zipche Phase				—	— Hocaba-Sotuta	Xcacel	Arrecife
1050	—		—	—					
1000	Late	—					—	—	—
950	Sotuta		Jotuto		Yaxuná IV	Oro			
900	—	Copo 2 Phase	—	Late Yumcab				Chemuyil	Ribera
850	Early	—							
800	Sotuta	Late	Chacpel						
750		Copo I Phase							
700									

association with eastern and western Cehpech ceramics at settlements such as Chichén Itzá (see the ceramic section in this chapter and Brainerd 1958: 43; Bey et al. 1992), Isla Cerritos (Chacpel ceramic complex, see Robles 1988: 67–68), Yulá (Anderson 1998, Table 1), and Yaxuná (Yaxuná IV ceramic complex, Suhler et al. 1998: 177–180).

Despite the spatial restriction of Sotuta ceramics to central and north-central Yucatán between A.D. 750/800 and 900, evidence demonstrates that Sotuta ceramics were totally contemporaneous with the western Cehpech materials of Dzibilchaltún (Copo I ceramic complex and early phase of Copo II) and Ek' Balam (early phase of the Yumcab ceramic complex). On the other hand, Sotuta ceramics were also totally contemporaneous with the eastern Cehpech ceramics of Cobá (early phase of Oro ceramic complex), Xelhá (Chemuyil ceramic complex), and San Gervasio in Cozumel (Ribera ceramic complex) (Table 22.3).

If current data support a total overlap between A.D. 750 and 900, the overlap occurred when northern Yucatecan settlements were transformed into complex regional states. However, not all of these regional states achieved that complexity at the same time. For instance, Dzibilchaltún, Ek' Balam, and Cobá reached their apogees between A.D. 750/800 and 900/1000 and these settlements controlled northwestern, northeastern, and central-eastern Yucatán respectively, whereas Chichén Itzá, Uxmal, and possibly Tiho reached their apogees toward the end of the ninth or during the tenth century A.D. It seems that the transformation of Chichén Itzá and Uxmal into complex regional states occurred at least fifty years after the apogees of Dzibilchaltún, Ek' Balam, and Cobá, or in other words, when the occupations at Dzibilchaltún and Ek' Balam had been reduced drastically, and when the territorial control of eastern Yucatán by Cobá had diminished tremendously.

At Dzibilchaltún some 7,560 structures were occupied between A.D. 700 and 1000 and the site "became one of the most populous and extensive communities in the Northern Lowlands" (Andrews V 1981: 326). However, toward the end of the Pure Florescent period (Copo 2 Phase, A.D. 830–1000), the occupation and building activity decreased at Dzibilchaltún due perhaps to the rise of Tiho, a settlement located fourteen kilometers to the south that "cast a shadow over Dzibilchaltún" (Andrews V 1981: 333). Tiho had massive platforms and architectural complexes with Pure Florescent architecture "similar in size and arrangement to the Monjas Quadrangle at Uxmal" (Andrews V 1981: 333). Tiho ceramics include the following Cehpech types: Muna Slate, Ticul Thin Slate, Teabo Red, Chumayel Red-on-slate, Sacalum Black-on-slate, Chum Unslipped, and Yokat Striated.

According to epigraphic texts and ceramic and architectural data during the middle of the ninth century A.D., Ek' Balam acquired not only its final layout, but also consolidated its domain over northeastern Yucatán. Ruler Ukit Kan Lek of Ek' Balam has been identified as the individual responsible for the apogee of the site, which he orchestrated late in the eighth or early in the ninth century A.D. In fact, Ukit Kan Lek ordered the construction of the acropolis and several of the buildings located at the site center of Ek' Balam (Vargas et al. 1999). Evidence of the construction activity is supported by the presence of Ek' Balam's second architectural style, which consists of "high quality Florescent-style architecture characterized by cut-stone veneer and cut-stone vaulting" associated with Chum Unslipped, Encanto Striated, and Muna Slate. These three Cehpech ceramic types account for 69 percent of the Late Classic and Terminal Classic ceramics found at the site (Bey et al. 1998: 115, also 114).

At Cobá construction activity included building the Nohoch Mul Group with its late causeway system, and the construction of Causeway 1, which links Cobá with Yaxuná (Benavides 1981a; Robles 1990). This building activity probably took place early in the Oro ceramic complex (A.D. 700/730—1100/1200; see Robles 1990: 131–217). In fact, Cobá Stela 20 dates to A.D. 780 and was found "incorporated into" the plaza floor of the Nohoch Mul Group (Robles and Andrews 1986: 66; see also Graham 1977: 60–61; Stuart 1975: 791). The construction of the Nohoch Mul Group plaza floor and the placing of Stela 20 in it could be interpreted in two ways: (1) these two events are contemporaneous and date to the end of the eighth century A.D., and (2) Stela 20 briefly predates the great construction activity of the Nohoch Mul Group, which probably dates between the eighth and ninth centuries A.D.

According to Robles (1990: 211–214) Sotuta ceramics such as Dzitas Slate (n= 200 sherds) and Balantun Black-on-slate (n= 350 sherds) were "recovered from sealed deposits beneath the plaza floor of the Nohoch Mul complex." The presence of Sotuta ceramics in contexts dating to the late eighth or ninth century A.D. of the Nohoch Mul Group suggests contacts between Chichén Itzá, Yulá, Yaxuná, and Cobá. The contacts between central and eastern Yucatán took place when Cobá expanded its territory by constructing Causeway 1, linking it with Yaxuná. Moreover, the construction of Causeway 1 may have occurred before the construction of the Great Terrace and associated buildings, or in other words, before the rise of Chichén Itzá as a regional state in A.D. 900.

I pointed out previously in this chapter that Sotuta ceramics were found at Chichén Itzá associated with Cehpech materials of western Yucatán and the ceramic type Akil Impressed of eastern Yucatán (Cobá). The finding of these ceramics in "old" Chichén Itzá and in the foundations of the West Colonnade (3D1) supports the argument that early phase Sotuta ceramics were associated with western and eastern Cehpech ceramics at the site before A.D. 900 (see also the Chacpel ceramic complex of Isla Cerritos in Gallareta et al. 1989 and Robles 1988).

The ceramics used during the Protoclassic, Early Classic, and the beginning of the Late Classic periods at Yulá show that this site maintained a close relationship with Yaxuná (Anderson 1998; Suhler et al. 1998). Nevertheless, toward the end of the Late Classic and during the Terminal Classic periods, the interaction of Yulá changed from south to north, that is, Yulá was influenced by its northern neighbor Chichén Itzá and eventually became one of its satellite sites. The Late Classic and Terminal Classic ceramics of Yulá are associated with the Sotuta complex of Chichén Itzá and include the following ceramic groups: Chichen Slate (Dzitas Slate, Balantun Black-on-slate, Timak Composite, Chacmay Incised, Balam Canche Red-on-slate), Chichen Unslipped (Piste Striated, Sisal Unslipped, Espita Appliqué), Chichen Red (Dzibiac Red, Chankom Black-on-red), Fine Orange Silho, and Tohil Plumbate (Anderson 1998: 158–162, Table 1).

According to Suhler et al. (1998: 177–179) archaeological investigations at Yaxuná have revealed a "mixture of eastern and western Cehpech influences." Although western Cehpech ceramics appeared in the beginning of Yaxuná IVa

(A.D. 730–900/950), eastern Cehpech became the dominant ceramics at the end of Yaxuná IVa. The occurrence of eastern Cehpech materials at Yaxuná is attributed to the economic, political, and territorial expansion of Cobá during the ninth century A.D. As a result of this expansion, Cobá engulfed Yaxuná within its territory and—besides the Cehpech ceramics shared by both sites—the 100-kilometer causeway linking Yaxuná with Cobá confirms that prior to the tenth century A.D. the latter site had successfully spread its realm in central Yucatán. In fact, Suhler et al. (1998: 177) date the 100-kilometer Sacbe 1 "to the Late Classic, rather than the Terminal Classic period as generally accepted."

The Yaxuná IVb period (A.D. 950/1000–1100/1200) is characterized by the presence of Chichén Itzá Sotuta ceramics at the site, "which led to the virtual conquest and termination of Cehpech Yaxuná" (Suhler et al. 1998: 178). An alternative interpretation is that the Sotuta ceramics are contemporaneous with western and eastern Cehpech, date before A.D. 900/950, and do not represent the "conquest and termination of Cehpech Yaxuná" by Chichén Itzá. In fact, Suhler et al. (1998: 179) indicate that "the presence of Sotuta wares in the 6F-68 termination materials has been greatly underreported." The presence of Cehpech and Sotuta materials associated with Pure Florescent architecture such as in structures 6F-68 and 6F-9 at Yaxuná could have been totally contemporaneous with architectural groups located to the south, southeast, and southwest of the Monjas Complex, El Castillo-sub, and the Temple of the Chacmool at Chichén Itzá. These groups also exhibit Pure Florescent architecture and are associated with the early phase occupation at the site.

In the Puuc region, sites such as Uxmal, Nohpat, Kabah, Sayil, Labná, and Xkipché rose between the eighth and ninth centuries A.D. as independent centers, and their ceramic component was basically Cehpech. According to Kowalski (1998: 416, see also 403), at the end of the ninth century A.D. Kabah and Nohpat "were incorporated in a political-military alliance in which Uxmal was the leading partner," and Uxmal used Chichén Itzá warriors to expand its domain over the Puuc region.

If by the end of the ninth century A.D. Uxmal had consolidated its internal structure and initiated its transformation into a regional capital, it was not alone in this process. Several kilometers to the east in central Yucatán, Chichén Itzá experienced the same transformation during the last half of the Terminal Classic period. Tiho may have replaced Dzibilchaltún as the regional capital of northwestern Yucatán during this time; however, systematic research focused on Tiho's role during the Terminal Classic period has not been carried out.

CHICHÉN ITZÁ AND ITS NORTHERN NEIGHBORS: A.D. 900–1050

As previously mentioned, during the late phase of the Sotuta ceramic complex (A.D. 900–1050), Chichén Itzá became a powerful regional capital in central Yucatán. The site controlled small settlements located at its periphery, secured an area between the north coast and central Yucatán (Andrews et al. 1989), established and controlled its own trade port in the northern coast (Andrews et al. 1988; Braswell 1997b; Gallareta et al. 1989), and expanded its realm along the eastern and western coasts of the Yucatán peninsula (Andrews and Robles 1985; Robles and Andrews 1986).

After A.D. 900 the Great Terrace and associated buildings functioned as the site center of Chichén Itzá. Several groups whose architectural pattern included a temple, altar, and gallery-patio were built surrounding the site center, and a concentric array characterized the internal structure of Chichén Itzá. Lincoln (1990: 578) used his survey data and personal field observations to acknowledge a "rough concentricity and infer a logical structure to the site plan" at Chichén Itzá. In fact, Lincoln recognized the Great Terrace as the site center, whereas the Initial Series Group, the Temples of the Three and Four Lintels, Platform Ho'Che, and the Temple of the Hieroglyphic Jambs were located at the site periphery. These groups exhibit neither massive architecture nor large monumental constructions that surpass or equal the architecture at the Great Terrace.

According to Kurjack (1974: 81), in the concentric pattern more substantial and larger architecture "seems to have been surrounded by less substantial construction." For instance, at Dzibilchaltún the concentric pattern is evident in the central group, the central aggregate, and the periphery. Most of the large and more substantial architecture is concentrated in the central group, which is 600 meters in diameter; the central aggregate is three square kilometers in area, and vaulted buildings as well as causeways are found in this area. Beyond the central aggregate, few vaulted buildings exist and they are "scattered in an almost random manner" (Kurjack 1974: 86, see also 89, 91–94; Andrews V 1981: 328–330). Other Maya sites organized in a concentric pattern include Cobá (Benavides 1981a: 190–197; Gallareta 1984: 114–119), Calakmul (Fletcher and Gann 1994: 87–116), and Caracol (Chase 1998).

My personal field observations and survey data collected at Chichén Itzá support Kurjack's definition as well as Lincoln's inference regarding a concentric structure in the ancient community of Chichén Itzá. This concentric structure is highly apparent when the site center and periphery are considered. In fact, the Great Terrace concentrates large and more substantial architecture, including architectural groups with vaulted buildings, while lesser architectural groups with fewer vaulted buildings have a more spaced geographical distribution at the periphery.

The best examples of large, substantial architecture at Chichén Itzá are found in the buildings standing on the Great Terrace, several of which seem to be larger versions of buildings with prototypes just to the south. For instance, El Castillo (2D5) and the Venus Platform (2D4) find their precedent in Structures 3C1 (the High Priest's Grave) and 3C3 (Venus Platform) of the Osario Group (Fernández 1996, 1999; Grube 1994: 345, Note 7; Schele and Freidel 1990: 356; cf. Coggins

1983: 57). El Mercado finds its precedent in Structures 5B17 and 5B19 of the Southwest Group, 5C11 of the Initial Series Group, and Structure 6E3, or Temple of the Hieroglyphic Jambs (Krochock 1997; also Ruppert 1943, 1950). The Great Ballcourt and its iconography can be related to the Monjas Ballcourt (4C14) and the Casa Colorada Ballcourt (3C10) (Bolles 1977: 73–81, 220–229; Krochock and Freidel 1994; Ruppert 1952: 49, Figures 124a, b, c; Tozzer 1957).

Architecture, hieroglyphs, and ceramics substantiate the fact that Chichén Itzá, a first-rank settlement, controlled some third-rank centers, such as Tikincacab and Chikché in the north, San Francisco in the east, Dzibiac in the west, Cumtún in the northwest, and Yulá in the south. Ten kilometers is the maximum distance separating these minor sites from the center of Chichén Itzá (Anderson 1998; Andrews et al. 1989; Krochock 1988, 1997; Love 1987). The specific function of each of the third-rank settlements surrounding Chichén Itzá is unknown; however, some probably functioned as quarries to obtain architectural and sculptural elements that were used at the regional capital (Winemiller 1996). For instance, a megalithic block of limestone was found at Cumtún, a site located six kilometers from Chichén Itzá and the place where Causeway 3 ends (Morris et al. 1931: 215–218, Figure 132a, b; Ruppert 1928: 307; Winemiller 1996). Causeway 3 begins on the northwestern corner of the Great Terrace, a few meters to the west of Structure 2D1, or the Great Ballcourt (see Ruppert 1952: Figure 151, where Causeway 3 is shown as "Sacbe 2").

Yulá was another third-rank settlement contemporaneous with Chichén Itzá. Excavations conducted at Yulá show that 90 percent of the ceramics are Sotuta and the main wares are represented in the ceramic sample recovered by Anderson (1998: Table 1). Cehpech ceramics from Yulá account for 10 percent of the sample and the ceramic types are similar to western and eastern Cehpech reported from Chichén Itzá (see Anderson 1998: Table 1, and compare with Lincoln 1990: 220 and Smith 1971: 15–30, 134, 162–163). At Chichén Itzá, Cehpech sherds represent less than 10 percent by frequency count of the ceramics uncovered at the site center and periphery, and western Cehpech outnumbers eastern Cehpech ceramics.

Results from investigations conducted between Chichén Itzá and Isla Cerritos show a majority presence of Sotuta ceramics in that area (Andrews et al. 1989; Kepecs 1998; Kepecs et al. 1994). Dzibiac Red and Silho Orange were found in central and western portions of the Chikinchel area near the Chichén Itzá–Isla Cerritos corridor (Kepecs 1998). At the inland sites of Loche and San Fernando, Dzibiac Red and Silho Orange "were collected in small quantities and were limited almost exclusively to central architecture," whereas at the coastal site of Emal located forty kilometers east of Isla Cerritos, these two ceramic types were found in "over half of the site's structures" (Kepecs 1998: 127–128).

Sites located in the Cupul area and west of the Chikinchel region probably functioned as way-stations in the transportation of objects (obsidian, turquoise, ceramics [Tohil Plumbate]) and natural resources (salt, marine resources) between the northern coast of Yucatán and Chichén Itzá (Andrews et al. 1989; Braswell 1997b; Carr 1989; Cobos 1989, 1996, 1998a; Kepecs and Gallareta 1995; Kepecs et al. 1994). Several of those settlements probably became way-stations when Chichén Itzá expanded its realm to the north and Isla Cerritos was transformed into a trade port of Chichén Itzá. Recalibrated radiocarbon dates associated with stratigraphic and ceramic evidence uncovered at Isla Cerritos show that Sotuta ceramics totally replaced Cehpech ceramics by A.D. 900 (Andrews et al. 1988; Gallareta et al. 1989; Robles 1988).

While Chichén Itzá successfully expanded into central and north-central Yucatán and along the coasts of the peninsula, its northern neighbors experienced different transformations, such as: a drastic reduction of the settlement at Dzibilchaltún and Ek' Balam, a dramatic decrease of Cobá's territory in central and eastern Yucatán, and the apogee of Uxmal in the Puuc region. Ceramics are good evidence of these transformations that affected northwestern, northeastern, central, north-central, and eastern settlements as well as the Puuc region toward the end of the Terminal Classic period. After A.D. 900 the contemporaneity between western and eastern Cehpech and Sotuta varied according to the region. Some areas experienced partial overlap whereas other regions lived a total overlap.

For instance, at Dzibilchaltún, Zipche 1 Phase "is defined partly by ceramics characteristic of the Mexican period at Chichén Itzá, such as Chichen Slate, Chichen Red, and Silho Orange" (Andrews V 1981: 334). The presence of Sotuta ceramics at Dzibilchaltún coincides with the use of Hunucma Slate (Puuc Slate), and these ceramics were found in buildings located at the center of Dzibilchaltún, whose construction dates to Copo 2 Phase. However, these buildings were reused by squatters during the Zipche 1 Phase.

The presence of Chichen Slate ware at Ek' Balam dates to the late phase of the Yumcab ceramic complex and is associated with what appears to be Ek' Balam architectural style III of the Terminal Classic period (Bey et al. 1998: 114–116). Sotuta ceramics at Ek' Balam account for .1 percent of the sample and it shows that the ceramic component of Ek' Balam was basically Cehpech. At a regional level, it seems that Chichén Itzá Sotuta ceramics and Ek' Balam western Cehpech ceramics coexisted during the Sotuta early phase. However, sometime during the second half of the Terminal Classic period, the occupation at Ek' Balam was significantly reduced and Cehpech ceramics continued into Hocaba, which corresponds with the Xtabay ceramic complex of the Postclassic period.

Suhler et al. (1998: 178) attributed the end of Yaxuná and Cobá to the military conquest of both sites by Chichén Itzá, which occurred during the Yaxuná IVb period (A.D. 950/1000–1100/1200). Previously in this article I argue that the presence of Chichén Itzá Sotuta ceramics associated with Cehpech and Pure Florescent architecture in Yaxuná predate the Yaxuná IVb period. Moreover, the Yaxuná IVa period is contemporaneous with the early phase of the Sotuta occupation in

Chichén Itzá, and I do not believe that the warrior forces of this site were responsible for the military conquest that ended Yaxuná and Cobá.

It has already been pointed out that the presence of Chichén Itzá in central Yucatán began by the eighth century A.D. However, the territorial expansion of the site, according to the ceramic and architectural evidence of Isla Cerritos, Yulá, and Chichén Itzá itself, suggests that by the tenth century A.D. Chichén Itzá controlled an area with a radius of at least ten kilometers surrounding the settlement, a great portion of the terrain between central Yucatán and the northern coast, and a broad sector of the Yucatán northern coast. The archaeological evidence also suggests that the expansionist action of Chichén Itzá focused on securing and consolidating its presence in the central, north-central, and the seacoast of Yucatán instead of revitalizing settlements that had initiated or were suffering a collapse, as was the case of Yaxuná and Cobá.

Sometime in the tenth century A.D., Cobá suffered a significant reduction in its territory, which extended from central to eastern Yucatán in the previous century. Cobá and Yaxuná were contemporaneous between A.D. 800 and 900/950, as the Oro and Yaxuná IVa ceramic complexes indicate. After A.D. 900 Cobá withdrew from central Yucatán, and this might have left Yaxuná isolated from its former ally. The ties between Yaxuná and Cobá were strong and the former depended on the latter. When Cobá began its collapse Yaxuná was also affected. Yaxuná and Cobá apparently underwent similar processes as Dzibilchaltún and Ek' Balam, and by the second half of the Terminal Classic period, these two settlements experienced a decrease in population and construction activity and the loss of controlled territories.

The collapse of Cobá and Yaxuná was probably happening when Chichén Itzá began its territorial expansion, although the internal causes that triggered the collapse of Cobá and Yaxuná are unknown. It is quite possible, however, that Chichén Itzá might have contributed to accelerate the collapse of these two sites. One of the ways in which Chichén Itzá could have indirectly participated in the collapse of Yaxuná and Cobá was to neither conquer nor revitalize them. Without the material presence of Chichén Itzá at Cobá and Yaxuná, the former site did not have to maintain, feed, or control the local populations. If my interpretation of the archaeological record is correct, the lack of Sotuta ceramics in period IVb of Yaxuná and at the end of the Oro ceramic complex of Cobá shows that the expansion program of Chichén Itzá did not include the territory located to the south and southeast of its southern border.

Cehpech ceramics from Yaxuná and Cobá continued into Hocaba Postclassic times. At Yaxuná the Postclassic occupation of the site is supported by the presence of burials, shrines, and Chen Mul Modeled incense burners (see Yaxuná V in Suhler et al. 1998: 179, Figure 14). At Cobá the end of the Oro ceramic complex is associated with Sotuta ceramics of the Pizá ceramic subcomplex represented by Espita Appliqué censers and hourglass Cumtún Composite censers (Robles

1990: 239–252). The Sotuta censers were found in an offering to Stela 11 and the offering was deposited at the beginning of Tases Seco ceramic complex, or around A.D. 1100/1200 (Robles 1990: 239).

Along the east coast of the Yucatán peninsula, Cobá's influence decreased in the tenth century A.D. Also tied to the downfall were El Meco (Hocaba-Sotuta ceramic complex; see Robles 1986) and Xelhá (Xcacel ceramic complex; see Canché 1992), whose ceramic components were Cehpech (Muna Slate, Vista Alegre Striated, Ticul Thin Slate). Eventually, an intrusion of Sotuta ceramics (Dzitas Slate, Piste Striated, Silho Orange) occurred, and this indicates the territorial expansion of Chichén Itzá to eastern Yucatán (Andrews and Robles 1985; Robles and Andrews 1986).

San Gervasio at Cozumel was not controlled by Cobá. On the contrary, San Gervasio was an independent center that used its own Cehpech ceramics, including Sombra Coarse and Vista Alegre Striated (see the Ribera ceramic complex in Peraza 1993: 138–243). San Gervasio's independent status changed when Sotuta ceramics (Piste Striated, Fine Orange, Tohil Plumbate) arrived at the site as a result of Chichén Itzá's expansion that overtook Cozumel (see the Arrecife-Sotuta ceramic complex in Peraza 1993: 244–306).

The rise of Uxmal as a regional capital in the Puuc region either occurred late in the ninth century A.D. or early in the tenth century. According to Kowalski (1998; see also Kowalski et al. 1996; Dunning and Kowalski 1994), if we accept that Uxmal reached its height between A.D. 850 and 950, this peak lasted until the middle of the tenth century A.D. which would place Uxmal as a site partially contemporaneous to Chichén Itzá. However, considering the limited amount of research conducted with Uxmal ceramics and their association with architecture, it is still possible that Cehpech and Sotuta totally overlapped at the site. Therefore, it would be plausible to date the end of Uxmal early in the eleventh century.

CONCLUSION

This paper has focused on Sotuta ceramics, the settlement patterns of Chichén Itzá, and the contemporaneity of this site and its northern neighbors during the Late Classic and Terminal Classic periods. Chronological as well as spatial considerations of each one of these three aspects confirm that Chichén Itzá arose as an important site at the end of the Classic period, and this process seems to have occurred in a period of approximately three centuries.

The data corroborate that Sotuta ceramics originated and were widely used in central and north-central Yucatán. Two interesting aspects of the data on Sotuta ceramics show that they were already in usage during the eighth century A.D., and in the particular case of Chichén Itzá, they do not seem to have replaced the Cehpech ceramics of the site. Unlike the ceramic evidence of Isla Cerritos and Yulá, whose Cehpech materials were replaced by Sotuta ceramics, the first important occupation of Chichén Itzá associates with the Monjas Complex, and the ceramic forms and types date this occupation between A.D. 750/800 and 900.

The virtual absence of Cehpech ceramics in Chichén Itzá, and the appearance and usage of the Sotuta materials in the site since the eighth century A.D., suggest that Chichén Itzá was not occupied before A.D. 700. This settlement probably housed individuals that migrated from the Izamal region located to the north/northwest of Chichén Itzá. These individuals brought with them their own pottery, which included the Dzitas and Sisal ceramic groups.

Sotuta ceramics can be associated with the early (the Monjas Complex) and late (Great Terrace) phases of occupation at Chichén Itzá. Besides pottery, architecture and the internal arrangement of Chichén Itzá corroborate that the settlement was organized around two different cores at the end of the Classic period. First, the center of the site was located in the Monjas Complex and, later on, in the Great Terrace with its enormous volume of construction and monumental architecture. The existence of two different chronological site cores at Chichén Itzá seems to have been very similar to Cobá, whose main occupations were centered at two distinct architectural complexes, the Cobá and Nohoch Mul Groups.

The data also show that the interaction between Chichén Itzá and other northern Yucatán settlements changed through time. Considering the different transformations that several regional capitals such as Chichén Itzá underwent, the fact that they neither evolved at the same pace nor at the same time is confirmed. Therefore, the chronology of Chichén Itzá has changed how it is perceived, from an isolated site to a settlement contemporaneous to other major regional capitals of northern Yucatán. Past and present interpretations of Chichén Itzá mirror the way in which data have been examined over the last two decades. For instance, the linear succession model was favored in the past. Now, we know of at least two ways in which Cehpech and Sotuta ceramics overlapped; Cehpech ceramics were thought to represent one single component and now we acknowledge at least two regional spheres.

To conclude, the achievements made in ceramic studies over the last twenty years are contributing significantly to a better understanding of the events that took place in northern Yucatán during the Late Classic and Terminal Classic periods. In other words, the cultural-historical reconstruction of the northern Maya lowlands is more complicated than previously thought, especially when ceramics dating between A.D. 700/750 and 1050/1100 are considered. Therefore, as new settlements and ceramics are investigated, and as long as we continue reanalyzing old ceramic type collections, our view of the northern Maya lowlands will become more complex. If this is the case, we still have a long way to go in understanding the transformations, transitions, and collapse of the Classic Maya in the archaeology of northern Yucatán.

ACKNOWLEDGMENTS

The surveying, mapping, and excavations conducted by the author at Chichén Itzá were funded in part by the Universidad Autónoma de Yucatán and the Instituto Nacional de Antropología e Historia between 1993 and 1996; the Middle American Research Institute of Tulane University (1994); the Sistema Nacional de Investigadores–CONACYT de México (1995 and 1996); the Foundation for the Advancement of Mesoamerican Studies, Inc. (1997). I thank Peter J. Schmidt, Lilia Fernández, Hettie Veneziano, Geoffrey Braswell, and Jennifer Briggs Braswell for their comments and support during the fieldwork at Chichén Itzá. I also thank E. Wyllys Andrews V and the reviewers of this book for their invaluable comments and suggestions. Any omission or error of fact is mine.

23

THE TERMINAL CLASSIC
IN THE MAYA LOWLANDS
ASSESSING COLLAPSES, TERMINATIONS, AND TRANSFORMATIONS

Arthur A. Demarest, Prudence M. Rice, and Don S. Rice

he nature of the end of the Classic period of lowland Maya civilization has been a matter of debate and speculation for more than a century. This can be attributed to a variety of issues, ranging from variation in broad theoretical paradigms, through an incomplete archaeological record for the critical ninth, tenth, and eleventh centuries, to insecure chronologies for the basic sequence of events in some regions.

DISAGREEMENT, DEBATE, AND REGIONAL FRAMES OF REFERENCE

Specific differences or ambiguities in the interpretation of chronology and culture-historical sequences continue to plague interpretation of the nature of the Classic to Postclassic transition from A.D. 750 to 1050. While ever more finely grained chronologies have been established for some regions, such as the Pasión and Petexbatun, in other zones, such as northern Belize, temporal periods are sometimes long and ill defined (e.g., "Tepeu 2-3," "Terminal Classic–Early Postclassic"), making comparisons and correlation difficult. In northern Yucatán, chronological variability in interpretations has been reduced as new stratigraphic, epigraphic, and iconographic evidence has been recovered (see Carmean et al., Suhler et al., Ringle et al., and Cobos, Chapters 19–22). Yet in other zones, such as the Copán Valley, recent chronological debates have generated widely divergent models of culture change at the end of the Classic era (e.g., Webster et al. vs. Fash et al., Chapters 11 and 12). It is hoped that the more refined sequences of some sites or regions will eventually allow cross-dating and alignment, eliminating the ambiguities in other regional culture-historical sequences.

Other disagreements have their basis in underlying theoretical positions or predispositions. Some scholars tend to interpret the record in their regions in terms of ecological processes or climatological events (e.g., Braswell et al., Chapter 9; Adams et al., Chapter 15; Gill 2000; Hodell et al. 1995). Others emphasize the impact of known or hypothesized political factors (e.g., O'Mansky and Dunning, Chapter 5; Fash et al., Chapter 12; Suhler et al., Chapter 20; Demarest 1992, 1996; Fash and Sharer 1991). Yet other recent studies have almost returned to J.E.S. Thompson's evaluative perspective in attributing the collapse at some centers to a failure of "moral authority" leading to "despair" and abandonment (Houston et al. 2001). Both chronological and theoretical disagreements seem to be most pronounced in the two chapters on the Copán Valley: Webster et al. (Chapter 11) argue for a gradual process of several centuries' change driven by ecological degradation, while Fash et al. (Chapter 12) describe a rapid, almost abrupt process of political crisis, collapse, and abandonment. Although the contrasting interpretations between these Copán Valley papers are focused on issues of dating, ceramic sequences, and other culture-historical details, the alternative views in this regional debate (and others in this volume) also tend to align with the established theoretical positions of the scholars involved toward emphasis of ecological, economic, or political factors in culture-historical interpretation.

In addition to contrasting chronologies, culture-histories, or general theoretical paradigms, the papers in this volume show an even wider range of divergence in their conceptions of the very nature of the transition from the Classic to the Postclassic societies of the Maya lowlands. For example, in one chapter, scholars working in northern Belize (Adams et al., Chapter 15) describe a "great collapse" as a dramatic climatological catastrophe, while others, working less than 100 kilometers to the south in central Belize (Chase and Chase, Chapter 2), reject the existence of a "collapse" or even a decline of Classic Maya society, seeing this notion as an interpretive delusion created by long-held misconceptions about the nature of Postclassic institutions and the complex roots of these institutions in Classic-period society.

Many of these disagreements about the very nature of the Terminal Classic transition, its pace, and its processes derive at least in part from confusion about terms, concepts, and frames of reference. As discussed in the first chapter of this volume, scholars tend to talk past each other about what constitutes a "decline," "collapse," or "transformation." This problem becomes manageable only if we clarify these terms as referring to *change in regional manifestations of Classic Maya civilization, particularly political systems and political ideology.*

Perhaps the greatest problem has been that each group of archaeologists working on the highly variable Classic Maya polities have tended to project the nature and processes in their own region of study as the universal model for culture change at the end of the Classic period. Most archaeologists have posited "causes" from the data in their particular regions or sites that could have been local factors of the specific kind of culture change observed in that area. Yet these processes were then proposed as a universal template for pan-lowland culture-history. Local economic and ecological conditions, and local or regional historical and political processes and events, were combined with pan-lowland problems or processes to generate the specific manifestations of the Classic to Postclassic transition in any given area. Furthermore, external factors or events (e.g., foreign intrusion or influence, climatological factors, etc.) may have affected only certain regions or have affected regions to differing degrees, while other external factors may have been of broader impact.

BEYOND GENERALIZATION, ISOLATIONISM, AND CATASTROPHISM: THE CONSTRUCTION OF LINKED REGIONAL CULTURE-HISTORIES

Among the examples of general projections of local evidence are arguments based on local environmental deterioration in the Copán Valley (e.g., Webster, Freter, and Gonlin 2000), a steep river valley with an environment unlike any other in the Maya world. Given its susceptibility to erosion and attendant problems and its uncertain culture-history, evidence from this zone does not project to other regions. On the other hand, many collapse models are myopically focused on local events without properly addressing other zones. Examples of this tendency include recent global projections of Yucatán drought (e.g., Gunn and Folan, 1981; Gill 2000), the proposed "moral" collapse at Piedras Negras (Houston et al. 2001), the alleged lack of significant change at some Belizean centers (e.g., Chase and Chase, Chapter 2; Pendergast 1985), and the purely trade-based models appropriate for some coastal areas (e.g., Sabloff and Rathje 1975a, 1975b). While culture-historical reconstructions should focus first on local evidence, scholars also should strive to discover the linkages between processes and events in a region or subregions and then compare them with adjacent areas.

For example, the collapse at Piedras Negras is almost simultaneous with the decline or abandonment of most major Pasión/Usumacinta-area sites (e.g., Yaxchilán, Palenque, Dos Pilas, Aguateca, and Cancuen). This collapse is probably part of a linked decline of the river trade system, perhaps caused by warfare and the rise of militaristic enclaves at Seibal and Altar breaking the exchange system in highland exotics (Demarest, Chapter 6; Demarest and Fahsen 2003). Conversely, the argument that there was no particularly significant change from the Classic to Postclassic period should not be based on continuity in some important centers in Belize, when other centers and zones nearby experienced notable depopulation, decline, or abandonment (e.g., compare Chase and Chase, Chapter 2; Adams et al., Chapter 15; Ashmore et al., Chapter 14; and Hammond and Tourtellot, Chapter 13).

Scholars should now be engaged in the process of comparing and linking the culture-histories of the centers in their regions, looking beyond their own sites and their preferred theories for explaining the historical sequence of changes and events. Comparison between regions can discern impact or effects between areas, be these through trade, war, migration, or stimulus diffusion. We hope that this volume will help instigate systematic region-by-region comparison, alignment, and culture-historical reconstruction. Only through such careful reconstruction will Maya archaeology advance beyond romantic befuddlement, myopic site focus, and/or leapfrogging from locally appropriate models to global projections of the explanation of *the* "Classic Maya collapse."

In this regard, some recent interpretations of (literally) global climatological change as "a drought-based explanation for the Classic Maya collapse" (Robichaux 2002) represent a retrogression to simplistic characterizations of both the nature of the Classic to Postclassic transition and the highly variable sequences of regional and subregional events, processes, changes, and continuities between A.D. 700 and 1100. This revival of catastrophism builds upon a fundamental misperception of the unity and nature of the Classic to Postclassic transition: e.g., "Between about A.D. 750 and 950 the Maya experienced a demographic disaster as profound as any other in human history" (Haug et al. 2003). As the chapters in this volume attest, the actual, detailed picture of events in the Terminal Classic could not be more variable and less susceptible to such broad characterizations.

Mischaracterizations of the complex nature and long duration (in some areas) of the Terminal Classic transition again result from global projection of local models and an incomplete understanding of the culture-historical record. It is not surprising that the chapters in this volume (9 and 15) and other recent publications (e.g., Dahlin 2002; Gunn and Adams 1981; Gunn and Folan 1981; Hansen et al. 2002) that propose drought/famine catastrophism are advanced by archaeologists working in a specific series of sites at the base of the Yucatán peninsula, an area highly susceptible to drought conditions. Global projection of models that might be appropriate to that poorly understood and sampled zone ignores the fact that the nature, timing, and specific evidence of Late and Terminal Classic change in other zones do not fit this proposed model (e.g., Demarest, Chapter 6; Masson and Mock, Chapter 17; Carmean et al., Chapter 19; Cobos, Chapter 22; see also Dahlin 2002, Robichaux 2002 for efforts at aligning drought evidence with a few other regions).

Note that these models also hypothesize two earlier uniform Terminal Preclassic and "Hiatus" (sixth-century) Maya lowland drought/famine catastrophes (e.g., Adams et al., Chapter 15; Gill 2000; Hansen et al. 2002), and tend to stereotype those variable periods and phenomena. Initial Classic declines did not occur in some areas, were a methodological creation of ceramic typologies in others (e.g., Lincoln 1985), and in the best-studied zones have been shown to be associated with anthropogenic (not climatological) environmental change resulting from massive Late Preclassic forest-clearing (Dunning et al. 1997; Dunning et al. 1998; Abrams and Rue 1988; Rue et al. 2002). Similarly, the presumed "hiatus collapse" might be primarily a political decline limited to Tikal and its alliance of centers due to their sixth-century military and political domination by the Calakmul hegemony (e.g., Martin and Grube 1994, 1995, 2000).

The lesson of these earlier disappearing "uniform catastrophes" is that pan-lowland hypotheses cannot precede the empirical compilation of reasonably complete regional culture-histories and the work of careful interregional comparisons of evidence on the sequence of events. This fundamental sequence of effort in constructing the history of any civilization cannot be avoided by site-focused isolationism, nor bypassed through the global projection of local events or the deus ex machina of catastrophism. Instead, we must systematically compare and link site sequences to understand subregional processes and variability, compare these to adjacent zones to reconstruct regional patterns, and then compare regions to begin reconstructing pan-lowland histories and correlating these to other zones in Mesoamerica.

At the time of the 1973 Maya collapse volume (Culbert 1973a), such systematic comparative efforts were premature, and the free-for-all of alternative theorizing on the collapse continued. This volume demonstrates, we believe, that the time has come to demand such systematic comparison in reconstructions of the Terminal Classic. In some zones, such as the Pasión and Usumacinta region and the Puuc area, we can already perceive linkages in local culture-histories (e.g., Demarest, Chapter 6; Carmean et al., Chapter 19). Yet in other regions, such as Belize and the Copán Valley, the reconstructions of different projects scarcely appear to reflect communication at all (cf. Chase and Chase, Chapters 2, 16; Ashmore et al., Chapter 14; Adams et al., Chapter 15; Masson and Mock, Chapter 17; Webster et al., Chapter 11; Fash et al., Chapter 12).

Nonetheless, the amount and quality of the last three decades of lowland excavation and regional studies make such systematic intersite and interregional comparison possible, and should be a prerequisite for future "collapse" or "transition" theorizing. It is our hope that the uneven efforts in this volume will initiate a new phase in studies of the Terminal Classic problem—a period of careful region-by-region communication, correlation, comparison, and, only then, synthesis.

THE PROTEAN TERMINAL CLASSIC: REGIONAL CULTURE-HISTORIES

In the decades to come, scholars will be searching for the broader patterning, parallels, and linkages between the regional perspectives on the Terminal Classic briefly summarized in this volume. Here, a cursory review of these regional syntheses can provide only an initial, highly subjective glimpse of this next comparative phase of study.

As observed above, one clear pattern is that of the chronological order of changes in material culture that define the Terminal Classic or Postclassic in different regions. The long-observed southwest to northeast "trend" of accelerated changes in the late eighth to tenth centuries (e.g., Bove 1981; Lowe 1985) seems to be verified by the culture-histories in this volume. Some scholars have interpreted this pattern as reflecting population movements in the late eighth and ninth centuries (e.g., Demarest, Chapter 6; Rice and Rice, Chapter 7; Carmean et al., Chapter 19; Suhler et al., Chapter 20). However, only in some regions do ceramic chronologies sharply subdivide the Late Classic and clearly demarcate the Terminal Classic (e.g., Foias 1997; Tourtellot and González, Chapter 4; O'Mansky and Dunning, Chapter 5; Demarest, Chapter 6). In Belize, as noted by Chase and Chase (Chapter 2), there are few non-elite ceramic markers to subdivide the Late Classic or distinguish it from the Terminal Classic. Poorly defined ceramic markers for many zones are a significant obstacle to interregional comparison and to the identification of common processes or related events. Yet in those regions, such as western Petén, where Tepeu 3 markers are most common and most clear, the changes at the end of the Classic period appear to be early and dramatic, and the Classic/Postclassic transition was disjunctive, rather than continuous (cf. O'Mansky and Dunning, Chapter 5; Demarest, Chapter 6; vs. Chase and Chase, Chapters 2 and 16).

The Pasión-Usumacinta Regions: Warfare, Status-Rivalry, Exotics Trade, and Early Collapse

Rapid changes in site sequences and material culture at the end of the Classic period were earliest and most pronounced in the west. Studies of the ninth-century cultural transformations by the Harvard Altar de Sacrificios and Seibal projects (e.g., Willey 1973, 1990) first observed the early and marked western shift to the Terminal Classic. While theories of foreign invasion and Mexican conquest have now been rejected, those projects elevated the debate on the Terminal Classic to a higher level of detail and intensity, and the issues they raised remain central to much of the research and debate described here. Tourtellot and González (Chapter 4) have updated and refined the interpretation of the Terminal Classic at Seibal and Altar.

Building on that research, the Vanderbilt projects completed large-scale multidisciplinary investigations from 1989 to 1996 that have allowed for one of the most detailed descriptions of eighth- to ninth-century changes available for any subregion (see Demarest 1997, 2004, for overviews). As a result of this forty-year series of projects, the sequence of events in the west is clearly subdivided into distinct intervals by ceramic and artifactual markers, linked to dated monuments. We cannot argue for demographic pressure, anthropogenic ecological deterioration, or climatological change as major factors in the early Petexbatun events. Ecological and settlement studies in this region have shown that in western Petén, the decentralized but complex agricultural regimes were well adapted to population levels (see O'Mansky and Dunning, Chapter 5, and Demarest, Chapter 6; Dunning et al. 1997; Dunning and Beach 2004). There is no evidence of increasing nutritional stress in the west in the centuries prior to, during, and after the collapse as determined by direct, intensive technical analyses of human and faunal osteology (e.g., Wright 1994, 1997a, 1997b; Wright and White 1996; Emery 1997, 2004; Emery, Wright, and Schwartz 2000). Therefore, the decline of polities in these regions in the late eighth and ninth centuries cannot be attributed to either population pressure or ecological circumstances.

Instead, the stresses of status-rivalry and intercenter warfare that began to intensify after A.D. 600 (Demarest and Fahsen 2003) had reached crisis level by A.D. 760, if not before, leading to warfare, depopulation, and a cessation of public architecture—first at Dos Pilas and later at Tamarindito, Arroyo de Piedra, and, finally, Aguateca. Between A.D. 760 and 830, major centers were abandoned one by one, and even the rural landscape became militarized with radical intersite population reduction and the fortification of hilltop villages (O'Mansky and Dunning, Chapter 5).

As described by Tourtellot and González (Chapter 4) and Demarest (Chapter 6), Seibal was fully engaged in the Petexbatun-region warfare of the late eighth and early ninth centuries. With its highly defensible location (Tourtellot 1988b: 432–436), access to water, and probable agricultural terraces in defended areas (Dunning et al. 1997: 261), Seibal was able to survive the eighth-century warfare, as did its small, lonely neighbor to the south at Punta de Chimino. During the A.D. 760–830 period, Group D at Seibal may have served as a defensive fortress with high parapets, probably sustaining palisades. Seibal was placed in a defensible position very similar to that of the Aguateca fortress (Tourtellot 1988b: 432–436; Tourtellot and González, Chapter 4; Demarest, Chapter 6). Similarly, Punta de Chimino, with its formidable natural and artificial defenses and protected field systems, held on to flourish in the Terminal Classic as the lone major center of the Petexbatun lake zone.

After A.D. 830 there is an introduction of Terminal Classic ceramic modes, new fine paste wares, and distinctive elements of iconography at the surviving enclaves at Altar, Seibal, Punta de Chimino, and perhaps others yet to be discovered. In Chapter 4, Tourtellot and González update and revise our understanding of the critical Terminal Classic of Seibal and the lower Pasión. Not only is Mexican or "foreign" invasion rejected, but, citing recent ceramic analyses and iconographic and epigraphic studies, they are able to trace the innovative aspects of the Pasión Terminal Classic to either the Petexbatun, central Petén, or the northern lowlands. The new architectural and sculptural elements at Seibal were not Mexican, but rather were an amalgam of traditional lowland Classic Maya traits combined into distinctive forms. The new *k'uhul ajaws* of Seibal appear to have had close ties to the central lakes area and later to the northern lowlands, two regions of the Maya world that were themselves linked by population movements and cultural ties in the Terminal Classic and Postclassic (Rice and Rice, Chapter 7; Jones 1998). The fine ware monochrome ceramics of the period were not imports but were local products using technologies introduced earlier into the Petexbatun from the west (Foias and Bishop 1997).

Tourtellot and González (Chapter 4) and Demarest (Chapter 6) argue that many of the unusual features in the sculptures, strange costumes, long hairstyles, and ubiquitous serpents were part of revitalistic experimentation with legitimating Maya ideologies. These symbol systems and exotic affiliations may have helped some elites pull together the fragmented politics and populations of the devastated Petexbatun. Recent studies have suggested that the adoption of a pan-Mesoamerican cult of the feathered-serpent deity, Quetzalcoatl, might have been part of this new amalgam (Ringle et al. 1998). Serpent iconography, circular temples, and other specific elements were adopted by the k'uhul ajaw at Seibal, in northern Belize, in the Puuc area, and at some central Petén centers—indicating communication and shared ideologies between rulers struggling to survive the events and crises of the ninth century (P. Rice 1983a, 1983b; A. Chase 1985b; Chase and Chase 1982; Ringle et al. 1998). Yet as Tourtellot and González point out here (Chapter 4), these experiments in government, styles, and legitimating ideologies were but a variant of the traditional Classic-period order. By the end of the tenth century, these also had failed, and Seibal, Altar, and Punta de Chimino declined and were abandoned.

Other centers in the west suffered an earlier fragmentation and collapse somewhat more comparable to the fall of Aguateca or to the fragmentation and decline at Copán than to the florescence of the Terminal Classic Pasión enclaves. In the eighth century, the hegemonies of centers such as Yaxchilán, Piedras Negras, and Palenque indicate a proliferation of elites, minor centers with new "holy lords," and division of power with subordinate *sahals* and other officials. These political developments were accompanied by intensified inter-elite state visits, alliance, warfare, and other forms of status-rivalry (see also Culbert 1991; Schele and Mathews 1991; Schele 1991; Mathews 1988; Mathews and Schele 1974). In the end, these centers in the west, such as Piedras Negras and Palenque, fell into decline after defeat and capture of their rulers by holy lords of rival or subordinate centers.

The loss of prestige and sacred authority of the western k'uhul ajaws would have accelerated as worsening stresses on the society raised doubts about the rulers' power with ancestors and supernatural forces (Demarest 1992; Houston et al. 2001). This loss of prestige may have been worsened by events upriver where endemic warfare in the lower Pasión would have partially restricted the flow of status-reinforcing exotics (such as quetzal feathers and jade) from their sources in the south. With a growing elite, proliferating independent dynasties, and intensified ritual and warfare, the kings, their courts, and their subordinate centers would have badly missed such exotic goods for the rituals, patronage, and tribute that were so critical to the formation and maintenance of power. At centers like Piedras Negras and Cancuen, the subordinate populations, literally "disenchanted" with their sacred lords and frustrated by a multitude of problems, gradually drifted away to rural areas (e.g., Johnston et al. 2001) or to more distant regions (Demarest, Chapter 6; Holley 1983; Houston et al. 2001; Webster et al. 1998).

The Terminal Classic Transition in Central and Far Northern Petén

In most areas of the Maya lowlands, the end of the Classic period was less abrupt than it was in the west. Indeed, the traditional concept of a dramatic "Classic Maya collapse" seems to apply *only* to the western region, perhaps the Copán/Motagua zone (at least in one chronology), and later, perhaps, to the far northern Petén/southern Campeche decline (although archaeology in that zone remains in its initial stages.) Fragmentation of political authority occurred, but it was accompanied in the central Petén by a very slow decline in population and architectural activity (Culbert and Rice 1990). Estimated population levels in Petén rose to a peak by the beginning of the ninth century (Culbert et al. 1990; Rice and Rice 1990). Some recent population estimates for "greater" Tikal are as high as 280,000 for A.D. 800 and for the entire northeast Petén region over 1.5 million (Turner 1990: 321). Contrary to previous assertions, we now know that such population levels could have been sustained by farming systems at Tikal, which included extensive use of sunken swamp "bajo" areas that surrounded the site zone (Kunen et al. 2000). Still, such high levels—combined with the growing burden of elite consumption, construction, and ritual display—would certainly have strained local resources and left little margin for periodic agricultural or political difficulties (e.g., Culbert 1988).

As described here by Valdés and Fahsen (Chapter 8), these stresses were apparent by, if not before, the ninth century, as some palaces began to be abandoned. By A.D. 830–850 population had begun to decline at major centers throughout the region, accompanied by a reduction in construction and monument erection. Rice and Rice (Chapter 7; P. Rice 2004) suggest that the decline in constructional activity at Tikal was in large part an anticipated transfer of ritual power in the middle of the 256-year calendrical cycle of the *may*. Tikal was a Late Classic *may* seat, a sacred capital city, and celebrated that status during the first half of its role by the regular construction of twin-pyramid complexes to celebrate *k'atun* endings every twenty years. After 128 years, around A.D. 810 or so, Tikal's role changed vis-à-vis other sites in the area for the last half of the *may* cycle. In the late ninth century, period-ending monuments, ceremonial architecture, and key rituals shifted out of Tikal to outlying secondary centers that would have served as k'atun seats, such as Uaxactún, Ixlú, Jimbal, and Xultún (see Rice and Rice, Chapter 7; Valdés and Fahsen, Chapter 8).

In the late ninth and tenth centuries, Eznab ceramics at Tikal and Uaxactún were impoverished, with few polychromes and a reduction in other elite markers (Valdés and Fahsen, Chapter 8). The simplified ceramic assemblage of this period, together with chronological markers of the Pasión region's Fine Orange and Fine Gray, were found with the household debris of the new occupants (Harrison 1970; Culbert 1973c). The diminished Eznab population at Tikal lived in the ruins of the site's earlier monumental architecture, much of which had ceased to host state rituals, feasts, or ceremonies (Valdés and Fahsen, Chapter 8; Culbert 1973c). Other temples and palaces may have been the scenes of formal termination rituals of architecture or monuments, burning, and the deposition of hundreds of broken vessels desacralizing previously holy places (e.g., Mock 1998d). The graffiti in Tikal's palaces show grisly scenes of warfare and sacrifice scratched into the plaster by untrained hands (Valdés and Fahsen, Chapter 8). The last Tikal stone monument was erected in A.D. 869 to commemorate the ending of a K'atun 3 Ajaw at 10.2.0.0.0.

Central Petén and particularly the lakes region experienced considerable demographic flux at this time, with groups moving both in and out. The ancestors of the Itza may have had their origins in central Petén and some groups moved northward into Yucatán during the Late and Terminal Classic (Boot 1996, 1997; Schele, Grube, and Boot 1998). At the same time, there is clear evidence of northern influences in the lakes region, including iconographic structure (clipped corners, braided borders, and multiple registers on stelae; Rice and Rice, Chapter 7) and architecture (mosaic mask facades, rounded pseudo-columns; Valdés and Fahsen, Chapter 8).

Terminal Classic ceramic assemblages from the various lake basins also indicate contacts with or immigration from the Pasión area, particularly evident at sites around Lakes Petén Itzá, Macanché, and Salpetén (P. Rice 1987c, 1996), and considerably less evident to the east around Lakes Yaxhá-Sacnab. The most prominent indicator of relations with southwestern Petén is the widespread presence of distinctive large, incurved-rim basins and carbonate-tempered ceramic types (Subín, Pantano). This, plus the presence of distinctive C-shaped structures, strongly supports the notion that groups fleeing the collapse of the Petexbatun and Pasión polities moved northward into the central Petén lakes area. It is noteworthy that excavations have revealed very little fine paste ware of the Fine Orange and Fine Gray ceramic groups. While imitations of these wares (P. Rice 1986) have been identified, it seems apparent that whatever contacts existed between the two areas did not include movement of fineware pottery.

Meanwhile, to the north in southern Campeche, Calakmul had been in slow decline since the beginning of the eighth century (Braswell et al., Chapter 9), perhaps at least partly a loss of prestige from military defeats. Both the Calakmul and more northern Río Bec regions of Campeche experienced great loss of population (Turner 1990). By A.D. 850 the centers there and in the surrounding hinterland had been reduced in population to 10 percent of their apogee levels of the late seventh century. At Calakmul in the Terminal Classic period, as at Tikal, populations concentrated near former public architecture. In the case of Calakmul, however, the remnants of leadership in the Terminal Classic adopted the combined temple-palace architectural form seen earlier at Caracol and characteristic of the contemporary Puuc centers of the north (Braswell et al., Chapter 9). These temple-palace combined structures may indicate a greater degree of economic involvement by the state (foreshadowing Postclassic patterns) because some of them also included workshops making lithic tools, textiles, and pottery (Braswell et al., Chapter 9). It is equally likely, however, that they reflect a drastic reduction of population and concentration of people and diverse activities on these high, defensible structures, as in the Petexbatun (O'Mansky and Dunning, Chapter 5; Demarest, Chapter 6). Climate change and drought might have been a major factor in the continued decline and lack of recovery in this zone (Braswell et al., Chapter 9; Hansen et al. 2002).

The evidence cited in this volume and elsewhere (e.g., Culbert and Rice 1990) does indicate a very substantial population decline in the western Petén and a more uneven decline in north-central Petén. Population dispersion and problems with chronological markers (Chase and Chase, Chapter 2) might account for a portion of this pattern in some regions. Reduced fertility and increased mortality may account for much of this change. Yet it seems increasingly probable that emigration from declining western and central Petén centers may have been a factor in changes elsewhere of the Terminal Classic period (Demarest, Chapter 6; Demarest and Escobedo 1997).

One element that has received little attention thus far concerns language change. The Classic lowland Maya are believed to have written and spoken two languages of the Mayan language family, Yukatekan and (western) Ch'olan, which are not closely related linguistically (Stuart et al. 1999, Houston et al. 2000, Justeson and Campbell 1997). Linguistic reconstructions (Hofling 1998) have indicated that around A.D. 1000, proto-Yukatekan began to differentiate into the four mutually intelligible dialects that are known today: Yukateko, Itzaj, Mopán, and Lakantun. Mopán is the most different from the others, suggesting that it diversified earliest, while Lakantun ("Lacandon") seems to have split more recently.

It is of interest to consider this process of language diversification in the context of the transformational processes of the Terminal Classic period, particularly the population movements identifiable by artifactual, iconographic, and architectural traits. The Itzaj (Hofling 1998) and Yukateko languages are very closely related, as is to be expected from the continuing close relations between central Petén and the northern lowlands beginning during the Early Classic period. All modern Itzaj speakers in San José, on the northwest shore of Lake Petén Itzá, trace their origins to the north (Hofling 1998), supporting the legendary return of the Itza to Petén from Chich'en Itza and Mayapán.

The Eastern Lowlands: Declines, Transitions, or Transformations

In the southeast, changes in the Terminal Classic period were complex and are still poorly understood. Fash et al. (Chapter 12) describe the political fragmentation of the Copán kingdom in the eighth century, followed by political collapse in the ninth. The intense competition manifest in ritual architecture, monuments, and more directly in warfare, reached a critical point in the mid-eighth century. In A.D. 738 Copán was defeated by Quiriguá, after which the Copán dynasty was revived by ruler Yax Pasah, who maintained only a shaky grasp on authority by sharing power with leaders in the Copán Valley. Also as with the Petexbatun and other regions, this fragmentation was followed within sixty years by the collapse of the elite center, with no public architecture or monuments raised after A.D. 822 (Fash et al., Chapter 12). A parallel political collapse occurred at their rival center of Quiriguá, where the last monument was raised in A.D. 810, although reduced constructional activity continued in the center (Sharer 1991).

Controversy and debate in this volume surround the issue of what exactly happened to the general population outside the center after the political collapse of Copán. Recall that the neighboring populations there were only marginally involved in the Classic Maya tradition. Ceramic and artifact styles and architecture at most minor centers remained in modified forms of non-Classic Maya southeastern regional traditions after the establishment of the Classic Maya elite ceremonial centers at Copán and Quiriguá in the fourth to fifth centuries. After the political collapse of these kingdoms or perhaps a Maya elite withdrawal from these southern valleys, these regions returned to local traditions of ceramics and artifacts and to a much lower level of political complexity (Manahan 1996, 1999; Sharer 1991; Fash and Stuart 1991; Webster and Freter 1990a, 1990b).

Disagreement concerns how long non-elite Classic Maya populations continued in these respective valleys, how rapidly populations declined, and how quickly artifact patterns changed from Classic to Postclassic styles. Some evidence from ceramic chronology and excavations has been interpreted as indicating a rapid collapse and decline of population after the end of the dynastic centers (Braswell 1992; Manahan 2000; Fash et al., Chapter 12), while chronology based on the obsidian hydration dating techniques argues for a much slower decline in the Copán Valley, with large populations only slowly diminishing over two to three centuries (Freter 1988, 1994; Webster and Freter 1990a, 1990b; Webster, Freter, and Gonlin 2000; Webster et al., Chapter 11). This type of disagreement over regional details in archaeology is common. In this case, its resolution has fewer implications for the nature of the *political* collapse of the Classic Maya than for interpretations of local populations' degree of dependence on the ideological or economic leadership of the k'uhul ajaw.

In southeastern Petén and Belize, events and processes in the period from A.D. 750 to 1000 were highly complex and completely variable. This region is occupied by speakers of the Mopán language, which apparently was the earliest to separate from Late Classic proto-Yukatekan. Laporte (Chapter 10) describes in the Mopán Valley and the Maya Mountains the decline of some centers in population and public construction, coeval with the expansion and florescence of other centers and beginnings of monument erection in the mid-eighth century. Centers such as Ixtonton, Ucanal, Sacul, and others flourished at the expense of their neighbors, concentrating power, population, and constructional activities and surviving for almost two centuries after the decline of many western and central Petén Classic Maya centers. A distinctive element of the Late and Terminal Classic in southeastern Petén is the continued use of the E-Group "observatory" (or "Public Ritual Complex," Laporte, Chapter 10) common to Late Preclassic/Early Classic k'atun celebration ritual in central Petén. These ties to central Petén are further supported by affiliation of the region's Terminal Classic ceramic complex, Ixmabuy, with the Tepeu 3 sphere (Laporte, Chapter 10). The Terminal Classic Mopán region centers absorbed into their new political formations influences from northern Yucatán in architectural facades, monument style, and ceramics (Laporte, Chapter 10).

Structurally, these events and processes were parallel to the earlier collapse or decline of centers in the far west, with the continuation of centers such as Seibal and Altar de Sacrificios. As with Altar and Seibal, some Terminal Classic states of southeastern Petén relied upon new styles in monuments, artifacts (and presumably, ideology) that were an amalgam of Classic Maya traits with new, often northern, influences. As at Seibal and Altar, the Terminal Classic florescence of centers such as Ixtonton and Ucanal also may have involved movement of refugees from surrounding collapsing centers seeking new leadership and security under these Terminal Classic states. The shifts in the Mopán Valley region, however, appear to be a more gradual, slow, and prolonged process. Also like those western centers, these innovative Terminal Classic states later declined, with reduced populations left by Postclassic times (Laporte, Chapter 10).

The seven chapters on Belizean sites and regions describe a similarly variable mosaic of some collapsing Classic centers and other flourishing states with new mixtures of styles and political structures. Between A.D. 750 and 950, some sites were rapidly abandoned, including both epicenters and their surrounding countryside (Adams et al., Chapter 15; Ashmore et al., Chapter 14; Hammond and Tourtellot, Chapter 13), while others were stable or even grew in population and epicenter construction (Adams et al., Chapter 15; Chase and Chase, Chapter 16). Still other centers such as Lamanai and some coastal sites simply carried on with great continuity, and changes in artifact styles and inter-regional contacts were incorporated into local traditions (e.g., Pendergast 1986a; Chase and Chase, Chapter 16). Some areas in northern Belize and on coastal islands, peninsulas, and lagoons experienced an irregular but pronounced increase in population at the end of the Classic period in the ninth to eleventh centuries. Again, this pattern suggests movement of populations, perhaps from the collapsing polities to the west (Adams et al., Chapter 15; Masson and Mock, Chapter 17; Andres and Pyburn, Chapter 18). Andres and Pyburn (Chapter 18) show how the use of coastal centers as refuges in times of radical change or disruption recurs in later episodes, including the conquest and Colonial periods. Some centers were then able to create successful mercantile enclaves linked to emerging coastal trade networks (Masson and Mock, Chapter 17; Andres and Pyburn, Chapter 18).

One example of an impressive, more aggressive regional polity in the Terminal Classic period in Belize is the kingdom of Caracol (Chase and Chase, Chapter 16). Despite shifts and changes, populations there continued to be high and monuments were erected until the very end of the ninth century (Chase and Chase 1987a, 1987b). There and at other northern Belize sites such as Nohmul (Chase and Chase 1982), monuments, architecture, and some artifacts show influence from the Terminal Classic polities of northern Yucatán (A. Chase 1985b). Yet other nearby kingdoms, such as Xunantunich and many smaller sites, were greatly depopulated or even completely abandoned (Ashmore et al., Chapter 14), and farther north some Classic-period occupations ended with episodes of warfare and mass sacrifice of captives. At Colhá, for example, a "skull pit" contained the skeletons of thirty sacrificed individuals heaped in a mass grave (Steele et al. 1980).

The overall picture in Belize was of a very complex mix of historical events and processes, as yet poorly understood, but certainly later than the western and central Petén declines. Yet in the Early Postclassic, Maya civilization flourished in many areas of Belize, with new economic and stylistic elements (Andres and Pyburn, Chapter 18; Masson and Mock, Chapter 17). It is still unclear whether the northern traits seen at this time reflect migrations, the intrusion of smaller elite groups, merchants or warriors, or the adoption by local elites of new ideas (see also A. Chase 1985b; Chase and Chase 1982, 1987a, 1987b). All of these factors may have been involved, because some sites such as Colhá and Nohmul register clear changes, while others such as Lamanai appear to have added elements to a tradition more continuous with Classic patterns (Pendergast 1986a; Chase and Chase, Chapter 2). Many sites, like Caracol, thrived in the Terminal Classic yet experienced a sharp decline by the eleventh century and the beginnings of the Postclassic era (Chase and Chase 1982, Chapter 16). Sites with continuing occupations, such as Lamanai, Chau Hiix, and growing centers on the coasts and cays of Belize, became part of a new, thriving Postclassic occupation with an emphasis on long-distance and coastal trade, inland-coastal exchange of products, and closer ties to the north and to other regions of Mesoamerica (Masson and Mock, Chapter 17; Andres and Pyburn, Chapter 18).

In Belize, the only consistency apparent is the disappearance of the Classic institution of divine kingship and the spectacular architecture and trappings of power evidenced in calendrically based ritual. Systematic site-by-site, subregion-by-subregion comparison and correlation of data must be undertaken for all of

Belize. The large number of sites excavated there in the past twenty years should yield a more comprehensible pattern of change. Scholars working there need to increase communication between their many projects, including alignment of chronologies and typologies and collaborative construction of subregional culture-histories.

The Northern Lowlands: Florescence and Conflict

The period from A.D. 750 to 1100, which had seen collapse or decline in many parts of the southern Maya lowlands, was arguably the period of greatest florescence in northern Yucatán. It is a complex period, still poorly understood, and this volume reflects the continuing debates on the chronology of the different developments there. All of the chapters here on the northern lowlands accept only slightly variable forms of a partial to near total "overlap" of the apogees of Chich'en Itza and the Puuc centers—with the eastern Cobá region declining only slightly earlier (Carmean et al., Chapter 19; Suhler et al., Chapter 20; Ringle et al., Chapter 21; Cobos, Chapter 22).

As summarized in those chapters, the Puuc centers began to grow in the mid-eighth century, to develop new architectural styles and motifs, and to introduce concepts from the Gulf Coast and Oaxaca, as well as from the lowlands to the south. At this time there was probably at least some migration of elites and populations from Petén and southern Campeche centers (Carmean et al., Chapter 19; Suhler et al., Chapter 20; see also Schele and Mathews 1998: 258–260). During this Terminal Classic period, Puuc centers grew, population dispersed into new and sometimes marginal areas, and new centers were established (Carmean et al., Chapter 19). As with Seibal, Caracol, and other centers that thrived, rather than declined, in the ninth century, the Puuc rulers of Uxmal and other centers drew upon an amalgam of new concepts and reoriented Classic-period imagery to legitimate power. Puuc architecture and sculpture also may have incorporated iconography of the cult of Quetzalcoatl, the feathered-serpent deity, which is even more prominent at the rival center of Chich'en Itza in central Yucatán (Ringle et al. 1998).

While initially a series of small kingdoms, Puuc centers developed larger regional alliances. Intensive warfare is attested by fortifications around the epicenters of Uxmal and other major Puuc sites and by scenes of battle in murals, graffiti, and artifacts (Carmean et al., Chapter 19; Walters and Kowalski 2000; Schele and Mathews 1998: 234–235). The rapid growth and immigration to this area, combined with status-rivalry and its associated costs in labor and conflict, may have created a political environment of rich display but with underlying stresses, similar to processes in the southwestern lowlands a century earlier. Yet in the north, the need for centralization of authority through alliance or conquest may have been even greater, given the reliance on careful cooperative husbandry of scarce water sources (Dunning 1992; McAnany 1990).

Faced with the problems and possibilities of rapid population increase and the end of inter-elite trade with the south, leadership in the Puuc region carried out large-scale and intensified architectural programs and campaigns of conquest (Carmean et al., Chapter 19). As with stress responses in the south in the eighth century, in the northern lowlands in the ninth and early tenth centuries rulers were investing in spectacular architecture, expansion of polities, and experimentation with new political formations. Puuc centers also experimented with new Mexican religious ideologies and with power-sharing arrangements involving councils of lineage heads (McAnany 1995; Ringle et al. 1998; Carmean et al., Chapter 19). As at Copán and elsewhere, *popol na* or council houses allowed rulers to confer with lineage heads and local leaders (Kowalski 1987, 1994; Kowalski and Dunning 1999). Such lineage councils or *multepal* forms of government were more evident at some Puuc centers, such as Xcalumkin, and would later become characteristic of Postclassic states (Carmean et al., Chapter 19; cf. Grube 1994b). We can speculate that these experiments may have been more successful in the Puuc region because long-distance trade along the Gulf of Mexico, inland-coastal trade, and water storage systems had helped a more flexible set of institutions of governance to evolve earlier there—institutions that were more directly involved in economics and subsistence.

Carmean et al. (Chapter 19) describe how by the late ninth and early tenth centuries, competition, warfare, and alliance had ended in the unification of all of the western Puuc cities under the leadership of the king of Uxmal, designated "Lord Chac," and his associates (see also Grube 1994b: 323–324; Schele and Mathews 1998). This ruler, through sharing power with other leaders, revived much of the symbolism and monuments of the Classic-period k'uhul ajaw institution of divine rulership. His expansionist efforts affected the Cobá sphere of influence to the east, where fortifications may have first been constructed around centers at this time (Suhler et al., Chapter 20; Ringle et al., Chapter 21; Carmean et al., Chapter 19). The chapters on Yaxuna (20) and Ek Balam (21), as well as other recent assessments (see Andrews and Robles 1985; Robles and Andrews 1986; Bey et al. 1997), describe a complex ninth-and tenth-century central Yucatec landscape of fortified centers, battles, and sieges (e.g., Suhler et al., Chapter 20; Suhler and Freidel 1998; Webster 1978), and shifting ceramic assemblages. Termination rituals of architectural destruction at some sites and subsequent occupation with western Cehpech Puuc ceramics may indicate that the conquest of these centers was one factor in the decline of the eastern hegemony of Cobá and that center itself (Chapters 20 and 21; cf. Andrews and Robles 1985; Robles and Andrews 1986).

Ultimately, however, the reign of Lord Chac and the Terminal Classic political hegemonies of the Puuc cities also declined. The stresses of intersite competition and population increase may have been exacerbated by drought (Hodell et al. 1995) and by conflict with the competing regional alliance of Chich'en Itza (Robles and Andrews 1986; Andrews and Robles 1985; Cobos, Chapter 22). Shortly after the reign of Lord Chac all monumental construction ceased, and by A.D. 950 the city was in full decline. Other great Puuc cities such as Sayil followed a similar trajectory and were largely abandoned by the end of the tenth century (Tourtellot et al. 1990; Tourtellot and Sabloff 1994). Even with innovative characteristics in economics and ideology, the Puuc centers and their modified form of Classic-period politics had declined by the eleventh century.

The expansion of the Puuc hegemony, the decline of the southern lowland kingdoms, and the initiation of the "Sotuta sphere" cult center and conquest state of Chich'en Itza were all reflected in central and eastern Yucatán and Quintana Roo in events and processes that are still poorly understood. Yet the chapters in this volume indicate that the *general* pattern is now clear. Cobá and its hegemonies declined only slightly later than the central lowland centers with which it had close ecological, ceramic, architectural, and sculptural similarities. Uxmal and the Puuc centers expanded at the expense of Cobá's sphere of influence, yet coeval with the expansion of the modified, distinctive, northern Yucatán hegemony of Chich'en Itza (Cobos, Chapter 22) marked by the presence of "Sotuta" ceramics and changes in architectural styles.

In Chapter 22 Cobos has marshaled and synthesized the recent evidence to demonstrate definitively a *near* "total overlap" model (Sabloff and Andrews 1986a; Robles and Andrews 1986; Lincoln 1986). Perhaps a mix of revitalization of Classic-period ideologies, foreign influences, participation in inter-regional commodity markets, and the creation of new cults and pilgrimage centers allowed Chich'en Itza to outlive its rivals (Carmean et al., Chapter 19; Freidel 1986d; Ringle et al. 1998). As the Cobá regional kingdom rapidly declined in the east, the western Puuc and northern Chich'en hegemonies came into conflict (Carmean et al., Chapter 19; Suhler et al., Chapter 20; Andrews and Robles 1986). The Puuc cities eventually lost this struggle—largely because of pressure and competition from Chich'en Itza.

Archaeologically, these struggles were fossilized in the chronological record by the destruction of epicenter architecture and formal "rituals of termination" involving the burning and burial of monuments and deposits of "desacralizing" broken ceramics in temple and palace contexts (Suhler et al., Chapter 20). Some of these sites continued to have significant occupations, but with new Sotuta ceramic styles (Cobos, Chapter 22; Suhler et al., Chapter 20; Andrews and Robles 1985; Robles and Andrews 1986). During this period, Terminal Classic Seibal, Altar de Sacrificios, Nohmul, Caracol, central and eastern Petén, and other areas show evidence of interaction with the north—with possibly even direct movements of elites to and from Chich'en Itza (Tourtellot and González, Chapter 4; Rice and Rice, Chapter 7; Laporte, Chapter 10; Chase and Chase 1982; A. Chase 1985b; Ball 1974b; Ringle et al. 1998; Kowalski 1989; Jones 1998).

Yet Chich'en Itza's ascendancy over its neighbors was followed within a century, perhaps within even just a few decades, by its own decline between A.D. 1050 and 1100, according to the most recent chronologies (Cobos 1998a, 1998b,

Chapter 22). One explanation for the Chich'en decline is Robles's and Andrews's speculation that the Itza polity was heavily dependent on predation and tribute. With the decline of the traditional Classic Maya centers of the Cobá area and the more innovative Puuc hegemony to the west, the lords of Chich'en found their flow of tribute resources and labor rapidly diminished (Robles and Andrews 1986: 89). Recent interpretations of climatic change and possible desiccation in the northern lowlands (Braswell et al., Chapter 9; Hodell et al. 1995) are hard to reconcile with the Puuc and the final Chich'en florescences. The alleged drought began just as these centers started to thrive and ended before their eleventh-century decline (Carmean et al., Chapter 19; Cobos, Chapter 22; Hodell et al. 1995). While climatic changes surely did have an affect on the complex culture history of these northern zones, the interplay among political changes, regional ecological and climatological systems, and general climate shifts appears to have been extremely complex and variable over the A.D. 800 to 1100 period—as it was throughout Maya prehistory (e.g., Demarest et al. 2003; Dunning and Beach, in press). In any case, the battling alliances of northern Yucatán in the Terminal Classic period represented the last stage in the end of the Classic Maya political and economic system. Chich'en may have delivered the final blow to revitalized, modified forms of the Classic-period political order.

TRANSFORMATIONS OF THE CLASSIC MAYA CIVILIZATION

Our goal in compiling this volume was neither to discover the "cause" of the Maya collapse nor to achieve consensus on the nature of the lowland Terminal Classic period. Instead, our objective was to compile summaries of the archaeo-logical evidence and the culture-histories excavated and interpreted at a broad range of lowland sites and areas over the last three decades. Our aims were empirical rather than theoretical, as we sought to expose and plot variability rather than belabor the rightness or wrongness of any particular theory, or generate new theories. Rather, we felt it would be useful to compile the data as a baseline for broader attempts in the future to chart areal and temporal trends and variability.

Bringing together such a mass of data has its obligations, of course: the need to make some sense of it. Future comparative research will complete needed systematic comparisons. Here, without trying to build an artificial and premature consensus, we offer some observations that might contribute to further evalua-tions of this period. These are directed broadly toward the general areas of politi-cal structure, ecology and population movement, chronology, and concepts.

The Classic Maya "Political Order"

All reconstructions of the Terminal Classic in the Maya lowlands postulate some changes in the Classic Maya political system, and even suggest that there could have been inherent structural problems that gave rise to the Terminal Clas-sic period. Unfortunately, this proposition is difficult to assess because there is still no widespread agreement as to what that Classic "political system" or "political order" actually *was*. Some concerns, however, can be dimly viewed in the flood of emerging data from epigraphy, ethnohistory, and archaeology.

One structural element found in many Classic Maya polities was the institution of the k'uhul ajaw. The centralization of much religious and political authority in divine shamanistic kings was a hallmark of many southern lowland states. Despite authority based heavily on ritual performance and intercenter warfare, the k'uhul ajawob had great power that sometimes also extended to clearly economic spheres.

Still, a very flexible system of royal succession allowed a son (not necessarily the eldest), a brother, another male relative, or, in some cases, even a queen to take the throne upon the death of the ruler. Such a flexible system of succession may have had advantages in assuring the presence of a suitable heir and, in most cases, one with the requisite lineage and personal traits needed to rule. Yet in this scenario, the flexible system of succession and the heavily ideological basis of power made the Classic political order unstable, with frequent struggles for succession to the throne fought both through warfare and in terms of other forms of status-rivalry (Webster 1998; Demarest 1992). Change in the political order of states sometimes occurred through usurpation by rivals for the throne, defeat by other states, and revolt and overthrow by rulers of subordinate states or secondary centers. All such blows to the dynastic order could have resulted in rapid changes in the prestige of the center and the control of tribute labor of its rulers—more so because royal power was based primarily on claims of supernatural and personal authority (Demarest 1992; Marcus 1993; Hammond 1991c)—and subroyal elites relied for power on their proximity to rulers and related forms of "cultural capital" (e.g., Bourdieu 1968; Inomata 2001).

Yet recent correlations of ethnohistorical, epigraphic, and archaeological data have discovered more specific sources for the apparently volatile dynamics of Maya states. While the k'uhul ajaw and a regal-ritual/theater-state–like ambiance constituted the core of Classic Maya political organization, along with power based in ideology and probable flexible succession, other elements can be explained more parsimoniously by a specific model. In particular, it can be shown (P. Rice 2004) that many aspects of Classic Maya political organization were based on the major cities ritually "seating" the *may,* a calendrical interval of 256 years consisting of thirteen k'atun cycles of twenty tuns (approximately twenty years) each, with each k'atun being seated in a subsidiary center within the *may* seat's realm. The seat of the *may* was a sacred city, *siyaj kan,* "born of heaven." Just as Bishop Landa (Tozzer 1941) reported sequential, overlapping roles of ritual authority for k'atun idols in Postclassic Yucatán, with transitions occurring on the half-k'atun of ten years, so the Classic *may* politico-calendrical cycle operated with overlapping seatings and transfers of ritual authority during the half-*may* of 128 years.

While generating great shifts in architectural investment and even in population distributions, the *may*-based political organization was inherently stable, having lasted from the Preclassic period up into Colonial times (P. Rice 2004; Edmonson 1979). It would also explain some of the instability that archaeologists have seen in the programmatic cycles of rotating power (i.e., *may* and k'atun seats) into and out of geo-politico-ritual authority every 128/256 years. Specifically, during the Classic period the *may* was seated at Tikal (and at other cities) in A.D. 426 (P. Rice 2004), which was the half-k'atun year before the ending of a K'atun 8 Ajaw ten years later, in 9.0.0.0.0. Moving forward 128 years, or half a *may*, brings us to A.D. 554, which marks the beginning of another 128-year period—Tikal's so-called "hiatus"—in which monuments were not erected. The next *may* seating at Tikal occurred in 682, another half-k'atun before a K'atun 8 Ajaw (in 9.13.0.0.0) and 256 years after the previous one. This Late Classic *may* seating, at Tikal at least, lasted until A.D. 938; the last half, or 128 years of it, beginning in 810, is known as the Terminal Classic or Maya "collapse." In both cases, the "instability" marked by the hiatus and the collapse is actually a preprogrammed transfer of ritual responsibility.

Whether through warfare, succession, or shifting of *may* capitals, changes in prominent rulers could lead to decline in construction activity and a contraction in the size of a center's hegemony of vassal centers and villages paying tribute in labor or goods. Even the largest and most prestigious centers were subject to these fluctuations, as seen in the sixth-century decline of Tikal after conquest by Caracol and Calakmul (Valdés and Fahsen, Chapter 8; Martin and Grube 2000), the decline of Calakmul's regional kingdom and inter-regional hegemony after A.D. 695, when Tikal ascended once again (Braswell et al., Chapter 9), and the shifting of power between Copán and Quiriguá in the eighth century (Fash et al., Chapter 12). Conversely, expansion of regional power could be brought about by success in alliance formation, war, and ritual by particularly charismatic kings. It could also be generated by the regional distribution of ideological (and political) power imposed by the *may*-cycle structures. More direct military expansionism has been documented by epigraphy and direct archaeological evidence (e.g., Demarest 1997; A. Chase and D. Chase 1996b; Martin and Grube 2000). In some cases, conquest provided tribute in exotics (e.g., O'Mansky and Dunning, Chapter 5; Demarest, Chapter 6) or even in basic subsistence goods (Dunning and Beach 2004). Yet in other cases in the Classic, Terminal Classic, and Postclassic periods, notable and profound shifts in settlement, architectural programs, monument erection, and even tribute sometimes resulted from the more orderly shifts imposed by the *may* cycle (see P. Rice 2004; Rice and Rice, Chapter 7).

The expansions and contractions in the northern lowland hegemonies of Uxmal and Chich'en Itza, described here in the chapters by Carmean et al. (19), Ringle et al. (21), Suhler et al. (20), and Cobos et al. (22), were based on modified forms of political organization (especially in the case of Chich'en Itza), several elements of which can be fit into 256-year cycles of the *may* (P. Rice 2004). Other shifts may be attributable to changes in economic and trade systems (Freidel 1986d; Sabloff

Table 23.1.

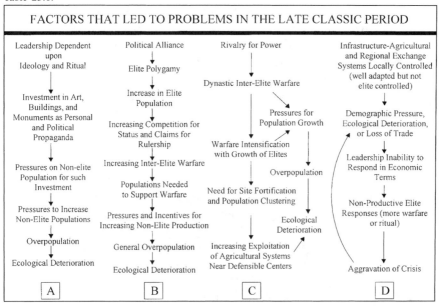

FACTORS THAT LED TO PROBLEMS IN THE LATE CLASSIC PERIOD

1977; Sabloff and Rathje 1975b) or to military victories. In some cases, these processes may have aligned due to the ideological advantage of incoming *may* capitals. As emphasized by analyses here and elsewhere (e.g., Andrews and Robles 1985; Robles and Andrews 1986) these northern lowland hegemonies can be regarded not so much as a new political order but rather as a modified version of that existing previously in the southern lowlands, minus the k'uhul ajaw or institution of divine kingship, and its highly visible architectural and artifactual products.

Intersite and Intrasite Competition

Features common to the various endings of the Classic-period political order may be identified and traced to common pressures and problems in Classic Maya society. In turn, the myriad manifestations of this period of culture change reflect (and help measure) the political and economic variability of Late Classic Maya civilization. In Table 23.1 we list just a few of the salient characteristics of many Classic Maya kingdoms. These are, of course, broad generalizations, some of which apply only weakly to specific polities (and all of which are subject to debate). The differing manifestations of culture change in different areas of the lowlands at the end of the Classic period result from different local responses to common challenges determined by regional conditions and varying external factors.

One issue raised (largely implicitly) in many of the chapters of this volume is the question of why Classic Maya rulers were generally unable to respond more effectively to preserve their political order and positions of power when confronted with the late eighth-and ninth-century internal stresses, climatic shifts, external competition, and population movements. We believe that the failure of many Classic Maya states to respond effectively to internal infrastructural stresses and external changes may have been due to the fact that ruling elites usually only weakly controlled major segments of economic infrastructure, such as subsistence management, production of utilitarian goods, or management of local settlement and exchange. Most Maya states were held together by the authority of the k'uhul ajaw of the capital center (the k'atun or *may* seat) with usually decentralized local, family, or community management of most aspects of the economy. Such a system would have had great strengths in terms of subsistence sensitivity to local microenvironmental features. Localized control was a key element in the success of the Classic Maya "managed mosaic" of subsistence systems (e.g., Fedick 1996a; Dunning et al. 1997; Dunning and Beach 2004). As Ashmore et al. (Chapter 14) point out, during the Classic period such community-level focus was also a strength in terms of social cohesion and community identity (see also Dunning 1992; McAnany 1990).

Elsewhere it has been argued that the unstable dynamics of expanding and contracting "galactic polities" and their hegemonies were merely the most spectacular versions of the ongoing status-rivalry that was a central characteristic of the Maya theater-states (e.g., Webster 1993, 1995; Tambiah 1977; Demarest 1992). This status-rivalry generated not only conflict and warfare but, more often, the extraordinary architecture, art, and monuments that were the settings for pageants, feasting, and rituals. These activities were the most common form of competition for the allegiance of subordinate elites and centers and the populace as a whole. Grand rituals, inter-elite visits and feasting, marriage alliance, and war were alternative paths to the charismatic power of the k'uhul ajaw.

Yet this apparent "status-rivalry" between centers during the Late Classic has recently been shown (P. Rice 2004, n.d.) often to result from either ritualized competition or actual "warfare" (or both) among centers to "seat" the k'atun. K'atun seats held considerable secular powers in terms of controlling tribute rights, land titles, and appointments to public office, at least during the early Colonial period (Edmonson 1979: 11, 1982: xvii). In the Late Postclassic and early Colonial periods, there was considerable competition and outright warfare among candidates for the honor of seating these cycles. In the case of k'atuns, of course, they cycled every twenty years, meaning that the fighting could have been relatively continuous, particularly viewed in "archaeological time." It also bears mention that during the Late Postclassic and early Colonial periods, the end of *may* cycles was accompanied by termination ritual: the city and its roads and idols were ritually destroyed at the end of the cycle and the city was abandoned (Edmonson 1979: 11). Some of the destruction of cities attributed to warfare in the Late Classic might have been the result of this sort of termination ritual (P. Rice 2004, n.d.).

In any event, almost all contributors to this volume have described intensification of the various forms of intersite competition in the Late Classic period. Increasing investment in architecture and monuments, reflecting intensified ritual, produced the beautiful art and ruins admired today, but they surely had a high energetic cost for the supporting populations of the Classic period. Alliance, warfare, and intersite visits also increased. Meanwhile, elite polygamy, a successful mode of extending power and forming alliances, could have exacerbated existing tensions by producing more heirs and competitors. The consequence, by the end of the Late Classic, was an increase in construction, ritual performance, and dynastic competition, all of which contributed to a staggering economic burden—but also resulted in the magnificent cities that centered the calendrical rituals assuring continuity of the Maya cosmos.

Environment, Demographics, and Migration

Many if not most theories about the end of the Classic Maya have stressed problems of demographic and ecological stresses at the end of the Classic period (e.g., Culbert 1973c; Turner and Harrison 1978; Harrison 1977; Culbert 1988; Sanders 1973; Adams 1973a; Santley et al. 1986; Culbert et al. 1990). Such analyses correctly point to the high population levels and densities in the Late Classic period as a major source of ecological stress on the productive, but fragile, rainforest agricultural system (e.g., Culbert and Rice 1990).

Yet we must also explain in specific terms how such rapid demographic growth occurred. The last fifty years of debate in social theory and archaeology have dismissed the Malthusian logic that nonwestern societies are unable to control their demography and simply grow uncontrollably (e.g., Cowgill 1975a, 1975b). Postprocessual critiques may be correct in arguing that the utilization of *assumed* universal principles of demographic pressure is a fallacy that may be created by the search for general principles or "laws" in processual approaches in archaeology (e.g., Watson et al. 1971; Hodder 1982). Yet the refutation of uncontrolled demographic growth as an inevitable force in human societies does not mean that it did not occur in particular episodes of culture-history. When arguments are made that it did occur, we should try to explain specifically *why* overpopulation and ecological stress were allowed to develop by leaders and populaces (as conscious actors). But this viewpoint begs the question of whether those actors were actually aware of overpopulation and its "stresses" on the system, and how archaeologists would recognize if they were. To seek such specific explanations of demographic stress in some regions we must turn to the more complex and variable economic, social, and political factors discussed for each region below.

In their discussion of the Classic end at Calakmul, Braswell et al. (Chapter 9) attribute the changes and population decline to a climatological change being experienced in various ways throughout Mesoamerica (see also Folan, Gunn, et al.

1983; Hodell et al. 1995; Gill 2000). These recent climatological theories, based on pollen cores from northern Yucatán (and more recently, Venezuela; Haug et al. 2003), are a subject of discussion and disagreement throughout this volume. While Adams et al. (Chapter 15) follow this interpretation, other chapters here (O'Mansky and Dunning, Chapter 5; Demarest, Chapter 6; Ringle et al., Chapter 21) and recent extensive paleoecological studies contradict the interpretation of the general end of Classic Maya civilization and the Terminal Classic as a period of widespread famine, disease, or other significant change in environment, nutrition, or health primarily due to climatic change (e.g., Emery 1997, 2004; Wright 1994, 1997a, 1997b, 2004; Emery, Wright, and Schwartz 2000; Wright and White 1996; see also Demarest, Chapter 6). Other chapters here (Carmean et al., Chapter 19; Ringle et al., Chapter 21; Cobos, Chapter 22) view probable drought in *some* areas as possibly having affected the later tenth-to eleventh-century decline of the northern Yucatán centers. In the far northern Petén and southern Campeche and Quintana Roo, climate change may have had regional manifestations and impact that accelerated collapse and prevented recovery. Yet in other areas, the local and regional impact of climatic shifts could have depended on regional ecological regimes, microclimatic variations, and political responses (e.g., Demarest et al. 2003; Dunning and Beach, in press). The timing, nature, and zones of earliest Terminal Classic changes suggest a secondary and later role for climatic change, but the issue is clearly subject to future debate. As with other factors, climate shifts may have been one element adding to the mosaic of collapses, transitions, and transformations that ended the Classic period cultural systems.

Another partial explanation for some regional demographic stresses and localized anthropogenic ecological deterioration may be seen in the chronological pattern of changes in the late eighth and ninth centuries. Processes of political fragmentation, demographic change, or loss of political complexity appear to have moved from west to east and south to north. This geographic pattern has been observed in many previous studies (e.g., Bove 1981; Lowe 1985) as indicative of the end of Classic Maya civilization. Change also appears to be more abrupt and dramatic in western Petén, with more gradual and later Terminal Classic processes in other regions. It is possible, then, that migration from western centers may have *added* population to other regions, perhaps with the unintended consequences of creating or exacerbating local ecological stress (see Demarest, Chapter 6).

Emigration from declining western and southern kingdoms could have further affected the demography of central Petén, Belize, and the northern lowlands in the ninth century (Demarest, Chapter 6; Rice and Rice, Chapter 7; Demarest and Escobedo 1998). The chapters here by Adams et al., Hammond and Tourtellot, Laporte, and Ashmore et al. (15, 13, 14, and 10, respectively) all describe erratic population increases in areas of Petén and Belize at the end of the Classic period. In some cases these increases were accompanied by florescence in construction activities, but generally they were followed by a disintegration of state systems (see especially Adams et al., Chapter 15; Hammond and Tourtellot, Chapter 13; and Ashmore et al., Chapter 14, on northern and central Belize). A somewhat later pattern of population growth and cultural florescence, followed by stresses and decline, has long been observed for the northern lowlands and, as here, has been attributed at least in part to emigration from the south (see Carmean et al., Chapter 19; Suhler et al., Chapter 20; Ringle et al., Chapter 21; Demarest, Chapter 6). In recent refugee and migration theory (Bellos 1997; Black 1998; Black and Vaughan 1993; Cohen and Denge 1998; Rogge 1987), it has been shown that radical population shifts usually lead to change, but the nature of that change depends upon a wide variety of variables.

THE TERMINAL CLASSIC TRANSITION

Many disagreements are about the very nature of the Terminal Classic transition, its pace, and the processes involved, and derive at least in part from confusion about concepts, terms, and frames of reference. It is worthwhile to recall some of the terms discussed in our introductory chapter. These clarify distinctions between, for example, "state" (a type of political organization) and "civilization" (a cultural "great tradition"), and "decline" and "collapse." In this context, it is evident that southern lowland Maya *civilization* did not "collapse" in the ninth century. However, a distinctive component of that civilization lying at the foundation of Maya state-level political organization—divine kingship, along with the elite-run social, political, and administrative hierarchies and economic support systems it entailed—could be said to have "collapsed" in the sense of "came to an end." Yet while this was happening, another variant form of state organization was developing, minus divine kingship but still retaining the Maya civilization's core mythic charter, belief system, multiple gods, and rituals designed to maintain their place in the universe. In other words, even after major catastrophes, traumas, and declines, these core elements of the civilization had the resilience to continue and be transformed into subsequent new configurations.

Current chronologies and concepts are outmoded and urgently need to be refined and reinterpreted. The concept of the Terminal Classic was developed and defined around 1965 on the basis of largely unpublished ceramic evidence, and was interpreted as a widespread or "horizon" phenomenon. Much the same evidence, from only eight sites or regions, primarily in the west, was the basis for the chronology of the 1970 Maya seminar addressing *The Classic Maya Collapse*. As Rands (1973a) makes explicit, the dates of the complexes are highly uncertain, which he has expressed by slanting lines covering spans of sixty years for both their beginnings and endings. The "collapse" of lowland Maya "civilization" itself, however, was seen as "a very specific problem, narrowly delimited in time and space" (Culbert 1973b: 3). Obviously, this assertion is now contradicted by the wide span of A.D. 750 to 1050 for Terminal Classic events and processes

(Figure 3.3). Subsequent investigations have only amplified the picture of regional and chronological variability. Extensive research in western and southwestern Petén is generating a far more fine-grained picture of the A.D. 600 to 1050 period, while chronologies in other areas remain relatively vague. Furthermore, ongoing explorations are exposing ever more regional variability in the actual events and processes that took place in this period. Specifically, the end of Classic-period kingdoms in western and southwestern Petén now appears to have been as dramatic, and perhaps more violent, than the original formulations, but elsewhere, the chronology, processes, and degree of continuity in Classic to Postclassic culture could not be more variable (and in some cases occurred more than two centuries later). Indeed, in some regions this period is better viewed as a "transition" and in others as a florescence, but in many regions continuities in central aspects of Maya politics, ideology, and economics are great between the Classic and Postclassic periods (see especially P. Rice 2004; Rice and Rice, Chapter 7; Chase and Chase, Chapter 2).

Still, we feel that it is not necessarily correct to assert (as Chase and Chase do in Chapter 2) that the notion of a Classic-period "collapse" or decline was the result of preconceived notions and biases against the "Postclassic," or purely methodological flaws. Rather, earlier generations of archaeologists had a sample that was very heavily skewed to western Petén, where Terminal Classic changes and disjunctions were indeed profound; in fact, most centers were rapidly abandoned and levels of population and political complexity never recovered in the west. Earlier scholars may have leaned too heavily for their Late to Terminal Classic interpretations on the western sites and on the record of the stelae-altar cult and its inscribed dates. The latter reliance was understandable before the widespread use of radiocarbon or obsidian dating hydration techniques. Recall also that at that time, ceramic chronologies were initially broad estimates (and, indeed, remain so in many regions).

CONCLUSIONS:
THE MOSAIC OF NINTH- TO ELEVENTH-CENTURY CHANGE

What earlier scholars were perceiving was not, however, a complete misperception of a "decline" or "fall" of Classic Maya civilization comparable to that of Rome. Rather, their oft-cited comparisons to the "fall" of the Roman Empire were not inaccurate; it was their stereotyped vision of the Roman decline that was incorrect! We now know that the decline and disappearance of Roman civilization was a complex and regionally highly variable process spanning several centuries (see, for example, Bowerstock 1988; Eisenstadt 1967; Gunderson 1976; Jones 1964; Tainter 1988). It was also never complete, with most aspects of Roman religion, writing, and political institutions (and even calendrics) surviving in the varied polities of Europe. The political disintegration of the western empire was marked by violence, invasions, and a rapid drop in levels of both population and political complexity. Recovery there was slow and delayed but the political landscape of western Europe was itself a highly variable mosaic of polities in the fifth to eighth centuries, some of which held closely to forms of "Roman" civilization. Meanwhile, in the east, Byzantine civilization flourished for many centuries, adapting and slowly transforming Roman concepts and institutions.

The papers in this volume demonstrate that the processes of decline, survival, and transformation of Classic Maya civilization were no less complex and variable. As with Rome, the western collapse (in this case, the southwestern collapse) was the earliest. After an interval of experimentation and failure, the great Classic-period cities of western Petén were replaced by rainforest with only scattered Postclassic occupations with little public architecture and no major centers. In stark contrast, the centers of the northern lowlands may have been politically and demographically bolstered by the southwestern collapse, and they experienced florescence and transformation. Meanwhile, in eastern Petén, Belize, and western Honduras, processes and events, yet poorly understood, appear to form a crazy quilt of continuities and discontinuities—rapid collapses, gradual declines, smooth transitions, or striking transformations. Recent revisions of our views on warfare (e.g., Demarest, Chapter 6; Webster 1993), political organization (e.g., Rice and Rice, Chapter 7; P. Rice 2004), ideology (e.g., McAnany 1990), and other aspects of Maya society have provided us with a much wider range of interpretive devices to understand and explain both the continuities and the changes in the lowland Terminal Classic landscape. The degree to which the perceived variability in Terminal Classic continuity or change reflects actual culture-history or methodological, theoretical, or interpretive disagreement is for the reader—and the future—to judge. What is certain, however, is that global theories of prime movers as the cause of a general, contemporaneous, and rapid collapse of the lowland cities no longer have explanatory force, because such a uniform general event never took place.

The term "collapse" or "fall" of a civilization is a colorful, but misleading, term. Unlike poetic metaphors that guide our colloquial descriptions of the trajectory of cultural traditions, civilizations do not "die." These anthropomorphic descriptions and organic models ignore the fact that a civilization is a complex configuration of institutions built upon a foundation of shared religious, political, and economic ideas and concepts. Even after major catastrophes, traumas, and declines, these elements can continue and be transformed into subsequent new configurations.

Beginning as early as the eighth century, Classic Maya kingdoms began to disintegrate into chaos (as with the Petexbatun), fragment into smaller units (as with the Copán Valley), or reinvent themselves with modified forms of the k'uhul ajaw institution of rulership (as with Seibal and Caracol). Refugees from collapsing western and southern political systems may have moved to the east, causing population increase in parts of Belize and Yucatán. In the north, the shift of southern trade routes to the north and Gulf Coast and an influx of southern populations may have initially provided preliminary advantages for innovative leadership, helping stimulate the Puuc florescence and the Chich'en Itza apogee. Anthropogenic or climatological deterioration may have been a factor in some subregions.

Yet note that *most* of the lowland evidence reported in this volume does *not* support theories of an ecologically driven pan-lowland collapse. The chronological ordering of changes at the end of the Classic period (as described in most chapters) occurred in a staggered sequence beginning with the western riverine kingdoms in areas of high rainfall with *no* evidence of climatic change, increased malnutrition, demographic stress, or reduced health. The sequence of events, the wealth of detailed historical and archaeological evidence, as well as regionally variable paleoecological findings, pose great problems for any simplistic theory. There is no shortcut, no way to avoid the sustained effort of the region-by-region construction and linking of culture-histories. The subsequent interpretation of these culture-histories must take into account the economic shifts, changing ideologies, political dynamics, population movements, and other complexities of the variable Late Classic to Postclassic landscape.

The Postclassic political and economic hegemonies that began to emerge in the eleventh century were distinct from Classic Maya civilization in the geographic distribution of their centers and populations, their trade networks, their involvement in international commodity economies, their artifactual assemblages, sculpture, and architecture. Tossing aside the outmoded debate over evaluative terms such as "decline" or "collapse," the ninth to eleventh centuries did mark a major change in archaeologically visible aspects of the lowland political and economic system, as well as population levels and distributions.

Most notable to generations of Mayanists, and to most of the descriptions in this volume, was the population decline or abandonment of many southern lowland centers, particularly in the western and far northern Petén. In the same period, the elaborate artifacts and architecture of the divine lords, the k'uhul ajaw, also disappeared throughout the entire Maya world. It is not correct to describe this change as a collapse or decline *of the Maya cultural tradition* or of "Maya civilization." What disappeared was the Late Preclassic– to Classic-period political system based on divine kingship and the extravagant symbolic system that it generated—and that later seduced two centuries of Mayanists with its elegant imagery of political legitimation.

The Maya tradition continued and flourished, but the distinctive configuration of features at the centers of the Classic-period lowland Maya had, indeed, "terminated." The details of this process, and especially its linkages to events and processes in the rest of Mesoamerica, remain uncertain—as seen in the debates and disagreements within this volume. Yet, finally, here we may have begun to perceive dimly the complex patterns of the continuities and the disjunctions of this Classic to Postclassic transition in the history of Maya civilization. The "mystery" is disappearing, but the hard work has just begun.

REFERENCES

ABBREVIATIONS

AA	*American Anthropologist*
AAA	American Anthropological Association
AAnt	*American Antiquity*
AM	*Ancient Mesoamerica*
BAR	British Archaeological Reports, International Series, Oxford, England
BDOA	Belize Department of Archaeology, Belmopan
CA	*Current Anthropology*
CCM	*Ceramica de Cultura Maya*
CIA	Congreso Internacional de Americanistas
CIW	Carnegie Institution of Washington
DO	Dumbarton Oaks Research Library and Collections, Trustees for Harvard University, Washington, DC
ECM	*Estudios de Cultura Maya*
HMAI	*Handbook of Middle American Indians* (Robert Wauchope, general editor). 15 volumes. University of Texas Press, Austin, 1964–1975
IDAEH	Instituto de Antropología e Historia, Guatemala City, Guatemala
IMS	Institute of Mesoamerican Studies, The University at Albany–SUNY, Albany, NY
INAH	Instituto Nacional de Antropología e Historia, México, D.F.
JAS	*Journal of Archaeological Sciences*
JFA	*Journal of Field Archaeology*
JWP	*Journal of World Prehistory*
LAA	*Latin American Antiquity*
LICM	*Los investigadores de la cultura maya.* UACM.
MAEFM	Mission Archéologique et Ethnologique Française au Mexique, México, D.F.
MARI	Middle American Research Institute, Tulane University, New Orleans, LA
NWAF	New World Archaeological Foundation, Brigham Young University, Provo, UT
PARI	The Pre-Columbian Art Research Institute, San Francisco
PMAE	Peabody Museum of Archaeology and Ethnology, Harvard University, Cambridge, MA
ROM	Royal Ontario Museum Toronto, Canada
SAA	Society for American Archaeology
SAR	School of American Research, Santa Fe, NM
Selz-Yaxuna	*The Selz Foundation Yaxuna Project: Final Report of the Field Season.* Southern Methodist University, Dallas
Simposio	*Simposio de investigaciones arqueológicas en Guatemala,* Museo Nacional de Arqueología e Etnologia. Ministerio de Cultura y Deportes, IDAEH, and Asociación Tikal
	IV Simposio, 1990 and *V Simposio, 1991,* ed. Juan Pedro Laporte, Héctor Escobedo, and Sandra Villagrán de Brady.

VIII–XI Simposios, 1994–1998, ed. Juan Pedro Laporte and Héctor Escobedo.
XII Simposio, 1998, ed. Juan Pedro Laporte, Héctor Escobedo, and Ana Claudia
M. de Suasnávar.
XIII Simposio, 1999, and *XVI Simposio, 2002,* ed. Juan Pedro Laporte, Héctor L.
Escobedo, Ana Claudia de Suasnávar, and Barbara Arroyo.
XIV Simposio, 2000, ed. Juan Pedro Laporte, Ana Claudia de Suasnávar, and
Barbara Arroyo.
XV Simposio, 2001, ed. Juan Pedro Laporte, Héctor L. Escobedo, and Barbara
Arroyo.

TARL	Texas Archaeological Research Laboratory, The University of Texas at Austin.
UACM	Universidad Autónoma de Campeche, México.
UAYM	Universidad Autónoma de Yucatán, Mérida, México.
UCLA	University of California, Los Angeles.
UM	University Museum, University of Pennsylvania, Philadelphia.
UMI	University Microfilms International, Ann Arbor, MI.
UNAM	Universidad Nacional Autónoma de México, México, D.F.

Abel-Vidor, Suzanne, Claude Baudez, Ronald Bishop, Leidy Bonilla Vargas, Marlin Calvo Mora,
Winifred Creamer, Jane Day, Juan V. Guerrero, Paul Healy, John Hoopes, Frederick W.
Lange, Silvia Salgado, Robert Stroessner, and Alice Tillet
1987   Principales tipos cerámicos y variedades de la Gran Nicoya. *Vínculos* 13(1–2): 35–
317.

Abrams, Elliot M.
1994   *How the Maya Built Their World: Energetics and Ancient Architecture.* University of
Texas Press, Austin.

Abrams, Elliot M., and David G. Rue
1988   The Causes and Consequences of Deforestation Among the Prehistoric Maya. *Human Ecology* 16(4): 377–395.

Acevedo, Renaldo, and Ana María Paz
1991   El patrón de asentamiento de Uaxactun en el clásico tardío. In *IV Simposio, 1988,* pp.
155–159.

Adams, Richard E.W.
1963   Seibal, Petén: una sequencia cerámica preliminar y un nuevo mapa. *ECM* 3: 85–96.
1971   *The Ceramics of Altar de Sacrificios.* PMAE Papers, vol. 63, no. 1.
1973a   The Collapse of Maya Civilization: A Review of Previous Theories. In Culbert 1973a,
pp. 21–34.
1973b   Maya Collapse: Transformation and Termination in the Ceramic Sequence at Altar de
Sacrificios. In Culbert 1973a, pp. 133–163.
1974   A Trial Estimation of Classic Maya Palace Populations at Uaxactun. In Hammond
1974, pp. 285–296.
1977a   (ed.) *The Origins of Maya Civilization.* SAR and University of New Mexico Press,
Albuquerque.
1977b   Rio Bec Archaeology and the Rise of Maya Civilization. In Adams 1977a, pp. 77–99.
1980   Fine Orange Pottery as a Source of Ethnological Information. In *Studies in Ancient
Mesoamerica,* ed. J. Graham, pp. 1–9. UMI.
1981   Settlement Patterns of the Central Yucatan and Southern Campeche Regions. In
Ashmore 1981a, pp. 211–258.
1983   Ancient Land Use and Culture History in the Pasion River Region. In *Prehistoric*

Settlement Patterns: Essays in Honor of Gordon R. Willey, ed. E. Z. Vogt and R. M.
Leventhal, pp. 319–335. University of New Mexico Press, Albuquerque.
1986   Río Azul: Lost City of the Maya. National Geographic 169(4): 420–451.
1990a   Archaeological Research at the Lowland Maya Site of Rio Azul. LAA 1: 23–41.
1990b   A Twenty Year Research Design for Classic Maya Lowland Civilization. Manuscript on
        file at the Center for Archaeology and Tropical Studies, San Antonio, TX.
1991   Prehistoric Mesoamerica, rev. ed., University of Oklahoma Press, Norman.
1999   Rio Azul, An Ancient Maya City. University of Oklahoma Press, Norman.

Adams, Richard E.W., and John L. Gatling
1964   Noreste del Petén; un nuevo sitio y un mapa arqueológico regional. ECM 4: 99–118.
        (Published in English 1986, in Rio Azul Reports, no. 2: The 1984 Season, ed. R.E.W.
        Adams, pp. 193–210. The University of Texas at San Antonio.)

Adams, Richard E.W., and Jane Jackson-Adams
2000   Río Azul Ceramic Sequence Summary: 1999. In Río Azul Reports no. 5: The 1987
        Season, ed. R.E.W. Adams, pp. 264–272. The University of Texas at San Antonio.

Adams, Richard E.W., and Richard C. Jones
1981   Spatial Patterns and Regional Growth Among Classic Maya Cities. AAnt 46: 301–322.

Adams, Richard E.W., and Woodruff D. Smith
1981   Feudal Models for Classic Maya Civilization. In Ashmore 1981a, pp. 335–349.

Adams, Richard E.W., and Aubrey Trik
1961   Temple 1 (Str. 5-1): Post-Constructional Activities, Tikal Reports No. 7. Museum
        Monographs, UM.

Adams, William Y.
1979   On the Argument from Ceramics to History: A Challenge Based on Evidence from
        Medieval Nubia. CA 20: 727–744.

Agurcia Fasquelle, Ricardo
1997   Le Temple du Soleil et son evolution au coeur de l'acropole de Copan. In Les Maya au
        pays de Copan, pp. 91–100. Skira Editore, Milan.
1998   Copán: Art, Science, and Dynasty. In Maya, ed. P. Schmidt, M. de la Garza, and E.
        Nalda, pp. 336–355. Rizzoli, New York.

Aimers, James J., Terry Powis, and Jaime Awe
2000   Formative Period Round Structures of the Upper Belize River Valley. LAA 11: 71–86.

Alvarez Aguilar, Luís Fernando, and Ricardo Armijo Torres
1989–   Excavación y consolidación de la Estructura III de Calakmul, Campeche.
1990   Información 14: 42–55. UACM.

Ambrosino, James N.
1995   Excavations at Structure 6F-68 and the Southwest Corner of Structure 6F-4. In Selz-
        Yaxuna 1994, pp. 11–17.
1996   Excavations at Structures 6F-4, 6F-68, and 6F-72. In Selz-Yaxuna 1995, pp. 23–40.
1997   A Desecrated Burial from Yaxuna, Yucatan, and Its Implications for Maya Gover-
        nance and Warfare. Paper presented at the 62nd Annual Meeting of the SAA, Nash-
        ville, TN.
1998   The Archaeological Deposit Associated with a Palace at Yaxuna, Yucatan: A Caution-
        ary Tale. Paper presented at the 63rd Annual Meeting of the SAA, Seattle.

Ambrosino, James, Traci Ardren, and Kam Manahan
2001   Fortificaciones defensivas en Yaxuná, Yucatán. In Yucatán a través de los siglos:
        memorias del simposio del 49 CIA, Quito, Ecuador, 1997, ed. R Gubler and P. Martel,
        pp. 49–66. UAYM.

Anan, Kofi
1997   Report of the Secretary-General on the Situation in Somalia. *Reports to the U.N. Security Council,* New York.

Anderson, Benedict
1987   *Imagined Communities.* Verso Press, London.

Anderson, Patricia K.
1998   Yula, Yucatan, Mexico. *AM* 9: 151–165.

Andres, Christopher R.
1998   The 1997 Excavations in Structure 1, Chau Hiix, Belize. In *Chau Hiix, Belize: 1997 Excavation Summary.* Interim Report submitted to the BDOA.
2000   *Caches, Censers, Monuments, and Burials: Archaeological Evidence of Postclassic Ritual Activity in Northern Belize.* Unpublished M.A. thesis, Department of Anthropology, Southern Illinois University Carbondale.

Andres, Christopher R., and Robert E. Fry
1997   Burials as Caches: Material and Ideological Links Between Lamanai and Chau Hiix, Belize. Paper presented at the 62nd Annual Meeting of the SAA, Nashville, TN.

Andrews, Anthony P.
1990   The Fall of Chichen Itza: A Preliminary Hypothesis. *LAA* 1: 258–267.
1993   Late Postclassic Lowland Maya Archaeology. *JWP* 7(1): 35–69.

Andrews, Anthony P., E. Wyllys Andrews V, and Fernando Robles Castellanos
2000   The Northern Maya Collapse and its Aftermath. Paper presented at the 65th Annual Meeting of the SAA, Philadelphia.

Andrews, Anthony P., Tomás Gallareta N., and Rafael Cobos
1989   Preliminary Report of the Cupul Survey Project. *Mexicon* XI (5): 91–95.

Andrews, Anthony P., Tomás Gallareta N., Fernando Robles C., Rafael Cobos P., and Pura Cervera R.
1988   Isla Cerritos: An Itzá Trading Port on the North Coast of Yucatán, Mexico. *National Geographic Research* 4: 196–207.

Andrews, Anthony P., and Shirley B. Mock
2002   New Perspectives on the Prehispanic Maya Salt Trade. In Masson and Freidel, pp. 307–334.

Andrews, Anthony P., and Fernando Robles C.
1985   Chichen Itza and Coba: An Itza-Maya Standoff in Early Postclassic Yucatan. In Chase and Rice 1985, pp. 62–72.
1986   (eds.) *Excavaciones arqueológicas en El Meco, Quintana Roo, 1977.* Colección Científica, INAH.

Andrews, Anthony P., and Gabriela Vail
1990   Cronología de sitios prehispánicos costeros de la península de Yucatán y Belice. *Boletín de la Escuela de Ciencias Antropológicas de la Universidad de Yucatán* 18(104–105): 37–66.

Andrews, E. Wyllys, IV
1960   Excavations at Dzibilchaltun, Northwestern Yucatan. *Proceedings of the American Philosophical Society* 104: 3: 254–265.
1965   Archaeology and Prehistory in the Northern Maya Lowlands: An Introduction. In *Archaeology of Southern Mesoamerica,* Part 1, ed. G. R. Willey, pp. 288–330. *HMAI.*
1970   *Balankanche, Throne of the Tiger Priest.* Pub. 32. MARI.
1973   The Development of Maya Civilization after the Abandonment of the Southern Cities. In Culbert 1973a, pp. 243–268.

Andrews, E. Wyllys, IV, and E. Wyllys Andrews V
1980 *Excavations at Dzibilchaltun, Yucatan, Mexico.* Pub. 48. MARI.

Andrews, E. Wyllys, V
1979 Some Comments on Puuc Architecture of the Northern Yucatan Peninsula. In Mills 1979, pp. 1–17.
1981 Dzibilchaltun. In *Archaeology,* ed. J. A. Sabloff, pp. 313–341. Supplement to *HMAI,* vol. 1, Victoria R. Bricker, gen. ed.
1995 The Decline of the Royal Compound at Copán, Honduras. Paper presented at the 94th Annual Meeting of the AAA, Washington, DC.

Andrews, E. Wyllys, V, and Cassandra R. Bill
n.d. A Late Classic Royal Residence at Copán. In *Copán: The History of an Ancient Maya Kingdom,* ed. W. L. Fash and E. W. Andrews. SAR Press, Albuquerque, NM (in press).

Andrews, E. Wyllys, V, William F. Doonan, Gloria E. Everson, Jodi L. Johnson, and Kathryn E. Sampeck
1999 Structure 10L-41, a Multifunctional Palace at Copán. In *Maya Palaces and Elite Residences: An Interdisciplinary Approach,* ed. J. J. Christie. Submitted to University of Texas Press, Austin.

Andrews, E. Wyllys, V, and Barbara W. Fash
1992 Continuity and Change in a Royal Maya Residential Complex at Copan. *AM* 3: 63–88.

Andrews, E. Wyllys, V, and Norman Hammond
1990 Redefinition of the Swasey Phase at Cuello, Belize. *AAnt* 55:3: 570–584.

Andrews, E. Wyllys, V, and Jeremy A. Sabloff
1986 Classic to Postclassic: A Summary Discussion. In Sabloff and Andrews 1986b, pp. 433–456.

Andrews, George
1967 *Comalcalco, Tabasco, Mexico: An Architectonic Survey of a Maya Ceremonial Center.* University of Oregon Press, Eugene.
1975 *Maya Cities: Placemaking and Urbanization.* University of Oklahoma Press, Norman.
1985 *The Architectural Survey at Sayil: A Report of the 1985 Season.* Unpublished manuscript, University of Oregon, Eugene.
1995 *Pyramids and Palaces, Monsters and Masks: The Golden Age of Maya Architecture, vol. I, Architecture of the Puuc Region and Northern Plains Areas.* Labyrinthos, Lancaster, CA.

Anovitz, Lawrence M., Michael J. Elam, Lee R. Riciputi, and David R. Cole
1999 The Failure of Obsidian Hydration Dating: Sources, Implications, and New Directions. *JAS* 26: 735–752.

Aoyama, Kazuo
1996 *Exchange, Craft Specialization, and Ancient Maya State Formation: A Study of Chipped Stone Artifacts from the Southeast Maya Lowlands.* Ph.D. dissertation, Department of Anthropology, University of Pittsburgh, PA. UMI.

Ardren, Traci
1997 *The Politics of Place: Architecture and Cultural Change at the Xkanha Group, Yaxuna, Yucatan, Mexico.* Ph.D. dissertation, Department of Anthropology, Yale University, New Haven, CT.
1998 Death Became Her: The Imagery of Female Power from Elite and Non-elite Burials at Yaxuna, Yucatan, Mexico. Paper presented at the 97th Annual Meeting of the AAA, Philadelphia.

Ardren, Traci, and Charles K. Suhler
    1999   The Origins of Chichen Itza. Paper presented at the 64th Annual Meeting of the
            SAA, Chicago.

Ardren, Traci, Charles Suhler, and David Johnstone
    1998   Evidence for Late Classic Conflict at Yaxuna: Warfare at the Borderlands. Paper
            presented at the 63rd Annual Meeting of the SAA, Seattle.

Arqueología Mexicana
    1997   Noticias. *Arqueología Mexicana* 5(25): 75.

Ashmore, Wendy
    1981a   (ed.) *Lowland Maya Settlement Patterns*. SAR and University of New Mexico Press,
            Albuquerque.
    1981b   Some Issues of Method and Theory in Lowland Maya Settlement Archaeology. In
            Ashmore 1981a, pp. 37–69.
    1988   Household and Community at Classic Quirigua. In *Household and Community in the
            Mesoamerican Past*, ed. R. R. Wilk and W. Ashmore, pp. 153–170. University of
            New Mexico Press, Albuquerque.
    1991   Site-planning Principles and Concepts of Directionality among the Ancient Maya.
            LAA 2(3): 99–226.
    1993   Settlement Archaeology at Xunantunich, Belize, Central America. Proposal submit-
            ted to the National Science Foundation, August.
    1998   Monumentos políticos: sitio, asentamiento y paisaje alrededor de Xunantunich, Belice.
            In Ciudad Ruíz et al. 1998, pp. 161–183.

Ashmore, Wendy, Samuel V. Connell, Jennifer J. Ehret, Clarence H. Gifford, L. Theodore Neff, and
    Jon VandenBosch
    1994   The Xunantunich Settlement Survey. In Leventhal and Ashmore 1994, pp. 248–280.

Ashmore, Wendy, and Richard M. Leventhal
    1993   Xunantunich Revisited. Paper presented at the Conference on Belize, University of
            North Florida, Jacksonville.

Ashmore, Wendy A., Edward M. Schortman, and Patricia A. Urban
    1987   The Classic Maya Fringe: Cultural Boundaries in the Southeast Maya Periphery. In
            Polities and Partitions: Human Boundaries and the Growth of Complex Societies, ed.
            K. M. Trinkhaus, pp. 157–178. University of Arizona Press, Tucson.

Atran, Scott
    1993   Itza Maya Tropical Agro-Forestry. *CA* 34: 633–700.

Aveni, Anthony F., and Horst Hartung
    1989   Uaxactun, Guatemala, Group E and Similar Assemblages: Archaeoastronomical Re-
            consideration. In *World Archaeoastronomy*, ed. A. F. Aveni, pp. 441–461. Cambridge
            University Press, Cambridge.

Awe, Jaime
    1992   Dawn in the Land Between the Rivers: Formative Occupation at Cahal Pech, Belize,
            and its Implications for Preclassic Development in the Maya Lowlands. Unpublished
            Ph.D. dissertation, Institute of Archaeology, University of London.

Ball, Joseph W.
    1974a   A Teotihuacan-Style Cache from the Maya Lowlands. *Archaeology* 27(1): 2–9.
    1974b   A Coordinate Approach to Northern Maya Prehistory: A.D. 700–1000. *AAnt* 39(1):
            85–93.
    1975   Cui Orange Polychrome: A Late Classic Funerary Type from Central Campeche,
            Mexico. *Contributions of the University of California Research Facility* 27: 32–39.

1976 Ceramic Sphere Affiliations of the Barton Ramie Ceramic Complexes. In Gifford 1976, pp. 323–333.

1977 *The Archaeological Ceramics of Becan, Campeche, Mexico.* Pub. 43. MARI.

1978 Archaeological Pottery of the Yucatan-Campeche Coast. *Studies in the Archaeology of Coastal Yucatan and Campeche, Mexico,* pp. 69–146. Pub. 46. MARI.

1979a Ceramics, Culture History, and the Puuc Tradition: Some Alternative Possibilities. In Mills 1979, pp. 18–35.

1979b The 1977 Central College Symposium on Puuc Archaeology: A Summary View. In Mills 1979, pp. 46–51.

1980 *The Archaeological Ceramics of Chinkultic, Chiapas, Mexico.* Papers of the NWAF, no. 43.

1982 The Tancah Ceramic Situation: Cultural and Historical Insights from an Alternative Material Class. In *On the Edge of the Sea: Mural Painting at Tancah-Tulum, Quintana Roo, Mexico,* ed. A. G. Miller, pp. 105–114. DO.

1983a Notes on the Distribution of Established Ceramic Types in the Corozal District, Belize, Central America. In *Archaeological Excavations in Northern Belize, Central America,* ed. R. V. Sidrys, pp. 203–220. Monograph XVII, Institute of Archaeology, UCLA.

1983b Teotihuacan, the Maya, and Ceramic Interchange: A Contextual Perspective. In *Highland-Lowland Interaction in Mesoamerica: Interdisciplinary Approaches,* ed. A. G. Miller, pp. 125–145. DO.

1987 A Preliminary Review of the Ceramic Situation in the Lower Mopan-Macal Triangle, Belize. Report submitted to the BDOA.

1993a *Cahal Pech, the Ancient Maya, and Modern Belize: The Story of an Archaeological Park.* San Diego State University Press, San Diego.

1993b Pottery, Potters, Palaces, and Polities: Some Socioeconomic and Political Implications of Late Classic Maya Ceramic Industries. In Sabloff and Henderson 1993b, pp. 243–272.

1994 Northern Maya Archaeology: Some Observations on an Emerging Paradigm. In Prem 1994, pp. 389–396.

Ball, Joseph W., and E. Wyllys Andrews V
1975 The Polychrome Pottery of Dzibilchaltun, Yucatan, Mexico: Typology and Archaeological Context. In *Archaeological Investigations on the Yucatan Peninsula,* ed. E. W. Andrews IV, pp. 227–247. Pub. 31. MARI.

Ball, Joseph W., and Jennifer J. Taschek
1989 Teotihuacan's Fall and the Rise of the Itza: Realignments and Role Changes in the Terminal Classic Maya Lowlands. In Diehl and Berlo 1989, pp. 187–200.

1991 Late Classic Lowland Maya Political Organization and Central-Place Analysis: New Insights from the Upper Belize Valley. *AM* 2: 149–165.

Bardsley, Sandra
1996 Benches, Brothers, and Lineage Lords of Copan. In *Eighth Palenque Round Table, 1993,* ed. M. G. Robertson, M. J. Macri, and J. McHargue, pp. 195–201. PARI.

Barrera Rubio, Alfredo
1980 *Mural Paintings of the Puuc Region in Yucatan.* In Third Palenque Round Table, 1978, Part 2, ed. M. G. Robinson, pp. 173–182. University of Texas Press, Austin.

1987 *Guia oficial: Uxmal.* INAH.

1990 El asentamiento prehispánico en el área de Uxmal, Yucatán. Paper presented at the First Maler Symposium on the Archaeology of Northwest Yucatán, Bonn.

Barrera Rubio, Alfredo, and José Huchim Herrera
1990 Architectural Restoration at Uxmal 1986–1987. *University of Pittsburgh Latin American Archaeological Reports* 1. University of Pittsburgh Press, Pittsburgh, PA.

580 REFERENCES

Barrera Vásquez, A., and Sylvanus G. Morley
1949   The Maya Chronicles. CIW Pub. 585, Contribution 48.

Barrientos Q., Tomás, Brigitte Kovacevich, Michael Callaghan, and Lucía Morán
2000   Investigaciones en el área residencial sur y suroeste de Cancuen. In Demarest and Barrientos Q. 2000, pp. 99–160.

Barth, Fredrik
1969   Introduction. In Ethnic Groups and Boundaries: The Social Organization of Cultural Differences, ed. F. Barth, pp. 1–38. George Allen & Unwin, London.

Bartlett, Harley H.
1956   Fire, Primitive Agriculture, and Grazing in the Tropics. In Man's Role in Changing the Face of the Earth, ed. W. L. Thomas, pp. 692–721. University of Chicago Press, Chicago.

Bateson, John H.
1972   New Interpretation of Geology of Maya Mountains, British Honduras. Bulletin of the American Association of Petroleum Geologists 56(5): 956–963.

Baudez, Claude F.
1983   (ed.) Introducción a la arqueología de Copán. Proyecto Arqueológico Copán. Secretaría de Estado en el Despacho de Cultura y Turismo, Tegucigalpa, Honduras.
1986   Iconography and History at Copán. In The Southeast Maya Periphery, ed. P. A. Urban and E. M. Schortman, pp. 17–26. University of Texas Press, Austin.
1989   The House of the Bacabs: An Iconographic Analysis. In Webster 1989, pp. 73–81.

Baudez, Claude F., and Pierre Becquelin
1973   Archéologie de Los Naranjos, Honduras. Collection Etudes Mésoaméricaines 2. MAEFM.

Bauer, Brian S.
1987   Sistemas andinos de organización rural antes del establecimiento de reducciones: el ejemplo de Pacariqtambo, Peru. Revista Andina 5(1): 197–210.
1992   The Development of the Inca State. University of Texas Press, Austin.

Beach, Timothy
1996   Estudios de catenas, fertilidad y fosfatos de suelos. In Demarest, Escobedo, and O'Mansky 1996, pp. 86–94.

Beach, Timothy, and Nicholas P. Dunning
1995   Ancient Maya Terracing and Modern Conservation in the Petén Rainforest of Guatemala. Journal of Soil and Water Conservation 50(2): 138–145.
1997   An Ancient Maya Reservoir and Dam at Tamarindito, El Petén, Guatemala. LAA 8: 20–29.

Becker, Marshall J.
1971   The Identification of a Second Plaza Plan at Tikal, Guatemala, and its Implications for Ancient Maya Social Complexity. Ph.D. dissertation, University of Pennsylvania, Philadelphia.
1979   Priests, Peasants, and Ceremonial Centers: The Intellectual History of a Model. In Hammond and Willey, pp. 3–20.
1982   Ancient Maya Houses and Their Identification: An Evaluation of Architectural Groups at Tikal and Inferences Regarding Their Functions. Revista Española de Antropología Americana 12: 111–129. Madrid.
1999   Excavations in Residential Areas of Tikal: Groups with Shrines. Monograph 104, UM.

Becquelin, Pierre
1994   La civilización Puuc vista desde la región de Xculoc. In Prem 1994, pp. 59–70.

Becquelin, Pierre, and Claude F. Baudez
1979   *Tonina, une Cité Maya du Chiapas.* Etudes Mésoaméricaines 6(1). MAEFM.

Becquelin, Pierre, and Dominique Michelet
1994   Demografía en la zona Puuc: el recurso del método. *LAA* 5: 289–311.

Bellos, Alex
1997   Shadow of the Warlords over Stricken Somalia. *Guardian*, July 4, 1997. London.

Benavides Castillo, Antonio
1981a   *Cobá: una ciudad prehispánica de Quintana Roo.* Centro Regional Sureste, INAH.
1981b   *Los caminos de Cobá y sus implicaciones sociales.* Colección Científica Arqueología, INAH.
1994   Edzna y el suroeste de la región del Puuc. In Prem 1994, pp. 121–132.

Bennett, Sharon
1993   1992 Burials from Yaxuna,Yucatan. In *Selz-Yaxuna 1992,* ed. C. Suhler and D. Freidel, pp. 144–164.
1994   The Burial Excavations at Yaxuna in 1993. In *Selz-Yaxuna 1993*, pp. 89–105.

Berger, Rainer, Suzanne DeAtley, Reiner Protsch, and Gordon R. Willey
1974   Radiocarbon Chronology for Seibal, Guatemala. *Nature* 252: 472–473.

Berlin, Heinrich
1953   *Archaeological Reconnaissance in Tabasco.* Current Reports 1(7). CIW.
1956   Late Pottery Horizons of Tabasco, Mexico. *Contributions to American Anthropology and History* 11(59): 95–153. Pub. 606. CIW.

Bevan, Bruce, and Robert J. Sharer
1983   Quirigua and the Earthquake of February 4, 1976. In *Quirigua Reports: Volume II,* ed. E. Schortman and P. Urban, pp. 110–117. Paper no. 12, Monograph 49. UM.

Bey, George J., III, Tara M. Bond, William M. Ringle, Craig A. Hanson, Charles W. Houck, and Carlos Peraza L.
1998   The Ceramic Chronology of Ek Balam, Yucatan, Mexico. *AM* 9: 101–120.

Bey, George J., III, Craig A. Hanson, and William M. Ringle
1997   Classic to Postclassic at Ek Balam, Yucatán: Architectural and Ceramic Evidence for Redefining the Transition. *LAA* 8: 237–254.

Bey, George J., III, Carlos Peraza, and William M. Ringle
1992   Comparative Analysis of Late Classic Period Ceramic Complexes of the Northern Maya Lowlands. *CCM* 16: 11–17.

Bey, George J., III and William M. Ringle
1989   The Myth of the Center. Paper presented at the 54th Annual Meeting of the SAA, Atlanta.

Bill, Cassandra R.
1997   *Patterns of Variation and Change in Dynastic Period Ceramics and Ceramic Production at Copán, Honduras.* Ph.D. dissertation, Department of Anthropology, Tulane University. UMI.
1998   Politics, Population, and Economy: The Effects of Late Classic Sociopolitical and Demographic Change on the Ceramic Production Industry at Copán. Paper presented at the conference Mayan Culture at the Millennium (Part I), Buffalo, NY.
2000   Tipología y análisis preliminar de la cerámica de Cancuen. In Demarest and Barrientos Q. 2000, pp. 161–216.

Bill, Cassandra, and Michael Callaghan
2001   Frecuencias relativas de los tipos y modos cerámicos en Cancuen. In Demarest and Barrientos Q. 2000, pp. 251–264.

Binford, Lewis R.
1989   *Debating Archaeology*. Academic Press, San Diego.

Bishop, Ronald
1994   Pre-Columbian Pottery: Research in the Maya Region. In *Archaeometry of Pre-Columbian Sites and Artifacts*, ed. D. A. Scott and P. Meyers, pp. 15–65. The Getty Conservation Institute, Los Angeles.

Black, Richard
1998   *Refugees, Environment, and Development*. Longman, Essex, England.

Black, Richard, and Vaughan Robinson (eds.)
1993   *Geography and Refugees: Patterns and Processes of Change*. Belhaven Press, London.

Blanton, Richard E.
1994   *Houses and Households: A Comparative Study*. Plenum Press, New York and London.

Blanton, Richard E., Gary M. Feinman, Stephen A. Kowalewski, and Peter N. Peregrine
1996   A Dual-Processual Theory for the Evolution of Mesoamerican Civilization. *CA* 37: 1–14.

Bloch, Maurice
1987   The Ritual of the Royal Bath in Madagascar: The Dissolution of Death, Birth and Fertility into Authority. In *Rituals of Royalty: Power and Ceremonial in Traditional Societies*, ed. D. Cannadine and S. Price, pp. 271–297. Cambridge University Press, Cambridge.

Bolles, John S.
1977   *Las Monjas: A Major Pre-Mexican Architectural Complex at Chichén Itzá*. University of Oklahoma Press, Norman.

Boot, Erik
1996   Recent Epigraphic Research on the Inscriptions at Chichen Itsa, Yucatan, Mexico. *Yumtzilob* 8(1): 5–27. Leiden, Germany.
1997   Kan Ek', Last Ruler of the Itsá. *Yumtzilob* 9(1): 5–22. Leiden, Germany.

Boucher, Sylviane
1990   Una revisión de la sequencia de cerámica preclásica en las regiones Chenes y Puuc. Paper presented at the First Maler Symposium on the Archaeology of Northwest Yucatán, Bonn.

Boucher, Sylviane, and Sara Dzul
1992   Cerámica pizarra temprana: algunos precursores y variantes regionales. *Memorias del Primer Congreso Internacional de Mayistas*, tomo II: 464–476. UNAM.
1998   La seriación tipológica preliminar de la cerámica del Proyecto Arqueológica Calakmul, Campeche (temporadas 1993–1997). Article submitted to *Saastun*. Universidad Mayab, Mérida, México.

Bourdieu, Pierre
1968   Outline of a Theory of Art Perception. *International Social Science Journal* 2 (4): 589–612.
1977   *Outline of a Theory of Practice*. Cambridge Studies in Social Anthropology 16. Cambridge University Press, Cambridge.
1990   *The Logic of Practice*. Translated by R. Nice. Stanford University Press, Stanford, CA.

Bove, Frederick J.
1981   Trend Surface Analysis and the Lowland Classic Maya Collapse. *AAnt* 46(1): 93–112.

Bowerstock, G. W.
1988   The Dissolution of the Roman Empire. In Yoffee and Cowgill 1988, pp. 165–175.

Brady, James E.
1994   Petexbatún Regional Cave Survey Artifacts. In *Petexbatún 6*, pp. 571–641.
1997   Settlement, Architecture and Cosmology: The Role of Caves in Determining the Placement of Architecture at Dos Pilas. *AA* 99: 602–681.

Brady, James E., Joseph W. Ball, Ronald L. Bishop, Duncan C. Pring, Norman Hammond, and Rupert A. Housley.
1998   The Lowland Maya "Protoclassic": A Reconsideration of its Nature and Significance. *AM* 9: 17–38.

Brady, James E., Ann Scott, Allan Cobb, Irma Rodas, John Fogarty, and Monica Urquizú Sánchez
1997   Glimpses of the Dark Side of the Petexbatun Project: The Petexbatun Regional Cave Survey. *AM* 8(2): 353–364.

Brain, James L.
1973   Ancestors as Elders in Africa—Further Thoughts. *Africa* 43: 122–133.

Brainerd, George W.
1958   *The Archaeological Ceramics of Yucatan*. Anthropological Records vol. 19. University of California, Berkeley.

Brandon, Joseph
1992   DP28: Pruebas de pala cerca de la muralla defensiva en Dos Pilas. In Demarest, Inomata, and Escobedo 1992, pp. 67–70.

Braswell, Geoffrey E.
1992   Obsidian Hydration Dating, the Coner Phase, and Revisionist Chronology at Copán, Honduras. *LAA* 3(2): 130–147.
1996a   Obsidian Hydration Dating. In *The Oxford Companion to Archaeology*, ed. B. Fagan, p. 537. Oxford University Press, New York.
1996b   El patrón de asentamiento y producción en la fuente de obsidiana de San Martín Jilotepeque. In *IX Simposio, 1995*, pp. 499–512.
1997a   El intercambio comercial entre los pueblos prehispánicos de Mesoamérica y la Gran Nicoya. *Revista de la Universidad del Valle de Guatemala* 6: 17–29. Guatemala City.
1997b   El intercambio prehispánico en Yucatán, México. In *X Simposio, 1996*, tomo 2, pp. 545–556.
1997c   La cronología y la estructura del colapso en Copán, Honduras. *LICM* 5(1):262–273.
1998a   El epiclásico, clásico terminal y posclásico temprano: una visión cronológica desde Teotihuacan, Chichén Itza, Kaminaljuyu y Copán. In *XI Simposio 1997*, pp. 803–806.
1998b   Trade, Procurement, and Population: Obsidian and the Maya of the Northern Lowlands. Paper presented at the 97th Annual Meeting of the AAA, Philadelphia.
2000   Industria lítica clase tallada: obsidiana. In Wurster 2000, pp. 208–221.
In press La producción y comercio de obsidiana en Centroamérica. In *Primer congreso de arqueología de Nicaragua*, ed. S. S. González. Instituto Nicaragüense de Cultura, Managua.

Braswell, Geoffrey E., E. Wyllys Andrews V, and Michael D. Glascock
1994   The Obsidian Artifacts of Quelepa, El Salvador. *AM* 5(2): 173–192.

Braswell, Geoffrey E., John E. Clark, Kazuo Aoyama, Heather I. McKillop, and Michael D. Glascock
2000   Determining the Geological Provenance of Obsidian Artifacts from the Maya Region: A Test of the Efficacy of Visual Sourcing. *LAA* 11 (3): 219–232.

Braswell, Geoffrey E., Michael D. Glascock, and Hector Neff
1996a   The Obsidian Artifacts of Group 10L-2, Copan: Production, Exchange, and Chronology. Paper presented at the 61st Annual Meeting of the SAA, New Orleans.

1996b   The P.A.C. II Obsidian Hydration Project at Copan: Why It Did Not Work. Paper presented at the 61st Annual Meeting of the SAA, New Orleans.

Braswell, Geoffrey E., Joel D. Gunn, María del Rosario Domínguez Carrasco, William J. Folan, and Michael D. Glascock
1988   Late and Terminal Classic Obsidian Procurement and Lithic Production at Calakmul, Campeche, Mexico. Paper presented at the 63rd Annual Meeting of the SAA, Seattle.

Braswell, Jennifer B.
1998a   Adaptación, supervivencia y fracaso en Belice durante el clásico terminal. In *XI Simposio, 1997*, pp. 721–728.
1998b   *Archaeological Investigations at Group D, Xunantunich, Belize.* Unpublished Ph.D. dissertation, Department of Anthropology, Tulane University, New Orleans.

Braudel, Fernand
1984   *The Perspective of the World. Civilization and Capitalism; 15th–18th Century,* vol. III. First English Translation by Siân Reynolds. Harper and Row, New York. (Originally published in French, *Le Temps du Monde,* Paris 1979.)

Broecker, Wallace S.
1995   Chaotic Climate. *Scientific American* 273: 62–69.

Brokaw, Nicholas V. L., and Elizabeth P. Mallory
1993   *Vegetation of the Rio Bravo Conservation and Management Area, Belize.* Manomet Bird Observatory, Box 1770, Manomet, MA.

Bronson, Bennett
1966   *Vacant Terrain.* Unpublished manuscript on file in the Tikal Room, UM.

Brumfiel, Elizabeth M.
1987a   Consumption and Politics at Aztec Huexotla. *AA* 89(3): 676–685.
1987b   Elite and Utilitarian Crafts in the Aztec State. In *Specialization, Exchange, and Complex Societies,* ed. E. M. Brumfiel and T. K. Earle, pp. 102–118. Cambridge University Press, Cambridge.

Bullard, William
1960   The Maya Settlement Pattern in Northeastern Peten, Guatemala. *AAnt* 25: 355–372.
1963   A Unique Maya Shrine Site on the Mountain Pine Ridge of British Honduras. *AAnt* 29(1): 98–99.
1964   Settlement Pattern and Social Structure in the Southern Maya Lowlands during the Classic Period. *Actas y Memorias,* XXXV CIA, México, 1962, vol. 1, pp. 278–287. México, D.F.
1965   *Late Classic Finds at Baking Pot, British Honduras.* Art and Archaeology Occasional Papers, no. 8. ROM.
1970   Topoxte: A Postclassic Maya Site in Peten, Guatemala. In *Monographs and Papers in Maya Archaeology,* ed. W. R. Bullard Jr., pp. 245–308. PMAE Papers, vol. 61, part IV, no. 2.
1973   Postclassic Culture in Central Peten and Adjacent British Honduras. In Culbert 1973a, pp. 221–241.

Bunzel, Ruth
1952   *Chichicastenango: A Guatemalan Village.* Pub. 22. American Ethnological Society, Locust Valley, NY.

Canché M., Elena
1992   *La secuencia cerámica de Xelhá, Quintana Roo.* Tesis de licenciatura, Facultad de Ciencias Antropológicas, UAYM.

Carmack, Robert M.
1981   *The Quiché Mayas of Utatlán: The Evolution of a Highland Guatemala Kingdom.*
        University of Oklahoma Press, Norman.

Carmean, Kelli
1991   Architectural Labor Investment and Social Stratification at Sayil, Yucatan, Mexico.
        LAA 2: 151–165.
1998   Leadership at Sayil: A Study of Political and Religious Decentralization. *AM* 9: 259–
        270.

Carmean, Kelli, and Jeremy Sabloff
1996   Political Decentralization in the Puuc Region, Yucatan, Mexico. *Journal of Anthro-
        pological Research* 52: 317–330.

Carr, Helen Sorayya
1989   Patterns of Exploitation and Exchange of Subsistence Goods in Late Classic–Early
        Postclassic Yucatan: A Zooarchaeological Perspective. Paper presented at the 54th
        Annual Meeting of the SAA, Atlanta.

Carr, Robert F., and James E. Hazard
1961   Map of the Ruins of Tikal, El Peten, Guatemala. Tikal Report no. 11. UM.

Carrasco Vargas, Ramón
1993   Formación sociopolítica en el Puuc: el sacbé Uxmal-Nohpat-Kabah. In *Perspectivas
        antropológicas en el mundo maya,* ed. M. J. Iglesias Ponce de León and F. Ligorred
        Perramon, pp. 199–212. Publicaciónes de la Sociedad Española de Estudios Mayas,
        no. 2.
1998   The Metropolis of Calakmul, Campeche. In *Maya,* ed. P. Schmidt, M. de la Garza, and
        E. Nalda, pp. 373–385. Rizzoli, New York.

Carrasco Vargas, Ramon, and Sylviane Boucher
1990   El palacio de Sayil (Estructura 2B1): un estudio cronológico. In *Mesoámerica y norte
        de México, siglo IX–XII,* ed. F. Sodi Miranda, pp. 59–85. INAH.

Carrasco Vargas, Ramón, Sylviane Boucher, Paula Alvarez González, Vera Tiesler Blos, Valeria
        García Vierna, Renata García Moreno, and Javier Vázquez Negrete
1999   A Dynastic Tomb from Campeche, Mexico: New Evidence on Jaguar Paw, a Ruler
        from Calakmul. *LAA* 10: 47–58.

Carrasco Vargas, Ramón, and Eduardo Pérez
1993   Los últimos gobernadores de Kabah. In *Eighth Palenque Round Table,* ed. M. Macri
        and J. McHargue, pp. 297–307. PARI.

Castañeda, Quetzil E.
1996   *In the Museum of Maya Culture: Touring Chichén Itzá.* University of Minnesota
        Press, Minneapolis.

Castellanos, Jeanette
1996   Resumen de resultados análisis cerámico, Punta de Chimino. In Demarest, Escobedo
        and O'Mansky 1996, pp. 140–183.

Cecil, Leslie G.
2001   *Technological Styles of Late Postclassic Slipped Pottery from the Central Petén Lakes
        Region, El Petén, Guatemala.* Ph.D. dissertation. Department of Anthropology,
        Southern Illinois University Carbondale. UMI.

Chappell, John, John Head, and John Magee
1996   Beyond the Radiocarbon Limit in Australian Archaeology and Quaternary Research.
        Antiquity 70(269): 543–552.

Chase, Arlen F.
1979   Regional Development in the Tayasal-Paxcaman zone, El Peten, Guatemala: A Pre-
         liminary Statement. *CCM* 11: 86–119.
1983   A Contextual Consideration of the Tayasal-Paxcaman Zone, El Peten, Guatemala.
         Ph.D. dissertation, Department of Anthropology, University of Pennsylvania. UMI.
1985a   Archaeology in the Maya Heartland: The Tayasal-Paxcaman Zone, Lake Peten,
         Guatemala. *Archaeology* 38(1): 32–39.
1985b   Troubled Times: The Archaeology and Iconography of the Terminal Classic Southern
         Lowland Maya. In *Fifth Palenque Round Table, 1983,* ed. M. G. Robertson and V. M.
         Fields, pp. 103–114. PARI.
1986   Time Depth or Vacuum: The 11.3.0.0.0 Correlation and the Lowland Maya Postclassic.
         In Sabloff and Andrews 1986b, pp. 99–140.
1990   Maya Archaeology and Population Estimates in the Tayasal-Paxcaman Zone, Peten,
         Guatemala. In Culbert and Rice, pp. 149–165.
1991   Cycles of Time: Caracol in the Maya Realm. In *Sixth Palenque Round Table, 1986,
         vol. VII,* ed. M. G. Robertson, pp. 32–42. University of Oklahoma Press, Norman.
1992   Elites and the Changing Organization of Classic Maya Society. In D. Z. Chase and A.
         F. Chase 1992b, pp. 30–49.
1994   A Contextual Approach to the Ceramics of Caracol, Belize. In D. Z. Chase and A. F.
         Chase 1994, pp. 157–182.
1998   Planeación cívica e integración de sitio en Caracol, Belice: definiendo una economía
         administrada del período clásico maya. *LICM* 6(1): 26–44.
Chase, Arlen F., and Diane Z. Chase
1983   *La ceramica de la zona Tayasal-Paxcaman, Lago Peten Itza, Guatemala.* Privately
         distributed by UM.
1985   Postclassic Temporal and Spatial Frames for the Lowland Maya: A Background. In
         Chase and Rice 1985, pp. 9–22.
1987a   *Investigations at the Classic Maya City of Caracol, Belize: 1985–1987.* Monograph 3,
         PARI.
1987b   *Glimmers of a Forgotten Realm: Maya Archaeology at Caracol, Belize.* University of
         Central Florida, Orlando.
1989   The Investigation of Classic Period Maya Warfare at Caracol, Belize. *Mayab* 5: 5–18.
1992   El norte y el sur: política, dominios y evolución cultural maya. *Mayab* 8: 134–149.
1994a   Details in the Archaeology of Caracol, Belize: An Introduction. In D. Z. Chase and A.
         F. Chase 1994, pp. 1–11.
1994b   Maya Veneration of the Dead at Caracol, Belize. In *Seventh Palenque Round Table,
         1989,* ed. M. G. Robertson and V. M. Fields, pp. 55–62. PARI.
1995   External Impetus, Internal Synthesis, and Standardization: E-Group Assemblages and
         the Crystallization of Classic Maya Society in the Southern Lowlands. In *The Emer-
         gence of Lowland Maya Civilization: The Transition from the Preclassic to Early
         Classic,* ed. N. Grube, pp. 87–101. Acta Mesoamericana no. 8, Berlin.
1996a   The Causeways of Caracol. *Belize Today* 10(3/4): 31–32.
1996b   A Mighty Maya Nation: How Caracol Built an Empire by Cultivating its "Middle
         Class." *Archaeology* 49(5): 66–72.
1996c   More than Kin and King: Centralized Political Organization among the Late Classic
         Maya. *CA* 37(5): 803–810.
1996d   The Organization and Composition of Classic Lowland Maya Society: The View from
         Caracol, Belize. In *Eighth Palenque Round Table, 1993,* ed. M. G. Robertson, M. J.
         Macri, and J. McHargue, pp. 213–222. PARI.
1998a   Late Classic Maya Political Structure, Polity Size, and Warfare Arenas. In Ciudad Ruíz
         et al. 1998, pp. 11–29.

1998b   Scale and Intensity in Classic Period Maya Agriculture: Terracing and Settlement at the "Garden City" of Caracol, Belize. *Culture and Agriculture* 20: 60–77.
2001   The Royal Court of Caracol, Belize: Its Palaces and People. In *Royal Courts of the Ancient Maya*, ed. T. Inomata and S. D. Houston, pp. 102–137. Westview Press, Boulder, CO.

Chase, Arlen F., Nikolai Grube, and Diane Z. Chase
1991   *Three Terminal Classic Monuments from Caracol, Belize.* Research Reports on Ancient Maya Writing No. 36. Center for Maya Research, Washington, DC.

Chase, Arlen F., and Prudence M. Rice (eds.)
1985   *The Lowland Maya Postclassic.* University of Texas Press, Austin.

Chase, Diane Z.
1981   The Postclassic Maya at Santa Rita Corozal. *Archaeology* 34(1): 25–33.
1982a   The Ikilik Ceramic Complex at Nohmul, Northern Belize. *CCM* 12: 71–81.
1982b   Spatial and Temporal Variability in Postclassic Northern Belize. Ph.D. dissertation, Department of Anthropology, University of Pennsylvania, Philadelphia.
1984   The Late Postclassic Pottery of Santa Rita Corozal, Belize: The Xabalxab Ceramic Complex. *CCM* 13: 18–26.
1985a   Between Earth and Sky: Idols, Images, and Postclassic Cosmology. In *Fifth Palenque Round Table, 1983,* ed. M. G. Robertson and V. M. Fields, pp. 223–233. PARI.
1985b   Ganned but not Forgotten: Late Postclassic Archaeology and Ritual at Santa Rita Corozal, Belize. In Chase and Rice 1985, pp. 104–125.
1986   Social and Political Organization in the Land of Cacao and Honey: Correlating the Archaeology and Ethnohistory of the Postclassic Lowland Maya. In Sabloff and Andrews 1986b, pp. 347–377.
1988   Caches and Censerwares: Meaning from Maya Pottery. In *A Pot for All Reason: Ceramic Ecology Revisited,* ed. C. Kolb and L. Lackey, pp. 81–104. Laboratory of Anthropology, Temple University, Philadelphia.
1990   The Invisible Maya: Population History and Archaeology at Santa Rita Corozal, Belize. In Culbert and Rice 1990, pp. 199–213.
1992   Postclassic Maya Elites: Ethnohistory and Archaeology. In D. Z. Chase and A. F. Chase 1992b, pp. 118–134.
1994   Human Osteology, Pathology, and Demography as Represented in the Burials of Caracol, Belize. In D. Z. Chase and A. F. Chase, pp. 123–138.

Chase, Diane Z., and Arlen F. Chase
1982   Yucatec Influence in Terminal Classic Northern Belize. *AAnt* 47(3): 596–613.
1988   *A Postclassic Perspective: Excavations at the Maya Site of Santa Rita Corozal, Belize.* Monograph 4, PARI.
1989   Routes of Trade and Communication and the Integration of Maya Society: The Vista from Santa Rita Corozal. In McKillop and Healy 1989, pp. 19–32.
1992a   Die Maya der Postclassic. In *Die Welt der Maya,* ed. Nikolai Grube, pp. 257–277. Verlag Philipp von Zabern, Mainz am Rhein, Germany.
1992b   Mesoamerican Elites: An Archaeological Assessment. University of Oklahoma Press, Norman.
1994   (eds.) *Studies in the Archaeology of Caracol, Belize.* Monograph 7, PARI.
1996   Maya Multiples: Individuals, Entries, and Tombs in Structure A34 of Caracol, Belize. *LAA* 7(1): 61–79.
1998   The Architectural Context of Caches, Burials, and Other Ritual Activities for the Classic Period Maya (as Reflected at Caracol, Belize). In Houston 1998, pp. 299–332.
2000   Inferences about Abandonment: Maya Household Archaeology and Caracol, Belize. *Mayab* 13: 67–77.

2002   Classic Maya Warfare and Settlement Archaeology at Caracol, Belize. *ECM* 22: 33–51.
n.d.   Contextualizing the Collapse: Terminal Classic Ceramics from Caracol, Belize. Paper presented at 65th Annual Meeting of the SAA, Philadelphia.

Chase, Diane Z., Arlen F. Chase, Christine D. White, and Wendy Teeter
n.d.   Human Skeletal Remains in Archaeological Context: Status, Diet, and Household at Caracol, Belize. Paper presented at 14th International Congress of Anthropological and Ethnological Sciences, Williamsburg, VA.

Chase, Sabrina M.
1992   South Group Plaza 1 and Nabitunich Plaza Group. In Leventhal 1992, pp. 35–55.
1993   Excavations at the San Lorenzo Group: The 1993 Testing Program and Plaza Group I. In Leventhal 1993, pp. 128–147.

Chepstow-Lusty, A. J., K. D. Bennett, V. R. Switsur, and A. Kendall
1996   4000 Years of Human Impact and Vegetation Change in the Central Peruvian Andes— with Events Paralleling the Mayas? *Antiquity* 70: 824–833.

Cherry, John F.
1987   Power in Space: Archaeological and Geographical Studies of the State. In *Landscape and Culture: Geographical and Archaeological Perspectives,* ed. J. M. Wagstaff, pp. 146–172. Basil Blackwell, Oxford, England.

Chinchilla Mazariegos, Oswaldo
1990   Operación DP14: investigaciones en el Grupo N5–6. In Demarest and Houston 1990, pp. 120–145.
1993   Mapeo en grupos habitacionales de Tamarindito. In Valdés et al. 1993, pp. 111–115.

Chocón, Jorge E., Heidy Quezada, and Héctor E. Mejía
1999   Acrópolis de El Chilonche: resultados de los sondeos y excavaciones. In *XII Simposio, 1998,* pp. 301–326.

Christaller, Walter
1972   How I Discovered the Theory of Central Places: A Report about the Origin of Central Places. In *Man, Space, and Environment,* ed. P. W. English and R. C. Mayfield, pp. 601–610. Oxford University Press, New York.

Ciudad Ruíz, Andrés, Yolanda Fernández Marquínez, José Miguel García Campillo, María Josefa Iglesias Ponce de León, Alfonso Lacadena García-Gallo, and Luis T. Sanz Castro (eds.)
1998   *Anatomía de una civilización: aproximaciones interdisciplinarias a la cultura maya.* Sociedad Española de Estudios Mayas, Madrid.

Clark, John E.
1991   Modern Lacandon Lithic Technology and Blade Workshops. In Hester and Shafer 1991b, pp. 251–265.

Clark, John E., and Dennis Gosser
1995   Reinventing America's First Pottery. In *The Emergence of Pottery: Technology and Innovation in Ancient Societies,* ed. W. K. Barnett and J. W. Hoopes, pp. 209–222. Smithsonian Institution Press, Washington, DC.

Clarke, David L.
1968   *Analytical Archaeology.* Methuen, London.

Cobos Palma, Rafael
1989   Shelling In: Marine Mollusca at Chichen Itza. In McKillop and Healy 1989, pp. 49–58.
1994   Preliminary Report on the Archaeological Mollusca and Shell Ornaments of Caracol, Belize. In D. Z. Chase and A. F. Chase 1994, pp. 139–147.
1995   *Katun and Ahau: Dating the End of Chichen Itza.* Unpublished manuscript on file, MARI.

1996   Shells from the Sea at Inland Maya Sites: A View from the Lowlands during the Late and Terminal Classic Periods. Paper presented at the 61st Annual Meeting of the SAA, New Orleans.

1998a   Chichén Itzá: análisis de una comunidad del período clásico terminal. *LICM* 6(2): 316–331.

1998b   Chichén Itzá y el clásico terminal en las tierras bajas mayas. In *XI Simposio, 1997*, vol. 2, pp. 791–799.

1999a   Fuentes históricas y arqueología: convergencias y divergencias en la reconstrucción del período clásico terminal de Chichén Itzá. *Mayab* 12: 58–70.

1999b   Chichén Itzá: nuevas perspectivas sobre el patrón de asentamiento de una comunidad maya. In *Trabajos de investigación arqueológica en Puerto Rico,* pp. 57–66. San Juan, Puerto Rico.

Coe, Michael D.

1978   *Lords of the Underworld: Masterpieces of Classic Maya Ceramics.* Princeton University Press, Princeton, NJ.

1993   *The Maya,* fifth ed. Thames and Hudson, New York.

Coe, William R.

1959   *Piedras Negras Archaeology: Artifacts, Caches and Burials.* Monograph 18, UM.

1965a   Tikal, Guatemala and Emergent Maya Civilization. *Science* 147: 1401–1419.

1965b   Tikal: Ten Years of Study of a Maya Ruin in the Lowlands of Guatemala. *Expedition* 8: 5–56.

1967   *Tikal: A Handbook of the Ancient Maya Ruins.* UM.

1975   *Tikal: guía de las antiguas ruinas.* Editorial Piedra Santa, Guatemala.

1990   *Excavations in the Great Plaza, North Terrace and North Acropolis of Tikal (Group 5D-2).* Tikal Report no. 14. UM.

Coggins, Clemency

1975   *Painting and Drawing Styles at Tikal: An Historical and Iconographic Reconstruction.* Ph.D. dissertation, Harvard University. Cambridge, MA.

1983   *The Stucco Decoration and Architectural Assemblage of Structure 1-sub, Dzibilchaltun, Yucatan, Mexico.* Pub. 40. MARI.

Coggins, Clemency C., and Orrin C. Shane

1984   *Cenote of Sacrifice: Maya Treasures from the Sacred Well at Chichen Itza.* University of Texas Press, Austin.

Cohen, Abner

1974   *Two-Dimensional Man: An Essay on the Anthropology of Power and Symbolism in Complex Society.* University of California Press, Berkeley.

Cohen, Anthony P.

1985   *The Symbolic Construction of Community.* Routledge, London.

Cohen, Mark, N., Kathleen O'Connor, Marie E. Danforth, Keith P. Jacobi, and Carl Armstrong

1997   Archaeology and Osteology of the Tipu Site. In *Bones of the Maya: Studies of Ancient Skeletons,* ed. S. L. Whittington and D. M. Reed, pp. 78–86. Smithsonian Institution Press, Washington, DC.

Cohen, Roberta, and Francis M. Deng

1998   *Masses in Flight: The Global Crisis of Internal Displacement.* Brookings Institution Press, Washington, DC.

Cohodas, Marvin

1985   Public Architecture of the Maya Lowlands. *Cuadernos de Arquitectura Mesoamericana* 6: 51–58. Facultad de Arquitectura, UNAM, México.

Cole, Monica M.
  1986   *The Savannas: Biogeography and Geobotany.* Academic Press, London.
Connell, Samuel V.
  1993   Chaa Creek: Reconnaissance. In Leventhal 1993, pp. 202–218.
  1995   Research at Chaa Creek in 1995: Developing Social Complexity in the Xunantunich Hinterlands. In Leventhal and Ashmore 1995, pp. 193–213.
  1997   1997 Research at Chaa Creek. In Leventhal 1997, pp. 116–146.
  1998   Merging the Variability Among Maya Minor Centers: Research at Chaa Creek, Belize. Paper presented at the 63rd Annual Meeting of the SAA, Seattle.
Cook, Patricia
  1996   Postclassic Ritual Among the Maya: A New Perspective from Chau Hiix, Belize. Paper presented at the 61st Annual Meeting of the SAA, New Orleans.
Cook, Patricia, and K. Anne Pyburn
  1995   Postclassic Occupation at Chau Hiix. Paper presented at the 60th Annual Meeting of the SAA, Minneapolis, MN.
Corzo, Lilian A., Marco Tulio Alvarado, and Juan Pedro Laporte
  1998   Ucanal: un sitio asociado a la cuenca media del río Mopan. In *XI Simposio 1997*, pp. 191–214.
Cojtí Cuxil, Demetrio
  1994   Políticas para la revindicación de los maya de hoy. Cholsamaj, Guatemala City.
Cowgill, George L.
  1975a   On Causes and Consequences of Ancient and Modern Population Changes. *AA* 77: 505–525.
  1975b   Population Pressure as a Non-Explanation. In *Population Studies in Archaeology and Biological Anthropology: A Symposium,* ed. A. C. Swedlund, pp. 127–131. SAA Memoirs, no. 30.
  1979   Teotihuacan, Internal Militarism and the Fall of the Classic Maya. In Hammond and Willey 1979, pp. 51–62.
  1988   Onward and Upward with Collapse. In Yoffee and Cowgill 1988, pp. 244–276.
Cowgill, George L., and Keith W. Kintigh
  1997   How Random Errors in Dates Increase Apparent Lengths of Intervals. Paper presented at the 62nd Annual Meeting of the SAA, Nashville, TN.
Cowgill, George L., and Norman Yoffee
  1988   Preface. In Yoffee and Cowgill 1988, pp. vii–x.
Coyoc Ramírez, Mario
  1985   El entierro de la tumba 1 de la estructura VII de Calakmul, Campeche, México. *Información* 9: 99–132. UACM.
  1989a   Los entierros en Calakmul, Campeche. Paper presented at the Primer Congreso Internacional de Mayistas, San Cristóbal de las Casas, México.
  1989b   *Reporte preliminar de las excavaciones de las estructuras 2, 3 y 7 de Calakmul. Temporada 1988–1989.* Centro de Investigaciones Históricas y Sociales, UACM.
Crane, Cathy J.
  1996   Archaeobotanical and Palynological Research at a Late Preclassic Community, Cerros, Belize. In Fedick 1996b, pp. 262–277.
Culbert, T. Patrick
  1973a   (ed.) *The Classic Maya Collapse.* SAR and University of New Mexico Press, Albuquerque.
  1973b   Introduction. In Culbert 1973a, pp. 3–19.
  1973c   The Maya Downfall at Tikal. In Culbert 1973a, pp. 63–92.
  1973d   Preface. In Culbert 1973a, pp. xiii–xiv.

1977   Maya Development and Collapse: An Economic Perspective. In Hammond 1977, pp. 509–530.

1988   The Collapse of Classic Maya Civilization. In Yoffee and Cowgill 1988, pp. 69–101.

1991   (ed.) *Classic Maya Political History: Hieroglyphic and Archaeological Evidence.* SAR. Cambridge University Press, Cambridge.

1992   La escala de las entidades políticas Mayas. In *V Simposio, 1991,* pp. 261–267.

1993a   *The Ceramics of Tikal: Vessels from the Burials, Caches and Problematical Deposits.* Tikal Report no. 25, Part A. Monograph 81. UM.

1993b   *Maya Civilization.* St. Remy Press and Smithsonian Institution, Washington, DC.

1997   *Eznab Complex Shapes: Chronological Shapes.* Unpublished manuscript

n.d.   Unpublished ceramic descriptions of Tikal types and complexes.

Culbert, T. Patrick, Laura J. Kosakowsky, Robert E. Fry, and William A. Haviland
1990   The Population of Tikal, Guatemala. In Culbert and Rice 1990, pp. 103–121.

Culbert, T. Patrick, and Don S. Rice (eds.)
1990   *Precolumbian Population History in the Maya Lowlands.* University of New Mexico Press, Albuquerque.

Curtis, Jason H., David A. Hodell, and Mark Brenner
1996   Climate Variability on the Yucatan Peninsula (Mexico) during the last 3,500 Years and Implications for Maya Cultural Evolution. *Quaternary Research* 46: 37–47.

Dahlin, Bruce H.
1976   An Anthropologist Looks at the Pyramids: A Late Classic Revitalization Movement at Tikal, Guatemala. Ph.D. dissertation, Temple University, Philadelphia.

1983   Climate and Prehistory on the Yucatan Peninsula. *Climatic Change* 5: 245–263.

1986   Los rostros del tiempo: un movimiento revitalizador en Tikal durante el período clásico tardío. *Mesoamérica* 7 (11): 79–112. Centro de Investigaciones Regionales de Mesoamérica, Antigua, Guatemala.

2000   The Barricade and Abandonment of Chunchucmil: Implications for Northern Maya Warfare. *LAA* 11(3): 283–298.

2002   Climate Change and the End of the Classic Period in Yucatan: Resolving a Paradox. *AM* 13(2): 327–340.

D'Altroy, Terence N., and Timothy K. Earle
1985   Staple Finance, Wealth Finance, and Storage in the Inka Political Economy, *CA* 26: 187–206.

Dark, Ken R.
1995   *Theoretical Archaeology.* Cornell University Press, Ithaca, NY.

de la Garza, Mercedes, Ana Luisa Izquierdo, María del Carmen León, and Tolito Fugueroa (eds.)
1983   *Relaciones histórico-geográficas de la gobernación de Yucatán: Mérida, Valladolid y Tabasco,* 2 vols. Instituto de Investigaciones Filológicas, Centro de Estudios Mayas. UNAM.

de Montmollin, Olivier
1989   *The Archaeology of Political Structure: Settlement Analysis in a Classic Maya Polity.* Cambridge University Press, Cambridge.

1995   *Settlement and Politics in Three Classic Maya Polities.* Monographs in World Archaeology no. 24. Prehistory Press, Madison, WI.

Deal, Michael
1988   Recognition of Ritual Pottery in Residential Units: An Ethnoarchaeological Model of the Maya Family Altar Tradition. In *Ethnoarchaeology Among the Maya Highlands of Chiapas, Mexico,* ed. T. A. Lee Jr. and B. Hayden, pp. 61–89. Papers of the NWAF no. 56.

Deevey, Edward S., Jr.
1978   Holocene Forests and Maya Disturbance near Quexil Lake, Peten, Guatemala. *Polskie Archiwum Hydrobiologii* 25: 117–129.

Deevey, E. S., Don S. Rice, Prudence M. Rice, H. H. Vaughan, Mark Brenner, and M. S. Flannery
1979   Mayan Urbanism: Impact on a Tropical Karst Environment. *Science* 206: 298–306.

del Mar de Pablo Aguilera, María
1991   El arte de la piedra, evolución y expresión. In *Oxkintok, una ciudad maya de Yucatán*, ed. M. Rivera Dorado, pp. 79–106. Misión Arqueológica de España en México. Madrid.

Demarest, Arthur A.
1989   Conclusiones. In Demarest and Houston 1989, pp. 225–233.
1990   Resumen de los resultados de la segunda temporada. In Demarest and Houston 1990, pp. 607–626.
1991   Conclusiones: Dos Pilas, la arqueología de una capital maya. In Demarest, Inomata, Escobedo, and Palka 1991, pp. 391–392.
1992   Ideology in Ancient Maya Cultural Evolution: The Dynamics of Galactic Polities. In *Ideology and Pre-Columbian Civilization*, ed. A. A. Demarest and G. W. Conrad, pp. 135–157. SAR.
1993   The Violent Saga of a Maya Kingdom. *National Geographic* 183(2): 94–111.
1996   War, Peace, and the Collapse of a Native American Civilization. In *A Natural History of Peace*, ed. T. Gregor, pp. 215–248. Vanderbilt University Press, Nashville, TN.
1997   The Vanderbilt Petexbatun Regional Archaeological Project 1989–1994: Overview, History, and Major Results of a Multidisciplinary Study of the Classic Maya Collapse. *AM* 8: 209–227.
2001   Nuevas evidencias y problemas teóricos en las investigaciones e interpretaciones sobre los orígines de las sociedades complejas en Guatemala. In *XIV Simposio, 2000*, pp. 445–460.
2004   *The Petexbatun Regional Archaeological Project: A Multidisciplinary Study of the Collapse of a Classic Maya Kingdom.* Vanderbilt University Press, Nashville, TN.

Demarest, Arthur A., and Tomás Barrientos Q. (eds.)
1999   *Proyecto Arqueológico Cancuen, informe preliminar no. 1, temporada 1999.* IDAEH and Department of Anthropology, Vanderbilt University, Nashville, TN.
2000   *Proyecto Arqueológico Cancuen, informe preliminar no. 2, temporada 2000.* IDAEH and Department of Anthropology, Vanderbilt University, Nashville, TN.
2001   *Proyecto Arqueológico Cancuen, informe preliminar no. 3, temporada 2001.* IDAEH and Department of Anthropology, Vanderbilt University, Nashville, TN.
2002   *Proyecto Arqueológico Cancuen, informe preliminar no. 4, temporada 2002.* IDAEH and Department of Anthropology, Vanderbilt University, Nashville, TN.

Demarest, Arthur, and Héctor Escobedo
1997   El Proyecto Arqueológico Punta de Chimino: objetivos, descubrimientos e interpretaciones preliminarias de la temporada de campo 1996. In *X Simposio, 1996*, pp. 381–384.
1998   Acontecimientos, procesos y movimientos de poblaciones en el clásico terminal y el colapso maya. In *XI Simposio, 1997*, pp. 699–712.

Demarest, Arthur A., Héctor Escobedo, and Matt E. O'Mansky (eds.)
1996   *Proyecto Arqueológico Punta de Chimino 1996, informe preliminar.* IDAEH and Department of Anthropology, Vanderbilt University, Nashville, TN.

Demarest, Arthur, and Federico Fahsen
2003   Nuevos datos e interpretaciones de los reinos occidentales del clásico tardío: hacía una visión sintética de la historia Pasión/Usumacinta. In *XVI Simposio, 2002*.

Demarest, Arthur A., and Stephen D. Houston (eds.)
   1989   *Proyecto Arqueológico Regional Petexbatún, informe preliminar no. 1, primera temporada 1989.* IDEAH and Vanderbilt University, Nashville, TN.
   1990   *Proyecto Arqueológico Regional Petexbatún. informe preliminar no. 2, segunda temporada 1990.* IDAEH and Vanderbilt University, Nashville, TN.

Demarest, Arthur A., Takeshi Inomata, and Héctor Escobedo (eds.)
   1992   *Proyecto Arqueológico Regional Petexbatún, informe preliminar no. 4, cuarta temporada 1992.* IDAEH and Vanderbilt University, Nashville, TN.

Demarest, Arthur A., Takeshi Inomata, Héctor Escobedo, and Joel Palka (eds.)
   1991   *Proyecto Arqueológico Regional Petexbatún, informe preliminar no. 3, tercera temporada 1991.* IDAEH and Vanderbilt University, Nashville, TN.

Demarest, Arthur, Nora María López, Robert Chatham, Kitty Emery, Joel Palka, Kim Morgan, and Héctor Escobedo
   1991   Operación DP28: Excavaciones en las murallas defensivas de Dos Pilas. In Demarest, Inomata, Escobedo, and Palka, pp. 208–241.

Demarest, Arthur A., Matt O'Mansky, Nicholas Dunning, and Timothy Beach
   2003   Catastrofismo, Procesos Ecologicos, ó Crisis Política: Hacia Una Metodología Mejor Para Interpretación de "Colapso" de la Civilización Clásica Maya. In *XVII Simposio de Investigaciones Arqueológicas en Guatemala,* ed. J. P. Laporte, B. Arroyo, H. Escobedo, y H. Mejia. Museo Nacional de Arqueología e Etnología, Guatemala.

Demarest, Arthur A., Matt O'Mansky, Q. Joshua Hinson, José S. Suasnávar, and Coral Rasmussen
   1995   Investigaciones en el Cerro de Mariposa y el Cerro de Cheyo. In Demarest, Valdés, and Escobedo 1995, pp. 473–489.

Demarest, Arthur A., Matt O'Mansky, Claudia Wolley, Dirk Van Tuerenhout, Takeshi Inomata, Joel Palka, and Héctor Escobedo
   1997   Classic Maya Defensive Systems and Warfare in the Petexbatun Region. *AM* 8(2): 229–253.

Demarest, Arthur A., José S. Suasnávar, Claudia Wolley, Matt O'Mansky, Joshua Hinson, Erin Sears, and Coral Rasmussen
   1995   Reconocimientos en sistemas defensivos de Petexbatun: la evidencia material de la guerra. In *VIII Simposio, 1994,* pp. 517–521.

Demarest, Arthur A., and Juan Antonio Valdés
   1995   Guerra, regresión política y el colapso de la civilización maya en la región de Petexbatun. In *VIII Simposio, 1994,* pp. 777–782.
   1996   Nuevos análisis e interpretaciones del colapso de la civilización maya en la región de Petexbatun. In *IX Simposio, 1995,* pp. 207–212.

Demarest, Arthur A., Juan Antonio Valdés, and Héctor Escobedo
   1995   *Proyecto Arqueológico Regional Petexbatún, informe preliminar no. 6, sexta temporada 1994.* IDAEH and Vanderbilt University, Nashville, TN.

Demarest, Arthur, Juan Antonio Valdés, Takeshi Inomata, Joel Palka, Héctor Escobedo, Stephen D. Houston, James Brady, Nicholas Dunning, Thomas Killion, Antonia Foias, Chris Beekman, Oswaldo Chinchilla, Robert Chatham, Inez Verhagen, Laura Stiver, and Kim Morgan
   1991   Conclusiones generales e interpretaciones de la temporada de campo de 1991 del Proyecto Arqueológico Regional Petexbatún: resumen y revisión general. In Demarest, Inomata, Escobedo, and Palka 1991, pp. 896–924.

DeMarrais, Elizabeth, Luis Jaime Castillo, and Timothy Earle
   1996   Ideology, Materialization, and Power Strategies. *CA* 37: 15–31.

Díaz Samayoa, Carolina, and Juan Antonio Valdés
    2000   Estructura M8-37. In *Informe final del Proyecto de Restauración Aguateca, enero–mayo 2000*, ed. J. A. Valdés, M. Urquizú, C. Díaz Samayoa, and H. Martínez, Programa de Desarrollo Sostenible de Petén BID-IDAEH, pp. 107–130. Report presented to IDAEH.

Diehl, Richard A., and Janet Catherine Berlo (eds.)
    1989   *Mesoamerica after the Decline of Teotihuacan, A.D. 700–900*. DO.

Digrius, Dawn Mooney, and Marilyn A. Masson
    2001   Further Investigations at Structure 1 (Subop 6), Caye Coco. In Rosenswig and Masson 2001, pp. 5–26.

Dillon, Brian D.
    1982   Bound Prisoners in Maya Art. *Journal of New World Archaeology* 5(1): 24–45.

Domínguez Carrasco, María del Rosario
    1992a   Exploraciones en el bajo El Laberinto de Calakmul, Campeche. Paper presented at the Segundo Congreso Internacional de Mayistas, Mérida, México.
    1992b   *El recinto superior del edificio VII de Calakmul, Campeche: una interpretación diacrónica de su desarollo desde el punto de vista de la arquitectura y el material cerámico*. Tésis de licenciatura, Escuela Nacional de Antropología e Historia, México.
    1994a   *Calakmul, Campeche: un análisis de la cerámica*. UACM.
    1994b   Tipología cerámica de Calakmul, Campeche, México. *Mexicon* 16: 51–53.
    1994c   El uso y función de la estructura VII de Calakmul, Campeche. *LICM* 2:55–67.
    1996   La cerámica de Calakmul, Campeche: una visión de su secuencia cronológica y cultural. *LICM* 3(2):503–521.

Domínguez Carrasco, María del Rosario, and William J. Folan
    1996   Calakmul, México: aguadas, bajos, precipitación y asentamiento en el petén campechano. In *IX Simposio, 1995*, vol. I, pp. 171–193.

Domínguez Carrasco, María del Rosario, William J. Folan, and Joyce Marcus
    1997   Calakmul, Campeche, México: un análisis sociopolítico de su centro urbano y su estado regional. *LICM* 6(2). (in press).

Domínguez Carrasco, María del Rosario, and Miriam J. Gallegos Gómora
    1989–   Informe de trabajo del Proyecto Calakmul, Campeche, 1984. Estructura 7.
    1990   *Información* 14: 56–84. UACM.

Domínguez Carrasco, María del Rosario, Joel D. Gunn, and William J. Folan
    1996   Calakmul, Campeche: sus áreas de actividades ceremoniales, cívicas y domésticas derivadas de sus materiales líticos y cerámicos. *LICM* 4:80–106.
    1998a   Calakmul, Campeche: sus áreas de actividades ceremoniales, cívicas y domésticas observadas en un análisis de sus artefactos de piedra. *LICM* 5(2):526–540.
    1998b   La cerámica y lítica de Calakmul, Campeche, México: un análisis contextual de las Estructuras I, II, III y VII. In *XI Simposio, 1997*, pp. 605–622.

Doonan, William F.
    1996   *The Artifacts of Group 10L-2, Copán, Honduras: Variation in Material Culture and Behavior in a Royal Residential Compound*. Unpublished Ph.D. dissertation, Department of Anthropology, Tulane University, New Orleans.

Duch Gary, Jorge
    1988   *La conformación territorial del estado de Yucatán*. Universidad Autónoma Chapingo, México.

Duncan, William N.
    1999a   Postclassic Mortuary Practices in Civic/Ceremonial Contexts in Petén, Guatemala. Paper presented at the 64th Annual Meeting of the SAA, Chicago.

1999b   Mortuary Practice in Ritual Contexts among the Postclassic Maya, Petén, Guatemala. Paper presented at the 69th Annual Meeting of the American Association of Physical Anthropologists, Columbus, OH.

2001   Understanding Ritual Violence in the Archaeological Record: Behavior Versus Meaning. Paper presented at the 66th Annual Meeting of the SAA, New Orleans.

Dunham, Peter S.
1993   The Search for the Forest of Jade. In *Spirit of Enterprise: The 1993 Rolex Awards,* ed. D. Reed, pp. 169–171. Buri International, Bern.

1996   Resource Exploitation and Exchange among the Classic Maya: Some Initial Findings of the Maya Mountains Archaeological Project. In Fedick 1996b, pp. 315–334.

Dunham, Peter S., Thomas R. Jamison, and Richard M. Leventhal
1989   Secondary Development and Settlement Economics: The Classic Maya of Southern Belize. In *Prehistoric Maya Economies of Belize,* ed. P. A. McAnany and B. L. Isaac, pp. 255–292. Research in Economic Anthropology, Supplement 2, JAI Press, Greenwich, CT.

Dunham, Peter S., and Keith M. Prufer
1998   En la cumbre del clásico: descubrimientos recientes en las montañas mayas en el sur de Belice. In *XI Simposio, 1997,* pp. 165–170.

Dunning, Nicholas P.
1989   *Archaeological Investigations at Sayil, Yucatan, Mexico: Intersite Reconnaissance and Soil Studies during the 1987 Field Season.* Anthropological Papers vol. 2. University of Pittsburgh, Pittsburgh, PA.

1991   El uso prehispánico de la tierra y la historia cultural de la región del Río de la Pasión: una re-examinación. In Demarest, Inomata, Escobedo, and Palka 1991, pp. 887–895.

1992   *Lords of the Hills: Ancient Maya Settlement in the Puuc Region, Yucatan, Mexico.* Monographs in World Archaeology No. 15. Prehistory Press, Madison, WI.

1993   El análisis de fosfato de la tierra arqueológica y el patrón agrícola en la región de Petexbatún. In Valdés, Foias, Inomata, Escobedo, and Demarest 1993, pp. 165–169.

n.d.   *A lo largo de la Quijada de la Culebra: ambiente y asentamiento de Xkipché, Yucatán.* INAH. Instituto Nacional de Antropología e Historia, México, D.F.

Dunning, Nicholas P., and George F. Andrews
1994   Ancient Maya Architecture and Urbanism at Siho and the Western Puuc Region. *Mexicon* 16: 53–61.

Dunning, Nicholas P., and Timothy Beach
1994   Soil Erosion, Slope Management, and Ancient Terracing in the Maya Lowlands. *LAA* 5: 51–69.

2000   Stability and Instability in Pre-Hispanic Maya Landscapes. In *Imperfect Balance: Landscape and Transformations in the Pre-Columbian Americas,* ed. D. Lentz, pp. 179–202. Columbia University Press, New York.

2003   Noxious or Nurturing Nature? Maya Civilization in Environmental Contexts. In *Continuity and Change in Maya Archaeology,* ed. C. Golden and G. Borgstede. New York: Routledge Press.

2004   *Ecology and Agriculture of the Petexbatun Region: An Ancient Perspective on Rainforest Adaptation.* Vanderbilt University Press, Nashville, TN.

Dunning, Nicholas P., Timothy Beach, Pat Farrell, and Sheryl Luzzadder-Beach
1998   Prehispanic Agrosystems and Adaptive Regions in the Maya Lowlands. *Culture and Agriculture* 20: 87–101.

Dunning, Nicholas, Timothy Beach, and David Rue
1995   Investigaciones paleoecológicas y los antiguos sistemas agrícolas de la región de Petexbatun. In Demarest, Valdés, and Escobedo 1995, pp. 505–521.

1997   The Paleoecology and Ancient Settlement of the Petexbatún Region, Guatemala. *AM* 8: 255–266.

Dunning, Nicholas, Timothy Beach, David Rue, and E. Secaira
1991   Ecology and Settlement in the Petexbatun Region. Paper presented at the 47th International Congress of Americanists, New Orleans.

Dunning, Nicholas P., and Jeff K. Kowalski
1994   Lords of the Hills: Classic Maya Settlement Patterns and Political Iconography in the Puuc Region, Mexico. *AM* 5: 63–95.

Dunning, Nicholas P., Leonel Paiz, Timothy Beach, and James Nicholas
1993   Investigación de terrazas agrícolas en Petexbatún: temporada 1993. In Valdés, Foias, Inomata, Escobedo, and Demarest 1993, pp. 171–181.

Dunning, Nicholas P., David J. Rue, Timothy Beach, Alan Covich, and Alfred Traverse
1998   Human-Environment Interactions in a Tropical Watershed: The Paleoecology of Laguna Tamarindito, El Petén, Guatemala. *JFA* 25: 139–151.

Dutton, Bertha P., and H. R. Hobbs
1943   *Excavations at Tajumulco, Guatemala.* Monographs of the SAR, no. 9.

Earle, Timothy K.
1989   The Evolution of Chiefdoms. *CA* 30: 84–88.
1997   *How Chiefs Come to Power: The Political Economy in Prehistory.* Stanford University Press, Stanford, CA.

Eaton, Jack D.
1980   Operation 2011: Investigations within the Main Plaza of the Monumental Center at Colha. In *The Colha Project: Second Season, 1980 Interim Report,* ed. T. R. Hester, J. D. Eaton, and H. J. Shafer, pp. 145–162. Center for Archaeological Research, The University of Texas at San Antonio.

Edmonson, Munro S.
1979   Some Postclassic Questions about the Classic Maya. *ECM* 12: 157–178.
1982   *The Ancient Future of the Itzá: The Book of Chilam Balam of Tizimin.* University of Texas Press, Austin.
1986   *Heaven Born Merida and its Destiny: The Book of Chilam Balam of Chumayel.* University of Texas Press, Austin.
1988   *The Book of the Year: Middle American Calendrical Systems.* University of Utah Press, Salt Lake City.

Ehret, Jennifer
1995   The Xunantunich Settlement Survey Test Pitting Project. In Leventhal and Ashmore 1995, pp. 164–192.
1998   Lineage, Land, and Loyalty: Implications of Ancient Maya Settlement Complexity in the Rural Hinterlands of Xunantunich, Belize. Paper presented at the 63rd Annual Meeting of the SAA, Seattle.
n.d.   *Lineage, Land, and Loyalty: Implications of Ancient Maya Settlement Complexity in the Rural Hinterlands of Xunantunich, Belize.* Ph.D. dissertation, Department of Anthropology, University of Pennsylvania, Philadelphia, in preparation.

Eisenstadt, Shmuel N.
1967   *The Decline of Empires.* Prentice Hall, Englewood Cliffs, NJ.
1968   *The Political Systems of Empires: The Rise and Fall of the Historical Bureaucratic Societies.* Free Press, New York.
1986   (ed.) *The Origins and Diversity of Axial Age Civilizations.* State University of New York Press, Albany.

Emery, Kitty
1992   Manufactura y uso de artefactos de hueso de animales en la región Petexbatún. In Demarest, Inomata, and Escobedo 1992, pp. 301–309.
1995a   Manufactura de artefactos de hueso en la región Petexbatun: un taller de producción de herramientas de hueso del sitio Dos Pilas, Petén, Guatemala. In *VIII Simposio, 1994,* pp. 315–331.
1995b   Excavaciones en el taller de Dos Pilas (Grupo L4-3). In Demarest, Valdés, and Escobedo, pp. 268–280.
1995c   Operación TA 34: sondeos en el Grupo R6-1. In Demarest, Valdés, and Escobedo 1995, pp. 117–122.
1997   *The Maya Collapse: A Zooarchaeological Investigation.* Ph.D. dissertation, Department of Anthropology, Cornell University, Ithaca, NY.
2004   *Ancient Fauna, Bone Industries, and Subsistence History of the Petexbatun Region.* Vanderbilt University Press, Nashville, TN.

Emery, Kitty F., Lori E. Wright, and Henry Schwarcz
2000   Isotopic Analysis of Ancient Deer Bone: Biotic Stability in Collapse Period Maya Land-use. *JAS* 27(6): 537–550.

Erasmus, Charles J.
1963   Thoughts on Upward Collapse: An Essay on Explanation in Archaeology. *Southwestern Journal of Anthropology* 24(2): 170–194.

Escobedo, Héctor
1991   *Epigrafía e historia política de los sitios noroeste de las montañas mayas durante el clásico tardío.* Tesis de licenciatura, Escuela de Historia, USAC, Guatemala.
1993   Entidades políticas del noroeste de las montañas mayas durante el período clásico tardío. In *VI Simposio, 1992,* pp. 3–24.
1994a   *Apuntes sobre las inscripciones de El Chal.* Informe, Atlas Arqueológico de Guatemala. IDAEH.
1994b   Investigaciones arqueológicas y epigráficas en Arroyo de Piedra: un centro secundario en la región Petexbatun. In *VII Simposio, 1993,* pp. 429–437.
1996   Operaciones PC32, 26, y 25: rescate arqueológico en las estructuras 2, 76, y 7 de Punta de Chimino. In Demarest, Escobedo, and O'Mansky 1996, pp. 9–27.
1997   Arroyo de Piedra: Sociopolitical Dynamics of a Secondary Center in the Petexbatun Region. *AM* 8(2): 307–320.

Escobedo, Héctor, and Juan Pedro Laporte
1994   Monumentos tallados de Ixtonton. In *Atlas Arqueológico de Guatemala* 2: 171–180. IDAEH.

Escobedo, Héctor, Lori Wright, Oswaldo Chinchilla, Stacey Symonds, and María Teresa Robles
1990   Operación DP8: investigaciones en "El Duende." In Demarest and Houston 1990, pp. 277–333.

Fahsen, Federico
1992   A Toponym in Waxactun. *Texas Notes on Precolumbian Art, Writing and Culture* 35: 1–3, Austin, TX.

Farriss, Nancy M.
1984   *Maya Society Under Colonial Rule: The Collective Enterprise of Survival.* Princeton University Press, Princeton, NJ.

Fash, Barbara W.
1992   Late Classic Architectural Sculpture Themes in Copan. *AM* 3: 89–104.

Fash, Barbara W., and William L. Fash Jr.
1996   Maya Resurrection. *Natural History* 105(4): 24–31.

Fash, Barbara W., William L. Fash Jr., Sheree Lane, Rudy Larios, Linda Schele, Jeffrey Stomper, and
    David Stuart
    1992   Investigations of a Classic Maya Council House at Copán, Honduras. *JFA* 19: 419–
            442.

Fash, William L., Jr.
    1983a   *Maya State Formation: A Case Study and Its Implications*. Unpublished Ph.D. disser-
            tation, Department of Anthropology, Harvard University, Cambridge, MA.
    1983b   Reconocimiento y excavaciones en el valle. In Baudez 1983, vol. 1, pp. 229–469.
    1986   History and Characteristics of Settlement in the Copan Valley, and Some Compari-
            sons with Quirigua. In *The Southeast Maya Periphery*, ed. P. A. Urban and E. M.
            Schortman, pp. 71–93. University of Texas Press, Austin.
    1988   A New Look at Maya Statecraft from Copan, Honduras. *Antiquity* 62: 157–169.
    1991   *Scribes, Warriors and Kings: The City of Copan and the Ancient Maya*. Thames and
            Hudson, London.
    1998   Dynastic Architectural Programs. Intention and Design in Classic Maya Buildings at
            Copan and other Sites. In Houston 1998, pp. 223–270.

Fash, William L., Jr., and Barbara W. Fash
    1990   Scribes, Warriors, and Kings: Ancient Lives of the Copán Maya. *Archaeology* 43(3):
            26–35.
    1996   Building a World-View: Visual Communication in Classic Maya Architecture. *RES*, ed.
            Francesco Pelizzi, Spring/Autumn: 127–147. PMAE.

Fash, William L., Jr., and Sheree Lane
    1983   El Juego de Pelota B. In Baudez 1983, vol. 2, pp. 501–562.

Fash, William L., Jr., and Kurt Z. Long
    1983   El mapa arqueológico del valle de Copán. In Baudez 1993, vol. 3, pp. 5–48.

Fash, William L., Jr., and T. Kam Manahan
    1997   The Ejar Phase: Final Testimonies from Copán. Paper presented at the 62nd Annual
            Meeting of the SAA, Nashville, TN.

Fash, William L., and Robert J. Sharer
    1991   Sociopolitical Developments and Methodological Issues at Copan, Honduras: A Con-
            junctive Approach. *LAA* 2: 166–187.

Fash, William L., and David S. Stuart
    1991   Dynastic History and Cultural Evolution at Copan, Honduras. In Culbert 1991, pp.
            147–179.

Fedick, Scott L.
    1988   *Prehistoric Maya Settlement and Land Use Patterns in the Upper Belize River Area,
            Belize, Central America*. Unpublished Ph.D. dissertation, Arizona State University,
            Tempe.
    1989   The Economics of Agricultural Land Use and Settlement in the Upper Belize Valley.
            In *Research in Economic Anthropology*, Supplement 4, ed. P. A. McAnany and B. L.
            Isaac, pp. 215–253. JAI Press, Greenwich, CT.
    1991   Chert Tool Production and Consumption Among Classic Period Maya Households. In
            Hester and Shafer 1991a, pp. 103–118.
    1994   Ancient Maya Agricultural Terracing in the Upper Belize River Area: Computer-aided
            Modeling and the Results of Initial Field Investigations. *AM* 5: 107–127.
    1995   Land Evaluation and Ancient Maya Land Use in the Upper Belize River Area, Belize,
            Central America. *LAA* 6: 16–34.
    1996a   An Interpretive Kaleidoscope: Alternative Perspectives on Ancient Agricultural Land-
            scapes of the Maya Lowlands. In Fedick 1996b, pp. 107–131.

1996b   (ed.) *The Managed Mosaic: Ancient Maya Agriculture and Resource Use.* University of Utah Press, Salt Lake City.

Fedick, Scott L., and Anabel Ford
1990   The Prehistoric Agricultural Landscape of the Central Maya Lowlands: An Examination of Local Variability in a Regional Context. *World Archaeology* 22: 18–33.

Fedick, Scott, and Karl Taube
1992   The Role of Radiocarbon Dating in Maya Archaeology: Four Decades of Research. In *Radiocarbon After Four Decades: An Interdisciplinary Perspective,* ed. R. E. Taylor, A. Long, and R. S. Kra, pp. 403–420. Springer-Verlag, New York.

Feeley-Harnik, Gillian
1985   Issues in Divine Kingship. *Annual Review of Anthropology* 14: 272–313.

Fernández Souza, Lilia
1996   *Asociaciones arquitectónicas en Chichén Itzá: la Plaza del Osario.* Tesis de licenciatura, Facultad de Ciencias Antropológicas, UAYM.
1997   Un contexto funerario en la Plaza del Osario. *Temas Antropológicos* 21(2): 264–279. Facultad de Ciencias Antropológicas, UAYM.

Fialko, Vilma
1988   Mundo Perdido, Tikal: un ejemplo de Complejos de Conmemoración Astronómica. *Mayab* 4: 13–21.

Fialko, Vilma, William J. Folan, Joel D. Gunn, and María del Rosario Domínguez Carrasco
1998   Land Use in the Peten Region of Guatemala and Mexico. Paper presented at the 63rd Annual Meeting of the SAA, Seattle.

Fischer, Edward F.
1999   Cultural Logic and Maya Identity: Rethinking Constructivism and Essentialism. *CA* 40: 473–499.

Fischer, Edward F., and R. McKenna Brown (eds.)
1996   *Maya Cultural Activism in Guatemala.* University of Texas Press, Austin.

Flannery, Kent V.
1972   The Cultural Evolution of Civilizations. *Annual Review of Ecology and Systematics* 3: 399–426.
1976   Contextual Analysis of Ritual Paraphernalia from Formative Oaxaca. In *The Early Mesoamerican Village,* ed. K. V. Flannery, pp. 333–345. Academic Press, New York.
1982   (ed.) *Maya Subsistence: Studies in Memory of Dennis E. Puleston.* Academic Press, New York.

Fletcher, Laraine A., and James A. Gann
1992   Calakmul, Campeche: patron de asentamiento y demografía. *Antropológicas* IIA, nueva época 2: 20–25. UNAM.
1994   Análisis gráfico de patrones de asentamiento, el caso Calakmul. In *Campeche Maya Colonial,* coord. William J. Folan, pp. 84–121. Colección Arqueología 3. UACM.

Fletcher, Lariane A., Jacinto May Hau, and Lynda Florey Folan
1987   *Un análisis preliminar del patron de asentamiento de Calakmul, Campeche, México.* Centro de Investigaciones Históricas y Sociales, Universidad Autónoma Campeche.

Fletcher, Laraine A., William J. Folan, Jacinto May Hau, and Lynda Florey Folan
2001   *Las ruinas de Calakmul, Campeche, México: un lugar central y su paisaje cultural.* UACM.

Florey Folan, Lynda, and William J. Folan
1999   Estructura 2 de Calakmul, Campeche (octubre de 1988 a mayo de 1989). Plataforma F. *Información* 16: 15–21. UACM.

Foias, Antonia E.
1992   Análisis preliminar de la cerámica del Petexbatún. In Demarest, Inomata, and Escobedo 1992, pp. 250–285.
1993   Resultados preliminares del análisis cerámico del Proyecto Petexbatun. *Apuntes Arqueológicos* 3: 37–54.
1996   *Changing Ceramic Production and Exchange Systems and the Classic Maya Collapse in the Petexbatun Region.* Ph.D. dissertation, Vanderbilt University, Nashville, TN.
2004   *Ceramics, Trade, and Exchange System of the Petexbatun: The Economic Parameters of the Classic Maya Collapse.* Vanderbilt University Press, Nashville, TN.

Foias, Antonia E., and Ronald L. Bishop
1994   El colapso maya y las vajillas de pasta fina en la región de Petexbatún. In *VII Simposio, 1993*, pp. 563–586.
1997   Changing Ceramic Production and Exchange in the Petexbatun Region, Guatemala: Reconsidering the Classic Maya Collapse. *AM* 8: 275–291.

Folan, William J.
1981   Comment on "The Late Postclassic Eastern Frontier of Mesoamerica: Cultural Innovation along the Periphery," by John Fox. *CA* 22: 336–337.
1988   Calakmul, Campeche: el nacimiento de la tradición clásica en la gran mesoamérica. *Información* 13: 122–190. UACM.
1991   La península de Yucatán en vísperas de la conquista: un modelo diacrónico de desarrollo y decaimiento. *Gaceta Universitaria*, año VIII, no. 41–42: 25–38. UACM.

Folan, William J., Lynda M. Florey Folan, and Juan Pablo Cauich Mex
1989   Estructura II-B, Calakmul, Campeche: informe de la temporada 1988–1989. Centro de Investigaciones Históricas y Sociales, UACM.

Folan, William J., and Silverio Gallegos Osuna
1992   Uso prehispánico del suelo. In *Programa de manejo. reserva de la biosfera, Calakmul, Campeche,* ed. W. J. Folan, J. M. García Ortega, and M. C. Sánchez González. 4 vols. Centro de Investigaciones Históricas y Sociales, UACM.

Folan, William J., Joel D. Gunn, and María del Rosario Domínguez Carrasco
2001   Triadic Temples, Central Plazas and Dynastic Palaces: A Diachronic Analysis of the Royal Court Complex, Calakmul, Campeche, Mexico. In *Royal Courts of the Ancient Maya, vol. 2: Data and Case Studies,* ed. T. Inomata and S. D. Houston, pp. 223–265. Westview Press, Boulder, CO.

Folan, William J., Joel D. Gunn, Jack D. Eaton, and Robert W. Patch
1983   Paleoclimatological Patterning in Southern Mesoamerica. *JFA* 10: 453–468.

Folan, William J., Ellen R. Kintz, and Laraine A. Fletcher
1983   *Coba: A Classic Maya Metropolis.* Academic Press, New York.

Folan, William J., Joyce Marcus, and W. Frank Miller
1995   Verification of a Maya Settlement Model through Remote Sensing. *Cambridge Archaeological Journal* 5: 277–283.

Folan, William J., Joyce Marcus, Sophia Pincemin, María del Rosario Domínguez Carrasco, Laraine A. Fletcher, and Abel Morales López
1995   Calakmul: New Data from an Ancient Maya Capital in Campeche, Mexico. *LAA* 6: 310–334.

Ford, Anabel
1985   Maya Settlement Pattern Chronology in the Belize River Area and the Implications for the Development of the Central Maya Lowlands. *Belcast Journal of Belizean Affairs* 2(2): 13–32.

1986   *Population Growth and Social Complexity: An Examination of Settlement and Environment in the Central Maya Lowlands.* Anthropological Research Paper Number 35. Arizona State University, Tempe.

1990   Maya Settlement in the Belize River Area: Variations in Residence Patterns of the Central Maya Lowlands. In Culbert and Rice 1990, pp. 167–181.

1991   Economic Variation of Ancient Maya Residential Settlement in the Upper Belize River Area. *AM* 2: 35–46.

1996   Critical Resource Control and the Rise of the Classic Period Maya. In Fedick 1996b, pp. 297–303.

Ford, Anabel, and Scott L. Fedick
1992   Prehistoric Maya Settlement Patterns in the Upper Belize River Area: Initial Results of the Belize River Archaeological Settlement Survey. *JFA* 19: 35–49.

Ford, Derek C., and Paul W. Williams
1989   *Karst Geomorphology and Hydrology.* Unwin Hyman, London.

Forsyth, Donald W.
1980   Report on Some Ceramics from the Peten, Guatemala. In *El Mirador, Peten, Guatemala: An Interim Report,* ed. R. T. Matheny, pp. 59–82. Papers of the NWAF no. 45.

1983   *Investigations at Edzná, Campeche, Mexico. Volume 2: Ceramics.* Papers of the NWAF no. 46.

1989   *The Ceramics of El Mirador, Petén, Guatemala: El Mirador Series, Part 4.* Papers of the NWAF no. 63.

1997   Ceramic Continuity and Change During the Terminal Classic in the Southern Maya Lowlands. Paper presented at the 62nd Annual Meeting of the SAA, Nashville, TN.

1999   Cambios y continuidades durante el clásico terminal en las tierras bajas del sur. *LICM* 6: 64–80.

Forsyth, Donald W., Bruce Bachand, and Clint Helton
1998   Investigaciones preliminares en varios sitios entre Nakbe y Wakna, Petén, Guatemala. In *XI Simposio, 1997,* pp. 87–100.

Fortes, Meyer
1958   Introduction. In *The Developmental Cycle in Domestic Groups,* ed. J. Goody, pp. 1–14. Cambridge University Press, Cambridge.

Foster, George M.
1965   The Sociology of Pottery: Questions and Hypotheses Arising from Contemporary Mexican Work. In *Ceramics and Man,* ed. F. R. Matson, pp. 43–61. Aldine, Chicago.

Fowler, William R., Jr.
1981   *The Pipil-Nicarao of Central America.* Unpublished Ph.D. dissertation, Department of Anthropology, University of Calgary, Canada.

Fox, John W.
1980   Lowland to Highland Mexicanization Processes in Southern Mesoamerica. *AAnt* 45: 43–54.

1981   The Late Postclassic Eastern Frontier of Mesoamerica: Cultural Innovation along the Periphery. *CA* 22(4): 321–346.

1987   *Maya Postclassic State Formation: Segmentary Lineage Migration in Advancing Frontiers.* New Studies in Archaeology, C. Renfrew and J. A. Sabloff, series eds. Cambridge University Press, Cambridge.

1989   On the Rise and Fall of Tuláns and Maya Segmentary States. *AA* 91: 656–681.

Fox, Richard
1977   *Urban Anthropology.* Prentice-Hall, Englewood Cliffs, NJ.

Freidel, David A.
    1981a   Continuity and Disjunction: Late Postclassic Settlement Patterns in Northern Yucatan. In Ashmore 1981a, pp. 311–332.
    1981b   The Political Economics of Residential Dispersion Among the Lowland Maya. In Ashmore 1981a, pp. 371–382.
    1986a   *Archaeology at Cerros, Belize, Central America.* Southern Methodist University Press, Dallas.
    1986b   Maya Warfare: An Example of Peer Polity Interaction. In *Peer Polity Interaction and Socio-Political Change,* ed. C. Renfrew and J. F. Cherry, pp. 93–108. Cambridge University Press, Cambridge.
    1986c   The Monumental Architecture. In *Archaeology at Cerros, Belize, Central America, vol. 1,* series eds. R. A. Robertson and D. A. Freidel, pp. 1–22. Southern Methodist University Press, Dallas.
    1986d   Terminal Classic Lowland Maya: Successes, Failures, and Aftermaths. In Sabloff and Andrews 1986b, pp. 409–430.
    1987   *Yaxuna Archaeological Survey: A Report of the 1986 Field Season.* Southern Methodist University, Dallas.
    1990   The Jester God: Beginning and End of a Maya Royal Symbol. In *Vision and Revision in Maya Studies,* ed. F. Clancy and P. D. Harrison, pp. 67–78. University of New Mexico Press, Albuquerque.
    1992   Children of First Father's Skull: Terminal Classic Warfare in the Northern Maya Lowlands and the Transformation of Kingship and Elite Hierarchies. In D. Z. Chase and A. F. Chase 1992b, pp. 99–117.
    1998   Sacred Work: Dedication and Termination in Mesoamerica. In Mock 1998d, pp. 189–193.

Freidel, David A., and Maynard B. Cliff
    1978   Energy Investment in Late Postclassic Maya Masonry Religious Structures. In *Papers on the Economy and Architecture of the Ancient Maya,* ed. R. Sidrys, pp. 184–205. Monograph VIII, Institute of Archaeology, UCLA.

Freidel, David A., and Richard M. Leventhal
    1975   The Settlement Survey. In Sabloff and Rathje 1975b, pp. 60–76.

Freidel, David A., and Jeremy A. Sabloff
    1984   *Cozumel: Late Maya Settlement Patterns.* Academic Press, New York.

Freidel, David A., and Linda Schele
    1988   Kingship in the Late Preclassic Maya Lowlands: The Instruments and Places of Ritual Power. *AA* 90: 547–567.
    1989   Dead Kings and Living Temples: Dedication and Termination Rituals among the Ancient Maya. In *Word and Image in Maya Culture: Explorations in Language, Writing, and Representation,* ed. W. F. Hanks and D. S. Rice, pp. 233–243. University of Utah Press, Salt Lake City.

Freidel, David A., Linda Schele, and Joy Parker
    1993   *Maya Cosmos: Three Thousand Years on the Shaman's Path.* William Morrow, New York.

Freidel, David A., Charles K. Suhler, and Rafael Cobos
    1992   *The Selz Foundation Yaxuna Project, Final Report of the 1991 Field Season.* Department of Anthropology, Southern Methodist University, Dallas.
    1998   Termination Ritual Deposits at Yaxuna: Detecting the Historical in Archaeological Contexts. In Mock 1998d, pp. 135–144.

Freidel, David A., and Charles Suhler
    1998   Visiones serpentinas y laberintos mayas. *Arqueología Mexicana* 6(34): 28–37.

Freter, AnnCorinne
1988   *The Classic Maya Collapse at Copán, Honduras: A Regional Settlement Perspective.* Ph.D. dissertation, Pennsylvania State University. UMI.
1992   Chronological Research at Copan. *AM* 3: 117–133.
1994   The Classic Maya Collapse at Copan, Honduras: An Analysis of Maya Rural Settlement. In *Archaeological Views from the Countryside: Village Communities in Early Complex Societies,* ed. G. M. Schwartz and S. E. Falconer, pp. 160–176. Smithsonian Institution Press, Washington and London.
1996   Rural Utilitarian Ceramic Production in the Late Classic Period Copán Maya State. In *Arqueología Mesoamericana: Homenajae a William Sanders, vol. 2,* ed. A. G. Mastache, J. R. Parsons, R. S. Santley, and M. C. Sierra Puche, pp. 209–230. INAH.
1997   The Question of Time: The Impact of Chronology on Copan Prehistoric Settlement Demography. In *Integrating Archaeological Demography: Multidisciplinary Approaches to Prehistoric Population,* ed. R. Paine, pp. 21–42. Center for Archaeological Investigations, Southern Illinois University Press, Carbondale.

Fried, Morton H.
1967   *The Evolution of Political Society: An Essay in Political Economy.* Random House, New York.

Fry, Robert E.
1969   *Ceramics and Settlement in the Periphery of Tikal, Guatemala.* Unpublished Ph.D. dissertation, University of Arizona, Tucson.
1985   Revitalization Movements among the Postclassic Lowland Maya. In Chase and Rice 1985, pp. 126–142.
1990   Disjunctive Growth in the Maya Lowlands. In Culbert and Rice 1990, pp. 285–300.

Furley, Peter A.
1992   Edaphic Changes at the Forest-Savanna Boundary with Particular Reference to the Neotropics. In *Nature and Dynamics of Forest-Savanna Boundaries,* ed. P. Furley, J. Proctor, and J. Ratter, pp. 91–118. Chapman and Hill, London.

Gallareta N., Tomás
1984   *Coba: forma y función de una comunidad maya prehispánica.* Escuela de Ciencias Antropológicas, UAYM.
1990   Proyecto de reconocimiento de Ichmul de Morley y del área intermedia hacia Ek Balam, Yucatán, México. Manuscript on file, CRY/INAH, Mérida, México.

Gallareta N., Tomás, and Anthony P. Andrews
1988   El Proyecto Arqueológico Isla Cerritos, Yucatán, Mexico. In *Boletín de la Escuela de Ciencias Antropológicas de la Universidad de Yucatán,* año 15, no. 89, pp. 3–16.

Gallareta N., Tomás, Anthony P. Andrews, Fernando Robles, Rafael Cobos, and Pura Cervera
1989   Isla Cerritos: un puerto maya prehispánico de la costa norte de Yucatán, México. *II Coloquio Internacional de Mayistas,* tomo II: 311–332. UNAM.

Gallareta N., Tomás, Lourdes Toscano Hernández, Carlos Pérez Alvarez
1995   *Programa de investigación del Proyecto Labná: temporada de campo 1995.* Propuesta al Consejo de Arqueología del INAH, 1995.

Gallareta N., Tomás, Lourdes Toscano Hernández, Carlos Pérez Alvarez, Rossana May Ciau, David Salazar Aguilar
1994   *Restauración e investigaciones arqueológicas en Labná: la temporada de campo de 1994.* Reporte al Consejo de Arqueología del INAH, 1995.

Gallenkamp, Charles
1985   *Maya: The Riddle and Rediscovery of a Lost Civilization,* third ed. Viking Press, New York.

Gann, Thomas
1900   Mounds in Northern Honduras. In *Nineteenth Annual Report, 1897–1898, Bureau of American Ethnology, Part 2*, pp. 661–692. Smithsonian Institution, Washington, DC.

Garber, James F.
1986   The Artifacts. In *Archaeology at Cerros, Belize, Central America, Volume I*, ed. R. A. Robertson and D. A. Freidel, pp. 117–126. Southern Methodist University Press, Dallas.

1989   *The Artifacts: Archaeology at Cerros, Belize, Central America, Volume II*. Southern Methodist University Press, Dallas.

1994   Appendix A: Cosmology and Sacred Landscapes: Settlement Patterns in the Belize Valley. In *The Belize Valley Archaeological Project: Results of the 1993 Field Season*, by James F. Garber, David M. Glassman, W. David Driver, and Pamela Weiss, pp. 30–47. Report submitted to the BDOA.

Garber, James F., W. David Driver, Lauren A. Sullivan, and David M. Glassman
1998   Bloody Bowls and Broken Pots: The Life, Death, and Rebirth of a Maya House. In Mock 1998d, pp. 125–133.

García Campillo, José Miguel
1991   Edificios y dignitarios: la historia escrita de Oxkintok. In *Oxkintok, una ciudad maya de Yucatán*, ed. M. Rivera Dorado, pp. 55–78. Misión Arqueológica de España en México, Madrid.

1992   *El modelo de gravedad en arqueología especial: problemas y resultados de su aplicación al período clásico maya del norte de Yucatán*. Manuscript on file, Departamento de América, Universidad Complutense de Madrid, Madrid.

Garduño A., Jaime
1979   *Introducción al patrón de asentamiento del sitio de Cobá, Quintana Roo*. Escuela Nacional de Antropología e Historia, INAH.

Garza Tarazona, Silvia, and Edward B. Kurjack
1980   *Atlas arqueológico del estado de Yucatán*. INAH.

1992   *Palenque, Chiapas eterno*. Gobierno del Estado de Chiapas, México.

Gates, Gary, and William J. Folan
1993   The Hydrogeologic Setting of the Aguadas in the Calakmul Biosphere Reserve, Campeche, Mexico. Paper presented at the 13th International Congress of Anthropological and Ethnological Sciences, Mexico.

Geertz, Glifford
1980   *Negara: The Theatre State in Nineteenth-Century Bali*. Princeton University Press, Princeton, NJ.

Gerry, John P.
1993   *Diet and Status among the Classic Maya: An Isotopic Perspective*. Unpublished Ph.D. dissertation, Department of Anthropology, Harvard University, Cambridge, MA.

Gibson, Eric
1986   *Diachronic Patterns of Lithic Production, Use, and Exchange in the Southern Maya Lowlands*. Unpublished Ph.D. dissertation, Department of Anthropology, Harvard University, Cambridge, MA.

Giddens, Anthony
1979   *Central Problems in Social Theory: Action, Structure and Contradiction in Social Analysis*. University of California Press, Berkeley.

1984   *The Constitution of Society: Outline of a Theory of Structuration*. University of California Press, Berkeley.

1987   *Social Theory and a Modern Sociology*. Polity Press, Cambridge.

Giesey, Ralph E.
1985   Models of Rulership in French Royal Ceremonial. In *Rites of Power: Symbolism, Ritual, and Politics Since the Middle Ages,* ed. S. Wilentz, pp. 41–64. University of Pennsylvania Press, Philadelphia.

Gifford, James C.
1976   *Prehistoric Pottery Analysis and the Ceramics of Barton Ramie in the Belize Valley.* PMAE Memoirs, vol. 18.

Gill, Richardson B.
2000   *The Great Maya Droughts: Water, Life, and Death.* University of New Mexico Press, Albuquerque.

Gilman, Antonio
1981   The Development of Social Stratification in Bronze Age Europe. *CA* 22: 1–23.

Glassie, Henry
1975   *Folk Housing in Middle Virginia.* University of Tennessee Press, Knoxville.

Glazer, Nathan, and Daniel P. Moynihan
1975   Introduction. In *Ethnicity: Theory and Experience,* ed. N. Glazer and D. P. Moynihan, pp. 1–26. Harvard University Press, Cambridge, MA.

Gonlin, Nancy L.
1993   *Rural Household Archaeology at Copán, Honduras.* Ph.D. dissertation, Pennsylvania State University. UMI.
1994   Rural Household Diversity in Late Classic Copan, Honduras. In *Archaeological Views from the Countryside,* ed. G. M. Schwartz and S. E. Falconer, pp. 177–197. Smithsonian Institution Press, Washington and London.

González, Jason J.
1998   *Domestic Architecture of Terminal Classic Seibal: Maya Identities, Transformations, and Culture Change.* Unpublished master's thesis, Department of Anthropology, Southern Illinois University Carbondale.

Goody, Jack
1958   The Fission of Domestic Groups among the LoDagaba. In *The Developmental Cycle in Domestic Groups,* ed. J. Goody, pp. 53–91. Cambridge University Press, Cambridge, MA.

Gordon, George Byron
1896   *Prehistoric Ruins of Copan, Honduras. A Preliminary Report of the Explorations by the Museum, 1891–1895.* PMAE Memoirs, vol. 1, no. 1. Harvard University, Cambridge, MA.

Graff, Donald H.
1991   Investigación preliminar de los asentamientos rurales en la zona Puuc, Yucatán. *Boletín del Consejo de Arqueología (México) 1990*: 135–137.

Graham, Elizabeth A.
1985   Facets of Terminal to Postclassic Activity in the Stann Creek District, Belize. In Chase and Rice 1985, pp. 215–230.
1987a   Resource Diversity in Belize and Its Implications for Models of Lowland Trade. *AAnt* 52(4): 753–767.
1987b   Terminal Classic to Early Historic Period Vessel Forms from Belize. In *Maya Ceramics,* ed. P. M. Rice and R. J. Sharer, pp. 73–98. BAR International Series 345(i). Oxford.
1991   Archaeological Insights into Colonial Period Maya Life at Tipú, Belize. In *Columbian Consequences, vol. 3: The Spanish Borderlands in Pan-American Perspective,* ed. D. H. Thomas, pp. 319–335. Smithsonian Institution Press, Washington and London.
1998   Mission Archaeology. *Annual Review of Anthropology* 27: 25–62.

Graham, Elizabeth A., Grant D. Jones, and Robert R. Kautz
1985   Archaeology and Ethnohistory on a Spanish Colonial Frontier: An Interim Report on the Macal-Tipu Project in Western Belize. In Chase and Rice 1985, pp. 206–214.

Graham, Elizabeth A., Logan McNatt, and Mark Gutchen
1980   Excavations in Footprint Cave, Belize. *JFA* 7: 153–172.

Graham, Elizabeth A., and David M. Pendergast
1989   Excavations at the Marco Gonzalez Site, Ambergris Cay, Belize, 1986. *JFA* 16: 1–16.

Graham, Ian
1961   A Newly Discovered Maya Site. *Illustrated London News* 238 (6351): 665–667 (April 22).
1963   Across the Peten to the Ruins of Machaquila. *Expedition* 5(4): 2–10.
1967   *Archaeological Explorations in El Peten, Guatemala.* Pub. 33. MARI.
1980   *Corpus of Maya Hieroglyphic Inscriptions, vol. 2, pt. 3: Ixkun, Ucanal, Ixtutz, Naranjo.* PMAE.
1986   Looters Rob Graves and History. *National Geographic* 169 (4): 453–460.
1992   *Corpus of Maya Hieroglyphic Inscriptions, vol. 4, pt. 2: Uxmal.* PMAE.

Graham, Ian, and Eric von Euw
1997   *Corpus of Maya Hieroglyphic Inscriptions, vol. 8, pt. 1: Coba.* PMAE.

Graham, John A.
1971   Non-Classic Inscriptions and Sculptures at Seibal. *Contributions of the University of California Archaeological Research Facility* 13: 143–153. Berkeley, CA.
1973   Aspects of Non-Classic Presences in the Inscriptions and Sculptural Art of Seibal. In Culbert 1973a, pp. 207–219.
1977   Monumental Sculpture and Hieroglyphic Inscriptions. In *Excavations at Seibal,* ed. G. R. Willey. PMAE Memoirs, vol. 17, no. 1.
1990   *Excavations at Seibal: Monumental Sculpture and Hieroglyphic Inscriptions.* PMAE Memoirs, vol. 14, no. 1.

Grieder, Terrence
1960   Manifestaciones de arte maya en la region de Petexbatun. *Antropología e Historia de Guatemala* 12(2): 10–23.

Grube, Nikolai
1994a   Epigraphic Research at Caracol, Belize. In D. Z Chase and A. F. Chase 1994, pp. 83–122.
1994b   Hieroglyphic Sources for the History of Northwest Yucatan. In Prem 1994, pp. 316–358.
1994c   A Preliminary Report on the Monuments and Inscriptions of La Milpa, Orange Walk Belize. *Baessler Archive, neue folge, Band* XLII: 217–238.
1999   Epigraphic Details on Maya Warfare. Paper presented at the Primera Mesa Redonda de Palenque, México.
n.d.   Epigraphic Research at Caracol, Belize: An Update. In *Investigations at Caracol, Belize: 1988–1996,* ed. Arlen F. Chase and Diane Z. Chase. Monograph 8, PARI (in preparation).

Grube, Nikolai, and Norman Hammond
1998   Rediscovery of La Milpa Stela 4. *Mexicon* 20: 129–132.

Grube, Nikolai, and Linda Schele
1987   *U Cit Tok,* the Last King of Copán. *Copán Note 21.* Copán Mosaics Project and the Instituto Hondureño de Antropología e Historia, Copán, Honduras.
1995   *The Workbook for the XIXth Maya Hieroglyphic Workshop at Texas, with Commentaries on the Last Two Hundred Years of Maya History.* Department of Art, University of Texas, Austin.

Guderjan, Thomas H. (ed.)
1991   *Maya Settlement in Northwestern Belize. The 1988 and 1990 Seasons of the Río Bravo Archaeological Project*. Maya Research Program, San Antonio, TX, and Labyrinthos, Culver City, CA.

Guderjan, Thomas H., and James F. Garber
1995   *Maya Maritime Trade, Settlement, and Populations on Ambergris Caye, Belize*. Maya Research Program, San Antonio, TX, and Labyrinthos, Culver City, CA.

Guderjan, Thomas H., James F. Garber, and Herman A. Smith
1989   Marine Trade on Ambergis Key, Belize. In McKillop and Healy 1989, pp. 123–134.

Guderjan, Thomas H., Michael Lindeman, Ellen Ruble, Froyla Salam, and Jason Yaeger
1991   Archaeological Sites in the Rio Bravo Area. In Guderjan 1991, pp. 55–88.

Gunderson, Gerald
1976   Economic Change and the Demise of the Roman Empire. *Explorations in Economic History* 13: 43–68.

Gunn, Joel D., and William J. Folan
1981   Climatic Change, Culture, and Civilization in North America. *World Archaeology* 13: 87–100.
1996   Tres ríos: una superficie de impacto climatológico global interregional para las tierras bajas de los mayas del suroeste. *LICM* 4:57–79.

Gunn, Joel D., William J. Folan, and Hubert R. Robichaux
1994   Un análisis informatívo sobre la descarga del sistema del Río Candelaria en Campeche, México: reflexiones acerca de los paleoclímas que afectaron a los antiguos sistemas mayas en los sitios de Calakmul y El Mirador. In *Campeche maya colonial*, ed. W. J. Folan, pp. 174–197. UACM.
1995   A Landscape Analysis of the Candelaria Watershed in Mexico: Insights into Paleoclimates Affecting Upland Horticulture in the Southern Yucatan Peninsula Semi-Karst. *Geoarchaeology* 10: 3–42.

Haas, H., J. Devine, R. Wenke, M. Lehner, W. Wollfi, and G. Bonani
1987   Radiocarbon Chronology and the Historical Calendar in Egypt. In *Chronologies in the Near East*, ed. O. Aurenche, J. Evin, and P. Hours, pp. 585–606. BAR no. 379.

Hall, I.H.S., and J. H. Bateson
1972   Late Paleozoic Lavas in Maya Mountains, British Honduras, and Their Possible Regional Significance. *Bulletin of the American Association of Petroleum Geologists* 56(5): 950–956.

Hakovirta, Harto
1986   *Third World Conflicts and Refugeeism: Dimensions, Dynamics and Trends of the World Refugee Problem*. The Finnish Society of Sciences and Letters, Helsinki.

Hamblin, Robert L., and Brian L. Pitcher
1980   The Classic Maya Collapse: Testing Class Conflict Hypotheses. *AAnt* 45(2): 246–267.

Hammond, Norman
1974   (ed.) *Mesoamerican Archaeology: New Approaches*. University of Texas Press, Austin.
1975   *Lubaantun: A Classic Maya Realm*. PMAE Monographs, no. 2.
1976   Maya Obsidian Trade in Southern Belize. In *Maya Lithic Studies: Papers from the 1976 Belize Field Symposium*, ed. T. Hester and N. Hammond, pp. 71–81. Special Report no. 4. Center for Archaeological Research, University of Texas at San Antonio.
1977   (ed.) *Social Processes in Maya Prehistory: Essays in Honour of Sir J. Eric Thompson*. Academic Press, New York.

1980   Prehistoric Human Utilization of the Savanna Environments of Middle and South America. In *Human Ecology in Savanna Environments*, ed. D. R. Harris, pp. 73–106. Academic Press, London.

1981   Settlement Patterns in Belize. In Ashmore 1981a, pp. 157–186.

1982   *Ancient Maya Civilization.* Rutgers University Press, New Brunswick, NJ.

1983   Lords of the Jungle: A Prosopography of Maya Archaeology. In *Civilization in the Ancient Americas: Essays in Honor of Gordon R. Willey*, ed. R. M. Leventhal and A. L. Kolata, pp. 3–32. University of New Mexico Press, Albuquerque, and PMAE.

1985   The Emergence of Maya Civilization. *Scientific American* 255(2): 106–115.

1991a   (ed.) *Cuello: An Early Maya Community in Belize.* Cambridge University Press, Cambridge.

1991b   The Discovery of La Milpa. *Mexicon* 13: 46–51.

1991c   Inside the Black Box: Defining Maya Polity. In Culbert 1991, pp. 253–284.

1995   Ceremony and Society at Cuello: Preclassic Ritual Behavior and Social Differentiation. *The Emergence of Classic Maya Civilization,* ed. by Nikolai Grube, pp. 49–60. Acta Mesoamericana 8, Verlag von Flemming, Möckmühl, Bonn.

Hammond, Norman, and Matthew R. Bobo
1994   Pilgrimage's Last Mile: Late Maya Monument Veneration at La Milpa, Belize. *World Archaeology* 26: 19–34.

Hammond, Norman, Catherine Clark, Mark Horton, Anne Pyburn, Laura Kosakowsky, Jan Seymour, Gary Clayton, Tony Lacamera, Carl Beetz, and Diane Z. Chase
1985   Excavations in the East Group of the Nohmul Ceremonial Centre. In *Nohmul: A Prehistoric Community in Belize: Excavations 1973–1983,* ed. N. Hammond, pp. 567–761. BAR no. 250.

Hammond, Norman, Laura J. Kosakowsky, Anne Pyburn, John Rose, Justine C. Staneko, Sara Donaghey, Mark Horton, Catherine Clark, Colleen Gleason, Deborah Muyskens, and Thomas Addyman
1988   The Evolution of an Ancient Maya City: Nohmul. *National Geographic Research* 4: 474–495.

Hammond, Norman, Gair Tourtellot, Sara Donaghey, and Amanda Clarke
1996   Survey and Excavation at La Milpa, Belize, 1996. *Mexicon* 18: 86–91.

1998   No Slow Dusk: Maya Urban Development and Decline at La Milpa, Belize. *Antiquity* 72: 831–837.

Hammond, Norman, Gair Tourtellot, Gloria Everson, Kerry Lynn Sagebiel, Ben Thomas, and Marc Wolf
2000   Survey and Excavation at La Milpa, Belize, 1998. *Mexicon* 22(2): 38–45.

Hammond, Norman, and Gordon R. Willey (eds.)
1979   *Maya Archaeology and Ethnohistory.* University of Texas Press, Austin.

Hampton, Janie (ed.)
1998   *Internally Displaced People: A Global Survey.* Earthscan Publications, London.

Hanks, William F.
1990   *Referential Practice: Language and Lived Space among the Maya.* University of Chicago Press, Chicago.

Hansen, Richard
1990   *Excavations in the Tigre Complex, El Mirador, Peten, Guatemala.* El Mirador Series, Part 3. Papers of the NWAF no. 62.

1991   The Road to Nakbe. *Natural History,* May: 8–14. The American Museum of Natural History, New York.

1992   *The Archaeology of Ideology: A Study of Maya Preclassic Architectural Sculpture at Nakbe, Peten, Guatemala.* Ph.D. dissertation, Anthropology Department, UCLA.

1996   El clásico tardío del norte de Petén. *Utz'ib* 2(1): 1–15. Asociación Tikal, Guatemala.

Hansen, Richard D., Steven Bozarth, John Jacob, David Wahl, and Thomas Schreiner
2002   Climatic and Environmental Variability in the Rise of Maya Civilization. A Preliminary Perspective from Northern Peten. *AM* 13(2): 273–295.

Hanratty, Catherine C.
1998   Excavation in the Str. 37 Courtyard (Blue Creek site). Paper presented at the 63rd Annual Meeting of the SAA, Seattle.

Harris, David R.
1980   Tropical Savanna Environments: Definition, Distribution, Diversity, and Development. In *Human Ecology in Savanna Environments,* ed. D. R. Harris, pp. 3–30. Academic Press, London.

Harris, Edward C.
1989   *Principles of Archaeological Stratigraphy,* second ed. Academic Press, San Diego.

Harrison, Peter D.
1969   Form and Function in a Maya Palace Group. *Verhandlungen des XXXVIII Internationalen Amerikanistenkongressess,* vol. 1, pp. 165–172. Stuttgart-Munich.

1970   *The Central Acropolis, Tikal, Guatemala: A Preliminary Study of the Functions of Its Structural Components During the Late Classic Period.* Unpublished Ph.D. dissertation, Department of Anthropology, University of Pennsylvania, Philadelphia.

1977   The Rise of the Bajos and the Fall of the Maya. In Hammond 1977, pp. 470–508.

1998   *Lords of Tikal: Rulers of an Ancient Maya City.* Thames and Hudson, London.

Harrison, Peter D., and B. L. Turner II (eds.)
1978   *Pre-Hispanic Maya Agriculture.* University of New Mexico Press, Albuquerque.

Hassig, Ross
1985   *Trade, Tribute, and Transportation: The Sixteenth Century Political Economy of the Valley of Mexico.* University of Oklahoma Press, Norman.

1992   *War and Society in Ancient Mesoamerica.* University of California Press, Berkeley.

Haug, Gerald H., Detlef Günter, Larry C. Peterson, Daniel M. Sigman, Konrad A. Hughen, and Beat Aeschlimann
2003   Climate and the Collapse of Classic Maya Civilization. *Science* 299(5613): 1731–1735.

Haviland, William
1965   Prehistoric Settlement at Tikal, Guatemala. *Expedition* 7(3): 14–23.

1970   Maya Settlement Patterns: A Critical Review. *Archaeological Studies in Middle America.* Pub. 26. MARI.

1981   Dower Houses and Minor Centers at Tikal, Guatemala: An Investigation into the Identification of Valid Units in Settlement Hierarchies. In Ashmore 1981a, pp. 89–117.

1988   Musical Hammocks at Tikal. In *Household and Community in the Mesoamerican Past,* ed. R. R. Wilk and W. Ashmore, pp. 121–134. University of New Mexico Press, Albuquerque.

Haviland, William A., and Hattula Moholy-Nagy
1992   Distinguishing the High and Mighty from the Hoi Polloi at Tikal, Guatemala. In D. Z. Chase and A. F. Chase 1992b, pp. 50–60.

Healy, Paul F., Jaime J. Awe, Gyles Iannone, and Cassandra Bill
1995   Pacbitun (Belize) and Ancient Maya Use of Slate. *Antiquity* 69(263): 337–348.

Helmke, Christophe G.B.
n.d.   Molded-carved Vases as Indicators of the Social Status of Cave Users in the Terminal Classic. Paper presented at the 64th Annual Meeting of the SAA, Chicago.

Helms, Mary W.
1998   *Access to Origins: Affines, Ancestors, and Aristocrats.* University of Texas Press, Austin.

Henderson, John S., and Jeremy A. Sabloff
1993   Reconceptualizing the Maya Cultural Tradition: Programmatic Comments. In Sabloff and Henderson 1993, pp. 445–475.

Hermes, Bernard A.
1981   La cerámica arqueológica de Pataxte, Izabal: un análisis. Tesis de licenciatura, Universidad de San Carlos de Guatemala, Guatemala City.
1993   La secuencia cerámica de Topoxté: un informe preliminar. *Sonderdruck aus Beiträge zur Allgemeinen und Vergleichenden Archäologie* 13: 221–251. Verlag Philipp von Zabern, Mainz am Rhein, Germany.
2000   Industria cerámica. In Wurster 2000, pp. 164–201.

Hermes, Bernard, and Raúl Noriega
1998   El período postclásico en el área de la laguna Yaxha: una visión desde Topoxte. In *XI Simposo, 1997,* pp. 755–778.

Hermes, Bernard, Raúl Noriega, and Zoila Calderón
1997   Investigación arqueológica y trabajos de conservación en el edificio 216 de Yaxha. *Beiträge zur Allgemeinen und Vergleichenden Archäologie, Band* 17: 257–309.

Hervik, Peter
1999   The Mysterious Maya of National Geographic. *Journal of Latin American Anthropology* 4: 166–197.

Hester, Thomas R.
1985   (ed.) *Late Classic–Early Postclassic Transitions: Archaeological Investigations at Colha, Belize.* Final Performance Report to the National Endowment for the Humanities Grants R0 20534-83 and RO 20755. Center for Archaeological Research, The University of Texas at San Antonio. On file at TARL.

Hester, Thomas R., and Harry J. Shafer
1991a   (eds.) *Maya Stone Tools: Selected Papers from the Second Maya Lithic Conference.* Monographs in World Archaeology no. 1. Prehistory Press, Madison, WI.
1991b   Lithics of the Early Postclassic at Colha, Belize. In Hester and Shafer 1991a, pp. 155–162.
1994   The 1983 and 1984 Archaeological Investigations of the Colha Project. In *Continuing Archaeology at Colha, Belize,* ed. T. R. Hester, H. J. Shafer, and J. D. Eaton, pp. 1–6. Studies in Archaeology 16, TARL.

Hilton, Rodney
1985   Reasons for Inequality among Medieval Peasants. In *Class Conflict and the Crisis of Feudalism: Essays in Medieval Social History,* by Rodney Hilton, pp. 139–151. The Hambledon Press, London.

Hirth, Kenneth G.
1992   Interregional Exchange as Elite Behavior: An Evolutionary Perspective. In A. F. Chase and D. Z. Chase 1992b, pp. 18–29.

Hodder, Ian
1982   *Symbols in Action.* Cambridge University Press, Cambridge.

Hodder, Ian, and Clive Orton
1990   *Análisis espacial en arqueología.* Editorial Crítica, Barcelona.

Hodell, David A., Jason H. Curtis, and Mark Brenner
  1995   Possible Role of Climate in the Collapse of Classic Maya Civilization. *Nature* 75: 391–394.

Hofling, Andrew
  1998   The Language of the Inscriptions of Central Peten. Paper presented at the 63rd Annual Meeting of the SAA, Seattle.

Hodges, R.
  1987   Spatial Models, Anthropology and Archaeology. In *Landscape and Culture: Geographical and Archaeological Perspectives,* ed. J. M. Wagstaff, pp. 118–133. Basil Blackwell, Oxford.

Holley, George R.
  1983   *Ceramic Change at Piedras Negras, Guatemala.* Unpublished Ph.D. dissertation, Southern Illinois University Carbondale.

Holtman, Matthew
  1991   Evaluación preliminar de los artefactos de piedra pulida. In Demarest, Inomata, Escobedo, and Palka 1991, pp. 772–782.

Hopkins, Brian
  1992   Ecological Processes at the Forest-Savanna Boundary. In *Human Ecology in Savanna Environments,* ed. D. R. Harris, pp. 21–34. Academic Press, London.

Hosler, Dorothy, Jeremy A. Sabloff, and Dale Runge
  1977   Simulation Models and Development: A Case Study of the Classic Maya Collapse. In Hammond 1977, pp. 553–584.

Houck, Charles W.
  1996   Rural Survey at Ek Balam, Yucatan, Mexico: 1987–1995. Paper presented at the 61st Annual Meeting of the SAA, New Orleans.
  1998   Settlement and Sociopolitical Dynamics at Ek Balam: The View from the Hinterland. Paper presented at the 97th Annual Meeting of the AAA, Philadelphia.

Houk, Brett A.
  1996   *The Archaeology of Site Planning: An Example from the Maya Site of Dos Hombres, Belize.* Unpublished Ph.D. dissertation, Department of Anthropology, The University of Texas, Austin.

Houk, Brett A., Owen Ford, and Amy E. Rush
  1999   Fear and Loathing in Northwest Belize. Paper presented at the 64th Annual Meeting of the SAA, Chicago.

Houk, Brett A., and Hubert R. Robichaux (eds.)
  1996   *The 1996 Season of the Chan Chich Archaeological Project.* Center for Maya Studies, San Antonio, TX.

Houston, Stephen D.
  1983   Warfare Between Naranjo and Ucanal. In *Contributions to Maya Hieroglyphic Decipherment,* ed. S. D. Houston, pp. 31–39. Human Relations Area File, New Haven, CT.
  1986   Problematic Emblem Glyphs: Examples from Altar de Sacrificios, El Chorro, Rio Azul, and Xultun. *Research Reports on Ancient Maya Writing,* no. 3. Center for Maya Research, Washington, DC.
  1987a *Deciphering Maya Politics: Archaeological and Epigraphic Perspectives on the Segmentary State Concept.* Manuscript on file, Yale University, New Haven, CT.
  1987b *The Inscriptions and Monumental Art of Dos Pilas, Guatemala: A Study of Classic Maya History and Politics.* Ph.D. dissertation, Yale University, New Haven, CT.
  1987c Notes on Caracol Epigraphy and Its Significance. In A. F. Chase and D. Z. Chase 1987a, pp. 85–100.

1991   Appendix: Caracol Altar 21. In *Sixth Palenque Round Table, 1986,* ed. M. G. Robertson and V. M. Fields, pp. 38–42. University of Oklahoma Press, Norman.

1993   *Hieroglyphs and History at Dos Pilas: Dynastic Politics of the Classic Maya.* University of Texas Press, Austin.

1998   (ed.) *Function and Meaning in Classic Maya Architecture: A Symposium at Dumbarton Oaks, 7th and 8th October 1994.* DO.

Houston, Stephen D., Robert Chatham, Oswaldo Chinchilla, Erick Ponciano, and Lori Wright
1990   Mapeo y sondeos en Tamarindito. In Demarest and Houston 1990, pp. 369, 392.

Houston, Stephen D., Hector Escobedo, Mark Child, Charles Golden, and René Muñoz
2001   Moral Community and Settlement Transformation among the Classic Maya: Evidence from Piedras Negras, Guatemala. In *Social Construction of Ancient Cities,* ed. M. L. Smith. Smithsonian Institution Press, Washington, DC.

Houston, Stephen D., and Peter Mathews
1985   *The Dynastic Sequence of Dos Pilas, Guatemala.* Monograph 1. PARI.

Houston, Stephen D., John Robertson, and David Stuart
2000   The Language of Classic Maya Inscriptions. *CA* 41(3): 321–356.

Houston, Stephen D., and David Stuart
1990   Resultados generales de los estudios epigráficos del Proyecto Petexbatún. In Demarest and Houston 1990, pp. 568–577.

1996   Of Gods, Glyphs and Kings: Divinity and Rulership Among the Classic Maya. *Antiquity* 70: 289–312.

Houston, Stephen D., David Stuart, and Karl A. Taube
1989   Folk Classification of Classic Maya Pottery. *AA* 91: 720–726.

1992   Image and Text on the "Jauncy Vase." In *The Maya Vase Book,* vol. 3, ed. J. Kerr, pp. 499–512. Kerr Associates, New York.

Huchim, Jose Herrera, and Lourdes Toscano Hernández
1999   El Cuadrangulo de los Pajaros de Uxmal. *Arqueología Mexicana* vol. VII, no. 37: 18–23.

Ichon, Alain, and Rita Grignon
1981   *Archéologie de Sauvetage dans la Vallée de Río Chixoy, no. 3: El Jocote.* Institut d'Ethnologie, Paris.

Inomata, Takeshi
1991   Reconocimiento alrededor de Aguateca. In Demarest, Inomata, Escobedo, and Palka 1991, pp. 405–410.

1995   *Archaeological Investigations at the Fortified Center of Aguateca, El Petén, Guatemala: Implications for the Study of the Classic Maya Collapse.* Unpublished Ph.D. dissertation, Department of Anthropology, Vanderbilt University, Nashville, TN.

1997   The Last Day of a Fortified Classic Maya Center: Archaeological Investigations at Aguateca, Guatemala. *AM* 8: 337–351.

2001   The Power and Ideology of Artistic Creation: Elite Craft Specialists in Classic Maya Society. *CA* 42(3): 321–350.

2004   *Aguateca: Warfare and the Collapse of a Classic Maya Center.* Vanderbilt University Press, Nashville, TN.

Inomata, Takeshi, and Laura R. Stiver
1998   Floor Assemblages from Burned Structures at Aguateca, Guatemala: A Study of Classic Maya Households. *JFA* 25: 431–452.

Inomata, Takeshi, Stacey Symonds, Chris Beekman, and Stephen D. Houston
1990   Investigaciones arqueológicas en Aguateca. In. Demarest and Houston 1990, pp. 393–422.

Inomata, Takeshi, and Daniela Triadan
  2000   Craft Production by Classic Maya Elites in Domestic Settings: Data from Rapidly Abandoned Structures at Aguateca, Guatemala. *Mayab* 13: 57–66.

Inomata, Takeshi, Daniela Triadan, Erick Ponciano Alvarado, Richard E. Terry, Harriet F. Beaubien, Alba Estela Pinto, and Shannon Coyston
  1998   Residencias de la familia real y de la élite en Aguateca, Guatemala. *Mayab* 11: 23–39.

Jennings, Joseph N.
  1985   *Karst Geomorphology*. Basil Blackwell, Oxford.

Johnson, Allen W., and Timothy Earle
  1987   *The Evolution of Human Societies: From Foraging Group to Agrarian State*. Stanford University Press, Stanford, CA.

Johnston, Kevin J., Andrew J. Breckenbridge, and Barbara C. Hansen
  2001   Paleoecological Evidence of an Early Postclassic Occupation in the Southwestern Maya Lowlands: Laguna Las Pozas, Guatemala. *LAA* 12(2): 149–166.

Johnstone, Dave
  1994   Residential Excavations. In *Selz-Yaxuna, 1993 Field Season*, pp. 83–88.
  1998   Yaxuna Ceramics: Chronological and Spatial Relationships. In *Selz-Yaxuna, 1997 Season with Collected Papers*, ed. J. M. Shaw and D. A. Freidel, pp. 24–27.

Jones, A.H.M.
  1964   *The Later Roman Empire, 284–602: A Social, Economic and Administrative Survey*. Basil Blackwell, Oxford.

Jones, Christopher
  1969   *The Twin-Pyramid Group Pattern: A Classic Maya Architectural Assemblage at Tikal, Guatemala*. Ph.D. dissertation, University of Pennsylvania. UMI.
  1991   Cycles of Growth at Tikal. In Culbert 1991, pp. 102–127.
  1996   *Excavations in the East Plaza of Tikal*. Tikal Report, no. 16. UM.

Jones, Christopher, and Linton Satterthwaite
  1982   *The Monuments and Inscriptions of Tikal: The Carved Monuments*. Tikal Report no. 33, pt. A. Monograph 44. UM.

Jones, Grant D.
  1984   Maya-Spanish relations in sixteenth century Belize. *Belcast Journal of Belizean Affairs* 1(1): 28–40.
  1989   *Maya Resistance to Spanish Rule: Time and History on a Colonial Frontier*. University of New Mexico Press, Albuquerque.
  1998   *The Conquest of the Last Maya Kingdom*. Stanford University Press, Stanford, CA.

Jones, Martin, Peter J. Sheppard, and Doug G. Sutton
  1996   Modeling Archaeological Soil Temperatures in New Zealand. *International Association for Obsidian Studies Bulletin* 17: 6–7.

Jones, Sian
  1997   *The Archaeology of Ethnicity: Constructing Identities in the Past and Present*. Routledge, London.

Justeson, John S., and Lyle Campbell
  1997   The Linguistic Background of Maya Hieroglyphic Writing: Arguments Against a "Highland Maya" Role. In *The Language of Maya Hieroglyphs,* ed. M. J. Macri and A. Ford, pp. 41–67. PARI.

Karbula, James W.
  1989   *Spatial Analysis of Seven Maya Centers in the Northeastern Peten*. Unpublished M.A. thesis, Department of Anthropology, University of Texas at San Antonio.

Kelley, David H.
1976   *Deciphering the Maya Script.* University of Texas Press, Austin.

Kelley, Martha C. S., and Roger E. Kelley
1980   Approaches to Ethnic Identification in Historical Archaeology. In *Archaeological Perspectives on Ethnicity in America: Afro-American and Asian-American Culture History,* ed. R. L. Schuyler, pp. 133–143. Baywood Publishing, Farmingdale, NY.

Kepecs, Susan
1998   Diachronic Ceramic Evidence and Its Social Implications in the Chikinchel Region, Northeast Yucatan, Mexico. *AM* 9(1):121–136.

Kepecs, Susan, Gary Feinman, and Sylviane Boucher
1994   Chichen Itza and Its Hinterland, a World-Systems Perspective. *AM* 5: 141–158.

Kepecs, Susan, and Tomás Gallareta N.
1994   Una visión diacrónica de Chikinchel y Cupul, noreste de Yucatán, México. *Memorias del Segundo Congreso Internacional de Mayistas,* pp. 275–293. UNAM.

Kertzer, David I.
1988   *Ritual, Politics, and Power.* Yale University Press, New Haven, CT.

Killion, Thomas W.
1990   Cultivation Intensity and Residential Site Structure: An Ethnoarchaeological Examination of Peasant Agriculture in the Sierra de los Tuxtlas, Veracruz, Mexico. *LAA* 1: 191–215.

Killion, Thomas W., Jeremy Sabloff, Gair Tourtellot, and Nicholas Dunning
1989   Intensive Surface Collection of Residential Clusters at Terminal Classic Sayil, Yucatan, Mexico. *JFA* 18: 273–294.

Killion, Thomas, Inez Verhagen, Dirk Van Tuerenhout, Daniela Triadan, Lisa Hamerlynck, Matthew McDermott, and José Genovés
1991   Reporte de la temporada 1991 del recorrido arqueológico intersitio de Petexbatún (RAIP). In Demarest, Inomata, Escobedo, and Palka 1991, pp. 588–645.

King, Eleanor, and Daniel Potter
1994   Small Sites in Prehistoric Maya Socioeconomic Organization: A Perspective from Colha, Belize. In *Archaeological Views from the Countryside: Village Communities in Early Complex Societies,* ed. G. M. Schwartz and S. E. Falconer, pp. 64–90. Smithsonian Institution Press, Washington and London.

King, R. B., I. C. Baillie, T.M.B. Abell, J. R. Dunsmore, D. A. Gray, J. H. Pratt, H. R. Versey, A.C.S. Wright, and S. A. Sisman
1992   *Land Resource Management of Northern Belize.* Natural Resource Institute Bulletin 43. Overseas Development Natural Resources Institute, Chatham Maritime, Kent, England.

Kolata, Alan
1993   *The Tiwanaku: Portrait of an Andean Civilization.* Basil Blackwell, Cambridge.

Kosakowsky, Laura J., Kerry Sagebiel, Norman Hammond, and Gair Tourtellot III
1998   En la frontera: la cerámica de La Milpa, Belice. In *XI Simposio, 1997,* pp. 659–666.

Kowalski, Jeff Karl
1987   *The House of the Governor: A Maya Palace at Uxmal, Yucatan, Mexico.* University of Oklahoma Press, Norman.
1989   Who Am I Among the Itza?: Links Between Northern Yucatan and the Western Maya Lowlands and Highlands. In Diehl and Berlo 1989, pp. 183–185.
1994   The Puuc as Seen from Uxmal. In Prem 1994, pp. 93–120.
1998   Uxmal and the Puuc Zone: Monumental Architecture, Sculptured Façades and Politi-

cal Power in the Terminal Classic Period. In *Maya,* ed. P. Schmidt, M. de la Garza, and E. Nalda, pp. 401–425. Rizzoli, New York.

1999   (ed.) *Mesoamerican Architecture as a Cultural Symbol.* Oxford University Press, New York.

Kowalski, Jeff Karl, Alfredo Barrera R., Heber Ojeda M., and José Huchim H.

1994   Archaeological Excavations of a Round Temple at Uxmal: Summary Discussion and Implications for Northern Maya Culture History. In *Palenque Round Table, 1993,* ed. M. J. Macri and J. McHargue, pp. 281–296. M. G. Robertson, gen. ed. PARI.

Kowalski, Jeff Karl, and Nicholas Dunning

1999   The Architecture of Uxmal: The Symbolics of Statemaking at a Puuc Maya Regional Capital. In Kowalski 1999, pp. 273–297.

Kray, Christine A.

1997   *Worship in Body and Spirit: Practice, Self, and Religious Sensibility in Yucatán, México.* Unpublished Ph.D. dissertation, Department of Anthropology, University of Pennsylvania, Philadelphia.

Krejci, Estella, and T. Patrick Culbert

1995   Preclassic and Classic Burials and Caches in the Maya Lowlands. In *The Emergence of Lowland Maya Civilization: The Transition from the Preclassic to Early Classic,* ed. N. Grube, pp. 103–116. Acta Mesoamericana No. 8, Berlin.

Krochok, Ruth

1988   *The Hieroglyphic Inscriptions and Iconography of the Temple of the Four Lintels and Related Monuments, Chichen Itza, Yucatan, Mexico.* Unpublished M.A. thesis, University of Texas, Austin.

1990   Iconographic Investigations. In *Yaxuna Archaeological Survey: A Report on the 1989 Field Season and Final Report on Phase One,* ed. D. Freidel, C. Suhler, and R. Krochock, pp. 12–15. Southern Methodist University, Dallas.

1997   *A New Interpretation of the Inscriptions on the Temple of the Hieroglyphic Jambs, Chichén Itzá.* Texas Notes on Precolumbian Art, Writing, and Culture. Austin.

1998   *The Development of Political Rhetoric at Chichen Itza, Yucatan, Mexico.* Ph.D. dissertation, Southern Methodist University, Dallas.

Krochock, Ruth, and David A. Freidel

1994   Ballcourts and the Evolution of Political Rhetoric at Chichén Itzá, Yucatán, México. In Prem 1994, pp. 359–375.

Kubler, George A.

1975   *The Art and Architecture of Ancient America,* second ed. Pelican, Baltimore.

Kunen, Julie L., T. Patrick Culbert, Vilma Fialko, Brian R. McKee, and Liwy Grazioso

2000   Bajo Communities: A Case Study from the Central Peten. *Culture and Agriculture* 22(3): 15–31.

Kurjack, Edward

1974   *Prehistoric Lowland Maya Community and Social Organization: A Case Study at Dzibilchaltun, Yucatan, Mexico.* Pub. 38. MARI.

1994   Political Geography of the Yucatecan Hill Country. In Prem 1994, pp. 308–315.

Kurjack, Edward B., and E. Wyllys Andrews V

1976   Early Boundary Maintenance in Northwest Yucatan, Mexico. *AAnt* 41: 318–325.

Kurjack, Edward B., and Silvia Garza T.

1979   Archaeological Settlement Patterns and Modern Geography in the Hill Country of Yucatan. In Mills 1979, pp. 36–45.

1981   Pre-Columbian Community Form and Distribution in the Northern Maya Area. In Ashmore 1981a, pp. 287–310.

Kurjack, Edward B., Rubén Maldonado C., and Merle Greene Robertson
  1991   Ballcourts of the Northern Maya Lowlands. In Scarborough and Wilcox 1991, pp.
          145–160.

Kus, Susan, and Victor Raharijaona
  1998   Between Earth and Sky There Are Only a Few Large Boulders: Sovereignty and
          Monumentality in Central Madagascar. *Journal of Anthropological Archaeology* 17:
          53–79.
  2000   House to Palace, Village to State: Scaling up Architecture and Ideology. *AA* 102: 98–113.

Lacadena, Alfonso, and Andrés Ciudad Ruíz
  1998   Reflexiones sobre la estructura política maya clásica. In Ciudad Ruíz, et al. 1998, pp.
          31–64.

Laporte, Juan Pedro
  1993   Patrón de asentamiento y población prehispánica en el noroeste de las Montañas
          Mayas, Guatemala. In *Perspectivas antropológicas en el mundo Maya,* ed. M. J.
          Iglesias Ponce de León and F. Ligorred Perramon, pp. 129–150. Sociedad Española de
          Estudios Mayas, Madrid.
  1994   Ixtonton, Dolores, Petén: entidad politica del noroeste de las montanas mayas. *Atlas
          Arqueológico de Guatemala no. 2.* Universidad de San Carlos, Guatemala.
  1995   Una actualización a la secuencia cerámica del área de Dolores, Petén. *Atlas Arqueológico
          de Guatemala no. 3,* pp. 35–64. IDAEH.
  1996   Organización territorial y política prehispánica en el sureste de Petén. *Atlas
          Arqueológico de Guatemala no. 4.* IDAEH.
  1998   Una perspectiva del desarrollo cultural prehispánico en el sureste de Petén, Guate-
          mala. In Ciudad Ruíz et al., 1998, pp. 161–183.

Laporte, Juan Pedro, and Marco Tulio Alvarado
  1997   Curucuitz, un centro arqueológico en el pinar de Dolores, Petén. *Utz'ib* 2(2): 1–23.

Laporte, Juan Pedro, Lilian Corzo, Héctor Escobedo, Rosa M. Flores, Isabel Izaguirre, Nancy Monterroso,
    Paulino Morales, Carmen Ramos, Irma Rodas, Julio Roldan, and Franklin Solares
  1993   La sequencia cerámica del valle de Dolores, Petén: las unidades cerámicas. *Atlas
          Arqueológico de Guatemala no. 1.* IDAEH.

Laporte, Juan Pedro, Lilian A, Corzo, Oswaldo Gómez, Carmen Ramos, Jaime Castellanos, Luisa
    Escobar, Irinna Montepeque, Heidy Quezada, Mynor Silvestre, and Rosaura Vásquez
  1999   Exploraciones arqueológicas en Calzada Mopan: Los grupos de la Acrópolis. Reporte
          no. 13, *Atlas Arqueológico de Guatemala.* IDAEH.

Laporte, Juan Pedro, and Héctor L. Escobedo
  1992   Ixtutz, centro rector al oeste del valle de Dolores, Petén. *Mexicon* 14(5): 90–98.

Laporte, Juan Pedro, Héctor L. Escobedo, Paulino Morales, Julio Roldan, Rolando Torres, Oswaldo
    Gómez, and Yolanda Fernández
  1994   Ixkun, entidad política del noroeste de las montañas mayas. *Mayab* 9: 31–48.

Laporte, Juan Pedro, and Vilma Fialko
  1990   New Perspectives on Old Problems: Dynastic References for the Early Classic at
          Tikal. In *Vision and Revision in Maya Studies,* ed. F. S. Clancy and P. D. Harrison, pp.
          33–66. University of New Mexico Press, Albuquerque.
  1995   Un reencuentro con Mundo Perdido, Tikal, Guatemala. *AM* 6: 41–94.

Laporte, Juan Pedro, and Oswaldo Gómez
  n.d.   Depósitos de materiales como actividad ritual en Tikal: nueva evidencia del inicio del
          clásico tardío. Paper presented at the 4th International Congress of Mayanists, Antigua,
          Guatemala, 1998.

Laporte, Juan Pedro, Oswaldo Gómez, and Lilian A. Corzo
1999 La cuenca media del río Mopan, Petén, Guatemala: su desarollo arqueológico. *Mexicon* 21(2): 33–39.

Laporte, Juan Pedro, and María Josefa Iglesias Ponce de León
1999 Más allá de Mundo Perdido: investigación en grupos residenciales de Tikal. *Mayab* 12: 32–57.

Laporte, Juan Pedro, and Paulino I. Morales
1994 Definición territorial en centros Clásicos de Tierras Bajas: una aplicación metodológica a la region de Dolores. In *VII Simposio, 1993,* pp. 247–273.

Laporte, Juan Pedro, Paulino Morales, Dolores Ballesteros, Benito Burgos, Lilian A. Corzo, Francisco de León, Edgar García, Mario Marroquín, Federico Reyes, Juan Ulises, Marco A. Urbina, and Mariana Valdizón
1995 Excavaciones en Ixcol, Dolores. Reporte no. 9, *Atlas Arqueológico de Guatemala no. 3,* pp. 65–104. IDAEH.

Laporte, Juan Pedro, Paulino I. Morales, and W. Mariana Valdizón
1997 San Luis Pueblito: un sitio mayor al oeste de Dolores, Petén. *Mexicon* 19(3): 47–51.

Laporte, Juan Pedro, and Heidy Quezada
1998 Un acercamiento al postclásico en el sureste de Petén. In *XI simposio, 1997,* tomo 2, pp. 729–754.

Laporte, Juan Pedro, and Carmen E. Ramos
1998 Sacul, Dolores, Petén: excavación, arquitectura y hallazgos. *Utz'ib* 2(4): 1–22.

Laporte, Juan Pedro, and Carlos R. Torres
1987 Los señorios del sureste de Petén. *Mayab* 3: 7–22.

Larios, Carlos Rudy, William L. Fash, and David S. Stuart
1994 Architectural Stratigraphy and Epigraphic Dating of Copan Structure 10L-22: An Exercise in the Conjunctive Approach. In *Seventh Palenque Round Table, 1989,* ed. M. G. Robertson and V. M. Fields, pp. 69–78. PARI.

Leach, Edmund R.
1966 Ritualization in Man in Relation to Conceptual and Social Development. *Philosophical Transactions of the Royal Society of London* 251: 403–408.

LeCount, Lisa J.
1992 Xunantunich Ceramics—1992. In Leventhal 1992, pp. 127–144.
1993 1993 Ceramic Research: Initial Investigations into Assemblage Variation. In Leventhal, 1993, pp. 218–249.
1994 Notes on Chronology: The 1994 Progress Report on Xunantunich Ceramic Research. In Leventhal and Ashmore 1994, pp. 218–249.
1996 *Pottery and Power: Feasting, Gifting, and Displaying Wealth among the Late and Terminal Classic Lowland Maya.* Unpublished Ph.D. dissertation, Department of Anthropology, UCLA.
1999 Polychrome Pottery and Political Strategies in Late and Terminal Classic Lowland Maya Society. *LAA* 10: 239–258.

LeCount, Lisa J., Richard M. Leventhal, Wendy Ashmore, Glenn Russell, and Michael Gottesman
1998 New Dates and Old Issues: Radiocarbon and Obsidian Hydration Dating of Late and Terminal Classic Maya Ceramic Phases from Xunantunich, Belize. Paper presented at the 63rd Annual Meeting of the SAA, Seattle.

LeCount, Lisa J., Richard M. Leventhal, Jason Yaeger, and Wendy Ashmore
2002 Dating the Rise and Fall of Xunantunich, Belize: A Late and Terminal Classic Lowland Maya Secondary Center. *AM* 13(1): 41–63.

Lee, Thomas A., and Carlos Navarrete (eds.)
1978　*Mesoamerican Communication Routes and Cultural Contacts.* Papers of the NWAF no. 40.

Leventhal, Richard M.
1983　Household Groups and Classic Maya Religion. In *Prehistoric Settlement Patterns,* ed. E. Z. Vogt and R. M. Leventhal, pp. 55–76. University of New Mexico Press, Albuquerque.
1992a　The Development of a Regional Tradition in Southern Belize. In *New Theories on the Ancient Maya,* ed. E. C. Danien and R. J. Sharer, pp. 145–153. Monograph 77. UM.
1992b　(ed.) *Xunantunich Archaeological Project: 1992 Field Season.* Report submitted to the BDOA.
1993　(ed.) *Xunantunich Archaeological Project: 1993 Field Season.* Report submitted to the BDOA.
1997　(ed.) *Xunantunich Archaeological Project: 1997 Field Season.* Report submitted to the BDOA.

Leventhal, Richard M., and Wendy Ashmore
1994　(eds.) *Xunantunich Archaeological Project: 1994 Field Season.* Report submitted to the BDOA.
1995b　(eds.) *Xunantunich Archaeological Project: 1995 Field Season.* Report submitted to the BDOA.
1996　(eds.) *Xunantunich Archaeological Project: 1996 Field Season.* Report submitted to the BDOA.
n.d.　Xunantunich in a Belize Valley Context. In *The Ancient Maya of the Belize Valley: Half a Century of Archaeological Research,* ed. J. F. Garber. University Press of Florida, Gainesville.

Leventhal, Richard M., and Lisa J. LeCount
1997　The Terminal Classic Social and Political Organization of Ancient Xunantunich. Paper presented at the 62nd Annual Meeting of the SAA, Nashville, TN.

Leyden, Barbara W., Mark Brenner, and Bruce H. Dahlin
1998　Cultural and Climatic History of Cobá, a Lowland Maya City in Quintana Roo, Mexico. *Quaternary Research* 49: 111–122.

Leyden, Barbara W., Mark Brenner, David A. Hodell, and Jason H. Curtis
1994　Orbital and Internal Forcing of Climate on the Yucatan Peninsula for the Past ca. 36 ka. *Paleogeography, Paleoclimatology, Paleoecology* 109: 193–210.

Leyden, Barbara W., Mark Brenner, Tom Whitmore, Jason H. Curtis, Dolores R. Piperno, and Bruce H. Dahlin
1996　A Record of Long- and Short-term Climatic Variation from Northwest Yucatan: Cenote San Jose Chulchaca. In Fedick 1996b, pp. 30–50.

Lincoln, Charles
1985　Ceramics and Ceramic Chronology. In *A Consideration of the Early Classic Period in the Maya Lowlands,* ed. G. R. Willey and P. Mathews, pp. 55–94. Pub. 10. IMS
1986　The Chronology of Chichen Itza: A Review of the Literature. In Sabloff and Andrews 1986b, pp. 141–196.
1990　*Ethnicity and Social Organization at Chichén Itzá, Yucatán, México.* Ph.D. dissertation, Harvard University, Cambridge, MA.

Longyear, John M., III
1952　*Copan Ceramics: A Study of Southeastern Maya Pottery.* Pub. 597. CIW.

Looper, Matthew
1995　*The Political Strategies of Butz'-Tiliw at Quirigua.* Ph.D. dissertation, Art Department, University of Texas at Austin. UMI.

López de la Rosa, Edmundo, and Adriana Velázquez Morlet
1992 El patron de asentamiento de Oxkintok. In *Misión Arqueológica de España en México*, ed. M. Rivera Dorada, pp. 201–249. Ministerio de Educación y Cultura, Madrid.

López Varela, Sandra J.
1989 *Análisis y clasificación de la cerámica de un sitio maya del clásico: Yaxchilán, México*. BAR no. 535.
2000 A Ceramic View of the Political History of Pomoná and Yaxchilan During the Terminal Classic. Paper presented at the 65th Annual Meeting of the SAA, Philadelphia.

Loten, Stanley, and David M. Pendergast
1984 *A Lexicon for Maya Architecture*. Monograph 8. ROM.

Lothrop, Samuel K.
1924 *Tulum, an Archaeological Study of the East Coast of Yucatan*. Pub. 335. CIW.
1926 *Pottery of Costa Rica and Nicaragua*. Contributions from the Museum of the American Indian, Heye Foundation, vol. 8, New York.

Love, Bruce
1986 Proyecto de mapeo de Yulá: Chichén Itzá. *Boletín de la ECUADY* 15 (86): 44–52. Mérida, México.

Lowe, John G.W.
1985 *The Dynamics of Apocalypse: A Systems Simulation of the Classic Maya Collapse*. University of New Mexico Press, Albuquerque.

Lucero, Lisa J.
1992 Problems in Identifying Ceramic Production in the Maya Lowlands: Evidence from the Belize River Area. *Memorias del Primer Congreso Internacional de Mayistas*, vol. 2: 143–154. Centro de Estudios Mayas, UNAM.

Lundell, Cyrus L.
1937 *The Vegetation of Peten*. Studies of Mexican and Central American Plants, I. Pub. 478, vol. 9. CIW.

Mackie, Euan W.
1961 New Light on the End of the Classic Maya Culture at Benque Viejo, British Honduras. *AAnt* 27(2): 216–224.

MacKinnon, J. Jefferson, and Susan M. Kepecs
1989 Prehispanic Saltmaking in Belize: New Evidence. *AAnt* 54: 522–533.

Maler, Teobert
1908 *Exploration of the Upper Usumacinta and Adjacent Regions*. PMAE Memoirs, vol. 4, no. 1.

Malpass, Michael A.
1993a (ed.) *Provincial Inca: Archaeological and Ethnohistorical Assessment of the Impact of the Inca State*. University of Iowa Press, Iowa City.
1993b Provincial Inca Archaeology and Ethnohistory: An Introduction. In Malpass 1993a, pp. 1–13.
1993c Variability in the Inca State: Embracing a Wider Perspective. In Malpass 1993a, pp. 234–244.

Manahan, T. Kam
1995 *The Nature of the Classic Maya Collapse at Copán, Honduras*. Unpublished M.A. thesis, Department of Anthropology, Northern Illinois University, DeKalb.
1996 The Nature of the Classic Maya Collapse at Copán: New Insight from a Domestic Perspective. Paper presented at the 61st Annual Meeting of the SAA, New Orleans.

2000   Reexaminando los días finales de Copán: nuevos datos de la fase Ejar. In *XIII Simposio, 1999,* pp. 1149–1155.

Mann, Michael
1986   *The Sources of Social Power, vol. I: A History of Power from the Beginning to* A.D. *1760.* Cambridge University Press, Cambridge.

Marcus, Joyce
1973   Territorial Organization of the Lowland Classic Maya. *Science* 180: 911–916.
1976   *Emblem and State in the Classic Maya Lowlands: An Epigraphic Approach to Territorial Organization.* DO.
1982   Review of "Maya Archaeology and Ethnohistory," ed. N. Hammond and G. R. Willey. *Ethnohistory* 29: 224–227.
1987   *The Inscriptions of Calakmul: Royal Marriage at a Maya City in Campeche, Mexico.* Museum of Anthropology Technical Report no. 21. University of Michigan, Ann Arbor.
1992   Political Fluctuations in Mesoamerica. *National Geographic Research and Exploration* 8: 392–411.
1993   Ancient Maya Political Organization. In Sabloff and Henderson 1993b, pp. 111–183.
1995   Where is Lowland Maya Archaeology Headed? *Journal of Archaeological Research* 3: 3–53.
1996   The Importance of Context in Interpreting Figurines. *Cambridge Archaeological Journal* 6: 285–291.
1997   Calakmul's Geopolitical Context as Seen from New Hieroglyphic Texts. Paper presented at the 62nd Annual Meeting of the SAA, Nashville, TN.
1998   The Peaks and Valleys of Archaic States. In *Archaic States,* ed. G. M. Feinman and J. Marcus, pp. 59–94. SAR.

Marcus, Joyce, and William J. Folan
1994   Una estela más del siglo V y nueva información sobre Pata de Jaguar, gobernante de Calakmul, Campeche, en el siglo VII. *Gaceta Universitaria,* año IV, no. 15–16: 21–26. UACM.

Martin, Simon
1996   Calakmul y el enigma del glifo Cabeza de Serpiente. *Arqueología Mexicana* 3(18): 42–45.
2000   Los señores de Calakmul. *Arqueología Mexicana* 7(42): 40–45.

Martin, Simon, and Nikolai Grube
1994   *Evidence for Macro-Political Organization Amongst Classic Maya Lowland States,* Manuscript, London/Bonn.
1995   Maya Superstates. *Archaeology* 48(6): 41–46.
2000   *Chronicle of the Maya Kings and Queens: Deciphering the Dynasties of the Ancient Maya.* Thames and Hudson, London.

Mason, J. Alden
1939   *Archaeology of Santa Marta, Colombia: The Tairona Culture. Part II, Section 2.* Anthropological Series, vol. 20, no. 3, Field Museum of Natural History, Chicago.

Masson, Marilyn A.
1989   *Lithic Production Changes in Late Classic Maya Workshops at Colha, Belize: A Study of Debitage Variation.* Unpublished M.A. thesis, Department of Anthropology, Florida State University, Tallahassee.
1995   Understanding the Stratigraphic Context of the Maya Postclassic in Belize. *Geoarchaeology* 10(5): 389–404.
1997   Postclassic Maya Social Transformations: A Community Level Perspective from Laguna de On, Belize. *LAA* 8(4): 293–316.
1999   Postclassic Maya Lagoon Communities in Northern Belize. *JFA* 26: 285–306.

2000   *In the Realm of Nachan Kan: Postclassic Maya Archaeology at Laguna de On, Belize.* University Press of Colorado, Boulder.

2001   The Economic Organization of Late and Terminal Classic Period Maya Stone Tool Craft Specialist Workshops at Colha, Belize. *Lithic Technology* 26: 18–38.

n.d.   Fauna Exploitation from the Preclassic to the Postclassic Period at Maya Communities in Northern Belize. In *Maya Zooarchaeology,* ed. K. Emery. Institute of Archaeology, University of California Los Angeles Press, Los Angeles (in press).

Masson, Marilyn A., and David Freidel (eds.)

2002   *Ancient Maya Political Economies.* Altamira Press, Walnut Creek, CA.

Masson, Marilyn A., and Henry Chaya

2000   Obsidian Trade Connections at the Postclassic Maya Site of Laguna de On, Belize. *Lithic Technology* 25: 135–144.

Matheny, Raymond T.

1970   *The Ceramics of Aguacatal, Campeche, Mexico.* Papers of the NWAF no. 27.

Mathews, Peter

1985   Maya Early Classic Monuments and Inscriptions. In *A Consideration of the Early Classic Period in the Maya Lowlands,* ed. G. R. Willey and P. Mathews, pp. 5–54. Pub. 10. IMS

1988   *The Sculptures of Yaxchilan.* Unpublished Ph.D. dissertation. Department of Anthropology, Yale University, New Haven, CT.

n.d.   The Inscriptions on the Back of Stela 8, Dos Pilas, Guatemala. Unpublished manuscript, 1979.

Mathews, Peter, and Linda Schele

1974   Lords of Palenque: The Glyphic Evidence. In *Primera Mesa Redonda de Palenque,* pt. I, ed. M. G. Robertson, pp. 63–76. The Robert Louis Stevenson School, Pebble Beach, CA.

Mathews, Peter, and Gordon R. Willey

1991   Prehistoric Polities and the Pasión Region: Hieroglyphic Texts and Their Archaeological Settings. In Culbert 1991, pp. 30–71.

Maudslay, Alfred P.

1889–   *Biologia Centrali-Americana: Archaeology,* vol. 1. R. H. Porter and Dulau and Co.,
1902   London.

May Hau, Jacinto, Rogerio Couoh Muñoz, Raymundo J. González Heredia, and William J. Folan

1990   *El mapa de Calakmul.* Centro de Investigaciones Históricas y Sociales, UACM.

Mayer, Karl Herbert

1993   Recent Destruction at San Clemente, Peten. *Mexicon* 15(3): 49–50.

1994a   The Maya Ruins of Holtun, Peten. *Mexicon* 16(4): 48–49.

1994b   The Maya Ruins of La Blanca, Peten. *Mexicon* 16(5): 90–91.

McAnany, Patricia A.

1989   Economic Foundations of Maya Society: Paradigms and Concepts. In *Prehistoric Maya Economies of Belize,* ed. P. A. McAnany and B. L. Isaac, pp. 347–372. Research in Economic Anthropology, Supplement 4. JAI Press, Greenwich, CT.

1990   Water Storage in the Puuc Region of the Northern Maya Lowlands: A Key to Population Estimates and Architectural Variability. In Culbert and Rice 1990, pp. 263–284.

1991   The Structure and Dynamics of Intercommunity Exchange. In Hester and Shafer 1991a, pp. 271–293.

1993   The Economics of Social Power and Wealth among Eighth Century Maya Households. In Sabloff and Henderson 1993b, pp. 65–89.

1995   *Living with the Ancestors: Kinship and Kingship in Ancient Maya Society.* University of Texas Press, Austin.

McGovern, James O.
    1993   Survey and Excavation at Actuncán. In Leventhal 1993, pp. 100–127.
    1994   Actuncán, Belize: The 1994 Excavation Season. In Leventhal and Ashmore 1994,
            pp. 108–122.

McGuire, Randall H., and Michael B. Schiffer
    1983   A Theory of Architectural Design. *Journal of Anthropological Archaeology* 2: 277–303.

McKillop, Heather
    1989   Development of Coastal Trade: Data, Models, Issues. In McKillop and Healy 1989,
            pp. 1–18.
    1994   Ancient Maya Tree Cropping: A Viable Subsistence Adaptation for the Island Maya.
            AM 5(1): 129–140.
    1996   Ancient Maya Trading Ports and the Integration of Long-Distance and Regional
            Economies: Wild Cane Cay in South-coastal Belize. *AM* 7: 49–62.

McKillop, Heather, and Paul F. Healy
    1989   (eds.) *Coastal Maya Trade*. Occasional Papers in Archaeology, Trent University,
            Peterborough, Ontario, Canada.

McKinley, James C.
    1997   In One Somali Town, Clan Rule has Brought Peace. *New York Times,* June 22, 1997.

McMullen, David
    1987   Bureaucrats and Cosmology: The Ritual Code of T'ang China. In *Rituals of Royalty:
            Power and Ceremonial in Traditional Societies,* ed. D. Cannadine and S. Price, pp.
            181–236. Cambridge University Press, Cambridge.

McNeil, Cameron
    2000   Paleobotanical Remains from Early Classic Ritual Contexts at Copan. Paper pre-
            sented at the 65th Annual Meeting of the SAA, Philadelphia.

Mejía Amaya, Héctor E., Heidy Quezada, and Jorge E. Chocón
    1998   Un límite político territorial en el sureste de Petén. In *XI Simposio, 1997,* pp. 171–190.

Messenger, Lewis C., Jr.
    1990   Ancient Wind of Change: Climatic Settings and Prehistoric Social Complexity in
            Mesoamerica. *AM* 1: 21–40.

Michaels, George H.
    1987   *A Description of Early Postclassic Lithic Technology at Colha, Belize.* M.A. thesis,
            Department of Anthropology, Texas A&M University, College Station.
    1994   The Postclassic at Colha, Belize: A Summary Overview and Directions for Future
            Research. In *Continuing Archaeology at Colha, Belize,* ed. T. R. Hester, H. J. Shafer,
            and J. D. Eaton. TARL Studies in Archaeology no. 16.

Michaels, George H., and Harry J. Shafer
    1994   Excavations at Operation 2037 and 2040. In *Continuing Archaeology at Colha,
            Belize,* ed. T. R. Hester, H. J. Shafer, and J. D. Eaton, pp. 117–129. TARL Studies in
            Archaeology no. 16.

Michelet, Dominique
    1998   Del Proyecto Xculoc al Proyecto Xcalumkín: interrogacions acerca del la organización
            política en la zona Puuc. *ECM.*

Milbrath, Susan, and Carlos Peraza Lope
    2003   Revisiting Mayapan: Mexico's Last Maya Capital. *AM* 14(1): 1–46.

Miller, Arthur G.
    1977   "Captains of the Itza": Unpublished Mural Evidence from Chichén Itzá. In Hammond
            1977, pp. 197–226.

Miller, Bruce, and Carolyn Miller
    1994   Caracol: An Ecological Perspective. In D. Z. Chase and A. F. Chase, pp. 12–20.

Miller, Mary E.
    1986   *The Murals of Bonampak.* Princeton University Press, Princeton, NJ.
    1993   On the Eve of Collapse: Maya Art in the Eighth Century. In Sabloff and Henderson 1993b, pp. 355–413.

Miller, Virginia E.
    1989   Star Warriors at Chichén Itzá. In *Word and Image in Maya Culture: Explorations in Language, Writing, and Representation,* ed. W. F. Hanks and D. S. Rice, pp. 287–305. University of Utah Press, Salt Lake City.

Mills, Lawrence (ed.)
    1979   *The Puuc: New Perspectives.* Central College, Pella, IA.

Mock, Shirley Boteler
    1994a   *The Northern River Lagoon Site (NRL): Late to Terminal Classic Maya Settlement, Saltmaking, and Survival on the Northern Belize Coast.* Ph.D. dissertation, The University of Texas at Austin.
    1994b   Yucatecan Presence in Northern Belize Postclassic Ceramics at Colha. In *Continuing Archaeology at Colha, Belize,* ed. T. R. Hester, H. J. Shafer, and J. D. Eaton, pp. 9–16. TARL Studies in Archaeology 16.
    1997a   Monkey Business at Northern River Lagoon: A Coastal-Inland Interaction Sphere in Northern Belize. *AM* 8: 165–183.
    1997b   Preliminary Observations on Postclassic Ceramics from Laguna de On Island. In *The Belize Postclassic Project: Laguna de On Island Excavations 1996,* ed. M. A. Masson and R. M. Rosenswig, pp. 61–67. Occasional Pub. no. 1. IMS.
    1998a   Ceramics from Laguna de On, 1996 and 1997. In *The Belize Postclassic Project 1997: Laguna de On, Progresso Lagoon, Laguna Seca,* ed. M. A. Masson and R. M. Rosenswig, pp. 193–202. Occasional Pub. no. 2. IMS
    1998b   Prelude. In Mock 1998d, pp. 3–18.
    1998c   La sal como impulsor y agitador en las comunidades mayas al final de la época clásica en las costas de Belize. In *La sal en México II,* ed. J. C. Reyes G., pp. 29–41. Secretaría de Cultura, Gobierno del Estado de Colima, Universidad de Colima Dirección General de Culturas Populares y Consejo Nacional para la Cultura y las Artes, Colima, México.
    1998d   (ed.) *The Sowing and the Dawning: Termination, Dedication, and Transformation in the Archaeological and Ethnographic Record of Mesoamerica.* University of New Mexico Press, Albuquerque.
    1999   (ed.) *The Northern Belize Coastal Project Interim Report 1999.* University of Texas, Institute of Texan Cultures, San Antonio.
    n.d.a   Pushing the Limits: Late to Terminal Classic Settlement and Economies on the Northern Belize Coast. In *Terminal Classic Socioeconomic Processes in the Maya Lowlands through a Ceramic Lens,* ed. S. López Varela and A. Foias. Cotsen Institute, UCLA.
    n.d.b   Betwixt Land and Sea: Saktunja, a Terminal Classic to Postclassic Site on the Northern Belize Coast. In *New Horizons in Maya Ceramics,* ed. H. I. McKillop and S. Boteler Mock. University Press of Florida, Gainesville.

Montejo, Victor
    1991   In the Name of the Pot, the Sun, the Broken Spear, the Rock, the Stick, the Idol, ad Infinitum and ad Nauseam: An Expose of Anglo Anthropologists' Obsessions with and Invention of Mayan Gods. Paper presented at the 1991 Annual Meeting of the AAA, San Francisco.

Montmollin, Olivier de
    1989   *The Archaeology of Political Structure: Settlement Analysis in a Classic Maya Polity.* Cambridge University Press, Cambridge.

1995   *Settlement and Politics in Three Classic Maya Polities.* Monographs in World Archaeology, no. 24. Prehistory Press, Madison, WI.

Morales, Paulino I.
1995a   *El Chal, un sitio arqueológico en la sabana de Petén central: una aproximación a su asentamiento.* Tesis de licenciatura, Escuela de Historia, USAC, Guatemala.
1995b   Patrón de asentamiento de El Chal, Petén: resultados preliminares. In *VIII Simposio, 1994,* pp. 587–604.
1997   El Muxanal: un sitio arqueológico de la sabana del centro de Peten. In *X Simposio, 1996,* pp. 445–462.

The Morbidity and Mortality Weekly Report (MMWR), http://www.cdc.gov/mmwr/. Centers for Disease Control and Prevention, Atlanta.

Morgan, Kim
1995   Investigación de la cancha de juego de pelota en Punta de Chimino: suboperación postclásica 14. In Demarest, Váldes, and Escobedo 1995, pp. 375–381.
1996   Excavaciones en las estructuras 72, 79, 80, and 81. In Demarest, Escobedo, and O'Mansky 1996, pp. 61–81.

Morgan, Kim, and Arthur A. Demarest
1995   Excavación de un depósito basural postclásico: suboperación PC17A. In Demarest, Váldes, and Escobedo 1995, pp. 388–393.

Morley, Sylvanus G.
1920   *The Inscriptions at Copan.* Pub. 219. CIW.
1937–   *The Inscriptions of Peten.* Pub. 437. CIW
1938
1946   *The Ancient Maya.* Stanford University Press, Stanford, CA.

Morley, Sylvanus G., and George Brainerd
1956   *The Ancient Maya,* third ed. Stanford University Press, Stanford, CA.

Morley, Sylvanus G., George E. Brainerd, and Robert J. Sharer
1983   *The Ancient Maya,* fourth ed. Stanford University Press, Stanford, CA.

Morris, Earl H., Jean Charlot, and Ann Axtel Morris
1931   *The Temple of the Warriors.* Pub. 406. CIW.

Murdock, George P.
1949   *Social Structure.* MacMillan, New York.

Murra, John V.
1980   *The Economic Organization of the Inka State.* Research in Economic Anthropology, Supplement. JAI Press, Greenwich, CT.

Nalda, Enrique, and Javier López Camacho
1995   Investigaciones arqueológicas en el sur de Quintana Roo. *Arqueología Mexicana* III (14): 12–25. Editorial Raíces, INAH.

Navarrete, Carlos, and Luis Lujan Muñoz
1963   *Reconocimiento arqueológico del sitio de "Dos Pilas," Petexbatun, Guatemala.* Cuadernos de Antropología 2. Facultad de Humanidades, Universidad de San Carlos, Guatemala City.

Neff, Hector
1984   *The Developmental History of the Plumbate Pottery Industry in the Eastern Soconusco Region, A.D. 600 through A.D. 1250.* Ph.D. dissertation, University of California, Santa Barbara.

Neff, Hector, and Ronald L. Bishop
1988   Plumbate Origins and Development. *AAnt* 53: 505–522.

Neff, L. Theodore
  1998   Precolumbian Lowland Maya Population Dynamics and Intensive Terrace Agriculture in the Xunantunich Area, Belize, Central America. Paper presented at the 97th Annual Meeting of the AAA, Philadelphia.
  1999   The Archaeology of Agricultural Intensification: A Study of Precolumbian Maya Agricultural Terracing in the Dos Chombitos Area, Belize. Ph.D. dissertation, Department of Anthropology, University of Pennsylvania, Philadelphia.

Neff, L. Theodore, Cynthia Robin, Kevin Schwarz, and Mary K. Morrison
  1995   The Xunantunich Settlement Survey. In Leventhal and Ashmore 1995, pp. 139–163.

Nelson, Diane
  1999   *A Finger in the Wound: Body Politics in Quincentennial Guatemala.* University of California Press, Berkeley.

Nicholson, Harry B.
  1960   The Mixteca-Puebla Concept in Mesoamerican Archaeology: A Re-examination. In *Men and Cultures,* ed. A.F.C. Wallace, pp. 612–617. University of Pennsylvania, Philadelphia.

Ochoa, Lorenzo, and Luis Casasola
  1978   Los cambios del patron de asentamiento en el área del Usumacinta. In *Estudios preliminares sobre los mayas de la tierras bajas noroccidentales,* ed. L. Ochoa, pp. 19–43. UNAM.

Oland, Maxine H.
  1999   Preliminary Analysis of Lithics from Caye Coco, Caye Muerto, and the Shores of Progresso Lagoon. In *Belize Postclassic Project 1998: Investigations at Progresso Lagoon,* ed. M. A. Masson and R. M. Rosenswig, pp. 145–156. Occasional Pub. no. 3, IMS.
  2000   Lithic Tool and Debitage Analysis from Caye Coco, Progresso Op 7, and Laguna Seca. In *Belize Postclassic Project 1999: Continued Investigations at Progresso Lagoon and Laguna Seca,* ed. R. M. Rosenswig and M. A. Masson, pp. 133–140. Occasional Pub. no. 5. IMS.

O'Mansky, Matt
  1996   The Classic Maya Collapse in the Petexbatun: Recent Investigations in Hilltop Fortresses. Paper presented at the 19th Midwest Conference on Mesoamerican Archaeology and Ethnohistory, Madison, WI.
  1999   Intersite Settlement in the Petexbatun Region, Guatemala: The Effects of Late Classic Period Maya Warfare on Non-Elite Populations. Paper presented at the 64th Annual Meeting of the SAA, Chicago.
  2003   *The Petexbatun Regional Survey: Settlement and Land Use in a Late Classic Maya Kingdom.* Unpublished Ph.D. dissertation, Department of Anthropology, Vanderbilt University, Nashville, TN.

O'Mansky, Matt, and Arthur A. Demarest
  1995   La temporada de reconocimiento de 1994 del subproyecto del patron de asentamiento entre sitios en la región de Petexbatun. In Demarest, Valdés, and Escobedo 1995, pp. 403–406.

O'Mansky, Matt, Q. Joshua Hinson, Robert Wheat, and Arthur A. Demarest
  1995   Investigaciones del transecto 4 oeste de Aguateca. In Demarest, Valdés, and Escobedo 1995, pp. 447–472.

O'Mansky, Matt, Q. Joshua Hinson, Robert Wheat, and Kay Sunahara
  1995   Investigaciones de transectos anteriores. In Demarest, Valdés, and Escobedo 1995, pp. 407–446.

O'Mansky, Matt, and Robert Wheat

1996a   Patrones de asentamiento al oeste de la península de Punta de Chimino. In Demarest, Escobedo, and O'Mansky 1996, pp. 116–130.

1996b   Asentamientos fortificados en el final del período clásico: ambiente bélico de Punta de Chimino. In Demarest, Escobedo, and O'Mansky 1996, pp. 131–139.

Orrego, Miguel, and Carlos Rudy Larios

1983   *Reporte de las investigaciones arqueológicas en el Grupo 5E–11 de Tikal.* IDAEH.

Ower, L. H.

1928   The Geology of British Honduras. *Journal of Geology* 36: 494-509.

Pagden, Anthony R.

1971   *Hernan Cortes—Letters from Mexico.* Grossman, New York.

Paine, Richard R., and AnnCorinne Freter

1996   Environmental Degradation and the Maya Collapse at Copán (A.D. 600–1250). *AM* 7(1): 37–47.

Paine, Richard R., AnnCorinne Freter, and David Webster

1996   A Mathematical Projection of Population Growth in the Copán Valley, Honduras, A.D. 400–800. *LAA* 7(1): 51–60.

Palka, Joel

1991   Operación DP19: excavación de la estructura L5-47 y sus alrededores. In Demarest, Inomata, Escobedo, and Palka 1991, pp. 123–136.

1995   *Classic Maya Social Inequality and the Collapse at Dos Pilas, Peten, Guatemala.* Ph.D. dissertation, Vanderbilt University, Nashville, TN.

1997   Reconstructing Classic Maya Socioeconomic Differentiation and the Collapse at Dos Pilas, Peten, Guatemala. *AM* 8(2): 293–306.

Peña C., Agustín, Sylviane Boucher, Heajoo Chung, David Ortegón Z., Gabriel Euan C., José Osorio L., and María Elena Peraza

1991   *Proyecto Chichén Itzá, informe preliminar 1990.* Informe mecanuscrito, Centro Regional Yucatán del INAH, Mérida, México.

Pendergast, David

1967   Occupation post-clásica en Altun Ha, Honduras Britanica. *Revista Mexicana de Estudios Antropológicas* 21: 213–224.

1969   *The Prehistory of Actun Balam, British Honduras.* Occasional Paper 16. ROM.

1970a   *A. H. Anderson's Excavations at Rio Frio Cave E, British Honduras (Belize).* ROM.

1970b   Tumbaga Object from the Early Classic Period Found at Altun Ha, British Honduras (Belize). *Science* 168: 116–118.

1971   *Excavation at Eduardo Quiroz Cave, British Honduras (Belize).* Occasional Paper 21. ROM.

1979   *Excavations at Altun Ha, Belize, 1964–70, vol. 1.* ROM.

1981a   Lamanai, Belize: Summary of Excavation Results: 1974–1980. *JFA* 8(1): 29–53.

1981b   Lamanai 1981(II): Buds, Sweat and Gears. *Royal Ontario Museum Archaeological Newsletter, n.s. 199.*

1982   *Excavations at Altun Ha, Belize, 1964–70, vol. 2.* ROM.

1985   Lamanai, Belize: An Updated View. In Chase and Rice 1985, pp. 91–103.

1986a   Stability Through Change: Lamanai, Belize, from the Ninth to the Seventeenth Century. In Sabloff and Andrews 1986b, pp. 223–249.

1986b   Under Spanish Rule: The Final Chapter in Lamanai's Maya History. *Belcast Journal of Belizean Affairs* 3(1 and 2): 1–7.

1988   Lamanai Stela 9: The Archaeological Context. *Research Reports on Ancient Maya Writing* 20–22: 1–8. Center for Maya Research, Washington, DC.

1990a   *Excavations at Altun Ha, Belize, 1964–70, vol. 3.* ROM.

1990b Up From the Dust: The Central Lowlands Postclassic as Seen from Lamanai and Marco Gonzales. In *Vision and Revision in Maya Studies,* ed. F. Clancy and P. D. Harrison, pp. 169–177. University of New Mexico Press, Albuquerque.

1991 The Southern Maya Lowlands Contact Experience: The View from Lamanai, Belize. In *Columbian Consequences,* vol. 3, ed. D. H. Thomas, pp. 336–354. Smithsonian Institution Press, Washington, DC.

1992 Noblesse Oblige: The Elites of Lamanai and Altun Ha, Belize. In D. Z. Chase and A. F. Chase 1992b, pp. 61–79.

1993 Worlds in Collision: The Maya/Spanish Encounter in Sixteenth and Seventeenth Century Belize. In *The Meeting of Two Worlds: Europe and the Americas, 1492–1650,* ed. W. Bray, pp. 105–143. The British Academy, London.

1998 Intercessions with the Gods: Caches and their Significance at Altun Ha and Lamanai, Belize. In Mock 1998d, pp. 55–63.

Peniche Rivero, Piedad
1973 *Comalcalco, Tabasco: su cerámica, artefactos y enterramientos.* Unpublished M.A. thesis, Universidad de Yucatán, Mérida, México.

Peraza L., Carlos
1992 *Estudio y secuencia del material cerámico de San Gervasio, Cozumel.* Tesis de licenciatura, Facultad de Ciencias Antropológicas, UAYM.

Pérez de Heredia Puente, Eduardo J.
1998 Datos recientes sobre la cerámica de Chichén Itzá. *LICM 6,* tomo II: 271–287. UACM.

Phillips, Philip, and Gordon R. Willey
1953 Method and Theory in American Archaeology: An Operational Basis for Culture-Historical Integration. *AA* 55: 615–633.

Piehl, Jennifer
2001 Status, Diet, and Nutrition: An Analysis of Human Remains from Group 10L-2, Copán. Paper presented at the 66th Annual Meeting of the SAA, New Orleans.

Piña Chan, R.
1978 Commerce in the Yucatec Peninsula: The Conquest and Colonial Period. In *Mesoamerican Communication Routes and Culture Contacts,* ed. T. A. Lee and C. Navarrete, pp. 37–48. Papers of the NWAF 40.

Pincemin, Sophia
1989 La cerámica de Calakmul. Paper presented at the Primer Congreso Internacional de Mayistas, San Cristóbal de las Casas, México.

1994 *Entierro en el palacio (la tumba de la estructura III, Calakmul, Campeche.* Centro de Investigaciones Históricas y Sociales, UACM.

1999 Calakmul, Campeche: informe de la temporada noviembre–diciembre de 1988. *Información* 16:85–118. UACM.

Pincemin, Sophia, Joyce Marcus, Lynda Florey Folan, William J. Folan, María del Rosario Domínguez Carrasco, and Abel Morales López
1998 Extending the Calakmul Dynasty Back in Time: A New Stela from a Maya Capital in Campeche, Mexico. *LAA* 9: 310–327.

Pollock, Harry E.D.
1936 *Round Structures of Aboriginal Middle America.* Pub. 471. CIW.

1965 Architecture of the Maya Lowlands. In *HMAI, vol. 2, part 1,* ed. R. Wauchope and G. R. Willey, pp. 378–440.

1980 *The Puuc: An Architectural Survey of the Hill Country of Yucatan and Northern Campeche, Mexico.* PMAE Memoirs vol. 19.

Pollock, Harry E.D., Ralph L. Roys, Tatiana Proskouriakoff, and A. Ledyard Smith
  1962   *Mayapan, Yucatan, Mexico.* Pub. 619. CIW.

Pollock, Harry E.D., and Gustav Strömsvik
  1953   Chacchob, Yucatan. *Current Reports no. 6.* CIW.

Ponciano Alvarado, Erick, Takeshi Inomata, Daniela Triadan, Alba Estela Pinto, and Shannon Coyston
  1998   Aguateca: evidencias de un abandono repentino en el clásico tardío. In *XI Simposio, 1997,* tomo 2, pp. 685–697.

Potter, Daniel R.
  1982   Some Results of the Second Year of Excavation at Operation 2012. In *The Colhá Project, Second Season, 1981 Interim Report,* ed. T. R. Hester, J. D. Eaton, and H. J. Shafer, pp. 98–122. Center for Archaeological Research, University of Texas at San Antonio, and Centro Studi e Ricerche Ligabue, Venice.

Potter, Daniel R., and Eleanor M. King
  1995   A Heterarchical Approach to Lowland Maya Socioeconomies. In *Heterarchy and the Analysis of Complex Societies,* ed. R. M. Ehrenreich, C. L. Crumley, and J. E. Levy, pp. 17–32. Archaeological Papers of the AAA, no. 6, Arlington, VA.

Prem, Hanns J.
  1991   The Xkipché Archaeological Project. *Mexicon* 13: 62–63.
  1994   (ed.) *Hidden among the Hills: Maya Archaeology of the Northwest Yucatan Peninsula.* Acta Mesoamericana 7, Verlag von Flemming, Möckmühl, Bonn.

Preucel, Robert W., and Ian Hodder
  1996   Communicating Present Pasts. In *Contemporary Archaeology in Theory: A Reader,* ed. R. Preucel and I. Hodder, pp. 3–20. Basil Blackwell Publishers, Oxford.

Pring, Duncan
  1976   Outline of Northern Belize Ceramic Sequence. *Ceramica de Cultura Maya* 9: 11–52.

Proskouriakoff, Tatiana
  1950   *A Study of Classic Maya Sculpture.* Pub. 593.
  1955   The Death of a Civilization. *Scientific American* 192: 82–88.
  1962   Civic and Religious Structures of Mayapan. In Pollock, Roys, Proskouriakoff, and Smith 1962, pp. 87–163.
  1993   *Maya History,* ed. R. A. Joyce. University of Texas Press, Austin.

Pugh, Timothy W.
  2001   *Architecture, Ritual, and Social Identity at Late Postclassic Zacpetén, Petén, Guatemala: Identification of the Kowoj.* Ph.D. dissertation, Department of Anthropology, Southern Illinois University Carbondale. UMI.

Puleston, Dennis E.
  1973   *Ancient Maya Settlement Patterns and Environment at Tikal, Guatemala: Implications for Subsistence Models.* Unpublished Ph.D. dissertation, Department of Anthropology, University of Pennsylvania, Philadelphia.
  1974   Intersite Areas in the Vicinity of Tikal and Uaxactun. In *Mesoamerican Archaeology,* ed. N. Hammond, pp. 303–312. Duckworth, London.
  1977   The Art and Archaeology of Hydraulic Agriculture in the Maya Lowlands. In Hammond 1977, pp. 449–467.
  1979   An Epistemological Pathology and the Collapse, or Why the Maya Kept the Short Count. In *Maya Archaeology and Ethnohistory,* ed. N. Hammond and G. R. Willey, pp. 63–71. University of Texas Press, Austin.
  1983   *Tikal Report No. 13: The Settlement Survey of Tikal.* Monograph no. 48. UM.

Pyburn, K. Anne

1990   Settlement Patterns at Nohmul: Preliminary Results of Four Excavation Seasons. In Culbert and Rice, pp. 183–197.

1991   Chau Hiix: A New Archaeological Site in Northern Belize. *Mexicon* XIII (5): 84–86.

1998   Smallholders in the Maya Lowlands: Homage to a Garden Variety Ethnographer. *Human Ecology* 26(2): 267–286.

1999   Ordinary People. Paper presented at the Annual Meeting of the American Anthropological Association.

n.d.   Proposal submitted to the National Science Foundation.

Quezada, Heidy

1996   Investigaciones de terrazas y grupos del clásico terminal: operación 30. In Demarest, Escobedo, and O'Mansky, pp. 56–60.

Quintana, Oscar

1996   Sitios Mayas menores en el noroeste del Petén, Guatemala: un programa regional de rescate del Proyecto Triángulo, Yaxha, Nakum, y Naranjo. *Sonderdruck aus Beiträge zur Allgemeinen und Vergleichenden Archäologie* 16: 227–262. Verlag Philipp von Zabern, Mainz am Rhein, Germany.

Rands, Robert L.

1967a   Cerámica de la región de Palenque, México. *ECM* 6: 111–147.

1967b   Ceramic Technology and Trade in the Palenque Region, Mexico. In *American Historical Anthropology, Essays in Honor of Leslie Spier,* ed. C. L. Riley and W. W. Taylor, pp. 137–151. Southern Illinois University Press, Carbondale.

1969   *Mayan Ecology and Trade: 1967–1968.* Research Records of the University Museum, Mesoamerican Studies, no. 2. Southern Illinois University Museum, Carbondale.

1973a   The Classic Maya Collapse in the Southern Maya Lowlands: Chronology. In Culbert 1973a, pp. 43–62.

1973b   The Classic Maya Collapse: Usumacinta Zone and the Northwestern Periphery. In Culbert 1973a, pp. 165–206.

1987   Ceramic Patterns and Tradition in the Palenque Area. In *Maya Ceramics: Papers from the 1985 Maya Ceramic Conference,* ed. P. M. Rice and R. J. Sharer, pp. 203–238. BAR no. 345(i).

Rands, Robert L., and Ronald L. Bishop

1980   Resource Procurement Zones and Patterns of Ceramic Exchange in the Palenque Region, Mexico. In *Models and Methods in Regional Exchange,* ed. R. Fry, pp. 19–46. SAA Papers no. 1, Society for American Archaeology, Washington, DC.

Rands, Robert, and Barbara Rands

1959   The incensario complex of Palenque, Chiapas. *AAnt* 25(2): 225–236.

Rapoport, Amos

1990   *The Meaning of the Built Environment: A Nonverbal Communication Approach,* second ed. University of Arizona Press, Tucson.

Rappaport, Roy A.

1971   Ritual, Sanctity, and Cybernetics. *AA* 73: 59–76.

Rathje, William L.

1971   The Origin and Development of Lowland Classic Maya Civilization. *AAnt* 36: 275–285.

1972   Praise the Gods and Pass the Metates: An Hypothesis of the Development of Lowland Rainforest Civilizations in Mesoamerica. In *Contemporary Archaeology,* ed. M. P. Leone, pp. 365–397. Southern Illinois University Press, Carbondale.

1973   Classic Maya Development and Denouement: A Research Design. In Culbert 1973a, pp. 405–456.

1975   The Last Tango in Mayapan: A Tentative Trajectory of Production-Distribution Systems. In *Ancient Civilization and Trade,* ed. J. A. Sabloff and C. C. Lamberg-Karlovsky, pp. 409–448. University of New Mexico Press, Albuquerque.

Rathje, William L., William Gregory, and Frederick Wiseman
1978   Trade Models and Archaeological Problems: Classic Maya Examples. In *Mesoamerican Communication Routes and Cultural Contacts,* ed. T. A. Lee and Carlos Navarrete, pp. 147–175. Papers of the NWAF.

Rathje, William L., and Jeremy A. Sabloff
1973   Ancient Maya Commercial Systems: A Research Design for the Island of Cozumel, Mexico. *World Archaeology* 5(2): 221–231.
1975   *A Study of Pre-Columbian Commercial Systems: The 1972–1973 Seasons at Cozumel, Mexico.* PMAE.

Redfield, Robert
1955   *The Little Community: Viewpoints for the Study of a Human Whole.* University of Chicago Press, Chicago.

Redfield, Robert, and Alfonso Villa Rojas
1934   *Chan Kom: A Maya Village.* University of Chicago Press, Chicago.

Reed, Nelson
1964   The Caste War of Yucatan. Stanford University Press, Stanford, CA.

Reents-Budet, Dorie
1994   *Painting the Maya Universe: Royal Ceramics of the Classic Period.* Duke University Press, Durham, NC.
1997   Los maestros pintores de cerámica maya. *Arqueología Mexicana* 5(28): 20–29. Editorial Raíces, INAH.

Reina, Ruben E.
1963   Chinautla, comunidad indígena Guatemalteca: estudio de las relaciones entre la cultura de comunidad y el cambio nacional. *Guatemala Indígena* 3: 31–150.
1967   Milpas and Milperos: Implications for Prehistoric Times. *AA* 69: 1–20.

Reindel, Markus
1997   Xkipché: un asentamiento maya en el norte de Yucatán, México. *Beiträge zur Allgemeinen und Vergleichenden Archäologie* 17. Verlag Philipp von Zabern, Mainz am Rhein, Germany.

Renfrew, Colin
1978   Trajectory, Discontinuity and Morphogenesis: The Implications of Catastrophe Theory for Archaeology. *AAnt* 43: 203–222.

Renfrew, Colin, and Paul Bahn
1996   *Archaeology.* Thames and Hudson, London.

Rice, Don S.
1986   The Peten Postclassic: A Settlement Perspective. In Sabloff and Andrews 1986b, pp. 301–344.
1988   Classic to Postclassic Maya Household Transitions in the Central Peten, Guatemala. In *Household and Community in the Mesoamerican Past,* ed. R. R. Wilk and W. Ashmore, pp. 227–247. University of New Mexico Press, Albuquerque.
1993a   Eighth-Century Physical Geography, Environment, and Natural Resources in the Maya Lowlands. In Sabloff and Henderson 1993b, pp. 11–63.
1993b   (ed.) *Latin American Horizons.* DO.

Rice, Don S., and T. Patrick Culbert
1990   Historical Contexts for Population Reconstruction in the Maya Lowlands. In Culbert and Rice 1990, pp. 1–36.

Rice, Don S., and Dennis E. Puleston
    1981   Ancient Maya Settlement Patterns in the Petén, Guatemala. In Ashmore 1981a, pp. 121–156.

Rice, Don S., and Prudence M. Rice
    1979   Introductory Archaeological Survey of the Central Peten Savanna, Guatemala. *Contributions of the University of California Archaeological Research Facility* 41: 231–277.
    1980   La utilización de las sabanas del Petén central por los maya clásicos. *Antropología y Historia de Guatemala 2 (II época)*: 69–80.
    1990   Population Size and Population Change in the Central Petén Lakes Region, Guatemala. In Culbert and Rice 1990, pp. 123–148.

Rice, Don S., Prudence M. Rice, and Grant D. Jones
    1993   Geografía política del Petén central, Guatemala, en el siglo XVII: la arqueología de las capitales mayas. *Mesoamérica* 14(26): 281–318.

Rice, Don S., Prudence M. Rice, and Timothy W. Pugh
    1998   Settlement Continuity and Change in the Central Petén Lakes Region: The Case of Zacpetén. In Ciudad Ruíz et al. 1998, pp. 208–252.

Rice, Prudence M.
    1979   The Ceramic and Non-ceramic Artifacts of Yaxha-Sacnab, El Petén, Guatemala. Part 1—The Ceramics: Section A, Middle Preclassic. *Ceramica de Cultura Maya* 11: 1–85.
    1983a   Serpents and Styles in Petén Postclassic Pottery. *AA* 85: 866–880.
    1983b   Reptilian Imagery and Vessel Function in Petén Postclassic Pottery: A Preliminary View. In *Fifth Palenque Round Table,* ed. M. G. Robertson, pp. 115–122. PARI.
    1984   Change and Conservatism in Pottery-Producing Systems. In *The Many Dimensions of Pottery: Ceramics in Archaeology and Anthropology,* ed. S. E. van der Leeuw and A. C. Pritchard, pp. 231–288. University of Amsterdam, Amsterdam.
    1986   The Peten Postclassic: Perspectives from the Central Peten Lakes. In Sabloff and Andrews 1986b, 251–299.
    1987a   Economic Change in the Lowland Maya Late Classic Period. In *Specialization, Exchange, and Complex Societies,* ed. E. M. Brumfiel and T. K. Earle, pp. 76–85. Cambridge University Press, Cambridge.
    1987b   Lowland Maya Pottery Production in the Late Classic Period. In *Maya Ceramics: Papers from the 1985 Maya Ceramic Conference,* ed. P. M. Rice, and R. J. Sharer, pp. 525–543. BAR no. 345.
    1987c   *Macanché Island, El Petén, Guatemala: Excavations, Pottery, and Artifacts.* University Press of Florida, Gainesville.
    1989   Reptiles and Rulership: A Stylistic Analysis of Petén Postclassic Pottery. In *Word and Image in Maya Culture: Explorations in Language, Writing, and Representation,* ed. W. F. Hanks and D. S. Rice, pp. 306–318. University of Utah Press, Salt Lake City.
    1996   La cerámica del Proyecto Maya-Colonial. In *Proyecto Maya-Colonial, geografía política del siglo XVII en el centro del Petén, Guatemala. Informe preliminar al IDAEH sobre investigaciones del campo en los años 1994 y 1995,* ed. D. S. Rice, P. M. Rice, R. Sánchez Polo, and G. D. Jones, pp. 247–323. IDAEH.
    1999   Rethinking Classic Lowland Maya Pottery Censers. *AM* 10: 25–50.
    2004   *Maya Political Science: Time, Astronomy, and the Cosmos.* University of Texas Press, Austin.
    n.d.   The Classic "Collapse" and Its Causes: The Role of Warfare? In *The Archaeological Contributions of Gordon R. Willey: A Contemporary Perspective,* ed. J. A. Sabloff and W. A. Fash, Jr. Norman: University of Oklahoma Press.

632   REFERENCES

Rice, Prudence M., Helen V. Michel, Frank Asaro, and Fred H. Stross
1985   Provenience Analysis of Obsidians from the Central Peten Lakes Region, Guatemala.
AAnt 50: 591–604.

Rice, Prudence M., and Don S. Rice
1979   Home on the Range: Aboriginal Maya Settlement in the Central Peten Savannas.
Archaeology 32(6): 16–25.
1985   Topoxte, Macanche, and the Central Peten Postclassic. In Chase and Rice 1985, pp.
166–183.
n.d.   The Final Frontier of the Maya: Central Petén, Guatemala, A.D. 1450–1700. In
Frontiers Through Space and Time: Interdisciplinary Perspectives on Frontier Stud-
ies, ed. B. J. Parker and L. Rodseth. University of Utah Press, Salt Lake City.

Ricketson, Oliver
1929   *Excavations at Baking Pot, Honduras.* Pub. 403. CIW.

Ricketson, Oliver, and Edith Ricketson
1937   *Uaxactun, Guatemala: Group E, 1926–1931.* Pub. 477. CIW.

Ridings, Rosanna
1996   Where in the World Does Obsidian Hydration Dating Work? *AAnt* 61: 136–148.

Ringle, William M.
1985   *The Settlement Patterns of Komchen, Yucatan, Mexico.* Unpublished Ph.D. dissertation, Department of Anthropology, Tulane University, New Orleans.
1999   Preclassic Cityscapes: Ritual Politics Among the Early Lowland Maya. In *Social*
Patterns in Pre-Classic Mesoamerica, ed. D. Grove and R. Joyce, pp. 183–223. DO.

Ringle, William M., and George Bey III
1992   The Center and Segmentary State Dynamics. African Models in the Maya Lowlands.
Paper presented at the Conference for Segmentary State Dynamics. Cleveland State
University, October 1992.
2001   Post-Classic and Terminal Classic Courts of the Northern Maya Lowlands. In *Royal*
Courts of the Maya, vol. 2: Data and Case Studies, ed. T. Inomata and S. D. Houston,
pp. 266–307. Westview Press, Boulder, CO.

Ringle, William M., George J. Bey III, Tara Bond-Freeman, Jeremy Campbell, and Katie Ainsworth
2000   Regional Hierarchy in Eastern Yucatan: The Case of Kumal, Yucatan. Paper presented at the 65th Annual Meeting of the SAA, Philadelphia.

Ringle, William M., George Bey III, and Carlos Peraza L.
1991   An Itza Empire in Northern Yucatán?: A Neighboring View. Paper presented to the
47th International Congress of Americanists, New Orleans.

Ringle, William M., George J. Bey III, and J. Gregory Smith
2000   *Investigaciones arqueológicas en los periféricos de Ek Balam, Yucatán: informe de la*
temporada 1999. Report submitted to INAH and the Ahau Foundation.

Ringle, William M., Tomás Gallareta Negron, and George J. Bey III
1998   The Return of Quetzalcoatl: Evidence for the Spread of a World Religion During the
Epiclassic Period. *AM* 9(2): 183–232.

Ringle, William M., and J. Gregory Smith
1998   *Report on the 1997 Field Season at Ichmul de Morley, Yucatan.* Reported submitted
to INAH.

Rivera Dorado, Miguel
1991   Ruinas, arqueólogos y problemas. In *Oxkintok, una ciudad maya de Yucatán,* ed. M.
Rivera Dorado, pp. 9–54. Misión Arqueológica de España en México, Madrid.
1994   Notas de arqueología de Oxkintok. In Prem 1994, pp. 44–58.

1996   *Los mayas de Oxkintok.* Ministerio de Educación y Cultura, Madrid.

Robertson, Donald
1970   The Tulum Murals: The International Style of the Late Post-Classic. In *Verhandlungen des 38th Internationalen Amerikanistenkongresses, vol. 2*, pp. 77–88. Munich.

Robertson, Merle Green
1986   Some Observations on the X'telhu Panels at Yaxcaba, Yucatan. In *Research and Reflections in Archaeology and History, Essays in Honor of Doris Stone,* ed. E. W. Andrews V, 87–111. Pub. 57. MARI.

Robertson, Robin
1983   Functional Analysis and Social Process in Ceramics: The Pottery from Cerros, Belize. In *Civilization in the Ancient Americas,* ed. R. M. Leventhal and A. Kolata, pp. 105–142. University of New Mexico Press, Albuquerque, and PMAE.

Robichaux, Hubert R.
1995   *Ancient Maya Community Patterns in Northwestern Belize: Peripheral Zone Survey at La Milpa and Dos Hombres.* Unpublished Ph.D. dissertation, Department of Anthropology, The University of Texas at Austin.
2002   On the Compatibility of Epigraphic, Geographic, and Archaeological Data, with a Drought-based Explanation for the Classic Maya Collapse. *AM* 13(2): 341–345.

Robin, Cynthia
1989   *Preclassic Maya Burials at Cuello, Belize.* BAR no. 480.
1996a   Rural Household and Community Development in the Xunantunich Hinterlands during the Late and Terminal Classic. Dissertation Improvement Grant proposal submitted to the National Science Foundation, August.
1996b   Xunantunich Rural Settlement Project—1996. In Leventhal and Ashmore 1996, pp. 151–172.
1997   Xunantunich Rural Settlement Project 1997. In Leventhal 1997, pp. 146–155.
1999   *Towards an Archaeology of Everyday Life: Ancient Maya Farmers of Chan Nòohol and Dos Chombitos Cik'in.* Ph.D. dissertation, Department of Anthropology, University of Pennsylvania, Philadelphia.
2000   Methods for Identifying Outdoor Living Spaces. In *Understanding Households, Household Activities, and Activity Areas: Developing Issues in the Method and Theory of Activity Areas and Domestic Archaeology,* ed. W. D. Middleton and L. Barba. Cotsen Institute Press, UCLA (in press).
2001   Peopling the Past: New Perspectives on the Ancient Maya. *Proceedings of the National Academy of Sciences* 98: 18–21.

Robles C., Fernando
1986   Cronología cerámica de El Meco. In *Excavaciones arqueológicas en El Meco, Quintana Roo, 1977,* ed. A. P. Andrews and F. Robles C., pp. 77–130. Colección Científica no. 158. INAH.
1988   Ceramic Units from Isla Cerritos, North Coast of Yucatan (Preliminary Results). *Ceramica de Cultura Maya* 15: 65–71.
1990   *La secuencia cerámica de la región de Cobá, Quintana Roo.* Colección Científica no. 184. INAH.
n.d.   Las esferas cerámicas Cehpech y Sotuta del apogeo del clásico tardío (c. 730–900 d.C.) en el norte de la peninsula de Yucatán. In *La producción alfarera en el México antiguo,* ed. N. González Crespo and A. García Cook. INAH.

Robles C., Fernando, and Anthony P. Andrews
1986   A Review and Synthesis of Recent Postclassic Archaeology in Northern Yucatan. In Sabloff and Andrews 1986b, pp. 53–98.

Rockmore, Matthew
  1998   *The Social Development of the Itzá Maya: A Reassessment of the Multiple Lines of Evidence.* M.A. thesis. Department of Anthropology, Southern Illinois University Carbondale.

Rodas, Irma
  1995   Pequeña investigacion de desbroce en la Plaza Principal de Dos Pilas. In Demarest, Váldes, and Escobedo 1995, pp. 281–285.

Rodas, Irma, and Juan Pedro Laporte
  1995   Aktun Ak'ab: una cueva asociada al sistema hidrológico de la cuenca del alto río Mopan. In *VIII Simposio, 1994,* pp. 629–650.

Roemer, Erwin, Jr.
  1984   *A Late Classic Maya Lithic Workshop at Colha, Belize.* Unpublished M.A. thesis, Department of Anthropology, Texas A&M University, College Station.

Rogge, John R. (ed.)
  1987   *Refugees: A Third World Dilemma.* Rowman and Littlefield, Totowa, NJ.

Roscoe, Paul B.
  1993   Practice and Political Centralization: A New Approach to Political Evolution. *CA* 34: 111–140.

Rosenswig, Robert M.
  1999   Looter's Trench Documentation in 1998 and a Brief History of Architectural Construction at Caye Coco, Belize. In *The Belize Postclassic Project 1998: Investigations at Progresso Lagoon,* ed. M. A. Masson and R. M. Rosenswig, pp. 125–135. Occasional Pub. no. 3. IMS.

Rosenswig, Robert M., and Marilyn A. Masson (eds.)
  2001   *Belize Postclassic Project 2000: Investigations at Caye Coco and the Shore Settlements of Progresso Lagoon.* Occasional Pub. no. 6. IMS.

Rovner, Irwin
  1975   *Lithic Sequences from the Maya Lowlands.* Unpublished Ph.D. dissertation, Department of Anthropology, University of Wisconsin, Madison.

Roys, Ralph L.
  1933   *The Book of Chilam Balam of Chumayel.* Pub. 438. CIW.
  1957   *The Political Geography of the Yucatan Maya.* Pub. 613. CIW.
  1967   *The Book of Chilam Balam of Chumayel.* University of Oklahoma Press, Norman.

Rue, David
  1986   *Palynological Analysis of Pre-Hispanic Human Impact in the Copán Valley, Honduras.* Ph.D. dissertation, Pennsylvania State University. UMI.
  1987   Early Agriculture and Early Postclassic Maya Occupation in Western Honduras. *Nature* 326: 285–286.

Rue, David, David Webster, and Alfred Traverse
  2002   Late Holocene Fire and Agriculture in the Copan Valley, Honduras. *AM* 13(2): 267–272.

Ruíz Guzmán, Roberto
  1998   *Las figurillas e instrumentos musicales de Calakmul, Campeche. Descripción, análisis e interpretación: una tentativa tipología.* Tesis de licenciatura, Escuela Nacional de Antropología e Historia, México.

Ruíz Guzmán, Roberto, Ronald L. Bishop, and William J. Folan
  1999   Las figurillas de Calakmul, Campeche: su uso funcional y clasificación sociocultural y química. *LICM* 7(1): 37–49.

Ruppert, Karl J.
1928   Report of Karl Ruppert on the Outlying Sections of Chichén Itzá. *Year Book* 27: 305–307. CIW.
1940   Special Assemblage of Maya Structures. In *The Maya and their Neighbors*, ed. C. Hay et al., pp. 222–231. Appleton Century, New York.
1943   *The Mercado, Chichen Itza, Yucatan.* Pub. 546, Contrib. 43. CIW.
1950   Gallery-patio Type Structures at Chichen Itza. In *For the Dean: Essays in Anthropology in Honor of Byron S. Cummings on His 89th Birthday*, ed. E. K. Reed and D. S. King, pp. 249–258. Hohokam Museums Association and Southwestern Monuments Association, Santa Fe and Tucson.
1952   *Chichen Itza: Architectural Notes and Plans.* Pub. 595. CIW.

Ruppert, Karl J., and John H. Denison
1943   *Archaeological Reconnaissance in Campeche, Quintana Roo, and Peten.* Pub. 543. CIW.

Ruppert, Karl, and A. Ledyard Smith
1955   Two New Gallery-Patio Type Structures at Chichen Itza. *Notes on Middle American Archaeology and Ethnology* vol. V, no. 122: 59–62. Department of Archaeology, CIW.
1957   *House Types in the Environs of Mayapan and at Uxmal, Kabah, Sayil, Chichen Itza, and Chacchob.* Current Reports 39. Department of Archaeology, CIW.

Ruz Lhuillier, Alberto
1953   *Uxmal: temporada de trabajos 1951–1952.* Centro de Yucatán, INAH.
1968   *Costumbres funerarias de los antiguos mayas.* Seminario de la Cultura Maya, UNAM.
1969   *La costa de Campeche en los tiempos prehispánicos: prospección cerámica y bosquejo historico.* Serie Investigaciones 18. INAH.

Sabloff, Jeremy A.
1970   Type Descriptions of the Fine Paste Ceramics of the Bayal Boca Complex, Seibal, Peten, Guatemala. In *Monographs and Papers in Maya Archaeology*, ed. W. R. Bullard Jr., pp. 357–404. PMAE Papers vol. 61, part IV, no. 2.
1973   Continuity and Disruption During Terminal Late Classic Times at Seibal: Ceramic and Other Evidence. In Culbert 1973a, pp. 107–131.
1975   *Excavations at Seibal: Ceramics.* PMAE Memoirs vol. 13, no. 2.
1977   Old Myths, New Myths: The Role of Sea Traders in the Development of Ancient Maya Civilization. In *The Sea in the Pre-Columbian World*, ed. E. P. Benson, pp. 67–97. DO.
1982   (ed.) Analyses of Fine Paste Ceramics. In *Excavations at Seibal, Department of Peten, Guatemala*, ed. G. R. Willey. PMAE Memoirs vol. 15, no. 2.
1986   Interaction among Classic Maya Polities: A Preliminary Examination. In *Peer Polity Interaction and Socio-Political Change*, ed. C. Renfrew and J. F. Cherry, pp. 109–116. Cambridge University Press, Cambridge.
1990   *The New Archaeology and the Ancient Maya.* New York: Scientific American Library.
1995   Archaeology: Drought and Decline. *Nature* 375(6530): 357.

Sabloff, Jeremy A., and E. Wyllys Andrews V
1986a   Introduction. In Sabloff and Andrews 1986b, pp. 3–13.
1986b   (eds.) *Late Lowland Maya Civilization: Classic to Postclassic.* SAR and University of New Mexico Press, Albuquerque.

Sabloff, Jeremy A., Ronald L. Bishop, Garman Harbottle, Robert L. Rands, and Edward V. Sayre
1982   *Analyses of Fine Paste Ceramics.* PMAE Memoirs 15(2).

Sabloff, Jeremy A., and John S. Henderson
1993a   Introduction. In Sabloff and Henderson 1993b, pp. 1–10.
1993b   (eds.) *Lowland Maya Civilization in the Eighth Century A.D.* DO.

Sabloff, Jeremy A., and William Rathje
   1975a   The Rise of a Maya Merchant Class. *Scientific American* 233(4): 72–82.
   1975b   (eds.) *A Study of Changing Pre-Columbian Commercial Systems: The 1972–1973 Seasons at Cozumel, Mexico.* PMAE Monographs no. 3.

Sabloff, Jeremy A., and Gordon R. Willey
   1967   The Collapse of Maya Civilization in the Southern Lowlands: A Consideration of History and Process. *Southwestern Journal of Anthropology* 23: 311–336.

Sackett, James R.
   1990   Style and Ethnicity in Archaeology: The Case for Isochrestism. In *The Uses of Style in Archaeology,* ed. M. W. Conkey and C. A. Hastorf, pp. 32–43. Cambridge University Press, Cambridge.

Sagebiel, Kerry Lynn
   1999   The La Milpa Ceramic Sequence: Evidence of Renewal and Growth in the Early Late Classic. Paper presented at the 64th Annual Meeting of the SAA, Chicago.

Sagebiel, Kerry, and Laura J. Kosakowsky
   1997   The Ceramic sequence of La Milpa, Belize. Paper presented at the 62nd Annual Meeting of the SAA, Nashville, TN.

Samayoa López, Jorge M.
   1996   Organización social: la evidencia arqueológica y el contraste teórico. Un caso específico. In *IX Simposio, 1995,* pp. 153–169.

Sanders, William T.
   1960   *Prehistoric Ceramics and Settlement Patterns in Quintana Roo, Mexico.* Contributions to American Anthropology and History, vol. 12, no. 60. Pub. 606.
   1973   The Cultural Ecology of the Lowland Maya: A Reevaluation. In Culbert 1973a, pp. 325–365.
   1977   Environmental Heterogeneity and the Evolution of Lowland Maya Civilization. In Adams 1977a, pp. 287–297.
   1981   Classic Maya Settlement Patterns and Ethnographic Analogy. In Ashmore 1981a, pp. 287–298.
   1989   Household, Lineage, and State at Eighth-Century Copan, Honduras. In Webster 1989, pp. 89–105.
   1992   Ranking and Stratification in Prehispanic Mesoamerica. In D. Z. Chase and A. F. Chase 1992b, pp. 278–291.

Santley, Robert S.
   1990   Demographic Archaeology in the Maya Lowlands. In Culbert and Rice 1990, pp. 325–344.
   1994   The Economy of Ancient Matacapan. *AM* 5(2): 243–266.

Santley, Robert S., Thomas W. Killion, and Mark T. Lycett
   1986   On the Maya Collapse. *Journal of Anthropological Research* 42(2): 123–159.

Sastry, Sheila
   2001   Excavations at Structure 19 (Subop 39), Caye Coco. In Rosenswig and Masson 2001, pp. 75–86.

Satterthwaite, Linton
   1951   Reconnaissance in British Honduras. *University Museum Bulletin,* vol. 16, no. 1: 21–37. UM.

Scarborough, Vernon L.
   1991a   *Archaeology at Cerros, Belize, Central America: The Settlement System in a Late Preclassic Maya Community,* vol. III, series ed. D. A. Freidel. Southern Methodist University Press, Dallas.

1991b   Water Management Adaptations in Non-Industrial Complex Societies: An Archaeo-logical Perspective. In *Archaeological Method and Theory,* vol. 3, ed. M. B. Schiffer, pp. 101–154. University of Arizona Press, Tucson.

1993   Water Management in the Southern Maya Lowlands: An Accretive Model for the Engineered Landscape. *Research in Economic Anthropology* 7: 17–69.

1994   Maya Water Management. *National Geographic Research and Exploration* 10: 184–199.

1996   Reservoirs and Watersheds in the Central Maya Lowlands. In Fedick 1996b, pp. 304–314.

1998   Ecology and Ritual: Water Management and the Maya. *LAA* 9: 135–159.

Scarborough, Vernon L., and Gary C. Gallopin
1991   A Water Storage Adaptation in the Maya Lowlands. *Science* 251: 658–662.

Scarborough, Vernon L., Matthew E. Becher, Jeffrey L. Baker, Garry Harris, and Fred Valdez Jr.
1995   Water and Land at the Ancient Maya Community of La Milpa. *LAA* 6: 98–119.

Scarborough, Vernon L., and David R. Wilcox (eds.)
1991   *The Mesoamerican Ballgame.* University of Arizona Press, Tucson.

Schele, Linda
1990   House Names and Dedication Rituals at Palenque. In *Vision and Revision in Maya Studies,* ed. F. S. Clancy and P. D. Harrison, pp. 143–157. University of New Mexico Press, Albuquerque.

1991   An Epigraphic History of the Western Maya Region. In Culbert 1991, pp. 72–101.

1995   *Some Suggestions on the Katun Prophecies in the Books of the Chilam Balam in Light of Classic Period History.* Texas Notes on Precolumbian Art, Writing and Culture no. 72. Austin, Texas.

1995   Some Speculations. *PARI Newsletter* 21: 4–5.

Schele, Linda, and David Freidel
1990   *A Forest of Kings: The Untold Story of the Ancient Maya.* New York: William Morrow.

1991   The Courts of Creation: Ballcourts, Ballgames, and Portals to the Maya Otherworld. In Scarborough and Wilcox 1991, pp. 289–316.

Schele, Linda, and Nikolai Grube
1994   Some Revisions to Tikal´s Dynasty of Kings. *Texas Notes on Precolumbian Art, Writing and Culture* 67: 1–9. Austin, Texas.

1995   *Notebook for the XIXth Maya Hieroglyphic Workshop at Texas: Late Classic and Terminal Classic Warfare,* transcription by Phil Wanyerka. Art Department, University of Texas, Austin.

Schele, Linda, Nikolai Grube, and Erik Boot
1998   Some Suggestions on the K'atun Prophecies in the Books of Chilam Balam in light of Classic-period History. In *Memorias del Tercer Congreso Internacional de Mayistas (9–15 de Julio, 1995),* pp. 399–446. Universidad Autonoma de México, Centro de Estudios Maya, México.

Schele, Linda, and Peter Mathews
1991   Royal Visits and Other Intersite Relationships Among the Classic Maya. In Culbert 1991, pp. 226–252.

1998   *The Code of Kings: The Language of Seven Sacred Maya Temples and Tombs.* Scribner, New York.

Schele, Linda, and Mary E. Miller
1986   *The Blood of Kings: Dynasty and Ritual in Maya Art.* Kimbell Art Museum, Fort Worth, TX.

Schiffer, Michael B.
1976   *Behavioral Archaeology.* Academic Press, New York.

1987   *Formation Processes of the Archaeological Record.* University of New Mexico Press, Albuquerque.

Schmidt, Peter J.
1978   Postclassic Finds in the Cayo District, Belize. *ECM* 10: 103–114.
1994   Chichén Itzá. *Arqueología Mexicana* 2(10): 20–25.

Schortman, Edward M.
1993   *Quirigua Reports III: Archaeological Investigations in the Lower Motagua Valley, Izabal, Guatemala.* University Museum Monographs, UM.

Schortman, Edward M., and Seiichi Nakamura
1991   A Crisis of Identity: Late Classic Competition and Interaction on the Southeast Maya Periphery. *LAA* 2: 311–336.

Schortman, Edward M., Patricia A. Urban, and Marne Ausec
1997   Politics with Style: Identity Formation in Prehispanic Southeastern Mesoamerica. Paper presented at the 96th Annual Meeting of the AAA, Washington, DC.

Schultz, Kevan A., Jason J. González, and Norman Hammond
1994   Classic Maya Ballcourts at La Milpa, Belize. *AM* 5: 45–53.

Shafer, Harry J., and Thomas R. Hester
1983   Ancient Maya Chert Workshops in Northern Belize, Central America. *AAnt* 48(3): 519–543.
1988   Preliminary Analysis of Postclassic Lithics from Santa Rita Corozal, Belize. Appendix III. In D. Z. Chase and A. F. Chase 1988, pp. 111–117.

Shanks, Michael, and Ian Hodder
1998   Processual, Postprocessual, and Interpretive Archaeologies. In *Reader in Archaeological Theory: Post-Processual and Cognitive Approaches,* ed. D. S. Whitley, pp. 69–95. Routledge, London.

Shanks, Michael, and Christopher Tilley
1987   *Re-Constructing Archaeology.* Cambridge University Press, Cambridge.

Sharer, Robert J.
1977   The Maya Collapse Revisited: Internal and External Perspective. In Hammond 1977, pp. 532–552.
1985   Terminal Events in the Southeastern Lowlands: A View from Quirigua. In Chase and Rice 1985, pp. 245–253.
1991   Diversity and Continuity in Maya Civilization: Quirigua as a Case Study. In Culbert 1991, pp. 180–198.
1993   *The Ancient Maya,* fifth ed. Stanford University Press, Stanford, CA.

Sharer, Robert J., and Arlen F. Chase
1976   New Town Ceramic Complex. In Gifford 1976, pp. 288–314.

Sharer, Robert J., William L. Fash, David W. Sedat, Loa P. Traxler, and Richard Williamson
1999   Continuities and Contrasts in Early Classic Architecture of Central Copan. In *Mesoamerican Architecture as a Cultural Symbol,* ed. J. K. Kowalski, pp. 220–249. Oxford University Press, New York and Oxford.

Sharer, Robert J., and Charles W. Golden
in press Kingship and Polity: Conceptualizing the Maya Body Politic. In *Maya Archaeology at the Millennium,* ed. C. Golden and G. Borgstede. Routledge Press, New York.

Sharer, Robert J., Loa P. Traxler, David W. Sedat, Ellen E. Bell, Marcello A. Canuto, and Christopher Powell
1999   Early Classic Architecture Beneath the Copan Acropolis: A Research Update. *AM* 10: 3–23.

Shaw, Justine
1998   *The Community Settlement Patterns and Residential Architecture of Yaxuna from* A.D. *600–1400.* Unpublished Ph.D. dissertation, Southern Methodist University, Dallas.

Sheets, Payson D.
1992   *The Ceren Site: A Prehistoric Village Buried by Volcanic Ash in Central America.* Case Studies in Archaeology Series, Harcourt Brace Jovanovich, Orlando, FL.
1997   Joya de Cerén. In *San Andrés y Joya de Cerén. Encuentro con las huellas de nuestros antepasados,* ed. R. Cobos and P. Sheets, pp. 63–93. Bancasa, San Salvador.

Shennan, Stephen J. (ed.)
1989   *Archaeological Approaches to Cultural Identity.* Routledge Press, New York.

Shepard, Anna O.
1948   *Plumbate—A Mesoamerican Trade Ware.* Pub. 573. CIW.

Shipley, Webster E., and Elizabeth A. Graham
1987   Petroglyphic Analysis and Preliminary Source Identification of Selected Stone Artifacts from the Maya Sites of Seibal and Uaxactun, Guatemala. *JAS* 14: 367–383.

Shook, Edwin M.
1990   Recollections of a Carnegie Archaeologist. *AM* 1(2): 247–252.

Sidrys, Raymond
1976   Classic Maya Obsidian Trade. *AAnt* 41(4): 449–464.
1983   *Archaeological Excavations in Northern Belize, Central America.* Institute of Archaeology Monograph 17. UCLA.

Sidrys, Raymond, and Rainer Berger
1979   Lowland Maya Radiocarbon Dates and the Classic Maya Collapse. *Nature* 277: 269–274.

Sidrys, Raymond V., and Clifford Krowne
1983   The Aventura Double Mouth Jar. In *Archaeological Excavations in Northern Belize,* ed. R. V. Sidrys, pp. 221–237.

Smith, A. Ledyard
1950   *Uaxactun, Guatemala: Excavations of 1931–1937.* Publication 588. CIW.
1962   Residential and Associated Structures at Mayapan. In Pollock, Roys, Proskouriakoff, and Smith, pp. 165–319.
1982   Major Architecture and Caches. *Excavations at Seibal, Department of Peten, Guatemala,* ed. G. R. Willey. PMAE Memoirs, vol. 15.

Smith, Carol A.
1974   Economics of Marketing Systems: Models from Economic Geography. *Annual Review of Anthropology* 3: 167–201.
1976a   Analyzing Regional Social Systems. In *Regional Analysis, vol. 2: Social Systems,* ed. C. A. Smith, pp. 3–20. Academic Press, New York.
1976b   Exchange Systems and the Spatial Distribution of Elites: The Organization of Stratification in Agrarian Societies. In *Regional Analysis, vol. 2: Social Systems,* ed. C. A. Smith, pp. 309–374. Academic Press, New York.

Smith, J. Gregory
1998a   Archaic Arenas of Negotiated Identity: Ethnic and Political Boundaries in Terminal Classic Northern Yucatán. Paper presented at the 97th Annual Meeting of the AAA, Philadelphia.
1998b   *Informe preliminar del Proyecto Transecto Chichen Itza-Ek Balam: temporada de campo 1998.* Report submitted to INAH.
1999   Ballcourts and Boundaries in the Chichén Itzá–Ek Balam Borderlands. Paper presented at the 64th Annual Meeting of the SAA, Chicago.

Smith, J. Gregory, William M. Ringle, and Tara M. Bond
  1998   Recent Research at Ichmul de Morley, Yucatan, Mexico, and Its Implications for Northern Lowland Maya Archaeology. Paper presented at the 63rd Annual Meeting of the SAA, Seattle.

Smith, Michael E.
  1987   Household Possessions and Wealth in Agrarian States: Implications for Archaeology. *Journal of Anthropological Archaeology* 6: 297–335.
  1992   Rhythms of Change in Postclassic Central Mexico: Archaeology, Ethnohistory, and the Braudelian Model. In *Archaeology, Annales, and Ethnohistory,* ed. A. Bernard Knapp, pp. 51–74. Cambridge University Press, Cambridge.

Smith, Robert E.
  1937   *A Study of Structure A-I Complex at Uaxactun, Peten, Guatemala.* Pub. 456. CIW.
  1955   *Ceramic Sequence at Uaxactun, Guatemala,* 2 vols. Pub. 20. MARI.
  1971   *The Pottery of Mayapan Including Studies of Ceramic Material from Uxmal, Kabah, and Chichen Itza,* 2 vols. PMAE Papers vol. 66.

Smith, Robert E., and James C. Gifford
  1966   *Maya Ceramic Varieties, Types, and Wares at Uaxactun: Supplement to "Ceramic Sequence at Uaxactun, Guatemala."* Pub. 28, pp. 125–174. MARI.

Smith, Robert E., Gordon R. Willey, and James C. Gifford
  1960   The Type-Variety Concept as a Basis for the Analysis of Maya Pottery. *AAnt* 25(3): 330–340.

Smyth, Michael P.
  1998   Before the Florescence: Chronological Reconstructions at Chac II, Yucatan, Mexico. *AM* 9: 137–150.

Smyth, Michael P., and Christopher D. Dore
  1992   Large-site Archaeological Methods at Sayil, Yucatan, Mexico: Investigating Community Organization at a Prehispanic Maya Center. *LAA* 3: 1–21.

Smyth, Michael P., Christopher D. Dore, and Nicholas P. Dunning
  1995   Interpreting Prehistoric Settlement Patterns: Lessons from the Maya Center of Sayil, Yucatan. *JFA* 22: 321–347.

Smyth, Michael, Christopher Dore, Hector Neff, and Michael Glascock
  1995   The Origin of Puuc Slateware: New Data from Sayil, Yucatan, Mexico. *AM* 6: 119–134.

Snow, David H.
  1988   Algunos probables efectos de cambios climáticos en las tierras bajas mayas. *Arqueología* 3. INAH.

Snow, Dean
  1997   Migration Theory and Archaeological Detection. Paper presented at the 62nd Annual Meeting of the SAA, Nashville, TN.

Spinden, Herbert J.
  1912   The Chronological Sequence of the Principal Monuments of Copán (Honduras). *Actas del 17 CIA,* 2: 357–363. Mexico, D.F.
  1913   *A Study of Maya Art: Its Subject Matter and Historical Significance.* PMAE Memoirs vol. 6.

Spindler, Konrad
  1994   *The Man in the Ice.* Harmony Books, New York.

Stanish, Charles
  1989   Household Archaeology: Testing Models of Zonal Complementarity in the South Central Andes. *AA* 91: 7–24.

Stanton, Travis
  1998   *Selz-Yaxuna:1997 Lab Season*. Unpublished manuscript in possession of the authors.
  1999   From Cetelac to the Coast: The Archaeology of Itza Expansion. Paper presented at the 64th Annual Meeting of the SAA, Chicago.

Steele, D. G., Jack D. Eaton, and A. J. Taylor
  1980   The Skulls from Operation 2011 at Colha: A Preliminary Examination. In *The Colha Project, Second Season 1980 Interim Report*, ed. T. R. Hester, J. D. Eaton, and H. J. Shafer, pp. 163–172. Center for Archaeological Research, University of Texas, San Antonio.

Stevens, Rayfred L.
  1964   The Soils of Middle America and their Relation to Indian People and Cultures. In *HMAI*, vol. 1, ed. R. C. West, pp. 265–315.

Stevenson, Christopher M., J. Carpenter, and B. E. Scheetz
  1989   Obsidian Dating: Recent Advances in the Experimental Determination and Application of Hydration Rates. *Archaeometry* 31: 193–206.

Stine, Scott
  1994   Extreme and Persistent Drought in California and Patagonia during Medieval Times. *Nature* 369: 546–549.

Stiver, Laura
  1992   La lítica del Proyecto Petexbatún: análisis de laboratorio, 1992. In Demarest, Inomata, and Escobedo 1992, pp. 286–296.

Stiver, Laura R., Michael D. Glascock, and Hector Neff
  1994   Socioeconomic and Historical Implications of Obsidian Source Analysis from Dos Pilas, Petexbatun Region, Guatemala. Department of Anthropology, Vanderbilt University, Nashville, TN.

Stross, Brian
  1998   Seven Ingredients in Mesoamerican Ensoulment: Dedication and Termination in Tenejapa. In Mock 1998d, pp. 31–39.

Stuart, David S.
  1984   *Epigraphic Evidence of Political Organization in the Usumacinta Drainage*. Unpublished manuscript in possession of the author.
  1986   The Hieroglyphs on a Vessel from Tomb 19, Rio Azul. In *Rio Azul Reports, no. 2, The 1984 Season*, ed. R.E.W. Adams, pp. 117–121. TARL.
  1990   Sondeos en Arroyo de Piedra. In Demarest and Houston 1990, pp. 353–368.
  1992   Hieroglyphs and Archaeology at Copan. *AM* 3: 169–184.
  1993   Historical Inscriptions and the Maya Collapse. In Sabloff and Henderson 1993b, pp. 321–354.
  1995   A Study of Maya Inscriptions. Unpublished Ph.D. dissertation, Department of Anthropology, Vanderbilt University, Nashville, TN.
  1996   Kings of Stone: A Consideration of Stelae in Ancient Maya Ritual and Representation. *Res* 29/30: 148–171.
  1997   Geroglifici e storia di Copán. In *I Maya di Copán*. Skire Editore, Milan.
  1998   "The Fire Enters His House": Architecture and Ritual in Classic Maya Texts. In Houston 1998, pp. 373–418.
  n.d.   The Texts of Temple 26: The Presentation of History at a Maya Dynastic Shrine. In *Copán: The History of an Ancient Maya Kingdom*, ed. W. L. Fash and E. W. Andrews. School of American Research Press, Albuquerque, NM.

Stuart, David, Stephen Houston, and John Robertson
  1999   *Recovering the Past: Classic Maya Language and Classic Maya Gods*. Maya Workshop Foundation, Austin, TX.

Stuart, George E.
1974   Riddle of the Glyphs. *National Geographic* 148(6): 768–791.

Stuiver, Minze, and Paula J. Reimer
1993   Extended 14C database and revised CALIB radiocarbon calibration program. *Radiocarbon* 35: 215–230.

Stuiver, Minze, Paula J. Reimer, Edouard Bard, Warren J. Beck, G. S. Burr, Konrad A. Hughen, Bernd Kromer, Gerry McCormac, Johannes van der Plicht, and Marco Spurk
1998   INTCAL98 Radiocarbon Age Calibration, 24,000 cal BP. *Radiocarbon* 40: 1041–1083.

Suasnávar, José Samuel
1995   Caxeba: un sitio rector en la cuenca del río Xaan, Dolores, Petén. In *VIII Simposio, 1994,* pp. 651–664.

Sugiyama, Saburo
1998   Termination Programs and Prehistoric Looting at the Feathered Serpent Pyramid in Teotihuacan, Mexico. In Mock 1998d, pp. 147–164.

Suhler, Charles
1996   *Excavations at the North Acropolis, Yaxuna, Yucatan, Mexico.* Unpublished Ph.D. dissertation, Southern Methodist University, Dallas.

Suhler, Charles, Traci Ardren, and David Johnstone
1998   The Chronology of Yaxuná: Evidence from Excavation and Ceramics. *AM* 9: 167–182.

Suhler, Charles, and David A. Freidel
1998   Life and Death in a Maya War Zone. *Archaeology,* May/June 1998.
1995   The Sack of Chichen Itza: Reinterpreting the Early Stratigraphic Excavations. Paper presented at the 1995 Maya Meeting, Austin, Texas.

Sullivan, Lauren, and Fred Valdez Jr.
n.d.   Late Preclassic Maya Ceramic Traditions in the Early Classic of Northwestern Belize. Manuscript to be submitted to *Latin American Antiquity.*

Sutro, Livingston D., and Theodore E. Downing
1988   A Step Toward a Grammar of Space: Domestic Space Use in Zapotec Villages. In *Household and Community in the Mesoamerican Past,* ed. R. R. Wilk and W. Ashmore, pp. 29–50. University of New Mexico Press, Albuquerque.

Swadesh, Maurice
1961   Interrelaciones de las lenguas mayenses. *Anales del INAH* 13(42): 231–267.

Symonds, Stacey
1990   Operación DP16: sondeos en el Grupo K5-2. In Demarest and Houston 1990, pp. 166–187.

Tainter, Joseph A.
1988   *The Collapse of Complex Societies.* Cambridge University Press, New York.

Tambiah, Stanley J.
1977   The Galactic Polity: The Structure of Traditional Kingdoms in Southeast Asia. *Annals of the New York Academy of Sciences* 293: 69–97.

Taschek, Jennifer J., and Joseph W. Ball
1992   Lord Smoke-Squirrel's Cacao Cup: The Archaeological Context and Socio-Historical Significance of the Buenavista "Jauncy Vase." In *The Maya Vase Book,* vol. 3, ed. J. Kerr, pp. 490–497. Kerr Associates, New York.

Taube, Karl
1989   The Maize Tamale in Classic Maya Diet, Epigraphy, and Art. *AAnt* 54: 31–51.
1994   The Iconography of Toltec Period Chichen Itza. In Prem 1994, pp. 212–246.

Tedlock, Barbara
1991   From Participant Observation to the Observation of Participation: The Emergence of Narrative Ethnography. *Journal of Anthropological Research* 47: 69–94.

Tedlock, Dennis
1992   The Popul Vuh as a Hieroglyphic Book. In *New Theories on the Ancient Maya*, ed. E. C. Danien and R. J. Sharer, pp. 229–240. UM.
1993   Torture in the Archives: Mayans Meet Europeans. *AA* 95: 139–152.

Teeter, Wendy Giddens
n.d.   Animal Utilization in a Growing City: Vertebrate Exploitation at Caracol, Belize. Paper presented at the Annual Meeting of the SAA, Nashville, TN.

Thompson, J. Eric S.
1938   Reconnaissance and Excavation in British Honduras. Pp. 16–17 in Annual Report of the Division of Historical Research, 1937–38. *Year Book* 37: 1–37. CIW.
1939   *Excavations at San Jose, British Honduras.* Pub. 506, CIW.
1940a   *Late Ceramic Horizons at Benque Viejo, British Honduras.* Contributions to American Anthropology and History no. 35. Pub. 528. CIW.
1940b   Problems of the Lowland Maya. In *The Maya and their Neighbors*, ed. C. L. Hay et al., pp. 126–138. Appleton-Century Co., New York.
1943   *Representations of Tlalchitonatiuh at Chichen Itza, Yucatan, and El Baul, Escuintla.* Notes 19, CIW.
1950   *Maya Hieroglyphic Writing: An Introduction.* Pub. 589. CIW.
1954   *The Rise and Fall of Maya Civilization.* University of Oklahoma Press, Norman.
1970   *Maya History and Religion.* University of Oklahoma Press, Norman.
1975   La expansión putun (Maya Chontal) en Yucatán y la cuenca del río de la Pasión. In *Historia y religión de los mayas*, ed. J. E. Thompson, pp. 21–62. Editorial Siglo XXI, México.

Thompson, J. Eric S., Harry E.D. Pollock, and Jean Charlot
1932   *A Preliminary Study of the Ruins of Cobá, Quintana Roo, Mexico.* Pub. 424. CIW.

Thompson, L. G., E. Mosley-Thompson, J. F. Bolzan, and B. R. Koci
1985   A 1,500-Year Record of Tropical Precipitation in the Ice Cores from the Quelccaya Ice Cap, Peru. *Science* 229: 971–973.

Tiesler Blos, Vera, María del Rosario Domínguez Carrasco, and William J. Folan
1999   Los restos humanos de contextos funerarios y extrafunerarios de Calakmul, Campeche, México. In *XII simposio 1998*, pp. 731–759.

Tourtellot, Gair
1983   An Assessment of Classic Maya Household Composition. In *Prehistoric Settlement Patterns*, ed. E. Z. Vogt and R. M. Leventhal, pp. 35–54. University of New Mexico Press, Albuquerque.
1988a   Developmental Cycles of Households and Houses at Seibal. In *Household and Community in the Mesoamerican Past*, ed. R. R. Wilk and W. Ashmore, pp. 97–120. University of New Mexico Press, Albuquerque.
1988b   *Excavations at Seibal, Department of Peten, Guatemala. Peripheral Survey and Excavation: Settlement and Community Patterns*, ed. G. R. Willey. PMAE Memoirs, vol. 16.
1990   Burials: A Cultural Analysis. *Excavations at Seibal, Department of Peten, Guatemala*, ed. G. R. Willey. PMAE Memoirs, vol. 17, no. 2.
1993   A View of Ancient Maya Settlements in the Eighth Century. In Sabloff and Henderson 1993b, pp. 219–241.

Tourtellot, Gair, III, Amanda Clarke, and Norman D.C. Hammond
1993   Mapping La Milpa: A Maya City in Northwestern Belize. *Antiquity* 67: 90–108.

Tourtellot, Gair, III, and John Rose
   1993   *More Light on La Milpa Mapping: Interim Report on the 1993 Season.* The La Milpa Archaeological Project. Department of Archaeology, Boston University, Boston.

Tourtellot, Gair, III, John J. Rose, Nikolai Grube, Sara Donaghey, and Norman Hammond
   1994   More Light on La Milpa: Maya Settlement Archaeology in Northwestern Belize. *Mexicon* 16: 119–124.

Tourtellot, Gair, and Jeremy Sabloff
   1994   Community Structure at Sayil: A Case Study of Puuc Settlement. In Prem 1994, pp. 71–92.

Tourtellot, Gair, III, Jeremy A. Sabloff, and Kelli Carmean
   1992   "Will the Real Elites Please Stand Up?" An Archaeological Assessment of Maya Elite Behavior in the Terminal Classic Period. In D. Z. Chase and A. F. Chase 1992b, pp. 80–98.

Tourtellot, Gair, Jeremy Sabloff, and Michael Smyth
   1990   Room Counts and Population Estimation for Terminal Classic Sayil in the Puuc Region, Yucatan, Mexico. In Culbert and Rice 1990, pp. 245–262. University of New Mexico Press, Albuquerque.

Tourtellot, Gair, Jeremy Sabloff, Michael Smyth, L. Val Whitley, Stanley Walling, Tomas Gallareta Negrón, Carlos Perez Alvarez, George Andrews, and Nicholas Dunning
   1988   Mapping Community Patterns at Sayil, Yucatan, Mexico: The 1985 Season. *Journal of New World Archaeology* 7(2/3): 1–24.

Tourtellot, Gair, Marc Wolf, Francisco Estrada Belli, and Norman Hammond
   2000   Discovery of Two Predicted Ancient Maya Sites in Belize. *Antiquity* 74(285): 481–482.

Tozzer, Alfred M.
   1907   *A Comparative Study of the Mayas and the Lacandones.* Macmillan, New York.
   1930   Maya and Toltec Figures at Chichen Itza. *Proceedings of the 23rd International Congress of Americanists,* pp. 155–164. New York.
   1941   *Landa's Relación de las Cosas de Yucatán.* PMAE Papers, vol. 4, no. 3.
   1957   *Chichen Itza and Its Cenote of Sacrifice: A Comparative Study of Contemporaneous Maya and Toltec.* PMAE Memoirs, vols. 11 and 12.

Tremaine, Kim J., and David A. Frederickson
   1988   Induced Obsidian Hydration Experiments: Investigations in Relative Dating. In *Materials Issues in Art and Archaeology,* ed. E. V. Sayre, P. Vandiver, J. Druzik, and C. M. Stevenson, pp. 217–278. Materials Research Society Symposium Proceedings 123. Materials Research Society, Pittsburgh, PA.

Trigger, Bruce
   1991   Distinguished Lecture in Archaeology: Constraint and Freedom—A New Synthesis for Archaeological Explanation. *AA* 93: 551–569.

Tschopik, Henry
   1951   An Andean Ceramic Tradition in Historical Perspective. *AAnt* 15: 196–218.

Turner, Billie Lee, II
   1983   *Once Beneath the Forest: Prehistoric Terracing in the Rio Bec Region of the Maya Lowlands.* Westview Press, Boulder, CO.
   1990   Population Reconstruction for the Central Maya Lowlands: 1000 B.C. to A.D. 1500. In Culbert and Rice 1990, pp. 301–324.

Turner, Billie Lee, II, and Peter D. Harrison
   1978   Implications from Agriculture for Maya Prehistory. In *Prehispanic Maya Agriculture,* ed. P. D. Harrison and B. L. Turner II, pp. 337–373. University of New Mexico Press, Albuquerque.

U.S. Committee for Refugees
2001   *World Refugee Survey 2001.* Washington, DC.

Valdés, Juan Antonio
1983   *Etude de Groupes D'Habitations du Centre Ceremonial Maya du "Mundo Perdido,"*
        Tikal, Guatemala. Ph.D. dissertation, University of La Sorbonne, Paris.
1985   Investigación habitacional de los cuadrantes perdido y corriental de Tikal: una
        formulación. *Antropología e Historia de Guatemala* VIII: 49–65. Guatemala.
1992   El Grupo 6C-15 de Tikal: conjunto ritual con implicaciones de complejidad social para
        el clásico tardío. *Estudios* 3: 57–72. Instituto de Investigaciones de la Escuela de
        Historia, Universidad de San Carlos de Guatemala.
1997   Tamarindito: Archaeology and Regional Politics in the Petexbatun Region. *AM* 8:
        321–335.

Valdés, Juan Antonio, and Federico Fahsen
1995   The Reigning Dynasty of Uaxactun During the Early Classic: The Rulers and the
        Ruled. *AM* 6: 197–219.

Valdés, Juan Antonio, Federico Fahsen, and Héctor Escobedo
1999   *Tumbas, reyes y palacios: la historia dinástica de Uaxactun.* Centro de Estudios
        Mayas, UNAM.

Valdés, Juan Antonio, Antonia Foias, and Oswaldo Chinchilla
1994   Tamarindito: un sitio con historia en la región de Petexbatún. In *VII Simposio, 1993,*
        pp. 439–452.

Valdés, Juan Antonio, Antonia Foias, Takeshi Inomata, Héctor Escobedo, and Arthur A. Demarest
        (eds.)
1993   *Proyecto Arqueológico Regional Petexbatún, informe preliminar, quinta temporada*
        1993. IDAEH and Vanderbilt University, Nashville, TN.

Valdez, Fred, Jr.
1987   *The Ceramics of Colha, Northern Belize.* Ph.D. dissertation, Department of Anthro-
        pology, Harvard University, Cambridge, MA.
1993   Appendix I. Ceramic Types from Laguna de On Shore. In *Changes in Maya Commu-*
        nity Organization from the Classic to Postclassic Periods: A View from Laguna de On,
        Belize, by M. A. Masson, p. 280. Ph.D. dissertation, Department of Anthropology,
        University of Texas at Austin.
1994   The Colha Ceramic Complexes. In *Continuing Archaeology at Colha, Belize,* ed. T.
        R. Hester, H. J. Shafer, and J. D. Eaton, pp. 9–16. Studies in Archaeology 16. TARL.

Valdez, Fred, Jr., and Richard E.W. Adams
1982   The Ceramics of Colha after Three Field Seasons: 1979–1981. In *Archaeology at*
        Colha, Belize: The 1981 Interim Report, ed. T. R. Hester, H. J. Shafer, and J. D. Eaton,
        pp. 21–30. Center for Archaeological Research, The University of Texas at San
        Antonio, and Centro Studi e Ricerche Ligabue, Venice.

Valdez, Fred, Jr., Richard E.W. Adams, Vernon Scarborough, Stanley Walling, and Nicholas Dunning
1997   *The Programme for Belize Archaeological Project: A Historical Overview.* Paper read
        at the 62nd Annual Meeting of the SAA, Nashville, TN. Available from Fred Valdez,
        Department of Anthropology, The University of Texas at Austin.

Valdez, Fred, Jr., Marilyn A. Masson, and Lenore Santone
1992   *Honey Camp—El Cacao Project: Summary of Investigations, 1991.* Report submit-
        ted to the BDOA.

Valdez, Fred, Jr., and Shirley Boteler Mock
1991   Additional Considerations for Prehispanic Saltmaking in Belize. *AAnt* 6(3): 520–525.

Valdez, Fred, Jr., Lauren A. Sullivan, and Thomas H. Guderjan
1995   Ceramics from Northern Ambergris Caye Sites. In Guderjan and Garber, pp. 95–112.

Vaillant, George C.
1927   *The Chronological Significance of Maya Ceramics.* Unpublished Ph.D. dissertation, Harvard University, Cambridge, MA.
1933   Hidden History: How a Little-Known Corner of Chichen Itza Adds a Page to the Story of Pre-Columbian Yucatan. *Natural History* 33(6): 618–628.

VandenBosch, Jon C., III
1992   Excavation of Rubble Mound Features in the Periphery. In Leventhal 1992, pp. 84–109.
1993   Investigations of San Lorenzo's Linear and Cobble Mounds. In Leventhal 1993, pp. 148–171.
1995   The Distribution of Households and their Lithic Economies in Rural Zones of Xunantunich. Paper presented at the First International Symposium on Maya Archaeology, Department of Archaeology, San Ignacio, Belize.

Van Tuerenhout, Dirk
1996   *Rural Fortifications at Quim Chi Hilan, El Peten, Guatemala: Late Classic Maya Social Change Seen from a Small Site Perspective.* Ph.D. dissertation, Tulane University, New Orleans.

Van Tuerenhout, Dirk, Hope Henderson, Paul Maslyk, and Robert Wheat
1993   Recorrido en la región de Petexbatún: Temporada 1993. In Valdés, Foias, Inomata, Escobedo, and Demarest 1993, pp. 81–87.
1994   Recorrido en la región de Petexbatún: Temporada 1993. In *VII Simposio, 1993,* pp. 215–222.

Varela Torrecilla, Carmen
1990   Un nuevo complejo en la sequencia cerámica de Oxkintok: el clásico medio. *Oxkintok* 3: 113–126, Madrid.
1996   La secuencia histórica de Oxkintok: Problemas cronológicos y metodológicos desde el punto de vista de la cerámica. *Revista Española de Antropología Americana* 26: 29–55. Servicio Publicaciones, UCM, Madrid.

Vargas de la Peña, Leticia, and Victor R. Castillo
2001   Ek Balam, el reino prehispánico de Talol. Paper presented at Congreso Internacional de Cultura Maya, Mérida, Yucatán, México.

Vargas de la Peña, Leticia, and Victor Castillo Borges
1999a   La acrópolis de Ek' Balam, el lienzo en él que plasmaron lo mejor de su arte sus antiguos pobladores. *Boletín informativo la pintura mural prehispánica en México* 10–11: 26–30.
1999b   Ek' Balam: ciudad que empieza a revelar sus secretos. *Arqueología Mexicana* 7: 37: 24–31.

Vargas de la Peña, Leticia, Victor Castillo B., and Alfonso Lacadena G.
1999   Textos glíficos de Ek' Balam (Yucatán, México): hallazgos de las temporadas de 1996–1998. *LICM* 7, tomo 1, pp. 172–187.

Viel, René H.
1983   Evolución de la cerámica en Copán: resultados preliminares. In Baudez 1983, vol. 1, pp. 471–549.
1993a   Copán Valley. In *Pottery of Prehistoric Honduras,* ed. J. S. Henderson and M. Beaudry-Corbett, pp. 12–19. Institute of Archaeology Monograph 35, UCLA.
1993b   *Evolución de la cerámica de Copán, Honduras.* Instituto Hondureño de Antropología e Historia, Tegucigalpa, Honduras, and Centro de Estudios Mexicanos y Centroamericanos, México, D.F.

1999   The Pectorals of Altar Q and Structure 11: An Interpretation of the Political Organization at Copán, Honduras. *LAA* 10: 377–399.

Villa Rojas, Alfonso
1934   The Yaxuna-Coba Causeway. *Contributions to American Archaeology* no. 9. CIW.

Vinson, George L.
1960   Las ruinas mayas de Petexbatun. *Antropología e Historia de Guatemala* 12(2): 3–9.

Vogt, Evon Z.
1961   Some Aspects of Zinacantan Settlement Pattern and Ceremonial Organization. *ECM* 1: 131–145.
1964   Some Implications of Zinacantan Social Structure for the Study of the Ancient Maya. *Actas y Memorias, XXXV CIA,* vol. 1, pp. 307–319. México, D.F.
1969   *Zinacantan: A Maya Community in the Highlands of Chiapas.* Belknap Press, Cambridge, MA.
1970   *The Zinacantecos of Mexico: A Modern Maya Way of Life.* Holt, Rinehart and Winston, New York.
1976   *Tortillas for the Gods: A Symbolic Analysis of Zinacanteco Rituals.* Harvard University Press, Cambridge, MA.
1993   *Tortillas for the Gods: A Symbolic Analysis of Zinacanteco Rituals.* University of Oklahoma Press, Norman.

von Euw, Eric
1977   *Corpus of Maya Hieroglyphic Inscriptions, vol. 4, part 1: Itzimpte, Pixoy, Tzum.* PMAE.

von Euw, Eric, and Ian Graham
1984   Xultun, La Honradez, Uaxactun. *Corpus of Maya Hieroglyphic Inscriptions,* vol. 5, part 2. PMAE.

Voss, Alexander, and Markus Eberl
1999   Ek Balam: A New Emblem Glyph from the Northeastern Yucatan. *Mexicon* XXI: 124–131.

Walker, Debra
1990   *Cerros Revisited: Ceramic Indicators of Terminal Classic and Postclassic Settlement and Pilgrimage in Northern Belize.* Ph.D. dissertation, Southern Methodist University, Dallas.

Walker, William H.
1995   Ceremonial Trash? In *Expanding Archaeology,* ed. J. M. Skibo, W. H. Walker, and A. E. Neilsen, pp. 67–79. University of Utah Press, Salt Lake City.
1998   Where Are the Witches of Prehistory? *Journal of Archaeological Method and Theory* 5: 245–308.

Walker, William H., and Lisa J. Lucero
2000   The Depositional History of Ritual and Power. In *Agency in Archaeology,* ed. M. A. Dobres and J. E. Robb, pp. 130–147. Routledge Press, London.

Walters, Rachel E., and Jeff Karl Kowalski
2000   Los murales de Mul-Chic, la guerra y la formación de un estado regional Puuc. In *La guerra entre los antiguos mayas: memoria de la Primera Mesa Redonda de Palenque,* ed. S. Trejo, pp. 205–223. Consejo Nacional para la Cultura y las Artes, INAH.

Warren, Kay B.
1992   Transforming Memories and Histories: The Meaning of Ethnic Resurgence for Mayan Indians. In *Americas: New Interpretive Essays,* ed. A. Stepan, pp. 189–219. Oxford University Press, New York.

Watanabe, John M.
 1992   *Maya Saints and Souls in a Changing World*. University of Texas Press, Austin.
 1995   Unimagining the Maya. Anthropologists, Others, and the Inescapable Hubris of Authorship. *Bulletin of Latin American Research* 14(1): 25–45.

Watson, Patty Jo, Steven A. LeBlanc, and Charles L. Redman
 1971   *Explanation in Archaeology: An Explicitly Scientific Approach*. Columbia University Press, New York.

Wauchope, Robert
 1938   *Modern Maya Houses: A Study of their Archaeological Significance*. Pub. no. 502. CIW.

Webb, Malcolm C.
 1964   *The Post Classic Decline of the Peten Maya: An Interpretation in Light of a General Theory of State Society*. Ph.D. dissertation, University of Michigan, Ann Arbor.
 1973   The Peten Maya Decline Viewed in the Perspective of State Formation. In Culbert 1973a, pp. 367–404.
 1975   The Flag Follows Trade: An Essay on the Necessary Interaction of Military and Commercial Factors in State Formation. In *Ancient Civilizations and Trade*, ed. J. A. Sabloff and C. C. Lamberg-Karlovsky, pp. 155–209. University of New Mexico Press, Albuquerque.

Weber, Max
 1958 (1930) *The Protestant Ethic and the Spirit of Capitalism*. Translated by Talcott Parsons. Charles Scribner's Sons, New York.

Webster, David A., and Nancy Gonlin
 1988   Household Remains of the Humblest Maya. *JFA* 15: 169–190.

Webster, David L.
 1976   On Theocracies. *AA* 78: 812–828.
 1977   Warfare and the Evolution of Maya Civilization. In Adams 1977, pp. 335–371.
 1978   Three Walled Sites of the Northern Maya Lowlands. *JFA* 5: 375–390.
 1979   *Cuca, Chacchob, and Dzonot Ake: Three Walled Northern Maya Centers*. Occasional Papers in Anthropology no. 11. Pennsylvania State University, University Park.
 1980   Spatial Bounding and Settlement History at Three Walled Northern Maya Centers. *AAnt* 45: 834–844.
 1989   The House of the Bacabs: Its Social Context. In *The House of the Bacabs, Copán, Honduras*, ed. D. L. Webster, pp. 5–40. Studies in Pre-Columbian Art and Archaeology no. 29. DO.
 1993   The Study of Maya Warfare: What It Tells Us about the Maya and What It Tells Us about Maya Archaeology. In Sabloff and Henderson 1973b, pp. 415–444.
 1998   Warfare and Status Rivalry: Lowland Maya and Polynesian Comparisons. In *Archaic States*, ed. G. M. Feinman and J. Marcus, pp. 311–351. School of American Research Press, Santa Fe, NM.
 1999   The Archaeology of Copán, Honduras. *Journal of Archaeological Research* 7: 1–53.
 2000   The Not So Peaceful Civilization: A Review of Maya War. *JWP* 14(1): 65–119.
 n.d.   Political Ecology, Political Economy, and the Culture History of Resource Management at Copán. In *Copán: The History of an Ancient Maya Kingdom*, ed. W. L. Fash and E. W. Andrews. School of American Research Press, Albuquerque, NM (in press).

Webster, David L., Barbara W. Fash, Randolph Widmer, and Scott Zeleznik
 1998   The Skyband Group: Investigation of a Classic Maya Elite Residential Complex at Copan, Honduras. *AM* 25: 319–343.

Webster, David L., and AnnCorinne Freter
 1990a   The Demography of Late Classic Copan. In Culbert and Rice 1990, pp. 37–62.

1990b   Settlement History and the Classic Collapse at Copan: A Redefined Chronological Perspective. *LAA* 1: 66–85.

Webster, David L., AnnCorinne Freter, and Nancy Gonlin
2000   *Copán: The Rise and Fall of an Ancient Maya Kingdom.* Harcourt College Publishers, Fort Worth, TX.

Webster, David L., AnnCorinne Freter, and David Rue
1993   The Obsidian Hydration Dating Project at Copán: A Regional Approach and Why It Works. *LAA* 4: 303–324.

Webster, David L., William T. Sanders, and Peter van Rossum
1992   A Simulation of Copan Population History and Its Implications. *AM* 3: 185–197.

Welsh, W. Bruce M.
1988   *An Analysis of Classic Lowland Maya Burials.* BAR International Series, 409.

Wenke, Robert J.
1991   The Evolution of Early Egyptian Civilization: Issues and Evidence. *JWP* 5: 3: 279–329.

West, Georgia
1999   Investigations at Structure 1, Caye Coco. In *The Belize Postclassic Project 1998: Investigations at Progresso Lagoon,* ed. M. A. Masson and R. M. Rosenswig, pp. 83–102. Occasional Pub. no. 3. IMS.

2002   Ceramic Exchange in the Late Classic and Postclassic Maya Lowlands: A Diachronic Approach. In Masson and Freidel 2002, pp. 140–196.

Whitley, David S.
1997   New Approaches to Old Problems: Archaeology in Search of an Ever Elusive Past. In *Reader in Archaeological Theory: Post-Processual and Cognitive Approaches,* ed. D. S. Whitley, pp. 1–34. Routledge, London.

Whitmore, Thomas J., Mark Brenner, Jason H. Curtis, Bruce H. Dahlin, and Barbara W. Leyden
1996   Holocene Climatic and Human Influences on Lakes of the Yucatan Peninsula, Mexico: An Interdisciplinary, Paleolimnological Approach. *The Holocene* 6: 273–287.

Wiessner, Polly
1990   Is There a Unity to Style? In *The Uses of Style in Archaeology,* ed. M. W. Conkey and C. A. Hastorf, pp. 105–112. Cambridge University Press, Cambridge.

Wilk, Richard R., and Harold L. Wilhite
1991   The Community of Cuello: Patterns of Household and Settlement Change. In Hammond 1991a, pp. 118–133.

Willey, Gordon R.
1956   Problems Concerning Prehistoric Settlement Patterns in the Maya Lowlands. In *Prehistoric Settlement Patterns in the Maya Lowlands,* ed. G. R. Willey, pp. 104–114. Viking Fund Pub. 23.

1972   *The Artifacts of Altar de Sacrificios.* PMAE Papers, vol. 64, no. 1.

1973   *The Altar de Sacrificios Excavations: General Summary and Conclusions. PMAE* Papers, vol. 64, no. 3.

1978   *Excavations at Seibal, Department of Peten, Guatemala: Artifacts.* PMAE Memoirs, vol. 14, no. 1.

1981   Maya Lowland Settlement Patterns: A Summary Review. In Ashmore 1981a, pp. 385–416.

1986   The Postclassic of the Maya Lowlands: A Preliminary Overview. In Sabloff and Andrews 1986b, pp. 17–52.

1990   General Summary and Conclusions. *Excavations at Seibal, Department of Peten, Guatemala,* ed. G. R. Willey. PMAE Memoirs, vol. 17, no. 4.

1997   Copán: Settlement, Politics, and Ideology. *Symbols,* Spring: 5–8, 37.

Willey, Gordon R., William R. Bullard Jr., John B. Glass, and James C. Gifford
    1965   *Prehistoric Settlement in the Belize Valley*. PMAE Papers, vol. 54.

Willey, Gordon R., T. Patrick Culbert, and Richard E.W. Adams
    1967   Maya Lowland Ceramics: A Report from the 1965 Guatemala City Conference. *AAnt* 32: 289–315.

Willey, Gordon R., and Richard M. Leventhal
    1979   Prehistoric Settlement at Copan. In *Maya Archaeology and Ethnohistory,* ed. N. Hammond and G. R. Willey, pp. 75–102. University of Texas Press, Austin.

Willey, Gordon R., Richard M. Leventhal, Arthur A. Demarest, and William L. Fash Jr.
    1994   *Ceramics and Artifacts from Excavations in the Copán Residential Zone*. PMAE Papers, vol. 80.

Willey, Gordon R., and Philip Phillips
    1955   Method and Theory in American Archaeology, II: Historical Development Interpretation. *AA* 57: 723–819.
    1958   *Method and Theory in American Archaeology*. University of Chicago Press, Chicago.

Willey, Gordon R., and Demitri B. Shimkin
    1973   The Maya Collapse: A Summary View. In Culbert 1973a, pp. 457–501.

Willey, Gordon R., and A. Ledyard Smith
    1969   *The Ruins of Altar de Sacrificios, Department of Peten, Guatemala: An Introduction.* PMAE Papers, vol. 62, no. 1.

Willey, Gordon R., A. Ledyard Smith, Gair Tourtellot III, and Ian Graham
    1975   *Excavations at Seibal: Introduction: The Site and Its Settings*. PMAE Memoirs, vol. 13, no. 1.

Williams, A. R.
    2002   A New Chapter in Maya History: All-Out War, Shifting Alliances, Bloody Sacrifices. *National Geographic* 202(4) ("Geographica" section).

Williams-Beck, Lorraine A.
    1995   The Linear Complex: An Interpretive Alternative for the Architectural Concept of Acropolis. Paper presented at the First International Symposium on Belize Archaeology, San Ignacio Cayo, Belize.
    1996   Federalismo y poder prehispánico en la provincia Ah Canul, Campeche, México. In *IX simposio, 1995,* tomo I, pp. 355–374.
    1998   *El domino de los batabob: el área Puuc occidental campechana*. UACM.

Williams-Beck, Lorraine A., and Tsubasa Okoshi Harada
    1998   Recent Archaeological and Ethnohistoric Research in the Ah Canul Province. *Mexicon* 20: 79–84.

Winemiller, Terance L.
    1994   Exploitation of Limestone Resources by the Ancient Maya at Chichén Itzá. Paper presented at the 61st Annual Meeting of the SAA, New Orleans.

Winemiller, Terance L., and Rafael Cobos
    1999   Chichén Itzá: New Beginnings and Endings. Paper presented at the 64th Annual Meeting of the SAA, Chicago.

Wingard, John D.
    1992   *The Role of Soils in the Development and Collapse of Classic Maya Civilization at Copán, Honduras.* Ph.D. dissertation, Pennsylvania State University. UMI.
    1996   Interactions Between Demographic Processes and Soil Resources in the Copán Valley, Honduras. In Fedick 1996b, pp. 207–235.

Wisdom, Charles
1940   *The Chorti Indians of Guatemala.* University of Chicago Press, Chicago.

Wolf, Eric R.
1999   *Envisioning Power: Ideologies of Dominance and Crises.* University of California Press, Berkeley.

Wolley, Claudia
1993   Sistema defensivo de Punta de Chimino, Petén. Tesis de licenciatura, Universidad de San Carlos de Guatemala, Guatemala.
1995   Excavación en muros defensivos entre Cerro de Bananas y Cerro de Cheyo en Aguateca: Operación CBA. In Demarest, Váldes, and Escobedo 1995, pp. 490–493.
1997   *Petexbatun Lithic Form, Function, Production, and Exchange: Implications for Economic Systems on the Eve of the Maya Collapse.* Ph.D. dissertation proposal, Department of Anthropology, Vanderbilt University, Nashville, TN.

Wolley, Claudia, and Lori Wright
1990   Punta de Chimino: sondeos en el sistema defensivo. In Demarest and Houston, pp. 423–436.

Wren, Linnea, and Peter Schmidt
1991   Elite Interaction During the Terminal Classic Period: New Evidence from Chichen Itza. In Culbert 1991, pp. 199–225.

Wright, Lori E.
1994   *The Sacrifice of the Earth? Diet, Health, and Inequality in the Pasión Maya Lowlands.* Unpublished Ph.D. dissertation, Department of Anthropology, University of Chicago, Chicago.
1997a   Biological Perspectives on the Collapse of the Pasión Maya. *AM* 8: 267–273.
1997b   Ecology or Society? Paleodiet and the Collapse of the Pasión Maya Lowlands. In *Bones of the Maya: Skeletal Studies of an Ancient People,* ed. S. Whittington and D. Reed. Smithsonian Institution Press, Washington, DC.
1997c   Intertooth Patterns of Hypoplasia Expression: Implications for Childhood Health in the Classic Maya Collapse. *American Journal of Physical Anthropology* 102(2): 233–247.
2004   *Nutrition, Diet, and Health at the Time of the Maya Collapse: Osteological Evidence from the Petexbatun.* Vanderbilt University Press, Nashville, TN.

Wright, Lori E., and Christine D. White
1996   Human Biology in the Classic Maya Collapse: Evidence from Paleopathology and Paleodiet. *JWP* 10: 147–198.

Wright, Rita
1991   Patterns of Technology and the Organization of Productions at Harappa. In *Harappa Excavations: 1986–1990: A Multidisciplinary Approach to 3rd Millennium Urbanism,* ed. R. H. Meadows, pp. 71–88. Monographs in World Prehistory no. 3, Prehistory Press, Madison, WI.

Wrobel, Gabriel D., Della C. Cook, and K. Anne Pyburn
1997   An Early Classic Maya Tomb at Chau Hiix Archaeological Site, Northern Belize. Paper presented at the 62nd Annual Meeting of the SAA, Nashville, TN.

Wurster, Wolfgang (ed.)
2000   *El sitio maya de Topoxté, investigaciones en una isla del lago Yaxhá, Petén, Guatemala. Materialien zur Allgemeinen und Vergleichenden Archäologie,* Band 57, Verlag Philipp von Zabern, Mainz am Rhein, Germany.

Yaeger, Jason
1992   Xunantunich Settlement Survey, Preliminary Report. In Leventhal 1992, pp. 110–126.

1994   The 1994 Excavations at San Lorenzo. In Leventhal and Ashmore 1994, pp. 123–148.

1995a   Changing Patterns of Community Structure and Organization: The End of the Classic Period at San Lorenzo, Cayo District, Belize. Dissertation Improvement Grant proposal submitted to the National Science Foundation, August.

1995b   The 1995 Excavations at San Lorenzo. In Leventhal and Ashmore 1995, pp. 112–138.

1996   The 1996 Excavations at San Lorenzo. In Leventhal and Ashmore 1996, pp. 123–150.

2000a   Changing Patterns of Social Organization: The Late and Terminal Classic Communities of San Lorenzo, Cayo District, Belize. Ph.D. dissertation, Department of Anthropology, University of Pennsylvania, Philadelphia.

2000b   The Social Construction of Communities in the Classic Maya Countryside. In *The Archaeology of Communities: A New World Perspective,* ed. M. A. Canuto and J. Yaeger, pp. 123–142. Routledge, London and New York.

Yaeger, Jason, and Samuel V. Connell
1993   Xunantunich Settlement Survey. In Leventhal 1993, pp. 172–201.

Yaeger, Jason, and Lisa J. LeCount
1995   Social Heterogeneity and Political Integration in a Terminal Classic Maya Community: Ongoing Research at San Lorenzo, Belize. Paper presented at the 60th Annual Meeting of the SAA, Minneapolis, MN.

Yates, Timothy
1989   Habitus and Social Space: Some Suggestions About Meaning in the Saami (Lapp) Tent c. 1700–1900. In *The Meaning of Things: Material Culture and Symbolic Expression,* ed. I. Hodder, pp. 249–262. Unwin Hyman, London.

Yoffee, Norman
1988   Orienting Collapse. In Yoffee and Cowgill 1988, pp. 1–19.

Yoffee, Norman, and George L. Cowgill (eds.)
1988   *The Collapse of Ancient States and Civilizations.* University of Arizona Press, Tucson.

Zapata Castorena, Alicia
1985   Los chultunes de Calakmul, Campeche: trabajos preliminares. *Información* 10: 81–104. UACM.

Zapata Castorena, Alicia, and Lynda Florey Folan
1989–1990 Investigaciones arqueológicas en la estructura I de Calakmul, Campeche. *Información* 14: 27–41. UACM.

Zapata Peraza, Renee L.
1986   Los chultunes de la región serrana de Yucatán. *Cuadernos de la Arquitectura Mesoamericana* 8: 17–24.

No author given
1992   South Tyrol "Ice Man." *Archaeometry* 34:2: 346–347.

CONTRIBUTORS

R.E.W. Adams (The University of Texas at San Antonio)

Christopher R. Andres (Indiana University)

E. Wyllys Andrews (Tulane University)

Traci Ardren (University of Miami)

Wendy Ashmore (University of California, Riverside)

George J. Bey III (Millsaps College)

Geoffrey E. Braswell (State University of New York at Buffalo)

Kelli Carmean (Eastern Kentucky University)

Arlen F. Chase (University of Central Florida)

Diane Z. Chase (University of Central Florida)

Rafael Cobos Palma (Tulane University and Universidad Autónoma de Yucatán)

Arthur A. Demarest (Vanderbilt University)

María del Rosario Domínguez Carrasco (Universidad Autónoma de Campeche)

Nicholas P. Dunning (University of Cincinnati)

Federico Fahsen (Universidad del Valle)

William L. Fash (Harvard University)

Laraine A. Fletcher (Adelphi University)

William J. Folan (Universidad Autónoma de Campeche)

Donald Forsyth (Brigham Young University)

Tara Bond Freeman (Southern Methodist University)

David Freidel (Southern Methodist University)

AnnCorinne Freter (Ohio University)

Michael D. Glascock (University of Missouri)

Jason J. González (Southern Illinois University Carbondale)

Joel D. Gunn (University of North Carolina)

Norman Hammond (Boston University)

Craig A. Hanson (Tulane University)

Charles W. Houck (Tulane University)

Brett A. Houk (SWCA Environmental Consultants)

Dave Johnstone (Humbolt State University)

Jeff Karl Kowalski (Northern Illinois University)

Juan Pedro Laporte (Universidad de San Carlos)

Abel Morales López (Universidad Autónoma de Campeche)

T. Kam Manahan (Vanderbilt University)

Marilyn A. Masson (State University of New York at Albany)

Ruth Mathews (The University of Texas at San Antonio)

Shirley Boteler Mock (University of Texas)

Matt O'Mansky (Vanderbilt University)

K. Anne Pyburn (Indiana University)

Don S. Rice (Southern Illinois University Carbondale)

Prudence M. Rice (Southern Illinois University Carbondale)

William M. Ringle (Davidson College)

H. R. Robichaux (University of the Incarnate Word)

Cynthia Robin (Northwestern University)

J. Gregory Smith (University of Pittsburgh)

Rebecca Storey (University of Houston)

Charles Suhler (Southern Methodist University)

Gair Tourtellot (Boston University)

Juan Antonio Valdés (Universidad San Carlos)

Fred Valdez Jr. (University of Texas)

David Webster (Pennsylvania State University)

Jason Yaeger (University of Wisconsin)

INDEX

Page numbers in boldface refer to figures and tables.

666

INDEX

674

INDEX

92–93, 130; Early Classic, 156; East Plaza Ballcourt, 142, 150; elite factions, 130; Emblem Glyph, 93, 130, 151; graffiti, 554; Great Plaza, 143, 150, 153, 159; Group 6C-12, 154; Group 6C-15, 153; Group 6D-20, 154; Group G, 143; hiatus, 189; hieroglyphic texts, 15; K'inich Nab Nal, 143; K'ul Mutul Ahaw, 151, 160; Lost World complex, 143, 145, 150, 153, 154, 159; Maler Palace, 143; "Man of Tikal," 142; market ballcourt, 142, 150; as *may* seat, 135–136, 553, 564; and Naranjo, 69; North Acropolis, 145; obsidian, 184; political organization, 110, 141, 147, 151, 159; population size, 150, 156, 158, 191, 553; Postclassic, 153; Proyecto Nacional Tikal, 150; rank size analysis of sites in region, **335**; regency, 151; regional state, 333, 334, 335; ruler Hasaw Kan K'awil I (also Jasaw Chan K'awiil; Ruler A, Ah Cacau), 142; ruler Hasaw Kan K'awil II, 141, 150, 156, 160, 191; ruler K'ak' Sih (Smoking Frog), 140, 144; ruler Nun Bak Chak (Shield Skull); ruler Siyah Kan K'awil II, 135, 144; ruler Toh Chak Ich'ak' (Great Jaguar Paw), 143, 159; ruler Yax Ain II, 143, 160; ruler Yik'in Kan K'awil (Ruler B), 142, 145; and Seibal, 69, 73, **74**; social complexity and trade, 23; and southeastern Petén, 201; Stela 11, **149**, 150; Stela 20, 145; Stela 24, 143, 145; Stela 31, 21; stelae, 134, 191, 554; Str. 3D-43, 153; Str. 5C-49, 142; Str. 5D-22, 142; Str. 5D-35, 142; Str. 5D-51, 159; Str. 5D-57, stucco frieze, 169; Str. 6C-50, 153; subsistence catchment area, 321; Temple I, 146, 153; Temple 1, Lintel 3, 169; Temple II, 153; Temple III, 150, 153; Temple III, Lintel 2, 143; Temple V, 142; Temple VI, 153; Terminal Classic occupation areas, 148, 150, 151, 192, 345, 361, 554; trash deposition in, 349; twin-pyramid complex, 71, 553; and

Uaxactun, 140; University of Pennsylvania Museum Tikal Project, 150, 156; and Xiw origins, 429; Yax Moch Xoc (founder), 144
Tikincacab, 539
Tilley, Christopher, 7, 13
Timak Composite type, 536
Tinaja group, type, 32, 35, 37, 39, 49, 173, 175, 181; at Caracol, **347**, **354**, 355, **356**; in northern Belize, 383, 386, 390, 392, 394, **395**; in southeastern Petén, 215, 216–217, 221, 222. *See also constituent types*
Tipu, 308, 322(n3), 405, 419, 422
Tlaloc, 271
Tohil Plumbate, 39, 46, 48, 235, 256, 276, 277, 282, 283, 286, 432, 504, 522, 536, 540, 542. *See also* Plumbate
Tolobojo complex, 35, **56**, 146, 222
Toltec: "horizon" at Copán, 283; influence at Chichén Itza, 44, 47, 82(n7), 455; prowling jaguar at Seibal, 61; trade, 434
Toniná: ceramics, 42; hieroglyphic texts, 15, 160; last dated monument, 190; Mon, 101, 289
Topoxté, ceramics, 35; obsidian, 184
Toro Gouged-Incised type, 217, 383
Toscano, Lourdes, 477
Tourtellot, Gair, 116, 288, 309, 327, 328, 360, 361, 377, 550, 551, 552, 567
Tozzer, Alfred P., 135
Trade, 181, 283, 571; coastal, 367, 372–373, 374, 379, 385, 400, 558, 560 (*see also* Gulf coast); and community specialization, 376; and development of middle class, 23; and elites, 362; in Pasión region, 93, 102, 118, 147; Postclassic, 23–24; reorganized, 229
Traino Brown type, 46, 167, 192–193(n1)
Trapeche group, 129
Trapiche Incised type, **356**
Trinidad, 43
Tsabak Unslipped-Striated type, 375, 393, 397, **398**
Tula, Ballcourt 1, 432

Tulum, 507, 516(n17)
Tumbaga, 520
Tunich Red-on-orange type, 385, 386, 392
Turner, Billie Lee, 156, 158
Turquoise, 513, 520, 539
Tutu Camp Striated type, 379, 392
Tutul Xiw. *See* Xiw
Twin-pyramid complex, 71, 134, 159, 553
Tzibana Gouged-Incised type, 394
Tzibanché jade, 289
Tzum, 430

Uaxactún, 553; Burial A-2, 145; burials, 360; causeway, 145; ceramics, 32, 34, 49, 50, **56**, 148, 344, 360 (*see also* Tepeu sphere); Chik'in Chakte title, 156; declining population, 154; Early Classic, 140; Group A, 145, 154, 156, 159; Group B, 144, 145, 154, 156, 159; Group E, 156; last monuments, 147, 154, 160; Main Plaza, 154, 156; metate source, 198; Plaza Plan 2, 159; Postclassic, lack of, 156; rivalry with Tikal, 140; ruler Chaan K'an Ko, 143, 144, 145, 146, 160; ruler K'al Chik'in Chakte, 141, 154, 156, 160; ruler Olom Chik'in Chakte, 154, 155; ruler Oxlahun Koxba, 144; settlement locations, 158; stelae, 142, 160; Stela 2, 144; Stela 7, 144, 145; Stela 8, 143, 144, 145; Stela 9, 145; Stela 11, 143, 144, 145; Stela 12, 150, 154, 156, **157**; Stela 13, 154, **155**; Stela 14, 143; Str. A-1, 145; Str. A-2, 154, 156; Str. A-4, 154; Str. A-5 (Shell-Kawak), 140, 146, 154; Str. B-2, 145; Terminal Classic occupation, 148, 154–156, 158; "Vase of the Initial Series," 145, 156
Uaxactun Unslipped ware, 214–215
Uayeb rituals, 497
Ucanal, 116, 202; burning, 160; and Calzada Mopan, 228; and Caracol, 228–229, 345; conflict, 155; Emblem Glyph, 224; home of Kan Ek', 69, 127; home of Wat'ul Chatel, 69, 78; and Ixkun, 224; monuments,

676